Handbook of Business Infor

HANDBOOK OF BUSINESS INFORMATION
A Guide for Librarians, Students, and Researchers

Diane Wheeler Strauss
University of North Carolina at Chapel Hill

1988
Libraries Unlimited, Inc.
Englewood, Colorado

LIBRARIES UNLIMITED, INC.
P.O. Box 3988
Englewood, Colorado 80155-3988

Library of Congress Cataloging-in-Publication Data

Strauss, Diane Wheeler.
    Handbook of business information.

    Includes bibliographies and index.
    1. Reference books--Business--Bibliography--Handbooks, manuals, etc. 2. Business--Information services --United States--Handbooks, manuals, etc. 3. United States--Government publications--Handbooks, manuals, etc. 4. Business--Data bases--Handbooks, manuals, etc. I. Title.
Z7164.C81S7796 1988   [HF5351]   016.33   88-23093
ISBN 0-87287-607-1 (alk. paper)

To Olga Wheeler,
With Love and Gratitude

CONTENTS

PART 2
Fields of Business Information

LIST OF ILLUSTRATIONS

INTRODUCTION

Every day in academic, public, and special libraries and information centers, the answers to an array of business reference inquiries are sought. In the course of a normal working day, a librarian may be asked to find the beta for a stock, to find the market share for Alpo™ dog food, or to compare the cost of living in Seattle with that in Boston. He or she may be asked about the Big Eight, fundamental analysis, 10-Ks, Ginnie Mae or Freddie Mac, and sinking funds. Although the seasoned business information specialist usually can handle such inquiries with ease, to the novice and nonspecialist they can be daunting. How can the answers be found when the questions themselves seem incomprehensible?

The *Handbook of Business Information* is intended to help defuse some of the anxiety that inexperienced researchers feel when searching for business information. Its purpose is twofold: to give librarians, students, and other researchers a grounding in business basics, and to identify, describe, and in many instances illustrate the use of key information sources. Each chapter begins with business fundamentals, introducing basic concepts and vocabulary that will enable the reader to comprehend better the requests for assistance and use more effectively the myriad of business information sources available. The chapter on stocks, for example, begins with a discussion of the major stock exchanges and measures of stock performance, while the accounting chapter first covers balance sheets, accounting principles, and financial ratios. Following such discussion, key reference works are considered. In many instances, descriptions of these sources are supplemented with representative illustrations from the works themselves.

The *Handbook* is divided into two main parts. The first eight chapters cover business information according to the formats in which it is made available: guides, bibliographies, and quick reference sources; directories; periodicals and newspapers; looseleaf services; government documents; statistics; vertical file materials; and databases and other types of electronic business information. Chapters 9 through 18 focus on specific fields of business, covering marketing; accounting and taxation; money, credit, and banking; investment (with separate chapters for stocks, bonds, mutual funds, and futures and options); insurance; and real estate. Additionally, aappendixes include a list of business acronyms and abbreviations; descriptions of selected government agencies, their publications, and government-issued economic indicators; and a list of free materials for business-oriented vertical file collections.

Certain themes are evident throughout this book. The first is the importance of government-issued sources in answering research inquiries. Accordingly, references to government documents, databases, and the usefulness of depository library collections and staff are scattered throughout the text. Also evident is a strong bias in favor of the acquisition and use of vertical file materials. Although such collections are viewed as old-fashioned by some, it remains as true today as it was 50 years ago that booklets, pamphlets, and other ephemera are not only inexpensive but also may contain information that is virtually impossible to find elsewhere. Potentially useful vertical file publications are identified in almost every chapter, and are compiled into a single list in appendix I. It is hoped that the list will promote the acquisition and use of such materials by librarians and the people they serve.

Certain limitations must be kept in mind when reading the *Handbook*. Change is so continuous in every facet of business practice and publication that, inevitably, some of the companies, organizations, publications, and databases described herein may have changed appreciably by the time of publication. The cutoff date for inclusion of most materials in the *Handbook* was December 1987.

The *Handbook* is not inclusive. A decision was made to relinquish broader but less intensive coverage of every facet of business in favor of a more thorough consideration of a limited number of fields. Accordingly, business topics that are widely covered in other sources or that are not conceptually difficult to master are omitted. Small business and management, for example, are not covered in this work. Foreign and international business practices and information sources are also excluded, but for a different reason. To give them the attention they deserve would require the publication of another book of this size. Finally, the sheer volume of publications and databases available on every business subject has required that this work be selective. Inevitably, some sources that may be particular favorites of readers may be missing. The author hopes, however, that the coverage of basic business concepts in the *Handbook* and the inclusion of many examples reprinted from major reference works will be sufficiently helpful to compensate for the aforementioned limitations.

Many people helped to make this work a reality, but there are three to whom I am particularly grateful. The first is Fred Roper, without whom I would never have begun this and many other business-related library projects. His support and encouragement have been invaluable. Equally so has been the assistance offered by two colleagues, Karen S. Seibert and Luke Swindler. Each read and made numerous suggestions for the improvement of the *Handbook*. Without their expertise and unfailing patience and kindness, this manuscript might never have been completed.

Writing this book has been a long-term process, and many others have been involved at different times. In its early days, Heather Cameron, Tim Dempsey, Chuck Gouge, Bill Schenck, Marcia Tuttle, and Martha Jane Zacchert were especially helpful. Since then, many colleagues have reviewed chapters, and I would like to thank them as well. They include Donna Cornick, Bob Hebert, Carson Holloway, Ridley Kessler, Pat Langelier, and David Taylor. Faculty in the University of North Carolina's Schools of Information and Library Science and Business Administration generously read parts of my work and made suggestions for their improvement. My thanks in particular go to Ray Carpenter, J. Finley Lee, and especially to Richard McEnally, who was kind enough to review all five investment chapters. Former students in the School of Information and Library Science provided assistance as well. Mike Van Fossen and Kim Amato helped with verification, and Mary Horton and Jamie Davis handled the microcomputer graphics. To all of these people and to my family, friends, and coworkers in UNC's Business Administration/Social Sciences Reference Department, my heartfelt thanks and appreciation.

Part 1
Formats of
Business Information

Get your facts first, and then you can distort
them as much as you please.

—Mark Twain

1

BASIC BUSINESS REFERENCE SOURCES

Accurate, timely business information is vital. Executives contemplating a plant relocation, for example, will consider such factors as corporate income tax rates, average weekly wages of workers, cost of living, climate, and community resources before making their decision. A marketing department will want to learn all it can about the economic and social characteristics of specific regions of the country so that it can decide how to boost sales or where best to launch a new product. Proprietors of new businesses may want to find out what kinds of assistance are available from government agencies, and prospective investors, to learn all they can about the outlook for and the recent successes (or failures) of specific companies. Each of these situations illustrates the importance of information for business decision making, planning, and problem solving, and each is answerable to a very large extent by consulting library business collections.

Librarians and researchers seeking business information, in fact, are confronted with an overwhelming number of books, periodicals, newspapers, government documents, databases, and other sources from which to choose. Examination of these sources will reveal that their quality varies considerably; some are superb, others are marginal at best. In order to succeed, the librarian or researcher must decide not only where to go for the desired information, but also how to select the best sources from the many that are available. This chapter lists and describes important business guides, bibliographies, and other finding aids; by consulting them, some of the best and most widely used sources of business information can be identified. Also included in this chapter are major reference sources—dictionaries, almanacs, encyclopedias, and handbooks—that can be used to answer requests for quick, factual information.

GUIDES

Bibliographic guides to business literature are abundant. Some focus on specific business activities such as marketing and accounting and others survey the entire range of business endeavor, but the best have certain characteristics in common. They provide an overview of the area being covered; they frequently describe characteristics typical of research in the field; and they list, annotate, and sometimes evaluate relevant sources in a variety of formats. This section describes bibliographic guides that encompass the entire range of business activities. More specialized, subject-oriented guides are presented in the chapters that follow.

Types of Business Guides

Business guides can be classified in a number of ways (see figure 1.1). They can, for example, be categorized by the breadth of coverage they provide. Comprehensive guides cover virtually all fields of business and may include handbooks and basic textbooks as well as reference sources, while selective guides may exclude all but reference materials or may omit coverage of certain subjects. A selective guide may, for example, exclude insurance, international trade, or operations research from discussion, or it may focus only on databases. Dictionary guides are compilations of lists of research materials in highly specialized areas such as robotics and beekeeping. While their level of subject specificity is valuable, dictionary guides lack the subject background provided by comprehensive and selective bibliographic guides. Finally, other guides are written with specific user populations in mind. They may be written for managers and executives, researchers, business students, or novice library users. Each is written for a designated user group, and describes the basic sources and research techniques most likely to be of interest to it.

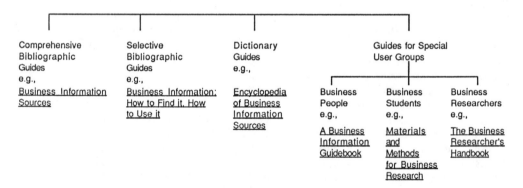

Fig. 1.1. Types of business guides.

No single guide, however thorough or well written, can possibly serve all needs. Titles representing each type of guide, therefore, are essential to all but the smallest and most selective business reference collections. Some of the most important ones are described below.

COMPREHENSIVE BIBLIOGRAPHIC GUIDES

Business encompasses so many different activities and is characterized by such rapid change that a truly comprehensive, up-to-date printed guide to the literature is impossible. There are, however, a few guides that provide thorough coverage of standard business reference sources and important texts, handbooks, and related works.

Daniells, Lorna M. **Business Information Sources.** Rev. ed. Berkeley, Calif.: University of California Press, 1985. 673p.

Vernon, K. D. C. **Information Sources in Management and Business.** 2nd ed. London: Butterworths, 1984. (Butterworths Guides to Information Sources). 346p.

Business Information Sources is widely acknowledged to be the most comprehensive guide available, indispensable to librarians and researchers alike. Written by Lorna Daniells, who has been both Business Bibliographer and Head of Reference at Harvard Business School's prestigious Baker Library, *Business Information Sources* (frequently referred to as "Daniells") lists and annotates an impressive array of books, periodicals, documents, databases, and other sources. It is divided into two main parts. The first, comprised of the opening eight chapters, describes basic business reference sources. It begins with a description of the types of libraries in which business reference services are provided, proceeds to identify sources of quick reference information, and discusses such basic reference formats as bibliographies, indexes and abstracts, government publications, doctoral dissertations, databases, microforms and cassettes, handbooks, and looseleaf services. Additional chapters discuss publications that track current business and economic trends, and that present domestic, foreign, and industry statistics. Also covered in this section are directories and investment sources.

The second part focuses on specific management functions, covering such topics as accounting, corporate finance and banking, international management, insurance and real estate, and marketing. Coverage in this section extends to textbooks, collections of readings, and books written for the practicing manager as well as reference sources and key trade and professional associations. Entries include essential bibliographic information and succinct, but thorough, annotations. Pagination is included for books and pamphlets, and entries for each periodical include the frequency of publication and the names of the indexing and abstracting services in which its articles are listed.

Business Information Sources is further enhanced by "A Basic Bookshelf," a chapter that lists and describes essential reference titles appropriate to a personal or small business library collection, and by a comprehensive author, title, and subject index.

Not all business publications, however, are included in Daniells. The emphasis is on English-language works published primarily in the United States. Two categories of materials—published proceedings and business casebooks—are specifically omitted, and coverage of government documents, databases, and materials suitable for vertical file collections is far from inclusive. Even so, this guide's scope and the quality of the information it contains are extraordinary. Its usefulness as a reference tool and as an aid to collection development is difficult to overestimate.

Information Sources in Management and Business, published in its first edition as *The Use of Management and Business Literature*, is a collection of bibliographic essays written by 14 British librarians, academicians, and business people. The book is in three parts. Part 1, "The Literature, the Library, and Bibliographical Tools for Finding Information," includes chapters by two noted business librarians, K. D. C. Vernon and Malcolm Campbell. Part 2 focuses on business information in various forms, with chapters on company information, statistical publications, online services and computer data banks, market research reports, and research in progress and unpublished material. Finally, part 3 includes literature surveys for the fields of accounting and corporate finance, organization studies, marketing, strategic management and planning, operations management, quantitative business analysis, and business law. A brief subject/title index is appended.

Several differences between *Information Sources in Management and Business* and *Business Information Sources* are worth noting. The first is that while both focus on English-language sources, Vernon's guide emphasizes British publications and business practices, while Daniells' emphasis is American. The difference in format is also notable: *Information Sources in Business and Management* is a collection of essays by a variety of experts, while *Business Information Sources* consists primarily of annotations, grouped together by subject. Further, while Vernon covers some subjects in greater depth, Daniells presents far more titles and covers more subject areas. Finally, the indexing in Daniells is far superior to that provided in Vernon's work.

A good case can be made for acquiring and using both guides. Daniells is perhaps most useful for a survey of major publications in a specific discipline or for a brief review of the contents of a particular title. Vernon, on the other hand, provides discussion and analysis that are particularly useful to someone in need of background information; its format and the lack of detailed indexing encourage more leisurely reading.

SELECTIVE BUSINESS GUIDES

The distinction between comprehensive and selective business guides is an arbitrary one. No guide is all-encompassing; but some, notably Daniells and Vernon, are more comprehensive than others, which limit their coverage by subject, information format, or type of library or information setting to which the sources listed are appropriate. Guides emphasizing specific subject areas are included in many of the chapters that follow. The titles listed below, however, selectively present sources relevant to several different fields of business.

> Lavin, Michael. **Business Information: How to Find It, How to Use It.** Phoenix, Ariz.: Oryx Press, 1987. 299p.

> Schlessinger, Bernard S., ed. **The Basic Business Library: Core Resources.** Phoenix, Ariz.: Oryx Press, 1983. 232p.

One of the best selective guides is Michael Lavin's *Business Information: How to Find It, How to Use It.* As its subtitle indicates, the guide emphasizes research techniques and basic business concepts as well as information sources. Lavin first introduces business information and basic finding aids, covering not only standard reference sources, but also identifying major characteristics of business information and the organizations from which it typically is available. The various published sources of company data are also considered, with chapters on business directories, registered trademarks, corporate finance, and basic investment information, advice, and analysis. Another section focuses on statistical information. In addition to chapters that identify general economic and industry statistics and describe many of the sources that contain them, it includes an extremely useful and interesting introduction to statistical reasoning and an excellent discussion of the decennial *Census of Population and Housing* and of population estimates and projections. Finally, four special topics—marketing, business law, tax law, and business information for job hunters and consumers—are treated at length. Title and subject indexes are also included.

Business Information is different from other guides in many important respects. Each chapter begins with an outline of the topics to be covered and the major sources to be discussed, and is followed by an explanation of the concepts necessary to understand each source. While far fewer titles are covered than in most other guides, those that are included are treated more thoroughly. Annotations, which vary in length from a single paragraph to more than a page, are thorough and are sometimes supplemented with reprints from the sources being discussed. Finally, each chapter concludes with a brief, annotated list of titles for further reading.

Although it is useful for identifying some of the best business reference books appropriate to medium-sized business library collections, Lavin is perhaps even better for its clear and well-written descriptions of basic research techniques and business concepts. It belongs in every business collection.

The Basic Business Library similarly seeks to identify business resources essential for small- and medium-sized libraries. It presents an annotated list of 156 core reference titles, including for each an annotation describing its authority and scope and evaluating its usefulness to libraries. A bibliography on business reference and business librarianship and a series of essays on business reference are also featured. *The Basic Business Library* perhaps is more useful for its collection of essays and its business reference bibliography than for the core list of titles it presents. More thorough and up-to-date information about these same publications can be obtained by consulting *Business Information Sources* or *Business Information: How to Find It, How to Use It*. The overview of business librarianship and library practices, however, justifies the acquisition of *The Basic Business Library* for most business reference collections.

The comprehensive and selective guides described above are most useful for descriptions of standard business publications and for general surveys of business literature. The librarian or researcher in quest of statistics on paper bag production or in need of information on the olive oil industry, however, will need to consult sources that provide more detailed subject indexing. Dictionary guides are particularly useful in such situations.

DICTIONARY GUIDES

A dictionary guide is a computer-generated list of publications, databases, and other information sources, usually arranged by very narrow and precise subject headings. The titles that follow are representative.

> Woy, James, ed. **Encyclopedia of Business Information Sources.** 6th ed. Detroit: Gale Research Co., 1986. 878p.

> Mayros, Van, and D. Michael Werner. **Business Information: Applications and Sources.** Radnor, Pa.: Chilton, 1983. 490p.

Long the standard dictionary guide, the *Encyclopedia of Business Information Sources* lists a wide variety of published reference sources, databases, trade and professional associations, research centers and institutes, and other information sources on over 1,100 business-related subjects. It is arranged alphabetically by topic, from "Abbreviations" and "Abrasives Industry" to "Zinc" and "Zoning." Each topic is subdivided by type of information sources available (e.g., almanacs, abstracts, bibliographies, encyclopedias, handbooks, financial ratios, and price and statistics sources), with full bibliographic citations and prices for most of the items listed. The addresses and telephone numbers of publishers are also included. The entry for the paper bag industry, shown in figure 1.2 (see page 8), is typical.

Business Information: Applications and Sources, compiled by Van Mayros and D. Michael Werner, can be used as an inexpensive supplement to the *Encyclopedia of Business Information Sources*. Mayros lists and annotates over 3,800 sources (including nearly 400 databases), and is divided into two major parts. In section 1, each of the chapters deals with a specific area within business. Banking, economics, and finance; marketing planning; sales planning; marketing and sales promotion; legal and legislative affairs; environmental, social, and political affairs; industrial and manufacturing planning; research and development; general management issues; and long-range strategic planning are included. Each chapter is subdivided into smaller units. The chapter on marketing and sales promotion, for example, contains sections on advertising trends, direct mail, management trends, marketing ideas, and public relations. Each begins with a general description of information characteristics of and applications typical to that field and is followed by a categorized listing of basic titles and listings of additional sources. Section 2 consists of six separate parts (general references, periodicals, databases, information services, U.S. government agencies and departments, and U.S. government publication sources) that provide bibliographic citations and annotations for each of the source titles listed in section 1. Titles are arranged alphabetically and current price information and the numeric codes for business information categories identified in section 1 are also included.

PAPER BAG INDUSTRY

DIRECTORIES

Sources of Supply: Buyers Guide. 300 N. Prospect Ave., Park Ridge, IL 60068. (312) 823-3145. Annual. $50.00.

PERIODICALS AND NEWSLETTERS

Paper, Film and Foil Converter. 300 W. Adams St., Chicago, IL 60606. (312) 726-2802. Monthly. $32.00 per year.

STATISTICS SOURCES

Converted Flexible Packaging Products. U.S. Bureau of the Census, Washington, DC 20233. (301) 763-4051. Quarterly and annual summary.

TRADE ASSOCIATIONS AND PROFESSIONAL SOCIETIES

Paper Bag Institute. Two Overhill Rd., Scarsdale, NY 10583. (914) 723-7610.

Paper Shipping Sack Manufacturers' Association. Two Overhill Rd., Scarsdale, NY 10583. (914) 723-6440.

Fig. 1.2. Typical entry in *Encyclopedia of Business Information Sources.* Selected from *Encyclopedia of Business Information Sources*, edited by James Woy (Copyright © 1986 by Gale Research Company; reprinted by permission of the publisher), 6th edition, Gale, 1986, p. 643.

Business Information also features an appendix that describes database retrieval systems, explains basic online search procedures, and defines key terms. A directory of database producers, an index to government publications, and a subject index are also included.

A comparison with the *Encyclopedia of Business Information Sources* may be useful. The *Encyclopedia* is more current, provides more precise subject indexing, and does not require the flipping from one section to the other necessary in *Business Information*. Unfortunately, it is also considerably more expensive; the current edition of the *Encyclopedia* costs over six times Mayros's price. In addition, Mayros is useful for its brief descriptions of information sources and applications in a variety of business fields and for its inclusion of literally hundreds of databases. Both the *Encyclopedia* and *Business Information* deserve a place in most business reference collections. When the book budget does not permit purchase of the *Encyclopedia*, however, Mayros is a useful, although less highly regarded, choice. Book selectors should be forewarned, however, that it has at least three spinoffs, publications that recycle some of the information it contains.[1]

To this point, the guides that have been presented have been intended for an array of prospective users. Other guides are written with specific user populations in mind.

GUIDES FOR SPECIFIC USER GROUPS

Some of the people who might benefit most from using a business library or consulting business information sources are often unaware of such resources. Accordingly, guides to sources of business information and to the libraries that contain them can serve an important function. Some are written specifically for business people and business students, and others for researchers. The following titles represent the guides intended for business practitioners and students.

Figueroa, Oscar, and Charles Winkler. **A Business Information Guidebook.** New York: AMACOM, 1980. 190p.

Johnson, H. Webster, Anthony J. Faria, and Ernest L. Maier. **How to Use the Business Library, with Sources of Information.** 5th ed. Cincinnati, Ohio: South-Western Publishing, 1984. 265p.

Piele, Linda J., John C. Tyson, and Michael B. Sheffey. **Materials and Methods for Business Research**. New York: Libraryworks, 1980. 209p.

A Business Information Guidebook is intended primarily for managers and small business people in need of information. Following a brief discussion of the rudiments of information retrieval and an introduction to such basic concepts as the Standard Industrial Classification system and census geography, the *Guidebook* presents over 80 different subject categories, under which relevant reference titles are listed and annotated. The topics covered include accounting, advertising, franchising, public relations, insurance, and who's who directories. Key books, periodicals, documents, and advisory services are listed under each subject heading, and each entry includes bibliographic information, pagination, a detailed descriptive annotation, and a separate section in which special features are identified. It concludes with a section on personal finance, in which such topics as securities, mutual funds, security dealers, investment companies, securities research, and the New York and American Stock Exchanges are covered.

The *Guidebook* makes no attempt to be comprehensive. Its compilers specify that it is intended for use as a quick reference source and finding aid, rather than as a definitive bibliographic treatment of the subject being investigated. Its annotations, however, are clear and concise and present a businessperson's, rather than a librarian's, perspective on why certain reference sources are important.

How to Use the Business Library is a practical guide, written by business faculty for students and practitioners. The first chapter instructs readers in basic library skills including the Library of Congress and Dewey Decimal Classification systems and the use of the card catalog, while subsequent chapters focus on specific information formats (periodical literature, databases, handbooks and yearbooks, directories, financial and investment services, and government publications). Chapters generally begin with a survey of the types of materials being covered, followed by lists and brief annotations of relevant reference works. As with the *Guidebook, How to Use the Business Library* is not written with the sophisticated researcher in mind. Its annotations and introductory remarks, however, can be useful to librarians and general library users as well as to more specialized business clientele.

Materials and Methods for Business Research was developed by librarians and faculty to serve as a workbook for students and is designed to familiarize them with and help them to use effectively basic business reference sources, statistical data, and government publications. It is specifically intended for use in library bibliographic instruction programs, and each chapter contains an assignment as well as a discussion of specific types of business information sources. *Materials and Methods for Business Research* also includes suggestions for developing effective research techniques and strategies and tips for identifying sources of information outside the library. It was published in three separate versions: a student's workbook, an instructor's manual, and a library edition, which combines the workbook with the manual.

Other guides are written for serious researchers. Since most of them are already familiar with the rudiments of library arrangement and use and with many basic reference techniques, coverage in these publications is usually more intensive. Often the focus will be on a specific aspect of business research rather than the whole gamut of available business information. The following titles typify guides that belong in this category.

Business Researcher's Handbook: The Comprehensive Guide for Business Professionals. 2nd ed. Washington, D.C.: Washington Researchers, 1983. 247p.

How to Find Information about Companies: The Corporate Intelligence Sourcebook. 5th ed. Washington, D.C.: Washington Researchers, 1987. 483p.

Law-Yone, Wendy. **Company Information: A Model Investigation.** Washington, D.C.: Washington Researchers, 1983. 242p.

Fuld, Leonard M. **Competitor Intelligence: How to Get It, How to Use It.** New York: Wiley, 1985. 479p.

Washington Researchers, a private information brokerage and consulting firm, has parlayed its experience and expertise into a series of helpful publications for researchers, executives, and information specialists. The *Business Researcher's Handbook* follows a workbook approach, leading readers through the entire information-gathering process. The first section deals with understanding the client's information request, determining the format of the report to be submitted, and drawing up a contract with the client. The second section emphasizes the research process itself. Although it does not cover specific reference titles, it outlines methods for learning about industries that are relatively foreign to the researcher, for getting started when knowledge about the designated topic is negligible, and for learning about a particular company in the shortest time possible. The real emphasis, however, is on acquiring information by interviewing experts in the field and on techniques for successful telephone interviewing. Other sections discuss how information should be organized, how to report the research results, and how to enhance client-researcher relations. Sample forms are included, and an appendix lists a wide variety of information sources that are often overlooked, including government reference centers; information hotlines; and local, state, federal, and other corporate and industry information sources. It also outlines how to find information about competitors, and describes free market surveys available from the federal government. While intended for researchers, the *Handbook* can also be used by librarians and others to learn about information available outside the traditional library setting.

How to Find Information about Companies is a practical guide to corporate information sources. It begins with a brief description of the "why and how" of company research, but the real emphasis is on information available from federal and state government agencies, local and regional sources, trade and professional associations, labor unions, and on sources of industry data and information about foreign companies. Two sections focus on library resources. The first, "Published Sources and the Library," contains an annotated publications list compiled by Lorna Daniells. The second, "How to Find Company Intelligence On-Line," includes a brief description of database searching, a listing of relevant database vendors, gateway systems, and publications, and descriptions of the "Top 100" databases for business intelligence. While *How to Find Information about Companies* includes more references to library resources and to specific titles than the *Business Researcher's Handbook*, the emphasis remains on external information sources, particularly those available from government agencies and industry experts.

Also featured are sections on ethical considerations of company investigators, antitrust implications of corporate research, and private sector corporate information services, including investigative services, credit reporting, and bond rating services. An index is appended.

For researchers interested in how to apply the knowledge gained through reading *How to Find Information about Companies* and the *Business Researcher's Handbook, Company*

Information: A Model Investigation is useful. Following suggestions for planning a company research investigation, the author presents a case study, using Perdue Farms, Inc., a privately held chicken-processing company. The case study illustrates the methodology for obtaining information on Perdue Farms, presents the research findings, and summarizes the sources used during the investigation. Although perhaps of less immediate practical benefit than the other Washington Researchers publications described above, *Company Information* makes fascinating reading, and can help librarians and students as well as researchers.

Competitor Intelligence: How to Get It, How to Use It deals with specific tools and techniques that can be used to gather information about companies. It treats information gathering as a three-step process. The first begins with establishing a foundation (understanding intelligence, assembling a research team, understanding the difference between basic and creative information sources, the traits of a good information gatherer, and developing a library of information sources) and proceeds to discussing research techniques. Several research checklists for beginners are included, illustrating typical research projects and presenting, in order of priority, sources worth checking. The second focuses on basic information sources, covering resources likely to be available in business libraries, including databases and publications. After consulting the traditional sources described in the second step, Fuld advocates the use of creative information sources, showing readers how items as diverse as corrugated boxes, boxcars, technical manuals, help-wanted ads, and telephone Yellow Pages can be used to learn about companies that might otherwise be difficult to research. The text is supplemented with charts, graphs, case histories, and the addresses and telephone numbers of publishers and database producers.

The above guides and others like them are invaluable. They provide readers with an introduction to basic business sources, concepts, and research techniques, and help to acquaint them with business information needs. They are not, however, intended to be nor should they be used as the sole sources of information about business publications and databases. Bibliographies are also important.

BIBLIOGRAPHIES

Business bibliographies come in a variety of formats and serve an assortment of users. Some present retrospective lists of significant publications in all languages. Others list only the most recent publications, and are limited by country. Some cover relatively narrow fields, such as agribusiness and cost of living, while others include titles for all fields of business. This section focuses on bibliographies that present information on current English-language publications primarily issued by American publishers. Some are aimed at librarians, and others at library users.

Librarians seeking to build or improve business collections can begin by consulting the guides previously mentioned. In many instances, they will also refer to some of the bibliographies listed below.

> New York Public Library. Research Library. **The Bibliographic Guide to Business and Economics.** New York: G. K. Hall, 1975- . Annual.

> Baker Library. **Recent Additions to Baker Library.** Boston: Baker Library, Harvard Business School, v. 13- , 1973- . Monthly.

> Baker Library. **Core Collection: An Author and Subject Guide.** Boston: Baker Library, Harvard Business School, 1969/70- . Annual.

> Baker Library. **Baker Library Mini-Lists.** Boston: Baker Library, Harvard Business School, 1975- . Annual.

The Bibliographic Guide to Business and Economics is a comprehensive listing, by author, title, and subject, of books, reports, conference papers, and miscellaneous publications in business, economics, finance, labor, and related fields cataloged by the Library of Congress and the New York Public Library. It is most useful for large business and research libraries wanting to assess their business holdings, but is usually too costly and too inclusive to be practical for smaller libraries.

More current information is available in *Recent Additions to Baker Library*, an inexpensive monthly acquisitions list. Arrangement is by broad subject area. Titles are listed rather than annotated, but occasionally an issue will highlight a specific publication or collection, and will describe it at length. New additions to Baker's core collection of some 4,000 English-language titles, considered to be of particular value to Harvard Business School students, are designated by asterisks. Baker Library also issues the annual *Core Collection* that lists all titles currently housed in the Baker Library Reading Room. While both *Recent Additions to Baker Library* and *Core Collection* are useful, many of the titles listed are most suitable for academic business libraries and large research collections.

Of more practical benefit to small- and medium-sized libraries are the series of *Baker Library Mini-Lists* on such topics as "Sources of Information for Industry Analysis," "Business Dictionaries," and "Sources for U.S. Financial and Operating Ratios." Each covers key titles, with an emphasis on current, English-language publications, is updated annually, and ranges from two to six pages in length. Brief introductions to the subject and suggestions for further research are included when appropriate. Baker Library is not, of course, the only library preparing such business bibliographies for the use of its patrons. They are available at many academic, public, and special libraries, and are usually free. Baker Library, however, sells its *Mini-Lists* for a nominal fee through its publications office and may be better equipped than most libraries to fill large numbers of requests for its bibliographies.[2]

Many librarians, however, prefer annotated lists. For them, the following sources are particularly helpful.

The Good Book Guide for Business: From the Publishers of the Good Book Guide and The Economist. New York: Harper & Row, 1984. 318p.

DiMattia, Susan S. "Business Books [Year]," **Library Journal.** Annual feature, published in March.

Geahigan, Priscilla, ed. "Quick Biz: Recent Books on Business and Economics Topics," **American Libraries.** Column. Monthly.

Wynar, Bohdan S., **American Reference Books Annual.** Littleton, Colo.: Libraries Unlimited, 1970- . Annual.

The Good Book Guide for Business, compiled by the editors of the British periodicals, *The Good Book Guide* and *The Economist*, is a selected, subjective list of the best and most immediately relevant business books. The World Business Environment, The Management of Organizations, The Individual in Business, Business as It Happened, and Reference are the broad categories under which titles are grouped. Each is divided into narrower subcategories and contains bibliographic citations, annotations, and cover photographs for the titles listed. Author/title and subject indexes are included, and a brief guide to buying business books is appended.

Every year, *Library Journal* publishes an article that surveys the past year's trends in business publishing and that lists and annotates some of the best books of the year. Written by a subject specialist – in recent years, by Susan S. DiMattia, a business information consultant – "Business Books" lists by subject both circulating and reference titles judged by the author to be superior or significant.

In October 1987, a new column was added to "The Source," *American Libraries*' monthly review of selected professional sources for current awareness. "Quick Biz" is a brief annotated list of timely business and economics titles. Sponsored by the Business Reference and Services Section (BRASS) of the American Library Association's Reference and

Adult Services Division, each "Quick Biz" column focuses on a particular topic, such as business ethics, government documents, or international marketing and lists and annotates current titles considered by the guest columnist to be important. In addition, Geahigan, the column editor, highlights and describes an "Item of the Month" – a publication, database, or other information resource likely to be of interest to business reference librarians.

The emphasis is different in *American Reference Books Annual* (*ARBA*). First, only reference works are included. Second, while "Business Books" and *The Good Book Guide* are selective, subjective lists of the most highly acclaimed titles, *ARBA* includes publications of varying quality. Some are first-rate, others are clearly inferior. What makes *ARBA* so useful are the detailed, critical reviews, some of which discuss the strengths and weaknesses of specific titles at considerable length. Each review is signed, and citations to earlier reviews in library journals are included. By including both so-called good and bad titles accompanied by thoughtful evaluations, *ARBA* allows librarians to make informed decisions about publications to avoid as well as those to collect.

Although standard library review publications such as *Library Journal, Choice,* and *Wilson Library Bulletin* publish reviews of current business publications, the following periodical is particularly useful for tips on business research techniques and for information about relevant publications.

> Special Libraries Association. Business and Finance Division. **Business and Finance Division Bulletin.** Kent, Ohio: Kent State University Library, Reference Department, 1958- . Triannual.

The *Business and Finance Division Bulletin* is the official newsletter of the largest division of the Special Libraries Association. Like most such publications, it includes news of Division activities and of its members, but what makes it most useful is its collection of articles, bibliographies, and suggestions for locating difficult-to-find information. An issue may, for example, explain business concepts such as *market share* and *beta coefficients* and then proceed to identify sources that contain them. The articles cover topics as diverse as "Using the Business Pages of the *New York Times*," "Selected Sources of Time Series and Forecasts," and "Sources for Ticker Symbols and Company Information." A regular column, "Recent U.S. Government Publications of Interest to Business and Finance Librarians," lists and annotates selected documents. The emphasis throughout is on practical information.

Readers are encouraged to share their experiences – both good and bad – in looking for specific types of information or in using new business publications. Occasionally, the Division's publisher relations committee will correspond with publishers about titles with which librarians are dissatisfied or which are essentially recycled versions of earlier works, and frequently the publishers' responses are printed in the *Bulletin*. Other features include descriptions of specific business libraries and reprints of bibliographies from contributing special, academic, and public libraries. The *Bulletin*, which is included with Division membership and is available to nonmembers at a nominal price, is a forum where business and finance librarians from a wide range of library settings can share their common interests and concerns. It is well worth the subscription price.

The titles that have been described above are basic reference sources that enable librarians and researchers alike to identify business publications relevant to their interests. Equally important, however, are reference sources that provide quick, factual information. This chapter concludes by examining four major categories of quick reference tools: dictionaries, almanacs, encyclopedias, and handbooks.

DICTIONARIES

Business vocabulary can at times be baffling to the uninitiated. The librarian confronted for the first time with such terms as *market segmentation, convertible debentures,* and *beta coefficient* or with such slang as *killer bees, Fannie Mae,* and *golden parachutes* may feel with some justification that standard English and business English are two different languages. Many standard English dictionaries are, in fact, weak in their coverage of business jargon. As a result, specialized dictionaries are essential to all business collections. Each field of business is represented by dictionaries specific to it. There are, for example, dictionaries of insurance, accounting, finance, and real estate. Many of these specialized dictionaries will be discussed in the chapters that follow.

General Business Dictionaries

Other business dictionaries provide more general coverage. Some of the best and most widely used general business dictionaries are listed below.

Rosenberg, Jerry M. **Dictionary of Business and Management.** 2nd ed. New York: Wiley, 1983. 631p.

Ammer, Christine, and Dean S. Ammer. **Dictionary of Business and Economics.** Rev. and expanded ed. New York: Free Press/Macmillan, 1984. 507p.

Greenwald, Douglas, comp. **The McGraw-Hill Dictionary of Modern Economics: A Handbook of Terms and Organizations.** 3rd ed. New York: McGraw-Hill, 1983. 632p.

The *Dictionary of Business and Management*, compiled by Jerry M. Rosenberg, defines some 10,000 terms from over 40 different fields of business, ranging from accounting to warehousing. Slang and acronyms are included in addition to standard business terms, and definitions are clear and succinct. The emphasis, as in most business dictionaries, is on current usage; derivations are not included. Appendixes present equivalent measures, Celsius and Fahrenheit equivalents, interest and income tables, foreign currencies, graduate business and management programs, quotations, and a chronology of major business and economic events in the United States. Rosenberg's *Dictionary of Business and Management* is one of the most comprehensive general business dictionaries and belongs in most libraries.

Christine Ammer and Dean Ammer's *Dictionary of Business and Economics* is another reference staple. Although it includes fewer terms than Rosenberg, its definitions are longer and are occasionally supplemented with charts, graphs, and formulas. The focus is also somewhat different. Economic theory, biographies of important economists, and relevant legislation are included as well as basic business concepts. Since there is considerable overlap between business practice and economic theory, the combination is a useful one. The authors also include a brief list of periodicals that contain economic and financial statistics and a selected bibliography of historically significant business and economics books.

No reference collection should be without *The McGraw-Hill Dictionary of Modern Economics*. As its subtitle indicates, it is arranged in two parts. The first lists and defines basic words, phrases, and concepts. Although the emphasis is on economics, many business terms are also included. Definitions range in length from a few sentences to a page or more, and are sometimes supplemented by tables, graphs, and other illustrations. Further, most entries include citations to sources that provide more detailed explanations of the concepts under consideration.

The second part is a listing of more than 200 important organizations. It includes trade and professional associations (the American Council of Life Insurance, for example, and the American Economic Association), federal and international government agencies (the

Bureau of Labor Statistics and the International Labour Organisation), research institutions (the University of Michigan's Institute for Social Research), and many other organizations. Entries in this section are at least a paragraph long, and frequently include the organization's address and significant publications about it or issued by it.

The dictionaries that have been discussed above are basic. Other general business dictionaries provide a slightly different focus.

Janis, J. Harold. **Modern Business Language and Usage in Dictionary Form.** Garden City, N.Y.: Doubleday, 1984. 506p.

Hendrickson, Robert. **Business Talk: The Dictionary of Business Words and Phrases.** New York: Stein and Day, 1984. 251p.

Most general business dictionaries present current definitions of terms but omit or treat cursorily the actual usage or derivation of words. *Modern Business Language and Usage in Dictionary Form* and *Business Talk* provide useful supplementary information.

Modern Business Language lists more than 3,500 words and phrases. For each, it includes a brief definition, followed by a sentence illustrating its proper use. A bibliography of general and specialized dictionaries, guides to English usage, style manuals, newspapers and periodicals, and books on communication and composition is appended.

Business Talk, described by its compiler as a "relaxed lexicon," focuses on the origins of colorful words and phrases from such fields of business as marketing, advertising, finance, accounting, management, and manufacturing. Such terms as *blue-chip stock, blue sky laws, tontine,* and *go-go-funds* are included. *Business Talk* is a mixture of standard business vocabulary, slang, and words and phrases drawn from fields other than business, and while it is intended as much for browsing as it is for quick reference, it is nonetheless useful for its descriptions of the derivations of many commonly used business terms.

Other general business dictionaries are written with special users in mind. They may, for example, be intended for business students or managers or small business people. Most of these dictionaries duplicate coverage of the titles already discussed, and while they are not absolutely essential, they are useful in some library settings.

The general business dictionaries discussed thus far are American publications. For coverage of British terms, some of which may be considerably different from American business language, a representative collection of British business dictionaries is also useful. A number of such publications are available. Two of the most widely used titles are listed below.

Johannsen, Hano, and G. Terry Page. **International Dictionary of Management.** 3rd ed. New York: Nichols Publishing, 1986. 370p.

Adam, J. H. **Longman Dictionary of Business English.** Harlow, Essex: Longman, 1982. 492p.

The *International Dictionary of Management* defines over 6,000 business and management terms, phrases, acronyms, and organizations. Somewhat similar coverage is offered in the *Longman Dictionary of Business English*, which lists and defines vocabulary from such fields as management, accounting and taxation, economic theory, shipping and insurance, and commercial law. Many of the definitions are, in fact, accompanied by "field labels" which identify the type of business activities to which the terms belong. An appendix, "Useful Information," presents data on weights, measures, and temperature; chemical symbols; countries of the world, showing for each its language(s) and currency; and international time differences.

Business vocabulary reflects the constant change characteristic of business. In addition, it makes frequent use of specialized jargon and slang, which are also subject to change. As a result, it is important that a collection of business dictionaries be as current as possible. The librarian who does not regularly update business dictionaries is doing library users a disservice. However, while there is no dearth of new business dictionaries, not all are worth collecting. Accordingly, librarians will want to consult many of the bibliographies and guides mentioned in the previous sections to identify some of the best and most useful dictionaries.

Multilingual Business Dictionaries

Although this book emphasizes American business practice, to ignore another type of business dictionary would be remiss: dictionaries that present business terms in a variety of languages. Unlike their general business counterparts, these dictionaries do not include definitions. They are used instead by business people who need to determine the English equivalent of a foreign term, or the foreign version of an English phrase.

Appleby, Barry Leon. **Elsevier's Dictionary of Commercial Terms and Phrases.** Amsterdam: Elsevier, 1984. 1083p.

Isaacs, Alan. **The Multilingual Commercial Dictionary.** New York: Facts on File, 1980. 486p.

Elsevier's Dictionary of Commercial Terms and Phrases brings together English, German, Spanish, French, and Swedish business terms and expressions. The *Dictionary* presents a "Basic Table," a numbered, alphabetic listing of terms in English followed by their foreign counterparts. It, in turn, is followed by separate alphabetical lists of English, German, Spanish, French, and Swedish words accompanied by the numeric designations used in the table. Someone encountering the phrase *gozar de buena reputación*, for example, could refer to the Spanish section and determine that the appropriate numeric designation is 3541. By turning to that number in the basic table, the researcher would learn that the English language equivalent is *to enjoy a good reputation.*

The Multilingual Commercial Dictionary includes commonly used terms in English, Spanish, French, Italian, and Portuguese. It is less comprehensive than *Elsevier's Dictionary* and its arrangement is somewhat different as well. *The Multilingual Commercial Dictionary* intermixes terms in all of the languages represented. Accordingly, *aboard* is followed by *abogado*, and *private sector* by *Privatunternehmen*. Each entry lists the key term in boldface type and is followed by its foreign-language equivalents.

For more intensive coverage of foreign business vocabulary, dictionaries that pair English terms with their equivalents in a specific foreign language are useful. A wide variety of such publications are available; there are, for example, English/German and English/Spanish dictionaries as well as similar works in other languages. While a comprehensive collection of all such dictionaries in every language is generally impractical, each library's collection should, of course, reflect the interests and needs of its own users.

Acronyms and Abbreviations Dictionaries

The language of business has its own unique vocabulary, filled with jargon and slang. It also makes frequent use of abbreviations and acronyms, and while some of these designations are commonly recognized, others can be baffling to the librarian or researcher new to the field. Offhanded references by patrons to M1, NASDAQ, GNMA, or CFTC are not unusual, and often a librarian must refer to a list of acronyms or abbreviations in order to comprehend fully a request for assistance.

Some of the most widely used business acronyms, included in this book, are listed in appendix A. A far more comprehensive list, however, is available in the following standard reference work.

Towell, Julie E., and Helen E. Sheppard, eds. **Acronyms, Initialisms & Abbreviations Dictionary.** 12th ed. Detroit: Gale Research Co., 1987. 3v.

The *Acronyms, Initialisms & Abbreviations Dictionary* lists over 420,000 acronyms, initialisms, abbreviations, contractions, alphabetic symbols, and "similar condensed appellations." Although all disciplines and fields are represented in the *Dictionary*, many of the items listed are drawn from business and trade or are directly relevant to it. The *Dictionary* is issued in three volumes. The first, which actually consists of three volumes, alphabetically lists acronyms and abbreviations and the words or phrases that they represent. Volume 2, *New Acronyms, Initialisms & Abbreviations*, is comprised of an interedition supplement to volume 1, and the third volume is a *Reverse Acronyms, Initialisms & Abbreviations Dictionary*. By consulting this most comprehensive of acronyms dictionaries, the full text counterparts of most such business designations can be readily identified.

ALMANACS

Almanacs are an essential part of any reference collection, making it possible to find quickly current information about a wide range of subjects. They may, for example, include summary country information, lists of award and prize winners, demographic and economic statistics, chronologies, and directories. Even such general titles as *The World Almanac* include a surprising amount of business information, but the following special almanac is particularly useful.

Levine, Sumner N., ed. **The Dow Jones-Irwin Business and Investment Almanac.** Homewood, Ill.: Dow Jones-Irwin, 1977- . Annual.

The Dow Jones-Irwin Business and Investment Almanac is a veritable cornucopia of business information. It is arranged in 22 main sections, each focusing on a specific aspect of the economy, business, or investment. Using it, readers can review the past year's business events, assess the recent performance of specific industries, identify the country's largest companies (or brokerage houses or public accounting firms), locate the closest Small Business Administration field office, or learn how to interpret a newspaper stock price table. It is filled with statistics, graphs, charts, glossaries, bibliographies, and directories. Each year, the *Almanac* adds new features. In the 1987 edition, for example, a list of America's most and least admired corporations, federal deficit projections, summaries of the 1986 tax law, and a list of state business assistance centers were included for the first time.

Although some of the information presented is original, most of it has been culled from other sources such as business and trade journals and government documents. Many of these primary sources are, in fact, common to libraries. The lists of largest companies, for example, are based on *Fortune*'s annual rankings. Researchers in need of the most current information would do well to consult the original source. The *Almanac* remains extremely useful, however, for finding quick factual information and for identifying the sources in which more detailed or more current information may be found. It is a basic business reference source.

ENCYCLOPEDIAS

Although many disciplines are represented by comprehensive, multivolume encyclopedias, business is not one of them. Instead, the emphasis is on single-volume works that deal with specific fields of business. Some of the best known of these publications are the *Encyclopedia of Banking and Finance*, the *Encyclopedia of Accounting Systems*, and the *Encyclopedia of Investments*. These and several other specialized encyclopedias will be discussed in later chapters, but it may be useful to consider here some titles that have more general applications.

Greenwald, Douglas. **Encyclopedia of Economics.** New York: McGraw-Hill, 1982. 1070p.

Heyel, Carl, ed. **The Encyclopedia of Management.** 3rd ed. New York: Van Nostrand Reinhold, 1982. 1371p.

As was mentioned earlier, there is considerable overlap between business and economics. The *Encyclopedia of Economics*, which contains articles on over 300 different topics, reflects this overlap. In addition to articles on economic theory, it includes many that are directly relevant to business, covering specific investment mediums, basic statistical measures of economic and business well-being, government agencies responsible for the regulation of business activities, and other topics. "Bond Rating Agencies," for example, describes the history of, basis for, and importance of such ratings and compares the rating categories used by Standard & Poor's and Moody's. Each article is signed, and frequently includes suggestions for further reading. Appendixes classify articles by economic field and present a chronology of "Economic Events, Technological Developments, Financial Developments, and Economic Thought," beginning with 400,000 B.C. ("Homo Sapiens") and ending in 1981 ("Supply-Side Economics Popularized"). Subject and name indexes are also included.

Because managers are required to understand the fundamentals of many different business operations, encyclopedias of management usually provide good, general syntheses of basic business concepts and practices. Although a number of such encyclopedias are available, one of the best is *The Encyclopedia of Management*. Articles cover different aspects of corporate planning, research and development, business logistics, manufacturing, market research, advertising, and sales in addition to management. The articles, which are arranged alphabetically from "Accounting" through "Zero Defects," may vary in length from a paragraph or two to several pages and usually include cross-references and citations to additional sources.

The *Encyclopedia* also contains a guide to "core subject" readings, listing under each topic relevant articles and the order in which they should be read. In addition, it lists universities and colleges accredited by the American Assembly of Collegiate Schools of Business (AACSB) and includes both an index and a bibliography of all sources cited in the main text of the *Encyclopedia*.

Both the *Encyclopedia of Economics* and *The Encyclopedia of Management* are useful for a general overview of business and for brief introductions to specific fields of business.

HANDBOOKS

The difference between single-volume encyclopedias and business handbooks is often negligible. Both are good sources of quick, factual information, but, as a rule, handbooks tend to cover fewer topics at greater length than do encyclopedias and often presuppose a basic understanding of the subject. The following title represents handbooks that survey an array of business activities.

Fallon, William K., ed. **AMA Management Handbook.** 2nd ed. New York: AMACOM, 1983. 1872p.

The American Management Association (AMA) is the premier professional association of managers in this country. Among other services, it offers several well-written and useful business titles through its publishing agency, AMACOM. The *AMA Management Handbook* is typical. Although the *Handbook* emphasizes management, it covers other topics as well: examples include manufacturing; purchasing, transportation, and physical distribution; marketing; information systems and technology; packaging; and public relations. Each of the chapters is written by an expert and includes graphs, charts, and sample forms. A detailed index is appended. Although the *Handbook* is somewhat more technical than the one-volume encyclopedias listed above, it also provides more thorough treatment of the subjects being discussed.

Most handbooks focus on specific business activities such as insurance and accounting. Several specialized handbooks will be discussed in chapters 9 through 18; still others can be identified by consulting standard business bibliographies and guides.

Although the basic reference sources that have been described in this chapter are important, they are by no means the only useful sources of business information. The next seven chapters will treat business information available in other formats, including directories, periodicals and newspapers, looseleaf services, government documents, statistics, vertical file materials, and databases.

NOTES

[1]*Business Information: Applications and Sources* is the most comprehensive of several computer-generated guides compiled by Van Mayros and D. Michael Werner. Readers should be forewarned that three additional titles—*Data Bases for Business, Guide to Information from Government Sources*, and *Information Sourcebook for Marketers and Strategic Planners*—are essentially spinoffs of *Business Information* and consist largely of extracts from it.

[2]Orders for the *Baker Library Mini-Lists* and other Baker Library publications must be prepaid. To obtain a current publications and price list, write to:

Publications Office
Baker Library
Harvard Business School
Soldiers Field
Boston, MA 02163

Dalinsky's Drug Store in Georgetown decides to merge with Fischetti's Meat Market in Bethesda. Dalinsky & Fischetti can't agree on which name to use, so they call the company the Great American Drug & Meat Company.... They take over the Aetna Curtain Company, Markay Life Insurance Company, Mary Smith Pie and Bakery Company, Winston Life Preserver Company, Washington Green Sox Baseball Club, the Norfolk (basketball) Warriors, and a bank, another bank, a mutual fund, a fried chicken franchise company....

—Dick Levin, *Buy Low, Sell High, Collect Early and Pay Late*

2

DIRECTORIES

BACKGROUND

Among the most frequently asked business reference questions are those involving the identification of the manufacturers of a particular product, the addresses and telephone numbers of specific companies, or the names of their key executives. Directories, which supply the answers to these and many other questions, are of prime importance in business reference. At a minimum, a good business directory will include the names, addresses, and telephone numbers of the companies it lists as well as the names of their chief executives and, often, a phrase or code describing the products or services offered by each company.

Business Establishments Not Listed

Many of the questions requiring the use of business directories are easy to answer. Verifying the address of Union Carbide's corporate headquarters or the name of the president of General Electric is reference service at its most basic. Not all such seemingly simple requests for business information, however, are so quickly satisfied. It is an inescapable fact of reference life that nearly two-thirds of all American businesses are not listed in standard, printed commercial directories. There are presently some 14.5 million business enterprises in the United States.[1] As shown in figure 2.1, the Fortune 500 companies, the top-rated, *blue-chip* companies with which everyone is familiar, are really just the tip of the iceberg.

Only one of the standard business directories found in most reference collections—Dun & Bradstreet's *Million Dollar Directory*—lists more than 1 percent of U.S. enterprises. The most comprehensive listing of American businesses is *Dun's Business Identification Service*, a microfiche collection of

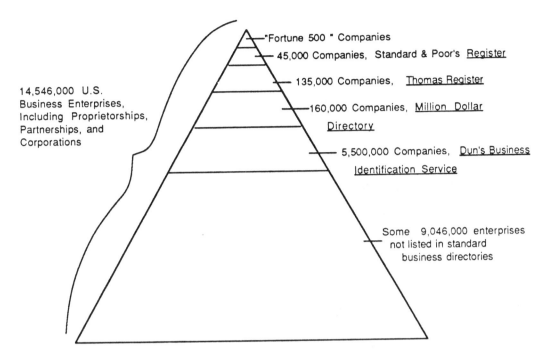

14,546,000 U.S. Business Enterprises, Including Proprietorships, Partnerships, and Corporations

"Fortune 500" Companies

45,000 Companies, Standard & Poor's Register

135,000 Companies, Thomas Register

160,000 Companies, Million Dollar Directory

5,500,000 Companies, Dun's Business Identification Service

Some 9,046,000 enterprises not listed in standard business directories

Fig. 2.1. U.S. business enterprises.

the names and addresses of all of the companies for which Dun & Bradstreet has credit reports, and it includes slightly more than one-third of all business enterprises. So, at least some of the time, printed directories will not answer what initially seem to be very simple requests for directory information.

In some instances, a company may not be listed because it is too small. A two-person accounting firm in Oshkosh, Wisconsin, is not likely to be included in any of the standard printed business directories. Neither enough people are employed nor enough money is earned for the firm to be included in a national or even a state directory. Furthermore, it provides a service rather than a product, and directory listings for businesses in the service sector are generally more difficult to find than for those in the manufacturing sector.

Public and Private Companies

Another important distinction must be kept in mind, the difference between public and private companies. A *public* or *publicly traded company* is one that sells stock to the public and that in effect is publicly owned. The federal government and most state governments have very strict laws about information that these companies *must* provide, both to the government and to stockholders. As a result, information on these companies is relatively easy to find.

A *private* or *privately held company*, also referred to as a *closely held* company, is one that does *not* sell stock to the public. It is usually exempt from the detailed reporting required of public companies and, as a result, information about many of these companies will be difficult to find. Some directories include information about the larger private companies, but as a rule, private companies are less often listed in directories than are public companies.

Parent Companies, Subsidiaries, Divisions, and Affiliates

Failure to find a company listing in a major national directory does not mean that one should give up. While the firm might be a small, privately held company about which nothing in print can be found, it is also possible that it is a subsidiary or a division of another, larger company. The librarian looking for the address of Giorgio, Inc., a perfume manufacturer, is contending with this problem. Clearly, Giorgio is well known; commercials for its products are regularly aired on television. One might reasonably expect to find it listed in all of the major national business directories. Not all directories include it, however, because it is a subsidiary of a larger company, Avon Products, Inc. In these days of corporate takeovers and conglomerates, it is entirely possible that the company being sought is owned by yet another company. And while *some* subsidiaries and divisions are cited separately in basic business directories, not all of them are.

Figure 2.2 presents some of the divisions and subsidiaries of the Coca-Cola Company. The business novice may be surprised to learn that Belmont Springs Water and Columbia Pictures are owned by Coca-Cola. As charts go, this is a simple one. Only three types of relationships are shown–parent company, subsidiary, and division. These are important concepts, terms employed frequently by library users, and it is essential to understand just what they mean.

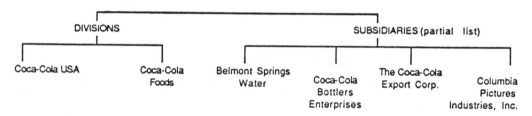

Fig. 2.2. The Coca-Cola Company.

A *parent company* is a company that operates and controls other separately chartered businesses. The Coca-Cola Company is the parent company for Belmont Springs Water and Columbia Pictures, for example, and RJR Nabisco is a parent company that owns and operates several separately chartered companies, such as Del Monte.

A *subsidiary* is a company that, although separately chartered, is owned or controlled by another company. Normally, the parent company owns at least 50 percent of its subsidiary's stock. If all of the stock is owned by the parent company, the subsidiary is referred to as *wholly owned*. Del Monte is a subsidiary of RJR Nabisco because, although it is a separately established business, RJR Nabisco owns and controls it. Subsidiaries began as separate businesses and have been acquired or taken over by the parent company. Columbia Pictures, for example, was incorporated in New York in 1924; it was not acquired by Coca-Cola until 1982. To further complicate matters, subsidiaries often have subsidiaries of their own. Del Monte, for example, has several subsidiaries, ranging from Banana Processors, Inc., to Southern Stevedoring Co., Inc. While major subsidiaries may be listed separately in some of the basic business directories, often it is necessary to consult special directories of subsidiaries in order to find information about them.

A *division* is a functional area or activity within the company. Unlike a subsidiary, it is not a separately chartered business. Coca-Cola USA and the Coca-Cola Foods Division are, for example, divisions of the Coca-Cola Company.

Finally, an *affiliate* is a separately chartered business whose shares are owned by one or more companies, with the level of ownership by any one company generally less than 50 percent.

Most of the time, directory inquiries will be for large companies which can be easily located. If, however, a company name does not sound familiar or if a search for it has proven unsuccessful, answers to the following questions should be sought.

1. *How big is the company?* Many publishers require that a company's assets, sales or number of employees must meet certain minimum standards in order for it to be listed.

2. *Is the company public or private?* Private companies are often not included in business directories; public companies usually are.

3. *What is the company's business?* Companies that manufacture or sell products are generally better represented in directories than are those that sell services.

4. *Is the company a subsidiary, a division, or an affiliate of another company?* If so, it may be necessary to consult a directory that lists them separately or links them with the appropriate parent companies.

With the answers to these questions in hand, the information search strategy can be modified, and other more specialized directories can be consulted, online directory files such as *Electronic Yellow Pages* can be accessed, or the information can be sought from government agencies and other organizations.

To reiterate: Most directory questions are simple to answer. With a few exceptions—usually caused by one or more of the above factors—they can be answered using the directories described in this chapter.

STANDARD INDUSTRIAL CLASSIFICATION SYSTEM

In addition to listing company addresses, telephone numbers, and officers, many directories also categorize companies by the activities in which they are engaged. Often these activities are designated by the use of a government-devised system of numeric codes, called the Standard Industrial Classification system (SIC). The SIC attempts to classify all business establishments by the types of products or services they make available. Establishments engaged in the same activity, whatever their size or type of ownership, are assigned the same SIC code.

SIC Hierarchy

The Standard Industrial Classification system is divided into 11 broad divisions, such as "Construction," "Retail Trade," and "Agriculture, Forestry, and Fishing." These divisions are subdivided into 99 two-digit major groups. Major groups are subdivided into three-digit individual groups, and individual groups into four-digit industry codes, the designation most often used in directories. As figure 2.3 (see page 24) indicates, the classification becomes more precise as more digits are added.

For example, one can move from Division D, "Manufacturing," to Major Group 20, "Food and Kindred Products," to Individual Group 206, "Sugar and Confectionery Products," to Industry Code 2067, "Chewing Gum," the SIC for establishments "primarily engaged in manufacturing chewing gum or chewing gum base" (see figure 2.4, page 24).

Someone seeking to identify the major manufacturers of chewing gum would simply turn to the SIC section of the directory and compile a list of all of the companies grouped under SIC code 2067.

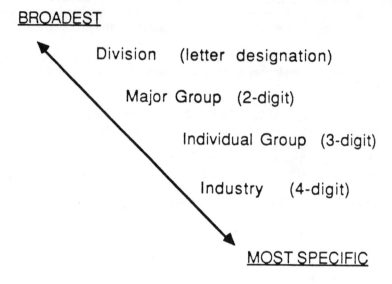

BROADEST

Division (letter designation)

Major Group (2-digit)

Individual Group (3-digit)

Industry (4-digit)

MOST SPECIFIC

Fig. 2.3. SIC hierarchy.

SIC Code	Categories (Levels)	Division, Group & Industry
Division D	Division	Manufacturing
20	Major group	Food and kindred products
206	Individual group	Sugar and confectionery products
2067	Industry	Chewing gum

Fig. 2.4. Example of the SIC hierarchy.

Figure 2.4 is a somewhat misleading example, because SIC 2067 is one of the few codes under which only one product is listed. More often, several related products will be grouped under the same four-digit industry code. For example, SIC 2032 is the industry code for "Canned Specialties," and examination of the products grouped under this code, shown in figure 2.5, reveals products as diverse as baby foods and tamales.

Thus, while SIC 2032 is the proper designation for canned baby foods, it is not safe to assume that *all* companies grouped under that code in directories manufacture baby foods. They do not. They may specialize in canned soup, or mincemeat, or chop suey, or any other canned specialty product. Librarians should keep these multiple-product entries in mind when using directories, realizing that in many instances a four-digit SIC code may be misleading. Good reference service requires not only that the proper SIC code be identified,

203   CANNED, FROZEN, AND PRESERVED FRUITS, VEGETABLES, AND
       FOOD SPECIALTIES

2032   **Canned Specialties**

Establishments primarily engaged in canning specialty products, such as baby foods, nationality speciality foods, and soups, except seafood. Establishments primarily engaged in canning seafoods are classified in Industry 2091.

Baby foods (including meats), canned	Macaroni, canned
Bean sprouts, canned	Mexican foods, canned
Beans, baked: with or without meat— canned	Mincemeat, canned
Broth, except seafood: canned	Nationality specialty foods, canned
Chicken broth and soup, canned	Native foods, canned
Chili con carne, canned	Pasta, canned
Chinese foods, canned	Puddings, except meat: canned
Chop suey, canned	Ravioli, canned
Chow mein, canned	Soups, except seafood: canned
Enchiladas, canned	Spaghetti, canned
Food specialties, canned	Spanish foods, canned
Italian foods, canned	Tamales, canned
	Tortillas, canned

Fig. 2.5. Products assigned SIC code 2032. Reprinted from the U.S. Office of Management and Budget, *Standard Industrial Classification Manual* (Springfield, Va.: National Technical Information Service, 1987).

but also that any other products sharing the same SIC code be noted. Often, a four-digit SIC code may include too many different products to be really useful.[2]

Although most directories that feature SIC listings also include a brief list and description of the SIC codes, by far the most detailed information can be found in the *Standard Industrial Classification Manual*, a basic business reference source.

U.S. Office of Management and Budget. **Standard Industrial Classification Manual.** Springfield, Va.: National Technical Information Service, 1987. 703p.

The *SIC Manual* consists of lists and descriptions, arranged by divisions, of industries, products, and services. Figure 2.5 is the *SIC Manual*'s entry for SIC 2032.

An alphabetical index lists all products and services featured in the main part of the *Manual*, including for each item its SIC code and the division to which it is assigned. Using it, one can determine the appropriate SIC for a particular product or service. If a description of the code itself is essential, or if one wants to find out what *other* products or services have been assigned the same SIC code, one can turn to the front of the volume.

Drawbacks to the SIC Codes

The *Manual* is intended to be revised every five years to coincide with publication of the economic censuses, with a major revision every ten years. Critics of the SIC system argue that it is too infrequently updated to reflect current business trends and technologies. This is, in fact, one of the system's most serious weaknesses. It fails to keep pace with and reflect the development of new industries and technologies. Another weakness—the imprecision of many four-digit SIC codes—was discussed earlier.

In an attempt to cope with obsolete and overgeneralized SIC codes, some business publishers have devised modifications to the SIC system. The one most commonly encountered in libraries is that developed by Predicasts, a Cleveland-based publisher of marketing data. The Predicasts system uses seven-digit SICs for a greater level of specificity and, when necessary, creates new codes for products for which there are no existing SIC codes.[3]

While the Standard Industrial Classification system has its flaws, it is nonetheless a useful scheme, making it possible to standardize the gathering and publication of information about the diverse business enterprises that characterize our economy. The frequent use of SIC codes in the standard business directories that follow attest to the system's continued importance and usefulness in spite of its faults.

BASIC BUSINESS DIRECTORIES

There are three standard business directories with which every reference librarian should be familiar. They are *Standard & Poor's Register of Corporations, Directors, and Executives*, the *Million Dollar Directory*, and *Thomas Register of American Manufacturers and Thomas Register Catalog File*. While not quite so well known, a fourth directory, the *Standard Directory of Advertisers*, is also helpful and is used heavily by those who are familiar with it. Each of these major business directories deserves close examination.

Standard & Poor's Register of Corporations, Directors, and Executives. New York: Standard & Poor's, 1928- . 3v. Annual, with supplements.

Million Dollar Directory. Parsippany, N.J.: Dun's Marketing Services, 1959- . 5v. Annual.

Standard Directory of Advertisers: Classified Edition. Wilmette, Ill.: National Register Publishing, 1915- . Annual.

Thomas Register of American Manufacturers and Thomas Register Catalog File. New York: Thomas Publishing, 1905- . 21v. Annual.

Standard & Poor's Register of Corporations, Directors, and Executives is a three-volume annual, kept up-to-date by three cumulated supplements. Volume 1 lists, by company name, some 45,000 businesses. Although a number of Canadian and international businesses are included, the emphasis is on American companies. Each listing includes company name, address, and telephone number; names and titles of principal officers; the names of the company's primary accounting, bank, and law firms; a description of and the SIC codes for the company's major products or services; and, when available, annual sales and number of employees. In addition, if the company is publicly held, the exchanges on which the company's stock is traded are also noted. Finally, divisions and subsidiaries are listed under the parent name unless they are so large that they merit a separate entry. The entry for Grantree Corporation, shown in figure 2.6, is typical.

Volume 2 is a biographical directory, which includes brief company affiliation and biographical information on 72,000 company officers, directors, and trustees. Usually included are year of birth, college attended and date of graduation, current position and business address, home address, fraternal memberships, and organizations and/or companies of which the individual is a director.

The third volume is comprised of indexes listing Standard Industrial Classification codes and the companies categorized under each code, a geographic index, lists of new additions to the directory, an obituary section, and a corporate family index that lists parent companies, divisions, subsidiaries, and affiliates.

Although the *Register* lists fewer companies than the *Million Dollar Directory* or *Thomas Register*, it lists many companies that the other directories do not contain. In addition, it often includes officers who are ranked further down the executive hierarchy than president or vice president. This can be particularly useful when looking for the name of a company sales director or purchasing officer.

*Chrm, Pres & Chief Exec Officer—Walker M. Treece
Exec V-P (Fin & Admin) & Treas—Gary A. Kisling
V-P (Rental)—Charles P. Murphy
V-P (Retail)—LaVern J. Bender
V-P (Rental Oper)—Zolman M. Cohen
V-P (Mktg)—G. Buck Fahland
Secy—J. Franklin Cable
Accts—Peat, Marwick, Mitchell & Co., Portland, Ore.
Primary Bank—First Interstate Bank of Oregon
Primary Law Firm—Miller, Nash, Wiener, Hager & Carlsen
Revenue: $74.90Mil   Employees: 1,100
Stock Exchange(s): NAS
        *Also DIRECTORS—Other Directors Are:
Raymond M. Alexander   Howell Appling, Jr.
Claire M. Gray   George E. Keck
R. H. Noyes, Jr.   Lyman E. Seely
BUSINESS: Furniture rental & sales
S.I.C. 7394

Fig. 2.6. Sample entry, *Standard & Poor's Register*. Reprinted by permission from *Standard & Poor's Register of Corporations, Directors, and Executives*, 1985 edition.

The *Million Dollar Directory* is another standard business directory, one whose scope and arrangement has changed several times during the past decade. At present, it consists of six volumes: five are included with the subscription and a sixth must be purchased separately. The first three volumes alphabetically list some 160,000 American companies having an indicated net worth exceeding $500,000; the fourth and fifth volumes are geographic and industry indexes. The sixth volume, "Top 50,000 Companies," lists those companies in volumes 1 through 3 with an indicated net worth of more than $1,850,000.

Each company listing in the *Million Dollar Directory* includes the name, address, and telephone number of the company; the company's state of incorporation; titles and names of key executives; categories of products and services offered; SIC code(s); approximate annual sales; and number of employees. Other data included are shown in the sample entry in figure 2.7.

D-U-N-S 00-479-7577
HOUSEHOLD UTILITIES INC (WI)
10 E Park Ave, Kiel, WI
Zip 53042   Tel (414) 894-2233
Sales 2MM   Emp 50
SIC 1711 3499 2599 5722 Heating & Ventilating
Contractor Mnfr Metal Horse Feeders & Stalls
FoodServing Carts & Ret Appliances
Bk Citizens State Bk
  Albert Deibele Sr   Ch Bd
  Albert J Deibele Jr   Pr
  Edward W Krueger Jr   VP
  Michael Steffen   VP
  Charles Deibele   VP Sec
  Eugene Beckman   Tr

Fig. 2.7. Sample entry, *Million Dollar Directory*. Reprinted by permission of Dun's Marketing Services from *Million Dollar Directory "Series,"* copyright 1987.

The first index, or "Series Cross-Reference by Geography" volume, lists businesses geographically by state and then by city or town. With this one can identify all of the major businesses (those having an indicated net worth of more than $500,000) in any city, ranging from New York to Hoople, North Dakota.

The second index volume, which lists businesses by industry classification, is equally important. By using it, one can identify the major manufacturers of specific products; by checking under SIC code 2067, shown in figure 2.8, one can compile a list of the major manufacturers of chewing gum in the United States.

2067 CHEWING GUM	
WRIGLEY WM JR CO° 410 N Michigan Ave Chicago, IL 60611	*P* 5345 *SIC* 2067
WARNER-LAMBERT CO 201 Tabor Rd Morris Plains, NJ 07950	*P* 5142 *SIC* 2834
TOPPS CHEWING GUM INC 254 36th St Brooklyn, NY 11232	*P* 4857 *SIC* 2067
SPANGLER CANDY CO° 400 N Portland St Bryan, OH 43506	*P* 4530 *SIC* 2065
FLEER CORP 10th & Somerville Ave Philadelphia, PA 19141	*P* 1803 *SIC* 2067

Fig. 2.8. Sample entry, "Industry" volume, *Million Dollar Directory*. Reprinted by permission of Dun's Marketing Services from *Million Dollar Directory "Series,"* copyright 1987.

Librarians are sometimes surprised to learn that Dun & Bradstreet does not actually sell its directories to subscribers; rather, it leases them. Unless special arrangements are made, the superseded editions must be returned to the publisher as soon as the new editions are received. Libraries that can make a strong case for retaining superseded editions – generally academic or research libraries that emphasize their importance for scholarly or historical research – are usually allowed to keep them. Each library must, however, receive permission from the publisher to do so. If the publisher agrees, the library must sign a contract promising that the superseded volumes will not be sent to other libraries and that they will be returned to the publisher should the subscription be cancelled.

This leasing arrangement is worth noting because, to some extent, it limits a library's options; subscribing to the *Million Dollar Directory* and other Dun & Bradstreet publications is an all-or-nothing proposition. Either they must be leased on an annual basis, or not at all; a library cannot choose to receive them every second or third year only. While this may not be a problem with the *Million Dollar Directory* – most libraries would choose to update it annually in any event – it can be a problem with some of the other more specialized Dun & Bradstreet directories for which annual updating may not always be feasible.

The *Standard Directory of Advertisers* is not nearly as well known as the *Million Dollar Directory* or *Standard & Poor's Register*, and lists far fewer companies. It is important, though, because it includes companies and organizations not listed in the other directories. The criterion for inclusion in the *SDA* is that the companies must allocate at least $75,000 in annual appropriations for either national or regional advertising campaigns. Companies that are too small to be included in the other basic business directories and some nonprofit organizations that advertise extensively are included in the *Standard Directory of Advertisers*. The 1987 edition, for example, lists organizations such as the U.S. Marine Corps and the Massachusetts State Lottery in addition to business enterprises. The entry for Elgin Watch International, in figure 2.9, is typical.

ELGIN WATCH INTERNATIONAL, INC.
(Div. of Elgin National Industries, Inc.)
33-00 Northern Blvd.
Long Island City, NY 11101
Tel.: 718-361-7720
Approx: Number Employees: 120
Mfr. Elgin, Waltham & Nelsonic Watches
Bernard Mermelstein (Chief Exec. Officer)
Steve Sack (V.P.-Sls.)
Robert Grossinger (V.P.-Mfg.)
Sidney Kaufman (Adv. Mgr.)

Advertising Agency:
Direct
(Appro.:.$500,000)
(Media: 4-8-10-15-16-19)
Distr.: Natl.

Fig. 2.9. Sample entry, *Standard Directory of Advertisers*. Reprinted by permission from *Standard Directory of Advertisers*, 1986 edition.

Each entry features information not found in the other directories, including annual advertising appropriations and type(s) of advertising media used, the advertising agency representing the company, and the names of key advertising, marketing, and sales executives. Companies are arranged by broad industry categories such as "Farm Equipment" and "Sporting Goods," with access facilitated by a company name index.

Another useful feature is the Tradename List, which lists brand names and the companies that own them. Since many business reference requests involve identifying the company that manufactures a specific brand, this list of 35,000 trade names can be very helpful. Using it, one can determine that *Golden Image* is the trade name for an imitation cheddar cheese produced by Kraft, that *Golden Grip* is the name for a line of bowling equipment manufactured by Brunswick, and that *Golden Light* cigarettes are manufactured by Lorillard.

Thomas Register of American Manufacturers and Thomas Register Catalog File is a multivolume annual that provides information on American manufacturers, distributors, and suppliers. Arrangement is in three main parts. Volumes 1 through 12 comprise the "Products and Services" section, with companies grouped by product and then by state and city. Thomas uses an arrangement called the *modified noun system*. Companies manufacturing animal cages, for example, are listed under "Cages: Animal," and those making tool chests are listed under "Chests & Cabinets: Tool." Sometimes a product may have several divisions. Buckle manufacturers, for example, are grouped under the following categories: army clothing, bag, bale tie, dog collar, jewelry, linemen's safety, plastic, safety, slide, shoe, steel, strap, and wire buckles! The entry for dog collar buckles in figure 2.10 (see page 30) is typical.

Volumes 13 and 14, the "Company Profiles" section, are the most heavily used volumes, alphabetically listing more than 123,000 companies. Compared to the other directories already discussed, the information given is rather brief, including only company name and address, telephone number, and products (see figure 2.11 on page 30). In some instances, a code rating the company's tangible assets is also featured. (Tangible assets are defined as anything that has physical, material substance, such as machinery, laboratory equipment, or stocks and bonds.)

BUCKLES: DOG COLLAR

AR: CONWAY
Leather Brothers, Inc. P.O. Box 1077-TR (Heavy Roller Buckles, Dees, Tuck Loops, Double Bar Buckles, Conway Buckles).. 1M+
CA: WILMINGTON
National Slide & Stamping Co. P.O. Box 877 ....NR
WIREWRIGHT CORP., THE 528-R N. Fries Ave. (ZIP 90744) (213—637-7400)..................................... 1M+
CT: MOUNT CARMEL
PARVA INDUSTRIES INC. 2974 Whitney Ave. (ZIP 06518) (203—248-5553)................................. 1M+
CT: NEWINGTON
Custom Metal Crafters, Inc. 817 N. Mountain Rd. .... 5M+
FL: OPA LOCKA
Sure-Snap South 4375 N.W. 128th St. (Snap Fasteners, Buckles, Clasps, Eyelets, Clips & Closure Hardware, Etc.)... 1/2M+
IL: ADDISON
Baron Manufacturing Co. 1200-T Capitol Dr. ...... 5M+
MA: CANTON
SX Industries Inc. 142T Will Dr. .... 1M+
NJ: LINDEN
Domar Buckle Mfg. Corp. P.O. Box 523, 2301 E. Edgar Rd. .... 1/2M+
NY: BROOKLYN
ALBEST METAL STAMPING CORP. 1 Kent Ave. (ZIP 11211) (Buckles, Rings, Wire Forms, Handbag Trimmings, Snaps & Clips) (718—388-6000) .. 10M+
NY: LONG ISLAND CITY
Plaxy Color, Inc. 11-01 40th Ave.................................NR
NY: NEW YORK
AMERICAN CORD & WEBBING CO., INC. 505-07 Eighth Ave. (ZIP 10018) (212—695-7340) .... 1M+
Axelrod, S. Co., Inc. 9 W. 30th St. (Metal Stampings, Castings, Rings, Swivels, Hooks) 1/4M–
Levin, Sam, Metal Accessories Corp. 236-T W. 26th St. ....NR
Sure-Snap Corp. 241 W. 37th St. (Snap Fasteners, Buckles, Clasps, Eyelets, Clips & Closure Hardware, Etc.)... 1/2M+
NY: WOODSIDE
Liberty Metal Products Co. 50-05 47th Av., P.O. Box 658-T.. 1M+
OH: ORRVILLE
Orrville Leather, Inc. P.O. Drawer 147-T................. 1M+
RI: PROVIDENCE
Rhode Island Buckle Co. 192-T Georgia Ave. ...... 1M+

Fig. 2.10. Sample entry, "Products and Services" volume, *Thomas Register*. Reprinted by permission from *Thomas Register of American Manufacturers*, 1987 edition.

LEATHER BROTHERS, INC., P.O. Box 1077-TR, Conway, AR 72032 (1M+) (IN AR Call: 501-329-9471)................................... Call Toll Free: 1-800-442-5522
(Leather & Nylon Pet Collars, Custom-Made Leather Goods, Pet Supplies, Horse Equipment, Belts & Belting, Strap Leather, Webbing, Rivets, Snaps, Dog Chains & Related Hardware)
(Ex.) (P.) L. Schrekenhofer; (G.M.) S. Schrekenhofer

Fig. 2.11. Sample entry, "Company Profiles" volume, *Thomas Register*. Reprinted by permission from *Thomas Register of American Manufacturers*, 1987 edition.

Volume 14 also includes a trademark index that can be used to identify manufacturers of specific products. When used in conjunction with the similar listing in the *Standard Directory of Advertisers*, many of the most frequently mentioned brands easily can be linked with their manufacturers.

Although company entries in both the "Products and Services" and "Company Profiles" volumes are normally rather brief, some companies have paid additional fees to include company logos or fuller product descriptions with their listings. Even more detailed information can be found in the "Thomcat Catalog File," volumes 15 through 21, which features the catalogs of 1,200 different companies. Information provided varies from company to company, but usually includes photographs, product specifications, and other data that can be extremely useful to suppliers, distributors, salesmen, and marketing specialists.

Standard & Poor's Register, the *Million Dollar Directory*, and *Thomas Register* are the most popular and heavily used of the national business directories. They are not, however, the only basic business directories. Others include *MacRae's Industrial Directory* and the *U.S. Industrial Directory*, as well as the *Standard Directory of Advertisers.* Researchers should be aware that while there is considerable overlap in coverage, each directory has its own unique features, and each lists companies not found in the other directories.

Companies not included in these standard directories may be too small, or based in another country, or part of a larger company. In these instances, one must consult special directories, some of which will be described later in this chapter. First, some of the guides that identify and list business directories will be mentioned.

GUIDES TO DIRECTORIES

Several of the basic business reference sources described in chapter 1 include information about directories. Other, more specialized directories are included in chapters focusing on specific subject areas such as accounting and banking. The *Encyclopedia of Business Information Sources* lists highly specialized as well as general directories. Using it, one can identify such diverse sources as the *Bee Researchers Directory, Wines and Vines Annual Directory*, and the *American Blue Book of Funeral Directors.* Although the titles are not annotated, price information is usually included in addition to standard bibliographic citations.

Marlow, Cecilia Ann, and Robert C. Thomas, eds. **The Directory of Directories.** 4th ed. Detroit: Gale Research Co., 1987. 2v. [Updated by *Directory Information Service*]

Klein, Bernard, ed. **Guide to American Directories.** 11th ed. Coral Springs, Fla.: B. Klein Publications, 1982. 560p.

The Directory of Directories, subtitled "An Annotated Guide to Approximately 9,600 Business and Industrial Directories, Professional and Scientific Rosters, Directory Databases, and Other Lists and Guides of All Kinds," groups directories under 16 broad subject categories such as "General Business Directories" and "Specific Industries and Lines of Business." In addition to annotations, entries include the publisher's address and telephone number, frequency of publication, number of pages, price, and other information useful in placing orders. The *Directory Information Service* supplements and updates the *Directory of Directories* between editions.

The *Guide to American Directories* lists nearly 7,000 trade, professional, and industrial directories. Each entry includes a brief annotation and the price of the directory at the time of publication. As with the *Directory of Directories*, arrangement is by subject classification, but much narrower categories, such as "Dairy, Egg, and Poultry Industries" and "Notions and Novelties," are used.

Examination of these guides will soon make one thing abundantly clear; few libraries have comprehensive or even representative directory collections listing all products, geographic areas, and types of companies. Such collections would be impossible for all but the largest and most affluent of business libraries. However, certain types of specialized directories are fairly common; these will be considered next.

SUBSIDIARIES, DIVISIONS, AND AFFILIATES

Some company divisions and subsidiaries do not merit separate entries in standard business directories. This is worth reemphasizing because many users (and some librarians) give up after unsuccessfully checking the standard business directories for specific companies. Failure to find a company listed in one of the basic directories does not mean that the desired information is not close at hand in a more specialized source. In many instances, the next logical step will be to check one or more of the directories that specialize in information about subsidiaries, divisions, and affiliates.

Directory of Corporate Affiliations. Wilmette, Ill.: National Register Publishing, 1967- . Annual.

America's Corporate Families: The Billion Dollar Directory. Parsippany, N.J.: Dun's Marketing Services, 1982- . Annual.

Two of the most heavily used sources are the *Directory of Corporate Affiliations* and *America's Corporate Families.* Each directory features lists of divisions and subsidiaries, but includes most information in the main section, which is arranged alphabetically by the name of the parent company. The entry for Hubbards Cupboard, Inc., in figure 2.12, taken from the *Directory of Corporate Affiliations*, is typical. Many corporations, of course, have subsidiaries and more divisions than are shown for Hubbards Cupboard. The entry for General Motors, for example, is over two pages long.

* 7790-000
HUBBARDS CUPBOARD, INC.
111-G Corporate Blvd.
South Plainfield, NJ 07080
Mailing Address: P.O. Box 3020
Edison, NJ 08818
Tel.: 201-769-7100 **NJ**
Approx. Sls.: $30,710,000 *Emp:* 325
Retail Convenience Foods, Cigars, Cigarettes & Tobacco; Video Film & Equip. Rental & Sales
S.I.C.: 2111; 5194; 2065; 5141; 5411
Alvin J. Rockoff *(Pres.)*
David Rockoff *(Chief Oper. Officer & Sec.)*
Arthur Kramer *(V.P. & Comptroller)*
Gerald H. Rockoff *(V.P. & Dir.-Site Devel.)*
Frederic S. Bear *(Pur. & Adv. Dir.)*
Board of Directors:
Alvin J. Rockoff
Arthur Kramer
David Rockoff
Gerald H. Rockoff

Divisions:

7790-003
Big A Provisions Div. **(1)**
54 B Brunswick Ave.
Edison, NJ 08817
Tel.: 201-287-5531
Groceries
S.I.C.: 5141
Hank Berger *(Gen. Mgr.)*

7790-001
Big A Tobacco Co., Div. **(1)**
54 B. Brunswick Ave.
Edison, NJ 08817 (NJ)
Tel.: 201-287-5531 (100%)
Emp: 9
Whl. Cigarettes, Tobacco & Candy
S.I.C.: 2111; 5194; 2065
Herman Berger *(Whl. Mgr.)*

7790-002
The First Row, Inc. **(1)**
2 W. Northfield Dr.
Livingston, NJ 07039 (NJ)
Tel.: 201-994-4099 (100%)
Emp: 3
Video Film Rental & Sls.; Video Equip. & Access. Sls.
S.I.C.: 3861
Gerald H. Rockoff *(V.P.)*

Fig. 2.12. Typical entry, *Directory of Corporate Affiliations.* Reprinted by permission from the *Directory of Corporate Affiliations*, 1987 edition.

By looking at the divisions listed in figure 2.12, one can see why these directories are so useful. Imagine that an irate customer wants to write to the person in charge of The First Row, Inc., about a defective videotape he recently purchased. We know from the entry that The First Row is a division of Hubbards Cupboard, Inc., and that The First Row's size (only three employees) makes it unlikely that it will be listed separately in any of the basic business directories. However, the patron does not know this, and may give up in frustration after failing to find it listed in *Standard & Poor's Register*, the *Million Dollar Directory*, or *Thomas Register*. The knowledgeable librarian who goes on to check subsidiary directories, however, will be successful.

While there is considerable overlap between *America's Corporate Families* and the *Directory of Corporate Affiliations*, each features some companies that are not included in the other. The *Directory of Corporate Affiliations* tends to include smaller companies, as well as branches and affiliates, which are not included in *America's Corporate Families*. However, *America's Corporate Families* lists over twice as many parent companies—some 8,600 as compared to the approximately 4,000 that are included in the *Directory of Corporate Affiliations*.

Who Owns Whom. London: Dun & Bradstreet International Ltd. Annual. [Separate editions for *Australasia & Far East; Continental Europe; North America;* and the *United Kingdom & Republic of Ireland*]

America's Corporate Families and International Affiliates. Parsippany, N.J.: Dun's Marketing Services, 1983- . Annual.

International Directory of Corporate Affiliations. Wilmette, Ill.: National Register Publishing, 1981- . Annual.

Directory of American Firms Operating in Foreign Countries. 11th ed. New York: World Trade Academy Press, 1987. 3v.

Other directories treat corporate ownership for multinational and foreign companies. A series called *Who Owns Whom* lists parents and subsidiaries in separate volumes for North America, the United Kingdom and Ireland, Continental Europe, and Australasia and the Far East. *America's Corporate Families and International Affiliates*, a companion volume to *America's Corporate Families*, and the *International Directory of Corporate Affiliations*, companion to the *Directory of Corporate Affiliations*, list foreign subsidiaries of U.S. parent companies and American subsidiaries of foreign parent companies. The *Directory of American Firms Operating in Foreign Countries* is used not only for standard subsidiary information, but also by those seeking employment abroad.

FOREIGN COMPANIES

Sometimes librarians will be asked to provide information on foreign companies.

Angel, Juvenal L., comp. **Directory of Foreign Firms Operating in the United States.** 5th ed. New York: World Trade Academy Press, 1986. 400p.

Arpan, Jeffrey S., and David A. Ricks. **Directory of Foreign Manufacturers in the United States.** 3rd ed. Atlanta: College of Business Administration, Georgia State University, 1985. 384p.

If the request is for an address for the corporate headquarters of a foreign company with American-based subsidiaries, the *Directory of Foreign Firms Operating in the United States* and the *Directory of Foreign Manufacturers in the United States* will be useful, as will the *International Directory of Corporate Affiliations* and *America's Corporate Families and International Affiliates*, mentioned in the preceding section.

If, however, the company has no U.S. subsidiaries, or if the information needed is a list of foreign companies manufacturing a particular product, consulting foreign and/or international directories will be necessary.

Directories that list the major business enterprises in specific countries can be tremendously useful, but they have drawbacks as well. Few libraries can afford to collect and keep current comprehensive collections of foreign business directories. They are expensive, and the level of demand for the information they contain often is not sufficient to justify their purchase. As a result, many libraries choose to collect foreign directories only for industrialized nations, or for those countries in which patron interest is particularly great. Two of the major publishers of foreign business directories are Dun & Bradstreet and Kompass. Dun & Bradstreet International, Ltd., publishes directories for Great Britain and Europe. Kompass presently issues directories for 17 countries, including Belgium, Singapore, and Sweden, with each directory usually published in the language of the country it represents. Thus, for all but the most linguistically accomplished researchers, scanning through the various Kompass directories may involve considerable guesswork. For countries not included in the series of directories issued by Dun & Bradstreet and Kompass, the librarian may have to identify publishers in specific countries, a process that can be time-consuming and often frustrating.

Since these directories typically cost between $200 and $300 each, only the most affluent libraries can afford comprehensive collections. As a result, many libraries will choose instead to collect international directories. Three of the most popular follow.

> **Principal International Businesses.** London: Dun & Bradstreet International, Ltd., 1974- . Annual.

> **Bottin International: International Business Register.** Paris: Didot-Bottin, 1895- . 2v. Annual.

> **Kelly's Business Directory.** East Grinstead, England: Kelly's Directories, 1880- . Annual. [Formerly *Kelly's Manufacturers and Merchants Directory*]

Principal International Businesses, a Dun & Bradstreet annual, provides information on more than 55,000 leading business enterprises in 133 different countries, ranging from Afghanistan to Zaire. The main section lists companies by country and then alphabetically by company name. Each entry includes company name and address, cable address or telex number, sales volume and number of employees (when this information is available), SIC code(s), and the name of the company's chief executive. If the company is a subsidiary, or if it imports or exports products, this information is also included.

Bottin International is another basic international directory, containing considerable information relating to international trade for each of the countries it covers. Arrangement is by country, with each country divided into two main sections. The geographical section includes general business and economic information about the country and its major cities. Included are country and city maps, trade statistics, lists of chief products and activities, legal holidays and business hours, and, for each important city, the addresses of its chamber of commerce, major advertising agencies, banks, newspapers and magazines, hotels and restaurants, and shipping and air lines. The second section lists leading exporters classified by specialty, such as tobacco or turpentine.

Kelly's Business Directory lists over 80,000 industrial and commercial enterprises. The directory is divided into three main sections: alphabetical, listing all British manufacturers, merchants, wholesalers, and firms; classified trade, grouping British enterprises by product or service provided; and international exporters and services arranged by products and subdivided by countries within continents. Although the focus is international, *Kelly's* real strength is its coverage of the British Isles.

STATE AND LOCAL DIRECTORIES

Many requests for business information require the use of directories that have far narrower geographic focuses than international or even national directories provide. State and local directories can be tremendously useful for locating information on companies too small to be included elsewhere. State industrial directories are published by a number of different organizations; state government agencies, trade associations, and commercial publishers are the most common. Although coverage will vary from one state to another, most directories include company name, address and telephone number, name of president or chief executive officer, approximate number of employees, and SIC or other product designation. While format is not always consistent, most directories usually include sections that arrange companies by city or county, by SIC or product, and by company name.

For many libraries, the collection of state directories will be limited to their own state's industrial directories. Larger business reference collections may include additional directories representing neighboring states or the most heavily industrial states. Some of the country's major business libraries include directories for all 50 states. State industrial directories are listed in both the *Directory of Directories* and the *Guide to American Directories*.

Two publishers, MacRae's and Manufacturer's News, Inc., compile and sell comprehensive collections of state industrial directories, making it possible to buy one, ten, or even fifty directories from one publisher. In many instances these commercially published directories cost considerably more than do those published by state government agencies, but to the librarian building a large state industrial directory collection, they offer the convenience of ordering from a single source, of automatic standing order plans (many government agencies and trade associations will not accept standing orders), and consistency of format. Another publisher, Colt, offers a microfiche library of state industrial directories. Again, the Colt collection offers convenience in ordering and updating state directory collections as well as savings in space, but since the fiche collection consists of copies of directories issued by many different public and private organizations, consistency of format is not one of its virtues.

While state industrial directories may provide adequate information on manufacturing establishments, they do not, as a rule, cover service industries or retailers. Although service directories for a few of the most populous states are now available, such directories are relatively rare. For information on service establishments, it may be necessary to consult a local directory. While only the largest metropolitan areas publish business directories — again, usually limited to manufacturing industries — almost all cities are represented by city directories. These annual or biennial publications include information on residents (most often, names, addresses, occupations, and homeowner/renter status) as well as classified sections which include information on local businesses.

Telephone directories are also useful for locating small business establishments, and since many libraries subscribe to *Phonefiche*, a microfiche collection of the white and yellow pages of telephone directories for many U.S. cities and towns, telephone directory information about small businesses located across the country may be readily available.

LISTS OF LARGEST COMPANIES

Librarians receive frequent requests for lists of largest companies. Since several sources rank companies by size, generally these questions are answered easily. The librarian, however, first should determine how the company's size is to be measured. Criteria used for ranking companies by size include annual sales, assets, profits, and number of employees; list makers use different criteria for compiling their lists. Two of the most frequently used lists are published as special issues of *Fortune* and *Forbes*.

The most widely consulted of these is the "Fortune 500," *Fortune*'s annual listing of the top 500 companies in the United States. The list, which usually appears in an April or May issue, uses annual sales volume to rank the 500 largest industrial companies. Each issue of the Fortune 500 also identifies "Who Did Best and Worst among the 500," using total return to investors, return on sales and assets, return on stockholders' equity, changes in sales, profits, sales per dollar of stockholders' equity and per employee, and money lost as criteria. Industry medians for each of 25 industries are included. Another section groups companies by industry categories and ranks them by 11 different measures. The Fortune 500 is an important list, because it is frequently used and cited. Many libraries, for example, try to collect annual reports for Fortune 500 companies because these are the companies for which information is most frequently sought.

In addition to the Fortune 500, *Fortune* publishes two additional lists. A June issue contains the "Service 500," a list of the 500 largest nonindustrial companies, and an August issue lists the 50 largest industrial corporations outside the United States. Although special issues of periodicals will be covered at length in the next chapter it is worth noting here that business periodical lists of largest companies can be extremely helpful to business researchers and to librarians. The Fortune 500 and the Fortune Service 500 are also available in the annual *Fortune Directory of U.S. Corporations.*

Another popular business magazine, *Forbes,* ranks and lists largest companies as well. *Forbes* calls its listing the "500s," because *Forbes* ranks companies not only by sales, as *Fortune* does, but also by other criteria, including assets, stock market value, and net profit. Separate lists using each of these criteria as determinants of company size are included in the *Forbes* annual directory issue. Another difference between the *Fortune* and *Forbes* lists is that, while the Fortune 500 is limited to industrial companies, the Forbes 500s include service companies (banks, insurance companies, airlines, and utilities) as well as manufacturers.

When the need is for a ranked list of several thousand companies, however, neither *Fortune* nor *Forbes* will suffice.

Dun's Business Rankings. Parsippany, N.J.: Dun's Marketing Service, 1982- . Annual.

Ward's Business Directory of Largest U.S. Companies. Belmont, Calif.: Information
   Access, 1961- . Annual.

Dun's Business Rankings presents the top 7,500 public and private U.S. companies, ranked both by number of employees and by sales volume. Separate sections make it possible to identify, for each state and for each of 152 industry categories, the companies with the highest sales volume and employing the greatest number of people. Entries are brief. In addition to company name, address, and telephone number, they include annual sales volume and rank, total number of employees and rank, number of employees at the location listed, primary SIC code, and, when applicable, the company's stock ticker symbol.

Ward's Business Directory of Largest U.S. Companies is different from *Dun's Business Rankings* in several important respects. First, it includes many more companies than are included in *Dun's. Ward's* lists 35,000 private companies with annual sales of $11 million or more and 7,000 public companies. Sales volume is the primary criterion used for rating companies. In addition, the main listings in *Ward's* are considerably more detailed than those in the Dun & Bradstreet directory. The entries include company name, address and telephone number, year founded, chief executive officer, annual sales, number of employees, SIC classification, selected financial and operating ratios, and other financial information.

Companies in *Ward's* are arranged in four sections. The first lists public companies, arranged within SIC codes by sales volume. The second combines both public and private companies, the third lists companies in zip code order by state, and the fourth lists them alphabetically with page references. In addition, *Ward's* presents ranked lists of the top 1,000 companies as determined by profit, sales volume, number of employees, high current ratios, and high capital expenditures. Two companion directories – *Ward's Business Directory of Major U.S. Private Companies* and *Ward's Business Directory of Major International Companies* – are also available.

TRADE DIRECTORIES

Many of the directories that already have been discussed list major companies under broad industry classifications. The businessperson seeking to identify companies under narrower product or service designations may need to consult a trade directory specializing in a particular industry or trade. Literally hundreds of such special directories are in print, each focusing on a specific industry. Some, such as those dealing with the petroleum, paper, textiles, and food industries, feature directories that rival standard business directories in size.

Others are considerably smaller, issued as paperbacks or even as pamphlets. Trade directories can be identified by using the guides to directories—the *Directory of Directories*, the *Guide to American Directories*, and the *Encyclopedia of Business Information Sources*—mentioned previously.

EMPLOYMENT DIRECTORIES

Business people and consumers are not the only ones who make frequent use of business directories. Another group is comprised of people in the job market who would like to enter the world of business. Frequently they use standard business directories to identify prospective employers. These sources, however, do not include the names and titles of personnel directors or any information about employee training programs or benefits. Such information can usually be obtained by consulting the following special employment directories.

CPC Annual. Bethlehem, Pa.: College Placement Council, Inc., 1951- . 3v. Annual.

The Career Guide/Dun's Employment Opportunities. Parsippany, N.J.: Dun's Marketing Services, 1983- . Annual.

Plunkett, Jack. **The Almanac of American Employers: A Guide to America's 500 Most Successful Large Corporations.** Chicago: Contemporary Books, 1985. 340p.

One of the most frequently used is the *CPC Annual*, which combines general articles concerning such aspects of the job search process as writing resumés with directories of major employers of engineering, science, computer, administrative, managerial, and general business personnel. Arrangement in the company directory sections is by company name. Each listing includes a brief description of the company, its employment opportunities, and employee benefits. Occupational, geographical, special employment, and employer indexes enhance access to the company listings.

The Career Guide contains information similar to that found in the *CPC Annual*, but lists more companies. Each entry includes an overview of the company itself, a list of the disciplines hired, a description of career development opportunities within the company, and employee benefits. Also included is the address to which employment inquiries should be sent and, in many instances, the name and title of the person to be contacted. The entry for Home Life Insurance Co., shown in figure 2.13 (see page 38), is typical. The main company listing section is supplemented by sections that list employers geographically and by broad (two-digit SIC) industry category, employer branch locations, and personnel consultants by state. Brief articles on job-hunting strategies and statistics indicating current employment patterns complete the directory.

The Almanac of American Employers is an inexpensive alternative to *The Career Guide*. For 500 companies "chosen specifically for their likelihood to provide long-lived jobs to the greatest number of employees" (p. 7), it lists and ranks salaries and employee benefits and assesses their financial stability. Each item of information about a company receives a point score. Companies are also assigned a composite score and rank. While interesting, some of the data used to rank companies are dated (salaries quoted, for example, are for 1983), but *The Almanac* is useful for its description of the type of business and number of employees and other general information about each company. Brief geographic, subsidiary, and brand-name indexes, and a series of appendixes that itemize pension plan considerations, suggest sources of additional company information, and present "Thoughts on Working for Big Business" are also included.

HOME LIFE INSURANCE CO*

New York, NY

Disciplines Hired Computer Science, Math/Statistics, Business Planning/Marketing, Accounting/Finance and Liberal Arts.

Company Overview Established in 1820, Home Life Insurance Company, Inc. is a multi-line insurance company.

Career Opportunities Home Life Insurance hires individuals for training positions in actuarial science, mathematics, underwriting, customer service, and computer science. Hiring is conducted through employment agencies, referrals, college recruiting, and advertisements in local newspapers for available positions.

Training and Career Development Employees gain experience through on-the-job and departmental training. Salesmen must also undergo a formal sales training program.

Additional Company Locations Home Life Insurance has locations in most major cities across the country.

Benefits Employee benefits include medical, health, hospital, life, and dental insurance, tuition reimbursement, and an investment plan.

Also Offered Summer Internships.

ADDRESS EMPLOYMENT INQUIRIES TO:

HOME LIFE INSURANCE CO*
253 Broadway
New York, NY 10007
Joseph Palya, Human Resources
(212) 306-2000

Fig. 2.13. Sample entry, *The Career Guide*. Reprinted by permission of Dun's Marketing Services from *The Career Guide: Dun's Employment Opportunities*, copyright 1987.

Although not directories per se, two books are extremely popular with people seeking jobs who would like additional information.

Moskowitz, Milton, Michael Katz, and Robert Levering, eds. **Everybody's Business: An Almanac. The Irreverent Guide to Corporate America.** New York: Harper & Row, 1980. 916p. [Supplemented by *Everybody's Business 1982 Update.* New York: Harper & Row, 1982. 64p.]

Levering, Robert, Milton Moskowitz, and Michael Katz. **The 100 Best Companies to Work for in America.** Reading, Mass.: Addison-Wesley, 1984. 372p.

Based on the premise that every company has its own distinctive style and personality, *Everybody's Business* attempts to reveal what makes each of 317 large U.S. companies unique. The corporate profiles, usually about two pages long, include basic information—sales and earnings figures, the company's "Forbes 500s" ranking, number of employees, and corporate brand names—as well as more subjective descriptions of the company's history, present management style, reputation, and public image.

Everybody's Business was published in 1980; most of the information it contains was gathered in 1979. Although a brief supplement was published in 1982, it, too, is dated and some of the information it contains is no longer accurate. Even so, the *Almanac* and the *Supplement* continue to be read widely for information that may be difficult to locate elsewhere. Here, for example, is an excerpt taken from the entry in *Everybody's Business* for *Reader's Digest*.

> Although many people in the magazine business change jobs frequently, most *Digest* staffers stay for years. For half a century, all employees have received year-end bonuses of approximately 15% of their salaries. The company subsidizes meals in the company cafeteria, where a full lunch ranges around $1 and the beverages are free. Everybody gets four weeks of vacation each year, and the whole operation shuts down every Friday in May, providing a month of three-day weekends. Working hours are a leisurely 8:30 to 4, with time off for lunch and coffee breaks. The company pays half the cost of any self-improvement course an employee takes, from Dale Carnegie to transcendental meditation; if the course is job related, the company pays for it all. (p. 394)

In addition to descriptions of how employees are treated, *Everybody's Business* often includes scathing commentary about corporate performance. It begins its description of Westinghouse, for example, in the following way.

> The nuclear reactor at Three Mile Island was *not* built by Westinghouse. That's the good news about this big Pittsburgh company. They run a distant second to General Electric in the electric equipment field, and their story in the last decade is a continuing tale of disasters, including an unsafe train-control system, defective turbine generators, broken contracts, and a nuclear power plant being built on the slope of an active volcano. It is a story that gives new meaning to the company's old slogan, "You can be sure if it's Westinghouse." (p. 632)

Patrons, particularly those seeking last-minute information about companies before job interviews, are much taken with *Everybody's Business*. While there is no doubt that it can provide useful and entertaining supplemental information about a company, its lack of currency can be a problem. Businesses fail, merge, consolidate. Corporate executives come and go. Policies change. As a result, patrons should be given *Everybody's Business* with the caveat that it is dated and may not always be accurate. Even so, it can be very useful, particularly for its description of corporate history, products, and public image.

In 1984, the editors of *Everybody's Business* compiled a new directory, *The 100 Best Companies to Work for in America*. Based on analyses of companies from the employees' viewpoint, it features the informal "insiders' look at" style found in *Everybody's Business*. It rates each company for pay, benefits, job security, chance for advancement, and ambience. In addition, each entry includes a description of the company's work environment, management style, and corporate personality. Mo Siegel, founder of Celestial Seasonings, is touted as "a guy with the moral conviction of Abraham Lincoln, the drive of Lee Iacocca, and the whimsey of E.T." (p. 41), and IBM's corporate personality is described as follows:

> IBM, more than any other big company, has institutionalized its beliefs the way a church does. They are expounded in numerous IBM internal publications to ensure that employees know what's expected of them. And they are reflected in codes of behavior, still in force even though the Watsons [founders of IBM] are no longer around. The Watsons insisted that sales persons wear dark business

suits and white shirts; that's no longer a strict regulation but most IBM salesmen continue to dress that way. The Watsons wouldn't permit drinking, on or off the job; today, an IBMer can drink off the job but anyone who drinks at lunch is expected to take the rest of the day off. (p. 157)

Although neither *Everybody's Business* nor *The 100 Best Companies to Work for in America* was published as a reference book, both are undeniably useful in this capacity. Directories are not the only sources of information about prospective employers. Annual reports, periodical articles, pamphlets, and books such as *Everybody's Business* should not be overlooked.

BIOGRAPHICAL DIRECTORIES

Sometimes, the need may be for information about an individual rather than a company. A salesman may want all of the data he can gather about a prospective client, a toastmaster may need personal background information to introduce an honored guest, or a small business woman may want to compile a mailing list of prominent business people in a particular location or industry. While standard biographical directories such as *Who's Who in America* and the *Who's Who* geographical series (*Who's Who in the Midwest, Who's Who in the South and Southwest*, etc.) include information about prominent executives, other more specialized biographical directories which focus solely on the world of business are also available and may list people not included in general biographical directories. In addition, *Standard & Poor's Register of Corporations, Directors, and Executives*, described in the section on basic business directories, incorporates a biographical directory as volume 2 of the three-volume set.

Reference Book of Corporate Managements. Parsippany, N.J.: Dun's Marketing Service, 1967- . 4v. Annual.

Who's Who in Finance and Industry. Chicago: Marquis Who's Who, 1936- . Biennial.

Ingham, John. Biographical Dictionary of American Business Leaders. Westport, Conn.: Greenwood Press, 1983. 4v.

Dun & Bradstreet also publishes a biographical directory, the four-volume *Reference Book of Corporate Managements*, which provides brief biographical information on thousands of principal officers and directors of more than 12,000 leading companies. Arrangement is by company name; volume 4, the "Cross-Reference" volume, includes an index of executives as well as the geographical and SIC indexes that are standard Dun & Bradstreet directory features.

The most widely used biographical business directory, however, is *Who's Who in Finance and Industry*, a biennial which lists over 22,000 North American and international business executives. Each biographical profile includes educational background, career history, political, civic and religious affiliations, special achievements, and personal data. The entry for Lee Iacocca, shown in figure 2.14, is typical.

A professional index, which lists biographees under more than 250 professional designations such as "Agricultural Products Executive" and "Real Estate Corporation Officer," makes it possible to identify key executives in a particular industry or field.

The patron looking for more detailed information on "historically significant" business people may wish to consult John Ingham's *Biographical Dictionary of American Business Leaders*. Although fewer than 1,000 entries are included, they are lengthier than those found in standard biographical directories and are generally accompanied by brief bibliographies. Appendixes in volume 4 make it possible to identify business leaders according to industry, company, birthplace, principal place of business activity, religion, ethnicity, year of birth, and gender. Coverage extends from colonial times to the present.

IACOCCA, LIDO ANTHONY (LEE), automotive mfr.; b. Allentown, Pa.,
Oct. 15, 1924; s. Nicola and Antoinette (Perrotto) I.; B.S., Lehigh U., 1945;
M.E., Princeton, 1946; m. Mary McCleary, Sept. 29, 1956; children—Kathryn
Lisa, Lia Antoninette. With Ford Motor Co., Dearborn, Mich., 1946-78,
successively mem. field sales staff, various merchandising and tng. activities,
asst. dirs. sales mgr., Phila., dist. sales mgr., Washington, 1946-56, truck
marketing mgr. div. office, 1956-57, car marketing mgr., 1957-60, vehicle
market mgr., 1960, v.p. Ford Motor Co., gen. mgr. Ford div., 1960-65, v.p. car
and truck group, 1965-67, exec. v.p. of co., 1967-68, pres. of co., 1970-78, pres.,
chief operating officer Chrysler Corp., Highland Park, Mich., 1978-79, chmn.
bd., chief exec. officer, 1979—. Wallace Meml. fellow Princeton. Mem. Tau
Beta Pi. Club: Detroit Athletic. Office: care Chrysler Corp 12000 Lynn
Townsend Dr Highland Park MI 48231*

Fig. 2.14. Sample entry, *Who's Who in Finance and Industry.* Copyright © 1985-86, Marquis Who's Who, Inc. Reprinted by permission from *Who's Who in Finance and Industry*, 24th edition.

Other, more specialized biographical business directories also exist, some published by professional and trade associations, others by commercial publishers. Some of the most widely used of these directories are described in the subject-oriented chapters that follow.

OTHER SPECIAL DIRECTORIES

The *Encyclopedia of Business Information Sources*, the *Guide to American Director-ies*, and the *Directory of Directories*, all mentioned earlier in the "Guides to Directories" section, list an almost overwhelming number of special business directories. These guides should be consulted whenever attempting to identify special industry and service-oriented directories. A few special directories are so regularly used, however, that they merit mention.

Koek, Karin E., and Susan Boyles Martin, eds. **Encyclopedia of Associations.** Detroit: Gale Research Co., 1956- . 4v. Annual.

Gill, Kay, and Donald P. Boyden, eds. **Business Organizations, Agencies, and Publi-cations Directory.** 3rd ed. Detroit: Gale Research Co., 1986. 2v. [Updated between editions by *Business Organizations, Agencies, and Publications. Supplement.*]

The first of these is the *Encyclopedia of Associations*. This standard reference work features brief information on over 18,000 "nonprofit American organizations of national scope," and includes sections on trade, business and commercial organizations, commodity exchanges, chambers of commerce, and other types of organizations relevant to business. Each entry includes the organization's address and telephone number, the name of the chief officer, founding date, and the number of members and staff. In addition, most entries in-clude brief descriptions of the organizations and lists of name changes, conference dates, and major publications.

Less essential than the *Encyclopedia of Associations* but still very useful is the *Business Organizations, Agencies, and Publications Directory.* Much of the information included in this directory is compiled from other sources, including the *Encyclopedia of Associations*, other Gale publications, and government documents. Although not a primary information source, it offers the undeniable convenience of access to a single directory rather than to several, disparate sources which may not all be close at hand. Large business reference col-lections and, alternatively, small libraries lacking access to the sources from which the infor-mation was gathered, may feature this directory in their collections.

Research and Technology

Directory of American Research and Technology. 21st ed. New York: Bowker, 1987. 756p. [Formerly *Industrial Research Laboratories of the United States.*]

While standard business directories list many companies that sponsor corporate research and development, these directories do not, as a rule, list company research and development centers, research laboratories, and their staff. That is why the *Directory of American Research and Technology* is so useful. It lists, by company name, laboratories and research and development centers for almost 6,000 parent organizations. Each entry, like the one shown in figure 2.15, includes name, address, and telephone number for the parent company, as well as the name and address of each laboratory, with names and titles of administrators, number of professional staff with doctorates, and number of support staff. Each entry concludes with a statement of the unit's chief research and development activity.

B90 **BECTON, DICKINSON & CO,*** Mack Centre 3, Paramus, NJ   (p)
07652. Tel: 201-967-3700
Chmn, Chief Exec Officer & Pres Wesley J Howe; *Exec VPres & Chief Operating Officer* Photios T Paulson; *VPres R&D* Donald S Hetzel
Professional Staff: 30 (Doctorates: 21). Technicians & Auxiliaries: 60
Fields of R&D: Basic and applied research in medical services, health care products and health sciences

.1   -**Becton, Dickinson Research Center*** (BDRC), PO Box   (pi)
112016, Raleigh, NC 27709. Tel: 919-549-8641
Dir Dr Roger E Wilsnack
Professional Staff: 43 (Doctorates: 11)—Bacteriology, biology, biomedical engineering, chemistry, electrical engineering, materials research, microbiology. Technicians & Auxiliaries: 56
Fields of R&D: Basic and applied research in biological sciences as related to public and private health care; multidisciplinary program in bacteriology, clinical biochemistry, radiobiology and pharmacology supporting medical problems and for improvement of product biological safety; biomedical engineering program concerned with the investigation and development of techniques and devices for life support instrumentation

Fig. 2.15. Sample entry, *Directory of American Research and Technology.* Reprinted with permission from *Directory of American Research and Technology, 20th edition.* Published by R. R. Bowker Company, a division of Reed Publishing USA. © 1986 by Reed Publishing USA, a division of Reed Holdings, Inc. All rights reserved.

In recent years, publishers have begun to compile even more specialized directories of high technology firms. The best known are the *Corporate Technology Directory* (Wellesley, Mass.: Corporate Technology Information Services), a three-volume set, and the *Directory of Public High Technology and Medical Corporations* (Philadelphia: American Investor Information Service). These publications, however, are too costly for many libraries. The *Directory of American Research and Technology* remains a good first choice.

Consultants

Only the largest consulting firms are listed in standard business directories. In order to identify individuals or organizations that offer consulting services, it is usually necessary to refer to special directories. Two such sources are in common use.

McLean, Janice, ed. **Consultants and Consulting Organizations Directory.** 7th ed. Detroit: Gale Research Co., 1986. 2v. [Updated between editions by *New Consultants*]

Dun's Consultants Directory. Parsippany, N.J.: Dun's Marketing Services, 1986- . Annual.

The *Consultants and Consulting Organizations Directory*, subtitled "A Reference Guide to Concerns and Individuals Engaged in Consultation for Business, Industry, and Government," features over 10,000 entries, arranged by broad subject category, such as "Marketing and Sales" and "Manufacturing/Industrial/Transportation Operations." Each entry includes the name of the principal executive(s), location of headquarters and branch offices, the organization's purpose, and recent publications, if any. Subject, personal name, industries served, and consulting firms indexes enhance access to the main section of the directory. *New Consultants*, a supplement issued twice between editions, brings the *Consultants and Consulting Organizations Directory* up-to-date.

Dun's Consultants Directory lists 25,000 consultants representing some 200 specialties, ranging from "Accounting" to "Wholesale." While it lists far more consultants than the *Consultants and Consulting Organizations Directory*, its entries include somewhat less information. Another difference is that the Gale publication is arranged by broad subject categories, and the Dun & Bradstreet directory, by consultant's name. Each, however, contains indexes that cross-reference the main section. Further, while there is considerable duplication between the sources, each contains listings that are unique. As a result, many libraries will choose to acquire both directories.

Trade Names

Wood, Donna, ed. **Trade Names Dictionary.** Detroit: Gale Research Co., 1976- . 2v. Annual. [Updated by *New Trade Names*]

Wood, Donna, ed. **Trade Names Dictionary: Company Index.** Detroit: Gale Research Co. 2v. Annual.

As mentioned earlier in this chapter, inquiries often involve linking a specific brand name with the company that owns it. Two sources of this information have already been described: the *Thomas Register of American Manufacturers* and the *Standard Directory of Advertisers*. Another important source is the *Trade Names Dictionary*, which lists almost 200,000 consumer-oriented trade names and the names of the companies associated with them. A companion directory, the *Trade Names Dictionary: Company Index*, lists for each company its major brands and trade names associated with it. The *Trade Names Dictionary* is supplemented by *New Trade Names*.

The directories discussed in this chapter are but a few of the hundreds of business directories in print. Directory information, furthermore, is not limited to printed sources. A growing number of directories are now available as computer databases, and this chapter concludes with a discussion of a few such directories.

ONLINE BUSINESS DIRECTORIES

Although online databases are described at length in chapter 8, it seems appropriate to consider briefly the growing number of business directories made available as online databases. Some duplicate printed directories. *Thomas Register Online*, for example, corresponds to volumes 1 through 13 of the printed *Thomas Register of American Manufacturers*. The *Million Dollar Directory* is made available online as *D&B-Million Dollar Directory*, and *Principal International Businesses*, as *International Dun's Market Identifiers*. Availability of these and other similar directories through database vendors has had and will continue to have profound collection-development implications. Libraries in which either floor space or book budget is inadequate to accommodate sizable directory collections can eliminate purchase of some printed directories and still have access via computer to the information they contain.

It is possible that, at some point, publishers will choose to make directories available only as online databases. Some directories, in fact, are already available only in this format. Typical of these is *Electronic Yellow Pages*, a series of databases that list businesses appearing in the Yellow Pages of over 4,800 U.S. telephone directories. Each database focuses on a different industry or group of industries, including construction, financial services, manufacturers, wholesalers, retailers, services, and professionals. A typical *Electronic Yellow Pages* entry includes name, address, and telephone number of the company or individual, a SIC code, and, usually, brief city or county information.

Often the cost of searching for specific company information by computer is less than the cost of purchasing equivalent printed directories. In addition, searching can offer considerable savings in staff time, and makes it possible to search by variables such as SIC codes and geographic location that are contained in each record. Clearly, directory databases will continue to grow in number and importance. The field is one in which change is continuous; any attempt to provide current comprehensive listings of computerized databases is all but impossible. Consultation of directories provided by database vendors, however, as well as of the commercially published database guides described in chapter 8 will help to identify many of the major online business directory databases presently available.

NOTES

[1]"Number of Returns, Receipts & Net Income, by Type of Business," Table 874, 1986 *Statistical Abstract of the United States* (Washington, D.C.: Government Printing Office, 1985), 517.

[2]The following articles discuss this problem and other shortcomings of the Standard Industrial Classification system.

> Ira Beth, "The SIC Code Needs Therapy," *Business Marketing* 69, no. 8 (August 1984): 50-53.

> John Courteos, "What's Wrong with the SIC Code ... and Why," *Business Marketing* 69, no. 12 (December 1984): 108-116.

> Jerry Reisberg, "An Expanded SIC Code: Let's Do It Ourselves!" *Direct Marketing* 50, no. 6 (October 1987): 148-151.

[3]While the Census Bureau does use seven-digit SIC codes in its economic censuses, most other government publications limit use of the SIC to four-digit industry codes.

All I know is just what I read in the newspapers.

— Will Rogers

3

PERIODICALS AND NEWSPAPERS

The world of business is not static. In the course of a year, many things can happen. Interest rates may skyrocket, new technologies be introduced, old products become obsolete, or stock prices plummet. Executives may retire, be fired, or abscond with company funds. Companies themselves may be victims of hostile takeovers or may in turn acquire companies. As a result, while directories and other reference books provide valuable information about fixed points in time, they are seldom completely up-to-date. For current information, business people turn to online databases, looseleaf services, periodicals, and newspapers. Of these, newspapers and periodicals are the most commonly used. This chapter seeks to examine various types of business periodicals and newspapers as well as representative examples of each and the indexes, abstracts, and online databases that provide access to them.

TYPES OF BUSINESS PERIODICALS

There are six main types of business periodicals. They are general business, trade, scholarly, consumer, government, and regional periodicals (see figure 3.1, page 46).

General Business Periodicals

General business periodicals provide broad coverage of the state of the economy and of commerce and industry. Although specific articles may treat different fields of business separately, the focus is broad, emphasizing overall trends and developments. *Business Week, Fortune,* and *Forbes* are general business periodicals: They are important and popular, and can be used to supplement standard business reference sources.

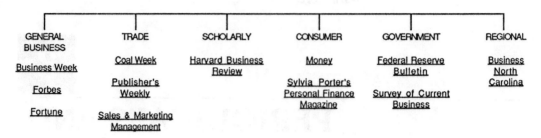

Fig. 3.1. Types of business periodicals.

Business Week. New York: McGraw-Hill, 1929- . Weekly.

Although *Business Week* may not, as its publishers advertise, show its readers how to "develop a silver tongue, a golden touch, and a mind like a steel trap," it does provide them with coverage of current conditions in national and international business and finance. It is a sort of business manager's *Time* or *Newsweek*, with concise, interesting, and frequently entertaining articles supplemented by statistics, graphs, photographs, and illustrations. Cover stories focus on subjects as diverse as artificial intelligence, capitalism in China, computer software, and baby boomers. Weekly news briefs generally fall into the following categories: Top of the News, International, Industries, Economic Analysis, Social Issues, The Corporation, People, Information Processing, Media, Marketing, Finance, Science and Technology, and Government. Also included each week are book reviews, editorials, and personal business advice. *Business Week* enjoys tremendous popularity; with a circulation of nearly 865,000 it is the most widely read of all business periodicals.[1]

In addition to the statistics that accompany many of its articles, *Business Week* also features a page of financial statistics in each issue. "Investment Figures of the Week" presents major financial indicators such as stock price and mutual fund indexes, technical market indicators, "leader" and "laggard" industry groups, and foreign exchange. Data include weekly, monthly, and annual figures and are usually for the period two weeks prior to the date of the issue being consulted. Strongest and weakest stocks and mutual funds are also identified.

Business Week also features a series of regularly recurring articles and issues. Annual articles include surveys of cigarette and liquor sales, labor negotiations, personal income, pensions, and industry forecasts. Although these articles are seldom more than three or four pages long, the information they contain is useful and may not always be easily available elsewhere. For example, the annual "Liquor Industry Scoreboard" article generally discusses factors responsible for growth or decline in liquor consumption in this country, and points to some of the ways in which distilleries plan to increase sales. It is accompanied by a table that ranks the top brands by sales for the past three years and rates their growth for a five-year period. For the business researcher trying to determine the market share for, say, Old Grand-Dad bourbon, or seeking to identify the five top-selling brands of scotch, this table can be tremendously useful.

In addition to these annual surveys, *Business Week* includes a Corporate Scoreboard series which provides information on domestic and foreign corporate and industry performance. The series includes the following.

Bank Scoreboard
    Ranks the top 200 U.S. banks, including data on assets, deposits, loans, and performance.

Corporate Balance Sheet Scoreboard
    Includes balance sheet data (assets and debts), with companies grouped by broad industry categories.

International Corporate Scoreboard
   Annual review of the financial performance of over 1,000 companies in some 60 countries. Arrangement is by country. Includes a list of the top 20 "giants" of foreign industry.

Investment Outlook Scoreboard
   Annual review of both personal and institutional investment outlooks. Lists for each of some 900 companies its stock price, dividend rate, earnings per share, and other detailed stock performance information.

Mutual Fund Scoreboard
   Reviews the investment performance of 385 equity mutual funds for the preceding year.

Pension Fund Scoreboard
   For the 200 largest companies, shows assets, total and vested benefits, net worth, vested funding position, assumed rate of return, and expense.

Quarterly Corporate Scoreboard
   Reviews financial performance (sales, profits, and growth) of some 900 U.S. companies, arranged by broad industry category. Also lists the 10 most profitable and least profitable companies and industries.

R & D Scoreboard
   Tallies annual research and development expenditures of over 800 companies, grouped by industry. Ranks and lists the top 15 companies in terms of sales dollars, and dollars per employee spent on research and development.

   Reference departments lacking immediate access to current issues of *Business Week* or preferring the convenience of consulting a single, consolidated source may wish to purchase the annual "Scoreboard Special," an issue that combines all of the Corporate Scoreboard series and the annual surveys (tobacco, liquor, industry outlook, executive compensation, etc.) into a single source. The low cost and potential usefulness of this issue make it a "best buy" for business reference collections of any size.[2]

Fortune. New York: Fortune Magazine, 1930- . Biweekly.

Fortune is the glossiest of the general business periodicals. Its popularity in the business community is undisputed; it is a key source of current information on all aspects of management, business, finance, and the economy. Each issue contains up to 10 regular features such as "News/Trends" and "Personal Investing," in addition to several special articles on such varied topics as farm price supports, abstinence, and baseball. Articles in *Fortune* are signed and generally longer than those appearing in *Business Week*, but are less likely to contain statistical data. Also missing are regular business and financial statistics pages.
   As with *Business Week*, *Fortune* publishes several special issues. Best known are the annual lists of largest companies, described in chapter 2. Other issues include "America's Most Admired Corporations," and "Deals of the Year" in January, "Products of the Year" and "Coups and Catastrophes" in December, and the "U.S. Business Hall of Fame" in March.
   Although *Fortune* is generally less useful than *Business Week* for answering statistical business reference questions, its biweekly profiles of up-and-coming executives and entrepreneurs, as well as of those elected to its business hall of fame, make it particularly useful as a source of current biographical information.

Forbes. New York: Forbes, Inc., 1917- . Biweekly.

Forbes is another important general business periodical. Like *Fortune* and *Business Week*, it includes regular columns and features such as company case histories, profiles of prominent business people, and investment commentary. Again, the scope is rather broad. Cover stories deal with topics as diverse as investment fraud and the plight of savings and loan associations. However, while *Fortune* and *Business Week* are intended primarily for business professionals, *Forbes* is written with the investor in mind. As a result, the focus is somewhat different. Rather than a single column on personal investments, for example, *Forbes* features several such columns of commentary and advice, each dealing with a specific investment medium and each written by an acknowledged expert in the field.

Like *Business Week, Forbes*' articles are frequently supplemented with statistics, and it, too, contains regular statistical features dealing with business and finance. The first of these is the "Forbes Index," which presents general business and economic statistics. It charts for a 14-month period eight main economic indicators—new housing starts, industrial production, manufacturers' new orders and inventories, personal income, unemployment claims, retail store sales, consumer prices, and consumer installment credit. The Forbes Index, which is a composite of these indicators, is charted for the past 15 years, with a close-up for the past 12-month period.

The "Forbes/Wilshire 5000 Review" charts stock price indexes over 12-month and 10-year periods, includes a brief summary of recent stock market activity, provides a close-up of equity markets, and tells its readers "Where the Action Is" and "What the Analysts Think."

Forbes publishes several special issues. In addition to its list of largest companies, the "Forbes' 500s" described in chapter 2, it publishes annual mutual fund, banking, insurance, and industry surveys, company growth predictions, a list of America's wealthiest individuals and families, and a special report on multinational corporations.

Together, *Business Week, Fortune,* and *Forbes* comprise the three most important general business periodicals and are essential to business collections in all libraries.

Trade Periodicals

General business periodicals are useful because they provide an overview of current business and economic conditions, but they seldom provide the depth of coverage required by a business researcher seeking detailed descriptive and analytic data for a particular industry. Someone looking for statistics pertaining to the meat-packing industry, for example, or for the latest information on packaging and advertising of prescription drugs would find little of value in *Fortune* or *Forbes*. In such situations, trade journals are often the best sources of information.

Almost every business endeavor is represented by at least one trade journal. "If there were just two guys in the world collecting and selling turkey buzzard eggs," writes Dick Levin, "you can be sure that one of the two would start a monthly *Turkey Buzzard Egg Dealers Journal* and start selling it to the other."[3] While turkey buzzard eggs are not yet actually covered in depth by any trade journal, the poultry business is well represented by such publications as *Poultry Digest, Poultry and Egg Marketing, Turkey World, Poultry Times*, and other titles. There are, in fact, hundreds of trade journals, each dealing with a specific business, industry, or profession. Some are issued by commercial publishers and others by trade and professional organizations. Most contain news of current developments in the field, reviews of past performance and forecasts for the future, descriptions of key companies and personalities, and buyers' guides and directories. They are, in short, veritable gold mines of highly specialized information, and can be invaluable to librarians and researchers seeking elusive statistics or esoterica. Typical examples of trade journals include *Broadcasting, Beverage World, Pit and Quarry, Sludge,* and *Sales & Marketing Management*.

Breadth and depth of trade journal collections vary considerably from library to library. A corporate information center may subscribe to all of the trade journals that reflect its company's interests, a public library may collect those relating to community industries and businesses, and an academic library may subscribe to those that support its curricula.

Scholarly Journals

Scholarly business periodicals focus on ideas rather than on the brief descriptions of present conditions, the recent past, or the near future found in general business periodicals and trade journals. Signed articles, based on research findings, are frequently lengthy and may include bibliographies. They may be theoretical or they may suggest new ways of dealing with existing business problems. They are publications of substance, whose value endures long after the somewhat ephemeral information in trade and general business periodicals has ceased to be of widespread interest.

Scholarly periodicals are often published under the sponsorship of learned societies, professional associations, or colleges and universities. Academic libraries are the heaviest subscribers to scholarly publications. While collections of these journals may be somewhat limited in special and public libraries, one such publication, the *Harvard Business Review*, is found in almost every library setting.

Harvard Business Review. Boston: Graduate School of Business Administration, Harvard University, 1922- . Bimonthly.

The *Harvard Business Review* is preeminent among scholarly business periodicals. Its popularity derives from the quality of its articles, authored by highly regarded scholars and business practitioners, and by their relevance to current business problems. Both its publisher and its readers view it as a continuing education tool for business executives. It is noted for the diversity of its articles, the eminence of its authors, and a combination of both the practical and the innovative. The *Harvard Business Review* is included in many of the business indexes and abstracts that will be described later in this chapter. It publishes its own annual author and subject index, as well as 5- and 10-year cumulative indexes. It can also be searched online as a full-text database through major database vendors.

Consumer Periodicals

Consumer-oriented periodicals, also known as personal finance magazines, are aimed at the general public. Usually glossy, these periodicals woo their readers with articles describing how to invest in stocks, bonds, and mutual funds, buy real estate, speculate in commodities, save money, and pay lower taxes. Often included are articles on successful investors, entrepreneurs, and self-made millionaires.

Although these periodicals make interesting reading, they are particularly valuable to reference librarians because of regular articles that describe investment mediums and mechanics in nontechnical terms and that list major information sources, particularly investment advisory publications. *Changing Times* is one of the oldest of these periodicals, and *Sylvia Porter's Personal Finance Magazine* is one of the newest. The most popular of all, however, is *Money*.

Money. New York: Time, Inc., 1972- . Monthly.

In addition to regular columns and features that include answers to readers' questions, recent developments on Wall Street, and articles describing the best brands of chocolates, ski gear, and other consumer goods, each issue of *Money* includes a special report section featuring a series of articles on specific topics such as real estate, income tax, and investments. Other articles deal with subjects as diverse as computer software, facelifts, the latest automobiles, and advice from financial planners and investment analysts. In addition, *Money* periodically rates the performance of mutual funds, of all New York Stock Exchange and American Stock Exchange common stocks, and of selected stocks traded over-the-counter.

Money regularly reviews investment advisory services and lists and describes publications that will be useful to prospective investors and entrepreneurs. "The Library Every Investor Needs,"[4] for example, annotates nine essential and ten supplementary money management titles, all of which belong in a good academic or public library business collection.[5] Reading *Money* will help librarians anticipate user demand for specific titles and, in some instances, will help to identify sources that should be added to the collection. Its descriptions and evaluations of investment advisory services are even more useful, since ratings of these services are not always readily available. Finally, *Money*'s explanation in lay terms of the newest investment mediums can help librarians keep abreast of recent trends and developments.

Government Periodicals

Business periodicals published by the federal government may at first glance seem to be drab cousins of their colorful, commercially published counterparts. Appearances to the contrary, however, they contain a wealth of information and can be of significant reference value to librarians and researchers. Although a few titles are described in this section, many more are available. They can be identified by consulting the following booklet.

King, Richard L., ed. **Business Serials of the U.S. Government.** Chicago: American Library Association, 1978. 38p.

Business Serials of the U.S. Government lists and annotates over 100 titles, chosen for inclusion on the basis of their usefulness as business reference sources. Arrangement is by broad subject category. Each entry includes a standard bibliographic citation as well as Superintendent of Documents classification and serial numbers, the Library of Congress card number, and an annotation which includes the source(s) in which the title is indexed, pagination, the kinds of illustrations typically included, the sources for the data reported, and a description of scope and coverage. Although *Business Serials* is somewhat dated, a revision by ALA's Reference and Adult Services Division's Business Reference and Services Section (BRASS) will soon be available.

While there are over 100 federally published business periodicals, the ones that follow are among the most highly regarded and heavily used.

U.S. Council of Economic Advisers. **Economic Indicators.** Washington, D.C.: Government Printing Office, 1948- . Monthly.

U.S. Department of Commerce. Bureau of Economic Analysis. **Business Conditions Digest.** Washington, D.C.: Government Printing Office, 1961- . Monthly.

U.S. Department of Commerce. Bureau of Economic Analysis. **Survey of Current Business.** Washington, D.C.: Government Printing Office, 1921- . Monthly.

U.S. Department of Commerce. Bureau of Economic Analysis. **Business Statistics.** Washington, D.C.: Government Printing Office, 1951- . Biennial.

The federal government is the world's largest collector and publisher of statistics, and many of them are first published in government periodicals such as *Economic Indicators*, *Business Conditions Digest*, and the *Survey of Current Business*. Of these, the most widely used is the *Survey of Current Business*, published monthly by the Commerce Department's

Bureau of Economic Analysis. Each issue is a comprehensive report on business activity and economic conditions and includes, in addition to articles on various aspects of commerce and the economy, a column describing the current business situation and statistical tables highlighting national income and product accounts. Each issue also presents some 2,500 different statistics series, grouped together under the following categories.

General Business Indicators
Commodity Prices
Construction and Real Estate
Domestic Trade
Labor Force, Employment, and Earnings
Finance
Foreign Trade
Transportation and Communication
Chemicals and Allied Products
Electric Power and Gas
Food and Kindred Products; Tobacco
Leather and Products
Metals and Manufactures
Petroleum, Coal, and Products
Pulp, Paper, and Paper Products
Rubber and Rubber Products
Stone, Clay, and Glass Products
Textile Products
Transportation Equipment

Together these statistics comprise the "Current Business Statistics" section in the center of each issue, easily identified by the blue paper on which it is printed. Whenever available, statistics are given monthly for the past 14-month period, with annual figures for the two preceding years included as well. The data for dairy products presented in figure 3.2 are typical.

April 1987		SURVEY OF CURRENT BUSINESS													S-21	
Unless otherwise stated in footnotes below, data through 1984 and methodological notes are as shown in BUSINESS STATISTICS: 1984	Units	Annual		1986											1987		
		1985	1986	Feb.	Mar.	Apr.	May	June	July	Aug.	Sept.	Oct.	Nov.	Dec.	Jan.	Feb.	Mar.
FOOD AND KINDRED PRODUCTS; TOBACCO—Continued																	
DAIRY PRODUCTS																	
Butter:																	
Production (factory)..........mil. lb.		1,247.8	1,207.6	119.4	120.2	121.7	116.0	92.0	81.5	72.3	79.2	84.6	84.0	100.9	109.2	97.8	
Stocks, cold storage, end of period..........do		205.5	193.0	ʳ242.4	283.3	ʳ305.0	ʳ330.8	342.8	337.6	304.4	279.6	253.3	ʳ218.5	193.0	206.6	ʳ231.6	254.5
Producer Price Index ....1967=100		217.1	223.0	212.9	212.9	213.2	213.4	214.0	220.4	234.9	234.8	236.0	ʳ235.3	235.1	211.3	210.5	211.9
Cheese:																	
Production (factory), total ....mil. lb.		5,024.9	5,225.8	398.7	462.7	461.0	480.5	459.1	439.3	424.9	414.8	425.4	397.6	435.8	413.6	400.9	
American, whole milk..........do		2,854.4	2,834.3	227.2	263.6	266.1	280.8	262.1	244.1	224.0	201.7	207.1	195.5	222.9	219.5	211.2	
Stocks, cold storage, end of period..........do		852.9	693.6	ʳ813.2	ʳ815.7	838.4	873.3	ʳ892.8	915.6	ʳ916.2	ʳ859.0	805.0	757.0	693.6	680.8	ʳ652.9	644.8
American, whole milk..........do		758.8	601.7	721.9	724.6	742.9	778.5	794.4	815.1	ʳ816.0	ʳ759.9	711.2	665.5	601.7	587.2	ʳ564.8	554.6
Imports..........do		302.5	311.4	37.2	20.9	17.5	19.9	24.5	24.6	23.1	25.8	30.7	33.2	31.3	14.4	15.5	
Price, wholesale, cheddar, single daisies (Chicago)..........$ per lb.		1.620	1.575	1.556	1.556	1.557	1.558	1.558	1.572	1.596	1.597	1.599	1.599	1.599	(ᵖ)		
Condensed and evaporated milk:																	
Production, case goods ....mil. lb.		635.3	569.0	43.5	50.2	52.6	53.8	49.8	49.3	47.8	46.6	44.9	42.8	44.6	39.8	41.1	
Stocks, manufacturers', case goods, end of period..........do		62.3	45.0	72.7	73.2	86.2	91.6	103.5	106.9	111.8	105.1	87.8	62.1	45.0	49.9	53.3	
Exports..........do		11.6	10.8	1.5	2.5	1.7	.4	.5	.3	.5	.5	.5	.6	.6	.2	.4	
Fluid milk:																	
Production on farms..........do		143,667	ʳ122,185	9,565	10,659	10,630	11,213	10,649	10,468	10,169	9,662	9,732	9,400	9,717	9,932	9,279	10,376
Utilization in manufactured dairy products..........do		83,023	82,977	6,721	7,495	7,733	8,000	7,445	7,156	6,612	6,309	6,272	5,734	6,371	6,468	6,304	
Price, wholesale, U.S. average ....$ per 100 lb.		12.75	12.42	12.40	12.20	12.00	12.00	11.90	12.00	12.20	12.70	13.10	13.40	13.40	13.30	ʳ12.90	ʳ12.60
Dry milk:																	
Production:																	
Dry whole milk..........mil. lb.		118.9	121.5	10.7	11.5	10.1	8.6	8.8	10.8	11.2	11.4	9.8	10.2	9.2	11.3	12.6	
Nonfat dry milk (human food)..........do		1,390.0	1,297.6	114.7	128.1	137.2	144.0	136.7	115.1	95.9	75.2	68.7	68.2	90.4	82.1	80.3	
Stocks, manufacturers', end of period:																	
Dry whole milk..........do		6.5	6.7	5.3	7.0	6.9	4.9	4.5	6.8	6.8	6.6	4.3	5.6	6.7	6.5	8.0	
Nonfat dry milk (human food)..........do		78.2	57.9	63.3	74.4	79.2	85.2	85.3	67.2	65.1	52.1	39.9	43.7	57.9	ʳ55.3	66.5	
Exports, whole and nonfat (human food)..........do		276.1	482.4	27.1	41.2	25.9	40.0	16.7	41.3	77.1	45.6	57.9	52.0	39.5	20.4	24.3	
Price, manufacturers' average selling, nonfat dry milk (human food)..........$ per lb.		.849	.810	.812	.807	.807	.810	.808	.807	.808	.808	.810	.816	.814	.802	.794	

Fig. 3.2. Typical listings, "Current Business Statistics," *Survey of Current Business*. Reprinted from U.S. Department of Commerce, Bureau of Economic Analysis, *Survey of Current Business* (April 1987).

The *Survey's* "Current Business Statistics" section is supplemented by *Business Statistics*, a biennial publication that contains historical statistics for most of the statistics series as well as more comprehensive and detailed methodological notes.

> U.S. Department of Labor. Bureau of Labor Statistics. **Monthly Labor Review.** Washington, D.C.: Government Printing Office, 1915- . Monthly.

> U.S. Board of Governors of the Federal Reserve System. **Federal Reserve Bulletin.** Washington, D.C.: Board of Governors of the Federal Reserve System, 1915- . Monthly.

Other government periodicals are more specialized. The *Monthly Labor Review,* for example, includes articles and statistics on employment and unemployment, work stoppages, prices and price indexes, and wages. The *Federal Reserve Bulletin* concentrates on money and banking, featuring articles and detailed banking, financial, and monetary statistics.

> U.S. Department of Commerce. International Trade Administration. **Business America.** Washington, D.C.: Government Printing Office, 1880- . Biweekly.

Not all government periodicals include statistics sections. *Business America* features articles on a wide range of subjects. Recent issues have included articles on changes in Mexico's import policy, China's telecommunications market, and the president's new trade policies. Each issue also includes such features as a calendar for world traders, reviews of books and reports, brief descriptions of foreign government actions affecting prospects for American business, and business opportunities. The description of a company seeking a partner to sell popcorn in Nigeria, shown in figure 3.3, is a typical entry from *Business America*'s "Trade and Investment" column. *Business America* also publishes annual lists of world trade fairs and foreign business holidays.

NIGERIA—Company seeking American joint venture partner to produce, process, and market popcorn in Nigeria—large-scale operation. Interested firms contact TREICO (international consultants), 93 Willets Drive, Syosset, N.Y. 11791, phone (516) 496-8740.

Fig. 3.3. Entry from "Trade and Investment Column," *Business America.* Reprinted from U.S. Department of Commerce, International Trade Administration, *Business America,* August 19, 1985.

The federal government is not the only government publisher of periodicals. Although space does not permit their inclusion, it should be noted that state, foreign, and international agencies also issue business periodicals which can be of considerable research value.

Regional Periodicals

The categories of periodicals previously discussed provide information on the national and international level. Economic statistics in government periodicals such as the *Survey of Current Business* are primarily for the United States. Corporations covered in general business periodicals such as *Fortune* are usually nationally prominent blue-chip companies.

Frequently, however, librarians are asked to provide information about small, private companies, or about state and local economic conditions. One valuable source of such information is comprised of the growing number of local, state, and regional business publications, categorized here as regional periodicals. Some, such as the *Boston Business Journal* and *New Orleans Business*, focus on specific cities; others, such as *Business North Carolina* and *Texas Business*, provide state coverage. Such publications typically include profiles of locally prominent business people, companies, and industries, and state and local economic indicators. At a minimum, a good business collection will include periodicals for the city and state in which it is located, and may extend to regional periodicals as well. Access to regional business periodicals is also available through such database vendors as BRS and DIALOG.

PERIODICAL DIRECTORIES

Literally hundreds of business periodicals are published every year. Some of the most popular ones, such as *Business Week, Money, Harvard Business Review*, and *Survey of Current Business*, are familiar to almost everyone. Others are not nearly so well known, and often librarians may be asked to help identify or provide information on such titles. For example, a businessman may want to identify trade magazines in which he can advertise his new line of waterbeds, or he may want to find the source that will best enable him to keep up with the latest developments in the home heating industry. In these situations, librarians frequently turn to periodical directories; the following are used often.

Ulrich's International Periodicals Directory. New York: Bowker, 1932- . 2v. Annual.

The Standard Periodical Directory. New York: Oxbridge Communications, Inc., 1964/ 65- . Biennial.

Gale Directory of Publications: An Annual Guide to Newspapers, Magazines, Journals, and Related Publications. Detroit: Gale Research Co., 1880- . Annual.[6]

Ulrich's is the most commonly used periodical directory. It lists nearly 71,000 periodicals from around the world, arranged by broad subject classification. In addition to a "Business and Economics" section, which includes listings for accounting, banking and finance, investment, and small business as well as general business and economics publications, *Ulrich's* also includes categories for specific industries and trades, such as building and construction, the clothing trade, and paints and protective coatings. Other fields of business such as advertising and real estate are listed separately.

Each entry includes title, frequency of publication, the publisher's name and address, and Dewey Decimal Classification. In addition, the entry usually includes the ISSN (International Standard Serial Number), circulation, subscription price, year first published, language of text, the presence of advertising and book reviews, and the names of the indexing and abstracting services in which the periodical is covered. A bullet symbol (•) is used to identify availability as an online database, and frequently the name(s) of the online vendor is listed as well. *Ulrich's* also includes a cross-index to subjects, a list of periodicals that have ceased publication, and a title index.

Ulrich's International Periodicals Directory is supplemented by *Irregular Serials and Annuals*, which provides similar data on serials, annuals, conference proceedings, and other publications issued irregularly or less frequently than twice a year, and by *The Bowker International Serials Database Update*, which updates the information in both *Ulrich's International Periodicals Directory* and *Irregular Serials and Annuals*. Information contained in the current editions of each of these sources is also available as an online database and on *Ulrich's Plus*, a compact optical disk database.

Although *The Standard Periodical Directory* contains fewer titles than does *Ulrich's* — some 60,000 compared to *Ulrich's* 70,800 — its coverage is limited to the United States and Canada. As a result, almost three times as many periodicals published in these countries are included as in *Ulrich's*. Titles listed include business, consumer, and trade magazines, newsletters, house organs, selected daily and weekly newspapers, yearbooks, and directories.

As with *Ulrich's*, arrangement of titles is by subject, with many general business, trade, and industry categories. In addition to the information contained in *Ulrich's*, *The Standard Periodical Directory* annotates the titles it lists, and includes information on the physical characteristics of periodicals, the names of their advertising, circulation, and art directors, and the prices of single issues.

The *Gale Directory of Publications*, formerly the *IMS/Ayer Directory of Publications*, lists newspapers, magazines, and trade journals published in the United States, Puerto Rico, and Canada. Unlike *Ulrich's* and the *Standard Periodical Directory*, the *Gale Directory* arranges serial titles by state and city, rather than by broad subject classification. The beginning of each state entry includes a brief description of the state, with demographic and publishing statistics, and is followed by city listings. All periodicals published in each city are listed alphabetically regardless of subject content. The listing for Milwaukee, Wisconsin, for example, includes titles as diverse as *The Milwaukee Journal*, one of the city's daily newspapers, *American Christmas Tree Journal, Building Operating Management, Farm Futures, Model Railroader, Sanitary Maintenance, Spare Time*, and *Singlelife Milwaukee*.

The arrangement of the *Gale Directory* requires several cross-indexes. They include an alphabetical title index; separate lists of agricultural, college, foreign language, Jewish, fraternal, black, and religious publications; newsletters; general circulation magazines; daily newspapers; daily periodicals; weekly, semiweekly, and triweekly newspapers; and trade and technical publications. Entries are not quite as comprehensive as those in the *Standard Periodical Directory*, but are useful for advertising rates and specifications for specific titles. Each of the directories mentioned above can be used to access major business and trade publications. Each has its strengths. *Ulrich's* includes more foreign-language titles and lists indexing and abstracting services in which specific periodicals are indexed. *The Standard Periodical Directory* features the most detailed descriptions of content and includes some advertising information, while *Gale* includes even more detailed information about advertising specifications and rates.

Another, more selective, publication is useful.

Fisher, William, comp. **Financial Journals and Serials: An Analytical Guide to Accounting, Banking, Finance, Insurance, and Investment Periodicals.** Westport, Conn.: Greenwood Press, 1986. 201p.

Financial Journals and Serials lists and annotates over 500 scholarly journals, popular periodicals, newsletters, house organs, and looseleaf services. Although it includes far fewer titles than the general periodical directories described above, it provides considerably more information for those it lists. In addition to a standard bibliographic citation, each entry includes the date the work was first published, title changes (and the dates each title was in effect), frequency of publication, 1984/85 subscription prices for individuals and libraries, availability of special issues, editorial and advertising policy, printed and online indexing services in which the title is included, the publication's target audience, and whether or not sample issues are available. In addition, most entries contain an evaluative annotation to help give the reader an indication of the potential value of the title for personal and library collections. A table of abbreviations and brief directories of printed indexes and abstracts, microform and reprint publishers, and online databases are also included. Arrangement is by subject, with geographic, title, publisher, and subject indexes.

GUIDES TO SPECIAL ISSUES

Earlier *Fortune, Forbes,* and *Business Week* were mentioned as periodicals that publish regularly recurring special issues. Many business, trade, and technical periodicals publish such issues, which normally fall into one of five broad categories: directories and buyers' guides, convention and exhibit reports, statistical reviews, industry reviews, and industry forecasts. The information these special issues contain is often unique or difficult to locate elsewhere; as a result, they can be enormously helpful to librarians and researchers. Many can be purchased separately, making it possible to order key issues and keep them close at hand in the reference collection.

Uhlan, Miriam, ed. **Guide to Special Issues and Indexes of Periodicals**. 3rd ed. New York: Special Libraries Association, 1985. 160p.

Sicignano, Robert, and Doris Prichard. **Special Issues Index.** Westport, Conn.: Greenwood Press, 1982. 309p.

The *Guide to Special Issues and Indexes of Periodicals* and the *Special Issues Index* list major business, consumer, and trade journals alphabetically by title. For each entry, publisher's address, frequency of publication, and annual subscription rate are given in addition to a listing of special issues, their cost if purchased separately, and the months in which they appear. The entry for *Advertising Age*, shown in figure 3.4, is typical.

```
20.   ADVERTISING AGE                        Weekly          $40.00
      Crain Communications
      740 Rush St.
      Chicago, IL   60611

      A.   March     Top Liquor Brands                     $ .75
                     Agency Income Issue                   $ .75
      B.   April     International Agency Profiles          $ .75
                     Coffee Consumption                    $ .75
      C.   May       Top 10 Syndicated TV Programs          $ .75
                     Latin Ad Agency Report                $ .75
                     Cold Cereal Report                    $ .75
                     Top 25 Market Research Companies      $ .75
      D.   June      Chewing Tobacco & Snuff Market         $ .75
      E.   July      Wine Industry Report                  $ .75
      F.   Aug       100 Leading National Advertisers       $ .75
      G.   Dec       100 Top Ad Markets                    $ .75
                     Cigarette Production & Consumption $ .75

           cl/ads, p/s ads(indexed ea. issue)
```

Fig. 3.4. Sample entry, *Special Issues Index. Special Issues Index: Specialized Contents of Business, Industrial, and Consumer Journals,* compiled by Robert Sicignano and Doris Prichard (Greenwood Press, Westport, Conn., 1982), p. 4. Copyright (©) 1982 by Robert Sicignano and Doris Prichard. Reprinted by permission of the publisher.

Users of these special directories should be forewarned that publishers may change the months during which specific special issues are published. Failure to find a special issue in the month indicated in either of these directories, therefore, does not necessarily mean that it is no longer being published.

PERIODICAL INDEXES AND ABSTRACTS

Indexing and abstracting services provide access to literally hundreds of general trade, scholarly, consumer, government, and regional business periodicals, enabling users to find recent information on a wide range of subjects. Some of the most popular business periodicals are indexed in general indexes such as *Readers' Guide to Periodical Literature* and *Public Affairs Information Service Bulletin*. Business indexes such as *Predicasts F&S Index United States, Business Periodicals Index*, and *Business Index* cover a broad range of business titles, while specialized indexes such as *Accountants' Index* and *Banking Literature Index* have a narrower focus. Chapters to come will cover specialized periodical indexes: the most commonly used business and general periodical indexes are discussed below. Readers should note that the following titles are by no means a complete listing of all indexes and abstracts in which business periodicals are cited; for more comprehensive listings, consult *Business Information Sources* or the listing of periodical indexes in *Ulrich's International Periodicals Directory*.

> **Readers' Guide to Periodical Literature.** New York: H. W. Wilson, 1900/04- . Semi-monthly with periodic cumulations.

> **Public Affairs Information Service Bulletin.** New York: PAIS, 1915- . Semimonthly with periodic cumulations.

The *Readers' Guide to Periodical Literature* indexes general interest periodicals published in the United States. Included among the business serials it indexes are *Black Enterprise, Business Week, Changing Times, Forbes, Fortune, Money, Monthly Labor Review*, and *Nation's Business*. In addition, many of the other periodicals it indexes also feature articles relating to business. As a result, *Readers' Guide* is a good source to consult when looking for popular, general interest business articles written with the lay person in mind. Indexing is by author and subject. A separate book review section is also included.

Public Affairs Information Service Bulletin, or *PAIS*, is more specialized and more scholarly than *Readers' Guide*. It focuses on current economic, social, and political considerations, and it indexes books, documents, conference proceedings, pamphlets, and reports in addition to periodicals. Arrangement in *PAIS* is by subject, with numerous cross-references. *PAIS* is useful not only for the articles indexed but also for its annual listing of directories and for its indexing of free and inexpensive pamphlets, many of which are extremely useful for vertical file collections.

> **Business Periodicals Index.** New York: H. W. Wilson, 1958- . Monthly, except July, with periodic cumulations.

> **Predicasts F&S Index United States.** Cleveland, Ohio: Predicasts, 1960- . Weekly, with monthly, quarterly, and annual cumulations.

> **Business Index.** Belmont, Calif.: Information Access, 1979- . Monthly microfilm index.

Business Periodicals Index is the basic business index, the one that has been published longest, is most popular, and is most likely to be found in a variety of library settings. It is a subject index and covers such fields as accounting, advertising and marketing, banking, chemicals, construction, cosmetic and drug industries, economics, electronics, finance and investment, industrial relations, insurance, management, personnel administration, public relations, regulation of industry, and specific businesses, industries, and trades. Also included are entries for prominent executives and companies, and a separate book review section. *BPI* indexes over 300 business periodicals, ranging from *ABA Banking Journal* to *World Oil*. Most are general business periodicals; trade journals are not well represented. Figure 3.5 illustrates a typical entry.

Income
  See also
  Capital gains
  Consumption (Economics)
  Farm income
  Gross national product
  National income
  Purchasing power
  Retirement income
  Underground economy
  Wages and salaries
  Wealth
Black income mirrors status in economy. A. F. Brimmer. il *Black Enterp* 17:33 S '86
The changing fortunes of young and old. G. J. Duncan and others. graphs *Am Demogr* 8:26-9+ Ag '86
The effects of H.R. 3838 and the Senate tax version on individual taxpayers in six cities. J. McGovern and J. E. Petersen. graphs tabs *Gov Finance Rev* 2:31-4 Ag '86
The right to smurf [gamblers structure bets to avoid reporting winnings] D. Seligman. *Fortune* 114:164 D 8 '86

Fig. 3.5. Typical entries, *Business Periodicals Index*. *Business Periodicals Index*, Copyright © 1987 by the H. W. Wilson Company. Material reproduced by permission of the publisher.

BPI's strength is its coverage of general business and management matters. It is less useful for the latest news on product and industry developments or for information on specific companies, particularly those not well known. Many librarians turn to *Predicasts F&S Index United States*, also known as *F&S*, for such information. *F&S* indexes over 750 periodicals. In addition to such general business titles as *Business Week* and *Fortune*, it also features business-oriented newspapers such as the *Wall Street Transcript*, special reports, and an array of trade publications including *Appliance Manufacturer, Health Industry Today,* and *World Cement. F&S*' strengths are new products and technological developments, corporate acquisitions and mergers, and social and political factors affecting business. The index is divided into two main sections, "Industries and Products," and "Companies."

F&S' Industries and Products section reports on new products, product demand and use, sales, market data, and general economic factors. Arrangement is by a numerical coding system, based roughly on the Standard Industrial Classification system described in chapter 2. The Predicasts code, however, contains more numbers and is thus more precise than its SIC counterpart. The *Standard Industrial Classification Manual*, for example, assigns SIC code 3714 to automotive brakes. Brakes, however, are not the only items listed. "Motor Vehicle Parts and Accessories," SIC 3714, includes over 50 different products, ranging from axles to windshield wipers. Although Predicasts begins with the same four-digit code, by adding two additional digits it is able to create a code, 371432, that is unique to automotive brakes. The advantages of such a system are obvious. Rather than having to read through entries for many different items, the researcher immediately is able to identify those for a specific product. In addition to greater specificity, the Predicasts codes are also more current and reflect the development of new products and technologies in a way that the infrequently revised SIC codes cannot. A section in the front of each issue contains an alphabetical index to the Predicasts codes that are used.

Figure 3.6 (see page 58) illustrates the arrangement of entries in the Industries and Products section. Each entry contains a brief description of the article, a journal abbreviation, and the date and pages on which the article appears. Predicasts uses heavy black dots to denote major articles so that researchers easily can identify those most deserving of attention.

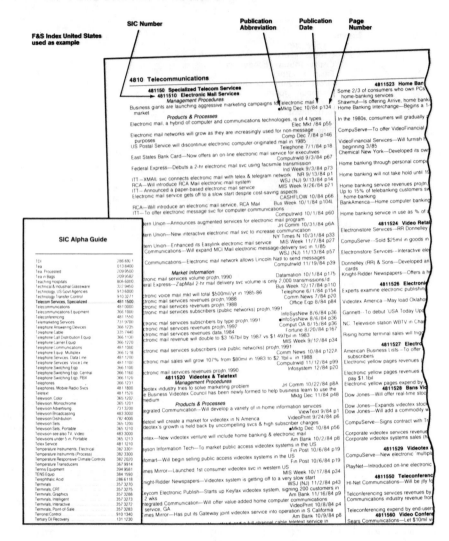

Fig. 3.6. Typical entries, *Predicasts F&S Index United States.* Reprinted by permission of Predicasts.

F&S' Companies section includes articles relating to mergers, sales and licensing agreements, company analyses, and forecasts of company sales and profits. Although arrangement is by company name rather than by Predicasts code, in all other respects the entries are similar to those found in the Industries and Products section.

Both *Business Periodicals Index* and *Predicasts F&S Index United States* are extremely useful. *BPI's* strength is in its coverage of management concepts and general business developments, while *F&S* is strongest for coverage of specific products and companies. Someone seeking articles on quality circles or on strategic planning, for example, would find *BPI* more useful, while someone interested in medical lasers or frozen yogurt would be wise to turn first to *F&S*. Each index supplements the other, and both are essential to a good business reference collection.

Business Index is a monthly microfilm index that is a cumulative, three-year index to over 800 business periodicals and newspapers. Although *Business Index,* which comes with its own microfilm reader, is expensive, it offers users the convenience of consulting a single index rather than several annual or monthly volumes. It is also somewhat more current than its printed competitors, and uses business slang and jargon as subject headings. It permits author as well as subject and company name access to the articles it lists. *Business Index*, however, is not without flaw. The quality of indexing is not as high as that of *Business Periodicals Index* or *Predicasts F&S Index*. Index terms are inconsistently used, standardization of company and organization names is sometimes lacking, and inaccurate citations are not uncommon. Even so, *Business Index* is popular with researchers, who appreciate its timeliness and convenience.

The most widely used business indexes, described above, can be found in many medium- and large-sized business library collections. Less common but very useful are two monthly business abstracting services. The first is *Business Publications Index and Abstracts* (Detroit: Gale Research Co.), derived from *Management Contents*, an online database. The second, *Predicasts Overview of Markets and Technology*, or *PROMT* (Cleveland, Ohio: Predicasts), abstracts articles from more than 1,000 sources and emphasizes new products and technologies, research, plant production, and sales and shipment. *PROMT* and the other Predicasts publications are also available as online databases.

NEWSPAPERS

Sometimes monthly, biweekly, or even weekly periodicals are not recent enough to satisfy current information needs. Although most business developments are eventually described in periodicals, they appear first in newspapers. The categories to which newspapers can be assigned roughly parallel those for periodicals. They include regular daily newspapers with business sections or pages, and special business and financial, trade, government, and employment opportunity newspapers (see figure 3.7). Each of these categories merits further discussion.

Fig. 3.7. Types of newspapers of interest to the business community.

Regular Daily Newspapers

Even the most modest daily newspaper includes a page or two of business information, usually consisting of news and feature articles about local businesses and tables of trading and price statistics for selected stocks, bonds, mutual funds, and commodities. Coverage is selective, with greatest emphasis being given to businesses and companies headquartered in the area. Some of the larger daily newspapers such as the *Chicago Tribune* and the *Washington Post* have excellent business sections. Coverage in the *New York Times* is outstanding. In addition to its lengthy "Business Section" in Sunday editions, the *Times* also publishes "Business Day" in its daily editions, a compilation of news, features, tables, and advertisements that fills most of the paper's second section. Coverage ranges from brief statements of corporate and executive news to detailed analyses of major financial developments and of specific industries. In many instances, the *New York Times* fills the need for news on industry trends, stock prices, and corporate developments. It is a resource that should not be overlooked.[7]

Business and Financial Newspapers

In addition to regular daily newspapers, most libraries subscribe to papers that specialize in providing in-depth coverage of current business, economic, and financial conditions. The *Wall Street Journal* is the best known and most important of these business and financial newspapers.

Wall Street Journal. New York: Dow Jones, 1889- . Daily, except Saturdays and Sundays.

Investor's Daily. Los Angeles, Calif.: Investor's Daily, Inc., 1984- . Daily, except Saturdays and Sundays.

The *Wall Street Journal* is indispensable. Its coverage of political, social, economic, and financial news makes it required reading for executives, business people, investors, and conscientious business reference librarians.[8] With an estimated readership of over 6 million, the *Journal* is an integral part of the daily business scene; every reference librarian should be familiar with it.

The *Journal* is divided into two sections. The first section contains major news articles, features, spot news, special reports, and the editorial page. The paper's front page follows a consistent format, with columns arranged according to the pattern shown in figure 3.8.

Also included in the first section are regularly recurring articles on leading economic indicators and business statistics. Although these statistics will be covered in chapter 5, it is worth noting here that government agencies and private organizations regularly compile statistics on such activities as capital spending, business failures, domestic car sales, and consumer prices. The *Journal* can be an excellent source of such current statistical data, which are published on a regular weekly, trimonthly, monthly, quarterly, or biannual basis.

The second section of the *Journal* includes a series of special reports for each day of the week ("Small Business," "Regions," "Real Estate," "Marketing," and "Technology"). In addition, the second section includes corporate, executive, and industry profiles, international news, classified advertisements, and columns such as "Abreast of the Market," "Heard on the Street," and "Your Money Matters." The most frequently consulted pages, however, are those that contain statistical tables for stocks and other investment mediums. The following are among the most important.

American Stock Exchange Composite Transactions
AMEX Bonds
Foreign Exchange
Futures Prices
Government Agency Issues
Listed Options Quotations
Mutual Fund Quotations
NASDAQ Over-the-Counter Markets
New York Exchange Bonds
New York Stock Exchange Composite Transactions

To the uninitiated, many of these tables can seem overwhelming. The print is small, numbers dense, and explanations cryptic. Fortunately, many secondary sources provide detailed explanations of the most important of these tables. For example, chapters 12 through 16 of this book include lengthy descriptions of stock, bond, mutual fund, futures, and options tables. In addition, the *Journal*'s publisher, Dow Jones, makes available a series of explanatory and promotional brochures describing information contained in the *Journal*.

Column 1. Daily feature, usually a general interest story. Subjects may include politics, law, foreign affairs, or education.

Column 2. "What's News: Business and Finance." A digest of corporate, industrial, and economic news reported elsewhere in the *Journal*. Page references to each full-length article are included.

Column 3. "What's News: World Wide." Summarizes major national and international news.

Column 4. Daily feature, often a tongue-in-cheek examination of such phenomena as prison rodeos, alligator scaloppine, and junk rock.

Column 5. "Special Reports," featuring a different topic each day of the week. Coverage is as follows:

Monday: "The Outlook." Broad coverage of business and the economy.

Tuesday: "Labor Letter." Includes labor-management relations, labor negotiations, and legislation.

Wednesday: "Tax Report."

Thursday: "Business Bulletin." Identifies and describes emerging trends.

Friday: "Washington Wire." Information on government activities of interest to the business community.

Column 6. News story, usually on business, economics, or finance.

Fig. 3.8. Columns on the *Wall Street Journal*'s front page. Cover reprinted by permission of the *Wall Street Journal* © Dow Jones & Company, Inc. 1982. All Rights Reserved.

Dow Jones established an Educational Service Bureau in 1947 to promote the use of the *Wall Street Journal* by college educators. Since then, the Educational Service Bureau and the publications it offers have grown significantly. There are now five regional offices, each making pamphlets available to librarians and educators.[9] These pamphlets are described in more detail in the chapter on vertical file materials, but it is worth noting here that many relate directly to the history of the *Wall Street Journal*, its current contents, and regularly featured statistical tables and measures of market performance.[10] They can be useful starting points for anyone seeking to learn more about this key business reference source.

Wall Street Journal Index. New York: Dow Jones, 1958- . Monthly, with annual cumulations.

The *Journal* is indexed in the *Wall Street Journal Index*, a monthly that provides subject and company name access to the final Eastern Edition. The index is divided into two main parts, "General News" and "Corporate News." The general news section uses subject and personal name headings, and entries under each heading provide brief synopses of the articles indexed. Researchers should be aware that sometimes the subject headings used in the general news section are too broad to be very useful. Someone looking for information on self-regulation in the accounting profession, for example, would have to scan through all of the articles indexed under "Accounting" (including articles on specific accounting firms, accounting principles and standards, and companies audited by accountants) in order to identify those on self-regulation. Subject indexing is not a strength of the *Wall Street Journal Index*.

The corporate news section is more useful. In addition to article summaries, entries in this section also include earnings and dividend information. The entry for the National Distillers & Chemical Corp., shown in figure 3.9, is typical.

NATIONAL DISTILLERS & CHEMICAL CORP.
RJR Nabisco Inc.'s Heublein Inc. unit agreed in principle to acquire Almaden Vineyards Inc., a unit of National Distillers & Chemical Corp., for an undisclosed price; analysts estimate the transaction value to be below $200 million. 1/7-6;3

The Energy Department ordered National Distillers & Chemical Corp. to repay overcharges, plus interest, stemming from alleged violations of price controls on natural gas liquids; firm estimated that the payments would total $200 million. 1/12-52;4

RJR Nabisco Inc. is expected to announce the sale of its Heublein Inc. unit to Grand Metropolitan PLC for an undisclosed price; move comes as a surprise because RJR Nabisco recently agreed in principle to buy Almaden Vineyards, a unit of National Distillers & Chemical Corp.; Almaden would be part of the Heublein sale. 1/16-3;4

James Schorr was named a corporate vice president and to the new position of president of firm's USI Chemicals division. 1/19-12;2

Net income Dec. 31 year $75,600,000 (2.21); net income Dec. 31 quar $33,300,000 (1.02). 1/30-28;7

Quar div $.55, 3/2; 2/10. 1/30-30;2

Fig. 3.9. Typical entry, "Corporate News Section," *Wall Street Journal Index*. Reprinted by permission of the *Wall Street Journal Index*, © Dow Jones & Company, Inc. 1987. All Rights Reserved.

The *Index* also includes closing Dow Jones Averages for the month or year being indexed, and since 1981 the annual volumes have also included an index to *Barron's*, another important Dow Jones publication.

Although the *Wall Street Journal* remains the undisputed favorite, a new business daily is gaining in popularity. The *Investor's Daily*, which began publication in 1984, contains less general news and fewer feature articles than does the *Journal*. Its emphasis is on investor information, and it includes some data not available in the *Journal*. Its daily stock tables, for example, include an earnings-per-share rank for each stock and measure its relative price strength and changes in its trading volume. In addition, it features more industry-specific information, and makes extensive use of graphics. In libraries in which neither user demand nor the materials budget are sufficient to accommodate two daily business newspapers, the *Journal* is still the best choice. The *Investor's Daily*, however, is a worthwhile addition to most larger business collections.

Barron's National Business and Financial Weekly. New York: Dow Jones, 1921- . Weekly.

Just as the *Wall Street Journal* is the most widely read business daily, so its sister publication, *Barron's*, is the most popular business weekly. Aimed primarily at investors, *Barron's* focuses on various investment mediums, and covers political, economic, and social news as it affects investments.

Barron's is divided into two main parts. The first consists of articles and regularly featured columns. The articles may include interviews with prominent financial analysts, investment officials, executives, or government leaders, or they may analyze the prospects for specific companies. Some articles appear on a regular basis. Every three months, for example, one issue assesses mutual fund performance for the past quarter, while another includes a cumulative author, title, and subject index to the articles and columns published that year. Three January issues include transcripts of a panel discussion in which editors and guest experts speculate about the investment outlook for the new year.

The columns, written by specialists, deal with different aspects of finance and investment. They include:

"Up and Down Wall Street"
   Focuses on trends in finance and investment.

"The Trader"
   Summarizes the past week's stock market activities.

"The International Trader"
   Covers foreign markets and the corporate, monetary, and political developments that affect them.

"Investment News & Views"
   Describes and analyzes three or four individual companies.

"Commodities Corner"
   Discusses one or two specific commodities.

"Current Yield"
   Covers fixed-income securities such as bonds.

"The Striking Price"
   Options and financial futures are discussed.

"The Ground Floor"
   The subject is real estate.

The second part of *Barron's* consists of statistics for the past week's market transactions. These weekly statistics, often filling 50 pages or more, are one of the most comprehensive collections of current statistics available. The second section not only contains weekly statistics for traditional investments, but also includes such indicators as interest rates on bank credit cards, and Southeby's Art Index, which compares current prices to those paid in 1975 for Old Master paintings, Chinese ceramics, and other *objets d'art*. In addition, various business and economic indicators and stock indexes are also included.

As with the *Wall Street Journal*, the Dow Jones Educational Service Bureau makes available pamphlets that describe *Barron's*, promote its use, and explain some of its recurring features and statistics.[11]

Media General Financial Weekly. Richmond, Va.: Media General Financial Services, Inc., 1971- . Weekly.

Media General Market DataGraphics. Richmond, Va.: Media General Financial Services, Inc., 1981. Weekly.

Dow Jones is by no means the only publisher of business and financial newspapers. Media General Financial Services, for example, publishes two weekly papers. Although the first, *Media General Financial Weekly*, includes news and a few columns, its real strength is in the statistics it publishes; "Market Digest," the second section, consists of as many as 80 pages of stock market statistics. *Media General Financial Weekly* is particularly useful for its composite industry statistics, and for the table in which it arranges stocks by industry group. An excerpt from this table is shown in figure 3.10.

Company-Page-Market	Close	Price Chg. Yr. to Date	Curr. P/E Ratio	EPS 12 Mth. Chg.	Div. Yld.	Ret. on Com. Eqty.	Company-Page-Market	Close	Price Chg. Yr. to Date	Curr. P/E Ratio	EPS 12 Mth. Chg.	Div. Yld.	Ret. on Com. Eqty.
	$	%	-	%	%	%		$	%	-	%	%	%
011 Aerospace Industries							**031 Auto Manufacturers**						
Boeing Co	11-N	46.13	- 9.8	11.3	4	3.0	13.8	Am Motors	6-N	4.25	47.8	NE	NE	.0	NE
Curtiss-Wright	19-N	60.75	15.4	13.1	NE	2.6	NE	Amertek	7-M	2.75	29.4	6.9	400	.0	5.0
Fairchild Ind	24-N	14.38	42.0	NE	NE	1.4	49.5	Athey Prods	8-M	13.75	31.0	12.9	20	.0	13.7
Gen Dynamics	28-N	64.25	- 5.2	NE	-100	1.6	NE	Chrysler Cp	15-N	40.75	65.1	6.8	0	2.5	26.3
Gen Motors H	28-N	45.38	17.5	NA	NC	1.4	NA	ESI Ind	24-A	6.75	28.6	24.1	- 59	.0	9.6
Grumman Corp	30-N	25.63	4.6	11.2	- 5	3.9	10.9	Ford Motor Co	27-N	100.00	77.8	6.6	68	3.0	22.1
Lockheed Corp	38-N	46.50	- 7.2	7.5	0	2.2	21.9	Ford of Can	27-A	140.00	27.0	NA	51	NA	9.4
Martin Marietta	39-N	45.13	16.8	12.4	- 23	2.2	24.0	Gen Motors	28-N	89.75	36.0	11.6	- 36	5.6	9.7
McDonnel Doug	40-N	68.50	- 3.9	10.7	- 18	3.4	9.8	Honda Motor	32-N	90.63	5.7	15.3	- 26	.8	19.2
Northrop Corp	45-N	44.25	12.7	48.6	- 80	2.7	4.6	Koenig Inc	36-O	1.00	23.1	NE	NE	.0	NE
Rockwell Intl	52-N	29.13	31.8	13.8	11	4.5	19.3	Mack Trucks	39-M	19.88	82.8	NE	NE	.0	NE
Singer Co	55-N	44.00	17.7	10.1	NC	.9	15.6	Oshkosh Truck	46-M	30.00	25.0	10.0	44	1.0	31.0
Utd Technol	63-N	46.75	1.6	NM	- 96	3.0	1.9	Spartan Motors	56-M	3.13	4.2	26.0	100	.0	10.3
								Subaru of Amer	58-M	13.50	- 29.9	6.9	15	2.8	29.8

Fig. 3.10. Typical listings, *Media General's* "Stocks by Industry Group" table. Reprinted by permission from the May 11, 1987 issue of *Media General Financial Weekly*.

Media General Market DataGraphics contains no news. It consists entirely of stock charts for specific companies, tables of detailed stock performance statistics, and statistical data for bonds, mutual funds, and options. Neither Media General newspaper contains advertisements, and neither features much in the way of explanatory text. Both presuppose a basic knowledge of stock market trading and are perhaps most popular with library users who prefer to make their own investment decisions without consulting the published advice or comments of analysts and other experts.

Wall Street Transcript. New York: Wall Street Transcript, 1963- . Weekly.

Quite a different approach is offered by the *Wall Street Transcript*, a weekly which consists of transcripts of roundtable discussions of specific industries and selected reports on specific companies prepared by brokers and securities analysts. Although no tabular statistics are included as in the Media General and Dow Jones newspapers, many of the reports on specific companies include tables, charts, and statistics. The *Wall Street Transcript* also includes "Chief Executive Review," which names and describes the top three or four chief executive officers in designated industries; "Technical Corner," which features technical analysis by major brokerage firms; and "Connoisseur's Corner," which discusses art as a medium of investment. Each issue also includes a cumulated index.

Journal of Commerce. New York: Twin Coast Publishers, 1827- . Daily except Saturdays and Sundays.

The *Journal of Commerce* is a specialized business newspaper. Emphasis in the *Journal* is on news and statistics pertaining to commodities such as coffee or fuel oil, and on foreign trade and freight transport. Although the *Journal* is not common to all libraries, those that subscribe to it should make full use of it for its detailed data on shipping and specific commodities. Listings of inbound and outbound ships and their scheduled ports of call, for example, and the weekly shipping timetable to world ports make it particularly useful for the business person who is interested in international trade.[12]

The above business and financial newspapers, although important, are but a sample of such papers presently being published. Others can be identified by consulting *Ulrich's*, the *Gale Directory of Publications, Business Information Sources*, and other bibliographic guides and directories. Subscription to these and other similar newspapers will, of course, be determined by the scope of the library's business collection, its users, and, not incidentally, the size of its materials budget.

Trade Newspapers

Trade papers, like their trade magazine counterparts, include news, statistics, and descriptions of developments in particular industries and trades that may be virtually impossible to locate elsewhere. Two of the best known are *Variety*, the entertainment industry's trade paper, and *Women's Wear Daily*, which covers retailing of women's and children's apparel and accessories. As with trade magazines, many can be identified by using the *Gale Directory of Publications*.

Government Newspapers

Although the *Congressional Record* is the best known of the government-published newspapers, it is by no means the only one. Another, *Commerce Business Daily*, is of considerable interest to the business community.

U.S. Department of Commerce. **Commerce Business Daily.** Washington, D.C.: Government Printing Office, 1954- . Daily, except Saturdays and Sundays.

Commerce Business Daily offers opportunities to business firms seeking to sell products or services to the federal government. Each day, it lists government procurement invitations, subcontracting leads, sales of surplus government property, and foreign business opportunities. In addition, it identifies government contracts that have already been awarded to specific companies, and describes research and development projects in which specific federal procurement officers may be interested.

The most widely read section is "U.S. Government Procurements," a shopping list for specific services, supplies, and equipment required by the government. One agency, for example, may be in the market for software maintenance and development support, while another may be looking for brooms or mattress covers. Each listing generally includes the name, address, and telephone number of the agency and its purchasing officer; a description of the work to be done or the item(s) being sought for purchase or rent; and the deadline for submitting bids. The entry shown in figure 3.11 is typical.

---

83 Textiles, Leather, Furs, Apparel and Shoe Findings, Tents and Flags

---

UNICOR, Fed Prison Ind Inc, US Penitentiary, Leavenworth, KS 66048, Contact Wallace Zelle
❶ 83 -- TICKING; COTTON, BLUE & WHITE 43" and 56" width finished to approved fire retardant treatment pr Fed Spec CCC-C-436D, dated 10-6-71. Laundry test specified in para 3.5 shall apply. Type II, class 2. Requirements for 43" are 360,000 ly. Requirements for 56" are 90,000 Ly. These requirements are approx. This is a requirements type contract with del as required for the six-month period of 2 Mar 87 thru 31 Aug 87. Date set for receipt of bids on IFB 3PI-70010 30 Jan 87. (351)

Fig. 3.11. Typical listing, *Commerce Business Daily*. Reprinted from *Commerce Business Daily* (Washington, D.C.: Government Printing Office).

Employment Opportunities Newspapers

National Business Employment Weekly. New York: Dow Jones. Weekly.

National Job Market. Kensington, Md.: NJM Inc. Biweekly.

An increasing number of newspapers and tabloids are devoted solely to the job market. The *National Business Employment Weekly*, for example, combines articles on such general topics as employment interviews and job search techniques with sections that list opportunities in a designated profession, such as engineering or marketing, or that include advertisements for franchising and distributorship opportunities. The bulk of the paper, however, is devoted to advertisements for specific business and management positions, compiled from the regional editions of the *Wall Street Journal*.

Another similar publication is *National Job Market*, a biweekly that reproduces job advertisements from several major newspapers. Most of the advertisements are for such business fields as management, accounting, marketing, and real estate.

Other, similar publications also exist. Such employment opportunities newspapers offer users the convenience of consulting a single source rather than combing through several different newspapers (not all of which may be available locally), but they lag behind the newspapers in which the advertisements are originally published and constitute a drain on the library's serials budget as well. They may be best suited to libraries serving colleges and universities that graduate a large number of business students.

NEWSPAPER INDEXES

Several of the periodical indexes discussed earlier in this chapter include some of the major business newspapers. *Business Index*, for example, indexes *Barron's*, the business section of the *New York Times,* the *Journal of Commerce, Variety,* the *Wall Street Journal,* and *Women's Wear Daily*. Since subject indexing in the *Wall Street Journal Index* is so broad, librarians and researchers should consider using *Business Index* whenever subject access to the *Journal* is needed.

Predicasts F&S Index United States indexes the *Wall Street Transcript* and the *Journal of Commerce*. It is also the most comprehensive printed index to trade papers.

Many major daily newspapers, such as the *Wall Street Journal*, the *New York Times*, and the *Washington Post* publish their own indexes and, in addition, can be accessed using *National Newspaper Index*, a monthly microfilm index compiled by the same company that publishes *Business Index*.

Although printed newspaper and periodical indexes are staples in many libraries, the use of online bibliographic databases to access articles has become increasingly commonplace.

PERIODICALS, NEWSPAPERS, AND INDEXES AVAILABLE ONLINE

Online databases are considered at length in chapter 8. It is worth mentioning here, however, that many of the publications that have been discussed in this chapter are available as online databases. *Barron's, Commerce Business Daily, Harvard Business Review, Investor's Daily,* and the *Wall Street Journal* can all be searched online as full-text databases. In addition, computerized versions of *Business Index, Business Periodicals Index, Predicasts F&S Index United States, National Newspaper Index,* and several other printed indexing services are available. All of the databases mentioned above and other, similar databases make it possible to search in minutes a wide range of periodicals and newspapers that might not otherwise be available in every library setting.

NOTES

[1]*Business Week* circulation figures were taken from the March 1987 CD-ROM disk for *Ulrich's Plus.*

[2]The 1987 edition of the *Business Week* "Scoreboard Special," for example, was published in April and could be purchased as a separate issue for $5.50.

[3]Dick Levin, *The Executive's Illustrated Primer of Long-Range Planning* (Englewood Cliffs, N.J.: Prentice-Hall, 1981), 182.

[4]Clint Willis, "The Library Every Investor Needs," *Money* 13, no. 10 (October 1984): 147-154.

[5]According to Willis, the nine essential money management titles are:

Blume, Marshall E., and Jack P. Friedman, eds. *The Complete Guide to Investment Opportunities.* New York: Free Press, 1984.

Engel, Louis. *How to Buy Stocks.* Boston: Little, Brown, 1982.

Julian Block's Guide to Year-Round Tax Savings. Homewood, Ill.: Dow Jones-Irwin. Annual.

Malkiel, Burton. *A Random Walk down Wall Street.* New York: Norton, 1981.

Miller's Personal Income Tax Guide. New York: Harcourt, Brace, Jovanovich. Annual.

Rachlin, Harvey, ed. *The Money Encyclopedia*. New York: Harper & Row, 1984.

Rolo, Charles. *Gaining on the Market*. Boston: Little, Brown, 1982.

Train, John. *The Money Masters*. New York: Harper & Row, 1980.

Weinstein, Grace. *The Lifetime Book of Money Management*. New York: New American Library, 1984.

In addition, Willis recommends these supplementary sources:

Brooks, John. *The Go-Go Years*. New York: E. P. Dutton, 1984.

_____. *Once in Golconda*. New York: Harper & Row, 1969.

Dreman, David. *The New Contrarian Investment Strategy*. New York: Random House, 1982.

Graham, Benjamin. *The Intelligent Investor*. New York: Harper & Row, 1965.

Mackay, Charles. *Extraordinary Popular Delusions and the Madness of Crowds*. Boston: L. C. Page, 1932.

Nessen, Robert. *More Money Now*. Boston: Little, Brown, 1984.

_____. *The Real Estate Book*. New York: New American Library, 1983.

Pring, Martin. *Technical Analysis Explained*. New York: McGraw-Hill, 1985.

Sarnoff, Paul. *Trading in Gold*. Cambridge, England: Woodhead-Faulker, 1980.

Smith, Adam. *The Money Game*. New York: Random House, 1968.

[6]Another publication, *The Serials Directory: An International Reference Book* (Birmingham, Ala.: EBSCO Publishing, 1986) is a relatively new entrant to the periodicals directory field. It is useful for its coverage of federal periodical titles and for an array of trade publications, but is not as widely held as the directories discussed in this chapter.

[7]For a more thorough analysis of the business pages of the *New York Times*, see Richard C. Reid, "Using the Business Pages of the *New York Times*." Part 1 appeared in the Winter 1987 issue of the Special Libraries Association's *Business and Finance Division Bulletin* (pp. 3-7), and part 2 on pp. 2-6 of the Spring 1987 issue.

[8]A survey of top industrial executives, described in the September/October 1981 issue of *Industrial Management*, rated the *Wall Street Journal* as the most frequently read of all business serial titles. (The others, listed in order of frequency, were *Business Week, Fortune, Forbes, Newsweek, Harvard Business Review,* and *Barron's*).

[9]Regional representatives of the Dow Jones Educational Service Bureau can be reached at:

Eastern Representative
Educational Service Bureau
Dow Jones & Company
P.O. Box 300
Princeton, NJ 08540

Southern Representative
3525 Piedmont Road, N.E., Suite 309
Six Piedmont Center
Atlanta, GA 30305

Midwestern Representative
One South Wacker Drive
Chicago, IL 60606

Western Representative
1701 Page Mill Road
Palo Alto, CA 94304

Pacific Representative
201 California Street, 6th Floor
San Francisco, CA 94111

[10]The following publications relating to the *Wall Street Journal* can be ordered, free of charge, from any of the regional representatives listed above: *How to Read Stock Market Quotations, Understanding Financial Data in the Wall Street Journal*, and the *Wall Street Journal Educational Edition*.

[11]The following *Barron's* pamphlets can be ordered, free of charge and in multiple copies, from the Dow Jones Educational Service: *The ABC's of Market Forecasting: How to Use Barron's Market Laboratory Pages* and *Barron's Educational Edition*.

[12]For a more thorough description of prices, statistics, and other information regularly featured in the *Journal of Commerce*, see Richard C. Reid, "Finding Prices and Statistics in the *Journal of Commerce*." Part 1 appeared in the Fall 1987 issue of the Special Libraries Association's *Business and Finance Division Bulletin* (pp. 4-8) and part 2 on pp. 9-14 of the Winter 1988 issue.

All Governments like to interfere; it elevates their position.

—Walter Bagehot, *Economic Studies*

4

LOOSELEAF SERVICES

Coverage of business reference sources in the preceding chapters has focused on information available in such traditional formats as bibliographies, directories, periodicals, and newspapers. They are formats common to all subject disciplines, as likely to be found in the humanities and social sciences as in business. While these types of publications are important to the business community as well, they fail to meet one of its most important requirements, the need for detailed, current information pertaining to relatively narrow subject fields. An accountant needing to keep abreast of the most recent amendments to the tax law or a personnel director in search of recent court decisions regarding dismissal of employees, for example, would find that neither *Business Week*, the *Wall Street Journal*, nor any of the other sources described in the preceding chapter would provide the level of detail required. Looseleaf services, however, satisfy the need for such highly specific, up-to-date information. They are all but unique to the fields of business and law and, in fact, often combine the two.

This chapter focuses on looseleaf services, describing and illustrating their arrangement and use. It begins with a brief summary of their history and development.

HISTORY AND DEVELOPMENT

Enactment of the federal income tax law in 1913, followed by the creation of the Federal Trade Commission in 1914, gave the first real impetus to the development of looseleaf services. In each instance, lawyers, accountants, and business people were required not only to know the law as it was originally enacted, but also to keep abreast of subsequent amendments, court cases, administrative regulations and rulings, and other developments. Looseleaf services, which culled relevant sections from multiple primary sources such as the *U.S. Code*, court decisions, the *Code of Federal Regulations*, and the *Federal Register*, and which could be revised simply by inserting or removing specified

70

pages from looseleaf binders, were ideal. They were both more up-to-date and more convenient to use than traditionally bound materials and, in some instances, made information accessible that was not otherwise widely available.

Reform legislation enacted during the New Deal era in the 1930s provided another spur to the growth of looseleaf services. Passage of such laws as the Social Security Act of 1935 and the Fair Labor Standards Act of 1938, as well as the creation of such government agencies as the Securities and Exchange Commission, the National Labor Relations Board, and the Federal Deposit Insurance Corporation, all had profound effects on the practice of business, leading to increased regulation of business and economic activity by the federal government. This expansion of the government's role was reflected in a corresponding increase in the volume of legislative, administrative, and judicial rulings, all of which changed frequently. Again, looseleaf services proved the ideal format for coping with both the volume and frequency of changes in the law relating to these fields. Services covering labor, securities, social security, and bankruptcy were among those inaugurated during the New Deal.

More recent legislation, much of it passed in the 1970s, has focused on consumer and employee safety, and on protection of the environment. Again, the initial enabling legislation was supplemented by amendments, court decisions, and rulings from such government regulatory organizations as the Environmental Protection Agency and the Occupational Safety and Health Administration. As in earlier years, new looseleaf services were created to help business people and professionals keep informed and up-to-date.

Today there are literally hundreds of looseleaf services, most of them falling into the categories shown in figure 4.1 (see page 72). While scope and arrangement vary from publisher to publisher and from title to title, some generalizations about looseleaf services can be made. First, they represent areas, such as taxation and labor, that are heavily regulated by government and in which changes are commonplace and frequent. Second, each specialized field covered by a looseleaf service is treated comprehensively. Included are all relevant primary source material, such as legislation, agency rulings and interpretations, judicial decisions, executive orders, and administrative rulings. Third, looseleaf services often include secondary data such as lists of pending legislation, citations to relevant periodical articles and books, editorial commentary, and the latest news on developments in the field. Fourth, the arrangement and detailed indexing of information in looseleaf services make them more convenient and easier to use than the myriad of primary sources from which the information is gathered. Looseleaf publishers, in fact, point out that many of the government agencies responsible for issuing rules and regulations and administering the law are among their best customers.

> Stupefyingly complex it may be, and riddled with ambiguities and outright errors, but the 1,200-page tax bill entitled the Deficit Reduction Act of 1984 is a source of delight at Commerce Clearing House, Inc. This obscure but improbably profitable Chicago company publishes timely legislative reports and authoritative reference works that are basic business tools for subscribers in law, accounting, and government. Thanks to tax laws so voluminous and arcane that even professionals cannot untangle them unaided, CCH has come to derive over half its $379-million annual sales from its tax products alone and now cheerfully counts the IRS as its largest customer. Apparently as bewildered as everyone else, the bureaucrats there buy millions of dollars of the company's tax publications annually.[1]

Finally, the relative ease and frequency with which looseleaf services are updated often make them the first place in which changes are reported. They are essential to libraries serving patrons who must keep abreast of statutory and regulatory business law.

Accounting and Auditing

Banking

Bankruptcy

Commercial Credit

Consumer Credit

Corporations

Energy

Environment

Estates

Fair Employment

Foods, Drugs, and Medical Devices

Labor and Employee Relations

Legislation

Occupational Safety and Health

Pensions and Compensation

Product Liability

Profit Sharing

Real Estate

Securities

Social Security

Taxation

Trade Regulation

Fig. 4.1. Fields represented by looseleaf services.

FORMAT AND CONTENTS

Looseleaf services consist of two main parts: a series of binders and the accompanying perforated sheets to be inserted in them. Beyond that, arrangement varies. Although some publishers use a cumulating method in which new sections are simply added to the old without any concurrent substitution or removal of pages, most services are kept up-to-date by adding new pages and removing those which are no longer current. Such looseleaf services are often called *reporters*. Depending on the complexity of the field being covered, a reporter may consist of a single looseleaf volume, or as many as a dozen or more; the *Standard Federal Tax Reporter*, for example, consists of 18 volumes and is said to weigh more than 70 pounds.

At a minimum, most looseleaf services consist of the following parts: a "how-to" section, the basic text, new matter, and a series of indexes and finding aids. Each merits further attention.

Introductory Section

Almost every reporter begins with several pages of instruction and description, which explain the scope of the reporter, its arrangement, and how to use it most effectively (see figure 4.2). The importance of understanding a specific service's basic structure and arrangement before beginning research cannot be overemphasized. Looseleaf services are complex, filled with legal and business jargon, and their text presupposes basic familiarity not only with the subject matter, but also with the ways in which the publishers have chosen to arrange it. Many of the questions concerning the contents and use of a specific looseleaf service can be answered simply by reading the introduction, which should be required reading for business reference librarians, serious researchers, and for those responsible for filing looseleaf services.

Basic Text

The bulk of each service is comprised of the basic text, consisting of statutes, regulations, rulings, court decisions, and editorial commentary. Contents are arranged by subject in sections divided by guide cards identifying each unit's contents. Some of the divisions in the *Trade Regulation Reports*, for example, include "Antitrust and Trade Regulation Law," "Business Practices—Trade Restraints and Monopolies," "Price Fixing," and "Selling below Cost." A table of contents appears at the beginning of each division, outlining the subjects to be found; in these contents pages as in the indexes, references are made to paragraph numbers rather than page numbers. The table of contents page for the "Fair Packaging and Labeling" division, shown in figure 4.3 (see page 74), is typical.

LABOR RELATIONS REPORTER®

May 11, 1987

HOW TO USE

BNA's
Labor Relations Reporter

The Labor Relations Reporter (LRR) offers three basic types of information:

1) **Case services** that publish *decisions* and *arbitration awards* rendered by federal courts, state courts, administrative agencies, and arbitrators. These case services are: **Labor Management Relations - Decisions of Boards and Courts, Labor Arbitration Reports, Wages and Hours Cases, Fair Employment Practice Cases,** and **Individual Employment Rights Cases**. Headnotes summarizing the important issues are printed with the full text of these decisions and awards, and the issues covered in each headnote are assigned numbers under the appropriate outline of classifications. The headnotes are reproduced, in classification-number order, in the *Cumulative Digest and Index (CDIs)* for each case service. These CDIs are housed in the Master Index Binder until consolidated in books covering several volumes of the service. The *Tables of Cases* list by title the cases in each volume of each case service, and are also housed in the Master Index Binder until reprinted in bound cumulative volumes.

2) **Reference manuals** contain editorial discussion, full text of significant state and federal laws and regulations, and directories to administrative agencies. These manuals include: **Labor Relations Expediter, State Laws, Wages and Hours Manual, Fair Employment Practices Manual,** and **Individual Employment Rights Manual**.

3) **News and Analysis** covers significant news, including information on economic developments and reports, and listing of upcoming conferences and meetings. The Analysis provides an in-depth discussion of important recent developments - leading court opinions or significant trends.

Section 1b

Vol. 125, No. 3
0148-7981/87/$0+.50

Fig. 4.2. Typical introductory page to a looseleaf service. Reprinted by permission from *Labor Relations Reporter*, copyright 1987, by the Bureau of National Affairs, Inc., 1231 25th Street, N.W., Washington, D.C.

FAIR PACKAGING AND LABELING

Table of Contents

Trade Regulation Reports **Contents**

Fig. 4.3. Typical sectional contents page, looseleaf service. Reproduced with permission from *Trade Regulation Reports*, published and copyrighted by Commerce Clearing House, Inc., Chicago, Illinois 60646.

General comments follow the divisional contents page. The table of contents for "Fair Packaging and Labeling," for example, is succeeded by an essay on practical business problems as they relate to packaging and labeling. The essay, in turn, is followed by a general description of the scope of the Fair Packaging and Labeling Act, and it by paragraphs focusing on specific parts of the law. Covered, for example, are package descriptions and size, cents-off and other types of savings claims, and ingredients labeling.

Figure 4.4 shows the entry for paragraph 7148, "Ingredients," typical of such entries. Each paragraph begins with a general description of the topic being considered; in this instance, the paragraph describes the scope of federal government control as it relates to current regulation of ingredients labeling. In addition to syntheses of current practice, such paragraphs generally include citations to other parts of the looseleaf service and to other sources. In paragraph 7148, for example, citations are made to other paragraphs in *Trade Regulation Reports*. Frequently specific laws, court decisions, and rulings are cited as well, and while paragraph 7148 includes only one such reference, it also summarizes part of a congressional committee report dealing with ingredients labeling.

Ingredients

[¶ 7148]   Scope of Controls

The label disclosure of the ingredients of consumer products other than foods may be required by the FTC and HEW (Fair Packaging and Labeling Act, Sec. 5(c)(3)). By regulation, the agencies could require that the label of a non-food product show (1) the common or usual name of the product, if any, and (2) the common or usual name of each ingredient when the product consists of two or more ingredients. The listing of ingredients in order of decreasing predominance also could be required. As a protective measure, however, the law provides that the disclosure of trade secrets cannot be required. The regulations would be issued on a product-by-product basis. See also the label requirement as to the identity of the product (¶ 7110) and FTC regulations (¶ 7226.04).

While the listing of ingredients in order of decreasing predominance could be required, there is no express authority for requiring the disclosure of ingredient percentages.

Such regulations can be issued only after the FTC or HEW determines that regulations other than those prescribed by Sec. 4 of the Fair Packaging and Labeling Act (relating to mandatory labeling requirements) are necessary (1) to prevent the deception of consumers, or (2) to facilitate value comparisons as to any consumer product. The regulation issuance procedure is described at ¶ 7182.

.60   **Prior law.**—"Existing law [Federal Food, Drug, and Cosmetic Act] with respect to foods requires that the label bear a statement of ingredients. Existing law with respect to drugs requires that the active ingredients be stated on the label (and in some cases all of the ingredients be stated on the label). However, there is no such requirement with respect to cosmetics or other consumer commodities such as detergents. This type of information may become very valuable to the consumer in making value comparisons. House Report No. 2076, Interstate and Foreign Commerce Committee, September 23, 1966.

Fig. 4.4. Typical paragraph, looseleaf service. Reproduced with permission from *Trade Regulation Reports*, published and copyrighted by Commerce Clearing House, Inc., Chicago, Illinois 60646.

Although frequent changes are made to the basic text to keep it up-to-date, most reporters also include supplementary "current matters" sections in which new developments are reported. These sections vary from one service to another, but generally include a regular bulletin or newsletter, lists of and status reports on new and pending legislation, and texts or summaries of recent court decisions and regulatory agency rulings and opinions. This layering of basic text material with separate sections containing the most recent information is also reflected in the indexing characteristic of looseleaf services.

Indexes and Finding Aids

Indexes provide immediate access to specific divisions and paragraphs. Most reporters include a basic subject index, supplemented by a current index, issued between revisions of the basic index. In some instances, the current index will be supplemented by yet another, even more up-to-date, index. For example, a full Commerce Clearing House index may consist of three separate parts, a "Topical Index," a "Current Topical Index," and "Latest Additions to the Current Topical Index." Clearly, a thorough subject search will require that *all* topical indexes be consulted.

> Reporter services make as much effort to keep their indexes current as they do to report current substantive information. Master indexes are interpaginated periodically and are also supplemented by current indexes. Frequently, however, several of the latest weekly reports will not yet be indexed and therefore specific finding aids of each separate issue will have to be consulted. When using any index, it is essential that dates of its coverage are noted.[2]

Additional finding aids provide alternative means of accessing information. Most looseleaf services include case tables, which can be searched by case name; citator tables, which list court decisions by name and include references to subsequent rulings and decisions in which prior court decisions have been cited; and numeric tables, which make it possible to search by public law numbers, ruling numbers, and other official numeric designations. In most instances, these sections include detailed explanations of their use; the astute researcher will read these as well as the service's introductory section before beginning work.

PUBLISHERS AND THEIR REPRESENTATIVES

Although many different looseleaf publishers are represented in law library collections, in business reference settings three publishers are dominant. They are the Bureau of National Affairs (BNA), Commerce Clearing House (CCH), and Prentice-Hall (P-H). Each issues services on a wide range of subjects, most of which are quite expensive and many of which essentially duplicate similar services published by the other companies. Unless the business reference collection is unusually comprehensive or affluent or serves a community of users in which comparing coverage in different services is important, usually one publisher predominates. Both Commerce Clearing House and Prentice-Hall, for example, publish federal tax reporters, but many business libraries subscribe to only one tax service.

Selection of a looseleaf reporter will to a large extent be based on satisfaction with other reporters from the same publisher, library user and staff preference, and cost. Almost as important, although less often verbalized, is the selecting librarian's satisfaction with the publisher's representative.

Many publishers depend on regional representatives to promote sales, handle renewals, and assist subscribers in the effective use of services. They can help librarians restore misfiled reporters to order, supply missing pages, and provide hands-on assistance in the use of specific services. In addition, some offer free on-site training sessions to library staff and users. These training sessions can be presented at different levels of comprehensiveness and complexity, taking the participants' skill and experience into account. Finally, representatives can supply booklets and pamphlets that describe looseleaf services and their use. Although these publications focus on the issuing company's products, they contain enough general information to be helpful to librarians and novice searchers.[3]

DIRECTORIES

Looseleaf services have become increasingly commonplace and, in recent years, have extended from treatment of business and law to other subjects, ranging from microcomputers to health care. Although looseleaf services are listed selectively in some of the basic business guides described in chapter 1, such listings are far from comprehensive. The librarian seeking information about the availability of looseleaf services on a particular subject or the contents of a specific reporter must turn to another publication, the *Directory of Business and Financial Services.*

> Grant, Mary McNierney, and Riva Berleant-Schiller, eds. **Directory of Business and Financial Services.** 8th ed. New York: Special Libraries Association, 1984. 189p.

The *Directory of Business and Financial Services,* first published in 1924, lists and annotates nearly 2,000 different services, many of which are published in looseleaf format. Entries are arranged by title, with subject, publisher, and geographic indexes. Each listing includes the publisher's name and address, a descriptive annotation, and an indication of format, size, and frequency of publication. Although prices are also included, they are useful primarily as benchmark figures, since they represent prices quoted prior to publication in 1984. The entry shown in figure 4.5 is typical.

421 FEDERAL TAXES

Prentice-Hall
Englewood Cliffs, NJ 07632

Comprehensive information on all federal taxes, including laws, regulations, court decisions, Tax Court decisions, administrative rulings, and interpretations. Indexed both by type of transaction and by IRS Code section number. Also includes a calendar of compliance dates, current decisions, summary charts, ideas for tax savings, and weekly report bulletins. Looseleaf in fourteen volumes. Weekly. $1015.

Fig. 4.5. Sample entry, *Directory of Business and Financial Services.* Reprinted by permission of the Special Libraries Association from the *Directory of Business and Financial Services,* 8th ed., 1984, p. 50.

ONLINE DATABASES

Some looseleaf services are available as online databases, making it possible to search by key words, case names, special publisher designations, and other variables. Most of these databases, however, are aimed at practitioners; searching of these files with librarians as intermediaries is rare in all but special or law library settings. This chapter concludes with a brief look at databases presently available from the three major publishers of looseleaf services.

Prentice-Hall serves as both database producer *and* vendor, making its databases available without the intervention of a commercial database vendor. Although the Bureau of National Affairs does use commercial vendors, most of its databases are accessible only through LEXIS and NEXIS. One BNA file, however, is available through DIALOG. It is

LABORLAW, which provides access to labor arbitration awards and labor and industrial relations decisions published in six BNA looseleaf services.[4]

Commerce Clearing House has lagged behind both BNA and Prentice-Hall in making online databases available. Its *CCH Tax Day*, which has accumulated digests of daily federal and state tax developments, is available through NewsNet, LEXIS, and WESTLAW, while another product, *CCH Access*, a complete federal tax database, is expected to become available in the near future.

NOTES

[1]Stratford P. Sherman, "The Company That Loves the U.S. Tax Code," *Fortune* 110, no. 11 (November 26, 1984): 58.

[2]*Reporter Services and Their Use* (Washington, D.C.: Bureau of National Affairs, 1979), 16.

[3]Commerce Clearing House's offering is *Today's Business and Tax Law* and is available free of charge in multiple copies. *Reporter Services and Their Use*, published by the Bureau of National Affairs and written for law students, is free only in single copies. For further information, the publishers or their local representatives should be consulted.

[4]The looseleaf services that comprise BNA's *LABORLAW* database are as follows: *Fair Employment Practice Cases, Labor Arbitration Reports, Labor Relations, Mine Safety and Health Cases,* and *Occupational Safety and Health Cases.*

I don't make jokes; I just watch the government and report the facts.

— Will Rogers

5

GOVERNMENT INFORMATION AND SERVICES

The preceding chapter on looseleaf services touched upon the government's role as regulator and overseer of many commercial activities. The concentration in this chapter is considerably broader, focusing on information and services made available to business by federal and state government agencies. The importance of such government support cannot be overestimated. Agencies compile and publish data, supply personal expertise, and, in many instances, provide financial assistance to individuals and organizations. The aim of this chapter is to provide an overview of the major types of business-related government information and services, and of the print and electronic sources that identify them.

FEDERAL GOVERNMENT INFORMATION

The federal government is widely acknowledged to be the world's largest gatherer and publisher of information. Once primarily available in paper copy, it is now published in other formats as well, including microfiche, computer tape, and microcomputer disk. Whatever the format, much of this information can be tremendously useful to the business community. In fact, there are many business fields in which government documents are the most comprehensive information sources available; no private, commercial publisher, for example, can possibly match the detailed demographic and socioeconomic data routinely gathered and published by the Census Bureau. Government documents play an indispensable role in answering inquiries business people are likely to make, whether they be for the cost of living in Chicago, or forecasts for the steel industry, or the number of families in Memphis living in air-conditioned houses. There are Department of Labor publications on the outlook for specific occupations, congressional hearings on trade regulations and the national debt, Interstate Commerce Commission statistics on trucking, and Small Business Administration documents on how to establish, operate, and promote small businesses. There are, in fact, very few subjects about which the federal government has not issued publications. Unfortunately, except for a few standard reference works such as the *Statistical Abstract* and the *Government Manual*, documents are often overlooked by patrons and sometimes even by librarians as important information sources.

Structure of the Government

Effective promotion and use of federal documents begins with an understanding of the organizational structure of the government. The Constitution created three branches of government: legislative, judicial, and executive. In addition, although not set forth in the Constitution, an unofficial fourth branch, comprised of independent agencies and government corporations, is commonly recognized (see figure 5.1).

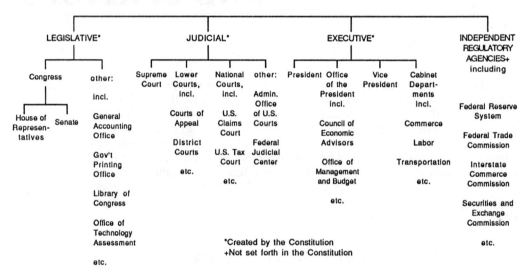

Fig. 5.1. Branches of the federal government.

LEGISLATIVE BRANCH

The legislative branch consists of both houses of Congress and several support organizations, such as the General Accounting Office and the Office of Technology Assessment. The publications of each reflect their varying purposes.

Congressional documents, for example, provide a record of information gathered and opinions shared and debated as well as laws enacted. The work of preparing and considering legislation is done largely by committee, and congressional committee publications such as committee prints (background information and studies prepared by staff for committee use), hearings, and reports contain a wealth of information. While there are few congressional committees whose activities do not affect business in one way or another, some, listed in figure 5.2, are particularly important. Copies of current committee prints, hearings, and reports can usually be obtained by contacting the Senate Document Room or by writing or calling the documents clerk of the committee itself. Since congressional documents are printed in limited supply, it may be necessary to borrow older ones from nearby depository libraries or to acquire reprints from commercial publishers.

House	Senate	Joint
Agriculture	Agriculture, Nutrition, and Forestry	Economic
Armed Services	Armed Services	Taxation
Banking, Finance and Urban Affairs	Banking, Housing and Urban Affairs	
Education and Labor	Commerce, Science, and Transportation	
Energy and Commerce	Energy and Natural Resources	
Interior and Insular Affairs	Environment and Public Works	
Merchant Marine and Fisheries	Finance	
Public Works and Transportation	Labor and Human Resources	
Science and Technology	Small Business	
Small Business		
Ways and Means		

Fig. 5.2. Congressional committees pertaining to business.

Support organizations in the legislative branch include the Congressional Budget Office, the Office of Architect of the Capital, and the U.S. Botanic Garden. The agencies in this category with most relevance to business, however, are the General Accounting Office, the Government Printing Office, the Library of Congress, and the Office of Technology Assessment.

The General Accounting Office, or GAO, is an independent, nonpolitical agency responsible for auditing government agencies, and for making recommendations to Congress on how to improve the efficiency and effectiveness of government programs. The GAO responds to legislation directing it to analyze and evaluate specific programs and to requests for assistance from congressional staff; its findings are published in reports to Congress, many of which are publicly available.[1] Reports can cover broad topics, such as foreign investment in the United States and the financial condition of American agriculture, or they may focus on narrower topics such as deteriorating airport runways and abuses of black lung benefits.

The Government Printing Office, or GPO, executes printing and binding orders placed by Congress and by other government agencies. In addition, it prepares catalogs, and distributes and sells government documents. Its activities are more fully described in the section on government publishers that follows.

Although the Library of Congress was established to serve the information needs of Congress, its considerable resources are also available to the public. These include collections that make it the world's largest library, and access to a number of services, some of which are listed later in this chapter.

The Office of Technology Assessment (OTA) was created by the Technology Assessment Act of 1972 to "help Congress anticipate and plan for the consequences of technology."[2] Its basic function is to provide congressional committees with studies that identify the social, economic, and physical consequences that may accompany various policy decisions relating to the use of specific technologies, such as nuclear power and robotics. These studies are issued as OTA reports, and are available from the GPO. Many treat issues of concern to business; a sampling of recent reports includes such titles as *Automation of America's Offices, Computerized Manufacturing Automation,* and *Intellectual Property Rights in an Age of Electronics and Information.*

JUDICIAL BRANCH

The Judiciary is comprised of the Supreme Court and the U.S. Courts of Appeals, and District and Territorial Courts. In addition, it includes national courts such as the U.S. Tax Court and the U.S. Court of International Trade. Finally, two support agencies, the Administrative Office of the U.S. Courts and the Federal Judicial Center, complete the roster of organizations in this branch.

Compared to the legislative and executive branches, the judicial arm of the government is not a prolific publisher. The documents it issues are primarily court decisions. While these decisions can have tremendous impact on how business is conducted, requests for the legal information they contain are generally handled by law libraries and in documents departments rather than in more general library settings.

EXECUTIVE BRANCH

The executive branch consists of the president, the executive office of the president, the vice-president, and 13 cabinet departments. While the duties of the president and vice-president themselves require no discussion, the other executive agencies merit examination.

The executive office of the president is comprised of various advisory and administrative support agencies. Those that are particularly important to business are the Council of Economic Advisers, the Council on Environmental Quality, the Office of Management and Budget, and the Office of the U.S. Trade Representative.

The Council of Economic Advisers is responsible for analyzing the economy and for advising and recommending policies to the president that promote economic growth and stability. It also assists in the preparation of two very important recurring documents, *Economic Indicators,* a monthly compilation of economic statistics prepared for the Congress' Joint Economic Committee, and the annual *Economic Report of the President.* The council's own annual report, not incidentally, is bound with the president's report and comprises the bulk of the document. In 1987, for example, the president's report was 8 pages long, and the council's, 360.

The main purpose of the Council on Environmental Quality is to formulate and recommend national policies to improve the environment. These recommendations are based on a continuing analysis of the environment and any changes or trends that affect it, as well as on a review and appraisal of government programs to determine their contributions to sound environmental policy. Many of its findings are published. Council documents in recent years have covered such topics as urban sprawl, energy alternatives, desertification, and acid rain. Like that of the Council of Economic Advisers, its annual report is filled with an impressive array of information and statistical data, ranging from the pollutant standard for urban air quality to the status of whale stocks. As with most other Council on Environmental Quality publications, the annual report is available from the Government Printing Office.

The Office of Management and Budget is charged with several responsibilities. They include reviewing the organization and management of the executive branch, developing and promoting interagency coordination and cooperation, helping the president prepare the budget, and supervising and controlling its administration. In addition, OMB is responsible for planning program performance evaluations, and for keeping the president informed of work proposed, initiated, and completed by government agencies. Although it issues documents on a wide range of subjects, some of the most heavily used titles are the *Budget of the United States Government* and its satellite documents such as the *Budget in Brief* and *Special Analysis of the Budget of the United States*, as well as the *Catalog of Federal Domestic Assistance*, which lists and describes federal assistance programs available to organizations and individuals.

The Office of the U.S. Trade Representative is responsible for administering trade agreements and coordinating trade policy. It periodically issues documents such as the *U.S. National Study on Trade in Services* and *A Preface to Trade*, a good introduction to U.S. international trade policy and policy making.

In addition to the agencies mentioned above, several commissions, committees, boards, and task forces are established periodically by the president to conduct fact-finding missions. Most publish their findings, and many relate to business and the economy.

Although the Departments of Commerce, Labor, and Treasury are particularly important, each of the 13 executive departments affects business in some way. Appendix B lists the departments, their primary responsibilities relating to business, and selected agencies and publications. Each department publishes a wide array of reports, periodicals, statistics, and information for the general public, most of which are available from the Government Printing Office. Each department also employs a complement of subject specialists who are generally quite willing to share their expertise and, in addition, each has at least one public affairs or information office.

Many departments have regional or field offices, established to provide assistance to designated regions of the country. The Department of Labor's Bureau of Labor Statistics, for example, has regional offices in 8 different cities; the Census Bureau, in 12. One of the easiest ways to determine the location of the closest field office is by consulting the *United States Government Manual*. Although it is described in more detail later in this chapter, it is worth noting here that the *Manual* provides quick access to the addresses and telephone numbers of such offices, the areas they serve, and, in many instances, the names of their administrators.

INDEPENDENT AGENCIES AND GOVERNMENT CORPORATIONS

The *United States Government Manual* lists over 50 different independent government organizations authorized by the president or by congress. Some, such as the Federal Trade Commission and the Interstate Commerce Commission, are regulatory agencies. In many instances, the activities they oversee and regulate are commercial ones; as a result, these agencies touch upon business in a very real and constant way. Others, such as the Federal Deposit Insurance Corporation, are government-established corporations. Whatever their designation, these agencies comprising the unofficial fourth arm of the government routinely gather and publish statistics, research findings, and agency regulations and decisions. They are prolific publishers. The agencies with greatest impact on business activities are listed in appendix C.

This overview of federal government structure attests to its complexity and diversity. There are literally hundreds of government departments, committees, bureaus, commissions, and agencies. Most are described in the official directory of federal organization, the *United States Government Manual*.

U.S. National Archives and Records Administration. Office of the Federal Register. **United States Government Manual.** Washington, D.C.: Government Printing Office, 1935- . Annual.

The *United States Government Manual* provides comprehensive information on independent, legislative, executive, and judicial agencies. Each agency listing generally includes a brief description of its history, programs and activities, and a list of its principal officials. Its address and telephone number and those of its regional and district offices are also included. In addition, each entry features a "Sources of Information" section that lists the names and telephone numbers of departments responsible for public information, contracts and grants, publications, and employment. Organization charts for major departments and agencies are included and a list of abolished and transferred agencies is appended. Name, subject, and agency indexes complete the *Manual.* This inexpensive directory is, in fact, a treasure trove of information, an indispensable guide to the federal government. It belongs in every reference collection.

Although the *Manual* provides an overview of the legislative branch, it is not the most comprehensive congressional information source. That distinction belongs to another federal publication, the *Official Congressional Directory.*

U.S. Congress. Joint Committee on Printing. **Official Congressional Directory.** Washington, D.C.: Government Printing Office, 1809- . Annual.

Prepared for the use of Congress members and their staff, the *Official Congressional Directory* is useful to anyone who requires information about the legislative branch of the government or about executive, judicial, independent, and private organizations whose activities affect Congress. It includes a listing of congressional committees and subcommittees, their staff, and the members of Congress who serve on them; a biographical section arranged by state; and an alphabetical listing of legislators, their office addresses and telephone numbers, and the names of their administrative and executive assistants. Information on embassies, diplomats, and international organizations is also included. Using the *Directory,* one can find the name of the ambassador from Botswana, determine when a senator's term of office will expire, and compile a list of OECD member countries. Like the *United States Government Manual,* the *Official Congressional Directory* is a basic reference source. Together they provide detailed and comprehensive access to most government organizations.

In government as in business, however, change is commonplace. Programs and responsibilities change, new departments and agencies are created, and old ones reorganized or even abolished. Thus, as with many annual business directories, these government directories sometimes lag behind. One solution is to supplement them with commercially published directories issued more frequently. Below are two of the most commonly used commercial publications.

Federal Executive Directory. Washington, D.C.: Carroll Publishing, 1980- . Bimonthly.

Federal Yellow Book. Washington, D.C.: Monitor Publishing, 1976- . Quarterly.

Both the *Federal Executive Directory* and the *Federal Yellow Book* provide directory access to federal agencies and key executives. While much of the information is garnered from federal telephone directories and the *United States Government Manual,* the commercial directories are considerably narrower in their approach, limiting data to names, addresses, and telephone numbers. Their advantage is their relative currency. One is updated bimonthly, the other quarterly, and as a result they sometimes reflect more accurately current government organization and staffing than do the government annuals. Subscriptions to the *Federal Executive Directory* and the *Federal Yellow Book,* however, cost several times the purchase price of the *United States Government Manual* and the *Official Congressional*

Directory. Whether the currency of the information they contain compensates for their cost is a decision that must be made in each library setting.

Federal Government Publishers

The federal government, as we have seen, is complex and diverse, a "colossus [that] dwarfs all other private or public activities."[3] Moreover, each agency in the government is involved in activities that often result in the publication of documents for public information and use. Documents take many different forms and their intellectual content varies widely, but most are made available through two major government publishers, the Government Printing Office and the National Technical Information Service. Consideration of these and of the other types of federal publishers is in order. As shown in figure 5.3, four major categories can be identified.

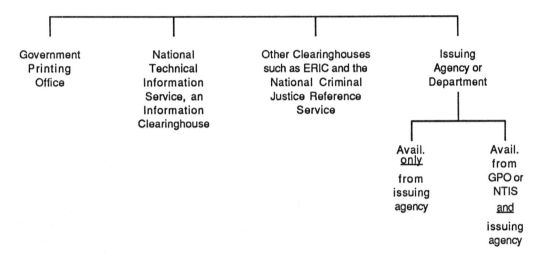

Fig. 5.3. Publishers of federal government documents.

GOVERNMENT PRINTING OFFICE

Although it began as the printer for Congress and is officially an agency of the legislative branch, the Government Printing Office's activities have long since expanded to make it the primary source for printing, distribution, and sales of federal government documents. Each year, it publishes thousands of items and makes many of them available through a network of depository libraries and a sales program.

Depository Libraries

The GPO distributes many of the documents it publishes to over 1,350 libraries, called *depository libraries* or *depositories*. The depository system was created to ensure public access to documents, and each depository library "is designated to receive, without charge on a deposit basis, government publications issued by governmental agencies, except those determined by the issuing agencies to be required for official use only or for strictly administrative or operational purposes ... [or] classified for reasons of national security."[4] Four points should be emphasized. First, depository libraries do not pay for the documents they receive. Second, although housed in the library, the documents do not really belong to the library; they are there "on deposit." The federal government has the right to ask for their return at any time. Third, the depository program exists to make documents available to the public. Although definition of public availability varies from one depository library to another, at a minimum, it means that *anyone* has the right to use, on site, any document held by the library. Fourth, not all GPO-published documents are sent to depository libraries; a distinction is made between *nondepository* documents, which are not sent to depositories, and *depository* documents, which are.

There are two types of depository libraries, regional and selective. The country's 50 regional depositories, listed in appendix D, are required to receive and keep permanently all documents that have been designated as depository items. In addition, regional depository staffs are expected to provide interlibrary loan and reference service and other types of assistance, both to the public and to other libraries in their region. Many regionals have been depositories since the late nineteenth or early twentieth century. As a consequence of their extensive collections and their strong service orientation, they are usually excellent providers of information, advice, and assistance.

Selective depository libraries can choose the documents that they want to receive; unlike the regionals, they are not required to accept and house every depository document published by the Government Printing Office. In addition, with the approval of the regional depository library in their area, they can discard unwanted documents. As a result, there is considerable variation in the breadth and depth of selective depository collections. Some rival regional depositories in size and scope; others are considerably narrower. There are presently some 1,300 selective depository libraries in the United States and, like their regional depository counterparts, they provide access to and assistance in the use of their documents collections.

Although most nondepository library business reference collections include a core of basic business sources published by the federal government, depository libraries provide access to more specialized sources and to GPO titles that are no longer in print. Library staff and users would do well to become acquainted with collections, service policies, and documents librarians at nearby depository libraries. They constitute a rich information source, one that can be of particular benefit to business librarians and researchers. A complete list of selective and regional depository libraries can be obtained by writing to the Government Printing Office.[5]

GPO Sales Program

Nondepository libraries wishing to build documents collections of their own or to acquire specific government publications, however, usually purchase them from the Government Printing Office's Superintendent of Documents. Three options are available. The one most frequently used is the GPO's mail and telephone order program. Using it, a library can order specific documents on an item-by-item basis. In some instances, standing orders can be placed for such popular and recurring titles as the *United States Government Manual* and the *Statistical Abstract of the United States.* Prepayment for all orders is required, and may be handled by check, by major credit card, or by establishing a deposit account with the Government Printing Office.[6]

In addition to the order service, there are five GPO bookstores in the Washington, D.C., area and in 20 other cities across the United States, each of which stocks and sells approximately 1,500 of the GPO's most popular titles.[7] In addition, librarians can acquire federal documents through commercial bookdealers, jobbers, and document delivery services. Usually, however, the choice is to order documents from the GPO by mail or by telephone.

GPO Bibliographies and Lists

Documents published by the Government Printing Office can be identified by consulting one or more of the GPO's bibliographies and lists. Among the most important are the *Monthly Catalog of United States Government Publications, U.S. Government Books, New Books, Subject Bibliographies,* and *Government Periodicals and Subscription Services, Price List 36.* Each merits attention.

> U.S. Superintendent of Documents. **Monthly Catalog of United States Government Publications.** Washington, D.C.: Government Printing Office, 1895- . Monthly, with monthly and annual indexes.

"The *Monthly Catalog*," writes Yuri Nakata, "is to government publications what the *Cumulative Book Index* is to general book publications."[8] It records and indexes documents received by the Government Printing Office from all arms of government—legislative, judicial, and executive branches, and independent and regulatory agencies as well. Arrangement of documents included in the *Monthly Catalog* is by issuing agency. All Department of Commerce publications, for example, are grouped together regardless of subject, as are those of the Department of Labor, the Federal Trade Commission, and other agencies. Entries are detailed and, as shown in figure 5.4, include information that facilitates ordering them from the Government Printing Office or the issuing agency, or that will help to access them through a depository library. Although the preliminary pages of each issue of the *Monthly Catalog* describe its contents and use in some detail, a few major points are worth noting.

86-11037

C 3.134/2-2:986
USA statistics in brief. [Washington, D.C.] : U.S. Dept. of Commerce, Bureau of the Census : [For sale by the Supt. of Docs., U.S. G.P.O., Supt. of Docs., U.S. Govt. Print. Off., Washington, D.C., 20402
   v. ; 14 x 51 cm. folded to 14 x 11 cm.
   Annual
   $1.00
   Began with 1972. Title from cover. Previously classed: C 3.134/2:St 2/ Shipping list no.: 86-211-P. 1986. Description based on: 1980. ●Item 151 S/N 003-024-06367-1 @ GPO Supplement to: Statistical abstract of the United States ISSN 0081-4741
   1. United States — Statistics — Periodicals. I. United States. Bureau of the Census. OCLC 02289219

Fig. 5.4. Sample entry, *Monthly Catalog of United States Government Publications.* Reprinted from the 1986 *Monthly Catalog of United States Government Publications.*

Each document is assigned an entry number, used in the indexes to identify specific documents by author, subject, title, and other designations. The entry number begins with two digits indicating the year of the *Monthly Catalog* in which it is listed, followed by a hyphen and the remaining identifying numbers. In the main section of the *Monthly Catalog*, the entry number is located at the top left of the listing for each item. In figure 5.4, for example, the entry number is 86-11037.

Each item is also assigned a Superintendent of Documents classification number, listed in boldface at the top center of each entry. The Superintendent of Documents classification system is one that focuses primarily on the identity of the issuing agency, rather than on the document's subject. It also designates publication type, series number (if any), and includes a number or other designation for the specific document. The Superintendent of Documents classification for *USA Statistics in Brief*, a Census Bureau publication, is C3.134/2-2:986, and it reflects the following hierarchical arrangement.

C   = Designation for the Department of Commerce, the parent department

C3   = Designation for the Bureau of the Census, part of the Department of Commerce

.134   = Designation for the *Statistical Abstract of the United States*, an annual Census Bureau publication

.134/2   = Indicates that the title is one of the regular supplements to the *Statistical Abstract*

.134/2-2 = Designation for a specific supplement, *USA Statistics in Brief*

:986   = Year of publication of the specific edition of *USA Statistics in Brief* being cited

Thus, the Superintendent of Documents classification number C3.134/2-2:986 indicates that the document is issued by the Census Bureau, which is a part of the Department of Commerce, and that it is the 1986 edition of *USA Statistics in Brief*, which is supplement number 2 to the *Statistical Abstract*. Although many librarians and researchers seldom use the Superintendent of Documents classification system, it is used frequently in depository library collections. Having the Superintendent of Documents numbers available when inquiring about or asking to borrow specific documents from depository libraries can be extremely helpful to the depository staff and may lead to faster service.

One should note two additional bits of information before calling upon depository libraries for assistance. As mentioned earlier, not all GPO-published documents are designated as depository documents. Those that are include heavy black dots, or bullets (•), in the main listing. Regional depository libraries—required to receive and keep *all* depository documents—should have all of these bulleted documents. Selective depository libraries, on the other hand, may have only a limited number of such publications. In addition, many documents formerly published in paper copy are now available only in microfiche. An increasing number of entries include the notation, "distributed to depository libraries in microfiche." Requests for assistance from depository libraries should, whenever possible, indicate whether the document being sought is published by the GPO in paper copy or microfiche. Finally, it is never safe to assume that a particular document, simply because it is not a depository item, will be unavailable at depository libraries. Many depositories have extensive holdings of nondepository documents collections purchased from commercial publishers such as Readex and Congressional Information Service.

When the choice is to acquire documents rather than to borrow them from another library, other information is necessary. In many instances, documents can be ordered from the Superintendent of Documents; their availability from the GPO at the time of printing is usually indicated in the main entry, as shown in figure 5.4. Also included are the price and the GPO sales stock number, preceded by the letters S/N. For example, *USA Statistics in Brief* is available from the GPO for $1.00, and its stock number, the number used to order it, is S/N 003-024-06367-1. Mail order forms are included in the preliminary pages of each issue of the *Monthly Catalog*.

A document's inclusion in the *Monthly Catalog* does not guarantee its availability from the Government Printing Office. Some must be ordered from the issuing agencies themselves. Many Census Bureau publications, for example, are sold by the Bureau's Data User Services Division rather than by the GPO. If neither a stock number, price, nor the phrase "For sale by the Supt. of Docs." appears in an entry, it is safe to assume that it will have to be requested from the issuing agency.

In summary, the following information is necessary when attempting to borrow or acquire documents listed in the *Monthly Catalog*.

Borrowing from a Depository	Ordering from the GPO	Requesting from Issuing Agency
Is it a depository item? (i.e., does it have a black dot?)	Is it for sale from GPO? (i.e., does it say "For sale by Supt. of Docs"?)	What is the title? Publication date? Is there an author? Is a price given? Be as specific as possible.
Is it in paper copy or microfiche?	How much does it cost?	
What is its SuDocs classification?	What is its stock number?	

Since the main section of the *Monthly Catalog* is arranged by government agency, indexes that permit other means of identifying and accessing material are extremely important. The *Monthly Catalog* features seven such indexes.

Author Index	Alphabetically lists personal authors, editors, co-authors, corporate authors, and conferences
Title Index	Alphabetically lists titles, series titles, and sub- or alternate titles
Subject Index	Alphabetically lists subjects derived from Library of Congress subject headings
Series/Report Index	Alphabetically lists report numbers and series statements
Contract Number Index	Alphabetically lists contract, grant, and project numbers associated with technical report publications
Stock Number Index	Numerically lists Superintendent of Documents sales stock numbers
Title Keyword Index	Alphabetically lists important words from the titles

Indexes are included in each issue, and are cumulated semiannually and annually. The *Monthly Catalog* can also be searched as an online database through such major database vendors as DIALOG and BRS.

Although the *Monthly Catalog* is the most comprehensive listing of GPO publications, it is not always the best source for building business reference collections, particularly in small- and medium-sized libraries. In these settings, other sources, such as *U.S. Government Books, New Books,* and the GPO's *Subject Bibliography* series, may be more helpful.

U.S. Government Books. Washington, D.C.: Government Printing Office, 1982- . Quarterly.

New Books. Washington, D.C.: Government Printing Office, 1982- . Bimonthly.

U.S. Government Books is a catalog of popular and bestselling government books and periodicals. It annotates and lists by subject almost 1,000 documents, titles such as the *Franchise Opportunities Handbook, How to Prepare for Workplace Emergencies,* and *Selling to the Military.* In addition to the category, "Business & Industry," other areas of interest to business librarians and researchers include Agriculture, Careers, Computers & Computer Science, Consumer Aids, Housing, Science & Technology, and Transportation. In addition to the annotation, each entry includes publication date, number of pages, price, GPO stock number, and, in most instances, the Superintendent of Documents classification number. As with the *Monthly Catalog,* order forms and instructions are included in each issue. Free copies of *U.S. Government Books* can be obtained by writing to the Superintendent of Documents.[9]

New Books is a current awareness tool, particularly useful for librarians and researchers who would like to keep abreast of the most recent titles issued by the Government Printing Office. Organization is by subject, and then alphabetically by title. Although annotations are not included, *New Books* includes an order form and ordering instructions with each issue. Libraries and individuals can be placed on the mailing list to receive free copies of *New Books* by writing to the Superintendent of Documents.[10]

U.S. Superintendent of Documents. **Subject Bibliography Index** (SB599). Washington, D.C.: Government Printing Office, 1985. 8p.

The Government Printing Office also publishes a series of brief bibliographies that list popular pamphlets and brochures by subject. At present, there are over 250 such bibliographies, all of which are listed in the *Subject Bibliography Index.* Bibliographies of particular interest to the business community include the following titles.

Accounting and Auditing (SB42)

Agricultural Research, Statistics, and Economic Reports (SB162)

Banks and Banking (SB128)

Business and Business Management (SB4)

Employment and Occupations (SB44)

Energy Management for Consumers and Businesses (SB303)

Foreign Investments (SB275)

Foreign Trade and Tariff (SB123)

Government Specifications and Standards (SB231)

How to Sell to Government Agencies (SB171)

Insurance (SB294)

Labor-Management Relations (SB64)

Marketing Research (SB125)

Occupational Safety and Health (SB213)

Patents and Trademarks (SB21)

Personnel Management, Guidance, and Counseling (SB202)

Prices, Wages, and the Cost of Living (SB226)

Shipping and Transportation (SB40)

Small Business (SB307)

Statistical Publications (SB273)

Taxes and Taxation (SB195)

For each document listed, the *Subject Bibliography* includes its title, date, pagination, Superintendent of Documents number, GPO stock number, and price. Many titles are annotated. Although the *Subject Bibliographies* and the *Index* are depository items and available in most documents collections, individuals and other libraries can acquire their own free copies by writing to the Superintendent of Documents.

Government Periodicals and Subscription Services. Price List 36. Washington, D.C.: Government Printing Office, 1974- . Quarterly.

Government Periodicals and Subscription Services, also known as *Price List 36*, is a catalog that lists over 500 serial titles and subscription services available from the Government Printing Office, including such titles as *Economic Indicators, Monthly Labor Review,* and *Survey of Current Business*. Entries are arranged by title, and usually include current prices, stock numbers, Superintendent of Documents classification, and, when applicable, the bullet symbol used to identify depository items. Many entries include annotations. In addition, each issue of *Price List 36* lists new and discontinued serials, as well as those with titles that have changed since the preceding issue of the price list. Like other GPO documents, these serials can be ordered by mail or by telephone. Free copies of *Price List 36* are available from the Superintendent of Documents.

Although the above bibliographies are among the most important lists of documents published by the Government Printing Office, they are by no means the only ones. The *Consumer Information Catalog*, described in chapter 7, lists free and inexpensive government booklets for the general public, while the GPO microfiche catalog, *Sales Publications Reference File*, lists titles currently in print and for sale by the Superintendent of Documents. Still other bibliographies are compiled by commercial publishers.

Although the Government Printing Office is the principal printing agency of the federal government, it does not publish and sell all federal documents. Further, although its sales program offers some 25,000 popular titles and some 500 serial titles, it does not as a rule keep or sell publications that are no longer current.

Other government agencies are also involved in publication of documents, usually more specialized than those available through the GPO. One of the most important of these agencies is the National Technical Information Service.

NATIONAL TECHNICAL INFORMATION SERVICE

The National Technical Information Service (NTIS), an agency of the Department of Commerce, is the central source for public sale of government-sponsored research, development, and engineering reports, and for sales of technical reports prepared by foreign governments and by local government agencies (see figure 5.5 on page 92). Reports collected and sold by the NTIS fall into one of 22 broad categories, ranging from "Aeronautics" to "Space

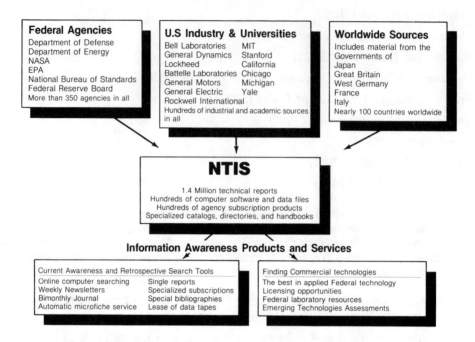

Fig. 5.5. National Technical Information Service (NTIS). Reprinted from National Technical Information Service, *Guide to NTIS* (Springfield, Va.: NTIS, 1987).

Technology." While most of the reports it sells are purely scientific or technical, an increasing number fall into its "Behavioral and Social Science" category, which includes such business-related fields as Administration and Management, Economics, Human Factors Engineering, Man-Machine Relations, and Personnel Selection, Training, and Evaluation.

When compared to the Government Printing Office, however, the NTIS has a much narrower focus. No congressional hearings or government regulations or consumer-oriented publications are included. There are other differences between the agencies. The Government Printing Office sells only current titles. The possibility of obtaining a 10- or even a 5-year-old document from the Government Printing Office is remote. The National Technical Information Service, on the other hand, offers access to all of the documents received since its inception, almost two million titles in all. Some 80,000 of the most popular NTIS titles are kept in stock; the rest are held as microform masters from which copies can be made as demand arises. Another difference is that the Government Printing Office subsidizes the printing and sale of its documents, which are very inexpensive. The NTIS, in contrast, is required by law to operate on a cost-recovery basis. As a result, there is considerable difference between the prices of NTIS and GPO documents. Finally, while the Government Printing Office has established a network of designated depository libraries, there is no NTIS equivalent. Although many research and technical libraries comprehensively collect NTIS documents, their collections are not part of a government-sponsored system.

NTIS documents are available in a wide variety of formats, including paper copy, microfiche, and microfilm, and, in many instances, computer tape and microcomputer disk. Orders can be placed by mail or by telephone, or documents can be purchased from NTIS sales units in Springfield, Virginia, and Washington, D.C. As with the GPO, payment can be by check, credit card, or deposit account.

Government Reports Announcements & Index (GRA&I). Springfield, Va.: NTIS, v.75- . 1975- . Semiweekly.

Government Reports Announcements & Index is the most comprehensive bibligrapy of NTIS documents, roughly analogous to the GPO's *Monthly Catalog*. Published biweekly, each issue abstracts and indexes some 2,500 new titles. Arrangement is by broad subject category, and then by narrower subcategory. Within each subcategory, each entry includes an abstract number, an order number, indication of format and availability, a price code, the report's title, the names of its corporate sponsor(s) and personal author(s), report and contract numbers, and an abstract. Each issue of *GRA&I* also contains indexes that permit access by keyword, personal author, corporate author, contract or grant number, and NTIS order or report number. Also included are detailed order information and order forms. *Government Reports Announcements & Index* can also be searched as an online database. Available through major database vendors, it is usually known as "NTIS."

Government Reports Annual Index (GRAI). Springfield, Va.: NTIS, v. 75- . 1975- . Annual.

The National Technical Information Service also publishes *Government Reports Annual Index*, a cumulative index to the 26 issues of *GRA&I* published annually. For libraries with extensive documents collections or serving clientele with a continuous, ongoing need for a wide array of scientific and technical information, both *GRA&I* and *GRAI* are basic bibliographic sources.

In many libraries, however, the need is neither so continuous nor so broad. A patron may want to keep up-to-date only in a designated subject area, or may want only to search for NTIS documents at one particular time. In these situations, other NTIS bibliographies may be more helpful.

Abstract Newsletters. Springfield, Va.: NTIS, 1978- . Weekly.

NTIS' *Abstract Newsletters* include summaries of recently received technical reports. There are 26 different newsletters in the series, each issued weekly, including such titles as *Administration & Management, Business & Economics,* and *Manufacturing Technology.* While the titles in the *Abstract Newsletters* are occasionally somewhat more current than those in *Government Reports Announcements & Index*, the *Newsletters* do not include titles that are not also listed in *GRA&I*. Their advantage for smaller libraries with narrower research interests is that they offer greater subject precision at lower annual subscription rates than does *GRA&I*.

Sometimes the need is for a comprehensive literature search on a specific topic rather than for ongoing, current information. In such a situation, purchase of an *NTIS Published Search* might be considered. The *Published Searches* are bibliographies resulting from online computer searches of *NTIS* and other scientific and technical databases. Each bibliography deals with a specific subject, such as fiber optics or lasers. Presently over 3,000 such bibliographies are available from NTIS for the same set fee.[11] A catalog of *Published Searches*, which lists searches by topic and includes dates of coverage and other information, is available from the NTIS.[12] Not all such searches are current, however. Some may be two or even three years old. In many instances, librarians with access to and experience in searching the online version of NTIS may prefer to conduct their own database searches to ensure that coverage is complete and up-to-date. Moreover, many library computer searches will cost less than the NTIS published searches.

Another NTIS product, *Selected Research in Microfiche* (*SRIM*), enables libraries to place standing orders for full-text copies of reports in specific subject areas, such as Management Information Systems and Personnel Management. NTIS is also a central source for federally generated computer software and bibliographic and numeric databases, and, in addition, provides customized information services to individuals and organizations. Free booklets describe these NTIS activities and products at length.[13]

FEDERAL INFORMATION CLEARINGHOUSES AND DEPOSITORY PROGRAMS

Both the Government Printing Office and the National Technical Information Service have extensive and wide-ranging publishing programs. While the GPO is the government's major publisher and the NTIS the major information clearinghouse, they are by no means the only collectors and disseminators of government information. There are approximately 300 additional federal information clearinghouses, information centers, and depository programs. Most focus on specific research or program areas, such as energy, aging, or education, and many collect and print both government and private-sector publications. Two of the best known clearinghouses are the Educational Resources Information Center and the National Criminal Justice Reference Service; two of the best known depository programs are those administered by the Patent and Trademark Office and by the Census Bureau.

ISSUING DEPARTMENTS AND AGENCIES AS PUBLISHER

In the past, many agencies distributed their own documents and issued their own publications catalogs to anyone who requested them. Recent cutbacks in government publishing programs, however, have been reflected in a corresponding reduction in the number of free catalogs and documents available to the public from these agencies. Access to some documents is now possible only through the Government Printing Office or the National Technical Information Service. Other publications, however, are still available from the issuing agencies, and in some instances exclusively from them. For example, as was mentioned earlier, the best sources for congressional documents are generally the issuing congressional committees and the Senate Document Room.

Almost every agency has an information office, designated to handle public inquiries and to distribute descriptive brochures and free publications. A call to this office will often yield valuable information about the publishing program of the agency, the availability of popular documents, and, in many instances, publications lists. The names and telephone numbers of information offices for executive departments and for independent government organizations are included in appendixes B and C; offices for other government agencies can be found in the *United States Government Manual*.

TRENDS IN FEDERAL PUBLISHING

Publishing activities of the federal government change from year to year and, more notably, from one administration to the next. Emphasis in recent years has been on reducing federal expenditures, which has been reflected in the government's publishing program. Many documents formerly available in paper copy, for example, are now available only in microfiche, a format significantly less expensive to produce. In addition, many documents serial titles have been discontinued. These not only include some of the publications catalogs mentioned in the preceding section, but also many periodicals and statistical series relevant to business researchers. Also under consideration as a means of curtailing government expenditures is the *privatization* of federally produced information. Privatization, defined as "the transfer of ownership of assets, and consequently, the responsibility for supplying goods and services from the public sector to the private sector of the economy,"[14] means that commercial publishers would bear the brunt of publishing costs but would also be entitled to earn profit on the government titles they published. One privatization issue presently under consideration is transferring NTIS operations to the private sector. Understandably, documents librarians are concerned about such a change, which would mean that many documents formerly available at cost would be priced to earn profit as well as to cover publishing expenses. Another concern is that commercial publishers might choose to issue only those documents deemed to be of widespread, popular interest; those with only limited appeal might be casualties of a commercial publishing program. Also under consideration is the publication and distribution of federal information using computer technology, both by the government and by the private sector. Whatever the resolution of these issues, there is no doubt that it will have a significant impact on documents, libraries, and the people who use them.

Another pattern should also be noted. Since government publications are in the public domain—that is, since they are not copyrighted—there are no restrictions on copying the information they contain. Accordingly, federal documents have sometimes been reproduced and issued under the imprints of commercial publishers. In some instances, the publishers have reformatted and repackaged the material so that it is both more attractive and easier to use; in others, publications are exact duplicates. While some advertisements indicate that such titles were originally issued as federal documents, many do not. Someone contemplating purchase of a commercial publication that sounds suspiciously like a document might do well to wait for the reviews; it is all too easy to purchase a title that costs considerably more than and may be an older version of a document that is already a part of the library's collection. Some documents are particularly attractive to commercial publishers. *The Franchise Opportunities Handbook*, for example, makes frequent appearances under the guise of commercially published titles.

Many commercially published sources, however, are very useful. Particularly important are guides to federal documents literature, bibliographies, and lists or reviews of documents publications. Some representative titles are included in the section that follows.

COMMERCIALLY PUBLISHED GUIDES, BIBLIOGRAPHIES, AND PERIODICALS

Guides

The volume and scope of published federal information can overwhelm the uninitiated at times. One good way to begin the quest for such information is by consulting a guide to federal documents. Two of the best are *Introduction to United States Public Documents* and *Using Government Publications*.

Morehead, Joe. **Introduction to United States Public Documents.** 3rd ed. Littleton, Colo.: Libraries Unlimited, 1983. 309p.

Sears, Jean L., and Marilyn K. Moody. **Using Government Publications.** Vol. 1: *Searching by Subject and Agencies*, 228p.; Vol. 2: *Finding Statistics and Using Special Techniques*, 240p. Phoenix, Ariz.: Oryx Press, 1985-86.

A proper understanding of documents and documents librarianship begins with familiarity with the structure of the government and with federal publishing programs. Although both have been covered briefly in this chapter, *Introduction to Public Documents*, which is used as a textbook in many documents courses, treats them in greater depth. It describes the publications and activities characteristic of each branch of the government as well as the history, responsibilities, and role of the Government Printing Office and the Superintendent of Documents. Depository libraries and legal and technical report literature are also covered. *Introduction to Public Documents* provides an authoritative overview of federal production and distribution of documents as well as of the types of publications issued by specific government agencies. It is a basic documents information source.

Using Government Publications focuses less on publishing programs than on practical search strategies and research techniques used to locate documents on specific subjects.

Each chapter deals with a different topic; those particularly relevant to business include Foreign Countries, Occupations, Selling to the Government, Business Aids, Tax Information, Economic Indicators, Business and Industry Statistics, Income, Earnings, Employment, Prices, Consumer Expenditures, Foreign Trade Statistics, Projections, Budget Analysis, Technical Reports, Patents and Trademarks, and Standards and Specifications. Each chapter is grouped into subcategories of similar or related material, each with a checklist of titles providing full bibliographic information and Superintendent of Documents classification numbers. Narrative descriptions of the titles are included in each section, and many chapters are enhanced by the use of sample pages from the documents cited. Relevant indexes, databases, and other specialized sources are also listed.

Using Government Publications is particularly helpful to librarians and researchers confronted for the first time with inquiries about subjects with which they have only limited familiarity; *Introduction to United States Public Documents*, on the other hand, is most useful for developing a sense of the types of publications that are available from the government, of the basic indexes used to identify them, and of the history and development of various federal publishing programs. Taken together, they provide an outstanding introduction to documents and to the types of business-related reference and research inquiries that documents can answer.

Bibliographies

Commercial publishers also publish documents bibliographies. Three of the most popular are the *Guide to Popular U.S. Government Publications, Government Reference Books*, and *Government Reference Serials*.

Schwarzkopf, LeRoy C. **Guide to Popular U.S. Government Publications.** 2nd ed. Littleton, Colo.: Libraries Unlimited, 1986. 432p.

_____. **Government Reference Books.** Littleton, Colo.: Libraries Unlimited, 1968/ 69- . Biennial.

_____. **Government Reference Serials.** Littleton, Colo.: Libraries Unlimited, 1988. 344p.

The *Guide to Popular U.S. Government Publications* lists and annotates free or inexpensive federal documents of current or long-standing popularity. Arrangement is by broad subject category, such as Business and Industry, and each entry includes full bibliographic information, an annotation, price, and when applicable, Superintendent of Documents classification and stock numbers. The *Guide* also includes common government acronyms and a list of selected agency publications catalogs.

Government Reference Books is a biennial listing of key reference sources issued by the Government Printing Office, an annotated guide to atlases, bibliographies, catalogs, dictionaries, directories, guides, handbooks, indexes, manuals, and other reference publications issued during the two-year period covered. Most titles are grouped together by subject; the section on economics and commerce, for example, includes titles categorized by such subject designations as employment and labor and government assistance and procurement programs. In addition to the bibliographic citation and annotation, each entry includes the Superintendent of Documents classification, *Monthly Catalog* entry number, stock number, and price. Since most of the titles listed are depository documents, *Government Reference Books* can be used to identify sources that are likely to be held at regional depository and large selective depository libraries.

Government Reference Serials describes reference periodicals and serials distributed by the U.S. government to depository libraries. It includes serials formerly included in *Government Reference Books*, adding titles issued more frequently, as well as those published less frequently. As a companion volume to *Government Reference Books*, it is arranged in the same four main sections (general reference, social sciences, science and technology, and humanities). Bibliographic citations include LC card numbers, OCLC numbers, ISSNs, *Monthly Catalog* entry numbers, GPO sales stock numbers and subscription list ID numbers, and prices. Also included are series notations, agency publication numbers, depository item numbers, and the publishing history of the serial.

In addition to being the world's largest publisher of printed sources, the federal government is also the world's largest producer and supplier of computerized databases and data files. As computer technology becomes increasingly commonplace, librarians and the people they serve often choose to supplement or even replace printed data with that available in electronic format. Some federal databases are available through standard online database vendors. Still others can be accessed through government agencies, their contractors, or designated centers, or can be purchased outright from the federal government. One of the best ways to identify such government-produced data files is through use of the *Federal Data Base Finder*.

> Zarozny, Sharon, ed. **Federal Data Base Finder: A Directory of Free and Fee-Based Data Bases and Files Available from the Federal Government.** 2nd ed. Chevy Chase, Md.: Information USA, 1986. 368p.

The *Federal Data Base Finder* lists and describes over 4,200 federal databases, computer tapes, and microcomputer disks available from the government and private contractors. Each entry includes the name of the database, a description of its contents and scope, price, and contact information including the agency address, telephone number, and, in many instances, the name of an information or subject specialist. The *Federal Data Base Finder* is a basic aid for researchers and librarians in search of government-generated machine-readable data. It is well worth acquiring.

Periodicals and Indexes

Although periodicals published by the Government Printing Office are listed in the *Monthly Catalog*, their contents are not. Accordingly, many documents departments and large research libraries subscribe to the *Index to U.S. Government Periodicals*, a commercially published index to nearly 200 federal serial titles.

> **Index to U.S. Government Periodicals.** Chicago: Infordata International Inc., 1970- . Quarterly, with annual cumulations.

The *Index* lists articles by author and subject, with each entry featuring a standard bibliographic citation. The entries shown in figure 5.6 (see page 98) are typical. Each issue also includes a list of periodical abbreviations used, accompanied by their full titles, Superintendent of Documents classification numbers, and symbols indicating whether the periodicals are depository items, or if they are titles not distributed by the Government Printing Office.

Some of the most popular government periodicals are also indexed in standard indexes such as *Business Periodicals Index* and *Public Affairs Information Service Bulletin. BPI*, for example, includes such widely read titles as *Business America,* the *Federal Reserve Bulletin*, and the *Monthly Labor Review*; and *PAIS*, such periodicals as *Business Conditions Digest, Economic Indicators,* and the *Survey of Current Business.* In addition, *PAIS* also identifies other relevant documents for its readers. Under the heading, "Employment," for example, a recent issue included not only books, periodical articles, and pamphlets, but also congressional hearings, Census Bureau and Equal Employment Opportunity Commission publications, and international and state documents. In recent years *PAIS* has begun to include Superintendent of Documents classification numbers and stock numbers and prices to facilitate the purchase or interlibrary borrowing of the federal documents listed.

TECHNOLOGY
China's economic experiment: from Mao to market. Jan
  S. Prybyla, il, ref Prob Commun 35 1 21-38 Ja-F 86-
  089
Economic interpretation of hedonic methods. Jack E.
  Triplett, Surv Cur Bus 66 1 36-40 Ja 86-101
Editor's note. Seldon P. Todd, Jr., J Rehab Res 23 1 v-
  viii Ja 86-311
Employment lessons from the electronics industry. John
  A. Alic and Martha Caldwell Harris, ref, gr Mon Labor
  Rev 109 2 27-36 F 86-069
FA 53 system automation officer. William O. Hunt, il, tab,
  gr Sold Sup J 13 1 10 Ja-F 86-301
Fluidized bed combustion: technology thrives on "junky"
  fuel. Monitor 5 25 1+ D 12 85-304
Highlights of 1985 NASA activities. NASA Act 17 1-2 3-
  8 Ja-F 86-072
Interactive use of videodiscs in interpretation. Ken Yellis,
  il Trends 22 4 43-45 85-241

Fig. 5.6. Typical entries, *Index to U.S. Government Periodicals.* Reprinted with permission from the *Index to U.S. Government Periodicals*, January-March 1986 issue.

Many professional publications identify important new documents. *RQ*, the publication of the American Library Association's Reference and Adult Services Division, includes "Government Information," a column that identifies and describes documents pertaining to specific subjects and that annually lists notable documents. Each issue of the Special Libraries Association's *Business and Finance Division Bulletin* includes a list of recent documents of interest to business librarians and their clientele. Other professional journals include similar features. In addition, there are two specialized documents periodicals with which librarians should be familiar.

Government Publications Review: An International Journal of Issues and Information Resources. New York: Pergamon Press, v. 9- . 1974- . Bimonthly.

Documents to the People. Chicago: American Library Association, Government Documents Round Table, 1972- . Quarterly.

Government Publications Review is a bimonthly scholarly journal devoted entirely to international, foreign, federal, state, and local documents, their production and distribution, and to documents librarianship. Often an issue will focus on a single topic, and the last issue of each year includes a listing of that year's notable documents. Although *Government Publications Review* is an integral part of many depository and research library collections, it is too specialized for many smaller libraries, which may find that its anticipated use does not justify the cost of a subscription.

Documents to the People, the official publication of the American Library Association's Government Documents Round Table, is considerably less expensive. Although it is a newsletter rather than a scholarly journal, it contains much valuable information, including descriptions of recently issued federal, international, and state documents, news about federal publishing and distribution programs, and lists of user guides and bibliographies available from other libraries. Its modest subscription price makes it affordable and worthwhile reading for anyone interested in building and maintaining a good documents reference collection.

To this point this chapter has focused on published information sources. Equally important, however, are the large number of government services available to business people, many of which are described in the following section.

FEDERAL GOVERNMENT SERVICES TO BUSINESS

The federal government spends billions of dollars annually, much of it for the accumulation of information and specialized expertise. The budget for publicizing the availability of such information and knowledge, however, is negligible. As a result, information and services that might contribute to productivity and profit are underutilized. Further, while many librarians have helped to increase awareness and use of published government information, they have not been equally successful in helping business people make good use of government services.

There are literally hundreds of special programs and services available to business, ranging from counseling to special loans. While the actual number and scope of such services change from one administration to the next, there are at most times services available that fall into one or more of the following categories: government referral; provision of specialized reference and research assistance; expert consultations; loans and financial aid; purchase of goods and services from the private sector; counseling; and training, seminars, and workshops. Each merits further attention.

Government Referrals

The government is often viewed with some justification as a vast, bureaucratic maze, complicated, confusing, and intimidating. For librarians and researchers in search of special information or assistance, the first question often is not where to find it, but rather how to find out where to find it, preferably with a minimum of telephone calls or correspondence. Several referral offices have been established within the government to direct citizens to the appropriate agencies.

Almost every government agency features an information or public affairs office. Staff members in these offices are informed about the programs, services, and expert staff that comprise the agency and generally provide quick and accurate referral to the individual or office best suited to answer an inquiry. Appendixes B and C include the names and telephone numbers of public affairs offices in executive departments and independent government agencies relevant to business; a more comprehensive listing of government information offices is included in the *United States Government Manual.*

Sometimes it is difficult to determine just which agency to contact. In such a situation, three main referral services are available. They are the Department of Commerce's Roadmap Program, a network of Federal Information Centers, and the Library of Congress' National Referral Center.

The Roadmap Program is one of the services offered by the Commerce Department's Office of Business Liaison. Designed specifically for business people, this program provides quick reference and referral assistance, directing callers to the proper authorities for legislation, regulations, and government programs, services, and policies pertaining to business. In addition, it publishes a number of free reports on current business topics, copies of which are available from the Business Liaison Office. It also publishes *Lost? Need Directions? Roadmap Leads Business to the Answers in the Federal Government Maze*, which describes the Roadmap Program, and *Business Services Directory*, which describes business services available from the Department of Commerce. Both are free.[15]

Less specialized referral service is available from the Federal Information Centers located in cities across the country. Part of the General Services Administration, the centers provide direct assistance to people with questions about government regulations, programs, and services. Their most important function is to serve as a central source of referral to other government agencies. Someone with questions about the impact of the Gramm-Rudman-Hollings Act, for example, might be referred to the Office of Management and Budget, and someone with queries about government benefit programs, to the Social Security Administration. In addition, the centers also can provide more regionally specific information for callers in the areas served by each center. Federal Information Centers operate in over 30 major metropolitan areas, with toll-free telephone service available in most major cities.[16]

A fourth referral service, the Library of Congress's National Referral Center, once provided similar assistance, directing the public to government and private organizations with specialized information. Recent budget cuts, however, have drastically reduced its services. Although the National Referral Center no longer provides telephone referral service, it continues to maintain the National Referral Center Register, a database of government and private organizations that produce and are willing to share specialized information. The database can be searched at the Library of Congress and is also available through the DOE/RECON and MEDLARS online computer systems. While written requests for referral assistance will be answered, they are no longer handled by National Referral Center staff but are added to reference staff workloads; as a result such letters are not always answered quickly. Anyone seeking immediate referral service is advised to contact the Roadmap Program or one of the agency information offices or Federal Information Centers.

Even with the expert referrals provided by public affairs officers, Federal Information Centers, the Roadmap Program, and the National Referral Center Register, mistakes are inevitable. As a result, researchers are advised to expect their calls to be transferred and to repeat their inquiries at least once, to remain patient, and to persevere.

Special Reference and Research Assistance

Sometimes local library collections and resources are not sufficient to answer requests for specialized reference and research assistance. The government offers such specialized assistance through federal libraries, document rooms, telephone hotlines and recordings, and information offices.

Federal libraries comprise a tremendous information asset, offering unique collections and resources and highly skilled staff. Most routinely answer mail and telephone inquiries, and many are open to the public. Particularly important to business people and business librarians are the Commerce Department, Census Bureau, Labor Department and Treasury Department Libraries, and the Library of Congress.

Evinger, William R. **Directory of Federal Libraries.** Phoenix, Ariz.: Oryx Press, 1987. 288p.

Federal libraries are listed in several of the publications described later in this section, but one of the most complete and up-to-date listings is that found in the *Directory of Federal Libraries*, which lists and describes more than 1,700 federal libraries and information centers. In addition to standard directory information, each listing includes the names of contacts, lists of special collections, database services offered, and the availability of services to the public.

While libraries are useful primarily for published information and guidance in using it, federal document rooms offer an abundance of unpublished information, much of it specifically related to economics and business. Document rooms are listed and described in *Information U.S.A.* (discussed later in this chapter) and include such facilities as the Agency for International Development's Development Information Center, which provides access to documents about overseas AID projects, and the Trademark Search Room of the Patent and Trademark Office, which contains trademark registrations back to 1881. Service in most document rooms is generally limited to providing the resources for on-site consultation and copying. Copying policy and rates vary from one document room to another, but are also cited in *Information U.S.A.*

The government also maintains several telephone lines for information and assistance. The Commodity Futures Trading Commission, for example, has a hotline that provides information on commodity brokers, and the General Accounting Office has a telephone line for "whistle blowers" who want to report fraud, waste, or mismanagement. In addition, some lines offer recorded messages that provide current information. Economic news and highlights of the day are provided by the Department of Commerce and the Joint Economic Committee; press release information, by the Department of Labor; and dates for auction of government securities and auction results, by the Treasury Department. *Information U.S.A.* includes a list of these telephone numbers and the information they provide.

Expert Consultations

"For any problem that you may face either professionally or personally," writes Matthew Lesko, "there is likely to be a free expert on the federal payroll who has spent years studying the very same subject."[17] These experts provide special assistance that, were it being sought from a private consultant, might cost hundreds or even thousands of dollars. Their areas of expertise range from stratospheric research to health care; for business, the most frequently consulted experts are those specializing in industry analysis, foreign markets, and the collection and analysis of statistical data.

The Census Bureau, for example, regularly publishes *Telephone Contacts for Data Users*, a list of specialists in such economic and demographic areas as income statistics, mineral industries, minority business, and trends in marital status and living arrangements. Each entry provides the name of the office specializing in a particular field, the name of the contact person, and the telephone number. The list is particularly useful for librarians confronted with questions about the methodology of collecting, processing, and analyzing census data, and for clarification or expansion of such data. A free copy of *Telephone Contacts for Data Users* can be gotten from the Census Bureau.[18]

Many industry analysts are employed by the Census Bureau and are listed in its *Telephone Contacts for Data Users*. Still others are employed by the Commerce Department's International Trade Administration. Although such experts are not listed in the *United States Government Manual*, other sources provide this information.

U.S. Department of Commerce. International Trade Administration. **U.S. Industrial Outlook.** Washington, D.C.: Government Printing Office, 1960- . Annual.

Who Knows: A Guide to Washington Experts. 8th ed. Washington, D.C.: Washington Researchers, 1986. (Business Research Series). 425p.

The *U.S. Industrial Outlook* contains industry analyses and statistical data for over 350 manufacturing and service industries. Although chapter 13 describes the *Outlook* at length, note here that most of the industry analyses include the name, office, and telephone number of the industry expert, making it both a useful source of industry information and a guide to specialists.

Who Knows is not limited to industry experts, but lists government specialists in other fields as well, including the names, titles, office addresses, and telephone numbers of some 10,000 Washington experts. A condensed version of *Who Knows* is published as *Who Knows about Industries & Markets* (Washington, D.C.: Washington Researchers, 1986), and is available for less than half the cost of the original volume. In most libraries, however, the broader scope of *Who Knows* will offset its purchase price.

As American businesses become increasingly involved in overseas trade, their need for current and reliable information about foreign trade opportunities, economic conditions abroad, and foreign government regulation of commerce has grown accordingly. Valuable information in government documents can be enhanced and supplemented by consulting with country specialists in the federal government. Usually located in the Departments of

Commerce, Agriculture, and State, such experts are listed in *Who Knows,* described above, and are also included in a condensed version of that title, *Who Knows about Foreign Industries & Markets.*

Although experts can be found in almost every government agency, the ones most often consulted by business people are found in such Department of Commerce organizations as the International Trade Administration and the Bureau of Economic Analysis, as well as in the Departments of Labor, Agriculture, and the Treasury, and in the Small Business Administration.

Loans and Financial Assistance

More than 1,000 different federal assistance programs are available to individuals and organizations, over 200 of which are intended to promote the development and continued financial well-being of business enterprises. These include loans from the Small Business Administration, grants from the Economic Development Administration, and insurance from the Overseas Private Investment Corporation. Such programs are listed and described in the following sources.

> U.S. Office of Management and Budget. **Catalog of Federal Domestic Assistance.** Washington, D.C.: Government Printing Office, 1971- . Annual, with semiannual update.

> Lesko, Matthew. **Getting Yours: The Complete Guide to Government Money.** 3rd ed. New York: Penguin Books, 1987. 368p.

> U.S. Congress. Senate. Committee on Small Business. **Handbook for Small Business: A Survey of Small Business Programs of the Federal Government.** 5th ed. Washington, D.C.: Government Printing Office, 1984. (Senate Document 98-33). 228p.

The most comprehensive listing of federal assistance programs is contained in the *Catalog of Federal Domestic Assistance.* The *Catalog* is the basic reference source of financial assistance programs, including grants, loans, loan guarantees, scholarships, mortgage loans, insurance, and nonfinancial assistance and services. Arrangement is by agency and then by the numbers assigned to specific programs. Each entry generally includes a statement of program objectives, types of assistance available, potential uses and use restrictions, eligibility requirements, the application and award process, assistance considerations, and post-assistance requirements. In addition, the entries list information contacts and relevant regulations, guidelines, and documents literature.

The *Catalog* also includes subject, agency, program, applicant eligibility, and functional indexes, as well as a deadline index that lists program numbers and titles and the dates by which funding agencies must receive applications.

Getting Yours is, to a certain extent, a commercially published version of the *Catalog of Federal Domestic Assistance.* Although it borrows liberally from the *Catalog,* it condenses and simplifies information, thus making it easier to use and less intimidating to the casual user than its federally published counterpart. While it does not provide the same level of detail as the *Catalog,* its entries generally contain enough information to help a patron begin the quest for government financial assistance. Further, since *Getting Yours* uses the same numeric program identification scheme as the *Catalog,* moving from *Getting Yours* to the *Catalog of Federal Domestic Assistance* for additional or more up-to-date information is simple.

The *Handbook for Small Business* briefly describes federal programs designed to assist small business enterprises, listing a wide range of financial, management, technical assistance, and economic development programs. Arrangement is alphabetical by department or agency, and each entry generally includes a description of the organization itself, highlights of the programs it offers, and contacts for additional information.

Government Purchase of Goods and Services

In 1955, the U.S. government adopted a policy of relying on private industry whenever possible to supply needed goods and services. Agency requirements vary tremendously, ranging from high technology weaponry to painting and dry cleaning. There are two main categories of government purchasing. The first includes general items, such as office equipment and janitorial services, items for which the General Services Administration is the main purchaser. The second category consists of special, mission-oriented goods and services required by individual agencies. The Government Printing Office, for example, needs a constant supply of paper and ink, the Department of the Army needs weapon systems, and the U.S. Forest Service, insecticides and fire-fighting equipment. In all, there are approximately 15,000 buying offices among government agencies. Many are listed in the *United States Government Manual*, and can be found at the end of each listing under the heading "Contracts."

Other sources, both private and commercial, provide more specific information. Three of the most important of such information sources are *Doing Business with the Federal Government, Commerce Business Daily*, and the Business Service Centers established by the General Services Administration.

U.S. General Services Administration. **Doing Business with the Federal Government.** Washington, D.C.: Government Printing Office, 1986. 48p.

Commerce Business Daily. Washington, D.C.: Government Printing Office, 1954- Daily, Monday-Friday.

Doing Business with the Federal Government is a good introduction to federal purchasing programs. It explains the principles and procedures of government procurement, discusses the paperwork required, and indicates the range of products and services needed by each agency. *Commerce Business Daily* (chapter 3) lists current opportunities to sell goods and services to the government, subcontracting leads, and contracting awards.

In addition, the General Services Administration has established Business Service Centers in 12 different cities.[19] The centers provide advice on doing business with the federal government, offer counseling, and sponsor business seminars, workshops, and meetings.

Finally, the Small Business Administration serves as a middleman in procuring government contracts. In many instances, federal government agencies make contracts for purchase of goods or services with the Small Business Administration, and the SBA subcontracts them to small businesses. Usually, these contracts are for $10,000 or less.

Counseling

In addition to making specialists available for consultation by mail or by telephone, many government agencies also offer free counseling service. The Small Business Administration, for example, offers on-site analyses of specific small businesses and makes suggestions for their improvement, using active and retired business executives who are volunteer members of the Service Corps of Retired Executives (SCORE) and the Active Corps of Executives (ACE). The International Trade Administration's district offices, listed in the *United States Government Manual*, counsel and advise prospective and practicing exporters about opportunities for overseas trade and financing, marketing, and promotion of specific products. The Occupational Safety and Health Administration will visit businesses unable to afford private consultants, identifying hazardous work conditions in need of correction.

These are but a few of the opportunities for free counseling available to business people. Library users in need of such services would do well to contact the Commerce Department's Roadmap Program or one of the field offices of the Small Business Administration or the

International Trade Administration. *Information U.S.A.*, described in the next section, also lists and describes many counseling opportunities.

Training, Seminars, and Workshops

Opportunities to enhance business-related skills through special training, seminars, and workshops abound. As with counseling services, the best way to identify such government offerings is through initial consultation with field offices of the Department of Commerce or the Small Business Administration, or by scanning *Information U.S.A.* or the *United States Government Manual.*

A sampling of government-sponsored continuing education programs includes Small Business Tax Workshops offered by the Internal Revenue Service, which cover business taxes and highlight tax benefits and obligations connected with small business. Workshops sponsored by the Census Bureau Data User Services Division introduce participants to basic census concepts and products. Census Bureau offerings include "Using Socioeconomic Census Data," "Census Bureau Economic Programs," and "Statistical Resources for Librarians and Information Specialists."[20] Small Business Administration field offices cosponsor business management courses in cooperation with local educational institutions, chambers of commerce, and trade associations; the International Trade Administration conducts conferences and seminars regarding export opportunities and procedures; and the General Services Administration conducts workshops on selling to the government.

As with many other government services, the main problem is not lack of educational opportunities but rather lack of public awareness of them. Librarians can help by developing a sensitivity for situations in which government services might be appropriate, by acquiring directories and lists of such services, and by actively publicizing them. In addition, public and academic libraries can heighten awareness of continuing education opportunities by cosponsoring workshops and seminars with federal government field offices, or with state and local government agencies.

Directories of Government Services

Although the *United States Government Manual* alludes to services provided to the public by specific agencies, it does not describe them in detail. One way to learn more about such services is by calling an agency field office, the agency's public information office, or one of the government referral agencies listed earlier in this chapter. Another way to begin is by consulting one of the commercially published directories of government services. Two of the most popular directories follow.

Lesko, Matthew. **Information U.S.A.** Rev. ed. New York: Viking Press, 1986. 1120p.

D'Aleo, Richard J. **FEDfind.** 2nd ed. Springfield, Va.: ICUC Press, 1986. 480p.

Although much of their information is also provided in the *United States Government Manual*, the directories offer significant advantages. Format and/or detailed indexing in both, for example, permit detailed subject access, virtually impossible in the *Manual.* In addition, while the *Manual* lists major agency publications, the commercial directories are more inclusive and annotate many of the titles they contain. The major drawback to the directories, aside from cost, is that they soon become dated. As a consequence, these and similar, commercially published directories should be used with the caveat that the agencies, specialists, and telephone numbers listed may no longer be accurate. Whenever possible, they should be used in conjunction with the *Manual*, which is revised annually.

STATE GOVERNMENT INFORMATION AND SERVICES

State government agencies, like their federal counterparts, are key providers of information and services to business. They publish statistical compendia, research findings, market surveys, annual reports, and other documents, provide access to information about locally based companies, and offer counseling and technical assistance to new and relocating businesses. Unfortunately, such sources and services are underutilized by those who might most benefit from them. The sections that follow highlight some of the most important types of publications and services provided by state government agencies.

Published Information

Publishing programs and policies regarding document distribution and sales vary from state to state. Most, however, publish a wide range of titles. While blue books, legislative handbooks, and statistical abstracts are the most commonly used state document reference sources, others can make equally valuable contributions to business reference. Most states generally publish employment and unemployment statistics and economic indicators monthly or at least several times a year. In addition, glossy brochures designed to lure prospective businesses and tourists salt propaganda with useful information, and directories provide access to government officials, state manufacturing industries, and trade and professional associations. Some of the types of business information commonly published by state government agencies are listed in appendix E.

The potential value of many state documents, however, is offset by their elusiveness. The issuing agencies themselves do not always publicize documents or include them in depository or sales programs; often one agency does not know what another—frequently involved in allied activities—is publishing. As a result, librarians seeking to build and maintain core collections of state document reference materials must rely on printed bibliographies and consultation with state documents librarians and state government agencies. Each of these methods of identifying source material deserves further consideration.

BIBLIOGRAPHIES OF STATE DOCUMENTS

One of the best ways to review broad categories of documents, either by subject or by issuing state, is by consulting one of the bibliographies compiled by David W. Parish.

Parish, David W. **State Government Reference Publications: An Annotated Bibliography.** 2nd ed. Littleton, Colo.: Libraries Unlimited, 1981. 355p.

_____. **A Bibliography of State Bibliographies, 1970-1982.** Littleton, Colo.: Libraries Unlimited, 1985. 280p.

State Government Reference Publications classifies documents into nine broad subject categories and assigns a separate chapter to each. The categories are Official State Bibliography; Blue Books; Legislative Manuals and Related References; State Government Finances; Statistical Abstracts and Other Data Sources; Directories; Tourist Guides; Audiovisual Guides, Atlases and Maps; and Bibliographies and General Reference Sources. Each entry includes the document title, date, pagination, and issuing agency as well as a brief annotation and, when available, its price. In addition, *State Government Reference Publications* includes a bibliography of suggested readings, a listing of state document reference tools, a core list of state publications by broad subject category including typical state agencies and titles, and author, title, and subject indexes.

A Bibliography of State Bibliographies, 1970-1982 lists, by state and then by broad subject category, bibliographies compiled and published by state government agencies over a 12-year period. Bibliographies listed under Economy/Economics, Employment, Energy, Environment, Equal Opportunity, Planning, and Technology are particularly relevant to business. Entries in *A Bibliography of State Bibliographies* are similar to those in *State Government Reference Publications*. Using it, one can identify, on a state-by-state basis, free and inexpensive documents pertaining to business.

While the above bibliographies are useful, they do not identify recently issued documents. Generally, three main sources are consulted to keep up with current publications. They are *Public Affairs Information Service Bulletin*, checklists issued by individual states, and the *Monthly Checklist of State Publications*.

Public Affairs Information Service Bulletin lists selected state documents along with books, federal documents, pamphlets, and periodical articles. Although it lists only a fraction of published state documents, most of the ones included have popular appeal or research value.

Librarians and researchers seeking to identify a broader range of such publications, however, would be well advised to consult documents checklists issued by state agencies and the Library of Congress.

Almost every state publishes an official checklist of publications. Some are issued monthly, others less frequently or even irregularly, but most are free and offer a good way of identifying some of the most important state documents and the agencies that publish them. Some states issue agency- or subject-specific checklists as well. Alabama, for example, publishes the *Alabama Planning Resource Checklist*; and Hawaii, *Current Hawaiiana*, a list of government and private publications about Hawaii. State checklists are listed and described in *State Government Reference Publications*.

> U.S. Library of Congress. Exchange and Gift Division. **Monthly Checklist of State Publications.** Washington, D.C.: Government Printing Office, 1910- . Monthly.

The *Monthly Checklist of State Publications* lists, by state and issuing agency, official state publications received by the Library of Congress. Entries include standard bibliographic information, but lack annotations. Usually, however, a person has enough information to place orders for documents or borrow them from other libraries. Annual author and subject indexes are included, and periodicals are listed in the June and December issues.

Neither state checklists nor the *Monthly Checklist of State Publications* list all state documents, however, and should be viewed as selective rather than comprehensive lists. Bibliographic control of state documents is virtually impossible. When the printed sources described above are inadequate, consultations with the closest state documents librarian or with state agencies themselves are sometimes helpful.

STATE DEPOSITORY LIBRARIES

Although there is significant variation from one state to another, most have designated specific libraries as state document depositories. Often the state library is named the official depository, and distributes duplicate copies of the documents it receives to other state depository libraries, usually large research and public libraries. In addition, some of these same libraries collect documents from other states, sometimes received through exchange programs. Documents librarians at these institutions can be extremely helpful in providing information about and, in some instances, lending state documents.

STATE AGENCIES

As was mentioned earlier, many documents are excluded from state depository programs. If a search for information fails to produce desired results after consulting bibliographies, checklists, and state documents librarians, a final option is to contact the agency itself. Often the necessary data are at hand and will be forwarded promptly. As with such quests in the federal government, however, patience and perseverance are necessary.

Directories of State Agencies

Most state governments publish information about their structure, component agencies, and operations. State blue books, for example, include descriptions of agency organization, purpose, and functions, and state telephone directories list agency names, addresses, telephone numbers, and key officials. Most libraries collect such publications for their home state, but few acquire those issued by other states. As a result, the following commercially published directories are frequently used to provide similar information about other states.

National Directory of State Agencies. Bethesda, Md.: National Standards Association, 1974-75- . Annual.

State Executive Directory. Washington, D.C.: Carroll Publishing, 1980- . Triannual.

Book of the States. Lexington, Ky.: Council of State Governments, 1935- . Biennial.

The *National Directory of State Agencies* lists agencies by state and by functional category. Entries in each of these sections include names, addresses, telephone numbers, and the names of agency directors and executives. In addition, the *Directory* includes lists of agency executives by name, state elected officials, and the names of standing legislative committees, their chairpersons, and telephone numbers. Also included are the names, addresses, and telephone numbers of more than 85 national associations representing state government officials.

The *National Directory of State Agencies* is published annually, and many state-issued blue books and telephone directories are issued annually or biennially. As a result, libraries needing to keep up-to-date with agency and personnel changes may want to subscribe to the *State Executive Directory*. Like its sister publication, the *Federal Executive Directory*, it provides current directory information including agency names, component offices, telephone numbers, and state officials.

The *Book of the States* is more than a directory. Although it includes some directory information, it is more commonly used for comparative state statistical and descriptive data. It provides information on the structure, financing, and functions of state governments, compares state policies, regulations, and statistics, lists major officials, and includes state profiles featuring basic reference information.

State Services to Business

Services offered to business by state agencies parallel those offered by the federal government. Many are described briefly in "State Sources of Money and Help to Start or Expand a Business," in *Getting Yours*, discussed earlier in this chapter. The following publication provides even more information.

National Association of State Development Agencies. **Directory of Incentives for Business Investment and Development in the United States: A State-by-State Guide.** 2nd rev. ed. Washington, D.C.: Urban Institute Press, 1986. 687p.

The *Directory of Incentives for Business Investment and Development in the United States* is a compilation of specific financial and tax incentives and special services offered by state government agencies to nurture existing in-state businesses and to attract new business and industry. It begins with a general discussion of such incentives, followed by a state-by-state listing, describing for each development bonds issued to help finance industry, state grants, and other financing; industrial training programs; basic business taxes and tax incentives; small business assistance; enterprise zones; and related economic incentives. For each program or service listed, the name, address, and telephone number of the appropriate government agency are included, and often the name of a contact person is provided as well. An index of incentives leads readers to states offering specific types of programs.

REFERRALS

Although not all states feature central referral offices or have public information offices for each agency, most offer referral through a central telephone information number, the governor's office, or the state library. In addition, many agencies that provide special assistance to businesses will help with referral to other agencies.

SPECIAL REFERENCE AND RESEARCH ASSISTANCE

State libraries provide special reference and research assistance, collections, and referral to other agencies and libraries. In addition, some states offer specialized technical assistance through technical information centers. Often housed in research libraries, these centers generally collect data, compile bibliographies, and provide research assistance pertaining to major industries represented in the state. The *Dow Jones-Irwin Business and Investment Almanac* includes a "State Information Guide" section that lists state technical assistance centers and other state government agencies relevant to business.

State regulation of business activities requires that many businesses and corporations file reports with the government. While many of these reports are not published as documents, they are available to the public at the state agency that collects them. Each state, for example, requires that a company file articles of incorporation which include information about the company, its location, and the nature of its business in order to incorporate. Other government filings include insurance company financial reports, complaints about companies or specific consumer products, environmental impact studies, and franchise information. Facilities for reading and often for copying some of these unpublished documents are available. Copying rates and policies, however, may vary from one agency to another.

EXPERT CONSULTATIONS

As with the federal government, state agencies employ specialists, many of whom are quite willing to share information, advice, and expertise. Identifying them, however, requires more diligence and persistence, since state-published or commercial lists of state experts are rare.

COUNSELING

Counseling, particularly for small businesses and for businesses proposing to move to the state, is readily available. Many state agencies work with volunteer counselors, university business faculty and students, and the private sector to provide such assistance.

WORKSHOPS AND TRAINING

Many state agencies sponsor workshops and training that encourage small business development and growth. These opportunities for continuing education are often made available locally, through community colleges, chambers of commerce, universities, and other organizations.

CONCLUSION

Many business librarians will work in settings in which only a few key documents reference sources are collected. The level of service provided, however, can be enhanced by greater awareness of the scope and diversity of publications and services offered by federal and state government agencies. In addition, although not covered in this chapter, international, foreign, and local government documents can provide information that is unique, timely, and relevant to business research.

NOTES

[1]GAO reports are available free of charge (with a maximum of four copies per report) and can be ordered from:

U.S. General Accounting Office
Document Handling and Information Services
P.O. Box 6015
Gaithersburg, MD 20760

[2]*United States Government Manual, 1985-86* (Washington, D.C.: Government Printing Office, 1985), 53.

[3]Joe Morehead, *Introduction to United States Public Documents*, 3rd ed. (Littleton, Colo.: Libraries Unlimited, 1983), 26.

[4]Yuri Nakata, *From Press to People: Collecting and Using U.S. Government Publications* (Chicago: American Library Association, 1979), 15.

[5]For a complete listing of selective and regional depository libraries, write to:

Superintendent of Documents
U.S. Government Printing Office
Washington, D.C. 20402

[6]For a useful outline and description of ordering procedures, see Thomas Gottschalk, "Guidelines for Ordering GPO Publications and Subscriptions," *Documents to the People*, 8, no. 1 (January 1980): 25-26.

[7]GPO bookstores are located in the following cities: Atlanta, Birmingham (AL), Boston, Chicago, Cleveland, Columbus (OH), Dallas, Denver, Detroit, Houston, Jacksonville (FL), Kansas City, Los Angeles, Milwaukee, New York, Philadelphia, Pittsburgh, Pueblo (CO), San Francisco, Seattle, and Washington, D.C. Addresses and telephone numbers for the bookstores are listed in the front of each issue of the *Monthly Catalog*.

[8]Nakata, 54.

[9]To receive a free copy of *U.S. Government Books*, write to the address shown in note 5 above.

[10]To be placed on the mailing list to receive *New Books*, write to the address shown in note 5.

[11]In 1987, packaged NTIS searches cost $45.00 each.

[12]The *Published Search Catalog*, PR-186/154, is available free from NTIS. To request the catalog, write to:

> National Technical Information Service
> 5285 Port Royal Road
> Springfield, VA 22161

[13]Librarians and researchers interested in the computer software, bibliographic, and numeric databases made available through NTIS can request the following free titles at the address shown in note 12.

> *Data Files Directory* (PR-629/154)
> *Data Files List* (PR-700/154)
> *Directory of Computer Software* (PR-261/154)
> *Diskette Titles List* (PR-771-1/154)
> *General Information Catalog* (PR-154/154)
> *NTIS Bibliographic Database Guide* (PR-253/154)
> *NTIS Computer Software* (PR-260/154)

[14]U.S. Congress. Joint Economic Committee. *Privatization of the Federal Government, Part I*. Hearings, 98th Congress, 1st session (Washington, D.C.: Government Printing Office, 1984), 1.

[15]For a free copy of the pamphlet, *Lost? Need Directions? Roadmap Leads Business to the Answers in the Federal Government Maze*, and of the *Business Service Directory*, write to:

> Roadmap Program
> Office of Business Liaison
> Room 5898-C
> Department of Commerce
> Washington, D.C. 20230

[16]For a free brochure describing the Federal Information Centers program, write or call the nearest Federal Information Center. The centers' addresses and telephone numbers are included in each edition of the *United States Government Manual*.

[17]*Information U.S.A.* (New York: Viking, 1983), 38.

[18]For a free copy of *Telephone Contacts for Data Users*, write to:

User Training Branch
Data User Services Division
Bureau of the Census
Washington, D.C. 20233

[19]Business Service Centers, listed in the *United States Government Manual*, are located in Atlanta, Boston, Chicago, Denver, Fort Worth, Kansas City, Los Angeles, New York, Philadelphia, San Francisco, Seattle, and Washington, D.C.

[20]For more information about Census Bureau workshops and seminars, contact the User Training Branch at the address shown in note 18.

In our society, loving dogs, cats and goldfish is OK. Saying a kind word for numbers qualifies you as being a little mad.

—Robert J. Samuelson, "The Joy of Statistics"

6

STATISTICS

Statistics are vital to decision making. They are particularly important in management, accounting, marketing, finance, and other fields of business, where they help to assess past performance, compare and appraise current activities, and make predictions about the future. Market researchers, for example, use statistical data to compare sales of one brand with another and to predict consumer demand for new products. Union leaders use them to document the need for increased wages to keep up with spiraling living costs, and personnel managers, to measure labor turnover and absenteeism. Statistics are, in fact, so essential to business that the ability to identify, provide access to, and, in some instances, assess the relative merits of statistical data is fundamental to good business reference service. This chapter considers basic business-related uses of statistics, the major compilers and publishers of statistical data, key types of business and economic statistics, and the sources that contain them. In addition, it examines some of the common pitfalls attendant to using such data.

MAJOR COMPILERS AND PUBLISHERS OF STATISTICS

The cost of collecting primary statistical data, particularly on a large scale, is so great that usually only the biggest or wealthiest organizations can afford to do so. Most businesses depend upon secondary statistical data generated by government agencies, trade associations, commercial publishers, and private research firms. Each of these types of organizations regularly compiles, analyzes, and publishes statistics. Familiarity with their statistics-gathering programs and representative publications is an important first step in providing statistical reference assistance.

Federal Government Agencies

The federal government is the greatest single supplier of statistics, spending an estimated 1.5 billion dollars annually to produce and publish them.[1] These data provide information on population, agriculture, energy and the

112

environment, employment and earnings, money supply, foreign and domestic trade, industrial activity, health, education, and many other subjects. Responsibility for collecting and analyzing such data is assigned to several different agencies within the government. Federal statistical organization, in short, is decentralized, with the diverse statistical activities of all agencies coordinated by the Office of Management and Budget's Office of Information and Regulatory Affairs. Agencies fall into three broad categories according to their principal statistical activities and responsibilities (see figure 6.1).

Central Coordinating Agency

(Office of Management and Budget's Office of Information and Regulatory Affairs)

GENERAL-PURPOSE STATISTICAL AGENCIES	ANALYTICAL AND RESEARCH AGENCIES	ADMINISTRATIVE AND REGULATORY AGENCIES
Bureau of the Census	For example:	For example:
Bureau of Labor Statistics	Bureau of Economic	Environmental Protection
National Center for Education	Analysis	Agency
Statistics	Council of Economic	Federal Trade Commission
Statistical Reporting	Advisers	Securities and Exchange
Service, USDA	Economic Research	Commission
National Center for Health	Service, USDA	Internal Revenue Service
Statistics		
Bureau of Justice Statistics		

Fig. 6.1. Statistical organization of the federal government.

GENERAL-PURPOSE STATISTICAL AGENCIES

These agencies collect, compile, and publish statistics in specific fields for general use. They account for a significant proportion of all federal statistical activity, and the data they supply are used by businesses, private organizations, government bodies, and individuals in many different settings. Demographic statistics published by the Census Bureau, for example, enable companies to gauge future demands for their products based on the race, age, sex, occupation, and educational levels of different segments of the population. They are also used to help companies decide where to relocate, to measure population growth and decline in different parts of the country, and to document significant changes in the composition of the population.

There are six general-purpose statistical agencies: the Bureau of the Census, Bureau of Labor Statistics, National Center for Education Statistics, Statistical Reporting Service of the Department of Agriculture, National Center for Health Statistics, and Bureau of Justice Statistics.

The Bureau of the Census is the largest, responsible for the collection, compilation, and publication of demographic and economic statistics. Its statistical programs fall into two main categories: (1) current programs, which produce the monthly, quarterly, and annual data contained in such publications as the *Current Population Reports* series and *County Business Patterns*, and (2) periodic censuses and programs mandated by law (see appendix F).

As a rule, data contained in the periodic censuses, which can be as much as 5 or even 10 years old, are updated by current Census Bureau publications. The *Census of Manufactures*, for example, is brought up-to-date by the *Annual Survey of Manufactures*, the *Current Industrial Reports* series, *Survey of Plant Capacity*, and *Manufacturers'*

Shipments, Inventories, and Orders. While useful, the current publications lack the detailed geographic, product, and demographic coverage common to censuses. In addition to censuses and surveys, the bureau also publishes such basic statistical compilations as the *Statistical Abstract of the United States* and the *County and City Data Book.*

Keeping up with census publications, the types of statistics they contain, and the formats in which they are available is no easy task. Fortunately, several guides and lists are available to help identify and simplify access to specific statistics sources.

> U.S. Bureau of the Census. **Census Catalog and Guide.** Washington, D.C.: Government Printing Office, 1946- . Annual.
>
> _____. **Monthly Product Announcement.** Washington, D.C.: Government Printing Office, 1981- . Monthly.
>
> _____. **Data User News.** Washington, D.C.: Government Printing Office, 1966- . Monthly.
>
> _____. **Catalog of Publications, 1790-1972.** Washington, D.C.: Government Printing Office, 1974. 591p.
>
> _____. **Guide to the 1982 Economic Censuses and Related Products.** Washington, D.C.: Government Printing Office, 1984. 78p.

The annual *Census Catalog and Guide* lists and annotates data products in print, microfiche, computer tape, and diskette formats. Coverage is usually for the past five years, and most annotations describe the geographic areas and time span covered in addition to the subject content (see figure 6.2).

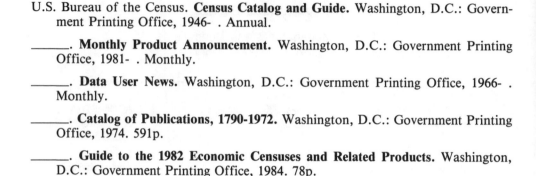

Cars and Trucks in the United States: 1970 to 1977 (Current Housing Reports, H-121, No. 17)

Cited in the 1984 Catalog.

Data time span—1970 to 1977.

Geographic areas covered—United States and regions.

Subject content—Contains statistics on vehicles per household, cars and trucks available, and average annual increase. Data are reported for regions and locations inside and outside standard metropolitan statistical areas (SMSA's) based on the Annual Housing Survey national sample in 1973, 1975, and 1977, as well as the 1970 census.

42 pp. 1983. $3.75.
Available from Customer Services (Publications).

Fig. 6.2. Sample entry, *Census Catalog and Guide.* Reprinted from U.S. Census Bureau, *Census Catalog and Guide 1985* (Washington, D.C.: Government Printing Office, 1985).

In addition, the *Catalog* describes various statistical programs conducted by the bureau, charts both current and periodic statistical series, and lists depository libraries, State Data Centers, and census regional offices. Ordering information and forms are also included.

The *Monthly Product Announcement* is a free list of recently released publications and data files.[2] Arrangement is by format, and then by subject, with each listing including the title, series number, price, and, when available, GPO stock number.

Data User News is the bureau's official newsletter. It covers new products and services, lists census-sponsored training opportunities available, and generally includes one or two feature articles in each monthly issue. Recent features have focused on such topics as plans for the 1990 census, sales of retail merchandise lines, work disability, American Indians, and the growing number of married women workers who earn more than their husbands. Often these articles are supplemented with maps, graphs, and statistical tables. As a result, *Data User News*, which publishes an annual subject index, can be used as a reference tool as well as a source for bibliographic verification.

The first census publications were issued almost 200 years ago. Since then, the breadth and depth of census enumerations have increased considerably. In addition, titles and frequency of census data collection have changed, and specific items have been added to or deleted from successive census questionnaires. Statistics about American agriculture, for example, were once included as part of the *Census of Population*; today, they comprise a separate census. Similarly, data on religious affiliation included in early censuses are no longer gathered and published. The retrospective *Catalog of Publications, 1790-1972* is useful for identifying specific publications and what they contain.

Finally, the Census Bureau also publishes guides to specific censuses. One of the most useful for business librarians and researchers is the *Guide to the Economic Censuses and Related Statistics*, which contains descriptions of the censuses that, taken together, comprise the Economic Census. It also includes introductions to the Standard Industrial Classification system and to basic geographic area concepts employed by the Census Bureau, and discusses such related statistical sources as *County Business Patterns*. A new edition is published for each census.

When neither the census documents at hand nor the publications described above are sufficient to answer research inquiries, other resources are available. As mentioned in the preceding chapter, federal regional depository library collections, which include most major census publications, can provide both invaluable reference and bibliographical assistance. In addition, a number of State Data Centers are available to help librarians, state and local government employees, and the general public.[3] Assistance can also be obtained by calling the closest Census Bureau regional office or one of the experts listed in the bureau's *Telephone Contacts for Data Users*, described in chapter 5.

Although most of this discussion of the Census Bureau's statistical programs has focused on resulting publications, print is not the only format in which such data are available. In many instances, they can also be purchased on tapes for mainframe computers, microcomputer diskettes, or can be accessed through major online database vendors. In addition, the bureau compiles special statistical tabulations to meet the stated needs of individual users. Such tabulations are made available on a cost-recovery basis, and are usually produced as computer tapes or printouts.

The Bureau of Labor Statistics (BLS) is the principal source of information on labor economics, supplying data on such subjects as the labor force, employment and unemployment, hours and earnings, productivity, work stoppages, and consumer and producer prices. As with the Census Bureau, the BLS makes its statistics available in a wide range of formats — monthly, quarterly, and annual publications, computer tapes, floppy disks, and online databases — and offers expert assistance through field offices and contacts at Washington headquarters.

Taken together, the Bureaus of the Census and Labor Statistics account for the government-produced statistics used most frequently by business researchers. Although data collected by the other general-purpose statistical agencies are used less widely, they also have direct business applications. The National Center for Education Statistics, for example, collects, analyzes, and publishes statistics on the condition of education, and the Department of Agriculture's Statistical Reporting Service does the same for current national and state agricultural statistics. The National Center for Health Statistics collects data to assess the health status of the population, to measure births, deaths, marriage, and divorce, and to identify health-care costs. Finally, the Bureau of Justice Statistics gathers and disseminates statistics on crime, criminal offenders and crime victims, and the operation of the justice system at all levels of government.

FEDERAL ANALYTICAL AND RESEARCH AGENCIES

These agencies use statistical data for economic analysis, estimates, and projections. Although some engage in direct collection of statistics, others draw upon data from other sources. Some of the most important, for business purposes, are the Council of Economic Advisers, the Bureau of Economic Analysis, the Economic Research Service, and the Federal Reserve System's Division of Research and Statistics. Their functions are described briefly in figure 6.3.

ADMINISTRATIVE AND REGULATORY AGENCIES

Finally, although statistics gathering and dissemination are not their primary functions, almost every administrative or regulatory agency produces valuable statistics as a byproduct of its administrative operations. The *Statistics of Income* series published by the Internal Revenue Service, for example, is extremely useful to market researchers attempting to assess corporate and personal income, and the shipping statistics published by the Interstate Commerce Commission are equally valuable to companies requiring information about shipping in the United States.

The statistical resources of the federal government are extensive and varied. Although once difficult to access, their identification has been considerably simplified by the publication of the *American Statistics Index* and other sources described later in this chapter.

State Government Agencies

Until recently, state agencies generally operated independently of the federal government in determining and carrying out their statistical programs. As a consequence, there was considerable variation in the scope of state statistical programs. Efforts are now being made to coordinate the data collected by federal, state, and local government agencies. This coordination has been most notable in the areas of population estimates, employment, and income. Many of these data are, in fact, collected by state and local government organizations and then submitted to the federal government for compilation and publication.

Still other statistics-gathering and publishing activities remain the sole province of state agencies. Although state publishing programs vary, at a minimum most publish statistical compendia as well as specialized statistics focusing on industrial development, employment and unemployment, and the state's economy.

AGENCY	PARENT ORGANIZATION	FUNCTION
Council of Economic Advisers	Executive Office of the President	Advises the President on economic developments, appraises economic policies and programs, and recommends policies for economic growth and stability.
Bureau of Economic Analysis	Commerce Department	Develops, prepares and interprets economic accounts (national and product, balance of payments, foreign investments, input-output, and wealth) and economic developments using these accounts. Also forecasts economic developments.
Economic Research Service	Agriculture Department	Carries on a program of research and analysis on domestic and international food and agriculture, natural resources, and rural people and communities.
Division of Research and Statistics	Board of Governors of the Federal Reserve System	Analyzes economic and credit conditions; is the primary source of statistics on money and banking.

Fig. 6.3. Federal analytic and research agencies relevant to business.

Trade Associations

Charged with keeping their members apprised of industry trends and developments, trade associations constitute another major supplier of statistics. These data are usually collected from association surveys or from reports submitted by member firms, and are published as annual, monthly, and even weekly statistical compilations. Although coverage varies, most include information on industry production, inventories, shipments, sales, and prices. Many also include employment information. The American Automotive Leasing Association, for example, uses reports submitted by members to compile its annual *Analysis of Costs and Related Information*, which covers operating and administrative costs, fleet composition, and leasing and rental activities. Member firms can use the data in the *Analysis* as benchmarks against which they can compare their own costs, profits, and activities. Similarly, the American Trucking Association publishes an annual *Financial Analysis of the Motor Carrier Industry*; the Association of Home Appliance Manufacturers issues a monthly statistical press release, *Major Home Appliance Factory Shipments*; and the Carpet and Rug Institute, an annual *Carpet and Rug Institute Industry Review*.

While these publications are intended primarily for association members, they can be invaluable to librarians and researchers in need of detailed industry data. Although a few association publications are distributed only to members, some are available free of charge to educational institutions, and many can be purchased from the associations themselves, trade publishers, or other sources. Not all association statistics are published, however. When printed sources fail to provide the information being sought, the association staff should be contacted for assistance.

Commercial Publishers

Commercial publishers issue a wide range of statistical data, some of it gathered through original research, but most of it culled from government agencies and trade associations. As mentioned in chapter 3, business periodicals and newspapers are important sources of such information, often including both general business and economic statistics and highly specialized industrial data. The monthly *Beverage Industry*, for example, features an annual survey of soft drink sales, and *American Banker* publishes lists of the largest banks, credit unions, and foreign banks operating in the United States. Dun & Bradstreet publishes two monthlies, *Monthly Business Failures* and *New Business Incorporations*, containing data that are regularly reproduced in such basic government-published sources as the *Statistical Abstract of the United States* and the *Survey of Current Business*.

In addition to statistics contained in periodicals and newspapers, many commercial publishers also issue statistical fact books and directories. Fairchild Publications, for example, publishes the *Electronic News Financial Fact Book and Directory* and *Fairchild's Textile and Apparel Financial Directory*, both of which contain business and financial information, while McGraw-Hill publishes a series of annual reports, including the *McGraw-Hill Annual Survey of Business' Plans for New Plants and Equipment* and the *McGraw-Hill Survey of Research and Development Expenditure*. One of the most widely used compilations is the looseleaf *Statistical Service*, published by Standard & Poor's.

As America has become increasingly statistics-conscious, the market for popular statistics sources has also grown. Most of these sources draw upon statistics generated and originally published by government agencies; some repackage the government data, making them simpler to use by providing explanations and tables that are easier to understand. Others use these data to publish guides to high-paying jobs, safe cities, and locations where quality of life is better than average. Such popular guides as the *Places Rated Almanac* and the *New Book of American Rankings* fall into this category.

Finally, some commercial publishers make detailed and highly sophisticated economic and business information available to their customers, either in print or, more commonly, as online databases, computer tapes, or diskettes. Chase Econometrics, for example, has created and maintains a whole series of domestic and international economic databases. The high cost of these data, however, generally precludes their use by all but the most affluent or highly specialized business collections.

Other Organizations

In addition to data gathered and published by federal and state government agencies, trade associations, and commercial publishers, statistics are also published by university research centers (often called bureaus of business and economic research), independent research organizations such as the Conference Board, Tax Foundation, and U.S. Travel Data Center, and business organizations such as stock and commodity exchanges, banks, accounting firms, and publicly traded companies.

BASIC STATISTICAL CONCEPTS

Familiarity with key statistical concepts enables librarians to understand more clearly requests for specific kinds of statistical information, and to anticipate problems that may arise when seeking or supplying such information. This section considers four statistical concepts—sampling, time series, forecasts and projections, and index numbers—that are basic to business statistics.

Sampling

Data about the population or some designated segment of it are tremendously important to business researchers, government agencies, and others. Ideally, such data should accurately reflect information collected from examination of each person in the population being studied. Surveying an entire population, however, is generally too time-consuming, difficult, and costly to be practical or even effective. As a result, researchers usually select a smaller, representative segment of the population for study and analysis and use the data gathered to make inferences about the entire population. This process is called *sampling*, and the representative segment of the population being measured is known as a *sample*. Sampling is not confined to demographic study; it is used whenever the universe being measured is too large to lend itself to analysis of each of its constituent units. Sampling techniques are often employed in the study of production, wages, sales, and other business-related activities as well as in analysis of the population.

The Census Bureau employs sampling as a means of gathering detailed information about the social and economic characteristics of the population. Every 10 years, for example, it sends questionnaires about population and housing to every household in the country. Most receive brief questionnaires, no more than two pages long. One household in six, however, receives a lengthier, six-page questionnaire that solicits additional information. Thus, while some portions of the *Census of Population* reflect enumeration or counting of almost every household in the United States, other parts are statistical inferences based on the results of the Census Bureau's one-in-six sample of households.

Other census publications are completely based on samples. *Selected Characteristics of Persons in Engineering*, a special study issued periodically as part of the *Current Population Reports* series, bases its statistics on a National Sample of Scientists and Engineers which in 1978 represented some 50 percent of the entire scientific and engineering work force. Other samples represent a considerably smaller proportion of the population.

When a sample is being used, reputable statistical publications will describe its composition and, in many instances, point out its limitations. Thus, the Census Bureau's introduction to *Selected Characteristics of Persons in Engineering* includes the following information.

> The statistics in this report are based on the 1978 survey in a series of biennial surveys known as the National Sample of Scientists and Engineers.... All persons in the National Sample were experienced workers who either had jobs in 1970 or were looking for jobs; new entrants into the labor force since 1970 were not included. Thus, almost all of the sample persons were 30 years old and over in 1978. In addition, the fields of science and engineering in the National Sample were limited to persons who met strict educational, occupational, and professional qualifications. For these reasons, persons in the 1978 National Sample represented approximately 1.5 million scientists and engineers, only a part of the Nation's total scientific and engineering work force.[4]

While the Census Bureau's survey of engineers might be useful for an overview of the field, and for its composition by age, sex, race, and engineering specialty, the data pertain only to established members of the engineering community. It would not be particularly useful and might even be misleading to someone seeking information on recent engineering graduates. As with all types of statistical information, careful perusal of the introductory textual matter and footnotes is essential to determine the scope and limitations of the data being presented.

Time Series Analysis

Sometimes statistics are gathered and published on a one-time basis. A market research firm, for example, may be commissioned to collect data on consumption of and preferences for different types of peanut butter. Such data meet specific needs, reflecting conditions at a fixed point in time. They result from a single research effort and are not updated on a regular basis.

Most situations call for regularly collected statistical data that reflect changes over time. Such numbers are called *time series* and are used to analyze changes in business conditions and the economy, including such items as income, prices, production, and consumption. Most time series consist of monthly, quarterly, or annual observations, and many are produced by the government. Such data are analyzed to identify patterns and, in some instances, to make forecasts about the future.

Many time series that are published weekly, monthly, or quarterly reflect predictable seasonal changes, caused by such factors as climate and school openings and closings. Building construction, for example, regularly shows a slowdown in winter months caused by adverse weather conditions and increases during temperate months. Retail sales are influenced by such holidays as Christmas and Valentine's Day, and unemployment rates generally increase during the summer when school is closed and decrease when school reopens.

Time series that are subject to such predictable seasonal variations are often presented in two different ways: unadjusted and seasonally adjusted. *Unadjusted time series* present data as they are collected without regard to fluctuations caused by regular seasonal changes. *Seasonally adjusted time series*, on the other hand, are "deseasonalized" so that, as near as possible, predictable seasonal changes are eliminated through statistical manipulation. The resulting seasonally adjusted data reflect changes not caused by normal seasonal variation, changes that are sometimes difficult to identify using unadjusted data.

Many statistical publications present both unadjusted and seasonally adjusted time series. The *Survey of Current Business*, for example, includes both. In order to be effective, librarians need to be clear about which type of information is being sought and to label the time series data they supply as either seasonally adjusted or unadjusted.

Forecasts and Projections

Informed speculation about the future is essential for business executives, who must regularly decide whether to increase production of existing products, develop new ones, or otherwise prepare for anticipated changes. Thus, while they often consult time series to assess recent trends and developments, they also use them to make predictions about the future, called forecasts or projections. While the terms are often used interchangeably, there is a difference between the two. *Forecasts* are short-term predictions based on the recent past, generally extending no more than two years into the future. Since they draw upon information about current conditions, which often do not change appreciably over a two-year period, forecasts can be quite accurate. *Projections* are predictions made about the more distant future. The Census Bureau, for example, has already published population projections for the year 2080. Projections cover a greater time span, which may include technological developments, man-made and natural disasters, and other events that may not have been anticipated at the time the projections were made. As a result, projections are more speculative and prone to error than forecasts.

> Extrapolations are useful, particularly in that form of soothsaying called forecasting trends. But in looking at the figures or charts made from them, it is necessary to remember one thing constantly: The trend-to-now may be a fact, but the future trend represents no more than an educated guess. Implicit in it is "everything else being equal" and "present trends continuing," and somehow everything else refuses to remain equal, else life would be dull indeed.[5]

Business forecasts and projections are published by a wide variety of sources, including government agencies, private research organizations, corporations, commercial publishers, and others, and are contained in many of the publications that are described later in this chapter.

Index Numbers

One way in which researchers can consider changes over time is by comparing statistics for one time period with another. They can, for example, compare the number of automobiles manufactured in the United States in 1988 with the number for 1978, or they can contrast the cost of a haircut or rent or groceries or other consumer goods for one period with another. One way to do this is to count the actual number of units being measured—dollars spent for rent, say, or number of cars rolling off the assembly line. Often, however, index numbers are used instead.

In its simplest sense, an *index number* is the ratio of one quantity to another, expressing a given quantity in terms of its value relative to a base quantity. Index numbers frequently are used to compare percent change over time, to measure relative changes in quantity, price, or value of an item or series of related items compared with a designated time, known as the *base period* or *base year*. The base period has a value of 100, and any changes from it represent percentages. Suppose, for example, that someone is preparing a report on the rising costs of hospital care. Upon consulting the *Statistical Abstract of the United States*, the researcher learns that an index of hospital room costs is available, that it uses 1967 as the base year, and that the index in 1985 was 710.5. This means that a hospital room cost 610.5 percent more than it did in 1967. In other words, any number over 100, the number assigned to the base year, reflects an increase; anything less than 100, a decrease. Had the index for hospital rooms been 90, it would have meant that costs had declined by 10 percent since the base year.

Although months or groups of years are sometimes used for base periods, the most commonly used base period is a year. Base years are chosen to provide a good base of comparison, and are thus relatively economically stable years. In the example used above, 1967 is the base year, and government tables showing this and other consumer prices include this notation: [1967 = 100].

Base years sometimes change. Price indexes published in 1967, for example, use a composite of the years 1947 to 1949 as the base. Librarians comparing index numbers for 1967 with 1986 must first determine that the base year being used for both sets of data is the same. *Historical Statistics of the United States* and the *Handbook of Basic Economic Statistics*, described later in this chapter, present data using constant base years.

The index number consulted most frequently in libraries is the Consumer Price Index (CPI), which is a composite of indexes relating to the prices of specific consumer goods and services and which is used as a primary measure of inflation. Since some misunderstanding on the part of library users about the nature and application of the CPI exists, further discussion of this important index is in order.

The *Consumer Price Index* is a monthly measure of the change in average prices over time of a fixed list (usually called a *market basket*) of goods and services. It is based on the average prices of some 400 different items purchased for daily living, items such as shoes, fuel, dairy products, bus fares, newspapers, and dental services.[6] Each item is assigned a weight to account for its relative importance in consumers' budgets. New cars, for example, may account for 4 percent of the index, while shoes may be less than 1 percent.

Prices for each of the items are collected by the U.S. Bureau of Labor Statistics in 85 areas across the country from a sample of 25,000 tenants, 20,000 homeowners, and 32,400 establishments. Some prices are collected monthly, and others are collected bimonthly. They are reported in the *CPI Detailed Report*, published monthly by the Bureau of Labor Statistics. In addition to a U.S. city average, the *CPI Detailed Report* includes price indexes for 28 selected cities and Standard Metropolitan Statistical Areas (SMSAs), shown in figure 6.4.

No. 800. CONSUMER PRICE INDEXES—SELECTED CITIES OR SMSA'S: 1970 TO 1984

[1967 = 100, except as noted. Annual averages of monthly figures. For coverage details, see headnote, table 795, and text, p. 468. Area is generally the standard metropolitan statistical area (SMSA), exclusive of farms. Los Angeles-Long Beach, Anaheim, CA is a combination of two SMSA's, and New York, NY-Northeastern NJ, and Chicago, IL-Northwestern IN are the more extensive standard consolidated areas. Area definitions are those established by the Office of Management and Budget in 1973, except for Denver-Boulder, CO which does not include Douglas County. Definitions do not include revisions made since 1973]

CITY/SMSA	ALL ITEMS									
	1970	1974	1975	1976	1977	1978	1979	1980	1981	1982
City average [1]	116.3	147.7	161.2	170.5	181.5	195.4	217.4	246.8	272.4	289.1
Anchorage, AK [2]	(NA)	133.9	152.3	164.1	175.0	187.5	207.0	228.2	246.5	260.1
Atlanta, GA	116.5	148.5	161.7	169.2	179.6	192.6	212.7	242.3	272.0	289.5
Baltimore, MD	117.0	152.4	165.2	173.9	185.9	199.6	218.2	250.3	273.6	285.8
Boston, MA	116.7	148.7	162.1	174.5	183.4	193.1	212.9	240.0	266.7	277.7
Buffalo, NY	116.1	149.5	161.8	170.6	181.7	193.0	211.3	235.6	257.6	267.2
Chicago, IL-Northwestern IN	116.3	146.1	157.6	165.1	175.6	190.7	214.6	245.5	269.0	287.4
Cincinnati, OH-KY-IN	115.7	146.3	160.3	170.1	182.2	199.1	223.8	254.0	272.1	293.5
Cleveland, OH	119.3	147.8	160.9	169.0	180.5	193.9	219.5	252.9	279.3	301.2
Dallas-Fort Worth, TX	117.8	145.3	158.2	167.7	180.2	194.0	218.6	255.6	284.9	301.3
Denver-Boulder, CO	(NA)	146.5	161.3	170.3	184.7	202.1	233.5	261.5	290.8	317.0
Detroit, MI	117.4	149.0	160.1	168.8	180.4	194.1	218.8	253.5	277.1	288.3
Honolulu, HI	114.2	141.9	155.0	162.8	171.0	184.1	204.6	228.5	252.4	267.6
Houston, TX	116.8	147.8	164.9	177.3	190.2	208.2	235.7	265.4	291.9	312.2
Kansas City, MO-KS	115.8	144.2	157.9	166.5	178.3	191.8	219.2	248.1	268.6	282.0
Los Angeles-Long Beach-Anaheim, CA	114.3	142.5	157.6	168.0	179.6	192.8	213.7	247.3	271.4	287.6
Miami, FL [3]	(NA)	(NA)	(NA)	(NA)	(NA)	104.5	114.8	130.8	145.8	155.8
Milwaukee, WI	115.8	144.1	157.0	167.1	177.9	192.3	218.8	251.5	280.1	296.3
Minneapolis-St. Paul, MN-WI	117.5	148.3	160.9	170.9	183.0	199.7	222.6	247.8	278.3	306.2
New York, NY-Northeast NJ	119.0	154.8	166.6	176.3	185.5	196.1	213.1	237.2	260.5	275.6
Northeast PA	116.3	151.1	164.7	170.9	179.9	191.9	210.7	237.1	264.1	273.8
Philadelphia, PA-NJ	117.8	151.6	164.2	172.4	183.5	194.3	213.6	241.4	266.0	279.0
Pittsburgh, PA	116.4	147.3	160.0	168.3	179.8	195.5	217.3	247.2	272.5	288.0
Portland, OR-WA	113.2	142.8	156.5	167.0	180.2	198.4	225.4	255.4	278.2	287.0
St. Louis, MO-IL	115.2	142.2	156.1	165.1	176.6	191.5	215.8	244.9	267.5	286.9
San Diego, CA	115.3	147.2	160.8	170.7	182.0	200.1	233.1	268.5	304.6	325.3
San Francisco-Oakland, CA	115.8	144.4	159.1	168.0	180.8	197.8	214.6	247.3	279.0	300.0
Seattle-Everett, WA	114.0	141.5	155.8	164.5	177.6	194.8	216.3	252.1	279.7	297.8
Washington, DC-MD-VA	117.6	150.0	161.6	171.1	183.0	197.0	218.6	244.7	267.3	281.9

Fig. 6.4. Consumer Price Indexes for selected cities and SMSAs. Reprinted from the 1986 *Statistical Abstract of the United States.*

The Bureau of Labor Statistics now publishes two official Consumer Price Indexes, known as the CPI-U and the CPI-W.[7] The CPI-U, or Consumer Price Index for All Urban Consumers, is the one most frequently cited by the media. It includes professional and technical workers, the unemployed, the self-employed, retired people, and others, and is designed to take into account some 80 percent of the noninstitutional civilian population. The CPI-W, or Consumer Price Index for Urban Wage Earners and Clerical Workers, is used primarily for calculating cost of living adjustments in labor contracts.

The Consumer Price Index is used as the primary measure of inflation for "escalator clauses," designed to maintain purchasing power, in contracts covering about 60 percent of unionized workers and many government workers as well. Library researchers use it to measure changes in living costs from one year to another. For example, in figure 6.4 the CPI for Milwaukee in 1982 was 296.3, showing an increase of 196.3 percent since 1967.

A common error is to compare one city's CPI with another's in order to determine which has a higher or lower cost of living. Someone moving from Milwaukee to Anchorage, for example, may be understandably concerned about comparative living costs. If he used the data in figure 6.4, showing a CPI of 260.1 for Anchorage and 296.3 for Milwaukee, he might incorrectly assume that it would cost less to live in Anchorage than in Milwaukee. Although both indexes measure price change since 1967, each measures price change in the designated area only. In other words, it might cost twice as much to live in Anchorage as in Milwaukee, but if prices paid for goods and services purchased in Anchorage in 1982 have increased by only 160.1 percent compared to those paid in 1967, Anchorage will have a lower Consumer Price Index than Milwaukee, where prices have increased by 196.3 percent. Comparing one city's CPI with that of another is virtually meaningless. Fortunately, another source permits such comparison between cities.

American Chamber of Commerce Researchers Association. **Inter-City Cost of Living Index.** Indianapolis, Ind.: ACCRA, 1981- . Quarterly.

The *Inter-City Cost of Living Index*, also known as *ACCRA*, measures current prices paid for consumer goods and services in 250 participating cities. Using it, someone can compare living costs in one city with another or can determine the actual dollar amounts paid for specific items, such as hamburger, haircuts, and apartment rent. Since the *Inter-City Cost of Living Index* is published specifically to permit comparison between cities, it is extremely useful to companies and individuals contemplating moving to another part of the country.

Three important differences between the Consumer Price Index and the Inter-City Cost of Living Index should be noted. First, the CPI measures change over time, with the base year equalling 100. The Inter-City Index, on the other hand, measures change *between* locations rather than change over time, with a national city average of 100 used as the base for comparison. A CPI of 250, in other words, means that it now costs 150 percent more to buy the same goods and services as it did in 1967 (or in any other base year designated), while an Inter-City Cost of Living Index of 116 means that it costs 16 percent more than the current national average to live in a specific city or town.

Second, while comparison of Consumer Price Indexes between specific cities is impossible, comparison of two or more cities to the national average using the Inter-City Index is simple. Using it, a researcher can determine that Huntsville's index of 94.7 means that it would cost 5.3 percent less than the national average to live there, and that Phoenix's index of 107.7 represents living costs 7.7 percent above the national average. Further, someone moving from Huntsville to Phoenix could expect to pay 13 percent more for consumer goods and services.

In addition to a national city average, the Consumer Price Index offers individual indexes for 28 major cities and SMSAs. The *Inter-City Cost of Living Index*, however, presents current data for 250 cities and towns. Someone considering a move to North Carolina, for example, would search the *CPI Detailed Report* in vain for a separate CPI for any North Carolina city. The *Inter-City Cost of Living Index*, however, lists 16 different North Carolina cities and towns.

The *Inter-City Cost of Living Index* is not without its flaws. One of the most significant is that many large urban areas are not represented; a recent issue excluded Chicago, Los Angeles, and Washington, D.C. In addition, the list of cities represented does not always remain constant from one year to the next. Thus, simply because a city is included in one issue, it is not safe to assume that it will be listed in subsequent issues. Another problem is that price data are based on reports submitted by participating cities' local chambers of commerce. The data presented are assumed to be reliable, but the American Chamber of Commerce Researchers Association itself warns readers against blind acceptance. "All price data which form the basis of the Index are obtained from sources deemed reliable, but no representation is made as to the complete accuracy thereof. They are published subject to errors, omissions, changes, and withdrawals without notice."[8] In spite of these drawbacks, the *Inter-City Cost of Living Index* is a popular, much-used, and generally reliable source that belongs in most business reference collections.

In addition to indexes that permit comparison between cities, the *Inter-City Cost of Living Index* includes a section that lists actual dollar amounts paid for specific consumer goods, ranging from the average cost of a movie and a pizza to a six-pack of Schlitz beer and a bottle of Bayer aspirin.

Another important BLS index, the Producer Price Index, is used to measure price changes in goods at various stages of production, ranging from raw materials such as logs and timber to finished products, such as furniture. Like the Consumer Price Index, the Producer Price Index appears in many different statistics sources, including the *Survey of Current Business* and the *Statistical Abstract of the United States.*

Other privately produced price indexes are considerably more fanciful. The Christmas Price Index, for example, measures changes from one year to the next in the prices paid for items mentioned in the popular "Twelve Days of Christmas" carol, including partridges, turtle doves, and gold rings. Another index, published by *Money*, calculates changes in prices for a "Me-Generation" market basket of designer brand products for upwardly mobile consumers, including Häagen-Dazs ice cream, goat cheese, bottled water, and jogging shoes.

ECONOMIC INDICATORS

In business libraries, some of the most frequently asked for statistics are those used to assess the state of the national economy. Dozens of statistics are commonly used for this purpose, but among the most important are the Gross National Product, Industrial Production, Leading Indicators, Personal Income, the Consumer and Producer Price Indexes, Retail Sales, Employment, and Housing Starts, all of which are described in Appendix G. All are issued on a regular basis by the government and are reported in newspapers, periodicals, and statistical reference sources. The economic indicators listed above, however, are by no means the only ones. Keeping abreast of such statistics, their frequency of issuance, and the sources in which they appear is not always easy. Fortunately, in recent years several fine directories to economic time series data have been published. Some of the best are listed below.

> Levine, Robyn E., and Felicia G. Kolp. **Selected Economic Statistics: Definitions, Sources of Current Information, and Historical Tables.** Rev. ed. Washington, D.C.: Congressional Research Service, Library of Congress, 1985 (Report No. 85-108C). 63p.

> Hoel, Arline, Kenneth W. Clarkson, and Roger LeRoy Miller. **Economics Sourcebook of Government Statistics.** Lexington, Mass.: Lexington Books, 1983. 288p.

> O'Hara, Frederick M., Jr., and Robert Sicignano. **Handbook of United States Economic and Financial Indicators.** Westport, Conn.: Greenwood Press, 1985. 224p.

> Lehmann, Michael B. **The Dow Jones-Irwin Guide to Using the Wall Street Journal.** 2nd ed. Homewood, Ill.: Dow Jones-Irwin, 1987. 282p.

Selected Economic Statistics, prepared by staff members at the Library of Congress' Congressional Research Service, lists and describes frequently requested economic statistics, those pertaining to economic growth, employment and income, monetary conditions, and federal finance. Each listing includes a lengthy definition, and identifies the issuing agency, frequency of issuance, and the sources in which the statistic appears. Tables from such sources as the *Economic Report of the President, Statistical Abstract of the United States, Survey of Current Business*, and the *Monthly Labor Review* present historical data, and concepts not covered in the other sources listed above – definition and determination of poverty level, for example, and the formula for changing base years for the Consumer Price Index are also included. Unfortunately, neither the Government Printing Office nor the National

Technical Information Service has published *Selected Economic Statistics*, and it is not easily available to the public. It can, however, be borrowed on interlibrary loan or requested from one's representative or senator, and is well worth the effort required to obtain it.

Although written for members of the business press, the *Economics Sourcebook of Government Statistics* can be invaluable to anyone seeking information on some 50 major economic time series. Statistics are grouped by type into six broad categories (measures of inflation, profits, interest rates and financial indicators, measures of employment, indicators of international finance and trade, and indicators of government influence), and each indicator within the designated category is covered separately and at length. Most entries are about three pages long, and describe the statistic, discuss its limitations and biases, list publications containing current and historical data, and cite the addresses and telephone numbers of government contacts. Bibliographies are frequently included. The *Economics Sourcebook of Government Statistics* is extremely useful for statistical reference service, and belongs in most business reference collections.

The *Handbook of United States Economic and Financial Indicators* lists more than 200 different time series, ranging from "Accession Rates, Manufacturing" to "Workweek, Average Manufacturing." Although entries are not quite as long as those in the *Economics Sourcebook* described above, they include a definition, an explanation of the derivation of the statistic, comments on its applications, and list its frequency, publisher, and the publication(s) in which it is announced. Two other differences distinguish the *Handbook* from the *Economics Sourcebook*. The first is that entries include a list of government and nongovernment periodicals in which the statistics regularly appear, and the second is that indicators published by trade associations, consulting firms, financial publishing companies, and other private organizations are also included. Figure 6.5 illustrates a typical entry.

```
Automotive Factory Sales
<DESCRIPTION>
The number of vehicles shipped and sold or billed to
customers, dealers, or allied divisions during a given month.
<DERIVATION>
Manufacturers report the number of vehicles (cars, trucks,
buses, taxicabs, hearses, ambulances, fire trucks, etc.)
shipped or billed during the month. These are tabulated by
class (passenger cars, trucks and buses, etc.) and then
totaled. Export sales are included. Sales to the federal
government are included except for tactical military
vehicles. Virtually the entire industry is covered.
<USE>
An especially good indicator of future consumer demand and a
measure of overall economic health
<PUBLISHER>
Motor Vehicle Manufacturers Association of the U.S.
<ANNOUNCED IN>
Automotive News
<ANNOUNCEMENT FREQUENCY>
Monthly
<CUMULATIONS>
TABLES
Ward's Repts Monthly, units
Bus Stats    Monthly and yearly, cum, units
SCB          Monthly and yearly, cum, units
Ward's Repts Quarterly and yearly, cum, units
MVMA         Yearly, cum, units
Stat Abstr   Yearly, cum, units
<MORE INFORMATION>
    U.S. Dept. of Commerce, Bureau of Economic Analysis,
Handbook of Cyclical U.S. Indicators, USGPO, Washington,
D.C., 1977.
```

Fig. 6.5. Typical entry, *Handbook of Economic and Financial Indicators*. Reprinted by permission from the *Handbook of Economic and Financial Indicators*, Greenwood Press, 1985.

An appendix of nonquantitative indicators is also included, and is particularly helpful to librarians confronted with questions about such purported measures of economic and financial well-being as the "Short-Skirt Index," which holds that rises and falls in women's hemlines are accompanied by similar actions in the stock market, the "Surly Waiter Index," and the "Drinking Couple Count." Like the *Economics Sourcebook*, the *Handbook of United States Economic and Financial Indicators* is a basic statistical reference source.

Many economic statistics are first issued in government news releases. After the initial release, many are subsequently published in the *Wall Street Journal*, a good source of current economic indicators. *The Dow Jones-Irwin Guide to Using the Wall Street Journal* focuses on some of the key statistics reported, describing what they measure, how they are computed, and when they appear in the *Journal*. In addition, the *Guide* provides information on how each statistic is used to track the economy, and includes excerpts from *Wall Street Journal* articles that illustrate the context in which specific statistics are used.

Government periodicals such as the *Survey of Current Business* and *Monthly Labor Review* are prime sources of economic statistics. *Economic Indicators*, a monthly prepared by the Council of Economic Advisers for the Congress's Joint Economic Committee, includes historic as well as current data. Researchers seeking current government statistics can also call the Congressional Research Services CRS Stats Line, a telephone recording, updated weekly, that lists current economic indicators.[9]

RELIABILITY OF STATISTICS

Users, writes Joe Morehead, sometimes attribute "the power and value of holy writ"[10] to statistics. No statistics, whatever their air of authority, deserve unquestioning acceptance. Some, in fact, are deliberately misleading. The advertising cliche, "Nine out of ten doctors surveyed prefer Brand X," is a good example. Clearly, sampling techniques were employed. The advertisers, however, do not document sample size in their commercial, nor do they describe how the sample was selected. Although the advertisement implies that a preponderance of all doctors prefer Brand X, it is entirely possible that the sample consisted of only 10 doctors, all of whom were employees of or stockholders in the company manufacturing Brand X. Further, the advertisers do not list the options the doctors could choose from when selecting Brand X. They might have been given alternate brands of the same product, or they might have been presented with choices that clearly were unacceptable. The numbers themselves are suspect, with the mention of doctors lending an air of credibility and respectability by flaunting what Darrell Huff, author of *How to Lie with Statistics*, calls the "O.K. name."

> Anything smacking of the medical profession is an O.K. name. Scientific laboratories have O.K. names. So do colleges, especially universities, especially ones eminent in technical work.... When an O.K. name is cited, make sure that the authority stands behind the information, not merely somewhere alongside it.[11]

The Pentagon's body counts during the Vietnam War and public opinion polls commissioned by politicians are also examples of statistics that are deliberately misleading. These examples lead to the first questions that astute librarians and researchers ask when reviewing statistical data. *Where did the data come from? Is the source unbiased, or does it have a vested interest in supplying data that will lead to one conclusion rather than another? Are the statistics self-serving?*

When, as near as possible, statistical objectivity has been ascertained, methodology needs to be examined. Most librarians are not statisticians, but by reading the table headers, footnotes, and any additional documentation, they can learn about some of the more obvious limitations of the data being presented.

It is important that users, whether primary or secondary users, know just how the data for a particular table were collected and analysed, what was included, and what was omitted. For instance, firms with under a certain number of employees may be omitted from tables of production or employment statistics, and certain industries may for one reason or another be omitted from more general tables. In regular tables the content or classification may change at some time; and errors or later information may mean that some regular tables (foreign trade statistics, for instance) are corrected in the cumulated figures published in the next or even a later issue. A new base year for time series will mean that one cannot use earlier tables of index numbers in the same context. Figures may be rounded up or rounded down in a table or series of tables, and if these figures are added together they can result in an inaccurate figure. Time series may be amended to allow for seasonal or other variations. Misinterpretations can be avoided if care is taken to read the explanatory notes or other matter which statisticians usually take trouble to provide in an effort to overcome these and other dangers.[12]

Statistics, in short, require careful scrutiny to determine both their reliability and their applicability to the research situation at hand. Such assessment presupposes the existence of statistical data, and this chapter concludes with consideration of some of the most important sources of statistical information.

STATISTICAL PUBLICATIONS

Statistical inquiries are endemic to business reference; with directory-related questions, they comprise the bulk of day-to-day business reference work in most libraries. Many statistical reference questions are simple to answer, requiring only the use of an almanac or some other basic reference source. Others are considerably more difficult, calling for perseverance and ingenuity. A few are impossible to answer, either because the data do not exist or because they are inaccessible to libraries. Privately commissioned market research studies, for example, fall into the last category. In most instances, though, statistics are available and can be identified by consulting the following sources.

Dictionaries and Encyclopedias

Theory has it that a good reference librarian can answer inquiries in any field, without benefit of the appropriate educational background or even rudimentary knowledge of the subject being studied. No reference librarian, however, can answer an inquiry unless he or she understands the question being asked. This is particularly true in the area of business and economics statistics, where jargon is commonplace and terminology foreign to the uninitiated. Fortunately, several dictionaries, encyclopedias, and other sources define basic terms and concepts. Some, in fact, have already been identified: Those discussed in the section on economic indicators include lengthy definitions of the statistics that they list. The *McGraw-Hill Dictionary of Modern Economics*, described in chapter 1, includes definitions, written so that lay people can understand them, of such basic statistical concepts as index numbers, sampling, and business cycles.

Other dictionaries and encyclopedias focus on statistics as an area of study, and are useful for definitions of less commonplace terms and concepts. Two of the most widely used publications are listed below.

Kendall, Maurice G., and William R. Buckland. **A Dictionary of Statistical Terms**. 4th ed., rev. and enl. London: Longman, 1982. 166p.

Kruskal, William H., and Judith M. Tanur, eds. **International Encyclopedia of Statistics**. New York: Free Press, 1978. 2v.

Since the publication of the first edition in 1957, *A Dictionary of Statistical Terms* has gained widespread acceptance as the standard dictionary of current statistical terminology. Nearly 3,000 entries are included, featuring brief definitions and, in many instances, equations and formulas. While focus in *A Dictionary of Statistical Terms* is on terms in current usage, coverage in the *International Encyclopedia of Statistics* is considerably broader. The *Encyclopedia* is a compilation of articles pertaining to statistics and statisticians culled from the 17-volume reference classic, the *International Encyclopedia of the Social Sciences*. However, the *International Encyclopedia of Statistics* is more than a reformatted version of the statistical portions of the *International Encyclopedia of the Social Sciences*. In addition to presenting articles as they originally appeared in that source, each entry includes a lengthy postscript that covers subsequent developments and a supplementary bibliography that updates the original. Some articles are new to the *Encyclopedia*. In all, over 70 articles on statistics and over 50 biographies of statisticians and others important to the development of statistics are included. The *International Encyclopedia of Statistics* may not be appropriate for every library reference collection, but in settings where statistical research and reference inquiries are commonplace, it is an invaluable addition, providing thorough coverage of the development of the study of statistics, statistical theories, and applications.

Until now, this chapter has focused on the study of basic statistical applications and on the presentation of statistical data in tables. Often, however, business people are called upon to present statistics in charts and graphs. Although the increasing availability of microcomputers and graphics software have simplified the mechanics of graphic presentation for many, others must continue to construct charts by hand. The encyclopedia below is representative of publications aimed at people who must prepare such charts.

Carlsen, Robert D., and Donald L. Vest. **Encyclopedia of Business Charts**. Englewood Cliffs, N.J.: Prentice-Hall, 1977. 886p.

The *Encyclopedia of Business Charts* describes the mechanics of preparing charts and illustrates their use with actual examples. The main section contains hundreds of examples, grouped together by broad category, such as "Inventories" or "Manpower" or "Financial Ratios." Each category includes a wide variety of styles, ranging from simple to complex. The second section, "Chartmanship," describes basic types of business charts and discusses their preparation, including such items as format and nomenclature, titles, notes, and data layout. The *Encyclopedia of Business Charts* and similar works are practical and useful additions to most business collections.

Guides and Indexes

Some of the publications described in earlier chapters can be particularly helpful in identifying and locating statistical data. Lorna Daniells' *Business Information Sources*, for example, devotes separate chapters to basic U.S. statistical sources, industry statistics, and foreign statistics and economic trends, and identifies additional statistical publications in chapters focusing on such business operations as accounting and marketing. Michael Lavin's *Business Information: How to Find It, How to Use It* includes a whole section on statistical information, with chapters on statistical reasoning, the Census of Population and Housing, population estimates and projections, general economic statistics, and industry statistics. The *Encyclopedia of Business Information Sources* offers a greater level of subject specificity, listing published sources of statistics pertaining to such topics as honey and zinc production, carpet imports, and peanut stocks. In addition, both the *Special Issues Index* and the *Guide to Special Issues and Indexes of Periodicials* (chapter 3) list trade journals and other periodicals that regularly feature special statistical reviews. *Data Sources for Business and Market Analysis*, described at length in chapter 9, devotes considerable attention to both government- and privately generated statistics sources. In addition to the titles listed above, several specialized statistical guides and indexes are also available. Although space does not permit consideration of them all, some of the most useful are listed below.

O'Brien, Jacqueline Wasserman, and Steven Wasserman, eds. **Statistics Sources**. 11th ed. Detroit: Gale, 1987. 2v.

American Statistics Index. Washington, D.C.: Congressional Information Service, 1973- . Monthly, with annual cumulations.

Statistical Reference Index. Washington, D.C.: Congressional Information Service, 1980- . Monthly, with annual cumulations.

Statistical Services Directory. 2nd ed. Detroit: Gale, 1984. 461p.

Sears, Jean L., and Marilyn K. Moody. **Using Government Publications. Volume 2: Finding Statistics and Using Special Techniques**. Phoenix, Ariz.: Oryx Press, 1986. 240p.

Statistics Sources, described by its publisher as a finding guide to statistics, provides subject access to data contained in compilations such as the *Statistical Abstract of the United States* and the United Nations' *Statistical Yearbook*, basic statistical publications from many organizations, and special statistical issues of professional, technical, and trade journals. Arrangement is alphabetical by subject, with over 20,000 subjects, ranging from "Abortions" to "Zoology – Degrees Conferred." One of the strengths of *Statistics Sources*, like its companion publication, the *Encyclopedia of Business Information Sources*, is the level of subject specificity it provides. Using it, one can determine sources of statistics for shipments of lawnmowers, beer production in Angola, and the rate of injuries in the textile industry. Coverage is international, and while U.S. government and United Nations publications predominate, many private, commercial, and foreign government publications are also included. Each entry features the name of the issuing organization, the publication title, and, when applicable, its date. Page numbers are not given.

Another useful feature is the extensive bibliography of key statistical sources that precedes the main section. It lists and annotates significant dictionaries, general sources and guides, almanacs, U.S. government and nongovernment publications, guides to online databases and machine-readable data files, and international sources.

Statistics Sources provides quick access to statistical publications, but it does not describe their contents. A series of statistical indexes published by Congressional Information Service remedy this lack. The first of these, the *American Statistics Index*, made its debut in 1973, considerably simplifying work for documents and business librarians and for researchers seeking federal statistical data. The *American Statistics Index*, or *ASI*, is a master guide to statistical publications of the federal government. It is published in two parts, an *Index Section* and an *Abstracts Section*.

The *ASI Index Section* contains a variety of separate indexes. The main index lists sources by subject and name. As shown in figure 6.6 (see page 130), index entries include brief notations of content, frequently cite the title of the publication in which the statistics are presented, and always provide an accession number for reference to the *ASI Abstracts Section* and to microfiche reproductions of those publications sold by Congressional Information Service. Numerous cross-references to related index terms are also included.

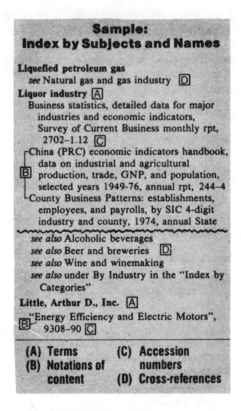

Fig. 6.6. Sample entry, *ASI Subject Index*. Copyright 1978 by Congressional Information Service, Inc. All rights reserved. Reprinted with permission.

In addition to the main subject index, the *ASI Index Section* also features an Index by Categories, which includes references to all publications that contain comparative tabular data broken down into designated geographic, economic, and demographic categories.[13] Although the main subject index provides more detailed subject access, the Index by Categories is useful when more specific information is being sought. General information on the national labor force, for example, is identified more easily through the Subject Index, while the Index by Categories is more helpful to identify publications pertaining to women in the work force. Figure 6.7 illustrates the use of one of the demographic categories in the Index by Categories to answer the question, "What segment of the total U.S. work force is comprised of married, college educated women?"

Once publications and their corresponding accession numbers have been identified, the *Abstract Section* can be consulted. Entries are arranged by accession number and, as shown in the second illustration in figure 6.7, include many of the features common to entries in the *Monthly Catalog of United States Government Publications*, such as Superintendent of Documents classification, item number, and when applicable, the *Monthly Catalog* entry number and/or the NTIS number. As in the *Monthly Catalog*, depository documents are designated by a bullet.

Information in *ASI*'s *Abstract Section*, however, is considerably more detailed than that in the *Monthly Catalog*. Every publication is annotated and, in many instances, specific tables or articles are listed and described separately. Each annotation provides full bibliographic data, describes the publication, and lists tables and articles.

Sample Category Search

QUESTION: "What segment of the total U.S. work force is comprised of married, college educated women?"

Step 1. Search the Index

Because the question calls for data broken down by specific demographic characteristics, the search begins in the Index by Categories:

DEMOGRAPHIC BREAKDOWNS

BY SEX

Labor and Employment
Age mandatory retirement from Civil Service, proposed abolishment, with data on retired Federal employees and Employment Service assistance recipients, by State, 1973-74, hearings, 21348-33
Aliens illegally in US, characteristics, employment experience, and participation in public programs, with some comparative data for alien commuters, 1976 rpt, 6408-30

Educational attainment of labor force, by employment and demographic characteristics, Mar 1976, 6746-1.193

NOTE: A list of 21 categories and 19 subject headings precedes the Index. In the above sample, other demographic categories that might have been checked, with equal results, were *By Educational Attainment* and *By Marital Status.*

Step 2. Note the accession number

This sample cites number **6746-1.193**.

Step 3. Locate and review the abstract

Under the number **6746-1**, a main abstract for a series of publications is found. The decimal number (**.193**) refers to an analytic abstract for an individual and specifically relevant report within this series.

Step 4. Obtain the publication

The abstract contains bibliographic data for use in obtaining the publication.

For more detailed information on how to use the *American Statistics Index* and *Abstracts,* refer to the "User Guide" in the most recent *ASI Annual,* or consult your librarian.

Congressional Information Service, Inc.
4520 East-West Highway, Suite 800
Bethesda, MD 20814

**6746
BUREAU OF LABOR STATISTICS:
MANPOWER AND EMPLOYMENT Publications in Series**

6746-1 SPECIAL LABOR FORCE REPORTS
●Item 768-R. † For individual bibliographic data, see below.
Spec. Labor Force Rpt. (nos.)
*L2.98:(nos.)

Continuing series of special reports on results of labor force surveys and analytical studies. Most reports also appear as articles in the *Monthly Labor Review,* but without the additional explanatory notes and detailed supplementary tables.
Reports received during 1977 are described below.

6746-1.193: Educational Attainment of Workers, Mar. 1976
[Rpt. 193. 1976. ii+26 p. ASI/MF/3]
By Kopp Michelotti. Report on educational attainment of the labor force as of Mar. 1976. Includes 5 summary tables and 14 detailed appendix tables showing the following data, all by years of school completed:
a. Labor force, by sex; selected years 1940-76.
b. Labor force status, by age and women's marital status; labor force participation and unemployment rates, by age; occupation; and industry. Data are by sex and race, Mar. 1976.

Fig. 6.7. Use of *ASI*'s Index by Categories. Copyright 1978 by Congressional Information Service, Inc. All rights reserved. Reprinted with permission.

Microfiche copies of publications listed in *ASI* are available from the publisher. Libraries can order ASI Microfiche Library collections that include all of the publications indexed. Alternatively, they can select fiche copies of nondepository publications only, or they can order specific documents as needed from the publisher's ASI Documents on Demand Service.

Finally, each volume of the *American Statistics Index* includes a lengthy introduction that describes the types of publications that are indexed, explains their arrangement, and presents search strategies highlighting effective use of this index. A shorter version, the "*ASI* Search Guide," is available in multiple copies to libraries, and is a good handout for library users.[14]

Arrangement is similar in the second major Congressional Information Service index, the *Statistical Reference Index* (*SRI*). As with the *American Statistics Index, Statistical Reference Index* is divided into index and abstract sections, with subject and category indexing provided in the *Index Section,* and publication descriptions, in the *Abstract Section.* The *SRI,* however, indexes and abstracts statistics contained in publications *not* issued by the federal government. It includes statistics published by private organizations such as trade associations, corporations, commercial publishers, and independent and university-affiliated research organizations. It also includes documents published by state government agencies. Focus is on publications "presenting business, industrial, financial, and social statistics of general research value and having national, regional, or statewide breadth of coverage."[15] Each entry includes an accession number, bibliographic information, a description of contents, and information for requesting or purchasing copies from the issuing source.

As with *ASI*, many of the publications listed in *SRI* are available from the publisher. However, while *ASI* documents are copied in their entirety, not all *SRI* publications are. Some are limited to designated statistical excerpts, and some, like the example shown in figure 6.8, are not available as part of the SRI Microfiche Library and must be ordered directly from the original publisher. However, in spite of these limitations, the SRI Microfiche Library permits access to many publications that otherwise would be difficult or time-consuming to acquire.

A7485
National Cotton
Council of America

A7485–1   COTTON COUNTS ITS
CUSTOMERS: The Quantity
of Cotton Consumed in Final
Uses in the U.S., Revised
1982-83 and Preliminary
1984
Annual. 1985. vi+110 p.
SRI/MF/not filmed

Annual report on cotton and other material consumption in textile product manufacture, by end use, 1982-84. Covers 92 detailed product categories in apparel, home furnishing, and industrial sectors.

Data are from textile manufacturers and Census Bureau.

Contains foreword and contents listing (p. iii-vi); 2 summary tables, including rankings of 92 major end-use product categories by cotton consumption, 1984 (p. 1-19); and 1 detailed table showing production, gray cotton material requirement, and total and cotton material consumption, by detailed end use within each product category, 1982-84 (p. 20-110).

Availability: National Cotton Council of America, Economic Services, PO Box 12285, Memphis TN 38182, members †, nonmembers $50.00, 40% discount to public and educational institution libraries; SRI/MF/not filmed.

Fig. 6.8. Sample abstract, *Statistical Reference Index*. Copyright 1986 by Congressional Information Service, Inc. (Bethesda, Md.). All rights reserved. Reprinted with permission.

A third Congressional Information Service index, the *Index to International Statistics*, provides access to and description of statistical publications of international intergovernmental organizations.

The *Statistical Services Directory* lists over 2,000 organizations, including corporations, professional and trade associations, foundations, and government agencies that are primary gatherers of statistical data in the United States and that provide statistical services to the public or to clients. Arrangement is alphabetical by organization name, and each entry includes the organization's name, address, and telephone number; the name of a contact within the organization; a description of its statistical programs and the subjects for which data are collected; the time period covered; the frequency of statistical releases; the formats in which they are available; and the cost of the publication or service. In addition, the *Statistical Services Directory* includes subject, geographic, contact name, and title indexes.

Finding Statistics and Using Special Techniques, volume 2 of *Using Government Publications*, lists and describes many of the most frequently used government statistics. Separate chapters are devoted to population and vital statistics, economic indicators, business and industry statistics, income, earnings, employment, prices, consumer expenditures, foreign trade, crime and criminal justice, energy, defense and military statistics, and projections. Each chapter lists basic sources, suggests search strategies for their use, and includes Superintendent of Documents classification and item numbers and *ASI* accession numbers in addition to standard bibliographic information. Sample pages from documents being discussed are frequently featured. In addition, techniques for conducting historical research, tracing legislative histories, budget analysis, and other types of special research are also included. Since the volume begins with chapters devoted to basic information about the publication, distribution, and arrangement of government documents, *Finding Statistics and Using Special Techniques* can be useful to librarians and researchers at any level of documents expertise.

Statistical Compilations

One of the best ways to begin the search for data is by consulting a statistical compilation. Comprised of data culled from many other sources, such publications can provide direct answers to many statistical reference inquiries and indirect access to sources that will answer others. Statistical compendia are published by international, foreign, federal, and state government agencies, commercial publishers, and other organizations. The following four such compilations are basic to business reference.

U.S. Department of Commerce. Bureau of the Census. **Statistical Abstract of the United States**. Washington, D.C.: Government Printing Office, 1878- . Annual.

U.S. Department of Commerce. Bureau of the Census. **Historical Statistics of the United States, Colonial Times to 1970**. Washington, D.C.: Government Printing Office, 1975. 2v.

The Handbook of Basic Economic Statistics. Washington, D.C.: Bureau of Economic Statistics, Inc., 1947- . Annual, with monthly supplements.

Standard & Poor's. **Statistical Service**. New York: Standard & Poor's, 1978- . One-volume looseleaf, with monthly supplements.

At every minute of every working day, hypothesizes one writer, a librarian somewhere is using the *Statistical Abstract of the United States*. Although this observation falls into the realm of an unsubstantiated statistic, there is no doubt that the *Statistical Abstract* is one of the most heavily used reference sources in any business or general reference collection. Published since 1878, the *Statistical Abstract* is the standard summary of social, political, and economic statistics for the United States. It is a compendia of data collected from over 220 different government and private agencies, with information grouped together by broad subject categories such as "Population," "Labor Force, Employment, and Earnings," and "Business Enterprise." Each chapter begins with a description of the data being presented, definitions of key terms and concepts, and, in many instances, consideration of the limitations and the general reliability of the data being presented. Sources providing information for earlier years and/or for local areas are frequently cited as well (see figure 6.9, on page 134).

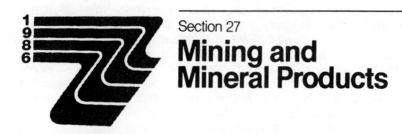

Section 27

Mining and Mineral Products

This section presents data relating to mineral industries and their products, general summary measures of production and employment, and more detailed data on production, prices, imports and exports, consumption, and distribution for specific industries and products. Data on mining and mineral products may also be found in Sections 29 and 33 of this *Abstract;* data on mining employment may be found in Section 14.

"Mining" comprises the extraction of minerals occurring naturally (coal, ores, crude petroleum, natural gas) and quarrying, well operation, milling, refining and processing and other preparation customarily done at the mine or well site or as a part of extraction activity. (Mineral preparation plants are usually operated together with mines or quarries.) Exploration for minerals is included as is the development of mineral properties.

The principal governmental sources of these data are the three-volume *Minerals Yearbook,* published by the Bureau of Mines, Department of the Interior, and various monthly and annual publications of the Energy Information Administration, Department of Energy. See text, Section 20 for list of Department of Energy publications. In addition, the Bureau of the Census conducts a census of mineral industries every 5 years. Non-government sources include the *Annual Statistical Report* of the American Iron and Steel Institute, Washington, DC; *Metals Week* and the monthly *Engineering and Mining Journal,* issued by the McGraw-Hill Publishing Co., New York, NY; *The Iron Age,* issued weekly by the Chilton Co., Philadelphia, PA; and the *Joint Association Survey of the U.S. Oil and Gas Industry,* conducted jointly by the American Petroleum Institute, Independent Petroleum Association of America, and Mid-Continent Oil and Gas Association.

Mineral statistics, with principal emphasis on commodity detail, have been collected by the Geological Survey or by the Bureau of Mines since 1880. Current data in Bureau of Mines publications include quantity and value of nonfuel minerals produced, sold or used by producers, or shipped; quantity of minerals stocked; crude materials treated and prepared minerals recovered; and consumption of mineral raw materials. The U.S. Mine Safety and Health Administration also collects and publishes data on workhours, employment, accidents, and injuries in the mineral industries, except petroleum and natural gas. In October 1977, mineral fuel data collection activities of the Bureau of Mines were transferred to the Energy Information Administration.

Censuses of mineral industries have been conducted by the Bureau of the Census at various intervals since 1840. Beginning with the 1967 census, legislation provides for a census to be conducted every fifth year for years ending in "2" and "7." The censuses provide, for the various types of mineral establishments, information on operating costs, capital expenditures, labor, equipment, and energy requirements in relation to their value of shipments and other receipts. Commodity statistics on many manufactured mineral products are also collected by the Bureau at monthly, quarterly, or annual intervals and issued in its *Current Industrial Reports* series.

In general, figures shown in the individual commodity tables include data for outlying areas, and may therefore not agree with summary table 1237. Except for crude petroleum and refined products, the export and import figures include foreign trade passing through the customs districts of United States and Puerto Rico, but exclude shipments between U.S. territories and the customs districts.

Historical statistics.—Tabular headnotes provide cross-references, where applicable, to *Historical Statistics of the United States, Colonial Times to 1970.* See Appendix I.

Statistics for States and metropolitan statistical areas (MSAs).—Data for States and MSAs may also be found in *State and Metropolitan Area Data Book 1985.* For cross-references, see Appendix VI.

Fig. 6.9. Typical introductory section to a chapter, *Statistical Abstract of the United States.* Reprinted from the *Statistical Abstract of the United States,* 1986 edition.

Since the chapters are usually several pages long, the most efficient way to identify the specific table needed is to consult the subject index. Unlike subject indexes in many government publications, that of the *Statistical Abstract* is superb. Using it, tables can be located that provide statistics on shipments and value of floppy disks and microwave ovens, volume of trading on the New York Stock Exchange, prices received by fishermen for tuna and cod, and hundreds of other subjects. When a fairly broad subject is being presented, subheadings are frequently used for greater precision.

The tables themselves provide basic statistics and, as shown in figure 6.10, frequently include definitions of terms or concepts as well as the source from which the statistics were derived.

No. 1398. DOMESTIC FRANCHISING—SUMMARY: 1970 TO 1985

[Franchising is a form of marketing or distribution in which a parent company customarily grants an individual or a company the right, or privilege, to do business in a prescribed manner over a certain period of time in a specified place. The parent company is termed the franchisor; the receiver of the privilege the franchisee; and the right, or privilege, the franchise. Excludes foreign outlets of U.S. companies]

ITEM	Unit	1970	1975	1978	1979	1980	1981	1982	1983	1984 [1]	1985 [1]
Number of franchised establishments...	1,000..........	396	435	452	452	442	442	439	442	455	481
Company-owned [2]	1,000..........	72	81	85	85	85	86	87	86	88	91
Franchisee-owned	1,000..........	324	354	367	367	357	356	352	355	367	390
Sales of products and services............	Bil. dol........	120	191	287	312	336	365	376	423	484	529
Company-owned [2]	Bil. dol........	23	29	44	39	47	51	55	59	64	70
Franchisee-owned	Bil. dol........	96	162	243	273	289	314	321	364	420	459
Average sales per establishment............	$1,000..........	302	439	635	690	760	824	856	958	1,064	1,099
Employment...................................	1,000..........	(NA)	3,511	4,496	4,605	4,668	4,878	4,927	5,165	(NA)	(NA)

NA Not available.   [1] Estimated by respondents to annual survey of franchisors.   [2] Represents establishments owned by the parent company.

Source: U.S. Dept. of Commerce, International Trade Administration, *Franchising in the Economy, 1983–85.*

Fig. 6.10. Sample table, *Statistical Abstract of the United States*. Reprinted from the *Statistical Abstract of the United States*, 1986 edition.

Other features should also be noted. A "Recent Trends" section uses tables, graphs, and charts to illustrate socioeconomic trends and for each item presents average annual percentage change. The appendixes include a description of metropolitan areas and a list of current metropolitan areas and their components, a discussion of statistical reliability and methodology, and a lengthy subject bibliography that lists important public and private sources of primary statistical data. Another appendix ties tables in the *Statistical Abstract* to corresponding tables in a companion publication, *Historical Statistics of the United States, Colonial Times to 1970.*

As a rule, most tables in the *Statistical Abstract* present national data. Occasionally regional and state breakdowns are given as well, and less often, some local information is included. Mainly, however, information is for the United States as a whole and other sources must be consulted for narrower geographic areas.

Most tables present information for the past 5 or 10 years; historical information is seldom presented. Someone who wanted to show how prices paid for consumer goods in 1888 compared with those paid in 1988, for example, would find that the *Statistical Abstract* lacked the necessary historical information. She would, however, find it in *Historical Statistics of the United States, Colonial Times to 1970* (see figure 6.11, on page 136). Issued by the Census Bureau as a periodic supplement to the *Statistical Abstract, Historical Statistics* also serves as a reference source and finding aid. Like the *Statistical Abstract*, it footnotes the sources from which tables are compiled and includes introductory remarks in most chapters that describe methodology employed and limitations, if any, of the data as presented.

The *Handbook of Basic Economic Statistics*, a commercially published sourcebook of key economic and statistical data produced by the federal government, includes over 1,800 different time series arranged by broad subject category. Statistics for the current and recent years are presented monthly or quarterly, with annual data for earlier years. Statistics date back to 1913 or to the first year thereafter for which the figures exist. One of the strengths of the *Handbook*, in fact, is that it makes several years of data available and presents them so that they can be compared easily. For example, it shows the Consumer Price Index from

1913 to the present, using 1967 as the base year. Using it, one can follow consumer price changes over decades, an impossibility with the *Statistical Abstract of the United States.*

CONSUMER PRICE INDEXES   E 135–173

Series E 135–166. Consumer Price Indexes (BLS)—All Items, 1800 to 1970, and by Groups, 1913 to 1970—Con.

[1967 = 100]

Year	All items	Food at home, total	Rent	House furnishings	Apparel, total	Year	All items	Year	All items	Year	All items	Year	All items	Year	All items	Year	All items
	135	137	150	155	156		135		135		135		135		135		135
1934	40.1	34.1	50.7	46.6	40.4	1912	29	1890	27	1868	40	1846	27	1823	36		
1933	38.8	30.6	54.1	42.4	36.9	1911	28	1889	27	1867	42	1845	28	1822	40		
1932	40.9	31.5	62.8	42.9	38.2			1888	27	1866	44	1844	28	1821	40		
1931	45.6	37.8	70.9	49.3	43.2	1910	28	1887	27			1843	28	1820	42		
						1909	27	1886	27	1865	46	1842	29	1819	46		
1930	50.0	45.9	73.9	54.7	47.5	1908	27			1864	47	1841	31	1818	46		
1929	51.3	48.3	76.0	56.2	48.5	1907	28	1885	27	1863	37			1817	48		
1928	51.3	47.7	77.8	56.8	49.0	1906	27	1884	27	1862	30	1840	30	1816	51		
1927	52.0	48.2	79.7	58.2	49.7			1883	28	1861	27	1839	32				
1926	53.0	50.0	81.0	59.6	50.8	1905	27	1882	29			1838	32	1815	55		
						1904	27	1881	29	1860	27	1837	34	1814	63		
1925	52.5	48.4	81.8	61.0	51.6	1903	27	1880	29	1859	27	1836	33	1813	58		
1924	51.2	44.7	81.5	62.3	52.6	1902	26	1879	28	1858	26			1812	51		
1923	51.1	45.1	78.6	63.4	53.1	1901	25	1878	29	1857	28	1835	31	1811	50		
1922	50.2	43.7	76.7	59.0	53.0			1877	29	1856	27	1834	30	1810	47		
1921	53.6	46.7	74.5	69.5	65.2	1900	25	1876	32			1833	29	1809	47		
						1899	25			1855	28	1832	30	1808	48		
1920	60.0	61.5	64.9	82.7	84.6	1898	25	1875	33	1854	27	1831	32	1807	44		
1919	51.8	54.6	55.2	67.4	71.1	1897	25	1874	34	1853	25			1806	47		
1918	45.1	49.0	51.0	53.5	53.6	1896	25	1873	36	1852	25	1830	32				
1917	38.4	42.6	50.1	41.6	39.6			1872	36	1851	25	1829	32	1805	45		
1916	32.7	33.1	50.5	35.6	33.0	1895	25	1871	36			1828	33	1804	45		
						1894	26			1850	25	1827	34	1803	45		
1915	30.4	29.4	49.9	31.9	30.1	1893	27	1870	38	1849	25	1826	34	1802	43		
1914	30.1	29.8	49.6	30.5	29.4	1892	27			1848	26	1825	34	1801	50		
1913	29.7	29.2	49.6	29.8	29.2	1891	27	1869	40	1847	28	1824	33	1800	51		

Fig. 6.11. Sample table, *Historical Statistics of the United States, Colonial Times to 1970.* Reprinted from *Historical Statistics of the United States, Colonial Times to 1970.*

Each issue of the *Handbook* features charts for selected economic indicators and a summary of monthly business and economic highlights. In addition, it includes introductory sections describing basic concepts and terms for each chapter. Footnotes identify the agencies from which data are drawn. The annual *Handbook* is updated by monthly supplements and, according to its publisher, presents current statistics for at least half of the series before they appear in official government publications.

The *Statistical Service,* a compilation of government and industry statistics published in looseleaf format by Standard & Poor's, is another major statistical compendium. The service is divided into three main parts, each of which merits further attention.

The *Security Price Index Record* section presents current and historical data on stock price indexes and averages as well as such other measures of securities market performance as stock and bond trading on the New York Stock Exchange, price-earnings ratios, yields, and stock price indexes for over 100 different industry groups. It is an excellent source of historic investment information and is often the only place in libraries where such data are easily available.

The *Business and Financial Basic Statistics* section consists of these parts, each concentrating on a specific industrial classification: "Banking and Finance," "Production Indexes and Labor Statistics," "Price Indexes," "Building and Building Materials," "Energy, Electric Power, and Fuels," "Metals," "Transportation," "Textile, Chemical, Paper," and "Agricultural Products." Each section is several pages long, and although data vary from one industry to the next, most feature statistics on employment, production, sales, income, inventories, and foreign trade. Tables in the "Building and Building Materials" section, for example, chart new construction activity and document residential housing permits, value of new construction, mortgage interest rates and debts outstanding, construction wages, and prices and shipment of specific building products.

Current Statistics supplements are published both annually and monthly; the monthly supplements are printed on yellow paper, and the annual, on white. Together, they bring data presented in the *Security Price Index Record* and the *Business and Financial Basic Statistics* sections up-to-date.

With the exception of the Standard & Poor's stock price indexes, which are discussed in the preliminary pages of the *Security Price Index Record*, the *Statistical Service* does not include descriptions of methodology or definitions of terms and concepts employed. To a certain extent, then, it presupposes a greater level of expertise than is assumed in the other statistical compendia discussed.

Although important, the above sources are by no means the only collections of statistical data. Other more specialized sources are equally important. Although space precludes listing them all, some important representative examples of more specialized statistical compilations are described below. Other sources are included in the subject-oriented chapters that follow.

> U.S. Bureau of the Census. **County and City Data Book, 1983**. Washington, D.C.: Government Printing Office, 1983 (*Statistical Abstract* supplement). 966p.
>
> _____. **State and Metropolitan Area Data Book, 1986**. Washington, D.C.: Government Printing Office, 1986 (*Statistical Abstract* supplement). 697p.
>
> U.S. Bureau of Labor Statistics. **Handbook of Labor Statistics**. Washington, D.C.: Government Printing Office, 1924/26- . Biennial (*BLS Bulletin*).
>
> U.S. President. **Economic Report of the President**. Washington, D.C.: Government Printing Office, 1947- . Annual.
>
> **Predicasts Forecasts**. Cleveland, Ohio: Predicasts, 1960- . Quarterly, with annual cumulative edition.

Data on state, city, and metropolitan areas are available in two Census Bureau publications issued periodically as supplements to the *Statistical Abstract*. They are the *County and City Data Book* and the *State and Metropolitan Area Data Book*.

The *County and City Data Book* is a compilation of statistics taken from the Economic Censuses and the Censuses of Population and Housing, Governments, and Agriculture, as well as from other government and private agencies. Data are arranged by subject in four main tables according to the geographic designations shown below.

Table	Geographic Coverage
A	Includes United States as a whole; geographic regions and divisions; and each state
B	Includes county-level data
C	Includes data for cities (incorporated places) with 25,000 or more inhabitants in 1980
D	Includes data for every place with 2,500 or more inhabitants in 1980

Although the *County and City Data Book* is almost 1,000 pages long, it includes only the above four tables. Each represents a different geographic area but covers a wide range of subjects. For new users, the incorporation of data on several different subjects into a single table can be confusing, and librarians should be prepared to help them use the *Data Book* to best advantage. Statistics are presented for population, health, housing, the labor force, income, the economy, and several other subjects. Preliminary pages describe concepts and data limitations, and offer notes on many of the items included in each table. The *County and City Data Book* is also available from the Census Bureau on computer tape and floppy disks.

A companion volume, the *State and Metropolitan Area Data Book*, presents similar information for metropolitan areas, central cities, and states and, like the *County and City Data Book*, includes detailed source notes and explanations.

Someone seeking statistics for a specific state, county, or city would also be well advised to consult the statistical handbook or abstracts issued by the appropriate states. Although many contain data derived almost exclusively from the statistical compendia described above, others offer statistics that are not available elsewhere.

As has already been shown, one way in which statistical compendia can reflect specialization is by limiting the data to specific geographic areas. Another type of specialization is by subject. Many government agencies and departments, for example, publish statistical handbooks and yearbooks reflecting their special interests and responsibilities. The Department of Agriculture produces the annual *Agricultural Statistics*, the Bureau of Mines, the *Minerals Yearbook*, and the Federal Bureau of Investigation, *Crime in the United States*. One of the most useful of such publications for business research is the *Handbook of Labor Statistics*, published by the Bureau of Labor Statistics.

The *Handbook*, which contains data from many BLS and Census Bureau publications, includes information on employment and unemployment, hours and earnings, occupational employment statistics, worker productivity, compensation, prices and living conditions, work stoppages, occupational injuries and illnesses, and foreign labor statistics. It also includes special labor force data on such subjects as work experience, school enrollment and educational attainment, and marital and family characteristics of the labor force. Technical notes are included for each of the subjects covered, and footnotes are appended to many tables. Those needing more recent information should refer to such BLS periodicals as the *Monthly Labor Review* and the *CPI Detailed Report*. If they are not available, any of the general statistical compilations described earlier can be consulted, as can the *Economic Report of the President*.

In addition to the president's annual message to Congress on the state of the economy and an accompanying report by the Council of Economic Advisers, the *Economic Report of the President* includes detailed tables of supplementary statistics on national income, production and business activity, prices, money stock, government finance, corporate profits and finance, agriculture, and international economic activity. Originating sources are cited and many of the figures date back 40 years or more.

The titles that have been described above cover fairly broad subject areas. Other compendia, particularly those issued by trade associations and commercial publishers, focus on narrower subject fields. Many are discussed at length in later chapters on marketing, accounting, banking, and investments.

Still other statistical compilations can be categorized by the time periods covered. Some present historical information. *Historical Statistics*, for example, includes statistics from colonial times to 1970, and *Business Statistics*, the supplement to *Survey of Current Business*, offers some 25 years of detailed business, economic, industry, and financial statistics. Some publications look to the future. The *U.S. Industrial Outlook* contains short-term forecasts for specific industries, and the Census Bureau regularly publishes population forecasts and projections. Another publication, *Predicasts Forecasts*, is useful both as a source of forecasts and projections and as a finding aid to other sources.

Published quarterly and cumulated annually, *Predicasts Forecasts* offers summary statistical data derived from government, commercial, and trade publications, with entries generally including short- and long-term projections (respectively designated by the letters S and L), estimated rates of annual growth, and the sources from which the projections were derived (see figure 6.12).

PREDICASTS

SIC	PRODUCT A	EVENT	PRODUCT B	YEARS B	YEARS S	YEARS L	QUANTITIES B	QUANTITIES S	QUANTITIES L	UNIT OF MEASURE	SOURCE JOURNAL	SOURCE DATE	PAGE	Annual Growth
Truck & Bus Tires														
30112 005	Truck & bus tires	shipments		85	–	90	7.	–	7.	mil units	Natl Rubber	11/ /85	3*	0.0%
30112 005	Truck tires	consump of	synthetic rubbers	–	86	06z	–	100	60.	index	R&P News	4/ 7/86	43*	-2.5%
30112 005	Truck tires	consump of	carbon black	85	87	90	19.6	18.6	18.2	% of prodB	R&P News 2	3/31/86	5*	-2.5%
30112 005	Truck tires	shipments		85	86	06z	31.9±	31.5	–	mil units	R&P News	1/20/86	2	-1.3%
30112 008	Light truck tires	shipments		85	86	06z	x.	x	+12	mil units	R&P News	4/ 7/86	43*	-1.3%
30112 015	Radial heavy truck tires	shipments	as % of all heavy truck tires	77	85	95	20.	50.	70.	% of total	R&P News 2	9/16/85	3*	3.4%*
30112 015	Radial truck tires	shipments	as % of all truck tires	–	86	06z	–	40	100.	% of total	R&P News 2	4/ 7/86	43*	4.7%
30112 035	Bias ply med-heavy truck tires	shipments		85	to	90	–	25	–	mil units	Tire Dealr	6/ /85	24*	– %
Truck & Bus Tires, OE														
30112 105	OE truck & bus tires	shipments		85	86	–	7.6	6.7	–	mil units	Elast	12/ /85	28*	-11.8%
30112 105	OE truck & bus tires	shipments		85	–	90	7.	–	7.	mil units	R&P News	11/18/85	1*	0.0%
30112 105	OE truck & bus tires	shipments		84	85	90	7.6	7.3	7.5	mil units	Rub Trends	9/ /85	39	0.5%*
30112 105	OE truck & bus tires	shipments		85	to	90	100.	93.	–	index	Tire Dealr	1/ /86	20*	-7.0%
30112 105	OE truck & bus tires	shipments		85	to	90	–	-6%	–	growth/yr	R&P News	1/13/86	14*	-0.6%
30112 108	OE low profile truck tires	shipments	% of all OE truck tires	85	86	85	30.	–	35. ?	% of total	Tire Dealr	6/ /85	19*b	– %
30112 112	Light truck tires	shipments		85	86	–	100.	100.	–	index	R&P News 2	1/20/86	2	0.0%
30112 112	Light truck tires,OE	shipments		–	86	–	–	3450	–	000 units	R&P News 2	1/20/86	2	– %
30112 122	Light truck radial tires	shipments		85	86	–	100.	100	–	000 units	R&P News 2	1/20/86	2	0.0%
30112 125	Light truck radial tires,OE	shipments	as % of all OE Lt truck tires	–	86	–	–	2587	–	000 units	R&P News 2	1/20/86	2	– %
30112 125	Light truck radial tires,OE	shipments		85	86	–	68	82	–	% of total	R&P News 2	1/20/86	2	20.6%
30112 132	Medium truck tires	shipments		85	86	–	10.3±	10.9	–	mil units	R&P News 2	1/20/86	2	5.8%
30112 132	Medium truck tires,OE	shipments		–	86	–	–	3.2	–	mil units	R&P News 2	1/20/86	2	– %
30112 145	Medium truck radial tires,OE	shipments		–	86	–	–	2.	–	mil units	R&P News 2	1/20/86	2	– %
Truck & Bus Tires, Replace														
30112 205	Replace truck & bus tires	shipments	(incl retreads)	84	85	90	49.4	50.	52.	mil units	Rub Trends	9/ /85	39	0.8%*
30112 205	Replace truck & bus tires	shipments		85	to	90	–	+1 %	–	growth/yr	R&P News	1/13/86	14*	1.0%
30112 205	Replace truck tires	shipments		85	86	–	33.	34.	–	mil units	Tire Dealr	6/ /85	77	3.0%
30112 208	Low profile replace truck tires	shipments	as % of replace hvy truck tires	85	–	85	12.	–	15. ?	% of total	Tire Dealr	6/ /85	19*b	– %
30112 208	Low profile replace truck tires	shipments	as % of replace hvy truck tires	–		90	–	–	40.	% of total	Tire Dealr	6/ /85	19*a	– %
30112 208	Replace med & heavy truck tires	shipments		83	84	85	11.5	11.	10.9	mil units	Tire Dealr	6/ /85	18	-2.6%
30112 212	Light truck tires,replace	shipments		83	84	85	18.	18.5	19.2	mil units	Tire Dealr	6/ /85	17	3.3%
30112 212	Light truck tires,replace	shipments		–	86	–	–	19.	–	mil units	R&P News 2	1/20/86	2	– %
30112 225	Light truck radial tires,replace	shipments		85	86	–	7.5	8.5	–	mil units	R&P News 2	1/20/86	2	13.3%
30112 225	Light truck radial tires,replace	shipments	as % of all lt truck replace tires	–	86	–	–	44	–	% of total	R&P News 2	1/20/86	2	– %
30112 225	Light truck radial tires,replace	shipments	as % of all lt truck replace tires	–	86	–	–	44.	–	% of total	R&P News 2	1/20/86	2	– %
30112 225	Light truck radial tires,replace	shipments	as % of all truck replace tires	–	86	–	–	44.	–	% of total	R&P News 2	1/20/86	2	– %
30112 232	Medium truck tires,replace	shipments		–	86	–	–	11.2	–	mil units	R&P News 2	1/20/86	2	– %
30112 235	Medium truck radial tires,replace	shipments		–	86	–	–	6.3	–	mil units	R&P News 2	1/20/86	2	5.0%
30112 235	Medium truck radial tires,replace	shipments		85	86	–	100.	105	–	index	R&P News 2	1/20/86	2	– %
Tires NEC														
30113 002	Tires ex car & truck incl retreads	consump of	carbon black	85	87	90	15.4	15.6	15.2	% of prodB	R&P News 2	3/31/86	5*	-0.3%
30113 125	Off-road tires	shipments		85	86	–	110.	105.	–	mil units	Elast	12/ /85	28*	-4.5%
30113 125	Tractor & implement tires	shipments		85	86	–	1.9	1.9	–	mil units	Elast	12/ /85	28*	0.0%
30113 138	OE tractor & implement tires	shipments		84	85	90	1.	1.1	1.4	mil units	Rub Trends	9/ /85	39	4.9%*
30113 138	OE tractor & implement tires	shipments		85	to	90	–	+8.4%	–	growth/yr	R&P News	11/18/85	1*	8.4%
30113 138	Replace tractor & implement tires	shipments		84	85	90	2.6	2.7	2.9	mil units	Rub Trends	9/ /85	39	1.4%*
30113 139	Farm rear tires	shipments		85	86	–	750.	750.	–	000 units	Elast	12/ /85	28*	0.0%
30113 139	Radial farm rear tires	shipments		85	86	90	70.	70.	–	000 units	Elast	12/ /85	29*	28.6%
30113 148	OE mobile home tires	shipments		84	85	90	1432	1500.	1650.	000 units	Rub Trends	9/ /85	39	1.9%*
30113 148	OE mobile home tires	shipments		85	to	90	–	+3.1%	–	growth/yr	R&P News	11/18/85	1*	3.1%
30113 148	Replace mobile home tires	shipments		84	85	90	40.	40.	50.	000 units	Rub Trends	9/ /85	39	4.6%*
30113 158	OE industrial & utility tires	shipments		84	85	90	8.6	8.2	8.8	mil units	Rub Trends	9/ /85	39	1.4%*
30113 158	Replace industrial & utility tires	shipments		84	85	90	4.6	4.3	4.7	mil units	Rub Trends	9/ /85	39	1.8%*
Tread Rubber & Tire Sundries														
30115 008	Die size rubber	used in	tire retreading & repair	84	85	86	81.	70.4	69.	mil lbs	Tire Dealr	5/ /86	42*	-2.0%*
30115 008	Master batch rubber	used in	tire retreading & repair	84	85	86	76.4	72.	71.	mil lbs	Tire Dealr	5/ /86	42*	-1.4%*

Fig. 6.12. Sample entries, *Predicasts Forecasts*. Reprinted by permission of Predicasts.

Arrangement is by Predicasts product code, a variant of the Standard Industrial Classification system, and each issue of *Predicasts Forecasts* includes an alphabetical list of products and events (business and economic activities) and the numbers assigned to them. In addition, articles that are considered by the publishers to be key market articles are identified by the use of the # symbol in the citations. Although government sources are cited, many of the forecasts are derived from trade publications.

Using the second entry shown in figure 6.12, one can determine that consumption of synthetic rubbers for the production of truck tires (product code 30112 005) is expected to decline by about 40 percent from 1986 to 2006, with a predicted annual decline of some 2.5 percent. The data were taken from page 43 of the April 6, 1986 issue of *Rubber & Plastics News*, a biweekly trade magazine published by Crain Communications.

The focus in *Predicasts Forecasts* is primarily on products and business activities, but some of the initial pages in each issue present general economic and demographic forecasts as well. A companion publication, *Worldcasts*, presents similar data for countries other than the United States.

Although they are expensive, both *Predicasts Forecasts* and *Worldcasts* can be extremely useful to librarians and researchers in search of projections and forecasts for specific products and their components. In libraries where such information is infrequently required, searching the online versions may be a less expensive and equally satisfactory alternative to subscribing to the printed versions.

Periodicals

Periodicals, particularly those published by the federal government, contain tables of recurring statistical data. Some of the most important of these periodicals and the types of data they contain are listed in appendix H.

NUMERIC DATABASES AND DATA FILES

Many of the publications listed and described in this chapter are available in electronic, as well as print, format (see chapter 8 for description of numeric databases and data files). Demographic statistics, for example, are available in *CENDATA*, a Census Bureau product, and in *Donnelley Demographics*, a commercially produced file. The Bureau of Labor Statistics has produced time series databases for producer and consumer prices and employment and earnings, and *Predicasts Forecasts* and *Worldcasts*, as mentioned earlier, can also be searched online.

A growing number of data sets are also being produced on floppy disks for use with microcomputers, and a few are now available on compact optical disk.

NOTES

[1]U.S. Office of Management and Budget, *Federal Statistics; a Special Report on the Statistical Programs and Activities of the United States Government, Fiscal Year 1986* (Washington, D.C.: Government Printing Office, 1986), 1.

[2]To be placed on the mailing list for a free subscription to the Census Bureau's *Monthly Product Announcement*, write to:

> Data User Services Division
> Customer Services (Publications)
> Bureau of the Census
> Washington, D.C. 20233

[3]Through the State Data Center program, the Census Bureau has appointed some 1,300 organizations — usually local agencies or academic centers — to receive Census Bureau products for their states to be made available for public use. Although centers vary from one state to another, most have specially trained staff to assist users in accessing information from the Census Bureau, and many provide special data services not available from the bureau itself. State Data Center agencies are listed in the *Census Catalog and Guide*, and are frequently profiled in *Data User News*.

[4]U.S. Bureau of the Census, *Selected Characteristics of Persons in Engineering: 1978* (Washington, D.C.: Government Printing Office, 1984), 1.

[5]Darrell Huff, *How to Lie with Statistics* (New York: Norton, 1954), 140.

[6]In order to decide what items to include in the Consumer Price Index, the Bureau of Labor Statistics periodically conducts an extensive survey of consumer spending habits.

[7]Until 1978, when the Consumer Price Index for All Urban Consumers, or CPI-U, was introduced, the Consumer Price Index was limited to prices paid by urban wage earners. The pre-1978 Consumer Price Index, in other words, is roughly analogous to the Consumer Price Index for Urban Wage Earners and Clerical Workers, or CPI-W.

[8]American Chamber of Commerce Researchers Association, *Inter-City Cost of Living Index* (First Quarter 1986): i.

[9]The telephone number for the Congressional Research Service's CRS Stats Line (still working as of December 1987) is 202-287-7034.

[10]Joe Morehead, "The Uses and Misuses of Information Found in Government Publications," in *Collection Development and Public Access of Government Documents* (Westport, Conn.: Meckler, 1981), 62.

[11]Huff, 123.

[12]Joan Harvey, "Statistical Publications for Business and Management," in *Information Sources in Management and Business*, 2nd ed. (London: Butterworths, 1984), 136.

[13]The *American Statistics Index*'s Index by Categories uses the following categories for indexing comparative statistical data:

Geographic	**Economic**	**Demographic**
Census Division	Commodity	Age
City	Federal Agency	Disease
Foreign Country	Income	Educational Attainment
Outlying Area (U.S. Territories)	Individual Company or Institution	Marital Status
Region	Industry	Race and Ethnic Group
SMSA or MSA	Occupation	Sex
State		
Urban-Rural		
Metro-Nonmetro		

Entries within each of the categories listed above are arranged by subject under any of 19 different subheadings. Although most pertain at least indirectly to business, the most directly relevant subheadings are "Banking, Finance, and Insurance," "Industry and Commerce," "Labor and Employment," and "Prices and Cost of Living."

[14]Congressional Information Service, publisher of the *American Statistics Index, Statistical Reference Index,* and *Index of International Statistics*, makes free "Search Guides" available to libraries. The guides describe the scope and applications of each of the indexes, and can be gotten from an area sales representative or:

> Congressional Information Service, Inc.
> 4520 East-West Highway, Suite 800
> Bethesda, MD 20814

[15]*1985 Statistical Reference Index*, viii.

A librarian ordinarily collects pamphlets as unhesitatingly as a little dog runs out and barks at a buggy. The dog could not give any reason for it; but all of his ancestors have done it; all the curs of his acquaintance do it; and he has done it himself from his earliest recollections.

— Charles A. Cutter

7

VERTICAL FILE COLLECTIONS

Cutter's comments to the contrary, most librarians are well aware of why they collect pamphlets. They are spurred by reason rather than reflex, seeking to build and maintain vertical file collections of current, inexpensive, and often unique sources of information. This chapter weighs the advantages and disadvantages of vertical file collections for business reference, describes basic types of materials generally included in such collections, and lists bibliographic sources that are particularly helpful for identifying these materials.

First, a definition. Traditionally, the *vertical file* denotes "a collection made up primarily of pamphlets and clippings which are housed vertically in filing cases or similar containers."[1] Although pamphlets and clippings may predominate, they are by no means exclusive. Other types of materials may include corporate annual reports, advertisements, charts, posters, maps, even postcards. All are gathered together, usually arranged by subject, with a minimum of processing.

ADVANTAGES OF VERTICAL FILE COLLECTIONS

Pamphlets and other vertical file items are compact. This is important not only in terms of space savings, but also in terms of user acceptance. Someone who would balk at a thick and imposing book might be eager to get—and use—the same information presented in capsule form. A novice investor, for example, might be far less intimidated by reading about the stock market in a glossy pamphlet than he would by a scholarly treatise on investing. Full service brokerage houses know this and, as a consequence, make many such pamphlets available to investors.

Pamphlets focus on a small segment of knowledge. *The Dow Jones Averages*, a four-page pamphlet published by Dow Jones, is a case in point.[2] Instead of dealing with stock trading generally, it focuses on just one measure of stock market activity—stock averages. Further, it deals with only one set of averages, the Dow Jones averages. Although a sophisticated researcher or an experienced investor might find coverage in this pamphlet superficial and simplistic, for others it would be exactly right. Students writing term papers, for example, or inquisitive librarians or novice investors might find it extremely useful and informative.

Vertical files often house material that contains information that is difficult to find elsewhere. Dipping into such collections one might find corporate histories, buyers' directories, statistics on coffee drinking and gasohol consumption, guides for doing business abroad, and surveys of consumer attitudes toward cameras and skin care products. In some instances, the information may be too esoteric to receive frequent use. When such pamphlets are needed, however, they can be a godsend. Laventhol & Horwath's annual *U.S. Lodging Industry*, for example, presents detailed statistics on the nationality of hotel guests, average room rates, use of credit cards for payment, beverage and food sales, and operating expenses.[3]

> A pamphlet that tells how to estimate the board foot volume of trees in a woodlot may not be called for every day. But when a patron does ask for this information, his need is real and immediate. He will go away marveling at the crackerjack librarian who was able to produce the necessary facts at a moment's notice.[4]

Pamphlets are useful because they are compact, concise, easy to understand, and contain unique information. Another advantage is that they provide current information that can supplement and update encyclopedias, dictionaries, and other reference works. A pamphlet on a new investment medium, for example, will appear in print long before a book on the same subject is published.

Pamphlets and other vertical file materials are usually inexpensive. Many, in fact, are free, costing only the postage required to order them and the staff time required to select, process, and maintain them. Lack of financial constraint makes it possible to order titles with only limited appeal and, conversely, to order multiple copies of items likely to be in great demand. Finally, just as low cost enables librarians to be less cautious in selecting material, it also reduces inhibitions about weeding items that are dated, inaccurate, or otherwise inappropriate. A sense of freedom pervades both the selection and weeding of vertical file materials.

These are some of the advantages offered by vertical file collections. Such benefits are particularly important in business reference, where the need for current information is great, and where requests for unusual and hard-to-find information are commonplace. Some of the major types of suppliers of vertical file materials in business are discussed in the section that follows.

MAJOR SUPPLIERS OF VERTICAL FILE MATERIALS

Vertical file materials relating to business are abundant. Some of the major suppliers of these items are trade associations, corporations, banks and accounting firms, securities exchanges and brokerage houses, commercial publishers, and federal, state, and foreign government agencies. Each merits further attention.

Trade Associations

A trade association performs many different functions. It keeps its members informed of economic, political, and technological developments that may affect the industry it represents, compiles industry statistics, and seeks to promote the interests of its members and to enhance its image with the general public. It achieves many of these goals through a publications program, making directories, newsletters and bulletins, handbooks, and statistical annuals available to its members and to others. In addition, many trade associations publish a series of informational pamphlets, posters, and brochures intended for the general public.

For the librarian seeking to build a collection of information sources relating to a specific industry, these publications can be extremely useful. A vertical file collection on the dairy industry, for example, would be enhanced by the publications of the National Dairy Council, as well as by the Milk Industry Foundation's *Milk Facts* and *The Latest Scoop*, a statistical annual published by the International Association of Ice Cream Manufacturers. Other industries are equally well represented by trade association publications. The Motor Vehicle Manufacturers Association publishes *MVMA Motor Vehicle Facts and Figures*, the Brazilian Coffee Institute issues *The Coffee Market in the United States and Canada*, the Aerospace Industries Association, *Aerospace Facts and Figures*, and so on. Publications range from comprehensive statistical sources to simple brochures intended for elementary school students.

Trade associations with extensive publishing programs frequently issue free catalogs. The Insurance Information Institute lists a whole series of publications in its catalog, *Educational Materials*, while the Food Marketing Institute, the American Trucking Associations, and the National Dairy Council, all prolific publishers, also issue catalogs.

The "Trade, Business and Commercial Organizations" section of the *Encyclopedia of Associations* is useful for identifying major trade associations and some of the titles they publish. Trade association publications are also listed in many of the general bibliographic sources discussed later in this chapter.

Corporate Publications

Many corporations have active publishing programs. In addition to the annual reports to shareholders which are mandatory for all publicly traded companies, they issue newsletters for distributors and suppliers, and public relations magazines and pamphlets intended to familiarize consumers with the company's major products and brand names, and to promote the company itself. Such publications are appropriate for vertical file collections.

Corporate annual reports, for example, are useful not only to prospective investors, but also to job hunters, suppliers, sales representatives, marketing researchers, and graphic designers. Such reports are available for the asking, and usually a single request to a company will ensure that a library will be placed on its mailing list to receive all future reports. Selection of corporate annual reports varies from one library to another, but will usually include companies headquartered in the area or those representing regionally important industries, and may extend to include all Fortune 500 companies as well.

Some corporate publications are aimed at prospective customers. Before it merged with Nabisco to become RJR Nabisco, R. J. Reynolds Industries published *RJR Archer Packaging*, a pamphlet that traced the subsidiary's history from its beginnings as a small tinfoil department in a tobacco company, described its current packaging technology, and solicited business. "Archer seeks out challenging assignments which have presented problems to other packaging suppliers," the pamphlet declared, and went on to present what it described as "a glimpse of the talents behind Archer's confidence in its ability to serve any customer's interests."[5]

The Dow Corning Corporation publishes a bimonthly, *Materials News*, in which new products such as acoustical mufflers and silicone brake fluid are described. Each issue contains product information cards enabling prospective clients to send for further details. In addition, Dow publishes *A Guide to Dow Corning Products*, which lists and describes company products and trademarks. Although both publications are intended to promote business, Dow Corning, like most other companies, will send them to librarians and educators as well.

Almost every large corporation selling consumer-oriented products features a publications or public relations department. The diversity of materials they publish is truly astounding, and includes posters, books, pamphlets, and charts. Growing in popularity are corporate-sponsored magazines, "slick and polished periodicals [that] are subtly designed to convey the message that their corporate sponsors are concerned and helpful companies."[6]

Pamphlets and brochures are even more common than consumer magazines. The Hershey Foods Corporation makes its corporate policy publicly available, and issues a one-page statement describing its current stance on advertising. In addition, for calorie counters it offers pamphlets containing nutritional information about Hershey products, and, for those who are not, collections of recipes. Hershey is not unique. Land O'Lakes, Inc., publishes pamphlets on dairy farming and food processing, the Hoover Company makes available booklets on the history and care of carpets and rugs, and Georgia-Pacific publishes brochures on forest products, pulp and paper, and conservation. Eli Lilly and Company, a pharmaceutical firm, annually surveys pharmacies and pharmacists, and publishes the results in two separate reports. The *Lilly Digest* is a survey of independent community pharmacists, with detailed operating and financial statistics, and the *Lilly Hospital Pharmacy Survey*, its counterpart for the hospital sector.[7] The Bowling Division of the Brunswick Corporation offers a series of pamphlets for small business people, including such titles as *Your Bowling Business; What It Is (and Can Be) Worth, Are You Running Your Business... Or, Is It Running You?*, and *The Name of the Game Is ... How to Make Money*.[8] The array of corporate pamphlets reflects the diversity of American economy; almost every facet of industry is reflected in such publications.

Some companies go beyond promotion and information to produce educational packages for elementary and secondary school and even college students. The Firestone Tire & Rubber Company, for example, publishes *Stretching Your Mind*, an elementary science investigation program about rubber, while Procter & Gamble Educational Services publishes a whole series of classroom materials, including multimedia teaching kits for secondary students focusing on consumer advertising, home economics, and personal hygiene. NCR's *Self-Instructional Catalog and Educational Publications* lists publications for use in high schools, colleges, technical schools, and industrial training programs.

The challenge for librarians, then, is not merely to identify corporate materials, but rather to select the ones that are best suited for their special needs. As with trade associations, many corporate publications are listed in such standard bibliographical sources as the *Vertical File Index* and *Public Affairs Information Service Bulletin*, described later in this chapter. Another source is also useful.

Norback, Craig. **Corporate Publications in Print**. New York: McGraw-Hill, 1980. 271p.

Corporate Publications in Print lists employee, corporate, and product information publications available from major American companies. Entries include company addresses and telephone numbers, the names of contact people, and instructions for ordering. Although *Corporate Publications in Print* is dated and is itself no longer in print, librarians with access to it will find it extremely helpful in identifying companies with active publishing programs.

Banks and Accounting Firms

The publications of banks and accounting firms constitute a rich source of vertical file material. The research departments of large banks, Federal Reserve Banks, and the Board of Governors of the Federal Reserve System are all prolific publishers. Bank-issued publications (see chapter 11) represent a wide array of types of materials, ranging from staff reports and economic forecasts to personal financial guides, from comic books to scholarly studies. Bank publications are often listed in standard bibliographies of vertical file materials, but one special catalog should also be mentioned.

Public Information Materials of the Federal Reserve System. 8th ed. New York: Federal Reserve Bank of New York, 1986. 47p.

Public Information Materials of the Federal Reserve System is a comprehensive guide to books, pamphlets, and audiovisual materials for educators, bankers, economists, and the public. Arrangement is by intended audience (general and specialized), and then by subject. Each entry includes a brief annotation, price information, and the name of the Federal Reserve Bank from which the title should be ordered. A sample entry is shown in figure 7.1.

Occasional Publications

Fed	Title	Description/Audience	Charge
Federal Reserve System: Structure and Function			
Phil	**A Banker's Day**	Guides the reader through an imaginary banker's typical day, including lending decisions dealing with customers and bank personnel. 1984/8 pp. *General public.*	*None*

Fig. 7.1. Sample entry, *Public Information Materials of the Federal Reserve System*. Reprinted from the 7th edition of the Federal Reserve Bank of New York's *Public Information Materials of the Federal Reserve System*.

Most major accounting firms also issue booklets and brochures. These include guides to doing business in foreign countries, reviews of tax reform legislation, financial and accounting information for specific industries, and pamphlets promoting careers in accounting. One of the best ways to begin building a collection of such accounting information is by requesting copies of publication lists from the national headquarters or local offices of the so-called Big Eight accounting firms. Coopers & Lybrand, for example, publishes an annual *Compendium of Published Material*, Touche Ross issues *In Print and In View*, and Deloitte Haskins & Sells, *Publications for Outside Distribution*. (The Big Eight accounting firms are listed in chapter 10.)

Securities Exchanges and Brokerage Houses

Many of the descriptive and promotional brochures published by stock and commodities exchanges and by securities brokers are described in chapters 12 through 16. Their value to library users and to librarians cannot be overemphasized. Merrill Lynch, Pierce, Fenner, & Smith's *How to Read a Financial Report* is a classic, as are such New York Stock Exchange publications as *The Language of Investing* and *Ten Questions to Ask before You Buy Stocks*. Most of these publications are available from local brokers and investment advisors.

Commercial Publishers

Commercial publishers often issue pamphlets that promote the books, periodicals, and newspapers they produce. Generally, these pamphlets fall into two categories, those issued by prominent business publishers and those distributed by the producers of consumer magazines.

Such major business publishers as Moody's and Standard & Poor's distribute free booklets that describe basic business concepts, define key terms, and proffer advice. Dun & Bradstreet publishes a pamphlet, *Business Failure Record*, that is an annual compilation of statistics on businesses that have failed. It also publishes a series called "Cost of Doing Business," which present key business ratios for corporations, partnerships, and proprietorships, as well as the booklet, *The Pitfalls in Managing a Small Business*.[9] Dow Jones, publisher of *Barron's* and the *Wall Street Journal*, has established Educational Service Bureaus that offer a wide range of pamphlets, from *The ABC's of Option Trading* to *How to Read Stock Market Quotations*.[10]

Publishers of consumer magazines such as *Time, Redbook,* and *Playboy* sponsor and publish market research studies about their readers' attitudes toward and preferences for specific products such as microcomputers and wine. Although intended primarily to attract prospective advertisers, they are also valuable information sources for students, librarians, and business people. These studies are occasionally listed in standard bibliographic sources, but are more often found in a publication of the Special Libraries Association's Advertising and Marketing Division.

> **What's New in Advertising and Marketing**. New York: Special Libraries Association, Advertising and Marketing Division, 1945- . 10 issues/year.

What's New in Advertising and Marketing lists and briefly annotates books, documents, pamphlets, and other materials. Publishers' addresses and prices are generally included, and free publications are so designated. *What's New* is particularly useful for identifying specialized materials that may not be listed elsewhere.

In addition, periodicals frequently offer free and inexpensive material to their readers. Many include product information cards that enable readers to send for additional information about advertised products and services.

Government Agencies

Federal, state, and foreign government agencies publish hundreds of pamphlets on business and the economy. In many libraries, particularly those that are documents depositories or that have large research collections, these publications are segregated into separate documents collections. Other libraries, however, choose to add them to their vertical files. There is no doubt that these inexpensive, abundant, and informative publications enrich such collections.

A sampling of federal documents from the vertical file includes such titles as the *Consumer Handbook on Adjustable Rate Mortgages, Checklist for Going into Business*, and the *ABC's of Publicity*. There are pamphlets for educators and economists, exporters and importers, consumers and small business people. Some are free, others are inexpensive, ranging from as little as 50 cents to a few dollars or more. Although the *Monthly Catalog of U.S. Government Publications* and *Government Reports Announcements & Index*, described in chapter 5, are the standard bibliographies of current government publications, other catalogs are particularly helpful for identifying the types of documents appropriate to vertical file collections. Other useful sources are *U.S. Government Books, New Books* (chapter 5), and the following.

> U.S. General Services Administration. **Consumer Information Catalog**. Washington, D.C.: Government Printing Office, 1971- . Quarterly.

Perhaps the most widely publicized listing of federal government publications is the *Consumer Information Catalog*, a collection of free and inexpensive pamphlets that can be ordered from the Consumer Information Center in Pueblo, Colorado. Arrangement in the *Consumer Information Catalog* is by subject, with each entry including an annotation, an ordering number, and a price. Most of the titles listed in the *Catalog* are good vertical file candidates.[11]

Some government organizations issue their own catalogs and publication lists. These lists can be requested from agencies such as the Publishing Division of the Department of Agriculture, the Food and Drug Administration, and the Department of Labor's Office of

Information and Public Affairs. The Federal Trade Commission, for example, publishes a whole series of free pamphlets, some of the most popular of which are listed in its leaflets, *FTC 'Best Sellers'* and *Best Sellers for Business*.[12]

A good way to identify these agencies is by consulting the *United States Government Manual*, which includes for each organization the name and telephone number of its main information office. Federal documents are also listed selectively in the *Public Affairs Information Service Bulletin*, described later in this chapter.

In recent years, state government agencies have published an increasing number of documents focusing on consumer affairs, business opportunities, and state economic conditions. For example, almost every state now has an office or department whose main function is to persuade business and industry to relocate in that state. These agencies publish handsome documents that praise their states and describe economic conditions favorable to new and relocated businesses. *There's Still a Place in America for Eagles: South Carolina* is typical of some of the undisguisedly promotional documents. "The eagles of industry are landing here," it states, and goes on to praise the state's labor force—"South Carolina workers come to *work* ... not to *stop* work," its liberal tax policies, ample energy supplies, and state-sponsored employee training programs.[13] Even such highly promotional publications, however, may contain nuggets of information that are useful. Further, most state agencies publish factual documents as well. Kentucky's Commerce Cabinet, for example, not only publishes *Kentucky & Co: The State That's Run like a Business*, but also issues such titles as *Guide to Kentucky Business Regulations and Services to Business, Financing Methods for Kentucky Business and Industry*, and *Kentucky Economic Statistics*. New York's Department of Commerce publishes *Tax Incentives and Financing Assistance for Industrial Location*, and Connecticut, *Connecticut Market Data, Connecticut's Top Financial Companies*, and *Connecticut's Top Industrials*.

Clearly, state agencies of economic and industrial development are valuable sources of publications about business and economic conditions. The librarian seeking to build a collection of pamphlets pertaining to particular states would do well to write them. In addition to corresponding with these agencies, librarians may wish to consult the documents checklists issued by individual states or the Library of Congress' *Monthly Checklist of State Publications*, described in chapter 5.

Just as state governments seek to attract new business and industry, so also do many foreign governments. One of the ways in which they attempt to do so is by publishing English-language magazines and newsletters describing different aspects of their economies. Some, such as *Italian Trade Topics*, are embassy publications, while others, such as *Colombia Today*, are published by foreign information offices. The Swedish Information Service is one of the most prolific of such publishers, issuing a whole series of leaflets on working life, social change, and the human environment in Sweden. Other useful foreign documents include fact books and statistical compilations. Some will be listed in *Public Affairs Information Service Bulletin*, but one of the best ways to begin collecting these titles is by contacting the information divisions of embassies and consular offices.

Other Sources

While the organizations listed above are some of the major suppliers of business-related booklets, pamphlets, and brochures, they are by no means the only ones. Other sources may include chambers of commerce, university research bureaus, commercial pamphlet publishers, voluntary organizations, and libraries. In addition, many articles appearing in throw-away magazines and newspapers can enjoy a second life in vertical file collections, as can postcards, advertisements, posters, and maps. Few library collections, in fact, so directly reflect the ingenuity, resourcefulness, and imagination of the librarians responsible for them.

BIBLIOGRAPHICAL SOURCES

Some of the specialized sources used to identify specific types of vertical file materials have been mentioned in the preceding section. There are, however, two standard bibliographical sources that are commonly used in selecting vertical file materials, the *Vertical File Index* and *Public Affairs Information Service Bulletin*. A third source, *Materials Available to Educators*, is equally useful although not nearly so well known.

Vertical File Index. New York: H.W. Wilson, 1935- . Monthly, except August.

Public Affairs Information Service Bulletin. New York: Public Affairs Information Service, Inc., 1915- . Monthly, with quarterly and annual cumulations.

Materials Available to Educators. Princeton, N.J.: Dow Jones & Co., Educational Services Bureau. Irregular.

Vertical File Index selectively lists pamphlets, books, catalogs, documents, charts, and posters. Arrangement is by subject, with title and subject indexes appended. Although coverage is perhaps most suitable for school libraries, many of the titles listed are also appropriate for public, academic, and special library business reference collections. Each entry, as shown in figure 7.2, includes full bibliographic information, price, and publisher's address. Some also include annotations.

> **Economic indicators**
> Indexes and indicators. (Ledger econ educ newsletter v 11 no 4) 4p 1985 Fed. Reserve Bank of Boston, Public Services Dept., 600 Atlantic Ave., Boston, MA 02106 free
> Facts and figures about the U.S. economy pour out of Washington every month, but newspapers, radio, and television usually focus on just a few. This article offers brief explanations of the economic statistics that seem to appear the most: the consumer price index; the unemployment rate; and the composite indexes of leading, coincident, and lagging economic indicators.

Fig. 7.2. Sample entry, *Vertical File Index*. *Vertical File Index* Copyright © 1986 by the H.W. Wilson Company. Material reproduced by permission of the publisher.

Public Affairs Information Service Bulletin, or *PAIS*, selectively lists current books, pamphlets, periodical articles, documents, and reports. *PAIS'* role as an index to periodicals was described in chapter 3; it is equally important as a selection tool for vertical file materials. Each item listed is included under as many as three or four subject or geographic headings, and both free and priced items are so designated. (Free items are preceded by asterisks; priced items, by daggers.) Figure 7.3 illustrates some of the types of entries common to *PAIS*.

The inclusion of many different types of publications in *PAIS* makes identifying vertical file materials more difficult than with the *Vertical File Index*, but the extra effort is generally offset by the relevance to business reference collections of many of the titles listed.

One of the best and perhaps least well known listings of vertical file materials is published in *Materials Available to Educators*, an annotated bibliography of free publications compiled by Dow Jones' Educational Services Bureau as a service to the academic community.[14] Titles are not limited to those published by Dow Jones; corporations, trade associations, and government agencies are among the other types of publishers represented in this booklet. Arrangement is by issuing organization, and then alphabetically by title. The listing for the American Paper Institute, shown in figure 7.4, is typical.

BUSINESS FAILURES
See also
Bank failures.
Bankruptcy.

Bruno, Albert V. and others. Why firms fail. il charts *Bus Horizons 30:50-8 Mr/Ap '87*
Experience of ten high technology firms founded in the 1960s in the San Francisco Bay area.

Keasey, Kevin and Robert Watson. The prediction of small company failure: some behavioural evidence for the UK. bibl tables *Accounting and Bus Research 17:49-57 Winter '86*
Whether trade credit specialists can utilize post 1981 Companies Act financial ratios to predict small company failure.

Statistics

* Business failure record, 1984 final, 1985 preliminary; a comparative statistical analysis of geographic and industry trends in business failures in the United States. Mohorovic, Tiziana, ed. ['86] 20p tables chart Free
—*Dun's Marketing Services*

BUSINESS FORECASTING
See also
Economic forecasting.

† Saunders, John A. and others. Practical business forecasting. '87 xii+340p bibls tables charts index (LC 86-19564) (ISBN 0-566-02516-7) $59.95—*Gower*

Fig. 7.3. Sample entry, *Public Affairs Information Service Bulletin*. Reprinted by permission of *PAIS*.

American Paper Institute, Inc.
260 Madison Avenue, New York, NY 10016

The Paper Industry in the U.S.
A one-page fact sheet about the paper industry, including data on manufacturing and converting plants, employees, wages and salaries, sales, taxes, capital expenditures, and pulp, paper and paperbound production, etc. *Single copies free.*

Sources of Information about the Paper and Allied Products Industry
This bibliography, with more than 100 entries, is a valuable guide to information sources about the paper and allied products industry. It provides a listing of the materials published by the American Paper Institute. Also included are trade journals, directories, books about paper and the paper industry, data available from government and international agencies, as well as names and addresses of other national associations serving the paper industry. *Single copies free.*

Fig. 7.4. Sample listing, *Materials Available to Educators*. Reprinted with permission of the Educational Service Bureau, Dow Jones & Company, Inc., 1986. All rights reserved.

In addition to the bibliographic sources mentioned above, library and other professional journals often include columns that list pamphlets and other vertical file materials. Below are some of the most commonly consulted titles.

"The Source: Selected Readings for Current Awareness," **American Libraries**. Chicago: American Library Association. Monthly.
Although not limited to pamphlets, this column occasionally lists free and inexpensive pamphlets, bibliographies, and reports.

Special Libraries Association. Business and Finance Division. **Business & Finance Division Bulletin**. Kent, Ohio: Kent State University Library, Reference Department, 1958- . Triannual.

Pamphlets are often included in the columns, "Recent U.S. Government Publications of Interest to Business and Finance Librarians," "Association Publications," and "Et Cetera...."

"Government Information," **RQ**. Chicago: Reference and Adult Services Division, American Library Association. Quarterly.

This column treats special subjects, such as government services to the elderly or publishes lists of notable documents. Titles are annotated, with price, Superintendent of Documents classification, and stock number.

Special Libraries Association. Insurance and Employee Benefits Division. **Insurance and Employee Benefits Literature**. New York: Insurance and Employee Benefits Division, Special Libraries Association. Bimonthly.

Lists by subject titles relevant to insurance libraries. Many are free, and will be useful in more general library settings as well.

Many trade and consumer magazines also regularly feature lists of free and inexpensive pamphlet literature. Finally, several free publications are listed and described throughout this book and are cumulated in appendix I.

DISADVANTAGES OF VERTICAL FILE COLLECTIONS

Vertical file collections offer many benefits. This discussion would be both incomplete and misleading, however, if it did not also consider some of the costs and drawbacks of creating and maintaining such collections.

Because pamphlets are ephemeral and not widely advertised, considerable effort must go into identifying them while they are still current and in print. Building a solid collection requires substantial blocks of time, and may involve both professional and clerical staff. Further, the collection must be weeded regularly, another labor-intensive process. Files crammed with dated, inappropriate, and irrelevant materials are virtually useless.

In many libraries, only the librarian and other staff responsible for the vertical file make really good use of the material it contains. Others may use it only sporadically, often ignoring it when it might do the most good. Unless the librarian in charge is prepared to promote and publicize the vertical file by calling frequent attention to collection strengths and outstanding new titles, it will be underutilized and may not merit the staff time spent to maintain it.

The quality of pamphlets varies. Some are first-rate; others are not worth the space they occupy. Librarians may question the objectivity of such publications, and find some too blatantly promotional. Pamphlet literature, in short, is sometimes seen as "lacking in 'scholarly virtue.' "[15]

Most pamphlets are not cataloged. Instead, they are assigned broad subject headings and dropped behind the appropriate header in a file cabinet. Although this system has much to recommend it, particularly for patrons who are not inclined to use the card catalog, it can be frustrating for the librarian who may remember the name of the organization that issued a pamphlet, but not its title or the subject heading assigned to it. The use of commercial or in-house microcomputer databases, however, may do much to lessen this difficulty.[16]

A more serious problem is that pamphlets are fragile. They are easily damaged and easily stolen. Some librarians contend that patrons feel less inhibited about taking such materials for their own personal libraries than they would bound and cataloged books.

Pamphlets are usually unbound. They are thin little things, often with no backbone, so they do not stand up and show themselves on bookshelves or display racks. They accumulate dust, they curl with use, they disappear rapidly, for the reader seems often to feel that if it is a book it is not worth much to the library, although he may find it just what he wants and needs.[17]

These problems can be alleviated by ordering multiple copies, but if the delay in ordering replacements or added copies is too great, the needed pamphlets may be out of print.

Finally, librarians with vertical file collections comprised primarily of statistical data and with subscriptions to the *Statistical Reference Index* and the *American Statistics Index* microfiche collections, described in chapter 6, may find that their need for a vertical file has been diminished or even eliminated.

The costs and benefits of maintaining vertical file collections must be weighed carefully. Whether the staff time needed to select, process, publicize and weed such collections is offset by the timely and unique nature of the materials they contain is, of course, a decision that each library must make.

NOTES

[1]Shirley Miller, *The Vertical File and Its Satellites* (Littleton, Colo.: Libraries Unlimited, 1971), 11.

[2]For a free copy of the pamphlet, *The Dow Jones Averages*, write to the Dow Jones Educational Service Bureau. Addresses for Eastern, Southern, Midwestern, Western, and Pacific Representatives are listed in appendix I.

[3]To request a free copy of the annual *U.S. Lodging Industry*, write to:
Laventhol & Horwath
Executive Offices
1845 Walnut Street
Philadelphia, PA 19103

[4]Miller, 78.

[5]*RJR Archer Packaging* (Winston-Salem, N.C.: R.J. Reynolds Industries, n.d.), 3.

[6]David Mills, "Publications at No Charge Are Subtle Ads," *Wall Street Journal* (August 5, 1983): 1.

[7]To request free copies of the *Lilly Digest* and the *Lilly Hospital Pharmacy Study*, write to:
Eli Lilly and Company
Pharmaceutical Division
General Offices and Principal Laboratories
Indianapolis, IN 46285

[8]To request free copies of *Your Bowling Business, Are You Running Your Business...*, and *The Name of the Game Is: How to Make Money*, write to:
Brunswick Corporation
Bowling Division
69 W. Washington Street
Chicago, IL 60602

[9]Some of the free publications offered by Dun & Bradstreet are *Business Failure Record, Cost of Doing Business: Corporations, Cost of Doing Business: Partnerships and Proprietorships,* and *The Pitfalls in Managing a Small Business.* To request them, write to:

> Dun & Bradstreet
> 99 Church Street
> New York, NY 10007

[10]To request a free copy of the Dow Jones publication, *The ABC's of Option Trading,* write to one of the Educational Service Representatives listed in appendix I.

[11]A free copy of the *Consumer Information Catalog* can be obtained by writing to:

> Consumer Information Center
> P.O. Box 100
> Pueblo, CO 81002

[12]To request free copies of the leaflets, *FTC 'Best Sellers'* and *Best Sellers for Business,* write to:

> Federal Trade Commission
> 6th and Pennsylvania Avenue, N.W.
> Washington, D.C. 20580

[13]*There's Still a Place for Eagles: South Carolina* (Colombia, S.C.: South Carolina State Development Board, 1981), 2.

[14]*Materials Available to Educators* can be obtained, gratis, from the Dow Jones Educational Service Bureaus shown in appendix I.

[15]Tom Hodgson and Andrew Garoogian, "Special Collections in College Libraries: The Vertical File," *RSR* (July/September 1981): 77.

[16]Right on Programs, a commercial library software producer has, for example, devised a program called the *Vertical File Locater,* which enables users to identify a specific library's vertical file holdings by subject.

[17]Jennie M. Flexner, *Making Books Work; a Guide to the Use of Libraries* (New York: Simon and Schuster, 1943), 138.

For a decade, commercially available online databases have been kept literally in the closet. They were developed by a subculture of college professors, scientists, programmers, and librarians who rarely thought to initiate nonspecialists into their secret. Who else, indeed, would care enough about bibliographies, thesauri, and indexes? The answer is now becoming clear: business managers, owners, entrepreneurs.

—Doran Howitt and Marvin I. Weinberger, *Inc. Magazine's Databasics*

8

ELECTRONIC BUSINESS INFORMATION

Although most librarians would take issue with the implication in the above quotation that online database searching has been a well-guarded secret among an information "subculture" reluctant to initiate outsiders into its mysteries, it is undeniable that public interest in and enthusiasm for computer databases has grown tremendously in recent years. Business faculty and students, managers, small business people, and market researchers frequently tap into online computerized databases to gather information for many different projects. They may, for example, search directory databases to compile mailing lists; comb bibliographic databases for articles on such topics as employee motivation and performance, management style, and hostile corporate takeovers; or call up and manipulate the data contained in numeric files to determine the market for a particular product or to correlate one economic indicator with another. They may even use online services to invest in the stock market, make airline reservations, or submit tax returns. The number and diversity of such databases are astounding, with new databases and applications being introduced almost daily.

Further, while online databases are the type of electronic information with which librarians are most familiar, other forms of computer, or machine-readable, data files are becoming increasingly common. Statistical data sets, once available for use only on mainframe computers, are now offered for microcomputers as well, and a growing number of databases using microcomputers and laserdisk and compact optical disk technology permit unlimited, on-site searching. Microcomputers have, in fact, greatly expanded the types of data available and have made them more immediately accessible to researchers.

This chapter begins with a brief description of the various machine-readable storage technologies presently available, examines databases in a variety of formats, and discusses publications that aid in their identification and use.

MACHINE-READABLE STORAGE TECHNOLOGIES

Electronically stored information is referred to generically as *machine-readable data files* or *MRDFs*, and includes many different formats. Some, most notably magnetic computer tape, have been in use for nearly a generation. Others, such as data sets on magnetic disks for use with microcomputers, constitute a small but rapidly growing market for publishers, and still others, such as compact optical disks, have only recently become available. As shown in figure 8.1, computer storage technologies fall into two broad categories: those that store data on magnetic media, and those that use optical media.

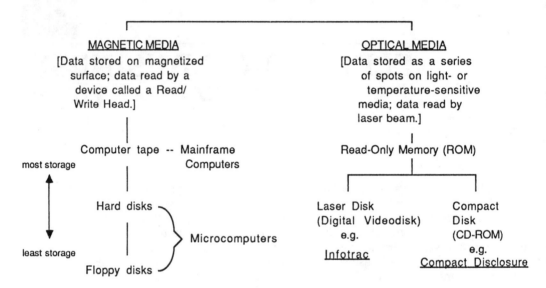

Fig. 8.1. Machine-readable information storage technologies.

Magnetic Media

Computer technology traditionally has employed magnetic technologies, with data stored on a magnetic surface. Computer tape for use with mainframe computers is the magnetic medium that has been used longest. Information stored on computer tapes include government-produced data files such as the *Census of Population* and *County Business Patterns*, commercially produced files, and those that are prepared in-house by scholars, researchers, and others. Such computer tapes are usually acquired by and stored in the computer departments of universities and colleges, corporations, and other research-oriented organizations. Generally, they are not available in libraries.

Other databases on magnetic tape are stored at remote locations and are usually made available to subscribers on a per-minute basis. These are the online databases mentioned earlier. The myriad of directory, bibliographic, numeric, and full-text databases available through such commercial database vendors as DIALOG Information Services, BRS Information Technologies, and ORBIT Search Service fall into this category.

Computer tapes are not the only type of magnetic storage technology. Magnetic disks, which are flat, circular, storage mediums coated with magnetic film, are also important. Both floppy and hard disks are used with microcomputers.[1] The most important difference between the two is their storage capacity; between 20 and 150 floppy disks would be required to match the capacity of one hard disk. Hard disk technology, however, is considerably more expensive.

Commercial publishers, government agencies, and educators are making an increasing number of data files available on floppy disks. Most are relatively small and are updated regularly. Typical of such data files are the *Directory of Public High Technology and Medical Corporations* (also available in print) and *Data Disk*, a series of economic, business, and financial indicators. In addition, some government databases prepared originally for mainframe computers are available on floppy disks as well. Such files, however, may require scores of floppy disks to store them and, as a result, can be cumbersome and unwieldly.

Although microcomputer hard disks are better suited for storage of small- and medium-sized databases, high cost, lack of portability, and technical complexity have generally precluded their use as a medium for issuing commercial database and directory information. Far more attention, in fact, has been given to a more recent type of information storage, which uses optical rather than magnetic technology.

Optical Media

Optical technology stores data as a series of spots on light- or temperature-sensitive mediums and uses a laser beam to read them. Although still in their early days, two types of optical storage technology are presently available.

LASERDISKS

Laserdisks, also known as digital videodisks, have the storage capacity of approximately 3,100 floppy disks. They can be used to store images and sound as well as text and numbers, and have been used for computer-aided instruction and simulation, entertainment, and distribution of databases. The most important laserdisk file presently available for business researchers is *InfoTrac*, a periodical and newspaper index that will be described later in this chapter.

COMPACT DISKS

Compact disks, also known as CD-ROMs, hold even greater potential for library use, and may emerge as one of the principal mediums for distribution of databases and other library reference and research sources. Databases previously only available online are now being offered on compact disk. Some, such as *Compact Disclosure* and *CD/Corporate*, are business databases and will be described later.

Although laser and compact disk storage technology are the types of optical media of most immediate interest to librarians and library users, other optical technologies are being developed as well. While they hold considerable promise for the future, they are not yet available for business library applications. Online databases, in fact, remain the most frequently accessed type of electronic business information.

ONLINE BUSINESS DATABASES

Online databases, as was mentioned earlier, are stored on magnetic tape and require the use of mainframe computers. Further, both tapes and the computers are housed at remote locations; databases made available through DIALOG, for example, are housed in Palo Alto, California, while those offered by BRS Information Technologies are in Latham, New York. Libraries and information centers access online databases at these distant locations by using telephone lines and computer terminals or microcomputers with modems and telecommunications software. Online databases are interactive; that is, they permit interaction between the searcher and the search program on the computer. Such direct communication allows the searcher to modify a search strategy as necessary in order to retrieve the desired information.

Database Producers and Vendors

Organizations that are responsible for creating databases are known as *database producers*. A database producer gathers information, edits it, and reproduces it in much the same way as publishers do. Many databases, in fact, were preceded by and continue to have printed counterparts; they are spinoffs of electronic publishing. As a result, some business publishers have also become database producers. Predicasts, for example, has produced a series of databases that correspond to its printed products, and Dun & Bradstreet offers electronic as well as printed versions of its directories. The major difference between database producers and publishers is that many producers do not market their databases to the public. Instead, they lease or sell them to database vendors.

Database vendors, in turn, supply the necessary hardware and software—mainframe computers and the programs to run them. In addition, they provide a certain level of standardization among the databases they offer, market them to the public, and supply customers with database descriptions, instructions, and training in their use. The most popular vendors in general library settings are BRS, DIALOG, ORBIT, and H.W. Wilson. Other vendors of interest to the business community are Dow Jones News/Retrieval, NewsNet, NEXIS, and I. P. Sharp Associates, Ltd. While each vendor offers some standardization in terms of basic commands and search protocol for its collection of databases, there is little standardization between vendors. The commands used in searching *ABI/Inform* on DIALOG, for example, are different from those used in searching it on BRS. In addition, the same database may have different names, or may cover different time spans or even have slightly different journal coverage. Few libraries use all vendors; more commonly, they select two or three of the major and one or two of the more specialized vendors.

Types of Databases

Business databases cover a wide range of subjects and are available in a variety of formats. They can be classified in many different ways; for example, by type of database producer. Some are commercial, others are government agencies, and still others represent professional associations and learned societies. Databases can also be categorized by the information they supply. Some are particularly useful for corporate financial data, others for product information. In this section, however, business databases are described in terms of the formats of business information that have been discussed in preceding chapters: directories, periodicals and newspapers, looseleaf services, government documents, statistical sources, and vertical file materials. Most of the databases that follow are general business databases; more specialized subject databases are covered in the chapters dealing with specific fields of business.

DIRECTORY DATABASES

Manually searching through directories to find the address for an elusive business enterprise or to identify the manufacturers of ball bearings, generators, or other products can be a tedious and time-consuming process. Online directory databases, as a result, are popular among business people who must compile mailing and telemarketing lists or who would like to learn quickly all they can about a specific company's executives, product lines, and brand names.

Many of the standard business directories described in chapter 2 have electronic counterparts (see figure 8.2). The *Million Dollar Directory*, for example, is available online as *D&B-Million Dollar Directory*, and *Thomas Register of American Manufacturers* as *Thomas Register Online*.

Type of Directory	Printed Version	Online Version	Comments
GENERAL BUSINESS	Dun's Business Identification Service (fiche)	Dun's Market Identifiers	Presents directory information for over 2 million public and private companies with a)10 or more employees or b)$1 million or more in sales. Comprehensive financial information included for ca. 700,000 companies. (An excerpt from the fiche).
"	Million Dollar Directory	D&B-Million Dollar Directory	Standard directory information for some 160,000 public and private companies with a minimum net worth of $500,000.
"	Standard & Poor's Register of Corporations, Directors and Executives	Standard & Poor's Register-Biographical	Corresponds to Vol. 2 of the Register. Provides biographical data on key executives affiliated with companies with sales of $1 million or more.
"		Standard & Poor's Register-Corporate	Derived from Vol. 1 of the of the Register. Presents standard business directory information for some 45,000 companies, usually with sales in excess of $1 million.
"	Thomas Register of American Manufacturers	Thomas Register Online	Covers over 134,00 public and private companies, which supply 50,000 classes of products and over 107,000 brand names.
AFFILIATIONS & DIVISIONS	Directory of Corporate Affiliations	Corporate Affiliations	Lists corporate divisions, subsidiaries, and affiliates in addition to parent co's.
INTERNATIONAL	Principal International Businesses	D&B-International Dun's Market Identifiers	Provides standard business directory information for more than 500,000 non-U.S. companies.

Fig. 8.2. Business directories and their online counterparts.

In addition, two useful directory files are based on sources not discussed in chapter 2.

Thomas New Industrial Products. New York: Thomas Publishing. Weekly updates.

Thomas Regional Industrial Suppliers. New York: Thomas Publishing. Quarterly reloads.

Prepared from new product press releases submitted to the monthly trade publication, *Industrial Equipment News, Thomas New Industrial Products* contains key technical information on new industrial products and systems. The database can be searched by product name, trade name and/or model number, performance specifications, product attributes and functions, SIC code, manufacturer's or distributor's name, and publication date. Using it, a researcher can monitor new product developments within a specific industry, compare similar products, and locate equipment that meets designated specifications. *New Industrial Products* is updated weekly.

A companion database, *Thomas Regional Industrial Suppliers*, is an index to the industrial products and services offered by some 325,000 companies, including for each a full list of products and services offered; an activity code specifying whether the product is manufactured, distributed, sold, or serviced by the firm; and, for many companies, trade names and the names and titles of key executives. The database, which is an online version of the *Regional Industrial Purchasing Guide*, lists companies according to 14 major U.S. industrial regions. *Regional Industrial Suppliers* is kept current by quarterly reloads; that is, the file is completely revised four times per year so that its information is as accurate and up-to-date as possible.

Other databases with corresponding printed publications provide financial as well as corporate directory information. Standard & Poor's and Moody's, for example, are now database producers as well as business publishers. Many such financial/directory databases will be described in the second section of this book.

Still other directory databases are unique; either they have no printed counterparts or the printed directories are only small portions of the databases themselves. Some of the most useful of these files are listed below.

Electronic Yellow Pages. Mt. Lakes, N.J.: Dun's Marketing Services. Quarterly reloads. (Includes the following databases: *Construction Directory, Financial Services Directory, Manufacturers Directory, Professionals Directory, Retailers Directory, Services Directory*, and *Wholesalers Directory*.)

Electronic Yellow Pages Index. Palo Alto, Calif.: DIALOG. Quarterly updates.

TRINET Company Database. Parsippany, N.J.: Trinet, Inc. Quarterly updates.

TRINET Establishment Database. Parsippany, N.J.: Trinet, Inc. Quarterly updates.

The family of seven *Electronic Yellow Pages* (*EYP*) databases, culled from the Yellow Pages of telephone directories and other sources, provides brief information on more than 8 million business establishments and professionals in the United States. Each database has a slightly different focus. The *Construction Directory*, for example, includes listings for builders, contractors, construction agencies, and heating, masonry, painting, and plumbing services. The *Financial Services Directory* provides directory information for banks, savings and loan associations and credit unions. Particularly useful are the *Professionals Directory* and the *Services Directory* files, which supply information that otherwise can be difficult to find. The *Professionals Directory*, for example, lists accounting, engineering, insurance, law, medical, and real estate professionals as well as hospitals, medical laboratories, and clinics throughout the United States. The *Services Directory* provides directory information for business, financial, office, and recreational services as well as hotels, motels, laundries, beauty and barber shops, employment agencies, and many other types of service establishments. Although the content varies slightly from one database to another, most *Electronic Yellow Pages* entries generally include the establishment's name, address, and telephone number, its SIC code, the county in which it is located, and employee and city size codes.

In some instances, it may be helpful to use the *Electronic Yellow Pages Index* before selecting one of the *EYP* databases. The *Index* consists of the SIC codes (and their text descriptions) included in the seven *EYP* files. By using it, a searcher can determine in which of the databases a specific SIC is included.

Two directory files produced by Trinet, Inc., provide more detailed corporate information. The first, *TRINET Company Databases*, draws upon trade journals, Census Bureau statistics, state and industrial directories, and other sources to present directory, marketing, and financial information for single- and multi-establishment companies employing 20 or more people. In addition to standard directory information, each listing includes primary and secondary SICs, number of employees and establishments, and, when applicable, ticker symbol and other special features (see figure 8.3). Researchers should be forewarned, however, that in the case of multi-establishment companies, the sales figures are aggregate statistics for the company as a whole rather than for each individual establishment. A companion database, the *TRINET Establishment Database*, presents similar information for branch locations.

```
DIALOG (VERSION 2)
DIALOG File 532: TRINET Company Database-4/87 Copr. TRINET Inc 1987

0189294     TRINET Number: 99002035
E I DU PONT DE NEMOURS
1007 MARKET ST
WILMINGTON, DE   19898

Telephone: 302-774-1000
County: NEW CASTLE
MSA: 9160   (WILMINGTON, DELAWARE-NEW JERSEY-MARYLAND)
Ticker Symbol: DD

Number of employees:         112,230
Number of establishments:        309

Manufacturing sales ($):     15,456,500,000
Nonmanufacturing sales ($):   3,275,600,000
Non-US sales ($):             8,415,900,000
Total sales ($):             27,148,000,000

Primary 4 digit SIC:
  2911 (PETROLEUM REFINING                   ) Sales ($):   5,785,300,000

Primary 3 digit SIC:
  291  (PETROLEUM REFINING                   ) Sales ($):   5,785,300,000

Primary 2 digit SIC:
  28   (CHEMICALS & ALLIED PRODUCTS          ) Sales ($):   8,334,400,000

Secondary SIC(s):
  2824 (ORGANIC FIBERS, NONCELLULOSIC        ) Sales ($):   2,387,700,000
  2821 (PLASTICS MATERIALS & RESINS          ) Sales ($):   1,531,900,000

This is:
  a PUBLIC Company
```

Fig. 8.3. Typical record, *TRINET Company Database*. Reprinted by permission of Trinet, Inc., and by courtesy of DIALOG Information Services.

Online business directories offer several advantages over their printed counterparts. The most important is that they permit access to information that might not otherwise be available. Not every library can afford to purchase the microfiche edition of *Dun's Business*

Identification Service or may have the *Regional Industrial Purchasing Guide* on hand; they may, however, be able to afford a few minutes of online time. Online directories also permit searching by more access points than do the printed directories. Further, some directory files are only available online. As a result, online directories can expand every library's collection of business directory information. In addition, online searching of directories may be more timely, permits greater flexibility in searching, offers some unique benefits (mailing labels, for example, can be printed), and saves researchers considerable time. Their popularity is well deserved.

PERIODICALS, NEWSPAPERS, AND INDEXES

Serials are well represented by online databases. Most fall into either of two categories: (1) electronic versions of the serials themselves, known as *full-text databases*, or (2) indexing and abstracting services, also known as *bibliographic databases*.

Full-text databases permit access to the complete text of articles and other publications, excluding any illustrations, tables, or figures that may be featured in the printed versions. Such databases are relatively recent entrants to the field of online searching, reflecting the increased information storage capacity offered by evolving computer technology. Full-text files offer two significant advantages over most traditional bibliographic databases. First, they expand the number of fields that can be searched. In addition to standard search fields (including, for example, author, title, subject descriptors, and keywords), the entire text of the article can be searched. New concepts, jargon, and slang can be retrieved, a significant benefit in a field where change is frequent and jargon commonplace. The second advantage is that full-text databases make possible immediate and direct access to publications that may not be available locally.

Several types of publications are represented by full-text databases, including general encyclopedias, legal cases, and looseleaf services, but by far the greatest number of such files are serial titles. Some of the most significant full-text periodicals databases for business researchers are listed below.

Harvard Business Review. New York: Wiley. Bimonthly updates.

McGraw-Hill Business Backgrounder. New York: McGraw-Hill. Weekly updates.

Trade & Industry ASAP. Belmont, Calif.: Information Access. Monthly updates.

Business Dateline. Louisville, Ky.: UMI/Data Courier. Monthly updates.

The *Harvard Business Review* is particularly useful for its coverage of management issues, including such topics as strategic planning, entrepreneurship, productivity, innovation, and business ethics. Using the online version, in minutes one can identify and print out not only all of the articles by a particular author, but also those in which he or she is cited. While *HBR* articles by Peter Drucker, for example, are not too difficult to identify using standard printed or online bibliographic indexes, finding those in which he is mentioned is not always an easy matter. The full-text online *Harvard Business Review* makes this a simple task.

Not all articles in the *Harvard Business Review* database are available in full text. A core collection of some 700 selected articles published between 1925 and 1970 and all of the articles published between 1971 and 1975 are represented only by abstracts and bibliographic citations. Articles written since then, however, are available in full text. The *Harvard Business Review* is a good example of a database that represents just one title. Many files, however, contain the complete text of articles from a number of periodicals.

The *McGraw-Hill Business Backgrounder* offers full-text access to many of the business periodicals published by McGraw-Hill. These include the popular *Business Week* and such trade publications as *Aviation Week and Space Technology, Coal Age,* and *Metals Week*. At present, 16 such McGraw-Hill publications are available through *Business Backgrounder* on DIALOG, and over 30, through the NEXIS version. Such disparity illustrates the difference that may exist between similar databases offered by different vendors. Often one of the major vendors has exclusive rights to a specific database for a few years before it is made available through other vendors. As a result, coverage in specific databases is not always consistent.

Trade & Industry ASAP, for example, varies from one vendor to another, but at a minimum contains the full text of 125 trade journals and regional business periodicals, including such titles as *Air Transport World, California Business*, and *Supermarket News*. (A companion database, described below, permits bibliographic access to over 800 such publications.)

Business Backgrounder and *Trade & Industry ASAP* are particularly useful to librarians and researchers needing up-to-date information on a particular industry but lacking an extensive trade journals collection. In many cases, the cost of searching and printing out the complete text of an article online is far less than the corresponding staff costs of acquiring a copy through interlibrary loan or the fee charged by a document delivery service. This, coupled with the instantaneous availability of such articles, makes full-text databases valuable supplements to existing library resources.

Just as extensive, in-house trade journal collections are rare in most libraries, geographically diverse collections of regional business periodicals are equally unusual. In many settings, regional business periodicals are limited to those representing the library's home city and state and, in some instances, neighboring states. It is unlikely that many libraries in Montana will carry *New Orleans Business*, or that information centers in Connecticut will subscribe to the *Houston Business Journal*. Such regional periodicals, however, can be extremely useful. They frequently provide information about local businesses or about a city or state's economy that may be difficult to find elsewhere. Such information may help market researchers, sales people, jobseekers, and those planning to move to another part of the country. Although *Trade & Industry ASAP* contains the complete texts of articles from some 20 different regional serials, another database includes even more publications. *Business Dateline* offers immediate access to the complete texts of over 125 regional business periodicals, permitting searching by regional designations as well as by more traditional access points. Selected newspaper articles from such papers as the *Los Angeles Times, Providence Journal-Bulletin*, and *Tulsa World* recently have been added to the file. Just as the *McGraw-Hill Business Backgrounder* and *Trade & Industry ASAP* can effectively expand a library's trade journal collection, so also does *Business Dateline* broaden a library's business coverage of remote parts of the country.

The databases described above are electronic versions of periodicals; they do not, as a rule, provide access to business and industry newsletters. Many such publications, however, are available through NewsNet, a specialized database vendor. Although NewsNet provides access to several news wire services, it is most useful in libraries for its collection of trade, technical, financial, and tax newsletters that it offers in full text. Access to NewsNet can expand considerably a library's collection of industry-specific information sources. Using it, a person researching the entertainment industry can retrieve the contents of *Hollywood Hotline* and *Video Week*, while someone interested in recent aerospace developments can scan the latest issues of such newsletters as *Satellite Week, Space Business News*, and *Space Daily*.

Still other databases are full-text versions of newspaper articles and wire services. Such files are offered by many vendors. Newspapers available in electronic versions include *Barron's, Commerce Business Daily, Financial Times, Investor's Daily,* the *New York Times,* the *Wall Street Journal*, and the *Washington Post*. Most libraries and information centers do not have access to wire services except as online databases. Typical wire service databases include *UPI News*, which contains the complete text of articles carried on the United Press International wire service, and *Businesswire*, which presents the full text of news releases issued by corporations, universities, research institutions, and other organizations.

Bibliographic databases, often the electronic equivalent of periodical and newspaper indexing and abstracting services, are even more numerous than full-text databases. Although space does not permit consideration of all such files, the most widely used bibliographic business databases are discussed below.

Some bibliographic databases provide broad coverage of business issues, while others are considerably narrower, focusing on a specific industry or business activity. Among the general business databases, six predominate.

ABI/Inform. Louisville, Ky.: UMI/Data Courier. Weekly updates.

Management Contents. Belmont, Calif.: Information Access. Monthly updates.

Business Periodicals Index. New York: H.W. Wilson. Semiweekly updates.

PTS F&S Indexes. Cleveland, Ohio: Predicasts. Weekly updates.

PTS PROMT. Cleveland, Ohio: Predicasts. Weekly updates.

Trade & Industry Index. Belmont, Calif.: Information Access. Monthly updates.

For coverage of management, administration, and general business issues, *ABI/Inform, Management Contents*, and *Business Periodicals Index* are most useful. Of the three, only *ABI/Inform* does not have a printed counterpart. *ABI/Inform* divides the journals that it covers into two broad categories: (1) a core collection of 300 periodicals, which are fully indexed and abstracted, and (2) a second group of some 300 journals from which articles are chosen selectively, based on their relevance to management.

ABI/Inform is popular with users for several different reasons. The first is that it is the oldest, most comprehensive of the general business databases, with its coverage dating back to 1971. The second is that the quality of its indexing is generally quite high, and the third and possibly most important reason is that its abstracts are detailed and informative (see figure 8.4). Finally, *ABI/Inform*, perhaps for the reasons mentioned above, is available through many database vendors.

Management Contents is another important general business file. It provides cover-to-cover coverage (excluding book reviews and letters to the editor) of some 700 U.S. and English-language foreign business periodicals, newsletters, transactions, and proceedings. Although both *Management Contents* and *ABI/Inform* are general business databases with similar goals and emphases, there are several important differences between the two. The first is that *ABI/Inform's* coverage of periodical literature dates back to 1971, while *Management Contents'* does not begin until 1974. Another is that *ABI/Inform's* abstracts are generally more detailed than those offered by *Management Contents* (see figure 8.5). Finally, *ABI/Inform's* controlled vocabulary, a thesaurus of subject terms used for indexing, is about twice the size of *Management Contents'*, often permitting greater precision in subject searching.

Management Contents, however, has its own strengths. It covers some publications not included in *ABI/Inform*, most notably conference proceedings, transactions, business course materials offered by the American Management Association, and research reports. It also has a printed counterpart, Gale Research Company's *Business Publications Index and Abstracts*, described briefly in chapter 3.

ABI/Inform and *Management Contents* can be used to supplement one another in searches relating to general management topics. Analysis in *Databasics* indicates that an identical search on both databases reveals an "astonishingly small" overlap of no more than 10 percent.[2]

The online version of *Business Periodicals Index* is a relatively new database, less widely used at this time than either *ABI/Inform* or *Management Contents*. The reasons for this are fairly obvious. *BPI* is available through only one vendor, H.W. Wilson. Further, it lacks abstracts and dates back only to 1982. Still, for those accustomed to searching the printed index and with access to the periodicals it covers, it can be a useful online file. In addition, it can be used in conjunction with another recently developed Wilsonline product, the compact disk version of *Business Periodicals Index* described later in this chapter.

ABI/Inform, Management Contents, and *Business Periodicals Index*, however, do not provide strong coverage of specific industries and trades. For such information, *PTS F&S Indexes, PTS PROMT*, and *Trade & Industry Index* are particularly helpful.

AN 87-20356. 8706.
AU Kern-Richard.
TI Marketing Indianapolis: Sports and Statistics to Numb the Mind.
SO Sales & Marketing Mgmt. VOL: v138n7. PAG: 45-47, 3 pages. May
  1987.
CC 1120 8360.
DE Sports. Indiana. Urban-development. Economic-development.
  Economic-policy. Promotions-ADV.
AV ABI/INFORM.
AB The population of metropolitan Indianapolis grew 3.2% during the
  period 1980 to 1985, making it the 2nd fastest growing of 20
  midwestern metropolitan markets. In large part, the success of
  Indianapolis, Indiana, while many of its midwestern counterparts
  experienced population declines, is due to its recent involvement in
  amateur sports. Indianapolis has been selected as the site for
  1987's Pan American Games as well as a host of other prestigious
  amateur athletic events and many smaller events. Sports facilities
  that have been completed in recent years include the Indiana
  University Natatorium, the Track and Field Stadium, the Indianapolis
  Sports Center for tennis, Market Square Arena, and the 61,000-seat
  Hoosier Dome. The influx of people to the downtown area has
  resulted in numerous office, retail, and industrial developments,
  among them the renovated Union Station marketplace. Since 1983,
  restaurants have been opening in the downtown area at the rate of
  one per month. A demand for downtown housing has developed, and
  10,000 new and rehabilitated units are planned to be completed by
  the year 2000.
PT 02.
LG EN.
CD SMMAD.
YR 87.
JC CD-SAL.
IS 0163-7517.
PD 870500.

Fig. 8.4. Typical record, *ABI/Inform*. *ABI/Inform*, the business database, is a copyrighted product of UMI/Data Courier, 620 South Fifth Street, Louisville, Kentucky 40202. Full-text articles of most *ABI/Inform* abstracts are available from Data Courier for $9.50 each. Call 800/626-2823 (U.S.) or 800/626-0307 (Canada) for additional information or to order an article.

****

AN ACCESSION NUMBER: 03882198. 8703.
AU AUTHOR: Riche-Martha-Farnsworth.
TI TITLE: Americans at play.
SO SOURCE: American Demographics, v7, n8, Aug, 1985, p38(2).
DE DESCRIPTORS: Leisure-analysis. Recreation-analysis.
AB ABSTRACT: The 1984 Gallup Leisure Index found that swimming
  continues to remain the most popular sport in the United States,
  followed by bicycling. Four of the top ten sports have only been in
  the survey for the past two years: aerobics, calisthenics, jogging,
  and pool-billiards. Participation in sports and recreation hit a
  record high in 1984, owing to the fact that 30 percent of U.S.
  adults are aged 18 to 29, the group most active in sports. Sports
  participation increases with education level, and participation also
  tends to increase with affluence.

****

Fig. 8.5. Sample record, *Management Contents*. Reprinted by permission of Information Access Company and by courtesy of BRS Information Technologies.

PTS F&S Indexes is the electronic version of three different printed indexes: the U.S., European, and international editions of *Predicasts F&S Index*. Like the printed indexes, the database is most useful for its coverage of specific industries, products, and companies, drawn from some 2,500 trade journals, business newspapers and periodicals, and other publications. One of the interesting features of this and other Predicasts databases is that they can be searched by a series of numeric codes as well as by natural language. One can, for example, search for polyvinyl chloride by an SIC-based product code as well as by name. In addition, it is possible to search by numeric geographic codes and by two-digit hierarchical event codes, numbers assigned to specific business, economic, and government activities. The event code for corporate acquisitions and mergers, for example, is *15*, and for marketing *24*. Predicasts suggests using a combination of natural language and product, geographic, and event codes when searching its databases. Records in the *PTS F&S Indexes* are brief, limited to the name, date, volume, and pages of the journal in which the article appears, and a phrase or two summarizing its contents (see figure 8.6).

```
1886610
Hotel & Motel Management
May 18, 1987    p. 36    PROMT: 1647939    (United States)

Beer   consumption  rose   1.6% in 1986 vs 1985, though domestic
     brand sales rose only 0.5%
Liquor consumption has dropped 12.1% in the 10 yrs to 1986
Wine cooler sales rose 60% in 1986 vs 1985; 6 brands accounted
     for 92.4% of mkt

1USA  United  States  2082000  Beer  & Other Malt Beverages 65
     Sales & Consumption
1USA United States 2085000 Liquor 65 Sales & Consumption
1USA United States 2084050 Pop Wines 65 Sales & Consumption
```

Fig. 8.6. Sample record, *PTS F&S Indexes*. Reprinted by permission of Predicasts and by courtesy of DIALOG Information Services.

For more detailed annotations, another Predicasts database is available: *PTS PROMT*, which stands for *Predicasts Overview of Marketing and Technology*. *PROMT*'s abstracts, which are almost as long and as detailed as those offered by *ABI/Inform*, are particularly helpful because many libraries lack the trade publications from which the articles are drawn. In many instances, simply by scanning the abstract, it is possible to determine whether or not the article itself should be sought.

While *PROMT* provides more information about the publications that it does index, it covers only half of the titles included in the *PTS F&S Indexes* database. Accordingly, Predicasts recommends that a search be initiated in *PROMT* for detailed information and continued in *F&S Indexes* for broader coverage of periodicals and newspapers.

Trade & Industry Index is drawn from industry-specific articles included in *InfoTrac*, the laserdisk index produced by Information Access Company, and from the company's other databases, *Magazine Index* and *National Newspaper Index*. It supplements *Trade & Industry ASAP*, but offers no more than brief abstracts (and sometimes none at all) rather than the complete text of articles contained in *ASAP*. Further, unlike most of the other bibliographic business databases, *Trade & Industry Index* includes industry-related articles from general nonbusiness periodicals as well as from business publications. This can be frustrating or it can be useful, depending on the purpose of the search. A market researcher in quest of recent product information, for example, might find coverage in popular periodicals such as *Life* superficial and simplistic, but for a high school student or an undergraduate working on a term paper, it might be exactly right.

Although *PTS F&S Indexes, PTS PROMT*, and the *Trade & Industry Index* cover a wide range of industries, other databases have a narrower focus. Some, such as *Agribusiness* and *Biobusiness*, may treat a group of related industries, while others, such as *Coffeeline*, may deal exclusively with a single industry or industry component. Although space does not permit coverage of such files, it should be noted that they can be identified easily by consulting some of the database directories described later in this chapter.

LOOSELEAF SERVICES

As was mentioned in chapter 4, most electronic versions of looseleaf services are costly and not available through standard database vendors. They are, accordingly, most often used by specialists in law and accounting firms and the libraries that serve them. Librarians in other settings do not as a rule make frequent use of these files.

GOVERNMENT DOCUMENTS DATABASES

There are two major government-produced online databases, each representing one of the major federal government publishers.

GPO Monthly Catalog. Washington, D.C.: Government Printing Office. Monthly updates.

NTIS Bibliographic Database. Springfield, Va.: National Technical Information Service. Biweekly updates.

The *GPO Monthly Catalog* is the online version of the *Monthly Catalog of United States Government Publications*, the standard index to federal documents published by the Government Printing Office. Like its printed counterpart, it primarily lists executive and congressional documents, accompanied by their Superintendent of Documents classification and stock numbers and Library of Congress subject headings. Libraries interested in ordering documents identified through searches of either the printed or electronic version of the *Monthly Catalog* may wish to first consult another database, the *GPO Publications Reference File*, to determine that the documents are still in print and for sale. The *Reference File* corresponds to the microfiche *GPO Sales Publication Reference File* available in most depository libraries, and lists titles that are about to be published, are currently for sale, or have recently been discontinued.

The *NTIS Bibliographic Database* lists and abstracts government-sponsored research and development reports available through the National Technical Information Service. The database offers the same access points as its printed counterpart, *Government Reports Announcements & Index*, making it possible to search by author, corporate sponsor, title, keywords, and report, contract, and grant numbers. Its main advantage is the speed with which such access points can be searched.

Although the *GPO Monthly Catalog* and *NTIS Bibliographic Database* are the most heavily used and multidisciplinary of the federal government databases, they are by no means unique. There are, in fact, nearly 500 databases produced by or under the control of government agencies and still other government-related files that are commercially produced. Most focus on a specific subject area or government activity. One can, for example, search databases for patents and trademarks recorded in the *Official Gazette* of the U.S. Patent and Trademark Office, acquire tax forms and instructions from the Internal Revenue Service, or locate information in the *Congressional Record* and the *Federal Register*. Other files list overseas business opportunities and federal procurement contracts, and still others present a wide range of demographic and economic statistics. Such basic printed sources as the *Index to U.S. Government Periodicals* and the *American Statistics Index* are also available online. Although space does not permit consideration of these files, most can be identified by using the standard database directories described later in this chapter.

NUMERIC DATABASES

Statistics are vital to business, a basic part of research and analysis. Investors may want, for example, to follow changes in stock prices over time, executives to review the data contained in corporate balance sheets and income statements, and researchers to track economic and demographic trends. Although print and computer tape traditionally have been the media in which such data are available, they are now also being offered in other machine-readable formats, including online databases. Such databases are generally known as *numeric files*; that is, they are databases in which numbers rather than words predominate. In business, the most popular numeric databases present information on wages and prices, population trends, interest rates, securities prices, and the financial condition of specific companies.

Many numeric files are available through standard vendors and use the same search protocol and commands commonly used with directory, full-text, and bibliographic databases. There are, however, important differences between numeric files and other types of online databases. First numeric databases focus on the retrieval of a specific bit of information, such as the consumer price index in Atlanta in 1986 or the gross national product for the past decade. "From the outset," writes Patricia Souzzi, "you must know everything about the data, except what the actual numbers are. You are, then, *retrieving* the data, rather than searching to find out if it exists."[3] As a result, the documentation that accompanies and describes the contents of numeric databases is extremely important.

Another difference is that, even more than with other databases, it is essential to be able to assess the reliability of numeric databases and to determine their limitations, if any. Researchers need to be assured of their objectivity and reliability, just as they do with printed statistics.

With most databases, searchers use keywords as well as designated subject descriptors to identify sources or gather information. Keyword searching, however, is not particularly useful with most numeric databases and may even be detrimental to good results.

> Variations and/or changes in terminology can also cause problems in keyword searching. For example, the Standard and Poor's 500 Stock Price Index can also be called the "combined 500," the "composite 500," or just the "stock composite." The terms "stock," "price," and "index" may or may not be included, and the order of the terms can vary ("composite 500" or "500 composite"). Another illustration of the problems that can arise in keyword searching is with geographic names. Most obvious is the fact that many places have the same name (Kansas City, Kansas or Missouri).[4]

Once again, familiarity with the documentation is essential to identify the term, phrase, or abbreviation used to retrieve a certain item. In addition, many statistical databases use numeric codes to designate specific activities, geographic areas, or other concepts. The Predicasts databases, for example, include industry, geographic, and event codes. Such codes are also listed in the documentation, and can be extremely useful in constructing a precise computer search strategy.

Finally, one of the most attractive features of many numeric databases is that the statistics that they contain can be manipulated in order to derive new information. Some databases permit online manipulation and print out the results in tables or charts. Others do not have this capability, but the same results can be achieved by downloading the search onto a microcomputer disk and using standard microcomputer software to perform the necessary calculations and reformatting.

Many numeric databases are available. Some of the most important financial files will be described in the second section of this book, but the following are a few of the most useful economic and demographic databases.

CENDATA. Washington, D.C.: U.S. Bureau of the Census. Daily updates.

Donnelley Demographics. Mountain Lakes, N.J.: Donnelley Marketing Services. Annual reloads.

PTS U.S. Forecasts. Cleveland, Ohio: Predicasts. Monthly updates.

PTS U.S. Time Series. Cleveland, Ohio: Predicasts. Quarterly updates.

Econ Base: Timeseries & Forecasts. Bala Cynwyd, Pa.: The WEFA Group. Monthly reloads. (Formerly *Chase Econometrics*)

CENDATA is based on several Census Bureau publications. It contains data drawn from press releases, new product announcements, demographic and economic censuses, and the *Current Population Reports* series. In addition, it is not a purely numeric database; it offers text as well as numbers and hence is often classified as a *textual-numeric* file. *CENDATA*, which is offered through DIALOG, is available in two separate versions. One is a standard DIALOG database, assigned a file number and searched using DIALOG commands, while the other is a menu-driven system which prompts users with choices during the course of the search. The latter begins by offering them 16 major categories from which to choose (see figure 8.7).

Code   Category

01	Introduction to Census Bureau Products and Services
02	What's new in CENDATA
03	U.S. Statistics at a Glance
04	Press Releases
05	Census User News
06	Product Information
07	CENDATA User Feedback
08	General Data
09	Agriculture Data
10	Business Data
11	Construction and Housing Data
12	Foreign Trade Data
13	Governments Data
14	International Data
15	Manufacturing Data
16	Population Data

Fig. 8.7. Major search categories in *CENDATA*.

Although both *CENDATA* files contain the same data, they are searched differently. In addition, each is updated at different intervals. The standard file contains daily updates; the menu-driven counterpart is updated hourly as data releases warrant. Searchers in need of up-to-the-minute information or unfamiliar with *CENDATA* or with online searching generally are advised to begin by using the menu-driven system.[5]

Using *CENDATA*, one can obtain the complete texts of the 20 most recent Census Bureau press releases, print out tabular statistical data for mortgage rates, or get population estimates or the latest retail sales figures. *CENDATA* is a versatile and inexpensive database, particularly useful in libraries lacking extensive collections of Census Bureau publications or in which such information is in frequent demand.

Many of the statistics contained in the Census Bureau and other government-issued numeric databases are also available in commercially produced files.

Donnelley Demographics, for example, draws upon 1980 census data as well as on population estimates and projections prepared in-house by Donnelley Marketing Services. Data include age, sex, race, industry, occupation, marital status, number of families and households, education, housing and income, and are available for 1980 as well as for the current year and five years hence. The database covers all states, Standard Metropolitan Statistical Areas, cities, towns, and zip codes, as well as such marketing designations as Arbitron's Areas of Dominant Influence and A. C. Nielsen's Designated Market Areas.

Donnelley Demographics is particularly useful for its coverage of smaller cities and towns, areas for which finding information can be difficult. Figure 8.8, for example, shows part of its coverage of Chapel Hill, North Carolina. Although *Donnelley Demographics* is a relatively expensive database, librarians in small towns may find it well worth the cost to print out annually the demographic, business, and economic data for their communities. A copy at the reference desk can save hours of searching through printed sources for elusive local statistics.

```
DIALOG (VERSION 2)
DIALOG File 575: Donnelley Demographics 10/86 (Copr. 1986 DMIS)

0053989
CHAPEL HILL TOWN

Level:          City
State:          NC
City or Place:  CHAPEL HILL TOWN
```

	1980 Census	1986 Estimate	% Change 80 to 86	1991 Projection
Total Population	32,421	33,126	2.2%	32,989
Total Households	10,019	10,476	4.6%	10,480
Household Population	23,346	24,051	3.0%	23,914
Average Household Size	2.3	2.3	-1.3%	2.3
Median Household Income	$16,094	$25,644	59.3%	$34,027

	1980 Census Number	1980 Census Percent	1986 Estimate	1991 Projection
TOTAL POPULATION BY AGE	32,421	100.0%	33,126	32,989
0 - 5	1,340	4.1%	4.0%	3.9%
6 - 13	2,334	7.2%	5.7%	5.1%
14 - 17	1,249	3.9%	11.5%	10.9%
18 - 24	13,598	41.9%	27.0%	27.7%
25 - 34	5,638	17.4%	21.7%	17.4%
35 - 44	2,716	8.4%	11.3%	14.1%
45 - 54	1,839	5.7%	6.7%	8.1%
55 - 64	1,624	5.0%	5.3%	5.5%
65 +	2,083	6.4%	6.8%	7.3%

Fig. 8.8. Partial record, *Donnelley Demographics*. Copyright Donnelley Marketing Information Services. Reprinted by permission of Donnelley Marketing Information Services and by courtesy of DIALOG Information Services.

Predicasts, the Cleveland-based publisher, produces a range of numeric files. Each uses the geographic, product, and event codes mentioned in the descriptions of *PTS F&S Indexes* and *PTS PROMT*, but unlike those files, the emphasis is on statistical data rather than on text. *PTS U.S. Forecasts* is the online equivalent of *Predicasts Forecasts*, and *PTS International Forecasts*, of *Worldcasts*. Both are based on data drawn from trade journals, newspapers, government documents, special studies, and other sources, and the records in each typically contain historical base period data, short-term and long-term forecasts, and a citation to the original source (see figure 8.9).

```
1155664    Wld Fd&Drk  86/02/18  P7      United States
   Wine coolers. sales. .

          YEAR      MIL  $

          1984       220.
          1986       333.
          1990       800.


   GROWTH RATE= 24.0%
   CC=1USA    PC=2084049    EC=652
```

Fig. 8.9. Sample record, *PTS U.S. Forecasts*. Reprinted by permission of Predicasts and by courtesy of DIALOG Information Services.

PTS U.S. Time Series contains historical time series tables of data assembled by Predicasts from past issues of statistical publications. Statistics date back to 1957 if available, and cover population and the economy as well as production, foreign trade, agriculture, mining, manufacturing, and other business activities. Figure 8.10 shows a typical record, retrieved from a search for information on Predicasts product code 28443, hair care products.

```
239637    DrugTopics  85/07/01  P67    United States
   Men's hair spray. retail sales. .
              YEAR     MIL  $
              1965       87.1
              1966       89.2
              1967       91.8
              1968       93.5
              1969       96.2
              1970       98.0
              1971       98.8
              1972       99.9
              1973       93.9
              1974       87.3
              1975       87.3
              1976       83.4
              1977       82.9
              1978       85.6
              1979       88.8
              1980       93.2
              1981       89.5
              1982       98.0
              1983      103.9
              1984      114.2

   GROWTH RATE= -0.3%
   CC=1USA    PC=2844362    EC=654
```

Fig. 8.10. Sample record, *PTS U.S. Time Series*. Reprinted by permission of Predicasts from the *PTS Users Manual*.

Formerly known as *Chase Econometrics*, *Econ Base* contains a series of economic, financial, and industrial statistics for the United States and 30 other countries, culled from a variety of government sources. More than 10,000 time series are presented, dating back as far as 1948, with monthly, quarterly, or annual updates. Two-year forecasts are provided for 1,100 major economic indicators.

The numeric files described above are among the most important databases available through standard database vendors. Still others are offered by vendors, such as I. P. Sharp, that specialize in numeric databases. As with the selection of any other information resource, the choice of vendors and the databases they offer should reflect the needs and interests of library users and the ability of librarians and other information specialists to search them effectively.

VERTICAL FILE MATERIALS

Two bibliographic databases, each with printed counterparts, are particularly useful for identifying vertical file materials.

> **PAIS International**. New York: Public Affairs Information Service, Inc. Monthly updates.

> **Vertical File Index**. New York: H.W. Wilson. Biweekly updates.

PAIS International indexes printed materials dealing with business, economics, finance, government, international relations, and political science. Based on two printed publications, the *Public Affairs Information Service Bulletin* and *PAIS Foreign Language Index*, the database indexes pamphlets as well as other sources.

Vertical File Index, which only recently has become available through Wilsonline, covers current-interest pamphlets, nonbook materials, and selected periodical articles, government, and university publications. Each record includes title, publisher, year of publication, price and ordering instructions for pamphlets and, when appropriate, government publication code, out-of-print status, title series note, or the full bibliographic citation for periodical articles. Brief annotations are included for some pamphlets.

Developments in Online Searching

In the past few years, microcomputers have become increasingly important to online searching and in many libraries and information centers have replaced the dumb terminals formerly used for accessing databases. Microcomputer technology has, in fact, greatly expanded searching options.

> Micros offer a wide range of new capabilities to online searchers. Uploading preplanned search strategies, downloading searches, cleaning them up with a text editor, combining the results of several searches in a neat package, tracking database costs for accounting purposes, and recently, capturing search results at 2400 baud, are only a few of the advantages of using a microcomputer for online searching.[6]

One of the most important of these advantages for researchers is the ability to *download*, or store, data from an online search onto a microcomputer disk, using special software to reformat the stored search results. Such a process allows the searcher to edit the results and, in the case of numeric databases, to manipulate the data and print out graphic representations.

Another significant development has been the growth of end-user searching. *End-user searching* is basically self-service searching, done at home, at work, or in libraries by the person who needs the information, rather than by a librarian, information specialist, or other intermediary. The databases offered through end-user searching systems are generally easier to use than those offered through traditional database vendors. Most are menu-driven: They offer the searcher a range of options from which to choose and do not require that he or she be familiar with traditional search protocol and commands.

End-user searching has flourished among business people. Investors in search of financial information, for example, can access the electronic versions of *Barron's*, the *Wall Street Journal*, and *Media General Financial Weekly* through the Dow Jones News/Retrieval Service. Others search business periodical literature using standard bibliographic databases such as *ABI/Inform*. Often they use the end-user systems developed by two major database vendors, DIALOG and BRS. Both DIALOG's Knowledge Index and BRS After Dark are menu-driven and are considerably easier and less expensive to use than the vendors' standard search systems.

A comparatively new entrant to the end-user field is the DIALOG Business Connection (DBC). It, too, is a menu-driven system, but is different in many important respects from Knowledge Index and BRS After Dark. The most obvious difference is that it focuses solely on business information; none of the general, scientific, social science or humanities databases available on BRS After Dark and Knowledge Index are offered. In addition, the Business Connection emphasizes business data rather than business databases. "A DBC search begins by selecting a type of data rather than a database," writes Mick O'Leary, "and the user never does know which database is actually being searched."[7]

Searchers are given an initial menu of five broad information applications from which to choose: (1) corporate intelligence, which profiles companies, lists executives and major products, presents performance statistics, and highlights recent activities; (2) financial screening, which presents stock prices, financial ratios, balance sheets, income statements, and other financial data for publicly traded companies; (3) products and markets, which includes product and market-share information; (4) sales prospecting, which generates lists by location, SIC code, company size, and company status; and (5) travel planning, which permits access to the *Official Airline Guide Electronic Edition*.

Cost is another major difference between the DIALOG Business Connection and more traditional end-user systems. While such systems as Knowledge Index and BRS After Dark are less expensive than their standard, daytime counterparts, as a rule DBC not only costs more than other end-user systems but also is sometimes more costly than searches using standard online systems. As a result, the Business Connection is not likely to be offered in libraries or information centers. It is being marketed directly to the business community for use in offices or at home. It is, however, an extremely innovative system, one that may be a benchmark for future end-user systems.

> DBC is an impressive solution to the "last problem" of online information. The advantages of online access in terms of speed, efficiency, and searching power are profound, but the difficulties of complex command systems like DIALOG's have effectively limited online use to information specialists and a handful of others who have taken the trouble to acquire the necessary expertise. DIALOG hopes to fill this gap with DBC, a "bonehead" system that still has all the searching power that most people will ever need.[8]

While microcomputers have been extremely useful for both downloading and end-user searching, they have been even more important for the growth of other kinds of electronic business information, described in the following section.

OTHER TYPES OF ELECTRONIC BUSINESS INFORMATION

Online databases are not the only format in which electronic business information is available. It is also being offered on various types of disk products. Each of these formats deserves further consideration.

Laserdisk Databases

Although laserdisk technology has been used for other reference sources (most notably, *Grolier's Knowledge Disc*, a full-text version of the *Academic American Encyclopedia*), the product that has received most attention is *InfoTrac*, a bibliographic database. Produced by Information Access Company (IAC), *InfoTrac* indexes some 900 periodicals and newspapers. Although it frequently is described as an index to popular periodical literature, it is heavily weighted towards business. An estimated 75 percent of the titles presently included are general business, trade, and regional business periodicals.[9]

The database itself is stored on laserdisk, accessed by searchers at microcomputer stations. Up to six different user stations can be accommodated, with as many searches being run on the system or printed out at the same time.

InfoTrac is popular with library users because it is fast, easy to use, and usually free. No special training in search logic or commands is necessary. Instead, the searcher simply types in the subject to be searched. The system, which uses Library of Congress subject headings supplemented by IAC-assigned headings, often gives users additional, related subjects from which to choose. Someone typing in "Insurance," for example, would be presented with more than a score of *see also* references, including such topics as Insurance Policies, Reinsurance, and Risk Management.

The example shown in figure 8.11 points out many important features of *InfoTrac*. In addition to *see also* references, many *see* references are also included, referring users from a subject not in use to one which is. Someone typing in "Insurance, Police Malpractice," for example, would be directed to "Insurance, Police Liability." As shown in the illustration, most of the titles from which articles are indexed are business related, including such newspapers as the *Journal of Commerce* and such trade publications as *National Underwriter—Life and Health Insurance Edition*. Finally, many subject headings also have subheadings. "Insurance Policies," for example, includes "Adjustment of Claims Congresses" as one of its subdivisions.

```
INSURANCE, POLICE MALPRACTICE
   see
      INSURANCE, POLICE LIABILITY
   INSURANCE POLICIES
>=       Product-integrity cover essential: expert.  by
      Michael Bradford  Business Insurance v18-Oct 15'84
      p68(1)                                      17P4774
   =       Is biotechnology research insurable?  by Jeffrey
      L. Fox  Science v225-Sept 7'84 p1004(1)
   =       NCCI Workers' Comp Policy Revisions Examined.  by
      D. Forbes  Risk Management v31-July'84 p78.
   =       In defense of back-end UL charges. (universal life
      insurance)  by Claude Thau  National Underwriter -
      Life & Health Insurance Edition-March 10'84 p13(2)
      -ADJUSTMENT OF CLAIMS CONGRESSES
   =       Bhopal disaster likely to lead to tighter
      industrial coverage. (pesticides leak in Bhopal,
      India)  by Edwin Unsworth  Journal of Commerce and
      Commercial v362-Dec 14'84 p1A(2)
```

Fig. 8.11. Sample records, *InfoTrac*. Reprinted by permission of Information Access Company.

While *InfoTrac* is one of the most popular end-user products available, it is also one of the most controversial. Librarians fear that users may neglect to consult other, possibly more appropriate, printed indexes, and point to inaccuracies and inconsistencies in IAC's subject indexing. Others, however, feel that Information Access Company has become increasingly receptive to complaints about quality control and is genuinely trying to improve its accuracy.[10] Another problem centers around cost; a subscription to *InfoTrac* is expensive, and expenditures for paper and ink cartridges for the printers are significant. Many feel that these problems, however, are outweighed by *InfoTrac*'s resounding success with library users. Few end-user searching systems can match its popularity. A new version, *InfoTrac II* is now available on CD-ROM, the other major type of optical disk technology in current use.

CD-ROM Databases

A growing number of bibliographic and numeric databases are now being offered on compact disk. Most are intended for end-users, are menu-driven and, like *InfoTrac*, are popular with users. One reason is the relative ease with which they can be searched; another is that, at many libraries, CD-ROM database searches are free. For these reasons, many users are choosing to retrieve information from compact disk databases rather than from their online counterparts.

The number of business databases available on CD-ROM has increased steadily. Many, such as *Compact Disclosure* and *CD/Corporate*, offer detailed corporate financial information and will be described in chapter 13. *Business Periodicals Index*, however, is also available on compact disk. Like its printed and online counterparts, it indexes articles contained in general business periodicals. Like many CD-ROM databases, *BPI* is updated quarterly, and is thus less current than either the printed or online versions. It offers subscribers an interesting benefit, however. Anyone subscribing to the CD-ROM *Business Periodicals Index* can have unlimited free access to the online version available through Wilsonline. No database royalties are charged; the only additional cost is for telecommunication. Finally, *ABI/Inform* recently has been introduced in CD-ROM format as *ABI/Inform Ondisc*.

CD-ROM databases are not perfect, however. One problem is their cost; an annual subscription to a single CD-ROM database may cost as little as $900 or as much as $14,000. The same level of expenditure might subsidize a significant number of online searches or pay for subscriptions to multiple printed versions of many of the databases. Another drawback is that present technology limits searching to a single user at a time. While several different people might simultaneously search the printed copies of *Business Periodicals Index*, for example, only one person can use the CD-ROM version. In addition, many different CD-ROM databases may be competing for a limited number of CD-ROM search stations. Accordingly, people using *Psychological Abstracts, ERIC, Books in Print Plus*, and other files may make it impossible for business searchers to access databases at times that are convenient for them. Although the format and arrangement of compact disk databases encourages spontaneity, the lack of sufficient search stations may negate this advantage. In spite of these problems, however, compact disk databases are an exciting new development and reinforce the trend toward increasing end-user searching.

Microcomputer Data Disks

Another recent development is the growth and proliferation of nonbibliographic data stored on microcomputer disks. Such files include numeric and directory databases and, like the optical technologies, offer the opportunity for do-it-yourself searching at little or no cost to users.

Many such files are available on floppy disks, some produced commercially and others by government agencies. Commercially produced files include *Data Disk*, a collection of economic, financial, manufacturing, and sales data, *State Data Profiles*, and Value Line's *Value Screen*, a selective version of the *Value Line Investment Survey*. The federal government is a major supplier of data disks. The Bureau of Labor Statistics, for example, offers disks on economic growth, the labor force, and prices, while the Census Bureau sells microcomputer disk versions of *County Business Patterns*, the *County and City Databook*, and the *Census of Agriculture*. Still other files are available from the National Technical Information Service.

Although data disks are intended for end-users, they sometimes require skills that are not necessary for other types of end-user searching. Often they are used in tandem with special spreadsheet packages and may presuppose a basic knowledge of such software. Further, the quality of data disks and their accompanying documentation varies widely. Many Census Bureau files, for example, are downloaded excerpts from mainframe computer tapes and their documentation may focus on mainframe files and technology rather than on microcomputers. Some files require reformatting before they are ready for public use. Library staff must, as a result, invest considerable time to make the files and documentation useful to searchers, an expenditure not required for most other end-user searching systems. Further, because data disks are more difficult to learn to use, library staff must be on hand to provide initial training and resolve problems.[11]

In spite of these difficulties, however, microcomputer data disks can be extremely helpful to experienced researchers willing to invest the time necessary to learn to use them effectively. Accessing such files, one can retrieve a wide array of statistical information, print out graphs, maps, charts, or other illustrations, create databases, and support a variety of business applications.

INFORMATION SOURCES

The number of printed database guides, directories, periodicals, and other sources available reflects the growth of electronic business information. Some of the most important ones are discussed below.

Guides

Database guides traditionally have been written with librarians and information specialists in mind, but a growing number are now available for special user groups. Two of the best general business-related database guides follow.

Howitt, Doran, and Marvin I. Weinberger. **Inc. Magazine's Databasics: Your Guide to Online Business Information**. New York: Garland, 1984. 614p.

Hoover, Ryan E. **Executive's Guide to Online Information Services**. White Plains, N.Y.: Knowledge Industry, 1984. 296p.

Billed by its publisher as both a how-to manual and a reference guide, *Inc. Magazine's Databasics* combines general information about the process of online searching with analysis and comparison of specific databases. Some 100 files, arranged by broad subject classifications such as "Databases about Companies," "Stock Market Databases," and "Broad-Coverage Business Databases," are reviewed at length. In addition, general and specialized database vendors and computer hardware and peripherals are listed and described. Also featured are a bibliography of relevant publications, a directory and descriptions of major information brokers, and a chapter in which the future of online database searching is considered. *Databasics* is a thorough, thoughtful, and well-written introduction to the field, and although it is intended for managers and executives, it can be equally relevant to librarians, researchers, and information specialists.

Also useful is the *Executive's Guide to Online Information Services*. Like *Databasics*, it presents the rudiments of online searching, offers an overview of major online services, and categorizes and describes different business-related databases. Sample searches are also included. While *Databasics* is more comprehensive and covers databases more thoroughly, the *Guide* is also well written, free of jargon, and potentially helpful to a wide range of readers. Both titles, however, are somewhat dated, and statements about specific databases and vendors may no longer be accurate.

While the *Guide* and *Databasics* are useful for general introductions to online searching and surveys of relevant business databases, they do not deal with practical aspects of constructing search strategies or using specific databases. The guides below fill this need.

Ness, Dan. **Fast Facts Online: Search Strategies for Finding Business Information**. Homewood, Ill.: Dow Jones-Irwin, 1986. 548p.

Popovich, Charles J. **Business and Economics Databases Online: Environmental Scanning with a Personal Computer**. (Advanced Online Searching Series) Littleton, Colo.: Libraries Unlimited, 1987. 276p.

Fast Facts Online is a practical guide to business database searching. Initial chapters cover the basics, describing types of databases and producers, introducing Boolean logic, and suggesting techniques for developing and evaluating search strategies. Ness then arranges databases by 32 subject categories, ranging from World News to Management Techniques and Case Studies. Within each category, databases are assigned grades from A to C, reflecting the depth of coverage they provide. Further, databases in each grade level are grouped together by vendor. Information about each database includes its code, the first date covered, the number of records in the file, frequency of updates, geographic coverage, number of journals indexed, searchable fields, and database vendor. Databases offered by more than one vendor appear more than once within a category. This is a useful feature because, as was mentioned earlier, there can be considerable difference in coverage between vendors. *PTS PROMT* on DIALOG, for example, begins its coverage in 1971, but VuText's version dates back only to 1978, and that of BRS to 1980.

In addition, *Fast Facts* includes a section that lists databases alphabetically, with separate entries for each vendor offering them. *ABI/Inform*, for example, has separate listings for BRS, DIALOG, VuText, and Knowledge Index. Each includes general information about the database, and lists those subject categories for which it received grades of A, B, and C. *Fast Facts* is indexed, and includes a glossary and an annotated bibliography.

A different approach is used in *Business and Economics Databases Online*. Following a review of the environmental scanning process, in which social, technological, economic, and political factors are monitored as part of corporate strategic planning, Popovich describes basic microcomputer hardware and software and presents an overview of two database vendors, DIALOG and I. P. Sharp. Although experienced searchers may want to skip his coverage of Boolean logic, DIALOG, and basic search commands, those not familiar with I. P. Sharp will find this a useful introduction to an important numeric database vendor.

Subsequent chapters demonstrate the use of *Lotus 1-2-3* to graph out quantitative data, and suggest search methods (and specific databases) for retrieving social, technological, economic, and political information relevant to business. Discussion is enhanced by the frequent use of print screens (reproductions of data displayed on the microcomputer monitor) and by printouts of search results. A bibliography of online database directories and annotated, selected lists of business-related databases on DIALOG and of economic files on I. P. Sharp are also included.

In addition to the above sources, most database vendors and many database producers issue extensive guides to online searching. These publications are well worth acquiring, and are listed in such database directories as *Computer Readable Databases*.

Guides to other types of machine-readable information technology are also important. Although the market has yet to be flooded with guides to compact disk databases, a few good general guides to CD-ROM technology are available.

Lambert, Steve, and Suzanne Ropiequet, eds. **CD-ROM: The New Papyrus**. Redmont, Wash.: Microsoft Press, 1986. 619p.

Roth, Judith Paris, ed. **Essential Guide to CD-ROM**. Westport, Conn.: Meckler, 1986. 189p.

Miller, David C. **Special Report: Publishers, Libraries & CD-ROM: Implications of Digital Optical Printing**. Benecia, Calif.: DCM Associates, 1987. 99p.

Bowers, Richard A. **Optical Publishing Directory**. 2nd ed. Medford, N.J.: Learned Information, 1987. Looseleaf.

CD-ROM: The New Papyrus is a compilation of articles by computer hardware, software, and information specialists. Sections cover compact disk systems and CD-ROM production, design, publishing, applications, and resources. Although no business files are discussed and bibliographic and numeric databases are only one of the applications considered, *CD-ROM* is nonetheless useful as a basic introduction to the field.

The *Essential Guide to CD-ROM* is less theoretical, focusing on the basic concepts and principles of CD-ROM technology. Although reference tools and databases are not covered in detail, the *Guide* does describe briefly some of the sources that were available at the time it was compiled.

Special Report: Publishers, Libraries, and CD-ROM focuses on CD-ROM as a publishing medium, describing such applications as automobile parts catalogs, newspapers, advertising logos, and federal and state government environmental regulations on compact disk as well as more "traditional" library use of catalogs, databases, and quick reference sources on compact disk. A nontechnical explanation of compact disk technology is also included.

Finally, the *Optical Publishing Directory* combines a general discussion of the advantages and disadvantages of optical publishing and its outlook for the future with a glossary and profiles of major optical disk (primarily CD-ROM) products. Each profile includes the producer's name, address, and telephone number; the name of the original source; the type of product and its format; a description of hardware and software requirements; frequency of updates; and current price.

General guides to microcomputing are abundant. Most are either hardware specific or software specific. Although the scope of this book precludes extensive coverage of such publications, it should be noted that a number of them focus on specific business applications. Representative of these guides are such titles as *Forecasting Tools for the IBM PC* (Hasbrouck Heights, N.J.: Hayden, 1985), *Financial Analysis with Lotus 1-2-3* (Belmont, Calif.: Wadsworth Electronic Publishing, 1985), and *DBase II Programming: Making DBase II Work for Your Small Business* (Englewood Cliffs, N.J.: Prentice-Hall, 1984). Some guides, such as *Real Estate and Financial Applications Using SuperCalc* (Hasbrouck Heights, N.J.: Hayden, 1984) and *Preparing Your Business Plan with Symphony* (Englewood Cliffs, N.J.: Prentice-Hall, 1985), are accompanied by supplementary software packages. Considerable care should be exercised in acquiring microcomputer guides for library collections. Although they are abundant, the quality of the information they provide and their usefulness vary considerably.

Bibliographies

Many of the guides listed above include selective bibliographies of online, compact disk, and microcomputer sources, but another title, written specifically for librarians, should also be mentioned.

Young, Sayre Van. **MicroSource: Where to Find Answers to Questions about Micro-computing**. Littleton, Colo.: Libraries Unlimited, 1986. 220p.

MicroSource, written for "the harried librarian who is besieged by questions about microcomputers,"[12] annotates sources appropriate to medium-sized public and school libraries. Chapters cover computer literacy; the purchase of hardware, software, and user guides; telecommunications; computer languages; programming; and many other topics. Librarians in academic and special libraries, however, may find the chapters on software publishing guides, periodicals and indexes, directories, dictionaries, and vertical file materials even more useful. The annotations are thorough, and highlight the good and bad features of the works being considered.

Dictionaries and Thesauri

"Computerese," like business English, can be baffling to the uninitiated. A collection of comprehensive, up-to-date dictionaries, glossaries, and thesauri is essential, and should include general as well as more specialized dictionaries.

Rosenberg, Jerry M. **Dictionary of Computers, Data Processing, and Telecommunications**. New York: Wiley, 1984. 614p.

Edmunds, Robert A. **The Prentice-Hall Standard Glossary of Computer Terminology**. Englewood Cliffs, N.J.: Prentice-Hall, 1985. 489p.

The *Dictionary of Computers, Data Processing, and Telecommunications* lists and defines more than 10,000 terms relating to computers, data processing, home computers, information transmission, microcomputers, personal computers, programming languages, telecommunications, and word processing. Commonly used symbols, acronyms, and abbreviations are also included, and an English-Spanish-French language glossary is appended.

The Prentice-Hall Standard Glossary of Computer Terminology contains nontechnical definitions, designed to give readers an understanding of basic computing and information processing concepts as well as of jargon currently in use. In addition to words, the *Glossary* lists phrases and combinations of words, acronyms and abbreviations, and the names of important individuals, organizations, and products.

Other publications provide more specialized coverage.

Christie, Linda Gail, and John Christie. **The Encyclopedia of Microcomputer Terminology: A Sourcebook for Business and Professional People**. Englewood Cliffs, N.J.: Prentice-Hall, 1984. [336p.]

Byerly, Greg. **Online Searching: A Dictionary and Bibliographic Guide**. Littleton, Colo.: Libraries Unlimited, 1983. 288p.

The Encyclopedia of Microcomputer Terminology defines some 4,000 terms, many of which, like bar codes and robotics, have direct business applications. Definitions are fairly lengthy, and frequently include examples and cross-references. Many technical appendices and four glossaries (covering videodisk technology, bar codes, music synthesis, and word processing) are also included.

Online Searching offers concise definitions of standard online vocabulary as well as a classed bibliography of titles about online searching and specific databases. Although *Online Searching* is useful, even more important to searchers are the thesauri and user guides issued by database producers that contain the controlled vocabulary used in indexing. Since the controlled vocabulary varies from one database to another, a comprehensive collection of such publications for the files that are searched regularly is a necessity. Most can be identified by consulting the following directories.

Directories

A wide range of computer-oriented directories are available. Some focus on online databases, others on microcomputer software, and still others on manufacturers and suppliers of computing equipment. The directory with the broadest coverage, however, is the *Encyclopedia of Information Systems and Services*.

Lucas, Amy, and Kathleen Young Marcaccio, eds. **Encyclopedia of Information Systems and Services**. 7th ed. Detroit: Gale Research Co., 1987. 3v.

Another of the computer-generated dictionary lists in which Gale specializes, the *Encyclopedia* describes some 4,000 organizations, systems, and services involved in the production of electronic information. It is published in three volumes, with the first containing U.S. listings, the second, international, and the third, an array of indexes. Arrangement in the first two volumes is by organization name. Each entry generally includes the organization's address and telephone number; date established; name of its head; number and type of staff; name and relationship of affiliated organizations; description of its program, purposes, and functions; principal areas of interest; input sources, type and quantity of stored information; publications; microform and computer-based products and services; other services; and user groups and clientele for whom the services are intended. Also identified are new products and services being developed, name and title of the contact person, and other pertinent information. Organizations represented include database producers and vendors, bibliographic utilities, data collection and analysis firms, library and information networks, document delivery sources, professional and trade associations, and publishers.

The third volume contains not only a master index but also database, publications, software, functional, personal name, geographic, and subject indexes, greatly enhancing access for researchers.

Most directories are not so comprehensive. Some, for example, cover only online databases.

Directory of Online Databases. New York: Cuadra/Elsevier, 1979- . Quarterly.

Mayros, Van, and D. Michael Werner. **Data Bases for Business**. Radnor, Pa.: Chilton, 1982. 178p.

The *Directory of Online Databases* lists and describes 3,369 publicly available textual, numeric, and textual-numeric U.S. and foreign databases accessible through online vendors and service organizations. The main section is arranged alphabetically by database name. Each entry classifies the database by type, identifies its producer and the vendors through which it is available, describes its content, the language in which it is produced, its geographic coverage, time span, and the frequency of updates. The entry for *Donnelley Demographics* in figure 8.12 is typical.

DONNELLEY DEMOGRAPHICS

Type: Source (Numeric)

Subject: Demographics & Population

Producer: Donnelley Marketing Information Services, a company of The Dun & Bradstreet Corporation

Online Service: DIALOG Information Services, Inc.

Content: Contains demographic data, current-year estimates, and 5-year projections based on the 1980 U.S. Census of Population and Housing. Demographic data include total population, number of households, household size and median income, race, age, sex, occupation and employment, marital status and families, level of education, housing, and mobility. Data are available for cities, counties, states, ZIP codes, Metropolitan Statistical Areas (MSAs), Arbitron Areas of Dominant Influence (ADIs), A.C. Nielsen Designated Marketing Areas (DMAs), and the entire U.S.

Coverage: U.S.

Time Span: 1980 data, current-year estimates, and 5-year forecasts

Updating: Annually

Fig. 8.12. Typical entry, *Directory of Online Databases*. Reprinted by permission of the publisher from the *Directory of Online Databases*, vol. 8, no. 1, p. 113. Copyright 1987 by Elsevier Science Publishing Co., Inc.

Subject, producer, online service/gateway and telecommunication indexes are included. The *Directory* is regarded highly for the quality and usefulness of the information it provides.

Data Bases for Business combines general information about online searching with profiles of 400 databases. Most of the information it contains, however, is duplicated in the more comprehensive *Directory of Online Databases*. Further, libraries that hold Van Mayros's *Business Information: Applications and Sources* will find that *Data Bases for Business* is essentially an extract of the database portions of that publication. Accordingly, *Data Bases for Business* might be more useful in a business manager's or executive's office than in a library.

Some directories cover other types of machine-readable data files in addition to online databases. Below are two of the most useful.

Williams, Martha E., Laurence Lannom, and Carolyn G. Robins, eds. **Computer-Readable Databases; A Directory and Data Sourcebook**. Chicago: American Library Association, 1985. 2v.

Zarozny, Sharon, ed. **The Federal Data Base Finder**. 2nd ed. Chevy Chase, Md.: Information USA, 1987. 368p.

Published in two volumes, *Computer-Readable Databases* contains descriptions of some 2,800 databases. The *Science, Technology, Medicine* volume covers the hard sciences, medicine, engineering, and such related materials as the business aspects of science. The *Business, Law, Social Sciences, Humanities* volume presents files in the disciplines specified as well as general databases. Entries include basic information about the file, a description of its subject matter and scope, a list of data elements present, and the identification of available user aids (see figure 8.13, page 182). Name, author, subject, and producer indexes are also included.

The Federal Database Finder describes over 4,200 free and fee-based databases and data files available to the public. The *Finder* is divided into three main sections. One lists and describes databases; another focuses on computer tapes and microcomputer disks; and the third enumerates tapes and disks available from the Census Bureau, NTIS, and the National Archives and Records Administration. Descriptions are succinct and generally free of jargon, and frequently include the names and telephone numbers of contact people. As a result, the *Federal Data Base Finder* can be helpful to lay people and novice researchers as well as to experienced information specialists.

Vertical File Materials

Vertical file collections in many libraries can be enhanced by the addition of catalogs, product brochures, and pamphlets pertaining to microcomputers, databases, and software. Identifying such items, however, is not always easy. The *Vertical File Index*, for example, is estimated to list only one such item per issue.[13] *MicroSource*, described in the section on bibliographies, is particularly useful for its list of publications and publishers' addresses in the chapter, "Free and Easy—Catalogs, Pamphlets, and Other Inexpensive Resources."

Automotive News Data Bank

BASIC INFORMATION
Name: Automotive News Data Bank
Producer: Data Resources, Inc. (DRI), Data Products Division
  Headquarters
Frequency of database update: varies
Time span covered by database: 1965-70 to present
Approx. size 12/84: 3,000 time series
Approx. annual growth: unspecified
Corresponding print products: Automotive News (print and
  online versions not identical)
Language of database: English
Geographic coverage: USA and Canada
Sources of data: Crain Automotive Group, Inc.
Established policy for lease or license: yes
Processed for online searching by: producer
Special features: DRI data can be accessed through a series of
  software that can be used to perform various types of quanti-
  tative analyses and data display. DRI models are available for
  many of the econometric databases or the user may simulate
  these models and generate alternative forecasts based on his
  own assumptions. Display formats include simple printouts,
  reports or multicolored graphics. Users may download DRI's
  information for local processing through DATALINK and
  DataKITS software.

SUBJECT MATTER AND SCOPE
The Automotive News Data Bank details the status of the
U.S. automobile market at a nameplate level. Also available in
detail are statistics on Canadian car production, U.S. light-duty
truck sales, and imported car sales. Other concepts include: production, days supply, sales, option installations, prices, and physical specifications. Annual, quarterly, monthly, weekly, and ten-
day data are available.

Fig. 8.13. Typical entry, *Computer-Readable
Databases*. Reprinted with permission of the American
Library Association, entry taken from *Computer-
Readable Databases: A Directory and Data Source-
book*, edited by Martha E. Williams; copyright © 1985
by ALA.

NOTES

[1]Hard disks can also be used with mini- and mainframe computers as well as with microcomputers.

[2]Doran Howitt and Marvin Weinberger, *Inc. Magazine's Databasics* (New York: Garland,
1984), 100.

[3]Patricia Suozzi, "By the Numbers: An Introduction to Numeric Databases," *Database* 10,
no. 1 (February 1987): 18.

[4]See note 3 above.

[5]For an interesting article about *CENDATA, Donnelley Demographics*, and other demographic databases, see Diane Crispell, "The World of Demographic Data," *Database* 10, no.
2 (April 1987): 36-43.

[6]Nancy Gorman, "Downloading ... Still a Live Issue? A Survey of Database Producer Policies for Both Online Services and Laserdisks," *Online* 10, no. 4 (July 1986): 15.

[7]Mick O'Leary, "DIALOG Business Connection: DIALOG for the End-User," *Online* 10, no. 5 (September 1986): 15.

[8]Ibid., 20.

[9]Cynthia Hall, Harriet Talon, and Barbara Pease, "InfoTrac in Academic Libraries: What's Missing in the New Technology?," *Database* 10, no. 1 (February 1987): 52.

[10]For a defense of *InfoTrac*, see Ann Bristow Betron, "InfoTrac at Indiana University: A Second Look," *Database* 10, no. 1 (February 1987): 48-50.

[11]For some of the issues involved in making a collection of microcomputer data disks available to library users, see Diane Strauss, "A Checklist of Issues to be Considered Regarding the Addition of Microcomputer Data Disks to Academic Libraries," *Information Technology and Libraries* 5, no. 2 (June 1986): 129-32.

[12]Sayre Van Young, *MicroSource: Where to Find Answers to Questions about Microcomputers* (Littleton, Colo.: Libraries Unlimited, 1986), xii.

[13]Ibid., 136.

Part 2
Fields of
Business Information

Don't write with a peach, you'll get a wet letter. Nor should you write with a prune. Words will come out wrinkly and dopey. And blueberries? Worse yet. It would take you two boxes to write one postcard. That's how small they are. Let's face it; the only fruit you can write with is a banana. The BIC Banana. A fineline marker. Not to be confused with a ballpoint.

—Mel Brooks

9

MARKETING

Mel Brooks's famous television commercial for BIC pens is an appropriate way in which to begin this chapter because, in the minds of many lay people, marketing and advertising are synonymous. Marketing, however, is an extremely broad, complex, and important field of which advertising is just one part.

MARKETING BASICS

Marketing is a mix of activities, beginning with estimating the demand for products and leading to their development, pricing, distribution, and promotion. These activities can be reduced to four broad categories: product, price, place, and promotion.

Marketing Activities

Product planning involves the product itself as it is designed to appeal to a predetermined group of users or potential users. It includes decisions about package design, brand names and trademarks, warranties, and the development of new products. In 1984, for example, PepsiCo began test marketing a new product to see if user response merited full production and distribution.

> PepsiCo is test marketing Slice, a new caffeine-free soft drink with 10% real fruit juice. "Pepsi is the first major international corporation to use real fruit juice in a carbonated soft drink" says Jesse Meyers, publisher of *Beverage Digest*.
>
> The product is currently being tested in Rochester, NY and Tulsa, OK. By the end of the month, testing will continue in Colorado Springs and Pueblo, CO; Rockford, IL; Phoenix, AZ; Milwaukee, WI, and several other locations in Wisconsin, Meyers says. Nationwide distribution and the start-up of advertising will depend on the test results, says Steve Hauser, manager of marketing services at PepsiCo headquarters in Purchase, NY. The tests could take as long as a year.[1]

Test results were positive, and Slice became an official PepsiCo brand in 1984. By the end of 1985, it was available in 80 percent of the country, and by year-end 1986, enjoyed retail sales of 1 billion dollars.[2]

Marketers must also make a series of decisions relating to *pricing*, setting profitable and justified prices for their products. Other factors are at work here as well. The product's image is important and may be affected by its price. It would not do, for example, to set too low a price for a perfume intended for affluent consumers; they might ignore it or think it inferior and turn instead to more costly brands. Market demand and competitors' prices must also be considered. Finally, pricing is closely regulated and is subject to considerable public scrutiny.

Promotion involves personal selling, sales promotion, and advertising using print, broadcast, and other media. Even as Slice, the new soft drink, was being test marketed, decisions were being made about how to promote it if PepsiCo went into full-scale production.

> Marketers will use "We got the juice" as the advertising campaign slogan for Slice, which contains the juices of white grapes, pears, lemons, and limes. The target market for the product is "men and women, ages 18 to 34, who consider themselves active," Hauser says, noting that one of two TV commercials for the product has a segment showing adults "obviously in their 20s," working out in a gymnasium.[3]

Place refers not only to the geographic area in which the product is marketed, but also to the channels and marketing intermediaries through which the product moves, and the transportation employed en route to the final user. When Quaker Oats bought Stokely-Van Camp, for example, one of the products it acquired was Gatorade. It subsequently made a "place" decision to enlarge the geographic area in which Gatorade was actively marketed.

> Gatorade has been particularly popular in the Southeast and Southwest, where 60% of its sales are concentrated. Quaker said the new marketing plan will build on that strength, but Gatorade will also be reintroduced into non-Sunbelt markets through advertising and promotion.[4]

Marketing has grown increasingly important in the 1980s and according to *Newsweek*, it has become the "No. 1 business priority."[5] Marketing activities are undertaken by manufacturers of industrial and consumer products and by companies that sell services, but they are also increasingly commonplace to nonprofit organizations—libraries, art museums, charities, and political parties. Whatever the nature of the product or service, good marketing helps.

> The Kroger supermarket chain conducts 250,000 consumer interviews each year and, as a result, has added flower alleys and fresh-fish counters to its stores. Deere & Co. has turned its tractor showrooms into market research bureaus. Even the medical industry is trying out some marketing techniques. Hospitals are promoting their doctors' expertise as if it were a product, and physicians in private practice trying to reduce the boredom of waiting by installing video games and juice bars in their outer offices.[6]

Small businesses also depend on effective marketing to keep ahead. They, even more than large corporations, can ill afford costly errors based on faulty marketing decisions or inadequate information. Good marketing does not guarantee business success, but it eliminates unnecessary gambling and improves the odds.

Market Segmentation

Not all people want or can afford all products or services. Someone in the restaurant supply business, for example, would be as disinclined to buy an industrial lathe as an adolescent would be to buy a Cabbage Patch doll, and while that same teenager might yearn for a Ferrari, it is unlikely that he or she would be able to buy one. Marketers define their markets by attempting to identify particular segments of the population, people with "purchasing power and the authority to make purchase decisions,"[7] who are likely to want to buy the product. This process is called *market segmentation*; that is, dividing a larger, somewhat diverse market into smaller markets in which demand for a particular product or group of products is likely to be greater.

> Firms that can identify buyers with similar needs may be able to serve those market segments quite profitably. The market consisting of people who use toothpaste (almost everyone), for example, can be divided into a number of smaller segments, each consisting of people who have more in common: children who want a toothpaste that tastes good, parents who want one that will reduce cavities, young adults who seek sex appeal, and so on. The smaller, more homogeneous submarkets and serving those submarkets with your product, is called market segmentation.[8]

Although any characteristic that describes and distinguishes buyers may be useful for market segmentation, those most commonly used are geographic, demographic, psychographic, and sociographic.

GEOGRAPHIC

Consumers in different geographic regions may exhibit different buying behavior. Market research by automobile manufacturers, for example, has shown that certain styles and colors are more popular in some parts of the country than in others. Tastes may also vary. Campbell Soup Company, for example, makes its nacho cheese soup spicier for Texas and California than for other parts of the country. Campbell has, in fact, placed considerable emphasis on geographic segmentation.

> Instead of developing a single set of products and marketing programs to win over American consumers, Campbell has cooked up a new approach. It is tailoring its products, advertising, promotion, and sales efforts to fit different regions of the country—and even individual neighborhoods within a city.[9]

Climate, political boundaries, and population density are some of the factors considered in geographic market segmentation.

DEMOGRAPHIC

Demographic information is of key importance to marketers, who often segment their markets using such demographic variables as age, sex, race, income, marital status, and family size. A real estate developer considering sites for an exclusive retirement community, for example, would be particularly interested in the number of affluent adults aged 65 and older. Although current data would be important, so also would be historical statistics and projections for the future, reflecting past and anticipated trends. If statistics for the last 10 years showed an absolute decline in the number of adults 65 and older in a particular region, the developer would probably eliminate that region from the list of prospective sites for the retirement community.

Advertisers use demographic information to segment their markets as well. They identify the demographic characteristics of the people most likely to buy their products, and then direct their advertising to these people through the media that will most effectively reach them.

> Therefore, if demographic analysis shows that the heaviest usage for our product is by women who are married and under 35 years of age, with 2 or more children under 8 and a blue collar occupation by the head of the household, then we know who our market is and from this we can determine what appeals in our advertising will be most effective. Finally, we can find out those advertising media with similar demographics to reach our market most effectively with our message.[10]

PSYCHOGRAPHIC

Psychographic segmentation looks at the values, activities, interests, and opinions of the population, what we often call *lifestyle*. As with geographic and demographic segmentation, the variables are quantitatively measured, but unlike them, the numbers are not as easily (or as inexpensively) available.

> For some purposes, geographic and demographic market segmentation may leave something to be desired. For example, age is a commonly used demographic classification. From it, advertisements have defined the "youth market." However, the youth market may need a new definition. Is it really an age group, or is it a state of mind? The youth market overflows the traditional age brackets and today can be defined more meaningfully in terms of those who think young in any age bracket—that is, in terms of youthfulness, not youth. Even among youth within the demographic age bracket there is a wide range of differences. Consider, for example, the popular positions of the "preppy" and the "street-smart" youth. It can be seen, therefore, that differentiation could be based on values as well as demographics. Thus, there is an increasing interest by advertisers in using this new dimension to define market targets in terms of attitudes and activities.[11]

SOCIOGRAPHIC

Finally, sociographic segmentation looks at the social environment, including social class and culture, peer and reference groups, and family structure and decision making.

Usually marketers use a mix of geographic, demographic, psychographic, and sociographic factors to identify their market segment. As a result, marketing research, which gathers and analyzes such data, is extremely important.

Marketing Research

Marketing research covers a whole gamut of activities but, in essence, is the process of systematically gathering and analyzing information about marketing problems and potentials for use in making marketing decisions.

> Marketing research helps a firm to identify and evaluate market opportunities and to develop the effort needed to exploit it. It also helps to identify and solve problems. Marketing research is useful in a wide variety of activities, such as economic forecasting and sales forecasting, measuring market share, identifying market trends, measuring company and brand images, developing customer profiles, designing products and packages, locating warehouses and stores, processing orders, managing inventory, analyzing demand, measuring price perception and advertising effectiveness, analyzing audience characteristics, and scheduling advertisements.[12]

It includes various subsidiary types of research, such as product research, which involves market tests for new products such as PepsiCo's Slice, studies of package effectiveness, and identifying new markets for existing products. It includes market analysis, the study of the size, location, and other characteristics of the markets themselves. In measuring markets, *market share analysis*, which compares sales for one product brand against total sales for all brands of the product, is particularly important. Figure 9.1, for example, shows market share information for different brands of coffee.

Coffee market shares

If you look at the market share percentages coffee makers hold, the dominance of a few becomes evident. *Source: John C. Maxwell Jr.*

	1981	1982	1983	1984	1985
Regular coffee					
General Foods					
Maxwell House*	20.2	19.5	19.0	18.6	18.8
Master Blend	5.2	6.9	7.5	8.0	9.0
Sanka	3.5	3.7	3.9	4.7	4.6
Max-Pax & Brim	3.2	2.8	2.7	2.6	3.2
Yuban	1.6	1.3	1.0	0.7	0.6
Mellow Roast	0.8	0.6	0.5	0.4	0.3
Total	34.5	34.8	34.6	34.4	36.5
Procter & Gamble					
Folgers	24.0	23.6	24.9	26.2	27.0
Hills Brothers					
Hills Brothers	6.0	6.7	7.4	8.1	8.4
Chock Full O'Nuts	4.2	4.2	5.0	5.8	5.4
Coca-Cola					
Butternut	1.8	1.7	1.5	1.4	1.5
Maryland Club	1.0	1.0	1.0	1.0	1.0
Total	2.8	2.7	2.5	2.4	2.5
Subtotal	71.5	72.0	74.4	76.9	79.8
All others	28.5	28.0	25.6	23.1	20.2
Grand total	100.0	100.0	100.0	100.0	100.0

*Electra-Perk is roughly 6% all years.

Fig. 9.1. Coffee market shares. Reprinted with permission from *Advertising Age*, September 15, 1986. Copyright Crain Communications, Inc. All rights reserved.

Sales research is another important subset of marketing research and includes such activities as evaluating sales policies, setting sales quotas, and measuring the effectiveness of the sales staff. Consumer research studies consumer attitudes, reactions, and preferences, and advertising research evaluates the advertising program used to promote products, and includes copy and media research as well as the evaluation of advertising effectiveness. Finally, corporate and economic research are used to consider the product in the context of the company itself, which in turn is examined in the context of the economy as a whole.

Not all companies practice all types of marketing research. A survey of some 1,300 companies engaged in marketing research showed that the most common types of research activities were measurement of market potential, determination of market characteristics, market share analysis, sales analysis, competitive product studies, short-range economic forecasts, and research on new product acceptance and potential.[13]

PRIMARY AND SECONDARY DATA

Researchers use both primary and secondary data. Primary data are originated and gathered for the specific problem being considered. While the fit between data and problem is good, this advantage is offset by the time, cost, and skill it takes to collect primary data. Secondary data, on the other hand, are data that already exist. They are useful because they are often inexpensive and easy to obtain, but they, too, have drawbacks. The fit between marketing problem and secondary data may be none too good, and in some instances, the validity of the data may be questionable. They may be dated, or collected in an unreliable or biased manner.

Keeping these warnings in mind, market researchers are advised to inventory and use secondary information whenever possible.

> You must use the work previously done by other people if it is available, and if it is relative to your problem. Otherwise you could very likely be wasting time and money. An almost unlimited amount of material is available from hundreds of sources. You cannot make an exhaustive study of all of these publications, but some are easily obtainable and can be quite useful in the solution of your problems.[14]

Secondary information is provided by the government, by trade organizations and associations, and by commercial publishers. Most libraries are particularly strong in these areas, and constitute a rich source of secondary marketing information. Some major secondary information sources will be described later in this chapter.

More specialized than the rather general secondary sources described above are *"off-the-shelf" market research studies*. Although not tailor-made to meet a particular company's specific market research needs, they are often highly specialized and can be extremely useful, particularly to companies not prepared to embark on expensive primary research. Several types of off-the-shelf studies have been identified, including standard research reports, reports produced by securities analysts, and off-the-shelf surveys and audits. Most frequently, librarians will be asked to help identify standard market research reports.

Standard market research reports are generally produced from secondary information sources available at many libraries—census data and trade publications, for example—and from primary data gathered from interviews and investigation. The reports, which are generally 100 to 200 pages long, may cost as little as $200 or as much as $15,000 or more, depending on depth of coverage, data used, and expertise needed to compile the reports. Clearly, the cost of these publications will preclude their addition to most libraries. Although these reports fall outside the scope and budget of most collections, librarians should be able to help patrons identify them. Some trade publications and periodical indexes list selected reports, but one of the most comprehensive listings is contained in the following publication.

FINDEX; the Directory of Market Research Reports, Studies, and Surveys. Bethesda, Md.: NSA Directories, 1979- . Annual, with midyear supplement.

FINDEX includes some 11,000 consumer, market, and industry studies, polls, audits, and company reports. Arrangement is by broad industry and subject category, and each entry features title, description, publisher, date, number of pages, and price. Since most of the publications listed in *FINDEX* are not available in libraries, some librarians fear that its presence will confuse and ultimately frustrate library users. Whether or not librarians choose to add this title to their own collections, they should be aware that it exists, and that it can be found in many large business reference collections. *FINDEX* is also available as an online database.

Another way in which librarians can keep abreast of such reports is by asking to be put on the mailing list for *The Information Catalog*, a free, bimonthly publication published by FIND/SVP.[15]

The Information Catalog. New York: FIND/SVP. Bimonthly.

The Information Catalog is primarily an advertising device issued by one of the major publishers of off-the-shelf market studies. It combines descriptions of recently published market research studies, securities analysts' reports, newsletters and seminars, and books and reference sources. Prices, ordering information, and ordering cards are also included. Although many libraries will never acquire the reports it lists, the *Catalog* is useful for identifying current industry trends (see figure 9.2). Further, since FIND/SVP was the original publisher of *FINDEX*, readers unfamiliar with that publication can get a general idea of its coverage by scanning a few issues of the *Catalog*. Although *FINDEX* covers far more publications, the information it contains is quite similar to that available in the *Catalog*.

Good-For-You Snacks   ∎ NEW!
Segment boosts $23 billion snack industry.

Sales of snacks perceived as healthy grew 17% to $740 million last year, and expectations are that this is a segment which will continue to grow well into the 1990s. Snack firms are responding with new products, and repositioning existing ones.

FIND/SVP's study of "good-for-you" snacks examines granola bars, dried and dehydrated fruits, popcorn and a variety of less established but popular products (rice cakes, corn nuts, soy chips). Potato chip manufacturers' answers to healthy snacks are also included.

The study profiles main competitors in each category (Quaker Oats, General Mills, Ralston Purina, Carnation, Kellogg, Hershey, Del Monte, General Mills, Sunkist Growers/Lipton, Sun Diamond), as well as some of the up-and-coming smaller players. It includes current market share and sales figures and growth estimates through 1995. Consumer usage, product trends, advertising and promotional strategies are highlighted.
AA150   February, 1987   c. 200 pages $1,250

Fig. 9.2. Typical entry, *The Information Catalog*. Reprinted by permission of FIND/SVP from *The Information Catalog*, January/February 1987, p. 3.

Three of the major producers of off-the-shelf market research studies are Frost & Sullivan, Predicasts, and FIND/SVP. Another company, Fairchild, publishes research studies that are briefer, somewhat more superficial, and far less expensive. The focus is on retail trade, and specific reports cover such markets as footwear, major appliances and electric housewares, and athletic equipment and clothing. Libraries serving clientele with interest in retail trade may want to consider adding these inexpensive studies to their collections.

If neither secondary data nor off-the-shelf studies are sufficient, firms may need to generate primary research data. Techniques used for gathering primary data include surveys, observation, and field experiments.

1. *Surveys.* Answers to questions are sought through telephone or personal, face-to-face interviews, or through the mail. Generally, a specific list of questions or a questionnaire is prepared and mailed. Validity and reliability of these surveys are vital considerations.

2. *Observation.* Here the consumer is observed in the act of purchasing. Sometimes films are taken and analyzed. Candid camera is actually an observation technique.

3. *Field Experiments.* These may involve either the survey method, the observation method, or both. The main characteristic is a more rigorous research design, often using sample control groups and sophisticated statistical techniques.[16]

Although large companies with highly skilled marketing staff may elect to do their own primary marketing research, often they hire other companies to do it for them. A. C. Nielsen, for example, audits the sales of items sold at drugstores and grocery stores at the request of specific customers.

MARKETING ASSOCIATIONS

Marketers are interested in the activities of two major types of associations: trade and professional. Trade associations represent diverse and wide-ranging industries. The Health Industry Manufacturers Association, for example, serves manufacturers of medical devices, while the National Association of Brick Distributors represents distributors and dealers of bricks and other clay products. The Headwear Institute of America represents wholesalers and suppliers of men's hats, and the National Association of Diaper Services is composed of owners of diaper rental and laundry services. What these associations have in common in addition to the other services that they provide is that they commonly collect and compile data from their members that are extremely useful to market researchers. Sometimes the information collected is published and made available commercially, as with the *Annual Statistical Report* published by the American Iron and Steel Institute.

Often large associations have divisions or sections that focus on marketing, and some industries are represented by associations whose sole function is marketing. Some of these associations are the American Floral Marketing Council, the Bank Marketing Association, and the Automotive Market Research Council.

Trade associations provide unique and highly specialized information about specific industries and should not be overlooked by the conscientious market researcher or the librarian seeking to build a comprehensive collection in a particular industry or group of industries. Since standard bibliographic works do not ordinarily include these publications, it may be necessary to identify issuing associations using the *Encyclopedia of Business Information Sources*, the *Encyclopedia of Associations*, or *National Trade and Professional Associations of the United States*.

Professional marketing associations promote advertising and marketing, conduct research, set standards, and, in many instances, publish journals, directories, and bibliographies. Among these associations are the Marketing Science Institute, the Business/ Professional Advertising Association, and the Association of National Advertisers. Two of the most important are the American Marketing Association and the Advertising Research Foundation.

The American Marketing Association has some 46,000 members, including educators, marketing and marketing research executives, advertisers, and sales and promotion specialists. It offers conferences and seminars to its members, fosters research, and promotes the interests of its members. In addition, it publishes several periodicals, including the scholarly *Journal of Marketing Research*, the *Journal of Marketing*, which includes both scholarly and applied research, and a biweekly newsletter, *Marketing News*. It also publishes occasional books, monographs, and pamphlets on marketing as well as a series of bibliographies on key marketing topics such as marketing distribution, selling, and small business marketing. The AMA, the leading professional marketing association, includes local chapters and over 300 collegiate chapters in addition to the activities carried on at the national level.

The Advertising Research Foundation is a nonprofit organization whose membership is comprised of advertisers, advertising agencies, the media, and colleges and universities. Its purpose is

to further scientific practices and promote greater effectiveness of advertising and marketing by means of objective and impartial research; develop new research methods and techniques; analyze and evaluate existing methods and techniques, and define proper applications; establish research standards, criteria, and reporting methods.[17]

The Advertising Research Foundation compiles statistics and publishes the *Journal of Advertising Research* as well as bibliographies, monographs, and reports.

REGULATION OF MARKETING

Marketing is regulated at the federal, state, and local levels. Federal laws prohibit price fixing, false or misleading advertising, and deceptive packaging and labeling. Several agencies administer these laws and exercise some measure of control over marketing. Prime among these are the Federal Trade Commission (FTC), the Food and Drug Administration (FDA), and the Federal Communications Commission (FCC).

Federal Trade Commission

The Federal Trade Commission was established in 1914 as an independent administrative agency.

> Although the duties of the Commission are many and varied under the law, the foundation of public policy underlying all these duties is essentially the same: to prevent the free enterprise system from being fettered by monopoly or restraints on trade or corrupted by unfair or deceptive trade practices.[18]

The FTC issues advisory opinions, sets industry guidelines, and establishes trade regulation rules. It has jurisdiction over false and misleading advertising, and has a number of ways of dealing with advertisers involved in deceptive advertising.

> A simple procedure without formal complaint and hearings is to obtain a letter of voluntary compliance from an advertiser stating that the advertisement in question will be discontinued. After a formal complaint has been issued by the Commission, a consent order may be issued in which the advertiser agrees to stop the practice without an admission of guilt. If, through formal hearings, the FTC finds the advertiser guilty of deception, the FTC may issue an order to cease and desist from such practice. The Commission also publicizes the complaints and cease and desist orders it issues. This adverse publicity for the advertiser proves to be an important weapon for the FTC. When dealing with *alleged deception* in advertising, the FTC considers a number of questions. At each point, a decision is made to either drop the matter or proceed to another decision point until the matter is finally settled.[19]

In 1981, for example, the FTC issued a consent order to Ted Bates & Company, Inc., an advertising agency that was hired by Standard Brands to promote sales of one of its products, Fleischmann's margarine. In advertisements for Fleischmann's it was implied or represented that

a. When a doctor chooses margarine, chances are it's Fleischmann's;

b. Twice as many doctors recommend Fleischmann's margarine as any other margarine;

c. Twice as many doctors personally use Fleischmann's margarine as any other brand of margarine;

d. Twice as many doctors recommend and personally use Fleischmann's margarine as any other brand of margarine;

e. Every 15 seconds, a doctor recommends Fleischmann's margarine.[20]

The advertisements substantiated these claims by alluding to the results of "a recent survey." Upon investigation, the FTC found that the survey did not prove many of the claims made in the advertisement. It discovered that

   a.   Of those survey respondents who were asked the question, "Which brand(s) of margarine do you recommend?", most (84.5%) did not state that they recommended Fleischmann's margarine;

   b.   Of those survey respondents who were asked the question, "Which brand(s) of margarine do you recommend?", most (at least 67.5%) did not recommend a specific brand of margarine;

   c.   Of those survey respondents who were asked, "Do you use margarine at home? If yes, which brand?", most (82.2%) did not state that they personally use Fleischmann's margarine;

   d.   Of those survey respondents who were asked the question, "Do you use margarine at home? If yes, which brand?", nearly one-half (47.1%) did not state that they used margarine or were unaware of the specific name brand of the margarine they personally used;

   e.   The survey respondents neither were asked nor stated the frequency of their recommendations of Fleischmann's margarine to their patients or to anyone else.[21]

The resulting consent order required, among other things, that Ted Bates & Company cease referring to any test or survey of "experts" or "consumers" while making representations regarding the "performance, benefit, choice or superiority of a product, unless the referenced test or survey has been specifically designated, executed, and evaluated by experts and provides substantiation for the representations."[22] The firm was further barred from representing that survey respondents used a particular brand without disclosing that an equal or greater percentage of the respondents had not indicated any brand preferences. Ted Bates & Company was also required to maintain records substantiating advertising claims for a three-year period.

The FTC publishes a number of consumer guides and guidelines for business people to use. The FTC Manual for Businesses series, for example, includes guidelines on writing readable warranties, complying with FTC mail order rules, and advertising consumer credit.

Food and Drug Administration

The Food and Drug Administration, part of the Department of Health and Human Services, is a scientific regulatory agency that acts to ensure consumer protection against a broad range of products, primarily food, drugs, cosmetics, and medical devices. As with the Federal Trade Commission, the FDA is concerned with preventing deception through misrepresentation of these products. The FDA, however, concentrates on false labeling and misrepresentation, while the FTC focuses on false advertising. *Labeling* includes not only the physical label but also any printed material accompanying the product.

The FDA approves labeling for prescription medicines to assure that physicians are fully informed about the drugs they prescribe and, in recent years, has issued regulations requiring nutrition labeling on many foods. In addition, the FDA now requires that the ingredients used in cosmetics be listed on the product labels. It also requires that warnings be included on the labels of products that are potentially hazardous. In 1979, for example, it required that warnings be included on the labels of permanent hair dye products containing an ingredient found to cause cancer in laboratory animals.

While the FDA will not take action to correct individual complaints, it will attempt to correct the situation that causes them. The following describes the preliminary steps taken by the FDA against a so-called weight-loss cream.

> The latest twist in the body wrap bonanza is a product called LaCreme, a cream to be applied to parts of the body where loss of inches is desired.... A leaflet for the product claims: "Lose up to two inches from those problem areas in just one hour...."

> Promotional literature distributed to retail outlets, such as department stores and specialty salons, claimed that FDA had approved or classified LaCreme as a skin toner, tightener, and smoother. In truth, FDA had never been given an opportunity to evaluate the product and had no idea what it contained.

> FDA advised a distributor of LaCreme that, based on the product's labeling, it should be regulated as drug because it claimed to alter the size, shape, or conformity of the body—a drug function as defined by the federal Food, Drug and Cosmetic Act. When the distributor contended that LaCreme was a cosmetic and therefore not subject to safety and efficacy requirements, FDA replied that claims of even temporary reduction of body measurements were not appropriate to a cosmetic.[23]

At the time the article was written, the company that manufactured LaCreme had not replied to the FDA's comments, but many of the department stores that carried LaCreme stopped selling it.

Sometimes if the situation is not corrected, the FDA will confiscate the product. Companies found guilty of false labeling or misbranding are guilty of misdemeanors and may be subject to fine.

Like the Federal Trade Commission, the FDA publishes a number of reports, studies, pamphlets, guides, and serials for its primary constituency—consumers, business people, physicians, and others involved in the production, prescription, and consumption of drugs, medical devices, food, and cosmetics.

Federal Communications Commission

The Federal Communications Commission was established in 1934 as an independent federal agency. One of the FCC's major activities is the regulation of broadcasting by granting and revoking licenses.

> The FCC's guiding rule is that radio and tv must operate in the public interest, convenience, and necessity. Specifically, it concerns itself with the quality of advertising and seeks to prevent obscene, profane, fraudulent, and deceptive advertising, all of which are obviously not in the public interest, convenience, or necessity. For the same reason, it also concerns itself with the quantity of time devoted to advertising.

> The FCC may suspend the license of any radio or tv station that is transmitting profane or obscene words. This severe threat largely eliminates any violation of this sort, but it should be noted that profanity and obscenity are constantly subject to redefinition as social mores change. Fraudulent and deceptive radio and tv advertising, on the other hand, is generally handled by the FTC's taking action against the advertiser. When the FCC receives complaints against advertisers, it notifies the station, and the station usually sees that the advertiser corrects the situation. If the station ignores the complaint, the FCC takes this fact into consideration when the license comes up for renewal.[24]

Other Government Agencies

Although the FTC, FDA, and FCC are the major agencies involved in the direct regulation of marketing activities, other federal agencies are involved as well. The Postal Service, for example, regulates not only "obscene, scurrilous, or otherwise offensive" mail, but also regulates against the use of the mails to defraud.

The Bureau of Alcohol, Tobacco, and Firearms of the Treasury Department reviews proposed advertisements of alcoholic beverages for its approval or disapproval. If advertisements that raise its disapproval are not corrected to the bureau's satisfaction, it can revoke the producer's license to sell alcoholic beverages. In addition, considerable adverse publicity can be attached to these activities.

State and local laws also regulate marketing activities. These laws vary considerably from one locale to another in their content, quality, and depth of coverage, and as a result can be confusing. They are important, however, because most federal laws come into effect only when interstate commerce is involved.

MARKETING REFERENCE SOURCES

Marketing reference sources are abundant. They include many different types of materials—statistical sources, government documents, directories, and databases. Some of the best places to identify these items are the bibliographic sources listed below.

Guides and Bibliographies

There are two outstanding guides to the literature of marketing.

Frank, Nathalie D., and John V. Ganly. **Data Sources for Business and Market Analysis**. 3rd ed. Metuchen, N.J.: Scarecrow, 1983. 470p.

Goldstucker, Jac L., and Otto R. Echemendia. **Marketing Information: A Professional Reference Guide**. 2nd ed. Atlanta: Georgia State University, College of Business Administration, 1987. 436p.

The third edition of *Data Sources for Business and Market Analysis* lists virtually all of the major sources of external secondary marketing information. It includes chapters arranged by issuing organization (e.g., Census Bureau, professional and trade associations) and by publication type (e.g., services and directories). Each entry includes fairly detailed annotations and may be preceded by lengthy introductory sections. An index is included.

Marketing Information is intended as both a directory and a sourcebook for all areas of marketing. Part 1 is the directory, a guide to associations and organizations, arranged by broad subject classification such as "Research Centers" and "Continuing Education in Marketing." Although some of the information this section contains is available in such standard reference works as the *Encyclopedia of Associations* and the *United States Government Manual*, other parts include information that may not be readily available in small or medium-sized business reference collections. The entry for Market Research Corporation of America reprinted in figure 9.3 is taken from the "Marketing Research, Service, and Consulting Organizations" section of part 1.

Part 2 lists and briefly annotates books, manuals, directories, periodicals, newsletters, databases, and nonprint materials, arranged by subject areas such as pricing, physical distribution, and sales promotion. While Frank and Ganly's strength lies in its more thorough consideration of specific sources, replete with explanations and background information, Goldstucker's value comes from the detailed subject categories under which specific information sources are identified. Together, these guides provide almost comprehensive access to major sources of secondary marketing information and to the organizations that generate this information.

Market Research Corporation of America (MRCA)
4 Landmark Sq (2nd Floor)
Stamford CT 06901 (203) 324-9600

Dr David B Learner Pres
H C "Peter" Judd, Jr Sr VP Marketing
Jose Anstey VP Soft Goods Services

Comprehensive diary panel service—data, reporting, analysis. National Consumer Panel provides information on purchasing of food products, HBAs. Menu Census service—food preparation and consumption behavior. Soft Goods Service—consumer purchasing of textiles, apparel accessories. Local market panels, special studies available.

Branch Office

-Market Research Corporation
of America (MRCA)
2215 Sanders Rd
Northbrook IL 60062 (312) 480-9600
Channing Stowell, III VP Menu Census
Laurence N Gold VP National Consumer Panel
Dr I J Abrams VP Special Projects

Fig. 9.3. Sample listing, *Marketing Information*. Reprinted by permission from *Marketing Information: A Professional Reference Guide,* © 1982.

Two bibliographies are also useful.

Robinson, Larry M., and Roy D. Adler. **Marketing Megaworks: The Top 150 Books and Articles**. New York: Praeger, 1987. 211p.

What's New in Advertising and Marketing. New York: Special Libraries Association, Advertising and Marketing Division, 1945- . 10 issues/year.

Marketing Megaworks lists and annotates books and articles deemed to have had a significant impact on marketing study and research. Using citation analysis to identify major works published between 1972 and 1976 and the awarding of the *Journal of Marketing*'s Alpha Kappa Psi and Harold Maynard Awards to select articles published between 1975 and 1984, the authors describe 150 such "megaworks." The arrangement is by author, with annotations ranging from a few paragraphs to more than a page. A series of indexes enables readers to identify publications by title, publication date, and author. Although a subject index is lacking, other indexes permit identification of the most-cited authors, books, and articles and the identification of the recipients of the *Journal of Marketing* awards. *Marketing Megaworks* is a useful introduction to recent marketing literature, and can also serve as a tool for library collection analysis and development.

Another source, issued by the Special Libraries Association's Advertising and Marketing Division, is useful for identifying more current publications. *What's New in Advertising and Marketing* lists by subject new books, periodicals, and trade publications. It includes many titles that are free, usually summaries of market research or pamphlets issued by trade associations, as well as other specialized publications that are not regularly listed or reviewed in standard library selection publications. One issue, for example, included a book on American breweries, published by Bullworks, as well as a history of the Goodyear Company and the highlights of a *Fortune*-sponsored corporate communications seminar. In addition, it offered a personal computer study, an update of a study of the American health system, and a survey of promotional practices, all of which were free. For the librarian seeking to build a comprehensive collection about a particular industry or a broad-based marketing collection, this inexpensive publication is extremely helpful.

The American Marketing Association publishes a series of bibliographies, each dealing with a specific aspect of marketing, such as selling and sales management, and marketing and the black consumer. These publications are inexpensive and can be ordered directly from the AMA.

Dictionaries and Encyclopedias

Although most standard business dictionaries include definitions of key marketing terms, there are special dictionaries that focus solely on marketing or on some aspect of marketing, such as advertising.

Shapiro, Irving J. **Dictionary of Marketing Terms**. 4th ed. Totowa, N.J.: Rowman and Littlefield, 1981. 276p.

Imber, Jane. **Dictionary of Advertising and Direct Mail Terms**. New York: Barron's Educational Series, 1987. 514p.

Moss, Julie M., ed. **Ayer Glossary of Advertising and Related Terms**. 2nd ed. Philadelphia: Ayer, 1977. 219p.

Graham, Irvin. **Encyclopedia of Advertising**. 2nd ed. New York: Fairchild, 1969. 494p.

Beacham, Walton. **Beacham's Marketing Reference**. Washington, D.C.: Research Publishing, 1986. 2v.

Foremost among these is the *Dictionary of Marketing Terms*, which defines over 5,000 marketing terms, ranging from *abandonment of mark* to *zero population growth*. Special emphasis has been given to concepts from the behavioral sciences, marketing research, and managerial decision-making techniques, and definitions have been written with nonmarketing specialists in mind.

Advertising has such an extensive vocabulary of its own that several advertising dictionaries have been published. Two of the best are the *Dictionary of Advertising and Direct Mail Terms*, which alphabetically lists words and phrases used in broadcast, print, direct mail, trade, and classified advertising, and the *Ayer Glossary of Advertising and Related Terms*, which groups terms into a general section and into special sections dealing with television and radio, research, and printing.

Although dated, the *Encyclopedia of Advertising* is still useful to advertising practitioners and lay people. Its entries range from a sentence or two to several pages, and while its section on computers is obsolete and should be avoided, other sections remain useful. Its 1,100 entries describe everything from specific type styles to advertising slogans. Some illustrations are included.

Beacham's Marketing Reference is a collection of articles by experts. In all, some 200 different topics are covered, ranging from subliminal advertising to brand awareness, from market segmentation to channels of distribution. Each article follows a standard format, presenting an overview of the topics, followed by examples, discussion of benefits, implementation, evaluation, and a conclusion. In addition, small business applications are described, and relevant references, software, and databases are identified. Related topics and terms are also listed. *Beacham's* concludes with an appendix of software applications and an index that differentiates between principal and secondary sources. It is a publication well worth acquiring.

Directories

Most of the standard business directories described in chapter 2 will be of interest to marketers. The *Million Dollar Directory*, for example, and *Thomas Register of American*

Manufacturers are used heavily by sales, distribution, and market research staff. In addition, trade directories that focus on specific industries, such as the *Directory of Department Stores* and the *Directory of Electrical Wholesale Distributors*, are extremely important and can be identified using the *Directory of Directories* or the *Encyclopedia of Business Information Sources*.

Since standard business and trade directories were discussed at length in chapter 2, this section focuses on titles that deal specifically with marketing and advertising.

American Marketing Association. New York Chapter. **Green Book: International Directory of Marketing Research Houses and Services**. New York: The Association, New York Chapter, 1963- . Annual.

American Marketing Association. **International Membership Directory and Marketing Services Guide**. Chicago: The Association, 1983- . Annual.

Standard Directory of Advertising Agencies. Wilmette, Ill.: National Register Publishing, 1917- . Triannual.

One of the best known of these publications is the *Green Book: International Directory of Marketing Research Houses and Services*. The *Green Book* lists and describes services offered by major marketing firms. Foreign as well as U.S. marketing research firms are entered alphabetically in a single listing. Each entry includes the firm's address and telephone number, the names of its key officers, and a brief description of the services it offers. In addition to the main section, the directory includes a geographic listing, a principal personnel index, a computer programs listing, and a classification of companies by type of service offered.

The American Marketing Association's *International Membership Directory and Marketing Services Guide* lists and describes organizations offering many different types of marketing services. It identifies firms involved in marketing research, direct marketing, merchandising, audiovisual communications, advertising, health care marketing, public relations, and consulting. Organizations are grouped together by type of service, and each section has its own index. The *Roster* also includes alphabetical, geographical, and advertisers' indexes as well as a complete list of current AMA members.

The *Standard Directory of Advertising Agencies*, also known as the *Agency Red Book*, contains current information about 4,400 American advertising agencies and their branches, including their names and addresses, specialization, major accounts, and key staff members. Figure 9.4 (see page 202) illustrates the information included in each listing.

In addition to the main section, which is arranged alphabetically by advertising agency, the directory has geographical listings of agencies by states and by foreign countries, a list of the largest advertising agencies, and a special market index, which lists agencies specializing in black and hispanic markets and special fields, such as medical and resort and travel. It is an essential resource for those directly involved in advertising, and can be found in many business reference collections. Although three issues are published annually, smaller libraries may wish to limit their subscription to one per year.

Equally important is the *Standard Directory of Advertisers*, a companion directory described in chapter 2. It focuses on companies and other organizations that advertise, and includes trade names, the types of media used for advertising, the advertising agencies employed and, frequently, annual advertising budgets.

Periodicals

Marketers turn to periodical literature to keep current with news about specific industries of interest to them, with developments in marketing and allied fields, and with the economy generally. Some may subscribe to one or two key publications, while others have extensive periodicals collections at their disposal. This section begins by examining the indexes and abstracts used to identify relevant articles and concludes with discussion of some major periodicals in the field.

Standard Listing Elements

Explanation of Listing Elements

Indicates that the agency has
provided the information

Employees and Year Founded

*Association Membership, etc.
(See Index of Abbreviations)*

Agency's Specialization

Annual Billing with breakdown

Top Management

Creative/Marketing

Other

Account Executives

Branch Office

Accounts

  *(Companies serviced by ABC
  Advertising Co., Inc.)*

  (✔) *New account acquired since
  last issue of directory*

*

ABC ADVERTISING CO., INC.
  1234 Second St., Anywheretown, AK 55667
  Tel.: 456-339-0123

Emp.: 22   Year founded: 1963
National Agency Associations: AAAA—MCA
Agency Specializes In:
Approx. Annual Billing $7,800,000

Breakdown of Gross Billings by Media:
  Newsp.$1,170,000; Bus. Publs. $1,638,000; Farm
  Publs. $156,000;TV $2,262,000; Radio $1,560,000;
  Mags. $390,000; Outdoor $78,000; Transit $78,000;
  Collateral $468,000

A. A. Anderson .... Chm. Bd.
B. B. Brown .... Pres.
Bea Glaberson .... Exec. V. P.
C. C. Charles .... Sr. V. P.
Jean Jones .... V. P., Sec.-Treas.
John Smith .... V. P., Creative Dir.
Robert Robertson .... V. P. & Acct. Supvr.
Fritz Elliot .... Mktg. Dir.
Sydney Simms .... Copy Chief
Jeffrey Rotman .... Radio & TV Dir.
Frank Van Gogh .... Art Dir.
Guy Oas .... Mdsg. Dir.
Don Ellis .... Media Dir.
Bryan Firth .... Pub. Rel. Dir.
Clem Harris .... Time/Space Buyer
Carol Schneider .... Prod. Mgr.
M. M. Miller .... Librarian

Acct. Execs.: C. C. Charles, Edna Green, John Smith,
Robert Robertson

ABC Advertising Co., Inc.
  1010 Tenth Ave., Lavillage, HI 60309
  Tel.: 789-545-4545
  Elliot S. Miller .... V. P. & Gen. Mgr.

Adams Abrasive Systems, Inc., Minneapolis, MN Mfr. & Distr. of
  Metal Working Equip.
B.A.H. Industries, Inc., Boston, MA Chemicals, Oil & Gas
✔
Diamond Drilling, Inc., Butte, MT Oil Contractors
Elcon Industrial Gases, Murray Hill, NJ Oxygen Nitrogen
✔
Hatfield Products Co., Orange, CA Indus. Chemicals
National Plastics Co., Pittsburgh. PA Indus. Plastics
Regal Brass, Inc., Glenview, IL Couplings, Valves
✔
Wilson Devices Co., Los Angeles, CA Heavy Construction &
  Mining Prods.

Fig. 9.4. Typical listing, *Standard Directory of Advertising Agencies*. Reprinted by permission from *Standard Directory of Advertising Agencies*, Feb.-May 1986 edition.

For the most part, American marketers and librarians seeking articles on specific marketing topics will need to consult general business indexes (see chapter 3) such as *Business Periodicals Index*. The *Index*, for example, includes relevant articles under the headings, "Market Analysis," "Market Penetration," and "Market Statistics" as well as under headings relating to sales, marketing channels, and specific industries. It is particularly strong for articles about marketing per se, and for scholarly articles as well.

The best index for all-around market coverage, however, is *Predicasts F&S Index United States*. Its coverage of industries, products, and specific companies is unsurpassed. The Predicasts "product code" for marketing is 9914; additional digits added to the base code treat specific aspects of marketing. Pricing policy, for example, is 991417, sales planning is 991434, and television advertising research is 9914234. In addition, the category,

"Market Information" is often used as a subset of a particular product category. Use and arrangement of the *F&S Index* are described in chapter 3, but it is worth emphasizing here that for specific product marketing information, *F&S* is first-rate.

Predicasts Overview of Markets and Technology or *PROMT* (see chapter 3) is extremely useful for its coverage of new products and technologies, market trends, market share and statistics, government regulation, research and development, and general industry news. Unlike most Predicasts publications, which are arranged by SIC-based product codes, *PROMT* is arranged by broad industry categories, including such industries as drugs and pharmaceuticals, paper and pulp, and plastic products. Further, while it covers fewer articles than the *F&S Index, PROMT* offers abstracts. Some abstracts include statistics culled from the articles themselves.

Also worth consulting is the "General News" section of the *Wall Street Journal Index*, which generally includes several pages of articles indexed under such headings as "Advertising," "Marketing," and "Sales." Each Thursday edition of the *Journal* includes a feature on the first page of the second section focusing on some aspect of marketing—the marketing of military electronics, for example, or of gourmet TV dinners.

Marketing periodicals are abundant. Some deal with specific aspects of marketing, such as *Industrial Distribution, Journal of Consumer Research*, and *Direct Marketing Magazine*. Some, including the *Journal of Marketing* and the *Journal of Marketing Research*, are scholarly journals; and others, such as *Advertising Age, Retail Advertising Week, Sales & Marketing Management*, and *Women's Wear Daily*, are trade publications. Libraries may not collect all of these serials, but many subscribe to *Advertising Age* and *Sales & Marketing Management*.

Advertising Age. Chicago: Crain-Communications, 1930- . Weekly, except semiweekly the 4th weeks in March and September.

Sales & Marketing Management. New York: Bill Communications, Inc., 1918- . 16/year.

Advertising Age is a newspaper that provides current coverage of advertising and marketing news. It includes descriptions of current advertising campaigns, news of decisions of government regulatory agencies, consumer trends, and personnel changes in the industry. Issues have, for example, included reviews of television commercials by film critics Gene Siskel and Roger Ebert, analyses of political ads, and special reports on international marketing and advertising research. *Advertising Age* is particularly useful for the special issues it publishes, including those with information on top liquor brands, coffee consumption, leading ad agencies and market research firms, and market share for specific products.

Sales & Marketing Management covers all aspects of marketing—product development, packaging, place decisions, promotion, and pricing. It is a major publication, and includes articles on specific marketing activities and on individual companies as well as personnel changes and trade news. It is best known, however, for its annual market surveys, which are included as special issues. These include the two-part *Survey of Buying Power*, the *Survey of Selling Costs*, and the *Management Survey of U.S. Industrial and Commercial Buying Power*. These surveys are described in the following section.

Statistics

Good marketing research is based on current and reliable statistical data. Market segmentation, for example, requires the use of statistics to define geographic, demographic, psychographic, and sociographic boundaries for market segments. The selection of a new plant site will be influenced by statistics on population and labor conditions, while the final decision about the location of a new business such as a pizza franchise or a computer store may in large part be based on statistics regarding the location of other, similar businesses in the area and the age, income, and educational levels of the population. Statistics are, in short, vital for effective marketing research.

Statistics relating to consumers and to industrial users are indispensable tools in the hands of distributors and manufacturers.... Used correctly, these statistics will assist management in making sound business decisions in such areas as market shares, the allocation of advertising expenditures, the alignment of sales territories for the purpose of achieving maximum sales at minimum costs, and the selection of sites for plants, stores, or distribution centers.[25]

Marketing statistics fall primarily into two main categories: demographic and economic. Although trade associations and commercial publishers make statistical data available, their major producer is the federal government.

FEDERAL GOVERNMENT STATISTICS

One of the best ways to identify and locate federal statistical data is by using guides. Frank and Ganly's *Data Sources for Business and Market Analysis* includes considerable information on statistical publications relevant to market research. Another useful source is published by the federal government.

U.S. Dept. of Commerce. International Trade Administration. **Measuring Markets: A Guide to the Use of Federal and State Statistical Data**. Washington, D.C.: Government Printing Office, 1979. 101p.

Measuring Markets provides an overview of the major types of statistical data gathered, compiled, and published by federal and state government agencies. It is particularly useful to the novice researcher who needs to understand in a general way the types of statistics available and their potential uses. In addition to tables that list basic state and federal publications, it includes cases that demonstrate the application of federal statistics in market measurement. One, for example, describes the use made of census data to help a firm select a county in which to locate a new supermarket. Another discusses the use of statistics to analyze sales performance and to determine sales potential for a chain of shoe stores. Each of the 12 cases presented includes information on the marketing problem, data sources, and the procedure used to arrive at a solution, and is accompanied by tables that show relevant statistics culled from government publications.

Although *Measuring Markets* lists many key statistical publications, it is not intended to identify government sources containing specific statistics. Someone looking for statistics on sugar consumption or the export of automobiles, for example, would not find it particularly helpful. There are, however, two major guides providing access to specific government statistics.

The best of these is the *American Statistics Index*, which indexes, lists, and annotates statistical sources published by the federal government (see chapter 6). Since smaller libraries and those lacking extensive federal documents collections may not subscribe to the *American Statistics Index*, another statistical guide should be mentioned. *Statistics Sources* (chapter 6) lists statistics by subject. Its scope is broader than that of the *American Statistics Index*: It includes international, commercial, foreign, and trade statistics as well as those published by the federal government. Many of the sources listed, however, are federal documents.

Almost every statistic that the government publishes is significant for research relating to industrial and consumer markets. The ones that will be most consistently useful and most heavily applied fall into four main categories: population, income, employment, and sales.

Population statistics, gathered, compiled, and published by the Bureau of the Census, are available in great detail and are basic to most marketing research.

Population change affects such business activities as the production of homes and associated durable goods for new households being formed by young adults, as well as health care and leisure products for the retired and elderly. The location of retail firms near their markets, the definition of sales territories, and the choice of what products and services to offer depend on information about the potential customers.[26]

A manufacturer of lawn mowers, for example, might consult population statistics for data on the number of households and individuals and their geographic location. Also of interest would be the number of owner-occupied housing units. With these facts, the company would be able to estimate potential sales for its lawn mowers, an important first step in marketing research. The *Census of Population*, the *Census of Population and Housing*, and the *Current Population Reports* series are major sources of population statistics.

Income statistics, which indicate consumer buying power, are also made available by the Census Bureau, both in decennial census publications and in special reports and studies. Series P-60 of the *Current Population Reports*, for example, deals solely with consumer income, while Series P-23 frequently includes studies that feature income and socioeconomic data. The most detailed information, however, is published in the decennial censuses.

The Bureau of Labor Statistics, the Internal Revenue Service, and the Bureau of Economic Analysis all publish income data as well. Major publications issued by these agencies are described in chapter 6 and in appendixes B, C, F, and G.

Sales and employment statistics are indicators of company performance and market size, and can be put to many uses. They can, for example, be used to measure sales effectiveness.

A wholesale company can prepare from its sales record a tabular presentation of percentage of sales, by kind-of-business for each county within a state. A similar presentation can be prepared by using the data presented in the *Census of Wholesale Trade*. By comparing the two tabulations the company can isolate those areas in which it is above or below the norm of sales for the individual territories.[27]

Federal employment statistics are produced primarily by the Bureau of Labor Statistics and the Census Bureau; sales statistics are most frequently taken from the economic censuses, the *Survey of Current Business*, and related reports.

COMMERCIAL STATISTICAL PUBLICATIONS

Government publications are unrivaled for their depth and breadth of statistical information; no commercial publisher comes close to matching them. There are, however, some problems related to using documents. Many libraries and market researchers do not have a full complement of government statistical publications on hand, and for others, combing through several documents to gather data may be tedious and inefficient. In addition, some of the needed information simply may not be available from the government.

Commercially published marketing guides, based on government statistics but supplemented with publisher-generated statistical estimates, are extremely useful. Several are available, but the titles listed below are particularly important and can be found in most business reference collections.

Editor & Publisher Market Guide. New York: Editor & Publisher, 1924- . Annual.

Sales & Marketing Management. Survey of Buying Power. New York: Bill Communications, 1929- . Annual. (Part I presently a July issue, Part II, an October issue)

Survey of Buying Power Data Service. New York: Sales & Marketing Management, 1977- . Annual.

Rand McNally & Co. **Commercial Atlas & Marketing Guide**. Chicago: Rand McNally, 1876- . Annual.

The Sourcebook of Demographics and Buying Power for Every ZIP Code in the USA. Arlington, Va.: CACI, 1984- . Annual.

The *Editor & Publisher Market Guide* is an annual that gives detailed statistical data for U.S. and Canadian cities publishing one or more daily newspapers. It is divided into four main sections. The first section is a compilation of market ranking tables, based on publisher estimates for the current year showing population, disposable income, total retail sales, total food sales, and income per household. Within each category, entries are arranged by size. Thus, by consulting the "Disposable Income per Household" table, it is possible to identify those metropolitan statistical areas estimated by Editor & Publisher to have the highest disposable income (personal income less taxes) per household.

The second section is individual market surveys for U.S. cities, arranged alphabetically by state and then by city. A state map introduces the survey for each state, and pinpoints the location of daily newspaper cities, the state capital, county seats, and metropolitan statistical areas. The city market data, however, are most heavily used. In all, 14 different items are included for each city, as shown in the listing in figure 9.5 for Bad Axe, Michigan.

It is easy to see why this publication is so popular. Not only does it collect and present statistical data from many government publications, but it also includes data gathered and prepared by the publisher—current population estimates, for example, and the names of specific retail stores and shopping centers. Similar surveys follow for Canada's provinces and newspaper cities. Finally, the *Guide* concludes with sales, population, and income tables.

The *Survey of Buying Power*, another key marketing guide, is one of the three special issues of *Sales & Marketing Management*. It is issued in two parts: the first part, published in July, contains geographically oriented demographic, income, and retail sales statistics for metropolitan areas and counties. It also includes regional and state summary data, tables that rank metropolitan areas by population (general, specific ethnic groups, and specific age groups), number of households, households with effective buying income of $50,000 and over, total retail sales and sales for retail store groups. Section C, "Metro Areas, Counties, Cities" is most frequently used. Figure 9.6 (see page 208), the entry for Hawaii, is typical.

Although the categories used in the population and retail sales tables are self-evident, those used in the income table may need some explanation. "Effective Buying Income," or "EBI," is a classification developed by Sales & Marketing Management (but similar in concept to *disposable income*, a designation used in the *Editor & Publisher Market Guide* and in many other publications), and is defined as personal income less personal tax and nontax payments. In other words, EBI equals spending money, what is left to pay bills, invest, and buy consumer goods *after* taxes and other unavoidable payments—fines and fees—have been paid. Further elaboration is included in the *Survey*; but it should be noted that marketers, like most people, distinguish between the amount of money people earn and the amount they have to spend.

The Effective Buying Income tables also include a "Buying Power Index," or "BPI." The BPI is one of the *Survey*'s most widely used single market measures, particularly useful in estimating demand for mass market products. In reexamining the income table for Hawaii in figure 9.6, one can distinguish clearly between Honolulu County, which has an EBI of .3588, and all other counties in Hawaii, whose combined EBI is a much smaller .0423. Clearly, the most promising market for mass-appeal consumer products in Hawaii would be Honolulu.

Part 2 of the *Survey of Buying Power*, published as an October issue of *Sales & Marketing Management*, includes five-year projections for population, income, and retail sales by states and metropolitan areas. In addition, it has summary rankings for retail sales by major merchandise lines such as footwear and household appliances, as well as population, income, retail sales, and buying power figures for specific newspaper and television markets.

In 1977, Sales & Marketing Management began publishing the *Survey of Buying Power Data Service*. Although the publication consolidates information from both parts of the *Survey of Buying Power*, it also includes additional information and more detailed breakdowns for each category. The *Survey of Buying Power*, for example, lists the adult population by broad age group categories (18-24, 25-34, 35-49, 50 and over). Using the *Data Service*, however, one can determine the number of people, by sex, in nine different groups (0-5, 6-11, 12-17, 18-24, 25-34, 35-44, 45-54, 55-64, 65 and over).

BAD AXE

1 - LOCATION: Huron County, E&P Map D-4. 85 mi. to Port Huron, 60 mi. NE of Bay City.

2 - TRANSPORTATION: Railroads-Chesapeake & Ohio.
Motor Freight Carriers-2.

3 - POPULATION:
Corp. City 80 Cen. 3,184; E&P 85 Est. 3,284
CZ-ABC: (80) 3,184
RTZ-ABC: (80) 39,410
County 80 Cen. 36,459; E&P 85 Est. 36,367
City & RTZ-ABC: (80) 42,594

4 - HOUSEHOLDS:
City 80 Cen. 1,185; E&P 85 Est. 967
County 80 Cen. 12,764; E&P 85 Est. 13,155
CZ-ABC: (80) 1,185
RTZ-ABC: (80) 13,646
City & RTZ-ABC: (80) 14,831

5 - BANKS	NUMBER	DEPOSITS
Commercial	3	$165,900,000
Savings & Loan	1	$130,345,155

6 - PASSENGER AUTOS: County 19,654

7 - ELECTRIC METERS: Residence County 19,134

8 - GAS METERS: Residence County 9,650

9 - PRINCIPAL INDUSTRIES: Industry, No. of Wage Earners (Av. Wkly. Wage)-Machines 1,350 ($250); Food 30 ($190).

10 - CLIMATE: Min. & Max. Temp.-Spring 44-56; Summer 66-77; Fall 48-56; Winter 24-31.

11 - TAP WATER: Hard (22 gr. per gal.); Iron (0.2 parts per million).

12 - RETAILING: Principal Shopping Center-Downtown Bad Axe on Huron Ave. (open til 9 pm on Fri.).
Neighborhood Shopping Centers-Westland-3/4 mile on West Huron (4 stores); Northgate, 1/2 N on M-53 (9 stores).
Principal Shopping Days-Fri., Sat.
Stores Open Evenings-Fri.

13 - RETAIL OUTLETS: Department Stores-Sears; Polewach Stores; Kritzman's; Fishers Big Wheel; Montgomery Ward.
Discount Stores-Mill End Store; Norman's Discount Clothing; K mart.
Variety Stores-Glass; Ben Franklin; Dibble's.
Chain Drug Stores-Perry.
Chain Supermarkets-Farmer Jack; Spartan.

14 - NEWSPAPERS: HURON TRIBUNE (e-mon to fri) 9,154; Mar. 31, 1985 ABC.
Local Contact for Advertising and Merchandising Data: Dennis M. Mesnard, Adv. Dir., HURON TRIBUNE, 211 N. Heistermann, Bad Axe, MI 48413; Tel. (517) 269-6461.
National Representative: Hearst Advertising Service.

Fig. 9.5. Typical listing, *Editor & Publisher Market Guide.* Reprinted by permission of Editor & Publisher Co., Inc., from the 1986 *Editor & Publisher Market Guide.*

HAWAII

HAWAII SaMM ESTIMATES	POPULATION—12/31/85									RETAIL SALES BY STORE GROUP 1985					
METRO AREA County City	Total Population (Thousands)	% Of U.S.	Median Age of Pop.	% of Population by Age Group				Households (Thousands)	Total Retail Sales ($000)	Food ($000)	Eating & Drinking Places ($000)	General Mdse. ($000)	Furniture/ Furnish./ Appliance ($000)	Automotive ($000)	Drug ($000)
				18-24 Years	25-34 Years	35-49 Years	50 & Over								
HONOLULU	828.2	.3439	29.8	14.1	20.1	19.1	20.5	256.4	5,017,488	851,809	919,420	711,912	155,030	684,907	307,406
Honolulu	828.2	.3439	29.8	14.1	20.1	19.1	20.5	256.4	5,017,488	851,809	919,420	711,912	155,030	684,907	307,406
• Honolulu	394.7	.1639	33.0	12.4	20.5	18.9	26.8	141.0	3,632,950	550,472	740,174	525,019	125,242	393,485	202,773
SUBURBAN TOTAL	433.5	.1800	26.9	15.8	19.7	19.2	14.7	115.4	1,384,538	301,337	179,246	186,893	29,788	291,422	104,633
OTHER COUNTIES															
Hawaii	110.6	.0459	31.1	10.0	18.6	17.7	25.1	35.5	634,136	174,640	76,735	46,437	25,617	103,938	34,324
Kauai	44.8	.0186	31.6	9.4	18.6	17.7	26.0	14.0	314,247	88,372	47,867	18,513	9,568	37,354	16,163
Maui	87.7	.0364	31.4	10.0	19.8	18.0	24.9	28.1	717,126	166,705	127,602	66,483	27,339	70,229	30,749
TOTAL METRO COUNTIES	828.2	.3439	29.8	14.1	20.1	19.1	20.5	256.4	5,017,488	851,809	919,420	711,912	155,030	684,907	307,406
TOTAL STATE	1,071.3	.4448	30.1	13.2	19.9	18.8	21.5	334.0	6,682,997	1,281,569	1,171,624	843,345	217,554	896,428	388,642

HAWAII SaMM ESTIMATES	EFFECTIVE BUYING INCOME 1985							HAWAII SaMM ESTIMATES	EFFECTIVE BUYING INCOME 1985						
METRO AREA County City	Total EBI ($000)	Median Hsld. EBI	% of Hslds. by EBI Group: (A) $10,000-$19,999 (B) $20,000-$34,999 (C) $35,000-$49,999 (D) $50,000 & Over				Buying Power Index	**METRO AREA** County City	Total EBI ($000)	Median Hsld. EBI	% of Hslds. by EBI Group: (A) $10,000-$19,999 (B) $20,000-$34,999 (C) $35,000-$49,999 (D) $50,000 & Over				Buying Power Index
			A	B	C	D					A	B	C	D	
HONOLULU	10,194,917	29,532	21.4	25.2	18.8	22.5	.3588	Kauai	468,413	25,873	23.6	30.0	19.4	13.5	.0188
Honolulu	10,194,917	29,532	21.4	25.2	18.8	22.5	.3588	Maui	915,685	24,861	22.2	29.0	16.9	14.3	.0391
• Honolulu	5,410,029	27,729	22.1	25.0	16.5	22.2	.2075								
SUBURBAN TOTAL	4,784,888	31,671	20.4	25.6	21.6	22.9	.1513								
OTHER COUNTIES								TOTAL METRO COUNTIES	10,194,917	29,532	21.4	25.2	18.8	22.5	.3588
Hawaii	1,096,978	22,955	24.7	27.7	15.6	12.9	.0423	TOTAL STATE	12,675,993	28,140	21.9	26.1	18.3	20.4	.4590

Fig. 9.6. Sample listing, *Survey of Buying Power*. Reprinted by permission from the 1986 *Survey of Buying Power*.

While the *Data Service* does include more information than the *Survey of Buying Power*, it is also considerably more expensive. As a result, it is found most commonly in larger business reference collections and in libraries or information centers where the additional information it provides offsets the added cost.

Sales & Marketing Management publishes two additional special issues. One is the *Management Survey of U.S. Industrial and Commercial Buying Power*, which serves as a guide for industrial marketing and contains data on manufacturing activity on a county-by-county basis for over 450 SIC 4-digit industries. The other special issue is the *Survey of Selling Costs*. It includes current data on selling costs in major metropolitan areas, compensation of sales staff, costs of sales training per salesperson, sales incentives, and travel costs. The markets with highest and lowest sales costs are highlighted.

Rand McNally's *Commercial Atlas & Marketing Guide* brings together current economic, demographic, and geographic information. As with the other statistical guides mentioned above, many of the data elements included were taken from government statistical publications but have been reformatted and supplemented with publisher-generated maps and statistics.

National, regional, state, and area data are arranged at the front of the *Atlas* by broad subject category, such as transportation, communications, and population. The economic section is typical. In addition to a series of area maps highlighting major military installations, trading areas, retail sales, and manufacturing centers, it includes statistics on business and manufactures, retail trade, sales, and the largest corporations in the United States.

It is the "State Maps and U.S. Index of Statistics and Places by States," however, that comprises the bulk of the *Atlas*. The maps section features a large, two-page map for each state; the index section presents detailed information on specific places, condensing a surprising amount of information about each locale by using abbreviations and symbols.

The *Atlas* is a unique source of population estimates for unincorporated places. Of the more than 40,000 that it included in the 1987 edition, for example, only 3,400 were reported separately in the 1980 Census. (Although the inhabitants of unincorporated places were counted in the census, their communities were not reported as separate places, but were combined as sections of townships or county divisions.) Secured by means of an extensive annual survey of local authorities, including postmasters, chambers of commerce, planning officials, and municipal authorities, these data are extremely useful to business people interested in state and local rather than national markets.

Each section of the *Atlas* is preceded by an introduction summarizing the contents of that section and describing data sources used and concepts and terms employed.

The Sourcebook of Demographics and Buying Power for Every ZIP Code in the USA combines data from the two most recent decennial censuses with publisher-generated estimates and projections. The main section contains residential zip code data by state, showing for each its population and distribution by age groups; median age; race; number of households; housing profile; median household income; education; employment; distribution of households by income; and purchasing potential. The latter is determined by a purchasing potential index that measures consumer preferences for each of 13 major consumer product and service categories. In addition, the *Sourcebook* includes a business section that lists the five top-employing SIC codes for each zip code. State summary data, and SIC and FIPS (Federal Information Processing Standards) code appendixes are also included. Data contained in the *Sourcebook* are also available on diskette, and can be purchased on a state-by-state basis.

Although the above titles are among the most important commercially published statistical compilations, they are by no means the only ones. Standard bibliographic guides, such as *Data Sources for Business and Market Analysis, Marketing Information*, and *Business Information Sources* should be consulted for additional titles. People seeking commercially published statistics on more specific subjects should also consult such publications as the *Statistical Reference Index* and *Statistics Sources*.

TRADE STATISTICS

Trade associations, the materials they publish, and the sources that can be used to identify them were described earlier in this chapter. It is worth reemphasizing, however, that these associations collect and publish unique statistics about their members and the industries they represent, and that such associations should not be overlooked when searching for elusive statistical data.

The major producers of marketing statistics and some typical publications have been described. Using the marketing guides mentioned in this chapter and the statistical indexes discussed in chapter 6, librarians and researchers should be able to identify sources that present data on almost every subject. Consideration of marketing statistics, however, would not be complete without a look at one very important type of statistic, market share.

MARKET SHARE

One of the statistical requests that business reference librarians regularly encounter is for the market share for a particular product or company. "What is the market share for Folger's coffee?" a patron may ask, or "What is Kellogg's share of the market for cold cereals?" *Market share* is, quite simply, the ratio of sales for one company's product or product line to the total market sales of that product or product line, expressed as a percentage of the market. Market share can be determined for a specific brand—Froot Loops versus Cheerios, for example—or for one company's product line—Kellogg's share of the market for cold cereals versus General Foods' market share. The concept is not a difficult one; market share can be calculated whenever total sales and specific product (or company) sales information are available. Market share can be computed for local, state, national, and even international markets as long as the necessary sales information is at hand.

Unfortunately, market share is not always readily available. While the off-the-shelf market studies described earlier in this chapter frequently contain detailed market share data, they are too expensive for most libraries. Other sources, more likely to be found in libraries, contain only selective market share information. *Advertising Age*, for example, regularly features market share data for some nationally advertised brands.

   Ward's Business Directory of Largest U.S. Companies and *Dun's Business Rankings* include sales data by three- and four-digit SIC codes for public and some private companies. Although these directories do not give actual market share, it can be calculated easily by dividing the sales figure for a specific company into the total sales for the SIC category of which it is a part. Researchers should be forewarned, however, that it is an approximate figure at best. Many large companies are involved in the sale of a multitude of products and services, and sales figures presented are for the company as a whole rather than for the product(s) assigned the SIC code under which a company is listed. In addition, many companies too small to be included in the directories may also sell the same product or service. As a result, market shares derived from these publications are really little more than ballpark estimates.

   Although the sources mentioned above are useful, they have some drawbacks. Market share data are given for only a limited number of products and brands in *Advertising Age*, and the directories do not include market share for specific brands or for the market as a whole.

   Market share for specific products or brands may also be included in periodical articles, which can be identified using some of the indexes already discussed. The *Statistical Reference Index*, for example, describes many sources that include market share. *SRI* uses index terms *product rankings* and *corporate rankings* in lieu of market share. *Predicasts F&S Index United States* also lists articles that include market share information under the product subheading *market information*. An article in the *Wall Street Journal* on market share for spaghetti sauce, for example, is indexed in *F&S* under the market information section of "203360 Catsup & Other Tomato Sauces." Finally, *Business Periodicals Index* uses the subject heading "Market Share," and includes under it general articles on the concept of market share as well as articles on market share for specific products.

   Market share for a specific brand or product is influenced significantly by the effectiveness of the advertising that promotes it. Selection of the appropriate medium in which to advertise is an important part of the marketing process. The next section considers various advertising media and the printed sources relating to them.

Advertising Media

   Selection of the best media in which to advertise is no simple task. Each medium has special characteristics which the advertiser must keep in mind. However, before these characteristics are considered and an advertising plan drawn up, the following questions should be answered.

   To whom do I want to advertise? Who are the people that can use and benefit from what I sell? Or that influence what others buy?

   Where are these people? If your business is a local one, from what distance can you expect to attract buyers? If you are a manufacturer, what industries, trades, or professions offer the best possibilities?

   What kind of advertising message do I want to deliver? Is it best told in print? If so, what print medium? If a broadcast medium seems most suitable, would radio or television be better?[28]

   The prospective advertiser, in other words, needs to segment his or her market and then consider the best ways(s) of reaching it.

   There are three main categories of advertising media: print, broadcast, and direct mail. Descriptions of these media and the reference publications relevant to each follow.

PRINT MEDIA

The two main types of print media are newspapers and magazines. Both are used heavily by advertisers, but newspapers lead magazines and all other media in terms of advertising dollars spent. In 1981, for example, it is estimated that $17.446 billion was spent by newspaper advertisers, of which $9.631 billion was spent for retail advertisements, $5.062 billion for classified advertisements, and $2.753 billion for national advertising.[29] These statistics also show that most newspaper advertisements are for local rather than national businesses, products, and services.

Prospective newspaper advertisers usually want to know two things: characteristics of newspaper readers or of the area in which they live, and the cost of advertising in specific newspapers. Both types of information are readily available.

Characteristics of newspaper readers in a city are likely to be similar to the population as a whole. Although this is somewhat less true of cities in which more than one newspaper is published, it is axiomatic that the socioeconomic and general demographic characteristics of the population served by a newspaper will be of great interest to those who are considering advertising in it. As a result, many newspapers publish general marketing information— widely varying in depth and breadth—which they make available to prospective advertisers. Here, for example, is a description of market information available from the *Tampa Tribune*.

> *Tampa Bay Market and Media* is a 64-page booklet from the Tampa Tribune which breaks down a nine-county Tampa Bay market by metro rankings, population profiles, construction/airport activity, agriculture, finance, sports, education, tourism, and retail sales.[30]

Such publications generally are available free of charge from the issuing newspaper, and the librarian seeking to build a collection for a specific city or part of the country may want to consider sending for some of them.

Similar local information may be closer at hand, either in government publications or in such statistical guides as the *Editor & Publisher Market Guide*, which gives demographic and trade information for daily newspaper cities. The entry for Bad Axe, Michigan (figure 9.5), for example, might give a business person all of the information necessary about the area served by the *Huron Tribune*.

The other main factor affecting a marketer's decision to advertise in a specific newspaper is the cost of advertising in that newspaper. Since newspaper circulation is the basis for advertising rates and a major consideration in selecting a newspaper, credible circulation figures are essential. As a result, many newspaper publishers belong to the *Audit Bureau of Circulations*, a nonprofit association whose purpose is to audit and ascertain the veracity of circulation figures for newspapers and magazines published by its members. The letters "ABC" in the *Editor & Publisher Market Guide* and other publications indicate that the circulation figures presented have been verified by the Audit Bureau of Circulations. Although two other groups—the Business Publications Audit of Circulation, or BPA, and the Verified Audit Circulation Corporation—audit circulation figures, the ABC dominates this field.

Newspaper circulation figures can be found in many publications—the *Editor & Publisher Market Guide*, for example, and the *Gale Directory of Publications*—but coverage is most complete in the following source.

Newspaper Circulation Analysis, Part II of *Standard Rate & Data Service: Newspaper Rates and Data*. Wilmette, Ill.: Standard Rate & Data Service, 1957- . Annual.

Newspaper Circulation Analysis covers newspaper circulation and metro area, TV market, and county penetration. Although some general market area and demographic data are included, it is the circulation analysis that makes this such a useful reference source. Entries include daily and Sunday circulation figures, by county, for each newspaper. In addition, market data (households, consumer spending income, retail sales, and circulation) are featured. Although some advertising rates are included, an advertiser would be well advised to turn to the following companion publications for more detailed information.

Standard Rate & Data Service: Newspaper Rates and Data. Wilmette, Ill.: Standard Rate & Data Service, 1919- . Monthly.

Standard Rate & Data Service: Community Publications Rates and Data. Wilmette, Ill.: Standard Rate & Data Service, 1945- . Semiannual.

Newspaper Rates and Data is a monthly SRDS publication that includes rates for daily and weekly newspapers as well as for black, college and university, and religious newspapers, comics, and newspaper magazines. Figure 9.7, which gives national advertising rates and market data for the Annapolis *Capital*, is typical. A similar SRDS publication, *Community Publications Rates and Data*, gives advertising rates and specifications for shopping guides and weekly newspapers.

Magazines, the other print medium, can be divided into three main categories: consumer, farm, and trade publications. Each of these, in turn, has many different subdivisions. Standard Rate & Data Service, for example, lists over 60 "editorial content" classifications for consumer magazines, and 175 "market served" classifications for trade publications.

As with newspapers, circulation, characteristics of the reader population, and advertising costs are the major factors considered. Advertising rates vary widely, based on the magazine selected and the type of advertisement to be placed—a full-page, four-color ad will, naturally, cost more than a 14-line black-and-white ad. A nationally circulated periodical with many readers will charge more than one with more limited circulation or more limited subject interest. In 1987, for example, it cost approximately $120,130 to place a full-page color ad in *Time*, which has an ABC-verified circulation of over 4 million, but only $14,290 to place a similar ad in *Mother Earth News*, which has a more limited readership. For local magazines, advertising rates are often comparable to those for newspapers.

Standard Rate & Data Service also publishes two main titles covering consumer, farm, and trade magazines.

Standard Rate & Data Service: Magazine and Agri-Media Rates and Data. Wilmette, Ill.: Standard Rate & Data Service, 1919- . Monthly.

Standard Rate & Data Service: Business Publications Rates and Data. Wilmette, Ill.: Standard Rate & Data Service, 1919- . Monthly.

Both *Consumer Magazine and Agri-Media Rates and Data* and *Business Publications Rates and Data* provide detailed information about magazines, including circulation, advertising rates, mechanical requirements, special issues, and advertising deadlines.

While advertising rates are significant and will be a major consideration in magazine selection, equally important is choosing one(s) in which reader characteristics most closely match the market identified for the product. The decision made to advertise a new line of cosmetics in certain women's magazines rather than, say, in automotive or fishing magazines may be a fairly simple one, but the next step must be to select the most appropriate women's magazines. Would *Vogue* or *Redbook* be better, or *Cosmopolitan* or *Working Woman*? In order to help advertisers decide, many magazines survey their readers for information about their income, occupations, education, and geographic location as well as about their attitudes toward and use of specific products. An ad in SRDS for *Fortune* highlights some salient readership characteristics for prospective advertisers. Its subscribers, claims *Fortune*, have an average income of $117,300, with the average value of their investment portfolios assessed at $504,400. Further, some 73 percent are college graduates, 46 percent are in top management positions, and 32 percent hold corporate directorships.[31]

Many national consumer magazines publish studies about specific products. *Newsweek*, for example, has published *Fragrances: How Executive Men and Women View and Use Fragrances at Work and Leisure*, as well as reports on the buyers of domestic and imported automobiles. Often these publications, which are frequently listed in the Special Libraries Association's publication *What's New in Advertising and Marketing*, are free to libraries.

Annapolis

Anne Arundel County—Map Location F-3
See SRDS Consumer market map and data at beginning of
the state.

CAPITAL
2000 Capital Dr., Annapolis, MD 21401.
Phone 301-268-5000.

Media Code 1 121 1245 3.00   **Mid 016675-000**
EVENING (except Sunday).
(Not published Jan. 1, July 4, Memorial Day, Labor Day,
Christmas or New Years Day).
Member: INAME; NAB, Inc.; ACB, Inc.

1. PERSONNEL
Chairman of the Board—Philip Merrill.
Publisher—Eleanor Merrill.
Business Manager—George Cruze.
Circulation Director—John R. Bieberich.
Adv. Dir.—Bernie Hoff.

2. REPRESENTATIVES and/or BRANCH OFFICES
Landon Associates, Inc.

3. COMMISSION AND CASH DISCOUNT
15% to agencies; no cash discount.

4. POLICY-ALL CLASSIFICATIONS
30-day notice given of any rate revision.
Alcoholic beverage and cigarette advertising accepted.

ADVERTISING RATES
Effective January 1, 1987.
Received December 11, 1986.

5. BLACK/WHITE RATES
Individual daily newspaper rates not made available.

6. GROUP COMBINATION RATES-B/W & COLOR
SAU flat, per inch 26.70
Above rate includes insertion of same copy, within 1 week
in Maryland Gazette (Wed. & Sat.) and Brooklyn News
(Wed.).
Inches charged full depth: col. 21; pg. 126.
Maryland Newspaper Network—see listing at beginning of
State. Suburban Washington Area Newspaper
Network—see listing at beginning of District of Columbia.

7. COLOR RATES AND DATA
5 day leeway required. No minimum.
Use b/w rate plus the following applicable costs:

	b/w 1 c	b/w 2 c	b/w 3 c
Extra	350.00	720.00	1,080.00

Closing dates: Reservations 10 days in advance: printing
material—1 week in advance. Cancellation date: 48 hours
in advance.

11. SPECIAL DAYS/PAGES/FEATURES
Best Food Day: Wednesday.

12. R.O.P. DEPTH REQUIREMENTS
Ads over 18 inches deep charged full column.

13. CONTRACT AND COPY REGULATIONS
See Contents page for location of regulations—items 1, 2,
3, 5, 6, 8, 10, 11, 12, 14, 18, 19, 20, 23, 26, 31, 32, 34,
35.

14. CLOSING TIMES
3 days before publication.

15. MECHANICAL MEASUREMENTS
**For complete, detailed production information, see
SRDS Print Media Production Data.**
PRINTING PROCESS: Offset.
6 col; ea 2-1/16; 1/8″ betw col.
Inches charged full depth: col. 21; pg. 126.

16. SPECIAL CLASSIFICATIONS/RATES
POSITION CHARGES
Guaranteed 50% extra.

17. CLASSIFIED RATES
For complete data refer to classified rate section.

20. CIRCULATION
DAILY
Net Paid—A.B.C. 9-30-86* (Newspaper Form)

	Total	CZ	TrZ	Other
Eve	39,848	17,097	10,773	11,978

(*) 26 weeks for period ending 9-27-86.
WEEKLIES
Net Paid & Non-Paid Sworn Combined 9-30-86

	Non-Paid	Paid	Total
Weeklies Comb	14,005	35,532	49,537

DAILY & WEEKLIES
Net Pd & Non-Pd A.B.C. & Sworn Comb.—9-30-86

	Non-Paid	Paid	Total
Total Comb	14,005	75,380	89,385

Max-Min CPM rate: Total Comb Max 9.41.
For county-by-county and/or metropolitan area
breakdowns, see SRDS Newspaper Circulation Analysis.

Fig. 9.7. Typical listing, *Standard Rate &
Data Service: Newspaper Rates and Data.*
Reprinted by permission of the publisher
from *Standard Rate & Data Service: Newspaper Rates and Data* 69, no. 4 (April 12,
1987): 411.

BROADCAST MEDIA

Radio and television are highly effective advertising media. Television, in fact, is second only to newspaper as the medium most often chosen to promote products and services. Broadcast advertising offers several advantages over print advertising. Radio and television programs are aimed at specific segments of the population, and the advertising that accompanies them can be aimed at these audiences. Broadcast media are also more flexible than print media, more responsive to quick changes.

> If you deal in seasonal products, you may be able to arrange for automatic advertising changes to match weather changes. Is it hot? Then your air conditioner advertisement goes on. Winter storm approaching? Advertise snow tires. Naturally, both broadcast media prefer reasonable notice of changes, but they can provide such sudden switches.[32]

The human voice, with its capacity to establish rapport with listeners and to convey urgency, is sometimes more persuasive than print. Finally, broadcast advertising is, in a sense, more democratic, making it possible for small as well as big businesses to establish the images they want to present.

> Little looks as "big" as big when everybody's limited to 60 (often 30) seconds or less. There are no other advertisements to overshadow yours—there is nothing comparable to the full page or double page color advertisement to detract prospects from your fractional page in print media. When your advertisement is broadcast, you've got the air on that station to yourself. With creative advertisements you can be as impressive as the largest of your competitors.[33]

Broadcast advertising is not without its disadvantages, however. Frequent repetition of advertisements is necessary, since potential customers can be reached only during the few seconds the message is being transmitted. Copy must be both brief *and* effective. Finally, planning for broadcast advertising is somewhat more difficult than for print since there is little standardization between broadcast stations. Nevertheless, these disadvantages are offset by the potential that broadcast ads offer for reaching a market and for saturating it with promotional messages.

Broadcast advertisers attempt to reach prospective buyers by selecting the media, station, program, and time most likely to reach the most appropriate audience. When considering a station, advertisers look at its coverage and its audience. *Coverage* refers to the geographical area where the station's signal can be heard, and *audience* refers to the number of people who actually watch or listen to that station or to a particular program on that station.

Just as verified circulation figures are crucial for print advertisers, so also are accurate audience statistics for broadcast advertisers. There are, however, some differences between circulation audits and audience measurement.

> Station and program audiences for radio and television are measured by privately owned research companies using different methods of collecting data. There are no nonprofit auditing organizations whose statements are fairly standardized, as for printed media. And, whereas the entire circulations of printed media are covered by audits, TV and radio audience measurements are based on *samples* of households or individuals in the population.[34]

Several firms offer audience measurement services; key among these are the Arbitron Ratings Company and the A.C. Nielsen Company.

Advertisers distinguish between network and spot announcements, or spots. *Network announcements* require buying air time from the network; *spot announcements* are bought on a station-by-station or market-by-market basis. They are further divided into fixed, preemptible, floating, and run-of-station spots.

> A *fixed spot* is guaranteed to be broadcast at a time you choose and contract for. A *preemptible spot* is "semi-fixed": you pay a reduced rate for the time you choose but risk being bumped by an advertiser willing to pay the higher fixed rate. You have little or no control over when a *floating spot* is broadcast; the station decides the time.... *Run-of-station* spots are broadcast whenever time is available, as decided by the station.[35]

Radio advertising is appealing for many different reasons. It is less expensive than television, and, because radio programming is designed to segment audiences, a much more closely defined audience can be reached than when using print media, particularly newspapers.

> Whereas there is usually only one newspaper in a market (except for the larger metro areas where there are several), there are many more radio stations in a market. With this growth in their number, radio stations have catered increasingly to specialized audiences through specialized program formats.... Thus, stations can deliver specific demographic segments such as teenagers, housewives, older adults, blacks, farmers and ethnic groups speaking foreign languages.[36]

Radio rates are based partially on radio coverage and audience. Another factor affecting rates is time of day. Radio is primarily a daytime and early evening medium, and categories, based on when most people are likely to be listening, have been assigned to different parts of the day. Although these categories are not standardized among all stations, the following classification is typical, with highest rates being charged for AA time slots, and lowest for D.

Class AA	Morning Drive Time	6:00 a.m. to 10:00 a.m.
Class B	Home Worker Time	10:00 a.m. to 4:00 p.m.
Class A	Evening Drive Time	4:00 p.m. to 7:00 p.m.
Class C	Evening Time	7:00 p.m. to Midnight
Class D	Night Time	Midnight to 6:00 a.m.

The most current radio advertising rates are published in a series of Standard Rate & Data Service titles.

Standard Rate & Data Service: Spot Radio Rates and Data. Wilmette, Ill.: Standard Rate & Data Service, 1929- . Monthly.

Standard Rate & Data Service: Spot Radio Small Markets Edition. Wilmette, Ill.: Standard Rate & Data Service, 1976- . Semiannual.

The first of these is *Spot Radio Rates and Data*, which profiles some 4,500 AM and 2,700 FM stations. Each issue includes SRDS's usual estimates of state, county, city and metro area market data as well as profiles of the individual stations themselves. The entry in figure 9.8 (see page 216) for WNRK in Newark, Delaware, is typical. A companion volume to *Spot Radio Rates and Data* is the semiannual *Spot Radio Small Markets Edition*, which lists radio stations in markets with populations of 25,000 or less.

WNRK
1964
NEWARK

N⁵B BROADCASTERS   **Radio**

Media Code 4 208 2000 3.00   **Mid 009112-000**
Arc Broadcasting, Inc.
Box 8152, Newark, DE 19714. Phone 302-737-5200.

PROGRAMMING DESCRIPTION
WNRK: Target audience 25-54. MUSIC: 60% music; 50% Adult Contemporary, 50% Oldies. AIR PERSONAL-ITIES handle daily contests & promos. NEWS: at :55; local at :25. SPORTS: at :60 & :30; high school, pro football, motor racing, & horse racing. FARM: M-F at 6:05 am. FEATURES: Swap Shop 12:10-12:55 pm M-F; Trivia 4x/day 6:40, 9:15 am, 12:45 & 3:40 pm; Ziggy Gorson's International Show Sun 3-6 pm; Frank Sinatra Sun 1-2:30 pm w/Al Campagnone. Rec'd 11/26/86.

1. PERSONNEL
Pres. & Gen'l Mgr.—Al R. Campagnone.
Sales Manager—Charles Ward.
Program Director—Mike Stevens.

3. FACILITIES
1,000 w.; 1260 khz. Directional.
Operating schedule: 6 am-7 pm. EST.

4. AGENCY COMMISSION
15%.

TIME RATES
No. 5 Eff 1/1/87—Rec'd 2/20/87.
AAA—Restricted times.
AA—Mon thru Sat 5-10 am & 3-7 pm.

6. SPOT ANNOUNCEMENTS

CLASS AAA—1-12 WEEKS

PER WK:	5 ti	10 ti	15 ti	20+
1 min	23.55	22.95	21.75	21.05
30 sec	18.85	18.35	17.45	16.85

CLASS AAA—13-52 WEEKS

	5 ti	10 ti	15 ti	20+
1 min	22.95	21.75	21.05	19.85
30 sec	18.35	17.45	16.85	15.95

CLASS AA ROTATOR—1-12 WEEKS

	5 ti	10 ti	15 ti	20+
1 min	21.05	20.45	19.85	18.75
30 sec	16.95	16.35	15.95	14.95

CLASS AA ROTATOR—13-25 WEEKS

	5 ti	10 ti	15 ti	20+
1 min	20.25	19.55	18.75	17.55
30 sec	16.15	15.65	14.95	14.05

CLASS AA ROTATOR—26-52 WEEKS

	5 ti	10 ti	15 ti	20+
1 min	19.55	18.75	17.55	17.05
30 sec	15.65	14.95	14.05	13.65

CLASS AA ROTATOR—52 WEEKS

	5 ti	10 ti	15 ti	20+
1 min	18.70	17.55	17.05	16.35
30 sec	14.95	14.05	13.65	13.05

15 sec: 60% of 1-min.

7. PACKAGE PLANS

50-50, 1 MINUTE—1/2 AAA, 1/2 AA

PER WK:	5 ti	10 ti	15 ti	20+
1-12 wks	18.55	17.55	16.75	16.05
13-52 wks	17.55	16.75	16.05	15.15
26-51 wks	16.05	15.15	14.55	14.05
52 wks	15.15	14.55	14.05	13.45

50-50, 30 SECONDS—1/2 AAA, 1/2 AA

1-12 wks	14.85	14.05	13.35	12.85
13-52 wks	14.05	13.35	12.85	12.15
26-51 wks	12.85	12.15	11.65	11.25
52 wks	12.15	11.65	11.25	10.75

10/15 sec: 60% of 1-min.

8. PROGRAM TIME RATES

	1 hr	1/2 hr
Ea	158.20	94.90

(CR)

Fig. 9.8. Typical listing, *Standard Rate & Data Service: Spot Radio Rates and Data.* Reprinted by permission of the publisher from *Standard Rate & Data Service: Spot Radio Rates and Data* 69, no. 5 (May 1, 1987): 108.

Another very useful publication is *Broadcasting/Cablecasting Yearbook*, a standard reference work and a comprehensive directory to all aspects of broadcasting.

Broadcasting/Cablecasting Yearbook. Washington, D.C.: Broadcasting Publications, Inc., 1935- . Annual.

In addition to its radio section, the *Broadcasting/Cablecasting Yearbook* includes sections that survey the broadcasting industry, profile television and cable stations, and focus on programming, professional services, technology, advertising and marketing, and satellites. Since the *Yearbook* may be more common in library collections than the SRDS publications, it merits close examination. The sample entry from the radio section reprinted in figure 9.9 shows the type of information included in each listing.

WOF(AM)—(1) Oct 8, 1946: (2) 1000 khz; 1 kw-D, 250
w-N, DA-D. (L-KQSL) (CP: 5 kw-U). Stereo. (3) Box
1000 (99999). (909) 555-1000. TWX: 909-999-9999. (4)
General Broadcasting Corp. (group owner; acq 7-20-
69). (5) Net: ABC/E, AP, Mountain State Network. Rep:
Jones & Company, Penn State. Format: MOR, C&W.
Spec prog: Sp 3 hrs wkly. ■ (6) John Jones, gen mgr;
David Smith, chief engr. ■ (7) Rates: $14; 13.50; 14;
12.50.

WOF-FM—(1) October 1959: (8) 101.1 mhz; 3 kw. Ant
300 ft. Stereo. (9) Dups AM 50%. Format: C&W. ■ (10)
WOF-TV affil. ■ (7) Rates: $8.50; 7; 8.50; 7.

Fig. 9.9. Typical radio station listing,
Broadcasting/Cablecasting Yearbook.
Reprinted with permission from the 1987
Broadcasting/Cablecasting Yearbook.

Television advertising is big business. There are more than 87 million homes in this country with at least one television set, and, according to A.C. Nielsen statistics for 1985, the average American home watches television for 7 hours and 10 minutes a day.[37] Small wonder that advertisers turn to TV to promote their products. Television advertising, however, is usually very expensive.

The average 30-second prime-time network television announcement now costs $100,000 (spots on a top-rated series cost $200,000; low-rated spots average about $80,000). An estimated 120 million people watched the 1987 Super Bowl telecast. Thirty-second announcements during that event cost $600,000. Thirty-second announcements on individual TV stations range from $15,000 in top-rated specials in major markets to as low as $10 in the second-hundred markets.[38]

As in radio, television stations divide their broadcasting day into parts, based on when people are most likely to be watching. The categories and terms they employ, however, are different; they generally call their classifications *daytime, early fringe, prime, late fringe,* and *weekend.*

Time of day is one of the variables determining television advertising rates. Another has to do with the station's coverage and its audience. Broadcasters and advertisers may refer to a station's *rating,* or to its *audience share.* Both are measures of its effectiveness, and are based on the *households using television index,* or HUT. The HUT is simply the percentage of households in a designated area with the television set turned on. In a sample of 2,000 households with television, if 800 of these sets are turned on, the HUT would be 40. A station's *rating* is the percentage of households in a sample turned to a specific station at a specific time. If 400 households out of the sample of 2,000 report turning to a particular station during the specified time period, that station would have a rating of 20 percent usually expressed as 20.0 rating points. Finally, a station's *share of audience,* or share, is calculated by dividing the individual station's rating by the HUT. Thus, using the above example, dividing the station's rating of 20.0 by the HUT of 40.0, yields an audience share of 50 percent for the station. These concepts are employed for specific programs as well as for stations, with prime-time network programs ranked by rating and audience share. For the week ending June 14, 1987, for example, "Family Ties" and the "Cosby Show" were ranked first and second, with respective ratings of 23.4 and 22.3 percent, and audience shares of 42 and 41 percent.[39]

There are several television rate books and directories.[40] Some of the most important are described below.

Standard Rate & Data Service: Spot Television Rates and Data. Wilmette, Ill.: Standard Rate & Data Service, 1947- . Monthly.

Television & Cable Factbook. Washington, D.C.: Television Digest, Inc., 1945- . 2v. Annual.

Spot Television Rates and Data profiles individual television stations, state networks and groups, and national networks and groups. The entry for station KVTV in Laredo, Texas, in figure 9.10 is typical.

KVTV
(Airdate December 28, 1973)
LAREDO

CBS Television Network

Media Code 6 245 1525 0.00   Mid 007843-000
K-SIX Television, Inc.
2600 Shea St., Box 2039, Laredo, TX 78040. Phone 512-
    723-2923.
1. PERSONNEL
    Pres. & Gen'l Mgr.—Vann M. Kennedy.
    Station Manager—J. Dickey.
2. REPRESENTATIVES
    Seltel, Inc.
3. FACILITIES
    Video 85,100 w., audio 17,000 w.; ch 13.
    Antenna ht.: 920 ft. above average terrain.
    Operating schedule: 5:30-2 am. CST.
4. AGENCY COMMISSION
    15% to recognized agencies on time only.
5. GENERAL ADVERTISING See coded regulations
    Affiliated with CBS Television Network.
    Programs sold in combination with KZTV Corpus Christi.
    See that listing.
6. TIME RATES
        No. G-12 Prog. rates eff 1/2/87—Rec'd 1/30/87.
10. PROGRAM TIME RATES
    AA—7-10:30 pm.
    A—4-7 pm & 10:30 pm-midnight.
    B—Time not otherwise specified.
    C—Sun sign-on-noon.

	AA	A	B	C
1 hr	1400	750	500	275
1/2 hr	850	450	275	175
1/4 hr	500	300	...	...
5 min	...	...	175	...

11. SPECIAL FEATURES
                    COLOR
    Schedules network color, slides and live.
    Equipped with 2" high band VTR plus 3/4" cassette.

Fig. 9.10. Typical listing, *Standard Rate & Data Service: Spot Television Rates and Data*. Reprinted by permission of publisher from the May 15, 1987 issue of *Standard Rate & Data Service: Spot Television Rates and Data*.

A comparison of listings for individual stations in *Spot Television Rates and Data* reveals the lack of standardization between stations in defining rate categories. Station KVTV, for example, uses the designations AA, A, B, and C for spots, with AA assigned to prime time commercials and C the designation for spots broadcast on Sundays between sign-on and noon. Other stations use other designations, often combinations of letters and numbers. Although the categories are not really comparable, it helps to remember that the first category the station lists will always be the most desirable in terms of broadcast time and advertiser control (and thus most expensive), and that the last will be the least desirable and the least expensive.

The Television section of *Broadcasting/Cablecasting Yearbook* lists all U.S. and Canadian television stations. A typical listing is shown in figure 9.11.

WOF-TV—(1) ch 2, 200 kw vis, 20 kw aur, ant 500t/300g. (CP: ant 750t/550g). **(2)** April 13, 1952. **(3)** Box 100, 99999. (909) 555-1000. TWX: 909-999-9999. **(4)** Licensee: WOF Bcstg Co. (acq 7-20-69). **(5)** Ownership: See Acme Stns, also Nwspr. ■ **(6)** CBS, NBC. Sp 2 hrs wkly. Rep: Jones, Tri-State. Wash atty: Goltz & Stick. ■ **(7)** Jud Jones, pres & gen mgr; D. Spark, chief engr. ■ **(8)** On 6 CATV's—20,000 subs. On 10 trans. **(9)** Co-owned WOF-AM-FM. ■ **(10)** Rates: $100; 83; 70.

Fig. 9.11. Typical television station listing, *Broadcasting/Cablecasting Yearbook*. Reprinted with permission from the 1987 *Broadcasting/Cablecasting Yearbook*.

In addition to these individual station entries, the *Yearbook* includes metro area maps showing in which counties metro area stations are viewed; a listing of cable television systems that includes data on number of subscribers, installation fees, and monthly charges; and producers and distributors of programs. A section on networks lists divisions and the major executives in each, as well as network-affiliated stations. The Technology section lists equipment manufacturers and distributors. Using it, one can identify manufacturers of studio monitors, cameras, and lighting systems. Similarly, by consulting the Professional Services section, one can find television brokerage services, media financing specialists, consultants, and attorneys specializing in communications law. Finally, the Advertising & Marketing section lists advertising agencies handling major radio and television accounts as well as radio and television advertising representatives.

The *Television & Cable Factbook* is another standard television directory. It is published in two volumes, *Stations* and *Cable & Services*. The *Stations* volume provides detailed information on every TV station in the U.S., Canada, and major foreign markets. Each station is given a full-page listing, including station coverage maps, market data, personnel, advertising rates, technical data, and engineering, sales, and legal consultants.

The *Cable & Services* volume lists cable systems, including for each system listed its address, the names of its local manager and chief technician, subscriber counts and subscriber fees, franchise fees and expiration dates, and ownership information. In addition to data on cable systems, the volume includes information about important services relating to the television industry, such as market and audience research organizations and manufacturers of television equipment.

DIRECT MAIL

Direct mail, which includes all forms of advertising sent through the mail, has certain advantages over other media. One of the most important is that it offers the advertiser the potential for selling to individuals, identifiable by name and address and possibly other characteristics rather than to broad groups of potential buyers having certain demographic or psychographic characteristics in common. Using carefully chosen mailing lists – compiled by the advertiser or purchased or rented from mailing list brokers – one can target the advertising to specific individuals. Print and broadcast advertising are scattergun media; direct mail, in contrast, is a pinpoint medium.

> The strongest reason for using direct mail is the degree to which you can select your audience, or readership. You can select people in any or all sections of the country. For consumer products, you can select them by sex, age, income, educational levels, occupation, recreational interests, or almost any characteristic you wish. (An extreme illustration of this is that for one state there is a list of men 6 feet tall or more and weighing at least 215 pounds). For industrial goods, you can address mail to companies selected by industry size, or to industrial business people, or to employees by their titles or functions.[41]

Selectivity is not the only advantage. Another is greater flexibility—direct mail advertising does not have the same limits on space or format as other media, and can be mailed at any time. The advertiser is not constrained by publishing deadlines or broadcast schedules. Finally, some claim that direct mail advertising receives more attention since it is a single message rather than one in a series of competing messages in print or broadcast media.

> At the moment of reception, or when a piece of direct advertising reaches the reader, it has his complete attention without any distracting elements. It will stand or fall on its own appeal just as will any other advertisement, but at least it will have a better chance because there is less competition for the reader's attention.[42]

Effective direct mail advertising begins with a good mailing list. Although some prefer to compile their own, many others use lists supplied to them by mailing list companies or mailing list brokers. For example, while a local, independently owned hardware store might construct its own mailing list, comprised of previous customers and neighborhood residents, the manufacturer of a line of hardware supplies intended for national distribution might purchase or rent a mailing list of hardware wholesalers. The manufacturer might limit the list further to directors of purchasing or sales managers working for hardware wholesalers.

When the decision is not to compile an in-house mailing list, advertisers must then consider outright purchase of a list from a mailing list company that compiles and sells its own list, or rent it from a mailing list broker who offers lists compiled by other organizations. These may include lists of subscribers, for example, and membership lists. For business people interested in direct mail advertising, one publication is particularly important.

Standard Rate & Data Service: Direct Mail Lists and Data. Wilmette, Ill.: Standard Rate & Data Service, 1967- . Bimonthly.

Mailing list compilers and brokers can be identified using SRDS's *Direct Mail Lists and Data*, which profiles over 50,000 different mailing lists. The main section is divided into three categories: business, consumer, and farm lists. Each of these categories, in turn, features several market classifications under which lists are arranged. One of the business classifications, for example, is "Industrial Purchasing," while representative consumer classifications are "Boating and Yachting" and "Senior Citizens."

Entries for specific mailing lists include a brief description of the list, rates, source(s) from which the list was compiled, method of addressing, and use restrictions. The profile for the Spark of Life Mail Order Buyers, a list composed of superstitious mail order buyers, reprinted in figure 9.12 (see page 221), is typical. *Direct Mail Lists and Data* also includes a Title/List Owner Index, a Subject/Market Classification List, and sections that profile co-op mailing and package insert programs.

Advertising Expenditures

Data on advertising expenditures by companies with big advertising budgets are readily available. Some of the sources already described include such information. *Advertising Age*, for example, lists leading national advertisers and their annual advertising expenditures, and the *Standard Directory of Advertisers* often includes figures on media expenditures for each company. Another series of publications, the BAR/LNA Multi-Media Service, deserves mention.

Company/Brand $. New York: Leading National Advertisers, 1974- . Quarterly.

Class/Brand $. New York: Leading National Advertisers, 1974- . Quarterly.

Ad $ Summary. New York: Leading National Advertisers, 1973 -. Quarterly.

SPARK OF LIFE MAIL ORDER BUYERS
Media Code 3 584 6966 0.00   Mid 020723-000
National Reporter Publications, Inc.
1. PERSONNEL
List Manager
MGT. Associates, Inc., 4676 Admiralty Way, Suite 421,
Marina del Rey, CA 90292. Phone 213-822-4911.
2. DESCRIPTION
Buyers of pendants, charms, books, etc. for health,
wealth and happiness.
Average unit of sale 9.95.
3. LIST SOURCE
Space ads and direct mail.
4. QUANTITY AND RENTAL RATES
Rec'd September, 1986.

	Total Number	Price per/M
Total list (1985-86)	120,836	50.00
Hotline (0-3 months)	20,000	55.00

Selections: ZIP Code, 5.00/M extra; state, SCF, 2.50/M
extra; keying, 1.00/M extra.
5. COMMISSION, CREDIT POLICY
20% commission to all recognized list brokers.
6. METHOD OF ADDRESSING
4/5-up Cheshire labels. Pressure sensitive labels, 5.50/M
extra. Magnetic tape (9T 800/1600), 15.00 nonrefundable
fee.
7. DELIVERY SCHEDULE
Two weeks from receipt of order.
8. RESTRICTIONS
Sample mailing piece required for approval.
9. TEST ARRANGEMENT
Minimum 5,000.
11. MAINTENANCE
Updated monthly.

Fig. 9.12. Typical listing, *Standard Rate & Data Service: Direct Mail Rates and Data.* Reprinted by permission of the publisher from *Standard Rate & Data Service: Direct Mail Rates and Data* 21, no. 2 (March 14, 1987): 1441.

The first of the titles in this series is *Company/Brand $*, which lists company (and some brand) expenditures for advertising in seven different media: magazines, newspaper supplements, spot television, network television, cable television, network radio, and outdoor advertising. The companies featured include not only advertising giants such as Procter & Gamble and General Motors, but also cities, banks, radio and television stations, and associations such as the American Astrological Association and the National Pork Producers Council. For companies that advertise several different products, there may be separate listings for each product. Following the main entry for Procter & Gamble, for example, there are separate listings for nearly 200 different products, ranging from Acta throat soothers to Zest deodorant soap.

The second title, *Class/Brand $* is published quarterly in two parts: *Class/Brand QTR$* and *Class/Brand YTD$*, with the first containing quarterly statistics, and the second, year-to-date statistics. In this publication, brands are grouped alphabetically within each of the Leading National Advertisers' (LNA's) product classes, showing brand expenditures for each medium. *Class/Brand $* is particularly useful when one wishes to compare advertising expenditures for different brands of the same product.

Arrangement in *Ad $ Summary* is alphabetical by brand name. While its companion volumes, *Company/Brand $* and *Class/Brand $*, list advertising expenditures for each medium as well as total media expenditures, *Ad $ Summary* lists only total media expenditures. Types of media used to advertise each product, however, are designated. The publication also lists top advertisers, as well as the top 10 brands in each of LNA's product classes.

Online Databases

Marketing activities are so pervasive that there are few business databases in which they are not covered. General business files such as *ABI/Inform* and *Management Contents* cite a wide range of articles pertaining to the field. Predicasts databases, such as *PTS PROMT, PTS F&S Indexes*, and *PTS U.S. Forecasts*, are all useful for such information. Some of the numeric databases, including *CENDATA, Econ Base,* and *Donnelley Demographics*, are particularly important for market researchers, as are such industry-specific databases as *Coffeeline* and *Biobusiness*.

Some databases focus primarily on marketing-related activities. Some, such as *Arbitron Radio and Arbitron TV Database, College Market Database*, and *Nielsen Retail Index* are available through vendors used only by the most specialized libraries and information centers. Still others, however, can be accessed through standard database vendors.

Frost & Sullivan Research Report Abstracts. New York: Frost & Sullivan. Monthly updates.

FINDEX. Bethesda, Md.: National Standards Association. Quarterly reloads.

Industry Data Sources. Belmont, Calif.: Information Access Company. Monthly updates.

PTS Marketing and Advertising Reference Service. Cleveland, Ohio: Predicasts. Weekly updates.

Trademarkscan-Federal. North Quincy, Mass.: Thomson & Thomson. Weekly updates.

Frost & Sullivan Research Reports, produced by a major publisher of off-the-shelf market studies, provides access to the company's research reports for the past 10 years. Each record includes the bibliographic citation, price, list of products covered, and an abstract. Although the abstracts concisely describe the reports, they do not contain data extracted from them. Full text copies of the reports are available from Frost & Sullivan, but their cost – generally between $800 and $1,600 per report – precludes their addition to most libraries. As a result, the file's usefulness is limited in public and academic library settings.

Similar information is available in *FINDEX*, the online version of the printed directory discussed earlier in this chapter. *FINDEX*, however, is broader in scope, listing and describing industry and market research reports issued by several different publishers.

Industry Data Sources permits SIC as well as subject access to industry-specific newsletters, yearbooks and factbooks, special issues of periodicals, and other sources that contain marketing and financial information.

While the databases mentioned above are useful for information about specific industries and products, *PTS Marketing and Advertising Reference Service* (*MARS*) focuses primarily on news in the marketing and advertising industry. It indexes and abstracts more than 100 periodicals and is particularly useful for information about brand names and advertising slogans, consumer attitudes, public relations, consumer goods and services, market research techniques, and specific advertising agencies.

Even more specialized information is available in *Trademarkscan-Federal*, a database that contains information about some 800,000 federally registered trademarks. The database is used primarily for screening new trade names to ensure that they are not already in use for similar products or services, for stimulating new ideas, and for gathering competitive intelligence. The database recently has been enhanced by the capacity to display actual graphic representations, including logos, symbols, and stylized writing. Since an estimated 30,000 registered trademarks consist only of designs unaccompanied by text, this is an important new feature.

NOTES

[1]"Slice Has the Juice," *Sales & Marketing Management* 133 (August 13, 1984): 20.

[2]*The New Generation: Growth Opportunities and Business Strategies...; PepsiCo, Inc., 1986 Annual Report* (Purchase, N.Y.: PepsiCo, 1987), 8-10.

[3]See #1 above.

[4]"Gatorade's Second Wind," *Sales & Marketing Management* 133 (July 2, 1984): 20.

[5]"To Market, to Market," *Newsweek* (January 9, 1984): 70.

[6]Ibid.

[7]Louis E. Boone and David L. Kurtz, *Contemporary Marketing* (Hinsdale, Ill.: Dryden Press, 1974), 112.

[8]Frederick A. Russ and Charles A. Kirkpatrick, *Marketing* (Boston: Little, Brown, 1982), 109.

[9]"Marketing's New Look: Campbell Leads a Revolution in the Way Consumer Products Are Sold," *Business Week* (January 26, 1987): 64.

[10]Marvin I. Mandell, *Advertising*, 4th ed. (Englewood Cliffs, N.J.: Prentice-Hall, 1984), 146.

[11]Ibid., 147.

[12]William F. Schoell and Thomas T. Ivy, *Marketing: Contemporary Concepts and Practices* (Boston: Allyn and Bacon, 1982), 229.

[13]William T. Ryan, *A Guide to Marketing* (Homewood, Ill.: Learning Systems Company, 1981), 9.

[14]George Breen and A. B. Blankenship, *Do-It-Yourself Marketing Research*, 2nd ed. (New York: McGraw-Hill, 1982), 21.

[15]To be put on the mailing list for *The Information Catalog*, write to:
FIND/SVP
625 Avenue of the Americas
New York, NY 10011

[16]Ryan, 12.

[17]*Encyclopedia of Associations* (Detroit: Gale Research Co., 1987), 25.

[18]*United States Government Manual, 1987/88* (Washington, D.C.: Government Printing Office, 1987), 568.

[19]Mandell, 92.

[20]U.S. Federal Trade Commission, *Federal Trade Commission Decisions, Findings, Opinions and Orders, January 1, 1981 to June 30, 1981* (Washington, D.C.: Government Printing Office, 1982), 221.

[21]Ibid., 222.

[22]Ibid., 220.

[23]Judith Willis, *About Body Wraps, Pills and Other Magic Wands for Losing Weight* (Washington, D.C.: Government Printing Office, 1982), p. 2. Reprinted from the November 1982 issue of *FDA Consumer.*

[24]Mandell, 95.

[25]U.S. Dept. of Commerce, International Trade Administration, *Measuring Markets: A Guide to the Use of Federal and State Statistical Data* (Washington, D.C.: Government Printing Office, 1979), iv.

[26]U.S. Dept. of Commerce, Bureau of the Census, *Population Statistics* (Washington, D.C.: Government Printing Office, 1981), 2.

[27]*Measuring Markets*, 5.

[28]U.S. Small Business Administration, *Selecting Advertising Media: A Guide for Small Business* (Washington, D.C.: Government Printing Office, 1977), 9.

[29]Mandell, 323.

[30]"Worth Writing For," in *Sales & Marketing Management's Survey of Buying Power* 137, no. 2 (July 28, 1986): A-53.

[31]*Standard Rate & Data Service: Business Publications Rates and Data* 69, no. 6 (June 24, 1987): 335.

[32]*Selecting Advertising Media*, 58.

[33]Ibid., 59.

[34]Ibid., 13-14.

[35]Ibid., 63-64.

[36]Mandell, 369.

[37]*Broadcasting/Cablecasting Yearbook* (Washington, D.C.: Broadcasting Publications, 1987), A-2.

[38]Ibid.

[39]"CBS, and Celtics, Come Up Short," *Broadcasting* 112, no. 25 (June 22, 1987): 42.

[40]For an interesting comparative review of television directories, see R. Errol Lam, "Tuning in the Television Directories," *Reference Services Review* 11, no. 2 (Summer 1983): 20-34.

[41]*Selecting Advertising Media*, 20.

[42]Richard S. Hanson, *The Dartnell Direct Mail and Mail Order Handbook*, 3rd ed. (Chicago: Dartnell, 1980), 29.

Never ask of money spent
Where the spender thinks it went.
Nobody was ever meant
To remember or invent
What he did with every cent.

—Robert Frost, "The Hardship of Accounting"*

10

ACCOUNTING AND TAXATION

This chapter introduces basic concepts and terminology in accounting and taxation as they apply to the use of publications, databases, and other sources in libraries and information centers. Although they are treated in separate sections, it should be noted that accounting and taxation are closely related, and that the study of one almost inevitably requires consideration of the other. Both have profound and long-lasting effects on the daily conduct of business and, as a result, are of interest to business and lay people as well as accountants and tax professionals.

ACCOUNTING BASICS

Accounting provides information used to assess the financial well-being of businesses and other economic entities, including government agencies and nonprofit organizations. Although it is frequently confused with bookkeeping, the latter is but one aspect of the entire accounting process. Accounting is, in fact, a financial information system. It begins with determining the raw data to be collected, proceeds to gathering, recording, analyzing, and verifying them, and culminates in communicating the data to interested parties. An important aspect of accounting is the objectivity with which the information is presented.

The essence of accounting is its special quality of neutrality. Accounting is financial map-making. It organizes, maps, and presents complex transactions and financial interrelationships in a reliable fashion. Not all information is necessarily useful. Of equal or greater importance is the accountant's assurance that the information is verifiable, objective, accurate, and has been compiled in an unbiased way.[1]

Accounting information is used within the organization to make decisions about finance, resource allocation, production, and marketing. It is also used externally by creditors, other businesses, investors, and by government agencies charged with monitoring business activities and organizations. Accounting, which has been called the language of business, is quantitative and is usually expressed in monetary terms.

Types of Accounting

The three major fields of accounting are private, public, and government accounting. *Private accounting* is carried on within a single organization, such as a corporation. It includes such specialties as managerial, financial, and tax accounting. Managerial accounting develops, produces, and analyzes data to be used for internal management decisions. It includes cost accounting, which concentrates on determining various unit costs, and internal auditing, which checks for fraud and waste and helps to ensure that proper accounting procedures are being followed. Financial accounting gathers and reports information for inclusion in published financial statements such as balance sheets and income statements included in corporate annual reports to shareholders, stock exchanges, and the Securities and Exchange Commission. Finally, tax accounting refers to recording and reporting corporate and income tax and tax liability. It is a complicated specialty that requires knowledge of current and past tax legislation, court rulings, and administrative decisions, as well as of accepted accounting practices that will minimize corporate tax liability.

While private accounting is essentially for the benefit and under the purview of a single organization, *public accounting* is, either directly or indirectly, for the benefit of the public. It offers independent professional accounting assistance to the public, and consists of three main specialties: auditing, management services, and tax services. The most important of these is auditing, the base upon which most public accounting rests.

Private accountants employed by companies and other organizations are responsible for preparing and documenting financial statements. It is the responsibility of the independent public accountant to examine these financial statements and verify their accuracy, completeness, and accordance with generally accepted accounting principles. This process, called *auditing*, includes several different steps. In addition to checking figures for accuracy, it may also involve reviewing contracts, agreements, minutes of directors' meetings, and other corporate documents. In addition, it may require interviewing or corresponding with bankers and other creditors, or conducting inventories. Upon completion of this process, the public accountant reaches a conclusion that becomes the auditor's report, expressed as an opinion. These opinions, which are more fully described in the section on basic accounting concepts, are accepted as authoritative by executives and managers within the company, and by creditors, stockholders, investors, and other businesses as well. Only Certified Public Accountants are allowed to conduct external financial audits for their clients.

Management services, another public accounting specialty, offers independent reviews of clients' accounting and management systems, with suggestions for their revision and improvement. Accountants may assess the availability and prudent use of financial and statistical information within the client's organization, monitor internal control systems devised to prevent losses through theft or waste, review internal accounting procedures for efficiency and effectiveness, consult on how to manage cash resources more profitably, or install or modify computerized accounting systems.

Finally, just as private accountants provide tax advice and assistance to the organizations for which they work, public accountants offer similar services to their clients. They prepare income tax returns, consult on tax problems, and help to plan tax programs. In addition to providing professional assistance with income taxes, public accountants also offer services pertaining to other types of taxes and tax-related issues, including property, foreign, and franchise taxes, and estate planning.

Public accounting firms range in size from sole practitioners to huge, multinational companies employing thousands of workers. The largest of these firms, frequently referred to as the Big Eight, are prestigious companies that dominate the accounting marketplace and enjoy high visibility and prominence.

> The sight of a clean-cut tuxedoed man presenting a sealed envelope to a dashing celebrity is the only vision most Americans have of The Big Eight at work. Millions, in fact, know only one of The Big Eight by name—Price Waterhouse—and think it is some sort of detective agency whose shining hour comes once a year on a glamorous television show. Something like a corporate Bert Parks.... Who are The Big Eight? For starters, they are huge multinational business organizations, the largest professional firms in the world and some of the most influential financial powers on earth. They are Arthur Andersen; Arthur Young; Coopers & Lybrand; Deloitte Haskins & Sells; Ernst & Whinney; Peat, Marwick, Mitchell; Price Waterhouse; and Touche Ross. Working through an intricate network of high-level contacts and special relationships, they operate at the seat of power and yet are often removed from the public eye.... Their scope of practice is sweeping, offering clients a vast smorgasbord of business services. Just a brief glance reveals a full menu indeed. The Big Eight are, among other things, auditors, accountants, executive headhunters, merger-makers, tax specialists, consultants, attorneys, lobbyists, expert witnesses, financial planners, actuaries, engineers.[2]

The third field of accounting is *government accounting*. Government agencies at all levels employ accountants in a wide range of positions. Their responsibilities parallel those of private and public accountants: They may prepare financial statements, audit the records of their own or other government agencies, contractors, or private citizens, or they may gather and present data that will help managers decide how best an agency should operate to meet its mandated responsibilities. At the federal level, for example, accountants in the Internal Revenue Service audit personal and corporate income tax returns, while those employed by the Defense Contract Audit Agency examine the records of private defense contractors. The General Accounting Office assists in investigations to determine the compliance of federal agencies with government policies and regulations, and monitors the expenditure of public funds. Similar accounting activities are carried on at the state and local level.

In summary, private, public, and government accounting are the three broad fields into which the profession falls. Although there is some overlap between the work performed in these areas, each has its own specialties. For all three fields, however, the generally acknowledged indication of professional competence is the Certified Public Accountant (CPA) certificate, which is described in the following section. Not all CPAs are employed by Big Eight accounting firms or practice as public accountants. Many work as private accountants for corporations and nonprofit organizations, and still others are employed by the government. CPA status, in other words, designates a certain level of competency and adherence to professional standards and ethics and does not necessarily mean that an accountant works in the field of public accounting.

Certified Public Accountants

The right to practice as a Certified Public Accountant is governed by individual state boards of accountancy. Although the rules vary, particularly as they relate to minimum educational and experiential requirements, all require that candidates must pass the Uniform CPA Examination. The exam, which is given in every state and U.S. territory each May and November, is prepared by the Board of Governors of the American Institute of Certified Public Accountants (AICPA). To pass it, candidates must prove competence in the application of accounting and auditing standards, procedures, and principles to practical accounting problems, and they must demonstrate an understanding of professional responsibilities. The two-day examination is rigorous, and many candidates do not pass it the first time. Each section, however, is graded separately, and candidates are permitted to take subsequent examinations until passing grades are achieved for all parts.

Libraries can assist prospective CPAs by acquiring publications that will help them prepare for and pass the examination. Some of the most useful sources are those published by the American Institute of Certified Public Accountants. Others are commercially published.

American Institute of Certified Public Accountants. **Information for CPA Candidates**. New York: AICPA, 1970. 54p.

_____. **CPA Examination, Official Questions and Unofficial Answers**. New York: AICPA (a supplement to the *Journal of Accountancy*), 1961- . Semiannual.

_____. **CPA Examination Questions and Unofficial Answers Indexed to Content Specification Outlines 1981-1985**. New York: AICPA, 1986.

Gleim, Irving N., and Patrick R. Delancy. **CPA Examination Review**. New York: Wiley, 2v. Annual.

Many candidates begin their preparation for the Uniform CPA Examination by consulting *Information for CPA Candidates*, a booklet which discusses the format and focus of each section of the exam.[3] In addition, it includes a statement on the purpose and general objectives of the Uniform CPA Examination, describes how the exam is compiled and graded, and suggests how to prepare for it.

CPA Examination, Official Questions and Unofficial Answers consists of all questions included in a specific exam, accompanied by unofficial answers and study references. *CPA Examination* includes detailed instructions for candidates taking the test, and lists future examination dates. An index by content specification, which enables readers to identify by number all of the questions dealing with a specific subject, is also included. Although issued as a supplement to the *Journal of Accountancy*, *CPA Examination, Official Questions and Unofficial Answers* can also be purchased separately or in two-year cumulations from the AICPA.

The American Institute of Certified Public Accountants periodically publishes a cumulative subject index to topics covered in earlier exams, *CPA Examination Questions and Unofficial Answers Indexed to Content Specification Outlines*. The index is particularly useful to candidates who are weak in certain areas and would like to improve their skills by studying the questions that focus on them. It also helps candidates to determine topics emphasized during past exams and to anticipate the direction future exams might take. The most recent edition indexes by subject (or content specification) multiple-choice questions, problems, and essays included in the 10 exams that were given from May 1981 through November 1985.

In addition to the publications issued by the AICPA, several commercially published sources are available. Typical of these is *CPA Examination Review*, an annual, two-volume work that includes study guides, suggestions for test taking, and other information in addition to the CPA questions and unofficial answers. Many of the answers included in this work are supplemented by examples and illustrations. Libraries in which there is heavy demand for materials relating to the Uniform CPA Examination can make a good case for acquiring one or more of the commercially published sources in addition to the official AICPA publications. In libraries where the demand is not so great, however, the AICPA titles should receive first consideration.

American Institute of Certified Public Accountants (AICPA)

The American Institute of Certified Public Accountants is the oldest and largest association of professional accountants in the United States. Governed primarily by boards and committees comprised of AICPA members, it promotes and maintains high professional and ethical standards, supports research, and represents the public accounting profession to government, the business community, and the general public. As was mentioned in the preceding section, it also prepares the uniform examination given to all CPA candidates. In addition, the AICPA publishes a wide range of professional accounting materials, including the *Journal of Accountancy, Accounting Trends and Techniques*, and *Industry Audit Guides*. Its library is responsible for compiling and publishing the *Accountants' Index*, a key index of periodical literature.

Basic Accounting Concepts

While it is beyond the scope of this book to delve deeply into accounting principles, practices, and procedures, three accounting concepts and their application to business reference service should be considered. These are the basic financial statements included in corporate reports, the standards followed by the accounting profession in presenting and interpreting data, and the financial ratios used to assess and compare one company with others in the same industry.

KEY FINANCIAL STATEMENTS

Although corporate annual reports and the financial statements extracted from them are common to library business collections, not all librarians and researchers are familiar or comfortable with the data they contain. This section focuses on two basic financial statements, the balance sheet and the income statement, as well as on the notes and auditor's report that accompany them.

The *balance sheet* is a status report that describes the financial condition of a company at a fixed point in time. The date designated for H.J. Heinz Company's balance sheet, for example, is April 30th, while Delta Air Lines' is June 30th. It is important to remember that the data being presented reflect conditions on the specified day only.

> The balance sheet turns out to be nothing more than a snapshot of the financial condition of a company *as of a given day*. The balance sheet is not a motion picture, or a history, or a forecast. Therefore, it does *not* show how the company got to that condition on that day, and it does *not* show where the company is heading. It simply puts a frame around one day and shows where the company is—right now.[4]

Balance sheets present information according to a designated format. The left side shows *assets*, or the company's financial resources. The assets held by Delta Air Lines and reflected in the balance sheet reproduced in figure 10.1 (see page 230), for example, include cash, supplies, property and equipment, and money owed the airline.

DELTA AIR LINES, INC.

Consolidated Balance Sheets June 30, 1986 and 1985

ASSETS	1986	1985
	(In Thousands)	
Current Assets:		
Cash	$ 61,315	$ 37,151
Accounts receivable, net of allowance for		
uncollectible accounts	425,912	489,300
Refundable income taxes	10,485	—
Maintenance and operating supplies, at average cost	35,503	35,297
Prepaid expenses and other current assets	49,660	52,446
Total current assets	582,875	614,194
Property and Equipment (Note 2):		
Flight equipment	4,174,632	3,985,796
Less—Accumulated depreciation	1,939,205	1,713,059
	2,235,427	2,272,737
Ground property and equipment	965,980	865,628
Less—Accumulated depreciation	390,324	325,618
	575,656	540,010
Advance payments for new equipment	323,399	169,780
	3,134,482	2,982,527
Other Assets:		
Investment in associated company (Note 9)	37,976	—
Funds held by bond trustees	7,677	9,927
Other	22,452	20,192
	68,105	30,119
	$3,785,462	$3,626,840

Fig. 10.1. Delta Air Lines' 1986 balance sheet: Assets. Reprinted with permission from *Delta Air Lines, Inc., Annual Report, 1986.*

The right side of a balance sheet presents two different kinds of information, liabilities and stockholders' equity. *Liabilities* are debts and other corporate obligations and, as shown in figure 10.2, may include such items as long- and short-term debt and income tax. *Stockholders' equity* is the total interest that shareholders have in a corporation. It is the company's net worth, derived by subtracting liabilities from assets, and is what stockholders would earn if the company were liquidated at its balance sheet value. Total stockholders' equity for Delta Air Lines on June 30, 1986, for example, was $1,301,946,000.

Three points about balance sheets are worth noting. First, the right and left sides are equal; they always balance. Balance sheets are, in fact, based upon the following equation:

$$\text{Assets} = \text{liabilities} + \text{stockholders' equity}$$

Second, most balance sheets include information for the preceding as well as the current year. In figures 10.1 and 10.2, for example, data are presented for 1985 as well as 1986. Finally, the notes that follow the balance sheet are an integral part of it, and should not be overlooked.

DELTA AIR LINES, INC.

LIABILITIES AND STOCKHOLDERS' EQUITY	1986	1985
	(In Thousands)	
Current Liabilities:		
Current maturities of long-term debt (Note 3)	$ 10,921	$ 2,632
Short-term notes payable (Note 5)	9,000	35,924
Commercial paper outstanding (Note 5)	41,055	132,771
Accounts payable and miscellaneous		
accrued liabilities	270,445	277,594
Air traffic liability	286,579	357,771
Accrued vacation pay	88,595	82,844
Transportation tax payable	39,342	44,649
Accrued income taxes	—	6,384
Total current liabilities	745,937	940,569
Non-Current Liabilities:		
Long-term debt (Note 3)	868,615	535,159
Other	38,949	46,170
	907,564	581,329
Deferred Credits:		
Deferred income taxes (Note 7)	427,339	447,866
Unamortized investment tax credits	150,594	166,501
Manufacturers credits	146,844	139,235
Deferred gain on sale and leaseback transactions	104,742	63,322
Other	496	924
	830,015	817,848
Commitments and Contingencies (Notes 2, 4, 9, 10 and 12)		
Stockholders' Equity (Note 6):		
Common stock, par value $3.00 per share—		
Authorized 100,000,000 shares; outstanding		
40,116,383 shares at June 30, 1986, and		
39,958,467 shares at June 30, 1985	120,349	119,875
Additional paid-in capital	93,333	86,168
Reinvested earnings	1,088,264	1,081,051
	1,301,946	1,287,094
	$3,785,462	$3,626,840

The accompanying notes are an integral part of these balance sheets.

Fig. 10.2. Delta Air Lines' 1986 balance sheet: Liabilities and stockholders' equity. Reprinted with permission from *Delta Air Lines, Inc., Annual Report, 1986.*

The second basic financial statement is the *income statement*. Also known as the *earnings report*, it shows how much money a company made—or lost—during the fiscal year being reported. While the balance sheet highlights financial conditions on a given date, the income statement reflects the entire year's activities and, as shown in figure 10.3 (see page 232), frequently includes data for earlier years. Taken together, the historic and current information in an income statement can be used to assess the company's progress and to make predictions about its future. As a result, income statements are frequently consulted by investors.

The two major items included in an income statement are revenues and expenses. *Revenues* consist of the money received for goods and services sold by the company. Revenues for Delta Air Lines, for example, come primarily from the provision of passenger and cargo air flight service. *Expenses* usually consist of overhead costs such as salaries, interest paid on loans, taxes, and other costs associated with the company's business. For Delta and other airlines, expenses also include aircraft fuel and maintenance, landing fees, and aircraft rent.

DELTA AIR LINES, INC.

Consolidated Statements of Income For the years ended June 30, 1986, 1985 and 1984

	1986	1985	1984
	(In Thousands, Except Per Share Amounts)		
Operating Revenues:			
Passenger	$4,132,284	$4,376,986	$3,963,610
Cargo	240,115	235,199	239,649
Other, net	87,663	71,930	60,472
Total operating revenues	4,460,062	4,684,115	4,263,731
Operating Expenses:			
Salaries and related costs	1,963,575	1,856,243	1,687,899
Aircraft fuel	796,883	892,182	938,189
Aircraft maintenance materials and repairs	91,590	66,022	66,397
Aircraft rent	68,518	57,090	12,365
Other rent	109,778	92,839	70,893
Landing fees	65,879	60,908	62,351
Passenger service	180,409	170,163	151,317
Passenger commissions	359,299	350,690	303,362
Other cash costs	425,723	422,840	413,086
Depreciation and amortization	363,920	349,128	346,480
Total operating expenses	4,425,574	4,318,105	4,052,339
Operating Income	34,488	366,010	211,392
Other Income (Expense):			
Interest expense	(79,113)	(84,081)	(128,065)
Less — Interest capitalized	23,758	22,028	18,263
	(55,355)	(62,053)	(109,802)
Gain on disposition of flight equipment	16,526	94,343	129,511
Miscellaneous income, net	7,775	6,863	9,114
	(31,054)	39,153	28,823
Income Before Income Taxes	3,434	405,163	240,215
Income Taxes Credited (Provided) — (Note 7)	2,228	(186,624)	(102,625)
Amortization of Investment Tax Credits	41,624	40,914	38,014
Net Income	$ 47,286	$ 259,453	$ 175,604
Net Income Per Common Share	$1.18	$6.50	$4.42

The accompanying notes are an integral part of these statements.

Fig. 10.3. Delta Air Lines' 1986 income statement. Reprinted with permission from *Delta Air Lines, Inc., Annual Report, 1986.*

By comparing revenues with expenses, the income statement reflects net profit or loss for the company for the year being reported. In addition, net earnings per share of common stock is usually included. In the income statement shown in figure 10.3, Delta's net income for 1986 was $47,286,000, and the net earnings per share, $1.18. Figures included for 1984 and 1985 give additional insight into the company's performance in 1986.

Detailed notes that clarify, qualify, and supplement data presented in the balance sheet, income statement, and other financial statements are also included in annual reports. Most offer information not contained in the text and should be examined carefully. Frequently they summarize significant accounting principles followed in preparing the financial statements, provide information on corporate operations and employee benefits, and describe pending lawsuits. The notes accompanying the financial statements in H.J. Heinz Company's annual report for 1986, for example, include the following information.

Star-Kist Foods, Inc., a wholly-owned subsidiary of H.J. Heinz Company, is a defendant together with two other tuna canners, Ralston-Purina, Inc., and Castle & Cooke, Inc., in a suit which was originally filed in February 1985.... The plaintiffs presently consist of owners of 21 tuna fishing vessels. The complaint alleges that defendants have engaged in price fixing and other violations of federal antitrust laws in connection with the purchase of raw tuna from the plaintiffs, for which they seek antitrust damages of $168 million, which, if proven, would be trebled to $504 million. Plaintiffs have also asserted in the same litigation state contract and tort claims for which they seek actual damages plus $78 million in punitive damages. Star-Kist Foods, Inc. is defending vigorously against this action and in November, 1985, filed its own antitrust and state law counterclaims against the plaintiffs.[5]

Clearly, the accompanying notes are an integral part of the financial statements presented, and require the same careful scrutiny as the statements themselves.

Following the notes that accompany the financial statements is a brief report submitted by the public accounting firm responsible for auditing the company's financial records. The auditors' report included in Delta Air Lines' annual report, shown in figure 10.4, is typical.

Auditors' Report

ARTHUR ANDERSEN & CO.

ATLANTA, GEORGIA

To the Stockholders and the Board of Directors of
    Delta Air Lines, Inc.:

    We have examined the consolidated balance sheets of DELTA AIR LINES, INC. (a Delaware corporation) and subsidiaries as of June 30, 1986 and 1985, and the related consolidated statements of income, stockholders' equity and changes in financial position for each of the three years in the period ended June 30, 1986. Our examinations were made in accordance with generally accepted auditing standards and, accordingly, included such tests of the accounting records and such other auditing procedures as we considered necessary in the circumstances.
    In our opinion, the financial statements referred to above present fairly the financial position of Delta Air Lines, Inc. and subsidiaries as of June 30, 1986 and 1985, and the results of their operations and the changes in their financial position for each of the three years in the period ended June 30, 1986, in conformity with generally accepted accounting principles applied on a consistent basis.

Arthur Andersen & Co.

August 15, 1986
(except with respect to Note 10,
as to which the date is
September 11, 1986)

Fig. 10.4. Auditors' report accompanying Delta Air Lines' 1986 annual report. Reprinted with permission from *Delta Air Lines, Inc., Annual Report, 1986.*

Just as physicians presented with the same set of symptoms may diagnose different ailments, so also may public accountants auditing the same financial statements reach different conclusions. For this reason, auditors' reports are presented as opinions. Usually the opinion is that the financial statements are fair, and that they have been prepared in conformity with generally accepted accounting principles. If circumstances warrant, the auditors can qualify their opinion for an exception taken or state an adverse opinion. It is rare, however, for a report to be issued with an adverse opinion. External audits, as mentioned earlier, are always conducted by independent CPAs in public accounting practice and, in the case of large, blue-chip companies, are usually conducted by one of the Big Eight accounting firms.

Corporate financial statements are included in annual reports, and they are also reproduced in such commercially published sources as Standard & Poor's *Corporation Records* and *Moody's Manuals*. As a result, familiarity with basic terms, concepts, and applications can be extremely helpful to librarians in understanding requests for assistance and in providing information to business researchers. One way to gain such familiarity is by studying *How to Read a Financial Report*, a booklet published for investors by Merrill Lynch, Pierce, Fenner, & Smith.[6] *How to Read a Financial Report* describes balance sheets and income statements, explains their constituent parts, and discusses their application to investment decisions.

Also useful is the *Special Edition Annual Report* offered to educators and librarians by Armstrong World Industries, Inc. The *Report* consists of Armstrong's most recent annual report to shareholders, accompanied by a brochure that explains and defines many of the terms and concepts employed, citing specific examples from the shareholders' report.[7]

Financial statements are covered in greater detail in accounting handbooks and textbooks, and in even more depth in such specialized sources as Leopold Bernstein's *Analysis of Financial Statements* (Homewood, Ill.: Dow Jones-Irwin, 1984), *Balance Sheet Basics* (New York: Franklin Watts, 1986), and *How to Read a Financial Report* (Cleveland, Ohio: Penton/IPC, 1983), a programmed learning guide to the fundamentals of financial reporting.

ACCOUNTING PRINCIPLES AND STANDARDS

Accounting principles are human creations. They are not, writes Stephen Moscove, "like the immutable laws of nature found in physics and chemistry,"[8] but are instead rules developed by the accounting profession to serve the needs of the business community, investors, and government. Also known as *standards*, accounting principles are fundamental guidelines that help to determine whether or not specific choices of ways to record accounting information are acceptable. Their purpose is to ensure that the financial statements prepared by accountants are relevant, reliable, and comparable.

Accountants use the phrase *generally accepted accounting principles*, or *GAAP*, to refer to the body of conventions, rules, and procedures that define accounting practices at a particular time. Thus, an auditor's assurance that the financial statements examined present information fairly and in accordance with generally accepted accounting principles means that the financial accounting procedures followed reflect the consensus of accountants and officials regarding proper accounting practices at the time the report was prepared.

Generally accepted accounting principles are not static. New accounting methods and conventions are developed as changes in the economy, law, business, and accounting warrant. Many gradually gain widespread acceptance and emerge as generally accepted accounting principles.

> The general acceptance of an accounting principle or practice usually depends on
> how well it meets three criteria: relevance, objectivity, and feasibility. A principle
> is *relevant* to the extent that it results in information that is meaningful and useful
> to those who need to know something about a certain organization. A principle

is *objective* to the extent that the information is not influenced by the personal bias or judgment of those who furnish it. Objectivity connotes reliability, trustworthiness. It also connotes verifiability, which means that there is some way of ascertaining the correctness of the information reported. A principle is *feasible* to the extent that it can be implemented without undue complexity or cost.[9]

Such acceptance is greatly influenced by government agencies, by professional organizations in accounting and related fields, and by academicians, securities analysts, bankers, other professionals, and major corporations.

Although many organizations have affected the formulation of accounting principles, the most important today are the Securities and Exchange Commission and the Financial Accounting Standards Board.

The Securities and Exchange Commission (SEC) was established by Congress in 1934 to regulate the nation's securities markets and to assure that investors have adequate information on which to base their investment decisions. Among other things, Congress empowered the SEC to establish the accounting principles to be followed by publicly traded companies in reporting their financial condition. Although the SEC has chosen to delegate much of that responsibility to professional accounting organizations such as the Financial Accounting Standards Board, its role in helping to set and enforce those principles should not be underestimated.

While the Securities and Exchange Commission has statutory authority to establish standards of financial accounting and reporting, it is the Financial Accounting Standards Board, or FASB, that is primarily responsible for setting generally accepted accounting principles for financial reporting. Established in 1973, the FASB consists of a substantial research staff and seven full-time board members appointed by the Financial Accounting Foundation. Like the foundation, the Financial Accounting Standards Board is independent of all other business and professional organizations. Its standards are recognized as authoritative and official by the Securities and Exchange Commission, the American Institute of Certified Public Accountants, and other organizations.

The Financial Accounting Standards Board issues three main types of accounting pronouncements. *Statements of Financial Accounting Standards* (SFAS) are authoritative statements that spell out current accounting standards. More than 70 SFAS have been issued, each dealing with a specific accounting topic. SFAS 45, for example, deals with accounting for franchise fee revenue, and SFAS 74, with accounting for special termination benefits paid to employees. In addition, the FASB issues *Statements of Financial Accounting Concepts*, publications that describe ideas and concepts that will guide the development of future accounting standards and that may provide the groundwork for a philosophical framework for financial accounting and reporting. Finally, as their name implies, *Interpretations of Statements of Financial Accounting Standards* explain, clarify, and sometimes amend previously issued statements of standards. Over 40 such interpretations have been issued. In addition, the FASB publishes *Technical Bulletins, Exposure Drafts, Discussion Memoranda*, and special research reports. All can be purchased separately from the FASB or acquired through subscription plans.[10]

Prior to the creation of the Financial Accounting Standards Board in 1973, the American Institute of Certified Public Accountants was responsible for promulgation of generally accepted accounting principles. From 1939 to 1959, the AICPA issued over 50 *Accounting Research Bulletins* (ARBs) and *Accounting Terminology Bulletins* through its Committee on Accounting Procedures. In 1960, the institute established the Accounting Principles Board (APB) to issue authoritative opinions and to publish research studies. Before its dissolution in 1973, the APB issued 31 *Opinions*, which were later adopted by the FASB as part of generally accepted accounting principles.

A wide range of publications, many of them looseleaf services that permit continuous updating, are available to keep accountants apprised of FASB and AICPA official pronouncements. Some of the most widely used are listed and discussed below.

FASB Accounting Standards – Current Text. New York: McGraw-Hill, 1982- . 2v. Looseleaf.

Miller, Martin A. **Miller Comprehensive GAAP Guide**. New York: Harcourt Brace Jovanovich, 1974- . Annual.

AICPA Professional Standards. Chicago: Commerce Clearing House, 1974- . 2v. Looseleaf.

FASB Accounting Standards – Current Text integrates FASB and AICPA pronouncements on financial accounting into a single two-volume text, including such items as the FASB's *Statements of Financial Accounting Standards, Interpretations of Statements of Financial Accounting Standards*, and *Technical Bulletins*, the AICPA Committee on Accounting Procedures' *Accounting Research Bulletins*, and the Accounting Principles Board's *Opinions* and *Interpretations*. Arrangement is alphabetical by subject, with sections in each volume including summaries of the topics covered, the standards themselves, glossaries, and interpretive materials. *FASB Accounting Standards – Current Text* is also available in an annual paperback edition from McGraw-Hill.

Similarly, *Miller Comprehensive GAAP Guide* presents generally accepted accounting principles in current use. In contrast to the official Financial Accounting Standards Board publication issued by McGraw-Hill, however, *Miller* has been rewritten to eliminate jargon and increase comprehension by using what its authors describe as "plain, understandable English."

AICPA Professional Standards includes standards that apply to other types of public accounting – most notably, management services and tax consulting – as well as those pertinent to financial accounting and auditing. It is a compilation of professional auditing and accounting standards currently in effect. The first volume, *U.S. Auditing Standards*, includes auditing principles in force, reports of the AICPA's Committee on Auditing Standards, and auditing interpretations. The second volume includes AICPA's bylaws and code of professional ethics, statements on standards for management advisory services and tax practice, and statements on quality control standards. Like *FASB Accounting Standards, AICPA Professional Standards* is also available in a paperback edition.

AUDITING STANDARDS

Another acronym common to accounting is *GAAS*, or *generally accepted auditing standards*. While GAAP refers to rules and conventions followed in presenting financial information, GAAS refers to the rules followed by public accountants in auditing clients' financial records. Generally accepted auditing standards are developed by the Auditing Standards Board of the American Institute of Certified Public Accountants, the senior technical body of the institute, responsible for issuing pronouncements on auditing matters. All CPAs are required to follow the rules and procedures set forth by the Auditing Standards Board. Just as an auditor's report verifies that generally accepted accounting principles have been followed, so also does it indicate that the auditor preparing the report has followed generally accepted auditing standards when reviewing the statements for accuracy. Both GAAS and GAAP are important. The auditor's statement that a financial report has been examined in accordance with GAAS and has been found to conform to GAAP is, as one writer notes, "about as nice a compliment as you can pay a financial statement."[11] Publications dealing with auditing standards are abundant. Two of the most widely used are listed below.

AICPA Professional Standards. Vol. I: *U.S. Auditing Standards*. Chicago: Commerce Clearing House, 1974- . Looseleaf.

Miller, Martin A. **Miller Comprehensive GAAS Guide**. New York: Harcourt Brace Jovanovich, 1982- . Annual.

U.S. Auditing Standards, the first volume of *AICPA Professional Standards*, deals with auditing standards and guidelines. It includes *Statements on Auditing Standards* issued by the Auditing Standards Board, covering such subjects as the training and proficiency of independent auditors, adherence to principles, and the circumstances under which auditors may issue adverse opinions. A topical index and appendixes are also included.

Like its GAAP counterpart, *Miller Comprehensive GAAS Guide* restates auditing standards in basic, jargon-free English. Arranged to correspond to the types of auditing or accounting services that CPAs provide to their clients, the annual paperback offers an inexpensive alternative to the more comprehensive and up-to-date service published by Commerce Clearing House.

RATIO ANALYSIS

Until now, discussion of basic accounting concepts has focused on accounting and auditing standards and on two important financial statements, the balance sheet and income statement. This section considers another basic concept, ratio analysis, and examines some of the sources that contain information used in ratio analysis.

Sometimes managers and executives, government officials, investors, and others use financial information just as it is presented in financial statements. Frequently, however, they convert it into ratios to facilitate comparison. For example, an investment analyst studying Delta Air Lines' balance sheet for 1986 (figures 10.2 and 10.3) might report that the company has current assets of $582,875,000 and current liabilities of $745,937,000. He might also convert those figures to a ratio, dividing current assets by current liabilities. In the case of Delta Air Lines, the ratio of current assets to current liabilities is .78 to 1. This ratio, called *Current Ratio*, gives a rough indication of a company's ability to pay its current debts. A firm with a Current Ratio of 2.5 to 1, for example, might be assumed to be better able to meet its financial obligations than one with a ratio of 1 to 1, or .78 to 1.

A ratio is simply one number expressed in terms of another. *Ratio analysis* is the study of relationships between and among various items on financial statements. Each ratio relates one item on the balance sheet (or income statement) with another or, more often, relates one element from the balance sheet to one from the income statement. Financial ratios are measures of corporate performance, and are particularly useful when compared with similar ratios for earlier years or with ratios for other companies in the same industry.

> Ratios give us two things: (1) a way of determining how we are measuring up to other folks who do the same kinds of the things we do for a living and (2) a method of examining our financial performance in an orderly way, moving through our operations step by step.[12]

As shown in figure 10.5 (see page 238), a number of financial ratios are in common usage, each serving as a yardstick against which a company can compare one aspect of current performance to earlier years or to the industry norm. When historical standards are used, the company's ratios are compared from one year to another. By looking at changes over time, it is possible to identify trends and to appraise current performance in the light of historical relationships. Data used in historic ratio analysis for a specific company can be obtained from its annual reports or from commercially published sources, such as those issued by Standard & Poor's, Moody's, and Value Line.

Ratio	Formula	Significance
Current ratio	Current assets ÷ Current liabilities	Test of debt-paying ability
Acid-test (quick) ratio	(Cash + Net receivables + Marketable securities) ÷ Current liabilities	Test of immediate debt-paying ability
Accounts receivable turnover	Net sales ÷ Average net accounts receivable	Test of quality of accounts receivable
Average collection period	Number of days in year ÷ Accounts receivable turn-over ratio	Test of quality of accounts receivable
Inventory turnover	Cost of goods sold ÷ Average inventory	Test of whether or not a sufficient volume of business is being generated relative to inventory
Total assets turnover	Net sales ÷ Average total assets	Test of whether or not volume of business generated is adequate relative to amount of capital invested in business
Equity ratio	Owners' (Stockholders') equity ÷ Total equities	Index of long-run solvency and safety
Earning power	Net operating earnings ÷ Operating assets	Measure of managerial effectiveness
Net earnings to stock-holders' equity	Net earnings ÷ Average stockholders' equity	Measure of what a given company earned for its stockholders from all sources as a percentage of the stockholders' investment
Earnings per share (of common stock)	Net earnings available to common stockholders ÷ Average number of shares of common stock outstanding	Tends to have an effect on the market price per share
Number of times interest is earned	Net earnings before interest and taxes ÷ Interest expense	Indicates likelihood that bondholders will continue to receive their interest payments
Number of times preferred dividends are earned	Net earnings after income taxes ÷ Preferred dividends	Indicates the probability that preferred stockholders will receive their dividend each year
Earnings yield	Earnings per share ÷ Current market price per share	Useful for comparison with other stocks
Price-earnings ratio	Current market price per share ÷ Earnings per share	Index of whether a stock is relatively cheap or expensive
Dividend yield	Dividend per share ÷ Current market price per share	Useful for comparison with other stocks
Payout ratio	Dividend per share ÷ Earnings per share	Index of whether company pays out large percentage of earnings as dividends or reinvests most of its earnings

Fig. 10.5. Summary of financial ratios. Reprinted by permission of publisher from R. F. Salmonsen, *A Survey of Basic Accounting*, 3rd ed., copyright © 1981, R. D. Irwin.

Industry standards, in contrast, involve a comparison of a particular company's ratios to those of other companies in the same line of business. Standards of comparison include ratios calculated from the financial statements of similar companies or average ratios for an industry. Industry ratios are available in several different sources, some of the most important of which are discussed below.

Robert Morris Associates. **Annual Statement Studies**. Philadelphia: Robert Morris Associates, 1923- . Annual.

Troy, Leo. **Almanac of Business and Industrial Financial Ratios**. Englewood Cliffs, N.J.: Prentice-Hall, 1971- . Annual.

Dun & Bradstreet Credit Services. **Industry Norms and Key Business Ratios: Library Edition**. New York: Dun & Bradstreet, 1982/83- . Annual.

Robert Morris Associates, the national association of bank loan and credit officers, has long been noted for its extensive work in ratio compilation and analysis. Each year, it collects financial statements submitted to member banks from current and prospective borrowers in many different industries. The statements are then compiled by industry category, and are published as Robert Morris Associates' *Annual Statement Studies*. Although it is designed primarily for commercial bankers who need to compare one company's performance with the industry norm to determine whether or not the company is a good credit risk, *Annual Statement Studies* is also used by business people, executives, researchers, students, and librarians.

Annual Statement Studies contains composite financial data on manufacturing, wholesaling, retailing, service, and contractor industries. Arrangement is by broad category, such as manufacturing, and then by industry group and line of business. For example, "Beverages," one of the industries included in the Manufacturing section, includes separate pages for "Bottled and Canned Soft Drinks and Carbonated Water"; "Flavoring Extracts and Syrups"; and "Wines, Distilled Liquors, and Liqueurs." Each line of business is represented by a page-long entry that includes detailed financial information and financial ratios (see figure 10.6 on page 240).

As shown in figure 10.6, a typical page in *Annual Statement Studies* consists of several vertical and horizontal columns and an almost bewildering array of figures. One of the easiest ways to understand the information that each entry contains is by using the center column to divide the left and right sides of the page, and to draw an imaginary horizontal line between the top of the page and the horizontal columns labeled "Ratios." Keeping these divisions in mind, some generalizations can be made about the information included for each industry.

The top part of the page begins with the name and Standard Industrial Classification of the industry being reported. In figure 10.6, for example, the industry is Electronic Computing Equipment Manufacturers, and the SIC is 3573. Most of the information presented in the top half of the page is taken from balance sheets ("Assets" and "Liabilities") and income statements ("Income Data"). Instead of being expressed in dollars and cents, however, each item is expressed as a percentage. Thus, 27.9, the number shown in the "Inventory" column for all companies reporting, indicates that corporate inventories constitute 27.9 percent of total corporate assets for the 227 computing equipment manufacturers reporting.

Other divisions on the page should also be noted. Data to the right of the center column, for example, are historic; data to the left, current. In addition, current data are categorized by asset size, grouped into four categories, ranging from companies with assets of less than $1 million to those with assets of from $50 to $100 million. Thus, of the 227 manufacturers of electronic computing equipment reporting in 1985, 38 had assets of less than $1 million; 98 had assets of between $1 and $10 million; 65 had assets of more than $10 million but less than $50 million, and 26 were in the top category. These categories are important, because they permit comparison between companies of roughly comparable size. A fifth column, marked "All," is the financial composite of all 227 companies reporting.

MANUFACTURERS - ELECTRONIC COMPUTING EQUIPMENT SIC# 3573　　111

Current Data					Type of Statement	Comparative Historical Data				
5	54	43	20	122	Unqualified					122
9	9	6	1	16	Qualified					16
11	14			25	Reviewed	DATA NOT AVAILABLE				25
9	4	1	2	16	Compiled					16
13	17	15	3	48	Other					48

102(6/30-9/30/84)　　125(10/1/84-3/31/85)

0-1MM	1-10MM	10-50MM	50-100MM	ALL	ASSET SIZE	6/30/80-3/31/81	6/30/81-3/31/82	6/30/82-3/31/83	6/30/83-3/31/84	6/30/84-3/31/85
38	98	65	26	227	NUMBER OF STATEMENTS	ALL 181	ALL 195	ALL 178	ALL 188	ALL 227
%	%	%	%	%	**ASSETS**	%	%	%	%	%
11.3	8.4	10.7	16.8	10.5	Cash & Equivalents	8.6	10.9	10.3	13.8	10.5
33.2	32.2	27.7	24.6	30.2	Trade Receivables - (net)	30.2	27.6	28.6	28.8	30.2
23.8	28.8	28.2	29.6	27.9	Inventory	33.7	30.2	28.3	25.8	27.9
1.6	2.9	1.4	3.5	2.3	All Other Current	2.1	3.4	2.5	3.1	2.3
69.9	72.2	68.1	74.3	70.9	Total Current	74.7	72.1	69.7	71.5	70.9
22.8	21.2	23.2	20.1	21.9	Fixed Assets (net)	18.4	19.3	23.2	21.5	21.9
.9	.9	1.8	.9	1.1	Intangibles (net)	1.2	1.2	1.4	1.0	1.1
6.5	5.7	7.0	4.7	6.1	All Other Non-Current	5.7	7.5	5.7	6.0	6.1
100.0	100.0	100.0	100.0	100.0	Total	100.0	100.0	100.0	100.0	100.0
					LIABILITIES					
11.2	10.7	8.0	3.9	9.2	Notes Payable-Short Term	8.5	7.5	6.7	6.7	9.2
3.5	2.6	1.7	.9	2.3	Cur. Mat.-L/T/D	2.4	2.3	2.3	3.0	2.3
18.5	17.0	10.8	8.6	14.5	Trade Payables	14.3	14.9	13.4	14.8	14.5
1.4	1.8	1.8	2.5	1.8	Income Taxes Payable	–	–	–	–	1.8
10.9	12.5	10.2	7.8	11.0	All Other Current	13.0	12.6	12.5	12.0	11.0
45.5	44.6	32.5	23.6	38.9	Total Current	38.2	37.4	34.8	36.4	38.9
12.7	11.2	10.4	7.8	10.8	Long Term Debt	12.3	12.7	12.3	11.2	10.8
.3	1.0	1.3	2.0	1.1	Deferred Taxes	–	–	–	–	1.1
1.3	2.3	2.5	1.2	2.1	All Other Non-Current	3.2	2.8	5.0	2.6	2.1
40.3	40.9	53.2	65.5	47.1	Net Worth	46.3	47.1	47.9	49.9	47.1
100.0	100.0	100.0	100.0	100.0	Total Liabilities & Net Worth	100.0	100.0	100.0	100.0	100.0
					INCOME DATA					
100.0	100.0	100.0	100.0	100.0	Net Sales	100.0	100.0	100.0	100.0	100.0
39.0	41.7	41.8	37.9	40.9	Gross Profit	40.2	41.2	40.3	40.1	40.9
32.5	34.9	36.4	27.3	34.1	Operating Expenses	30.1	34.2	34.5	34.3	34.1
6.5	6.8	5.4	10.5	6.8	Operating Profit	10.1	7.0	5.8	5.9	6.8
1.8	-1.5	1.2	.0	1.3	All Other Expenses (net)	1.3	.8	.9	1.2	1.3
4.6	5.3	4.2	10.5	5.5	Profit Before Taxes	8.8	6.1	4.9	4.6	5.5
					RATIOS					
2.2	2.4	3.9	4.4	2.8	Current	2.9	2.9	3.5	3.5	2.8
1.7	1.7	2.3	3.6	1.9		2.3	2.1	2.1	2.0	1.9
1.3	1.2	1.6	2.4	1.4		1.4	1.4	1.4	1.5	1.4
1.4	1.4	2.2	3.3	1.7	Quick	1.6	1.7	1.9	2.1	1.7
1.1	.9	1.3	1.7	1.1		1.1	1.0	1.1	1.1	1.1
.8	.6	.8	1.0	.7		.7	.7	.7	.7	.7
35 10.3	51 7.1	64 5.7	58 6.3	53 6.9	Sales/Receivables	53 6.9	50 7.3	51 7.2	49 7.4	53 6.9
54 6.8	70 5.2	81 4.5	81 4.5	72 5.1		68 5.4	64 5.7	65 5.6	68 5.4	72 5.1
74 4.9	94 3.9	111 3.3	94 3.9	94 3.9		85 4.3	89 4.1	79 4.6	91 4.0	94 3.9
27 13.5	65 5.6	104 3.5	107 3.4	69 5.3	Cost of Sales/Inventory	89 4.1	81 4.5	76 4.8	64 5.7	69 5.3
69 5.3	118 3.1	152 2.4	159 2.3	122 3.0		140 2.6	126 2.9	118 3.1	111 3.3	122 3.0
135 2.7	174 2.1	215 1.7	203 1.8	183 2.0		183 2.0	166 2.2	166 2.2	183 2.0	183 2.0
20 18.4	35 10.3	33 11.0	24 15.0	29 12.7	Cost of Sales/Payables	30 12.3	33 10.9	28 13.2	31 11.8	29 12.7
36 10.1	53 6.9	47 7.8	38 9.5	49 7.5		45 8.1	55 6.6	43 8.4	51 7.2	49 7.5
85 4.3	94 3.9	89 4.1	63 5.8	87 4.2		70 5.2	74 4.9	70 5.2	79 4.6	87 4.2
5.6	3.4	2.1	1.7	2.6	Sales/Working Capital	2.9	2.8	2.7	2.4	2.6
9.7	6.2	3.2	2.1	4.9		4.1	4.1	4.5	4.2	4.9
20.0	15.4	5.4	3.9	10.4		8.1	10.3	9.0	9.0	10.4
9.9	13.2	15.5	17.9	13.8	EBIT/Interest	13.0	11.7	9.8	13.1	13.8
(31) 4.6	(74) 3.4	(47) 4.6	(18) 6.1	(170) 4.4		(156) 5.4	(166) 3.5	(148) 3.1	(153) 4.0	(170) 4.4
1.2	1.2	-6.0	2.4	1.1		2.8	1.1	1.2	1.2	1.1
16.0	16.8	18.5	37.7	18.4	Cash Flow/Cur. Mat. L/T/D	16.7	13.0	27.9	18.9	18.4
(19) 4.9	(53) 5.3	(40) 7.4	(16) 7.9	(128) 6.2		(116) 6.1	(115) 3.6	(120) 7.3	(121) 3.9	(128) 6.2
1.1	2.2	.6	4.1	2.1		2.7	1.0	1.5	.9	2.1
.3	.3	.3	.2	.3	Fixed/Worth	.2	.2	.3	.3	.3
.6	.5	.4	.3	.5		.4	.4	.5	.4	.5
1.1	.9	.6	.5	.8		.7	.7	.8	.7	.8
.7	.7	.4	.3	.6	Debt/Worth	.7	.6	.5	.5	.6
1.4	1.3	.8	.5	1.1		1.2	1.1	1.1	1.0	1.1
2.9	3.8	1.5	.8	2.3		2.3	2.2	2.0	2.0	2.3
53.4	60.2	25.9	31.7	47.9	% Profit Before Taxes/Tangible Net Worth	51.9	44.0	39.7	41.6	47.9
(35) 26.6	(95) 25.0	(62) 15.2	20.2	(218) 21.2		(180) 30.3	(192) 23.7	(173) 21.3	(184) 17.0	(218) 21.2
5.8	2.8	-10.0	2.7	2.0		14.3	1.7	3.8	2.8	2.0
22.4	19.6	16.7	20.4	19.7	% Profit Before Taxes/Total Assets	20.7	21.2	18.8	16.8	19.7
12.4	8.3	7.0	14.3	9.0		13.5	10.3	8.6	8.6	9.0
1.0	1.1	-5.1	1.9	.6		5.4	.6	1.1	1.2	.6
18.7	15.5	8.8	8.3	12.6	Sales/Net Fixed Assets	19.6	17.4	13.2	13.4	12.6
11.6	8.4	5.7	6.4	7.6		10.1	8.9	8.2	7.4	7.6
6.6	5.0	3.5	4.5	4.9		6.4	5.4	4.6	4.6	4.9
2.9	2.1	1.4	1.5	2.1	Sales/Total Assets	2.1	1.9	2.0	2.0	2.1
2.5	1.6	1.1	1.2	1.5		1.6	1.5	1.5	1.4	1.5
1.7	1.1	.9	.9	1.0		1.3	1.1	1.2	1.0	1.0
1.8	1.5	2.5	2.3	1.8	% Depr., Dep., Amort./Sales	1.2	1.4	1.5	1.7	1.8
(35) 2.8	(76) 2.4	(56) 3.2	(24) 3.1	(191) 3.0		(161) 2.0	(168) 2.1	(158) 2.6	(166) 2.6	(191) 3.0
3.9	4.3	4.3	3.9	4.1		3.1	3.8	3.8	4.1	4.1
5.7	2.3			2.4	% Officers' Comp/Sales	3.3	2.3	2.0	3.2	2.4
(14) 9.0	(16) 3.7			(31) 5.8		(27) 7.1	(26) 4.3	(24) 5.5	(30) 5.3	(31) 5.8
13.1	6.6			10.0		10.4	8.5	7.9	8.1	10.0
49440M	562970M	1728698M	2168947M	4510055M	Net Sales ($)	4045380M	3910087M	3839166M	3720439M	4510055M
21533M	372107M	1437013M	1770070M	3600723M	Total Assets ($)	2918480M	3014996M	2856211M	3433102M	3600723M

M = $thousand   MM = $million
See Pages 1 through 13 for Explanation of Ratios and Data

Fig. 10.6. Typical listing, *Annual Statement Studies*. Reprinted by permission.

Also included in the "Current Data" section at the top of the page is a breakdown by type of financial statement and an indication of the periods being reported. The notations "102(6/30-9/30/84)" and "125(10/1/84-3/31/85)" indicate that 102 of the financial statements had fiscal dates falling between June 30 and September 30, 1984, and that the remaining 125 had fiscal dates falling between October 1, 1984, and March 31, 1985.

Columns to the right present consolidated historical data from earlier years. Note that historic financial information is not categorized by asset size of reporting companies and that the number of companies reporting may vary from one year to another.

The bottom part of the page consists primarily of 16 different financial ratios, ranging from Current Ratio to a ratio of officers' compensation divided by net sales. The ratios, their derivation, and applications are described in the preliminary pages of *Annual Statement Studies*; only the names of the ratios are listed, with accompanying data, in the entry for each industry.

For each ratio, three different values—the upper quartile, median, and lower quartile—are given. Robert Morris Associates describes the methodology used for computing these values.

> For any given ratio, these figures are calculated by first computing the value of the ratio for *each* financial statement in the sample.... In such an array of ratio values, the figure which falls in the middle between the strongest and the weakest ratios is the *median*. The figure that falls halfway between the median and the strongest ratio is the *upper quartile*. The figure that falls halfway between the median and the weakest ratio is the *lower quartile*.[13]

Robert Morris Associates uses medians and quartiles instead of average figures to better reflect the full range of ratio values within an industry. Median and quartile values are always shown in this order: upper quartile, median, and lower quartile. For companies manufacturing electronic computing equipment and with assets between $50 and $100 million, for example, the array for one ratio, Current Ratio, is 4.4, 3.6, and 2.4. In other words, 3.6 is the median Current Ratio, 4.4, the upper quartile, and 2.4, the lower quartile. Just as with the variety of asset size classes for companies in a particular industry, the three different ratio categories make it possible to assess more thoroughly corporate performance.

Additional numbers are presented in boldface type for three of the ratios relating to sales. For example, the entry for the Sales/Receivable Ratio for manufacturers of electronic computing equipment with assets of less than $1 million is:

35	10.3
54	6.8
74	4.9

The numbers in boldface, which are always to the left of the ratios to which they refer, are for days. Using the example shown above, the median Sales/Receivable Ratio, which measures the company's ability to collect its account receivables, is 6.8, the number of days, 54. The 6.8 ratio means that the median company has annual sales equal to 6.8 times its receivables. The boldface number to the left of the ratio represents a conversion of the Sales/Receivable Ratio into days. In the case of the Sales/Receivable Ratio, the days' receivable figure represents the number of days that pass, on average, between company billing and the receipt of payment. In the example shown above, the company collects its money approximately 54 days after billing.

For some ratios, additional numbers, enclosed in parentheses, are also included. Such numbers are used to indicate that not all of the companies in a particular asset size category reported the information in question.

In addition to the data presented for each industry, *Annual Statement Studies* includes explanations of balance sheet and income data, definitions of ratios, a listing of SICs covered, and a bibliography of sources of composite financial information for industries not included.

For the 340 industries covered, *Annual Statement Studies* is the most detailed information source of composite financial information available. It is a basic business reference tool; the time invested in learning what it contains and how to use it will reap ample returns. Robert Morris Associates cautions that the *Annual Statement Studies* be regarded only as a general guideline and not as an absolute industry norm. This is due to limited samples within categories, the categorization of companies by their primary Standard Industrial Classification (SIC) number only, and different methods of operations by companies within the same industry. For these reasons, RMA recommends that the figures be used only as general guidelines in addition to other methods of financial analysis.

The *Almanac of Business and Industrial Financial Ratios* is another basic source. Compiled annually from data collected by the Internal Revenue Service, the *Almanac* provides information on more than 250 different lines of business. As compared to the *Annual Statement Studies*, the *Almanac* covers fewer businesses and presents fewer ratios. Further, while *Annual Statement Studies* presents three different values (upper quartile, median, lower quartile), the *Almanac* includes only the industry average for each ratio. Finally, although both the *Almanac* and *Annual Statement Studies* are published yearly, data in the *Statement Studies* are more current. In contrast, information in the *Almanac* may be as many as four or even five years old.

If these were the only differences between the publications, the *Almanac* would be of negligible value. However, while the *Annual Statement Studies* covers more industries in greater depth, it lacks some of the features available in the *Almanac*. First, a greater number of companies in each line of business are represented in the *Almanac*, which is based on tax returns rather than on financial statements submitted to banks. The industry composite for manufacturers of computers in *Annual Statement Studies*, for example, is based on data from 227 firms, while the composite in the *Almanac* is based on tax returns from 861 companies. In addition, the *Almanac* uses a greater number of asset-size categories. In all, 12 different categories are used, ranging in size from "zero assets" to "$250 million and more." The *Almanac* also distinguishes between profit-making companies and those that are not. Each entry is two pages long, with the first page presenting composite data for all companies in the industry, and the second page limited to companies that earned a profit for the year being reported. In many instances, these features result in even greater precision than is possible with *Annual Statement Studies*. Consequently, most business libraries subscribe to both publications.

A third basic source, *Industry Norms and Key Business Ratios: Library Edition* presents composite financial information for over 800 different lines of business, arranged by Standard Industrial Classification. Based on data collected by Dun & Bradstreet for its credit reporting service, entries for each business include balance sheet and income statement information and 14 financial ratios. Although *Industry Norms and Key Business Ratios* does assign the same values to ratios as *Annual Statement Studies*, it does not categorize companies by asset size and generally includes less information for each line of business than either *Annual Statement Studies* or the *Almanac of Business and Industrial Financial Ratios*. Its real strength is in its timeliness and the wide array of industries it covers.

Only general data are supplied in the *Library Edition*. Although Dun & Bradstreet also publishes a series of industry volumes that include detailed geographic and asset-size breakdowns and offers microcomputer disk versions as well, they are costly and are not available in most libraries.

The three titles discussed above are among the most important sources of composite financial information, but they are by no means the only ones. Others include the Accounting Corporation of America's semiannual *Barometer of Small Business* and the Census Bureau's *Quarterly Report for Manufacturing, Mining and Trade Corporations*. The composite industry sources listed above, however, are not inclusive. Not every industry is covered. "If," as Dick Levin writes, "you manufacture corrugated steel pipe, maple flooring, or fabricated roof trusses, or if you install ceiling tiles,"[14] the composite sources may not be particularly useful. In such instances, the best recourse is to identify sources of financial and ratio information for a single industry or group of related industries. Such publications are commonly issued by trade associations, accounting firms, large corporations, government agencies, and universities. Of these, trade associations are perhaps the most important providers of financial data, covering businesses and industries that are not included elsewhere. A sample of titles indicates the scope and diversity of these publications. The *Annual Key Ratio Survey of the Folding Carton and Rigid Box Industry*, for example, is published by the National Paperbox and Packaging Association, while the Healthcare Financial Management Association publishes the *Hospital Industry Analysis Report*, and the National Automatic Merchandising Association, *Cost and Profit Ratios for Vending Operators*. Many of the association publications are inexpensive, and a few, when requested on library letterheads, are free.[15] Some association publications are annotated in the *Annual Statement Studies'* bibliography, "Sources of Composite Financial Data." An even more comprehensive listing of trade associations issuing industry ratio studies is included in *Ratio Analysis for Small Business*, which was published by the Small Business Administration in 1970. The booklet lists some 70 different trade associations, ranging from the American Association of Advertising Agencies to the Wine and Spirit Wholesalers of America, Inc.[16]

Not all libraries stock these specialized sources of financial information and accounting principles and standards. A number of more general publications are discussed below.

SOURCES OF ACCOUNTING INFORMATION

The literature of accounting is voluminous. It includes numerous handbooks, looseleaf services, periodicals, documents, and other sources, some written for accounting practitioners and others for non-accountants. This section considers many of the types of accounting information sources generally consulted, and lists and describes representative publications in each category. Readers should, however, keep in mind that the literature of accounting reflects continuing and continuous changes. As accounting theories, practices, and principles change, so also do many accounting sources.

Guides, Bibliographies, and Dictionaries

For librarians and researchers confronted for the first time with an accounting research problem, one of the best ways to gain familiarity with the literature is by referring to guides and bibliographies. Two guides are ordinarily consulted.

Demarest, Rosemary. **Accounting Information Sources**. Detroit: Gale Research Co., 1970. 420p.

Daniells, Lorna. "Accounting/Control and Taxation," **Business Information Sources**. Rev. ed. Berkeley, Calif.: University of California Press, 1985, pp. 178-304.

Accounting Information Sources is an annotated guide to the literature, associations, and government agencies concerned with accounting. Compiled by the former chief librarian at Price Waterhouse, the guide remains in print and in use despite its 1970 imprint date. Although many of the publications listed in the "Handbooks" and "Books" sections have been revised or superseded since *Accounting Information Sources* was published, other sections such as "Modern Accounting: Background" and "Governmental Regulations" remain useful. Also helpful are the appended lists of state boards of accountancy and state societies of CPAs. As with any other guide that has not been recently updated, however, care must be exercised to ensure that the information presented is still accurate. In spite of this major drawback, *Accounting Information Sources* remains the most comprehensive guide to accounting literature presently available.

More recent information can be found in "Accounting/Control and Taxation." This chapter from *Business Information Sources* lists and annotates accounting handbooks and textbooks, periodicals, indexes and abstracts, looseleaf services, and basic reference sources, and features sections that deal with specific types of accounting such as management, government, and financial accounting and auditing. Also included are sections on accounting systems for specific types of businesses, surveys of accounting practice, and accounting for multinational enterprises.

> U.S. Superintendent of Documents. **Accounting and Auditing**. Washington, D.C.: Government Printing Office, 1987. (Subject Bibliography 42). 2p.

Although the sources mentioned above are useful, they do not include many government documents. *Accounting and Auditing*, a brief bibliography published irregularly by the Superintendent of Documents, lists and annotates selected relevant federal documents. As with other bibliographies in the Superintendent of Documents' *Subject Bibliographies* series, entries include annotations, Superintendent of Documents classification numbers, GPO stock numbers, prices, and ordering information. While the emphasis is on government accounting, other subjects are also covered; accounting and auditing practices for small business, for example, are well represented. Like the other GPO Subject Bibliographies, *Accounting and Auditing* is free.[17]

The accounting profession has its own vocabulary and conventions. It includes many unique words and, in addition, uses familiar words in unique ways. As a result, most business reference collections supplement standard business dictionaries with specialized accounting sources. Some of the best known are listed below.

> Cooper, W. W., and Yuji Ijiri, eds. **Kohler's Dictionary for Accountants**. 6th ed. Englewood Cliffs, N.J.: Prentice-Hall, 1983. 574p.

> Estes, Ralph W. **Dictionary of Accounting**. 2nd ed. Cambridge, Mass.: MIT Press, 1985. 162p.

> Davidson, Sidney, Clyde P. Stickney, and Roman L. Weil. **Accounting: The Language of Business**. 4th ed. Glen Ridge, N.J.: Thomas Horton and Daughters, 1979. 121p.

Following publication of the first edition in 1952, Eric L. Kohler's *Dictionary for Accountants* became the standard, authoritative dictionary of accounting. Now in its sixth edition, two new editors have taken over responsibility for the dictionary and renamed it *Kohler's Dictionary for Accountants*. The *Dictionary* defines over 4,500 terms and concepts in accounting and related fields. Definitions vary from a sentence or two to several pages, and are frequently supplemented with graphs, charts, statistical formulas, and mathematical computations. Prominent accountants and important organizations are included as well as accounting terms. *Kohler's Dictionary* is a nearly encyclopedic source, and belongs in most business reference collections.

Less comprehensive but also possibly less intimidating to casual users, the *Dictionary of Accounting* and *Accounting: The Language of Business* offer clear and concise definitions of basic accounting terms and concepts. In addition, *Accounting: The Language of Business* also presents excerpts from financial statements included in annual reports for General Electric and Sears, accompanied by comments and notes from the dictionary's editors. It also includes a survey of the development and evolution of accounting standards and principles and lists principles in force at the time the dictionary was compiled. Both sources are widely used and common to library collections.

Handbooks and Encyclopedias

When more information is required than can be found in dictionaries, researchers frequently turn to handbooks and encyclopedias. Several such publications are available. Some deal with specialized fields of accounting and others are more general. Some are written for accountants, and some for managers, small business people, and others lacking accounting expertise.

Nickerson, Clarence B. **Accounting Handbook for Nonaccountants**. 3rd ed. New York: Van Nostrand Reinhold, 1985. 720p.

Edwards, James Don, et al. **How Accounting Works: A Guide for the Perplexed**. Homewood, Ill.: Dow Jones-Irwin, 1983. 374p.

Understanding basic accounting concepts, applications, and vocabulary greatly enhances the ability of managers and business people to communicate with accountants and to assess corporate financial well-being. Accordingly, a number of handbooks have been published to promote such understanding; Nickerson's *Accounting Handbook for Non-accountants* is one of the best. Its first 21 chapters are intended to help readers analyze and understand financial statements, with topics arranged to correspond to their order of appearance in balance sheets, income, and other financial statements. The remaining chapters focus on cost accounting and control, cost-volume-price relationships, pricing, long-range planning, and performance measurement. Chapters are generously illustrated with charts, graphs, and excerpts from annual reports, and include frequent references to pronouncements issued by the Financial Accounting Standards Board and its predecessor, the AICPA's Accounting Principles Board. Two appendixes are included. The first is a step-by-step presentation of the accounting cycle, the bookkeeping process that begins with opening a set of books and recording financial transactions, and that culminates in the preparation of financial statements. The second appendix reproduces a series of tables frequently used in the analysis of capital expenditures.

How Accounting Works covers both financial and managerial accounting. It explains the basic accounting cycle, inventory and cost, plant assessment and depreciation, financial statements, budgeting, cost accounting, capital budgeting, and other key concepts. Intended for self-study and for use in training and continuing education programs, *How Accounting Works* includes questions, exercises, business decision problems, and accompanying answers at the end of each chapter. Compound interest and annuity tables are appended.

Blensly, Douglas L., and Tom M. Plank. **Accounting Desk Book**. 8th ed. Englewood Cliffs, N.J.: Institute for Business Planning, 1985. 524p.

Ameiss, Albert P., and Nicholas A. Kargas. **Accountant's Desk Handbook**. 2nd ed. Englewood Cliffs, N.J.: Prentice-Hall, 1981. 438p.

Handbooks for the professional accountant are equally abundant. Generally they come in two sizes: desk books, intended for quick reference, and detailed, comprehensive sources which are often published in more than one volume. The *Accounting Desk Book* and the *Accountant's Desk Handbook*, for example, are two such ready reference sources, each highlighting topics of wide interest and appeal.

The more comprehensive handbooks treat accounting in greater depth, often providing history and background, explanations, and bibliographies that may be lacking in desk books. Four of the most popular comprehensive sources are listed below.

Burton, John C., Russell E. Palmer, and Robert S. Kay, eds. **Handbook of Accounting and Auditing**. Boston: Warren, Gorham & Lamont, 1981. [Kept current by *Accounting and Auditing Update Service*.]

Seidler, Lee J., and D. R. Carmichael. **Accountants' Handbook**. 6th ed. New York: Wiley, 1981. 2v.

Davidson, Sidney, and Roman L. Weil. **Handbook of Modern Accounting**. 3rd ed. New York: McGraw-Hill, 1983. 1358p.

Pescow, Jerome K., ed. **Accountants' Encyclopedia, Revised**. Englewood Cliffs, N.J.: Prentice-Hall, 1981. 2v.

Coverage in the above handbooks varies, but each treats in depth the theory and practice of accounting and their application to specific business problems. Publishers of the *Handbook of Accounting and Auditing* drew upon the expertise of the professional staff at

Touche Ross to compile a thorough treatment of general and specific areas of accounting and auditing, as well as of accounting for specialized industries. Other sections identify and discuss the Financial Accounting Standards Board and other major institutions of accounting, describe the legal environment within which accounting and auditing operate, and summarize recent research. Chapters in each section are signed, and include brief bibliographies. Also included are a consolidated bibliography of sources cited and a list by number and title of each major accounting pronouncement, including those of the AICPA, FASB, and the Accounting Principles Board. The *Handbook* is kept current through annual supplements issued by its publisher.

Coverage in the *Accountants' Handbook*, the *Handbook of Modern Accounting*, and the *Accountants' Encyclopedia, Revised* is also very thorough. All include lengthy, signed chapters written by experts, and are well regarded by accounting professionals. Since they are revised somewhat infrequently, however, they do not always reflect current accounting principles and practices. As a result, the *Handbook of Accounting and Auditing*, which is updated frequently, offers a clear advantage for those who must keep abreast of the most recent developments.

More specialized handbooks and encyclopedias are also available. Some deal with accounting practices as they relate to specific industries, others reproduce accounting forms, letters, and reports, and still others present mathematical tables and formulas. Titles representing each of these categories are discussed below.

Pescow, Jerome K., ed. **Encyclopedia of Accounting Systems**. Rev. ed. Englewood Cliffs, N.J.: Prentice-Hall, 1975. 3v.

Newman, Benjamin. **Forms Manual for the CPA: For Audit, Review, and Compilation of Financial Statements**. New York: Wiley, 1980. 574p.

Lipkin, Lawrence, Irwin K. Feinstein, and Lucile Derrick. **Accountant's Handbook of Formulas and Tables**. 2nd ed. Englewood Cliffs, N.J.: Prentice-Hall, 1973. 487p.

Johnson, James M. **Handbook of Depreciation Methods, Formulas, and Tables**. Englewood Cliffs, N.J.: Prentice-Hall, 1981. 704p.

The *Encyclopedia of Accounting Systems* examines accounting practices and systems as they relate to specific industries, businesses, professions, and nonprofit organizations. Each chapter covers a separate industry, and includes a general overview of the industry as well as a description of the basic design of the accounting system, data processing procedures, cost and payroll systems, plant and equipment records, and many other special features relating to the industry. The chapter on logging and lumber manufacturing, for example, includes a glossary of logging terms, an organization chart for a typical logging and lumber manufacturing company, sample tally and invoice forms, and examples of monthly operating reports. The *Encyclopedia* covers a wide assortment of industries and professions, ranging from flour milling and funeral directing to television broadcasting and real estate. Although somewhat dated, it is one of the most comprehensive compilations of industry-specific accounting systems and is still widely used.

Accounting practice requires the use of a wide array of specialized forms. The *Forms Manual for the CPA* reproduces and discusses forms as they relate to public accounting practice, including such documents as checklists, planning guides, audit program guides, questionnaires, confirmation forms and letters, illustrative reports, and many other forms commonly used by individual accounting practitioners and small and medium-sized public accounting firms.

Accountants are frequently required to draw upon tables, formulas, and mathematical computations in performing their work. Handbooks that present such information are of immediate practical benefit not only to accountants, but also to managers, executives, bankers, financiers, and others. The *Accountant's Handbook of Formulas and Tables* presents formulas for simple and compound interest, annuities, statistical sampling, index numbers, and time series. More specialized formulas covering inventory, depreciation, finance, pricing, marketing, cost and production, ratio analysis, and special situations are also included. Appendixes discuss the fundamentals of algebra and logarithms, and 14 different tables present data pertaining to present value, logarithms, square roots and reciprocals, sample size, random decimal digits, and many other topics.

The *Handbook of Depreciation Methods, Formulas, and Tables* is more specialized, focusing on situations in which specific depreciation methods may be used. Techniques for calculating depreciation of assets using formulas, tables, and computer programs are also presented.

The publications that have been listed and described above are but a few of the accounting handbooks available today. Library accounting reference collections should include these and other titles reflecting the wide range of accounting interests and abilities of their users.

Directories

Representation of accountants and accounting firms in the standard business directories discussed in chapter 2 is rather sparse. Although thousands of companies are included in the *Million Dollar Directory*, only about 100 are listed under SIC 8931, the designation for accounting, auditing, and bookkeeping services. While *Standard & Poor's Register of Corporations, Directors and Executives* includes the names of the principal accounting firms representing many of the companies it lists, it has fewer than 25 entries for accounting firms themselves. To identify accounting firms or locate accountants, it is usually necessary to consult specialized directories.

American Institute of Certified Public Accountants. **Accounting Firms and Practitioners**. New York: AICPA, 1977- . Biennial.

Who Audits America. Menlo Park, Calif.: Data Financial Press, 1976- . Semiannual.

Accounting Firms and Practitioners lists individual accounting practitioners, firms, and corporations whose partners are members of the American Institute of Certified Public Accountants. Arrangement is alphabetical by state, city, and name of accountant or accounting firm. The entries are brief, limited to name and address. The AICPA also publishes a biennial *List of Members*, and similar lists are generally available from state societies of Certified Public Accountants.

Who Audits America is a directory of publicly traded companies and the accounting firms that audit them. The first part of the directory focuses on the companies being audited. In addition to standard directory information, it designates the company's ticker symbol, the SIC for the primary product or service being sold, number of employees, corporate assets and sales, and the name of the accounting firm performing the audit for the period being covered. In addition, this section lists companies that have merged, been acquired, or changed their names since the last edition was published.

The second section of *Who Audits America* focuses on auditors. It is arranged in several different parts, including a ranked listing of auditors by total sales of audited companies; a list of the Big Eight accounting firms, citing for each clients with annual sales greater than $200 million; a national list of all other accounting firms; and state lists, showing for each auditor the names of client companies and their approximate sales.

Periodicals

The importance and pervasiveness of accounting in almost every facet of business is reflected in articles appearing in general business periodicals and newspapers. Accounting is also well represented by specialized periodicals, which are particularly valuable for their presentation of current accounting theory and practice. Although space does not permit identification or consideration of all accounting periodicals, two representative and widely read titles are discussed below.

> **Journal of Accountancy.** New York: American Institute of Certified Public Accountants, 1905- . Monthly.

> **Management Accounting.** Montvale, N.J.: National Association of Accountants, 1919- . Monthly.

The official journal of the American Institute of Certified Public Accountants, the *Journal of Accountancy* serves as the principal medium for the exchange of information and ideas by and for accounting practitioners. It includes articles on accounting, auditing, management advisory services, taxation, and related fields. Regular features include columns on microcomputer applications, recent tax developments, government and professional news, and a practitioners forum, in which working accountants discuss specific techniques and procedures. In addition, the *Journal* prints the complete texts of official pronouncements issued by the AICPA and the Financial Accounting Standards Board and regularly publishes book reviews and bibliographies. Although the *Journal* is included in most business and some general periodical indexes, it also publishes its own semiannual author and subject indexes as part of its June and December issues.

Management Accounting is the official journal of the National Association of Accountants, the professional organization representing management accountants in industry, public accounting, government, and teaching. Articles emphasize management accounting, and regularly cover such topics as cost accounting, manufacturing, budgeting, inventory, and productivity. Its "In the Library" column reviews titles recently received by and available on loan from its library to association members. Although *Management Accounting* publishes its own annual author and subject index, it is also included in general and business periodical indexes.

Some libraries choose to supplement their accounting periodicals or partially replace them with the *Accountants Digest*.

> **Accountants Digest.** Boca Raton, Fla.: Florida Atlantic University College of Business and Public Administration, 1935- . Quarterly.

The *Accountants Digest* presents outstanding articles selected from leading business and accounting journals. An issue typically focuses on a specific topic, with seven or eight articles dealing with related subjects. In addition, the *Digest* includes a section, "CPA Requirements," that lists by state minimum requirements for taking the Uniform CPA Examination, and another, "Current Status of Official Pronouncements," that lists outstanding statements, standards, and guidelines issued by U.S. and foreign accounting organizations.

Periodical Indexes and Abstracts

Major accounting periodicals are indexed in such standard business sources as *Business Index* and *Business Periodicals Index*. Two specialized indexes, held in most major business reference collections, are also available.

> **Accountants' Index.** New York: American Institute of Certified Public Accountants, 1920- . Quarterly, with annual cumulations.

> **Accounting Articles.** Chicago: Commerce Clearing House, 1965- . Looseleaf, updated monthly.

In 1921, the AICPA Library published the *Accountants' Index*, an author, title, and subject index to English-language books and periodicals received by the library since 1912. Following publication of the original volume, supplements were issued every two or three years until 1971, when it became an annual. Today, the *Accountants' Index* is issued quarterly with annual cumulations, and its coverage has expanded to include pamphlets, government documents, published proceedings, and speeches as well as books and periodical articles. Fields covered include accounting, auditing, data processing, financial reporting, financial management, investment, and taxation. Accounting practices for special industries, businesses, and professions are also covered, as are many general management topics. Cross-references are common, and, as shown in figure 10.7, many citations for books and pamphlets include the AICPA Library classification numbers to facilitate borrowing by association members and special libraries. The *Accountants' Index* is also available as an online database through ORBIT.

STOCKHOLDERS
See also Minority interests
Reports - To stockholders
Arthur Young. Questions at annual meetings of share-holders. New York, c1986. 19 p. [*223.4 A]
Baxt, Robert. Regulation of the use of proxies. (Company/commercial law) *Chartered accountant in Australia*, v. 56, May 1986, p. 64.
Bhagat, Sanjai. Effect of management's choice between negotiated and competitve equity offerings on shareholder wealth. *Journal of financial and quantitative analysis*, v. 21, June 1986, p. 181-96.
Hearth, Douglas. Divestiture uncertainty and shareholder wealth: evidence from the U.S.A. (1975-1982), by Douglas Hearth and Janis K. Zaima. *Journal of business finance & accounting* (Eng.), v. 13, Spring 1986, p. 71-85.
Peat, Marwick, Mitchell & Co. Shareholders' questions 1986. New York, c1986. 28 p. [*223.4 P]
Shareholder's right to call a meeting. (Company/commercial law) *Chartered accountant in Australia*, v. 56, June 1986, p. 58.
Touche Ross & Co. Questions shareholders will ask, 1986. New York, c1986. 34 p. [*223.4 T]
Wahl, Jack. Incentives for information acquisition, by Jack Wahl and Adrian E. Tschoegl. Ann Arbor, Mich., University of Michigan, Graduate School of Business Administration, Division of Research, 1984. 24 p. (*Working paper*, no. 398, Nov. 1984) [*720 W]
Wendell, Paul J. Preparing for shareholder questions. *SEC accounting report*, v. 12, April 1986, p. 1-2.

Fig. 10.7. Typical entries, *Accountants' Index*. Copyright © 1987 by the American Institute of Certified Public Accountants, Inc.

Accounting Articles is a looseleaf service, updated monthly, that identifies and abstracts articles from accounting and business journals as well as selected books and pamphlets. Arrangement is by broad topic and then by narrower subtopic and paragraph. As with other Commerce Clearing House looseleaf services, hierarchical numeric designations are used for specific topics. Figure 10.8 (see page 250) illustrates this arrangement.

Access is enhanced by topical and author indexes, with references in each being made to the appropriate numeric designation. For example, as shown in figure 10.9 (see page 250), the number 6600.97 would lead to the description of an article on managing the use of microcomputers.

Accounting Articles generally retains abstracts for some five or six years. Cumulated volumes of *Accounting Articles* are also available.

Looseleaf Services

Frequent changes in accounting practices, which in turn reflect changes in laws, regulations, and professional standards, make this a field in which looseleaf services are abundant. Many deal exclusively with accounting standards and principles; key examples have already been discussed in the sections on generally accepted accounting principles and

```
"Accounting Principles and Practices" - 100

"Statements and Reports" - 2000
    "Balance Sheet" - 2100
        "Current Assets and Liabilities" - 2100.19
        "Form of Balance Sheet" - 2100.35
    "Intangibles"  -  2100.50
 "Taxes"  -  2100.78
 "Income and Earned Surplus Statements" - 2200

"Cost Accounting" - 3000
```

Fig. 10.8. Numerical/topical arrangement, *Accounting Articles.*

Facing Up to the Challenges of Managing Microcomputers. Nigel Kelly. 59 Cost and Management (Canada), March-April 1985, pp. 42-44.—Poses the questions: Have the microcomputers in your organization been much less beneficial than intended when they were acquired? Do microcomputers consume too much money and time and produce too little benefit? If so, your organization may be losing the microcomputer revolution. The discussion describes the symptoms of the disease: too much time and effort spent in hardware maintenance: many inexperienced users of microcomputers having difficulty getting started; difficulties integrating microcomputer applications; technical problems in getting communication links, either point to point or networked; and excessive staff time in operating microcomputers.

¶ **6600.97**

Fig. 10.9. Sample entry, *Accounting Articles.* Reproduced with permission from *Accounting Articles*, published and copyrighted by Commerce Clearing House, Inc., 4025 W. Peterson Avenue, Chicago, Illinois 60646.

auditing standards. Others, on taxation, will be cited later in this chapter. Some other looseleaf services of interest to accountants include the following titles.

Accountancy Law Reports. Chicago: Commerce Clearing House, 1938- . 2v. Looseleaf.

SEC Accounting Rules. Chicago: Commerce Clearing House, 1968- . Looseleaf.

In addition to keeping abreast of current accounting principles and standards, accountants need to keep informed about laws and government regulations. Since state boards of accountancy regulate the practice of accounting, there can be considerable variation from one state to another. *Accountancy Law Reports* presents in two volumes state laws, rules, regulations, and court decisions affecting the practice of accounting in each state. Published in cooperation with the American Institute of Certified Public Accountants, *Accountancy Law Reports* sets out requirements by state and subject, with charts and checklists summarizing all state "right to practice" rules. It is a handy reference source for accountants who need to know about accounting as it is practiced in another state.

Although the Securities and Exchange Commission has delegated much of its responsibility for setting the standards for financial reporting and accounting, it nonetheless remains active in this sphere, issuing several series that affect financial accounting practice. Some of its most important publications are the *Accounting Series Releases*, or *ASR*s, which deal with specific aspects of accounting practice. *ASR*s and other SEC accounting-related publications such as *Bulletins* and *Guides for Registration Statements* are available in *SEC Accounting Rules*, a looseleaf service that presents and continuously updates all SEC rulings.

Other services, aimed primarily at smaller accounting firms and individual practitioners, present practical information and advice and are really the looseleaf equivalents of handbooks.

Management of an Accounting Practice Handbook. Fort Worth, Tex.: Practitioners Publishing Company, 1975- . 3v. Looseleaf.

Audit and Accounting Manual. Chicago: Commerce Clearing House, 1979- . Looseleaf.

Technical Practice Aids. Chicago: Commerce Clearing House, 1975- . 2v. Looseleaf.

Behrenfeld, William, and Andrew R. Bibel. **Accountant's Business Manual**. New York: American Institute of Certified Public Accountants, 1987- . Looseleaf.

The *Management of an Accounting Practice Handbook*, or *MAP Handbook*, is a three-volume looseleaf service that provides practical guidance and articles on developing an accounting practice and on administration, personnel, and management data. It includes more than 200 different forms, sample letters, worksheets, and other illustrations and, in addition, presents financial ratios, balance sheets, and financial statements for accounting firms of various sizes to evaluate performance and profitability. Practitioners Publishing Company also produces more specialized looseleaf services for accountants, including *Preparing Financial Statements, Compilation and Review Engagements,* and *Audits of Small Business*.

The *Audit and Accounting Manual*, published by Commerce Clearing House for the AICPA, explains and demonstrates audit techniques and procedures and provides practical advice on such subjects as audit approach and programs, internal control, and review and report processing. Each section contains extensive samples and illustrations, including such items as working papers, checklists, letters, and forms.

Technical Practice Aids provides practical guidance for dealing with specific accounting and auditing problems in conformity with current standards and procedures. It covers financial statement presentation, assets, liabilities and deferred credits, capital, revenue and expense, audit fieldwork, auditors' reports, and specialized industry and organizational problems. The second volume includes *Statements of Positions* issued by both the AICPA Accounting and Auditing Standards Divisions, and *Lists of Issues Papers* published by the AICPA Accounting Standards Division.

Accountant's Business Manual focuses on an array of general business, legal, and financial topics relevant to accounting practice rather than on accounting and auditing per se. Topics covered include legal forms of business organization (sole proprietorships, partnerships, corporations, S corporations), business financing and valuation, bankruptcy/insolvency, employment regulations, and estate planning. Each chapter features a bibliography in addition to explanations and definitions, and the addresses and telephone numbers of state government agencies are also included. A directory of key trade and professional organizations is appended.

Government Documents

Federal documents on accounting generally fall into three broad categories: "how-to" booklets and pamphlets for small business people and nonaccountants, procedural manuals for the audit of private government contractors, and studies and audits of government agencies themselves.

The most prolific publisher of accounting aids for nonaccountants is the Small Business Administration. Although other SBA publications are also useful, three of its publications that deal specifically with accounting are particularly helpful.

U.S. Small Business Administration. **A Handbook of Small Business Finance**, by Jack Zwick. 9th ed. Washington, D.C.: Government Printing Office, 1981 (Small Business Management Series No. 15). 57p.

_____. **Ratio Analysis for Small Business**, by Richard Sanzo. 4th ed. Washington, D.C.: Government Printing Office, 1977 (Small Business Management Series No. 20). 66p.

_____. **Cost Accounting for Small Manufacturers**, by R. Lee Brummet and Jack C. Robertson. 3rd ed. Washington, D.C.: Government Printing Office, 1979 (Small Business Management Series No. 9). 180p.

Published as a part of the SBA's Small Business Management Series, *A Handbook of Small Business Finance* sets forth the principles of financial management, describes such financial statements as the balance sheet and income statement, explains ratio analysis, and reviews ways of financing growth and working capital. Like the other titles in this series, it is written by an expert, and provides a brief introduction to basic accounting concepts.

Financial ratios are covered in greater depth in *Ratio Analysis for Small Business*. The document describes business ratios and how they work, discusses different types of ratios, describes sources of published ratios, and presents a case history showing ratio analysis in action. Although it is somewhat dated, particularly in regard to the section on published sources, *Ratio Analysis* remains a useful introduction to the subject.

Cost Accounting for Small Manufacturers presents a guide for setting up or revising cost accounting procedures. It includes sections on cost systems for different kinds of manufacturing plants, as well as on accounting for raw materials and purchased parts, labor, and overhead. Cost estimates, data processing, cost and profit analysis, and a bibliography of further references are also included. Although the section on electronic data processing is obsolete and the bibliography dated, the document is still useful for the general information on cost accounting that it presents.

Other SBA publications touch briefly upon specific accounting or bookkeeping operations. The SBA's Management Aids for Small Manufacturers Series, for example, includes such titles as *Basic Budgets for Profit Planning* and *Attacking Business Decision Problems with Breakeven Analysis*, while the Small Marketers Aids Series includes *Checklist for Profit Watching, Keeping Records in Small Business*, and *Analyze Your Records to Reduce Costs*. These and similar SBA publications make useful and popular additions to vertical file collections for many public and academic libraries.

Companies doing business with the Department of Defense may be interested in a publication issued by the Defense Contract Audit Agency, or DCAA.

U.S. Defense Contract Audit Agency. **DCAA Contract Audit Manual**. Washington, D.C.: Government Printing Office. Looseleaf.

Established in 1965, the Defense Contract Audit Agency has the right to audit the books and records of any private contractor having a negotiated contract of $100,000 or more with the Department of Defense. Its *DCAA Contract Audit Manual* prescribes auditing policies and procedures and presents guidelines and techniques for DCAA personnel. Although the *Manual* is far too specialized for most library collections, librarians and researchers should be aware that such a publication exists, and that it is available in most regional depository libraries.

The General Accounting Office, an agency of the legislative branch, is responsible for investigating and carrying out legal, accounting, auditing, and cost settlement functions of government programs and operations as assigned by Congress. Each year, it issues hundreds of reports and other publications that describe its findings.[18] Although GAO publications are included in the *Monthly Catalog of United States Government Publications*, they are also listed in indexes published regularly by the General Accounting Office.

U.S. General Accounting Office. **GAO Documents**. Washington, D.C.: Government Printing Office. Monthly.

———. **Reports Issued In [date]**. Washington, D.C.: Government Printing Office. Monthly.

GAO Documents is a comprehensive monthly listing of GAO audit reports, staff studies, memoranda, opinions, speeches, testimony, and Comptroller General decisions. It is organized into two parts, a citation section and an index section.

Entries in the citation section are detailed, including budget function and legislative authority as well as more standard bibliographic information and abstracts which present findings or conclusions as well as brief summaries. In addition, *GAO Documents* includes eight indexes: subject, agency/organization, personal name, budget function, GAO issue area (broad subject category), congressional, law/authority, and document number. All documents listed in *GAO Documents* are available in either paper copy or microfiche, and can be ordered by phone or by mail using the preaddressed request cards included in each issue.

Reports Issued In... is a free, monthly list of GAO reports arranged by broad subject areas, such as national defense, commerce, and income security. Each entry includes the title, GAO report number, and description of its contents[19] (see figure 10.10).

Retirement Before Age 65: Trends, Costs, and National Issues	GAO/HRD-86-86, July 16.
	This report shows that (1) the percentage of the population receiving employer-sponsored pensions at ages younger than 65 has increased rapidly, (2) individuals with employer-sponsored pension income have much lower labor-force participation rates than nonrecipients of the same age and sex, and (3) the resulting earlier retirement represents a potentially significant loss in federal revenues. These findings raise questions about the future financing of retirement benefits for persons who are living longer and retiring earlier. They also raise questions about federal policy concerning retirement eligibility age. Recent legislative changes have reduced incentives for early retirement and removed obstacles to older worker employment. Additional changes have also been proposed that would further remove some of the financial incentives to retire early in public and private plans. Uncertainty, however, over long-term economic and demographic projections raises questions as to what public policy changes may be needed.

Fig. 10.10. Sample entry, GAO's *Reports Issued....* Reprinted from the General Accounting Office's *Reports Issued in August 1986.*

Vertical File Materials

Free and inexpensive booklets about the profession and practice of accounting are generally quite easy to obtain. As was mentioned in the preceding section, government agencies such as the SBA and the GAO make many of their publications available to the public at little or no cost. Other suppliers include professional associations such as the National Association of Accountants and the American Institute of Certified Public Accountants. The AICPA, for example, offers a number of booklets and pamphlets available to its members, educators, and the general public. Most are listed and described briefly in AICPA's annual publications catalog. Several are available at no cost to libraries.[20]

In addition, major accounting firms regularly publish materials for actual and prospective clients on specific accounting practices. Price Waterhouse is perhaps the most prolific publisher of such items. Particularly useful to libraries is its "Information Guide" series, which includes booklets on business practices in foreign countries, as well as summaries of foreign exchange and tax requirements. Each guide to doing business describes the country's investment climate and covers factors that will affect commerce with the country, including exchange controls, regulatory agencies, investment incentives, banking and local finance, import restrictions and duties, legal forms of business, and labor relations and social security. Each booklet also describes auditing and accounting practices and requirements, the tax system, and corporate, individual, and other taxes levied. Although intended primarily for business people, the country guides also provide useful general information, including descriptions of the government, population and language, currency, working conditions, time zones, and statutory holidays. Other booklets in the series include *U.S. Citizens Abroad*, a guide to tax requirements for citizens working abroad; *Foreign Exchange Information; A Worldwide Summary*, which summarizes conditions in 96 different countries and territories; and the *World's Major Stock Exchanges; Listing Requirements*. Copies of these booklets, which make good additions to library vertical file and reference collections, can be requested from Price Waterhouse's Center for Transnational Taxation.[21] In addition, Price Waterhouse publishes other, more specialized sources: These include *Building a Better World of Financial Reporting* and *Personal Tax Strategy; A Guide to Year-End Planning*.[22]

Price Waterhouse is by no means the only Big Eight company involved in publishing. Each Big Eight firm issues a newsletter summarizing important trends and developments, and most also publish booklets and pamphlets on a wide range of subjects. Deloitte Haskins & Sells, for example, has published booklets for small and growing businesses on financing and exporting, and has recently begun an "Entrepreneur's Guidebook" series, which includes titles on how to raise venture capital, become a public company, and form research and development partnerships.[23] Arthur Andersen issues the monthly *Accounting News Briefs* and *Banking News Briefs* in addition to its quarterly *Chronicle*, and has also published several booklets on domestic as well as foreign tax issues, including such titles as *Yearend Tax Strategy for Individuals, Tax Shelters—the Basics*, and *Tax Economics of Charitable Giving*.[24] Although space does not permit a complete listing of the offerings of all Big Eight and other major accounting firms, librarians and researchers should be aware that a wide range of free booklets, newsletters, and pamphlets are available from them. Many are listed in *Public Affairs Information Service Bulletin* and *Accountants' Index*, and others can be identified by contacting the firm's local office or its corporate headquarters. The effort involved in identifying and ordering these titles is usually time well spent.

Online Databases

The online version of *Accountants' Index*, available through ORBIT Search Service, is the only database that is devoted solely to accounting. Many standard business databases, however, provide access to accounting information.[25] Further, many of the financial databases to be described in chapter 13 contain extracts of data from such basic financial statements as corporate balance sheets and income statements, and another, described in chapter 11, includes selected financial ratios for specific companies.

TAX BASICS

Librarians in almost every setting are called upon to provide information pertaining to taxation. This may range from supplying current federal and state income tax forms to stocking and providing assistance with looseleaf services that present and analyze the most recent tax laws, rulings, regulations, and court decisions. It may involve determining the existence or amount of sales tax levied in another state or the property tax rate in a particular city or town. Whatever the nature of such requests for assistance, the librarian's ability to understand and communicate with researchers about them will be enhanced by a basic understanding of the tax system and some of the key tax reference sources. This section briefly describes major types of taxes collected in this country, the government agencies responsible, and some of the tax sources most frequently consulted by lay people and tax professionals.

Governments levy taxes to promote certain economic and social objectives such as economic growth and full employment, to finance their operation, and to provide such public goods and services as education, a system of national defense, and a network of roads and highways. In the United States, taxes are imposed by state and local governments as well as by the federal government. As a result, there is considerable variety in the tax structures and tax rates levied in different places by different levels of government.

Kinds of Taxes

As shown in figure 10.11, there are two basic kinds of taxes, excise and property. *Excise taxes* are directly imposed on manufacturing, selling, or using certain merchandise or products, or on certain occupations or activities, such as obtaining a license or transferring property. An excise tax is a fixed, absolute charge, a fee that is levied regardless of the taxpayer's financial status or ability to pay. Anyone in the same tax district who buys a gallon of gasoline or a quart of whiskey, for example, can expect to pay the same tax regardless of his or her economic status. Estate, gift, and sales taxes are all excise taxes.

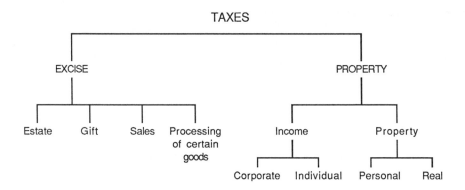

Fig. 10.11. Types of taxes imposed by governments.

Property taxes are imposed on the basis of the value of certain property, whether it be real estate, personal property, or individual or corporate income. Such taxes are also called *ad valorem* taxes to indicate that they constitute a percentage of the value of the items being taxed.

As mentioned earlier, the tax structures for state and local governments vary considerably. Some states tax personal income. Others do not. Most depend on excise taxes, particularly sales tax, but while one state may tax only luxury items, others will tax food and prescription drugs as well. Local governments impose different tax measures, but usually draw upon revenues raised from taxing real and personal property. While the federal government imposes gift, estate, and certain processing taxes, its most productive sources of revenue are personal income and corporate taxes, both of which are collected by the Internal Revenue Service.

Internal Revenue Service

The Internal Revenue Service (IRS) is responsible for administering and enforcing most federal tax laws and related statutes. Its activities include the determination, assessment, and collection of taxes, determination of pension plan qualifications and exempt organization status, and the issuance of rulings and regulations. In addition, it handles taxpayer complaints and provides taxpayer service and education. The IRS's service and education roles are particularly important to libraries, which may regularly acquire IRS forms and documents for their users and may occasionally refer them to regional and district offices for more specialized assistance.

The IRS will, for example, supply libraries with multiple copies of frequently used forms and instructions. Orders for such materials can be made by toll-free telephone or can be sent by mail to an IRS Distribution Center. In addition, the IRS publishes the following annual document that offers access to even more forms.

> U.S. Dept. of the Treasury. Internal Revenue Service. **Reproducible Federal Tax Forms for Use in Libraries**. Washington, D.C.: Government Printing Office. Annual (IRS Publication 1132).

Reproducible Federal Tax Forms is a compilation of forms and accompanying instructions for libraries to lend to their users for photocopying. It includes 100 different forms, or parts of forms, ranging from Form 1040EZ for single filers with no dependents to Schedule J, Form 1041, "Trust Allocation of an Accumulation Distribution." Arrangement is by form number, with subject and title indexes. Certain specially printed forms are not included, but may be ordered from the IRS Forms Distribution Centers listed on the inside back cover of the volume.

Librarians would be well advised to retain superseded editions of *Reproducible Federal Tax Forms*. Volumes for earlier years provide quick and convenient access to information and forms that might otherwise be difficult to find, and are especially popular with patrons who need to file amended tax returns for previous years. In addition to forms, the Internal Revenue Service publishes manuals, regulations, statistics, and decisions, some of which will be discussed later.

The IRS also offers free consultation by telephone regarding tax questions and problems. Telephone lines are often busy, however, particularly during the height of the tax preparing season, and callers are advised to be patient and persevere.

Other Government Agencies

Although the Internal Revenue Service is responsible for most of the federal taxes collected, another Treasury Department agency, the Bureau of Alcohol, Tobacco, and Firearms, is responsible for collecting revenues from the alcohol and tobacco industries.

In addition to federal agencies, each state has a department of taxation or revenue responsible for administering major taxes, including individual and corporate income taxes, and estate, sales, and other excise taxes. The names of state agencies, their tax rates, and the revenues they collect are included in several different sources, but one of the most convenient and readily accessible is *The Book of the States*. Even more detailed information is available in the *Multistate Corporate Tax Almanac*.

> Council of State Governments. **The Book of the States**. Lexington, Ky.: The Council, 1935- . Annual.

> **Multistate Corporate Tax Almanac**. Greenvale, N.Y.: Panel Publishers, 1984- Annual.

In addition to chapters on state constitutions, branches of government, elections, and management and administration, *The Book of the States* includes one on state finances. It provides an overview of the states' budget procedures, their revenue sources, expenditures, and debts. It also includes a summary of recent trends in state taxation, lists agencies responsible for administering different kinds of state taxes, and presents tables showing by state: excise tax rates, sales tax exemptions, and rates and exemptions on individual and corporate income tax returns. An article on state tax collection is followed by tables summarizing state government tax revenue by state and by types of tax collected.

The *Multistate Corporate Tax Almanac* uses charts to compare more than 33 different aspects of corporate taxation on a state-by-state basis, including such topics as tax audit procedures, treatment of foreign tax payments, and investment tax credit rules. In addition to a chart, each section includes a brief analysis and description of trends. The *Almanac* also features an overview of state tax legislation enacted in the preceding year, and a state tax information directory which lists for each state the telephone number of agencies to call for additional information on corporate and sales tax policy.

Just as taxes collected vary from one state to another, so also do services provided by state departments of revenue and taxation. At a minimum, however, most compile and publish pertinent statistics and, like the IRS, will make multiple copies of tax forms and instructions available to libraries.

Taxes collected by county, municipal, township, and special district governments vary so much that it is difficult to generalize about them. Brief information about taxes and tax rates imposed by local governments can often be found by consulting *Moody's Municipal & Government Manual*, described in chapters 12 and 13. More detailed information is contained in the Census Bureau's *Census of Governments*, which includes volumes on taxable property values and tax assessment and on the finances of school districts, special districts, county governments, and municipal and township governments. The Census Bureau also publishes a series of annual surveys of state and local finance. These include such titles as *City Government Finances, County Government Finances, Local Government Finances in Major County Areas, State Government Finances*, and *State Government Tax Collections*. The annual surveys and the *Census of Governments*, which is published every five years, are available at regional and many selective depository libraries.

Federal Tax Law and Administration

Taxes imposed in this country's early history were limited primarily to excise taxes, which were repealed whenever the government had enough money to meet its rather limited needs. During the Civil War, income as well as excise taxes were levied, but it was not until the early 20th century that income tax became a permanent part of our lives. In 1909, Congress passed the Sixteenth Amendment to the Constitution, permitting the imposition of federal income tax. In 1913, after ratification by three-fourths of the states, it became law.

As shown in figure 10.12 (see page 258), all three branches of the federal government are actively involved in the enactment and administration of tax law. The Joint Committee on Internal Revenue Taxation and the House Ways and Means and Senate Finance Committees are responsible for gathering information and holding hearings which may eventually be reported to Congress and culminate in the passing of new or amended tax legislation. Federal tax laws are referred to collectively as the Internal Revenue Code, or Tax Code.

The Treasury Department is responsible for administering the Tax Code. It issues interpretations of the Tax Code, called *Treasury Regulations*, which are available in many regional depository and law libraries.

The Internal Revenue Service, in addition to collecting taxes, enforcing tax law, and issuing rulings in response to requests for guidance, interprets *Treasury Regulations* and negotiates disputes with taxpayers.

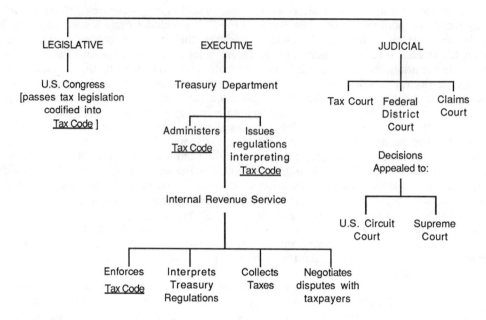

Fig. 10.12. Federal government involvement in taxation.

In the event that disputes between taxpayers and the IRS are not successfully negotiated, they can be taken to court. The Tax Court, federal district courts, and the Claims Court are empowered to hear cases involving the interpretation of tax law and its application in specific situations. Appeals are directed to U.S. Circuit Courts and to the Supreme Court.

The activities of these agencies of the federal government are important, because each is involved in amending or interpreting tax law. As amendments, rulings, regulations, interpretations, and court decisions are issued, they become part of the body of tax law and are in turn succeeded by rulings, regulations, interpretations, and court decisions pertaining to them. Such issuances are of vital concern to accountants, lawyers, and other tax professionals, who generally use looseleaf services to keep informed. Perhaps in no other field do looseleaf services play such an important role.

TAX PUBLICATIONS AND INFORMATION SOURCES

A wide range of frequently revised publications pertaining to taxation are available. Some are aimed at the general public, others at tax specialists. Clearly, the selection and inclusion of such publications in any library collection will reflect the interests and needs of its particular clientele. This section considers some of the main types of printed and electronic sources of potential interest to library users.

Dictionaries

In many libraries, the accounting and general business and economics dictionaries on hand will be sufficient to handle requests for definitions of tax terms. More specialized tax dictionaries do exist, however. The titles listed below are typical.

Westin, Richard A. **Lexicon of Tax Terminology**. New York: Wiley, 1984 (Wiley Law Publications). 845p.

U.S. General Accounting Office. **A Glossary of Terms Used in the Federal Budget and Related Accounting, Economic, and Tax Terms**. 3rd ed. Washington, D.C.: Government Printing Office, 1981. 136p.

Written primarily for lawyers, the *Lexicon of Tax Terminology* is also useful to accountants and other tax professionals. It lists and defines legal, technical, accounting, and slang terms, with entries ranging in length from a single sentence to a paragraph or more. References to the Internal Revenue Code, *Treasury Regulations*, and case law are frequently included, as are cross-references to related terms in the dictionary.

Although not nearly as comprehensive, *A Glossary of Terms Used in the Federal Budget and Related Accounting, Economic, and Tax Terms* offers clear, brief definitions, intended for the lay person. Terms are grouped by category, with cross-references from one section to another. In addition, the *Glossary* includes a brief description of the federal budget process, appendixes, and a bibliography of sources consulted. It is available free to academic and public libraries and government organizations, and can be purchased by others from the Government Printing Office for a nominal price.[26] Many of the guides described below also include definitions of frequently used terms.

Income Tax Guides

Issued annually to reflect current tax practice, income tax guides help individuals, accountants, lawyers, and others to identify, interpret, and prepare the necessary forms to be filed with federal and state agencies. Most are fairly general, summarizing federal income tax requirements as they apply to individuals, businesses, corporations, and organizations. Others have a narrower focus. They may be similar to those pertaining to federal tax but may deal with tax laws in specific states, or they may emphasize tax practices that apply to specific occupations or professions.

General guides fall into three categories: those published by the Internal Revenue Service itself, those issued by publishers of major looseleaf tax services, and popular guides. Some of the best are listed below.

U.S. Internal Revenue Service. **Your Federal Income Tax**. Washington, D.C.: Government Printing Office, 1943- . Annual.

_____. **Tax Information Publications**. Washington, D.C.: Government Printing Office, 4v. Annual.

Your Federal Income Tax is an IRS booklet that describes the types of tax returns that can be filed by individuals, including for each return step-by-step instructions and comments. It explains the tax laws that cover salaries, interest and dividends, capital gains, and other types of income, and discusses itemized deductions. Sample forms and schedules are included, as are numerous examples showing how tax law applies in certain situations. In addition, the booklet briefly summarizes important tax law changes, lists free publications available from the IRS, and includes toll-free telephone numbers to call for assistance. It, too, is available gratis from the IRS.

Although *Tax Information Publications* is not, strictly speaking, a guide, it provides information similar to that contained in guides in a somewhat different format. It is a four-volume compilation of the Internal Revenue Service's most frequently requested publications, including such titles as *Tax Information on Selling Your Home, Pension and Annuity Income*, and *Nonbusiness Disasters, Casualties, and Thefts*. Publications are arranged by IRS publication number, with subject indexes appended to each volume. *Tax Information Publications* also describes the IRS's Tele-Tax Information System and its taxpayer education and information programs, which will be discussed later in this chapter. Although most of the titles it includes are available free of charge to the public, *Tax Information Publications* is a convenient way for libraries to provide access to popular and much-used informational booklets for the current and preceding tax years.

Major publishers of looseleaf tax services also issue tax guides. As compared to those mentioned above, they are more technical, and may include citations to their corresponding looseleaf services, or to the Tax Code itself. The three most commonly used of these guides are published by Prentice-Hall, Commerce Clearing House, and the Research Institute of America.

Federal Tax Handbook. Paramus, N.J.: Prentice-Hall Information Services, 1947- . Annual.

U.S. Master Tax Guide. Chicago: Commerce Clearing House, 1943- . Annual.

Master Federal Tax Manual. New York: Research Institute of America, 1975- . Annual.

Although there are some differences, the above guides are quite similar in arrangement, format, and content. Each includes tax tables and schedules and a summary of recent tax developments. Like their looseleaf counterparts, each uses numeric paragraph designations rather than page numbers to refer to specific topics, and each is arranged by broad, topical chapters. All have detailed subject indexes and, in addition, include footnotes citing references to more detailed information contained in the corresponding looseleaf services. In addition, both the *Federal Tax Handbook* and the *Master Federal Tax Manual* include editorial observations, notes, and warnings about specific tax practices. These guides are quite inexpensive, and in many settings provide information sufficiently detailed to answer most tax-related inquiries. Libraries in which the need for information is more specific or highly specialized will, of course, need to subscribe to one or more of the looseleaf tax services.

The third major type of general tax guide consists of popular guides written for lay people. Such guides are in heavy demand at public and some academic libraries, particularly after major tax reform has been enacted. The quality of these guides can vary considerably, but two of the best are listed below.

Bernstein, Peter W., ed. **The Arthur Young Tax Guide**. New York: Ballentine, 1985- . Annual.

J. K. Lasser's Your Income Tax. New York: Simon & Schuster, 1937- . Annual.

Although most of the popular tax guides have been published for several years, one of the most-used guides in 1985 was the first edition of *The Arthur Young Tax Guide*, the only such guide issued by a Big Eight accounting firm. The *Guide* is an annotated version of the IRS publication, *Your Federal Income Tax*, described earlier in this section. In addition to the full text of the IRS guide, it includes additional explanations, examples, tax-saving tips, and tax planning suggestions.

J. K. Lasser's guide is one of the oldest. It includes several examples and special sections highlighting tax applications of interest to such groups as investors, veterans, homeowners, and business people. The publisher offers a free supplement that summarizes recent tax developments and contains examples of completed tax forms. The supplement, however, is not packaged with the guide, and must be requested from the publisher.

Specialized tax guides include those focusing on taxes levied by specific states or on tax practices most likely to be of interest to a specific professional or occupational group. The titles that follow are typical.

CCH Tax Law Editors. **Guidebook to North Carolina Taxes**. Chicago: Commerce Clearing House, 1972- . Annual.

Bernstein, Allen. **Tax Guide for College Teachers and Other College Personnel**. Washington, D.C.: Academic Information Service, 1973- . Annual.

The *Guidebook to North Carolina State Taxes* is representative of commercially published state tax guides. Intended as a quick reference source, it describes general provisions of state tax laws, regulations, and administrative practice, and includes tax tables and explanatory paragraphs. References are made throughout the *Guidebook* to relevant sections in CCH's *Standard Federal Tax Reporter* and in the corresponding state tax service, CCH's *North Carolina Tax Reports*. Key administrative officials in the Department of Revenue are listed by name and title, and a subject index is also included. Similar guidebooks are published for other states.

The *Tax Guide for College Teachers* focuses on tax laws, rulings, procedures, and forms most likely to pertain to academicians. Although it lacks the footnotes and legal references included in the guides issued by looseleaf publishers, it is more detailed than the popular guides, and is often comprehensive enough to serve the needs of individual faculty preparing returns.

Directories

Although there are few tax directories per se, many business, accounting, and government directories list tax practitioners and organizations. The *United States Government Manual*, for example, lists key officials and regional and district offices of the IRS, while the consultant directories described in chapter 2 include the names of selected tax specialists and consultants.

There is, however, a special directory that is used whenever information pertaining to tax-exempt organizations is sought: the *Cumulative List of Organizations*, compiled by the IRS.

> U.S. Dept. of the Treasury. U.S. Internal Revenue Service. **Cumulative List of Organizations Described in Section 170(c) of the Internal Revenue Code of 1986**. Washington, D.C.: Government Printing Office, 1954- . Annual.

The *Cumulative List* is a roster of organizations to which contributions are tax deductible. As shown in figure 10.13, each entry includes the organization's name and the city and state in which it is located. A coding system is also used which identifies each organization by type and limitation on deductibility. Three cumulative quarterly supplements update the annual *List* by citing organizations to be added. The supplements do not list organizations whose status has changed or that should be deleted from the *List*. A deletions list of organizations that no longer qualify is, however, published monthly in the *Internal Revenue Bulletin*.

Heart Love & Soul Inc., Niagara Falls, N. Y.
Heart Lung & Vascular Prevention and Education
   Center Inc., Chicago, Il. (4)
Heart Lung Institute of the East Bay, Oakland, Ca.
Heart Ministries Inc., Hutchinson, Ks.
Heart of America Bible Society Inc., Liberty, Mo.
Heart of America Bone Marrow Donor Registry Inc.,
   Until 8712, Raytown, Mo.
Heart of America Brangus Breeders Scholarship
   Foundation, Until 8612, Moberly, Mo.
Heart of America Chapter ABC Apprenticeship Trust
   Fund, Kansas City, Mo.
Heart of America Chapter Retired Officers Assoc,
   Kansas City, Mo. (6)
Heart of America Christian Justice Center Inc.,
   Overland Park, Ks.
Heart of America Crusades Inc., Kansas City, Mo.
Heart of America Genealogical Society and Library
   Inc., Kansas City, Mo.
Heart of America Indian Center, Kansas City, Mo.
Heart of America Kennel Club Inc., Kansas City, Ks.
Heart of America Pop Warner Football League, Until
   8612, Independence, Mo.

560

Fig. 10.13. Typical listings, *Cumulative List of Organizations*. Reprinted from the U.S. Internal Revenue Service's *Cumulative List of Organizations*, 1987 edition.

Periodicals, Newspapers, and Indexes

Since professional tax assistance is most frequently provided by accountants and lawyers, many serials in those fields contain articles on tax law, theory, and practice. In addition, almost every type of periodical described in chapter 3 regularly features tax-related articles. These articles are most evident in January issues and whenever major tax reforms are enacted. Taxation also has special periodicals of its own, ranging from special interest publications such as the *Real Estate Taxletter* and *Clergy Tax Tips* to serials with a much broader scope. Three such titles are discussed below.

National Tax Journal. Columbus, Ohio: National Tax Association–Tax Institute of America, 1948- . Quarterly.

The Journal of Taxation. New York: Warren, Gorham & Lamont, 1954- . Monthly.

Tax Features. Washington, D.C.: Tax Foundation, 1957- . Monthly.

The National Tax Association–Tax Institute of America is an association of some 2,000 accountants, economists, attorneys, government tax officials, academicians, and others with an interest in taxation. One of its major goals is to promote the scientific, nonpolitical study of taxation, and one of the key publications that it uses to meet this goal is its quarterly periodical, the *National Tax Journal*. The most scholarly of the titles discussed in this section, the *National Tax Journal* features articles by scholars and practitioners that report research, analyze and evaluate current national, state, and local tax policy, and treat other issues pertaining to government finance. Articles, which deal with topics as diverse as the relationship of inflation to corporate income and the impact of state taxation on fringe benefits for policemen and firemen, include abstracts and bibliographies and frequently contain formulas and graphs. One issue in each volume is devoted entirely to papers presented at the organization's annual symposium.

The Journal of Taxation is written by and for tax practitioners and focuses more on technical and methodological concerns. Articles are grouped by broad topics such as "Return Preparation" and "Accounting," and each issue includes an annotated list of new publications and an index to new court decisions and actions by the Internal Revenue Service. Although *The Journal of Taxation* is indexed in most business and many general periodical indexes, it also publishes its own subject/title and author indexes as parts of its June and December issues.

Tax Features, published monthly by the Tax Foundation and available free to libraries, is a newsletter that presents news and analytical articles on taxation and government spending.[27] It is particularly useful for its coverage of recent tax legislation and for its regular statistical features, which include annual articles on state and local tax collections, sales tax, individual income tax returns, and federal tax expenditures. Although the articles are neither so scholarly nor so technical as those appearing in the *National Tax Journal* and *The Journal of Taxation*, they are written with clarity and support the Tax Foundation's efforts to promote public awareness of and interest in government finance.

Almost all of the newspapers listed and described in chapter 3 include articles pertaining to taxation. As with periodicals, these are most numerous at the beginning of the year when taxpayers begin to think about taxes. Librarians can, in fact, help to facilitate preparation of tax returns by acquiring and retaining the issue of the *Wall Street Journal* that contains year-end prices for the securities it lists.

Tax articles are indexed in *Business Index, Business Periodicals Index,* the *Wall Street Journal Index, Public Affairs Information Service Bulletin*, and many other sources. In addition, Commerce Clearing House publishes a looseleaf service that indexes articles on federal taxation.

Federal Tax Articles. Chicago: Commerce Clearing House. Looseleaf, with monthly updates.

Federal Tax Articles is an annotated listing of articles, comments, and notes published in tax, accounting, legal, and other professional journals. It is similar in format and arrangement to Commerce Clearing House's *Accounting Articles*, described earlier in this chapter. In this instance, however, articles are grouped together under the section(s) of the Internal Revenue Code to which they apply. A "Current Articles" section presents the most recent articles, while a "Publishers & Publications" section lists the journals that are included, with current subscription information for each. Further access is provided by topical and author indexes.

Looseleaf Services

Taxation is a complex field, made particularly so by the diversity of taxes collected at each level of government and by the voluminous and frequently changing laws, regulations, and other government issuances pertaining to them. As a result, it is an area in which looseleaf services are abundant.

Although the nature and extent of looseleaf collections will vary from one library to another, most business reference collections will include at least one of the comprehensive federal tax services listed below. These multivolume services present and analyze tax law, court cases and decisions, and IRS administrative rulings. One tax practitioner, in fact, says that they are like patent medicine for tax researchers because they have something to treat almost any tax problem.[28]

Federal Tax Coordinator 2d. New York: Research Institute of America, 1970- . Looseleaf, with biweekly updates.

Federal Taxes. Paramus, N.J.: Prentice-Hall Information Services. Looseleaf, with weekly updates.

Standard Federal Tax Reporter. Chicago: Commerce Clearing House, 1913- . Looseleaf, with weekly updates.

The overlap between the *Federal Tax Coordinator 2d, Federal Taxes*, and the *Standard Federal Tax Reporter* is considerable. All include topical indexes, case tables, and numerical finding lists, permitting research by subject, case name, and numerical citation. Each, however, has certain unique characteristics and, as a result, has its own loyal following.

The *Federal Tax Coordinator 2d* is the easiest service to use, primarily because it features simple, nontechnical language in its explanations, and because it groups everything pertaining to a particular subject in a single chapter. Each chapter deals with a fairly broad topic, such as income tax deductions or estate tax, and each occupies its own volume. Further, each chapter begins with a description of the taxes normally collected, followed by a detailed table of contents. It, in turn, is followed by descriptions of problems in the designated area. Frequently the tax explanations include illustrations, observations, recommendations, and cautions. As shown in figure 10.14 (see page 264), citations to supporting authorities are included in footnotes at the bottom of each page.

Following the explanatory section is a verbatim reprint of all pertinent Tax Code and *Treasury Regulation* sections. Each volume concludes with a discussion of new developments that have occurred since the last revision of the text.

While the *Federal Tax Coordinator 2d* is particularly popular with novice tax researchers, professionals more often turn to *Federal Taxes* or the *Standard Federal Tax Reporter*. Although they are more technical and difficult to use, they are also generally perceived to be more timely, and to offer greater detail and more thorough analysis. Space does not permit detailed consideration of their respective contents, format, and arrangement, but such information is readily available in the descriptive and instructional booklets offered by their publishers.[29]

only the employee's share can be applied against his self-employment tax.[21] Whether an error was made is determined by the law and regulations of the taxable year, as interpreted by the latest authoritative ruling or decision.[22]

illustration: A pays $10 tax on an amount erroneously treated as wages, but which really is self-employment income subject to a $15 tax. If

assessment of the $15 self-employment tax is barred, no credit or refund of the $10 payment may be made. The payment must be offset against the $15 self-employment tax.

For the negligence and failure-to-file penalties involving the reporting and paying of self-employment tax, see ¶s V-2600 *et seq.* and V-2200 *et seq.* respectively.

A-6100. Specific Application of the Self-Employment Tax: Exemptions.

Unless engaged in a specifically exempt trade or business, all self-employed persons are subject to the self-employment tax. However, some persons or occupations must obey special rules in computing their liability.

A-6101. Self-employment tax of partners.

A partnership recognized as such for income tax purposes will be similarly treated for self-employment tax purposes.[1]

An association taxable under the income tax laws as a corporation is also treated as a corporation (not a partnership) under the self-employment tax law.[2] However, an unincorporated river pilots' association or a corporation formed to hold title to floating property, collect pilotage fees, pay expenses, and disburse net earnings from pilotage fees to its members, was held a partnership for self-employment tax purposes. The functions performed by the entity are not enough to constitute it as engaged in the business of piloting. Rather, the business of piloting is conducted by the pilots, with the association or corporation merely acting as their agent.[3]

A partner includes in self-employment earnings his share of the partnership income, as separately stated on the partnership return,[4] which arises from the trade or business of the partnership. If income from some source unrelated to the business is included in his share, it should be eliminated. Thus, wages earned by a partner outside of the partnership business, and turned over to the partnership in accordance with the partnership agreement, can't be included in self-employment earnings by the other partners.[5] (For 20% first year depreciation and other separately listed items, see below).

A partner picks up his share of the partnership business earnings regardless of his lack of active participation in the business.[6] Thus where a business passes to the former owner's widow and his children,

and a partnership is created, the distributive shares are self-employment income even though one or more of the members is inactive.[7]

Partners not recognized as such for income tax purposes, as in the case of certain family partnerships, would not be recognized for self-employment tax either.[8] On the other hand, a partnership invalid under state law but recognized as valid by the federal income tax law is considered valid under the self-employment tax law.[9]

When the partner's year is different from the partnership's, the partner picks up his share of the partnership earnings for the taxable year of the partnership which ends with or within his own taxable year. This is the same rule followed for income tax purposes.[10]

illustration: B files his return on the calendar year basis and his partnership uses the fiscal year ending Jan. 31. B includes his distributive share of partnership earnings and his guaranteed payments for the fiscal year ending Jan. 31, '82 in his return for the calendar year '82.

A partner's share of a passed through new jobs credit (forerunner of present targeted jobs credit) meant an increase in self-employment tax for a general partner. That's because the amount of the credit reduces the partnership's compensation deduction, thus "raising" the partnership's (and the partner's) distributed share of income for tax purposes.[11]

observation: The new jobs credit was the forerunner of the targeted jobs credit explained at ¶ L-15600 *et seq.* Apparently the targeted jobs credit

---

21. Rev Rul 78-127, 1978-1 CB 281.
22. Reg § 301.6521-2.
1. Reg § 1.1402(a)-2(f).
2. Reg § 1.1402(a)-2(f).
3. Rev Rul 54-614, 1954-2 CB 271.
4. Reg § 1.1402(a)-1(a); Reg § 1.1402(a)-2(d).
5. Rev Rul 54-223, 1954-1 CB 174.

6. Ellsasser, William Est, (1973) 61 TC 241.
7. Rev Rul 54-613, 1954-2 CB 269.
8. Reg § 1.1402(a)-2(f).
9. Rev Rul 54-75, 1954-1 CB 169.
10. Code Sec. 1402(a); Reg § 1.1402(a)-1(b)(5).
11. Hightower, Glenn, TC Memo 1982-559.

SEE DEVELOPMENTS AT END OF CHAPTER   **CODE & REGS PRECEDE DEVELOPMENTS**

Fig. 10.14. Sample page, *Federal Tax Coordinator 2d*. Reprinted by permission of The Research Institute of America, Inc. Copyright 1986.

In addition to the multivolume, comprehensive looseleaf services described above, a number of smaller, more highly specialized tax services are also available. These include titles that focus on a specific type of tax, such as sales or estate and gift tax, or that present state tax law in all 50 states or in a single state. These and other services are listed and described in the *Directory of Business and Financial Services*, discussed in chapter 4.

Government Publications and Services

Federal tax publications generally fall into three broad categories: (1) income tax guides and instructional booklets published by the Internal Revenue Service; (2) statistics compiled from tax returns; and (3) congressional publications, tax laws, regulations, and court decisions. While there is no government-issued bibliography that provides a full listing of all such publications, a Superintendent of Documents' subject bibliography lists current publications.

U.S. Superintendent of Documents. **Taxes and Taxation**. Washington, D.C.: Government Printing Office, 1987 (Subject Bibliography 195). 6p.

Taxes and Taxation, available free from the Government Printing Office, lists and sometimes annotates tax-related publications issued by the IRS, the Congress's Joint Committee on Internal Revenue Taxation, and other federal agencies. Emphasis is on titles of potential interest to researchers and tax practitioners rather than to the general public; lists of IRS tax information publications are not included. As with other bibliographies in this series, prices and Superintendent of Documents classification and stock numbers are also included.

Although the Government Printing Office has also compiled a list of general tax publications issued by the IRS (*Internal Revenue Service Tax Information Publications, Subject Bibliography 194*), the IRS offers lists that are both more current and more comprehensive.

U.S. Dept. of the Treasury. Internal Revenue Service. **Guide to Free Tax Services**. Washington, D.C.: Government Printing Office. Annual.

_____. **Catalog of Federal Tax Forms, Letters, and Notices**. Washington, D.C.: Government Printing Office. Annual.

The *Guide to Free Tax Services* lists and annotates taxpayer information publications, and describes special services available to taxpayers. These include a Tele-Tax program, which makes some 150 different prerecorded messages available. Messages cover such topics as tax credits for child care, business income, and how to choose a tax preparer, and can be reached by dialing the local or toll-free telephone numbers listed in the *Guide*.

Other services that are listed and described in the *Guide* include special assistance for disabled taxpayers, a walk-in service, and, when all else fails, the Problem Resolution Program. In addition, the Internal Revenue Service sponsors a Taxpayer Information Program, which makes audio tape cassettes, films, and speakers available, and Taxpayer Education Programs, which include Volunteer Income Tax Assistance, Tax Counseling for the Elderly, Small Business Workshops, Understanding Taxes, and Community Outreach Tax Assistance. Each of these programs is designed to teach people how to prepare their own tax returns. The *Guide* is particularly popular in public and academic libraries.

More specialized information is available in the *Catalog of Federal Tax Forms, Form Letters, and Notices*. It identifies and defines the purpose and use of various tax forms and the forms, letters, and notices that frequently accompany them. Copies of the documents themselves, however, are not included in the *Catalog*. Although written primarily for IRS employees, the *Catalog* is also used by accountants, attorneys, and other tax specialists.

Many of the most important IRS guides and instructional publications have been discussed in earlier sections of this chapter. Compilations of tax statistics, the second major type of federal tax publication, are described in the section that follows. Finally, while discussion of the myriad of laws, regulations, and court decisions that comprise the third major type of federal tax information is more appropriate to a legal text, a few such publications should be noted.

U.S. Dept. of the Treasury. Internal Revenue Service. **Internal Revenue Bulletin**. Washington, D.C.: Government Printing Office, 1954- . Weekly.

_____. **Internal Revenue Cumulative Bulletin**. Washington, D.C.: Government Printing Office, 1969- . Semiannual.

_____. **Bulletin Index-Digest System: Service 1-4. (Service 1 – Income Taxes; Service 2 – Estate and Gift Taxes; Service 3 – Employment Taxes; Service 4 – Excise Taxes)**. Washington, D.C.: Government Printing Office, 1978- . Basic manuals, with quarterly or semiannual supplements.

The *Internal Revenue Bulletin* lists and announces official IRS rulings and procedures, and publishes Treasury Decisions, Executive Orders, Tax Conventions, legislation, court decisions, and other items pertaining to taxation. Each issue is divided into four main parts: rulings and decisions based on the provisions of the 1954 Internal Revenue Code; treaties and tax legislation; administrative, procedural, and miscellaneous; and items of general interest. The highlights of each issue are described on its cover, and the first *Bulletin* for each month features an index to the preceding month's issues.

Twice a year, the weekly issues of the *Bulletin* are consolidated into a permanent, indexed source, the *Internal Revenue Cumulative Bulletin*. Each *Cumulative Bulletin* follows the same general arrangement as the weekly *Bulletin* but also includes a subject index, finding lists, a cumulative list of announcements relating to Tax Court decisions published in the *Bulletin*, and a list of tax practitioners (primarily attorneys and CPAs) who have been disbarred from or voluntarily consented to suspend preparing tax returns for a specified time period.

The *Bulletin Index-Digest System* consists of four services, each dealing with a different type of taxation: income, estate and gift, employment, and excise. Each service consists of a basic manual, covering more than 20 years, and a cumulative supplement, updated quarterly or semiannually. Together, they provide finding lists of items published in the *Bulletin*, digests of revenue rulings and procedures, and indexes of Public Laws, Treasury Decisions, and tax conventions.

Although the *Internal Revenue Bulletin* and the supplementary publications described above are most common in documents collections and law libraries, they are also included in many special and academic libraries with strong collections in accounting and public finance.

Statistics

Tax statistics generally fall into two main categories, those published by the government, and those issued by other organizations, including trade associations, research organizations, and commercial publishers. Statistics published by the government are frequently summarized or presented in condensed form in the *Statistical Abstract of the United States* and many of the statistical compilations described in chapter 6. There are, however, sources compiled by the IRS's Statistics of Income Division that provide more detailed information on federal taxes.

U.S. Dept. of the Treasury. Internal Revenue Service. **Statistics of Income Bulletin**. Washington, D.C.: Government Printing Office, 1981- . Quarterly.

_____. **Individual Income Tax Returns**. Washington, D.C.: Government Printing Office. Annual. (Statistics of Income series)

_____. **Statistics of Income, Corporation Income Tax Returns**. Washington, D.C.: Government Printing Office, 1916- . Annual. (Statistics of Income series)

_____. **Statistics of Income, Source Book, Partnership Returns**. Washington, D.C.: Government Printing Office. (Statistics of Income series)

The *Statistics of Income Bulletin* provides the earliest published annual financial statistics from various tax returns filed with the Internal Revenue Service. These statistics are presented in the *Bulletin's* "Selected Statistical Series" section, which includes current and historic statistics on individual income and business tax returns, as well as returns submitted by sole proprietorships, partnerships, and corporations. Other tables highlight gross IRS collections and receipts, excise taxes, and the use made of the IRS's assistance programs for taxpayers (see figure 10.15). In addition, the *Statistics of Income Bulletin* includes articles on a wide range of subjects, including demographic characteristics of taxpayers, high income tax returns, and environmental taxes.

Selected Statistical Series, 1970–86

Table 11.—Classes of Excise Taxes by Selected Fiscal Year, 1970–1985
[Money amounts are in thousands of dollars]

Selected class of tax	Taxes collected by fiscal year					
	1970	1975	1980	1983	1984	1985
	(1)	(2)	(3)	(4)	(5)	(6)
ALCOHOL TAXES, TOTAL	4,746,382	5,350,858	5,704,768	5,634,853	5,402,467	5,398,100
Distilled spirits	3,501,538	3,865,162	3,945,377	3,798,148	3,566,482	3,520,697
Wine	163,337	177,113	211,538	239,329	319,920	305,966
Beer	1,081,507	1,308,583	1,547,853	1,597,375	1,516,064	1,571,436
TOBACCO TAXES, TOTAL	2,094,212	2,315,090	2,446,416	4,139,810	4,663,610	4,483,193
Cigarettes	2,036,101	2,261,116	2,402,857	4,099,226	4,623,288	4,448,916
Cigars	56,834	51,226	39,500	33,716	30,372	24,294
MANUFACTURERS EXCISE TAXES, TOTAL ..	6,683,061	5,516,611	6,487,421	6,776,023	r10,107,930	10,020,574
Gasoline and lubricating oil[1]	3,517,586	4,071,465	4,326,549	4,953,267	9,020,413	9,062,630
Tires, tubes and tread rubber[2] ...	614,795	697,660	682,624	677,966	423,315	242,923
Motor vehicles, bodies, parts[3] ...	1,753,327	662,556	1,088,696	516,872	-14,777	N/A
Recreational products	53,427	84,946	136,521	132,672	132,448	166,666
Black Lung taxes	N/A	N/A	251,288	490,731	525,422	548,356
SPECIAL FUELS, AND RETAILERS TAXES, TOTAL[4]	257,820	404,187	560,144	831,196	r2,579,747	3,802,608
Diesel and special motor fuels ...	257,712	370,489	512,718	742,380	1,571,437	2,430,165
Trucks and buses	N/A	N/A	N/A	N/A	932,645	1,289,750
MISCELLANEOUS EXCISE TAXES, TOTAL ..	2,084,730	3,306,077	6,359,198	19,228,685	r13,319,322	11,044,833
Telephone and teletype[5]	1,469,562	2,023,744	1,117,834	1,048,317	2,034,965	2,307,607
Air transportation	250,802	850,567	1,748,837	1,898,786	2,456,712	2,589,818
Highway use tax	135,086	207,663	263,272	287,457	175,054	456,143
Foreign insurance[6]	8,614	19,458	74,630	-44,440	56,037	73,494
Exempt organization net investment income	N/A	63,828	65,280	112,380	146,806	136,153
Crude oil windfall profit	N/A	N/A	3,051,719	15,660,081	8,120,274	5,073,159
Environmental taxes (Superfund) ..	N/A	N/A	N/A	235,954	275,389	272,957

Fig. 10.15. Sample table, *Statistics of Income Bulletin*. Reprinted from U.S. Internal Revenue Service, *Statistics of Income Bulletin* (Spring 1986).

Although more detailed information is available, it is also less current. Most of it is contained in the IRS's Statistics of Income series, which includes separate volumes for individual, partnership, and corporate income tax returns. The individual and corporate income tax return volumes are published annually to cover a designated tax year, while the partnership volume is published less frequently and includes cumulative information. (A volume published in 1986, for example, covers the years 1957-83.) Each volume presents data on income and sources of income, number and characteristics of returns, amount of tax, deductions, exemptions, assets and liabilities, and other items.

Privately published compilations of tax statistics include those made available in *Book of the States*, the *Multistate Corporate Tax Almanac*, and other commercially published sources. Another useful compilation is issued by the Tax Foundation.

Facts and Figures on Government Finance. Washington, D.C.: Tax Foundation, 1941- . Annual looseleaf, with quarterly updates.

Facts and Figures on Government Finance contains almost 300 tables providing current and historic data on government revenues and expenditures at the federal, state, and local level. Each table cites the source(s) from which data were gathered and frequently date back for several years; some date back as far as 1902. A glossary and subject index are also included.

Many trade associations, particularly those representing industries that must pay special taxes, include relevant tax statistics in their publications. Typical of these are the Distilled Spirits Council's *Annual Statistical Review*, the American Trucking Associations' *Interstate Information Report: Truck Finance and Highway Finance*, and the Tobacco Institute's annual *Tax Burden on Tobacco*. Such industry-specific data can usually be identified by consulting the *Statistical Reference Index*.

Vertical File Materials

Many of the titles that have been discussed in this section are good candidates for vertical file collections. They are brief, revised frequently, and are free or inexpensive. Publications in the IRS Tax Information series, for example, make splendid additions to such collections.

Several privately published materials can be identified using the *Public Affairs Information Service Bulletin* or the *Vertical File Index*. As was mentioned in the section on accounting publications, many of the Big Eight firms publish booklets on taxation. Major reform in tax law frequently results in the publication of numerous guides to the amended law, issued by accounting firms, securities brokers, and other business organizations. Such publications are abundant and can be acquired easily.

Online Databases

Tax databases usually fall into three categories: (1) primary source databases that provide direct access to the rulings and regulations of the Internal Revenue Service; (2) secondary source databases that index business, legal, and general news articles relating to tax issues; and (3) collections of IRS forms and instructions.

Vendors of primary source databases include PHINet (Prentice-Hall Information Network), as well as WESTLAW and LEXIS, major legal database vendors. Databases made available through these vendors, however, are generally searched only in law libraries, selected special libraries, or by tax practitioners themselves.

Another database is more widely available.

Tax Notes Today. Washington, D.C.: Tax Analysts. Daily updates.

Tax Notes Today, produced by a prominent, nonprofit tax research organization, includes news stories, special reports and commentary by experts, and summaries of tax bills, IRS administrative documents, and tax cases from the Supreme Court, Tax Court, and Federal District and Appeals Courts. Each record has a headline, and most have lengthy, informative summaries as well. The database can be searched by document type, keywords, and subject.

Many of the databases described in chapter 8 are good sources of secondary tax information. *ABI/Inform*, for example, indexes both general business periodicals and such specialized titles as the *National Tax Journal* and *The Journal of Taxation*, while many of the Dow Jones News/Retrieval databases offer access to annotated or full-text articles on taxation.

Another type of secondary source database is roughly equivalent to looseleaf tax services. Although representative examples were listed and briefly described in chapter 4, it is worth repeating that such major looseleaf service publishers as Prentice-Hall and Commerce Clearing House also offer online versions of their services. Like the above primary source databases, however, these are most often searched by practitioners or in highly specialized library settings.

Finally, the Internal Revenue Service itself offers a database that provides online access to many of the printed forms and instructional booklets that are available through its Documents Distribution Centers. Time permitting, however, librarians and researchers will find it far more inexpensive to acquire printed copies of the forms from the IRS itself rather than to pay royalties to access the same information through commercial database vendors.

NOTES

[1]Martin Rosenberg, *Opportunities in Accounting Careers* (Lincolnwood, Ill.: VGM Career Horizons, 1983), 2.

[2]Mark Stevens, *The Big Eight* (New York: Collier, 1984), 2-3.

[3]For a free copy of the pamphlet, *Information for CPA Candidates*, write to:
> Examination Division
> American Institute of Certified Public Accountants
> 1211 Avenue of the Americas
> New York, NY 10036-8775

[4]Dick Levin, *Buy Low, Sell High, Collect Early and Pay Late; the Manager's Guide to Financial Survival* (Englewood Cliffs, N.J.: Prentice-Hall, 1983), 14.

[5]*H.J. Heinz 1986 Annual Report* (Pittsburgh, Pa.: H.J. Heinz, 1986), 58.

[6]For a free copy of the booklet *How to Read a Financial Report*, contact a local Merrill Lynch office or write to:
> Merrill Lynch, Pierce, Fenner, & Smith Inc.
> One Liberty Plaza
> 165 Broadway
> New York, NY 10080

[7]For free copies of Armstrong's *Special Edition Annual Report*, write to:
> Public Relations and Public Affairs Department
> Armstrong World Industries, Inc.
> P.O. Box 3001
> Lancaster, PA 17604

[8]Stephen A. Moscove, *Accounting Fundamentals for Non-Accountants.* Rev. ed. (Reston, Va.: Reston Publishing, 1984), 7.

[9]Robert Anthony and James S. Reese, *Accounting Principles*, 5th ed. (Homewood, Ill.: Irwin, 1983), 14.

[10]FASB's Basic Subscription plan includes *Statements, Interpretations, Technical Bulletins,* and *Status Reports*. The Comprehensive Subscription plan includes, in addition to the titles listed above, *Exposure Drafts, Discussion Memoranda*, and *Invitations to Comment*.

[11]James E. Kristy and Susan Z. Diamond, *Finance without Fear* (New York: AMACOM, 1984), 45.

[12]Levin, 106.

[13]Robert Morris Associates, *'85 Annual Statement Studies* (Philadelphia, Pa.: Robert Morris Associates, 1985), 7.

[14]Levin, 102.

[15]The following titles are representative of some of the free financial publications available from trade associations.

Air Transport
Air Transport Association of America
1709 New York Avenue, N.W.
Washington, D.C. 20006

Annual Report
American Bus Association
1025 Connecticut Avenue, N.W.
Washington, D.C. 20036

Cost and Profit Ratios for Vending Operators: Summary
National Automatic Merchandising Association
20 North Wacker Drive, Suite 3500
Chicago, IL 60606

Phonefacts
United States Telephone Association
1801 K Street, N.W., Suite 1201
Washington, D.C. 20006

[16]Librarians and researchers are advised to consult the *Encyclopedia of Associations* for current addresses of trade associations listed in *Ratio Analysis for Small Business*, which was published by the Small Business Administration in 1970.

[17]To request a free copy of the Superintendent of Documents bibliography, *Accounting and Auditing* (Subject Bibliography 42), write to:

> Superintendent of Documents
> U.S. Government Printing Office
> Washington, D.C. 20402

[18]Some of the general interest publications available free of charge from the General Accounting Office are:

> *United States General Accounting Office: Answers to Frequently Asked Questions,* 1979 (Accession No. 091614).

> *Managers, Your Accounting System Can Do a Lot For You; Accountants, You Can Do a Lot for Your Managers,* 1979 (Accession No. 091100).

Requests for these publications, which should include publication date and accession number as well as title, should be submitted to:

> General Accounting Office
> P.O. Box 6015
> Gaithersburg, MD 20877

[19]To be placed on the mailing list for the General Accounting Office's free, monthly publication, *Reports Issued In...*, write to the address shown in #18.

[20]Free pamphlets that are listed in the AICPA's 1986 publications catalog include:

Education Requirements for Entry Into the Accounting Profession (No. 876760)

Implementation of the Postbaccalaureate Education Requirement (No. 870265)

A Postbaccalaureate Education Requirement for the CPA Profession (No. 870250)

Academic Preparation for Professional Accounting Careers (No. 876744)

Careers in Accounting (No. 870104)

Supply of Accounting Graduates and Demand for Recruits (No. G00091)

Accounting: It Figures in Your Future (No. 870091)

Accounting Education—A Statistical Survey (No. G00020)

Why Graduate School for Professional Careers in Accounting (No. 872364)

The above titles should be requested from AICPA's Relations With Educators Division at the address shown in #3.

In addition, *What Does a CPA Do?*, *Choosing the CPA Firm That's Right for You*, and the association's annual catalog, *AICPA Publications*, can be requested at the same address.

[21]To request country guides from the "Information Guide" series, or to request other titles from the series such as *U.S. Citizens Abroad, Foreign Exchange Information,* and *World's Major Stock Exchanges*, write to:

> Price Waterhouse Center for Transnational Taxation
> 1251 Avenue of the Americas
> New York, NY 10020

[22]The free booklets, *Building a Better World of Financial Reporting* and *Personal Tax Strategy* can be ordered from Price Waterhouse's national office, as can *Price Waterhouse in Print*, which lists other free pamphlets and brochures.

[23]For free copies of *Exporting: Small and Growing Businesses*, and *Financing: Small and Growing Businesses* and titles in the "Entrepreneur's Guidebook' series (*Raising Venture Capital, Strategies for Going Public*, and *Forming R & D Partnerships*), contact a local office or write to:

> Deloitte Haskins & Sells
> 1114 Avenue of the Americas
> New York, NY 10036

[24]For free copies of *Yearend Tax Strategy for Individuals, Tax Shelters—the Basics*, and *Tax Economics of Charitable Giving*, and for subscriptions to *Accounting News Briefs* and *Banking News Briefs*, write to:

> Arthur Andersen & Co.
> 69 W. Washington Street
> Chicago, IL 60602

[25]For an interesting article about the use of online databases with accounting students, see Milton G. Ternberg, "BI for Accounting Students," *College & Research Libraries* (June 1985): 293-94.

[26]*A Glossary of Terms Used in the Federal Budget Process and Related Accounting, Economic, and Tax Terms* is available free to academic and public libraries and to government agencies. To request a copy, contact GAO at the address shown in #18.

[27]To request a free subscription to the monthly newsletter, *Tax Features*, write to:

> Tax Foundation
> One Thomas Circle, N.W., Suite 500
> Washington, D.C. 20005

[28]Allen D. Altman, "A Guide to Tax Research," *University of Miami Law Review* 22 (1968): 848.

[29]*Research in Federal Taxation*, which describes *Federal Taxes* and other Prentice-Hall looseleaf tax publications, can be obtained from an area sales representative or by writing to:

> Prentice-Hall Information Services
> 240 Frisch Court
> Paramus, NJ 07652

Commerce Clearing House's offering, *Finding the Answers to Federal Tax Questions*, similarly describes CCH looseleaf tax services, including the *Standard Federal Tax Reporter*. Local sales representatives can usually supply copies, or they can be requested from:

> Commerce Clearing House
> 4025 W. Peterson Ave.
> Chicago, IL 60646

Man to bank teller: I'll tell you what. You give me a thousand dollars and I'll give you a toaster.

— Wall Street Journal

MONEY, CREDIT, AND BANKING

The availability of money and credit has a profound influence on the way business is conducted. Whether a company chooses to expand operations or lay off employees, whether retail stores maintain large or small inventories, or whether real estate sales soar or plummet is to a very large extent determined by money supply, interest rates, and the financial institutions and government agencies responsible for both. This chapter begins by considering briefly the basic characteristics of money, monetary measures, and foreign exchange. It next covers commercial and consumer credit, and then proceeds to discuss such financial institutions as commercial banks, savings and loan associations, and credit unions, as well as such government agencies as the Federal Reserve System and the Federal Deposit Insurance Corporation. It concludes with the identification and description of key reference and research sources.

MONEY

One of the characteristics that distinguishes advanced cultures from more primitive ones is the widespread use of money, rather than barter, for the exchange of goods and services. Although one culture may designate wampum or fur pelts as money and another may choose gold and silver, money serves three major functions regardless of the forms it takes. First, money serves as the accepted medium of exchange; it is a tool to facilitate transactions. Second, it serves as a standard of value. In the United States, for example, librarians' salaries and television sets are priced by assigning dollar values to them. Finally, money serves as a store of value; it can be saved to permit future purchase of goods and services.

Money in the United States has evolved from such commodities as tobacco and gunpowder to the coins, paper currency, and demand deposits (checking accounts and other checkable deposits held by banks and thrift institutions) presently in use. While most lay people think of currency as comprising the bulk of our money supply, demand deposits are the most common form of money. Most payments today are made by check or by electronic transfer of funds from one account to another; few individuals or businesses use cash to pay for major purchases. Demand deposits and their role in the nation's money supply will be discussed at length in the section on banks.

Monetary System

Most countries have a monetary system comprised of the various kinds of money (for example, coins, currency, and demand deposits), the rules and regulations regarding their issuance and control, and the organizations responsible for them. The Constitution of the United States, for example, grants Congress the power to coin money and regulate its value. Congress has in turn delegated this money power to the Department of the Treasury and the Federal Reserve System and, through it, to commercial banks.

Monetary Measures

As economies become more complex, so also do their monetary systems, which is reflected in the way money is measured. The Federal Reserve System is responsible for collecting and publishing data on money supply in the United States. To do so, it has created a series of measures—M1, M2, M3, and L—that it uses to determine just how much money there is. Although this book does not delve deeply into the characteristics and uses of these alternative measures, please note here that the measures progress from M1, the narrowest definition of money supply, to L, the most inclusive, and that all are listed and defined in the Federal Reserve's most important periodical, the *Federal Reserve Bulletin*.

Foreign Exchange

The growth of foreign trade and travel is reflected in the increasing number of questions that librarians and researchers must answer regarding foreign money and its value relative to the dollar. Although any number of sources list foreign currencies, one title is particularly useful for detailed information.

> Cowitt, Philip P., ed. **World Currency Yearbook**. Brooklyn, N.Y.: International Currency Analysis, 1955- . Annual. [Formerly *Pick's Currency Yearbook*.]

For each country listed in the *World Currency Yearbook*, a discussion of its currency's history, transferability, recent developments, and administration is included, supplemented by annual statistics covering the past decade for currency circulation and official, free market, and, when applicable, black market exchange rates. Annual exchange rates are useful for tracking changes over time. Frequently, however, the need is for more current information. In such instances, the daily foreign exchange tables published in newspapers are the best place to begin. Although not all countries are represented in such tables, those in which trading is heaviest are included. As shown in figure 11.1, each listing contains the name of the country, its unit of currency, the number (or fraction) of dollars equal to that unit, and the number of units equal to one dollar. In the *Wall Street Journal*, figures are given for both the day specified and the preceding trading day.

```
                    Wednesday, September 9, 1987[1]

        The New York foreign exchange selling rates below apply
        to trading among banks in amounts of $1 million and more
        as quoted at 3 p.m. by Bankers Trust Co.  Retail transactions
        provide fewer units of foreign currency per dollar.[2]

                                                    Currency
                              U.S. $ equiv[5]       per  U.S. $[6]
        Country . . .[3]      Wed.      Tues.        Wed.      Tues.

        China (Yuan)[4]       .2687     .2687        3.722     3.722
        Japan (Yen)           .00745    .007075      141.95    141.35
        Lebanon (Pound)       .003540   .003540      282.50    282.50
        Norway (Krone)        .1516     .1520        6.5975    6.5800
```

1. Trading Day Being Reported. The day being reported is the business day prior to the newspaper publication date.
2. Wholesale Trade. Exchange rates represent wholesale transactions ($1 million or more) rather than retail transactions.
3. Country. The arrangement is alphabetical by country.
4. Unit of Currency, given in parentheses.
5. U.S. Dollar Equivalent. Number of (or fraction of) U.S. dollars comprising 1 unit of the currency being traded.
6. Currency Per U.S. Dollar. Number (or fraction) of foreign currency units equal to a dollar.

Fig. 11.1. Newspaper foreign exchange table.

CREDIT

Credit, usually defined as the promise to pay in the future in order to buy or borrow in the present, is an integral part of our economy. Consumers, corporations, businesses, even governments use credit on a regular basis. This section examines credit from two different perspectives: what a bank or other creditor looks for when deciding whether or not to grant credit, and what the prospective recipient, or debtor, seeks.

Creditworthiness

One of the major elements in determining whether or not to extend credit is the creditworthiness of the individual or organization seeking it. The granting of credit, in other words, is based on the creditor's confidence in the debtor's ability and willingness to repay the loan in accordance with the terms of the agreement. To determine creditworthiness, the creditor begins by considering three factors, sometimes called "the three C's": capacity, capital, and character.

Capacity is the debtor's present and future ability to meet financial obligations. In determining the capacity of a small business person to repay a loan, the creditor may take into account the applicant's business experience, general background, and demonstrated ability to operate a business profitably. Someone seeking a consumer loan, on the other hand, would be quizzed about his or her employment history and present level of debt.

The second factor is *capital*, the assets held by the debtor. Capital includes such items as savings accounts, securities portfolios, insurance policies, pension funds, and property, any of which might be used as collateral to secure the loan.

Capacity and capital help creditors to determine an applicant's ability to repay a loan. Equally important, however, is the applicant's willingness to repay, designated by creditors as *character*. Although character lends itself less easily to objective measurement than capacity or capital, certain factors such as the person's reputation, known associates, and credit history are considered to be important components of character. Of these, the most important to creditors is credit history.

CREDIT REPORTS

Creditors rely heavily on credit histories—records of how past debt obligations were handled—in order to make decisions about applicants. Such histories are contained in credit reports sold to banks and other organizations by credit bureaus and credit reporting services. Most credit bureaus are local. The credit reporting services, on the other hand, are large, national operations. Two of the best known credit reporting services are Dun & Bradstreet and TRW Information Services.

Dun & Bradstreet's "Business Information Reports" is a confidential rating service that presents credit histories and other information on some 5 million companies and businesses. A report may range in length from 1 or 2 pages to 20 or more, but includes the credit history, which notes outstanding debt, bills past due, late payments, and related data, as well as brief descriptions of the business and its key officers, current financial conditions, and banking information. In addition, special events such as burglaries or executive changes are noted, as are such public civil filings as lawsuits and tax liens. A credit rating assigned by Dun & Bradstreet is also included.

Two points about the "Business Information Reports" and other, similar credit reports should be noted. The first, and most important for libraries, is that such reports are sold only to financial organizations, businesses, and individuals with legitimate needs for them. They are not made available to business competitors, and they are not intended to be accessible to the public. As a result, except in libraries where access to the public is restricted, they are not a part of library collections.[1]

The second is that while the credit history itself is based on data supplied by creditors, some of the remaining information, such as the description of current financial conditions, is supplied by the company being rated, which is under no obligation to provide full or even accurate information.

TRW Information Services is one of Dun & Bradstreet's major competitors. Its Business Credit Services division calls its reports "Business Profiles"; and, like D & B's "Business Information Reports," they include such data as the company's location and officers, credit history, and business and financial records.

TRW is even better known, however, for its personal credit reports.

> For more than two decades that division has done a brisk business with a variety of banks, credit card companies, retailers, and other so-called credit providers, trying to weed deadbeats from good credit risks. TRW gets accounts receivable computer tapes, which detail consumer purchases made on credit.... TRW sorts this accounts receivable information, from some 20,000 different sources, and produces more than 130 million personal credit repayment history reports that are then sold back to the vendors on request.[2]

TRW is not the only compiler of personal credit reports. Many of them, in fact, are prepared or at least sold by local credit bureaus. Whether they are prepared locally or at some distant location, such reports generally include the person's name, address, and social security number; credit history; details concerning current and past employment; and such personal information as date of birth and number of dependents. Like their business counterparts, personal credit reports are intended primarily for financial institutions and other creditors, and are not available in libraries. Patrons who inquire about such reports, however, should be informed that, by law, they are allowed access to their own reports.

People who are curious about their credit standing and would like to examine their reports can do so for a small fee. For those who have been denied credit as a result of a bad report, the fee is waived. If the report is found to be in error, the issuing agency must amend it, and submit the revised version to the creditor(s) who originally requested the report.

Interest

While creditors are most interested in culling creditworthy applicants from those who are not, those same applicants are concerned with getting the best terms possible. Although the terms of a loan may include such factors as loan fees and service charges, the single most important item is interest. Interest is the price that borrowers pay to lenders for credit over specified periods of time; it is, in effect, a rental fee paid for the use of money. The amount of interest paid is based on a number of factors: the amount of the loan, the length of time involved, the repayment schedule, the interest rate, and the method used to calculate interest.

Interest rates usually depend on the supply of loanable funds and the demand for those funds. In addition, the rates may vary depending on the borrower. Two rates that are frequently referred to in business publications and broadcasts are the discount rate and the prime interest rate. Neither is available to ordinary borrowers. The *discount rate*, which will be described further in the section on the Federal Reserve System, is the interest charged on short-term loans made by Federal Reserve Banks to commercial banks that are members of the Federal Reserve System. The *prime interest rate*, on the other hand, is the rate commercial banks charge preferred customers, usually large corporations and business enterprises. Both discount and prime interest rates have an impact on the interest rates charged for all other types of loans, and both are regularly reported in the *Federal Reserve Bulletin* and other financial statistics sources.

By itself, however, the annual interest rate is not always an accurate indicator of what a loan really costs. More useful for comparative purposes is the *annual percentage rate*, or *APR*. The APR is the true cost of a loan and in some instances may be considerably higher than the annual interest rate. Suppose, for example, that someone wants to borrow $1,000 for one year at 6 percent interest. The most favorable terms for the borrower would be based on a single, annual simple interest payment; at the end of the year, the borrower would repay the creditor the $1,000 plus $60 interest. In this instance (and whenever the interest being paid is simple annual interest), the APR and the interest rate are identical.

If, however, the same person were offered a "discount" or an "add on" loan, the APR would exceed the annual interest rate. A discount loan is one in which the annual interest is deducted from the principal of the loan before the borrower receives it. The borrower, in other words, receives less than the principal but is being charged interest on the full amount.

> Let's borrow that same $1,000 for a year but this time from a bank. Say the annual interest rate is the same as you paid your friend, 6%. The bank would probably take out the $60 in the 6% annual interest—in advance. This is called a *discount loan*. Now, for openers, you receive only $940. Then you pay off $83.40 monthly to liquidate (pay off) the loan. Therefore, your *true cost* or *APR* is 11.8% on $1,000. Puzzled? Well, you were paying interest on $1,000 but had use of only $940, and not even that for the full year. Moreover, with your monthly payments reducing the principal amount of the loan, the average amount of your money at your disposal during the course of the year was $470.[3]

"Add on," another method of calculating interest, adds the annual interest to the principal at the outset and is thus somewhat more advantageous to borrowers than a discount loan, but less so than a simple interest loan. Once again, the APR is greater than the annual interest rate; the loan costs more.

> In this case, the 6% or $60 annual interest rate would be added to your principal sum of $1,000 at the outset. You pay back $88.30 a month, and your APR is 11.1%. Your monthly payments are a little bit higher, but your APR is slightly lower, and you have the use of more money—$1,000 versus $940—than you did with the discount loan.[4]

The point to be made here is not how to compute the APR, but to stress its importance. Creditors are required by law to disclose the APRs for all prospective credit transactions so that borrowers can compare the terms offered by one financial institution with those extended by another.

BANKS, THRIFTS, AND THE
FINANCIAL SERVICES INDUSTRY

The various business organizations offering services relating to financial resources are generally referred to as the financial services industry (see figure 11.2). A number of these organizations—commercial banks, savings and loan associations, savings banks, and credit unions—serve as intermediaries, accepting the deposits of some and extending credit to others. They are classified as *depository institutions*. Although the distinctions between the different types of depository institutions and other components of the industry have become increasingly blurred, each was originally formed to serve different functions and still retains certain emphases. This section concentrates on two main types of depository institutions— commercial banks and thrifts—and considers briefly other financial service organizations.

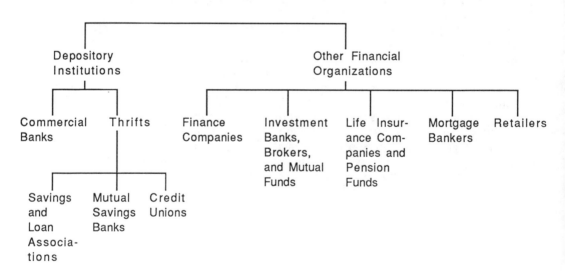

Fig. 11.2. The financial services industry.

Commercial Banks

There are over 14,000 commercial banks in the United States, ranging from small, nonspecialized operations to giant financial "department stores," with billions of dollars in deposits. All, however, share certain characteristics. First, each is a business whose main goal is to achieve profit by lending and investing the funds placed at its disposal.

> The individual commercial bank has much in common with the business firms with which it deals. Like many of them, the bank is a corporation. It has applied for, qualified for, and received a charter from the proper national or state government agency, empowering it to do business as stipulated in the charter.... The bank performs certain productive activities for which others are willing to pay; and in so doing, it incurs certain costs. In order to remain a going concern, it must experience a cash inflow from productive services rendered and from other sources that is sufficient for meeting all obligations as they become due, including all costs of doing business. Furthermore, its activities must provide an acceptable rate of return on investment. Usually a large fraction of a bank's income is in the form of interest on the claims it holds, particularly loans; while the two leading classes of bank costs are wages and salaries and interest paid on time deposits, that is, deposits not subject to check.[5]

Second, banks perform three functions: (1) they receive and hold deposits of funds from others; (2) they make loans or extend credit; and (3) they transfer funds by written orders of depositors.

Deposits of currency, checks, and bank drafts constitute the main source of funds available to commercial banks, typically accounting for some 90 percent of the funds that a bank has at its disposal. Deposits are categorized as time or demand. A time deposit is one in which the funds deposited can be withdrawn only after a specified lapse of time or designated future date. Although a number of types of time deposits are available, the two best known are certificates of deposit and savings accounts.[6]

Demand deposits, on the other hand, can be withdrawn at any time. They are available upon demand for immediate spending on goods and services, and are thus considered to be part of the nation's money supply. Checking accounts are the most common type of demand deposit; a depositor simply writes a check on his or her account to transfer funds to the organization or person requiring payment. With depositors writing and depositing checks every day, funds continuously flow into and out of banks.

Banks are not, however, required to keep on hand the full amount deposited. Under what is known as the fractional reserve system of banking, they must keep only a designated percentage of their deposits in cash and reserve accounts. The remainder can be used for investments and loans, commercial banks' major profit-making activities. Such activities are important not only to banks but to the economy as a whole, because they permit the creation of new demand deposits and thus contribute to the money supply. To illustrate, the following example is borrowed from a Federal Reserve Bank publication.[7]

Westside Bank receives a deposit of $1,000. It is required to keep a reserve of 15 percent, or $150; it can lend the remaining $850. The bank decides to lend the entire amount to Jake the Plumber, who deposits the loan into his checking account. Jake then visits Slick's Used Trucks to buy the pickup truck of his dreams which, coincidentally, happens to cost $850. He gets the truck, and Slick gets a check for $850. Slick takes the check to his bank, the Eastview Bank, where he deposits it into his checking account. Eastview Bank gains $850 in deposits. It, too, holds a reserve of 15 percent, so it keeps $127.50 on hand, leaving $622.50 to lend to Helen's Beauty Spa. Helen spends the entire $622.50 on new hair dryers, towels, and shampoo at Harry's Wholesale Beauty Supply Company. Harry deposits Helen's check at his bank, which will once again keep a 15 percent reserve and lend out the remaining 85 percent. It goes on and on. As the process continues, the original $1,000 deposit can expand to almost $6,700 in demand deposits.

Although banks can create new demand deposits by making loans, their ability to do so is greatly affected by the Federal Reserve System, which can increase or decrease legal reserve requirements (the percentage of total deposits that banks are required to keep available to make payments on demand) and can thus decrease or increase excess reserves available for lending and investing. This role will be discussed further in the section on the Federal Reserve System.

Commercial banks traditionally have emphasized the credit and deposit needs of businesses, rather than individuals. Further, since the bulk of a bank's money comes from demand deposits rather than savings accounts and other time deposits, the focus is on short-term loans rather than on long-term loans such as mortgages. Although commercial banks are now competing vigorously for individuals' business, other financial organizations historically have emphasized the banking and credit needs of individual consumers.

Thrift Institutions

Thrift institutions, or thrifts, received their name from the purpose for which they were originally established: to encourage thrift among the working class by providing places for them to deposit their savings and take out loans. Such organizations, accordingly, concentrated on savings accounts, residential mortgages, and other types of consumer credit. Three main types of thrift institutions evolved, each of which will be considered briefly.

SAVINGS AND LOAN ASSOCIATIONS

The savings and loan association, or S & L, is the predominant type of thrift institution. The first S & Ls, known as building and loan associations, were founded in the 19th century to help workers become home owners. People formed an association and regularly deposited their savings. As deposits grew, the association's members bid for mortgage funds.

> In early associations, members agreed to purchase shares of stock in the amount that they wished to borrow. The shares were paid for by regular, mandatory payments. When enough money was collected to make a loan, the loan was auctioned off among the association's members. The loan carried a fixed rate of interest, usually 6%, and the member bidding the highest number of discount points got the loan.... Meanwhile, each member continued to pay for his shares and, with the interest from the first loan, another was soon made.[8]

Although they no longer require that borrowers be members, savings and loan associations remain the major lenders for the purchase of homes and related types of real estate loans.

MUTUAL SAVINGS BANKS

Mutual savings banks are the oldest thrift institutions in the United States. Like savings and loan associations, they were established to promote financial security and thrift among workers, and have been active mortgage and real estate lenders. Whereas savings and loan associations have developed throughout the country, however, mutual savings banks have been concentrated largely in the northeastern United States. Further, while S & Ls, like commercial banks, can be either federally or state chartered, until a few years ago all mutual savings banks were chartered solely by state agencies.

CREDIT UNIONS

Credit unions are similar in many respects to the other thrift institutions already described. Like them, credit unions came into being in the United States in the 19th century to meet the needs of workers, "to take factory workers out of the clutches of 'loan sharks.' "[9] However, unlike savings and loans and mutual savings banks, credit unions will give loans only to members, who must share some common bond, such as place or nature of employment or institutional affiliation. Further, while the emphasis in the other types of thrifts has been on long-term mortgage lending, credit unions have tended to focus on short-term installment loans. Credit unions may be federally or state chartered, and most are also insured by federal or state agencies.

Other Financial Institutions

Depository institutions, however, are not the only components of the financial services industry. Other organizations include finance companies; investment banks, securities brokers, mutual funds and investment companies; life insurance companies and pension funds; mortgage banks; and retailers.

FINANCE COMPANIES

Finance companies finance both households and business firms and are, in fact, classified by the types of loans they make. Sales finance companies, for example, specialize in installment loans for the purchase of automobiles, home appliances, and other consumer durables; General Motors Acceptance Corporation, a General Motors unit that makes loans for the purchase of the company's automobiles, is an example of a sales finance company. Personal finance companies make personal loans, and business finance companies generally extend credit to business based on accounts receivable or sales of equipment. As a rule, loans made by finance companies are short term.

INVESTMENT BANKS, SECURITIES BROKERS, AND INVESTMENT COMPANIES

Although the subject of investing will be covered at length in the chapters that follow, it is worth noting here that three of the organizations most directly involved in investing are integral parts of the financial services industry.

Investment banks underwrite securities when they are first offered. When, for example, a corporation wants to raise money, it often issues stocks and bonds. These newly issued securities are then sold to investment banking firms, which in turn sell them to the public at a slightly higher price. Investment banks, in other words, buy large blocks of securities at wholesale prices and resell them at retail prices. Investment banks are different from commercial banks, which presently are prohibited by law from participating in the investment banking business.

Securities brokers act as agents for clients interested in the purchase or sale of stocks, bonds, and other securities. In recent years, some brokers have begun to offer new services that compete with commercial banks. Large, full-service brokerage houses, for example, now offer financial products that combine the features and benefits of credit cards, checking accounts, money market funds, and traditional securities trading accounts. They have, accordingly, become an increasingly powerful segment of the financial services industry.

Investment companies and mutual funds – organizations that pool the funds deposited by individual investors to buy diversified securities portfolios – have also grown tremendously in recent years. They, too, are in direct competition with commercial banks and have siphoned off some of the business formerly handled by banks.

LIFE INSURANCE COMPANIES AND PENSION FUNDS

The primary purpose of life insurance companies and pension funds is to provide financial security to individuals and households. Participants make periodic payments over long periods of time, in return for which they or designated beneficiaries will receive future payments. Insurance companies and pension funds, in turn, invest the money they receive in securities or use it to make loans.

MORTGAGE BANKS

Mortgage banks focus solely on residential and commercial real estate mortgages, and, like the organizations listed above, are major financial institutions (see chapter 18).

RETAILERS

Merchants and other retailers have extended credit to customers for years; retail credit cards, for example, long preceded such bank-issued competitors as Visa and MasterCard. In recent years, however, some retail operations have expanded significantly their role in the financial services industry. The most striking example is Sears, Roebuck and Company, which has acquired such financial operations as an insurance company, brokerage house, and mortgage banking firm. It has become a major financial force. Other retailers are beginning to follow Sears's example, although on a smaller scale.

FEDERAL RESERVE SYSTEM

Although it is by no means the only government agency involved in the regulation of banking activities, the Federal Reserve System is the most important. This section examines its structure, the services it provides, and its impact on the economy.

Organizational Structure

The Federal Reserve System, sometimes referred to as "the Fed," was established by Congress in 1913 to serve as the country's central bank. Its organizational structure is that of a pyramid (see figure 11.3). At its apex is the chairman of the central governing body, the Board of Governors. Based in Washington, D.C., the board consists of seven members appointed by the president with the advice and consent of the Senate. Each is appointed for a 14-year term and must represent a different Federal Reserve District, thus ensuring fair representation of regional interests. The president appoints one member of the board as chairman, and another as vice-chairman for four-year terms. Behind the scenes, the Board of Governors is assisted by financial experts, economists, and other support staffs.

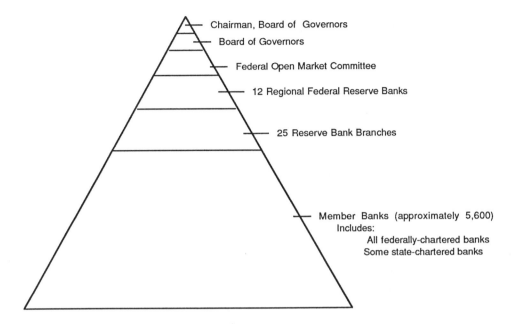

- Chairman, Board of Governors
- Board of Governors
- Federal Open Market Committee
- 12 Regional Federal Reserve Banks
- 25 Reserve Bank Branches
- Member Banks (approximately 5,600)
  Includes:
      All federally-chartered banks
      Some state-chartered banks

Fig. 11.3. The structure of the Federal Reserve System.

The board's duties include overseeing the operations of the 12 Federal Reserve Banks, supervising state-chartered member banks, approving changes in the discount rate, and setting reserve requirements for member banks. In addition, the governors serve on the Federal Open Market Committee, described below. The board also regulates the implementation of certain consumer credit protection laws and carries on public information activities, including publication of the monthly *Federal Reserve Bulletin*, staff economic studies, and other materials.

The Federal Open Market Committee (FOMC) is the Fed's most important policymaking body. Comprised of all seven members of the Board of Governors and 5 of the 12 regional Federal Reserve Bank presidents, this committee has become the forum at which monetary policy matters are discussed and decisions made.[10]

> Staff researchers from the banks and from the Board of Governors present data about variables reflecting the current and expected future health of the economy: changes in productivity activity, trade, employment, prices, and stocks of industrial commodities. The Committee must evaluate the evidence and determine the appropriate direction of policy.[11]

The FOMC is, in fact, considered so important that committee members are not the only ones in attendance. The seven remaining Federal Reserve Bank presidents not serving on the committee, Board of Governors staff members, and senior staff economists regularly attend the meetings, which are held every three or four weeks.

The next level of the Federal Reserve System consists of the regional Federal Reserve Banks and their branches. In all, there are 12 banks and 25 branches (see figure 11.4 on page 284). Each serves a designated district of the country, providing banking services to member banks in its district. Like the Board of Governors, each bank also provides an assortment of information materials, ranging from sophisticated statistical studies to comic books and filmstrips intended for grade school students.

Federal Reserve System Map

— Boundaries of Federal Reserve Districts
• Federal Reserve Bank Cities
★ Board of Governors of the Federal Reserve System
· Federal Reserve Branches: Buffalo, Cincinnati, Pittsburgh, Baltimore, Charlotte, Birmingham, Jacksonville, Miami, Nashville, New Orleans, Detroit, Little Rock, Louisville, Memphis, Helena, Denver, Oklahoma City, Omaha, El Paso, Houston, San Antonio, Los Angeles, Portland, Salt Lake City, and Seattle

Fig. 11.4. Federal Reserve Banks and their districts.

Finally, the last tier of the system is comprised of some 5,600 commercial banks. All nationally chartered (that is, those with *Federal* or *National* in their title) and most large state-chartered banks are members. Banks are required to comply with Federal Reserve regulations covering banking matters, but are entitled to certain services as well.

Services

The Federal Reserve System is a sort of "banker's bank," providing to member banks and the federal government services similar to those offered to the public by commercial banks. Federal Reserve Banks and their branches, for example, serve banks in their districts by holding their cash reserves and making short-term loans to them, charging the discount interest rate. The Reserve Banks also move currency and coin into and out of circulation.

The Federal Reserve Banks distribute paper money and coin to commercial banks to meet the public's need for cash. During periods of heavy cash demand, such as Christmas shopping season, banks obtain larger amounts of cash from the Federal Reserve Banks. When public demand for cash is light, banks deposit excess cash with the Federal Reserve Banks for storage. Currency and coin received at the Federal Reserve Banks is sorted and counted. Unfit paper money and coins are destroyed and replaced with new currency and coin obtained from the Treasury Department's Bureau of Engraving and Printing and Bureau of the Mint.[12]

Federal Reserve Banks issue Federal Reserve notes, the most common type of currency in circulation today. These notes are backed by assets held by Reserve Banks, consisting primarily of government securities and gold certificates.

The Fed also serves as a central check-clearing system. Each Reserve Bank receives checks from banks for collection, sorts them, sends the checks to the banks upon which they were written, and transfers payment for the checks through accounts at the Federal Reserve Bank.

Another service available to member banks is the national wire transfer of funds and securities using *Fedwire*, the Federal Reserve Communications System. Electronic payments of billions of dollars are made daily using Fedwire; nearly 100 trillion dollars are transferred over the Fedwire network annually.[13]

The Fed provides financial services to the U.S. government as well. The Federal Reserve System, through district Federal Reserve Banks, accepts deposits and issues checks for the U.S. Treasury. Payroll withholding taxes, for example, are deposited into the government's checking accounts at Federal Reserve Banks, while redemption fees for such items as U.S. Savings Bonds and food stamps are paid by transferring funds from the appropriate government accounts to the commercial banks at which they originally were redeemed. Finally, Reserve Banks handle the clerical work involved in selling and redeeming Government securities such as Treasury bills, notes, and bonds.

The Board of Governors and each Federal Reserve Bank employ research staff to gather and analyze economic data and interpret economic conditions and developments. Such data and the accompanying interpretations and projections are used by the Board of Governors, Federal Open Market Committee, and Federal Reserve Bank officers to make important administrative and policy decisions. They also serve to keep the public well informed. Most regional banks publish a monthly or quarterly journal devoted to basic research and analysis of current economic issues. Subscriptions are free to interested individuals and libraries, and generally can be obtained by writing to the issuing banks (see appendix I).

Monetary Policy

Even more important than the services it provides, however, is the Federal Reserve System's role in formulating monetary policy. By setting monetary policy, the Fed regulates the flow of money and credit, or money supply. Money supply is a key factor in economic stability. Too much money may lead to inflation; too little, to recession. As was mentioned earlier, the Fed continuously monitors economic conditions in the United States. Based on the data it gathers and analyzes, it recommends actions to encourage or discourage the ability of commercial banks to extend credit by increasing or decreasing the amount of credit available and by raising or lowering the cost of credit. In order to accomplish its goals, the Fed uses three main tools: reserve requirements, the discount rate, and the purchase and sale of government securities.

Reserves, it should be remembered, represent deposits not available for lending. By raising or lowering the amount of reserves that member banks are required to keep, the Fed can significantly affect the amount of credit that is available. In the example used earlier in this chapter, the reserve rate was set at 15 percent, enabling banks to lend 85 percent of their deposits. If reserve requirements were raised to 25 percent, however, the amount of credit available would decline significantly. Increasing reserve requirements reduces the amount of money available for loans and results in higher interest rates. Decreasing reserve requirements, on the other hand, allows banks to lend more and usually results in lower interest rates.

The discount rate charged by Reserve Banks on short-term loans to member banks can also affect lending. Raising or lowering the discount rate will discourage or encourage banks' borrowing from the Fed, which will in turn affect commercial banks' lending practices.

Finally, the Federal Reserve System, along with other organizations and individuals, buys and sells government securities in the open market. Unlike the others, however, the Fed does this to affect the supply of credit rather than for investment purposes. To illustrate, the Fed buys securities to increase reserves and stimulate lending, and sells them to decrease reserves and lending.

The System most often influences banks' reserves by selling or buying outstanding Government securities to or from dealers in transactions called open market operations. To lower bank reserves (and decrease potential lending), the Fed can sell securities from its holdings. Buyers pay for the securities with checks which, when cleared, reduce bank reserves. If the Fed wishes to increase reserves (and increase potential bank lending), it buys securities, paying the sellers by a check drawn against the Fed's own credit which, when deposited at a commercial bank, increases the bank's reserves.[14]

In summary, to stave off inflation, the Federal Reserve System usually raises reserve requirements and discount rates and sells government securities that it holds. To fight against recession—that is, to expand credit and increase borrowing—the Fed acts by taking the opposite actions. It lowers reserve requirements and discount rates and buys government securities. By making the policy decisions that result in these actions, the Fed contributes to the country's economic stability and growth.

OTHER FEDERAL AND STATE GOVERNMENT AGENCIES

The United States has a dual banking system. Banks and thrift institutions may be either federally or state chartered. As a result, both federal and state government agencies are involved in regulating and monitoring their activities.

Federal Agencies

The *Office of the Comptroller of the Currency*, part of the Treasury Department, is an integral part of the national banking system. As the administrator of national banks, the comptroller is responsible for chartering all national banks, for the conversion of state-chartered banks into national banks, and the establishment of branches by national banks. The Office of the Comptroller also supervises national bank operations, and is responsible for overseeing the regular examination of all national banks.

Each bank is examined periodically through a nationwide staff of approximately 1,800 bank examiners under the immediate supervision of six district deputy comptrollers and six district administrators. These examinations operate in the public interest by assisting the Comptroller in appraising the financial condition of the banks, the soundness of their operations, the quality of their management, and their compliance with laws, rules, and regulations.[15]

All banks belonging to the Federal Reserve System are required to be members of the *Federal Deposit Insurance Corporation (FDIC)*. The FDIC is an independent, self-supporting government organization that helps to promote the stability and safety of the banking system by insuring the deposits at commercial and savings banks. Prior to the establishment of the FDIC, a bank failure meant that depositors lost all or part of their savings. Today, in the case of such failure, the FDIC takes over the bank. The claim of each depositor (up to $100,000) is paid, either as a result of the FDIC's sale of the bank's assets or its auction of the failed bank's assets and liabilities to the highest bidder, who then is responsible for operating the bank.

Another way in which the FDIC contributes to the safety of the banking system is by requiring the improvement of banks that examination shows to be improperly managed. If corrective action is not taken, the bank's insurance is terminated. Loss of FDIC insurance requires a national bank to give up its charter and a state bank to withdraw from the Federal

System. Moreover, banks realize that public knowledge that they were no longer insured would be likely to lead to widespread deposit withdrawals and might culminate in bank failure.

Although commercial banks may be members of both the Federal Reserve System and the Federal Deposit Insurance Corporation, savings and loan associations, savings banks, and credit unions are excluded from membership. They are, however, served by other federal agencies patterned after the Fed and the FDIC.

The *Federal Home Loan Bank System* is to savings and loan associations what the Federal Reserve System is to commercial banks. Its primary purpose is "to provide a flexible credit reserve for member savings institutions engaged in home mortgage lending."[16] This system consists of three tiers: the Federal Home Loan Bank Board, 12 regional Federal Home Loan Banks, and some 5,000 member savings and loan associations.

The *Federal Home Loan Bank Board* (*FHLBB*) charters, supervises, and regulates savings and loan associations. It also operates the *Federal Savings and Loan Insurance Corporation* (*FSLIC*), which insures savings deposits. By providing insurance coverage, the FSLIC encourages deposits into savings and loan associations and thus promotes home ownership by increasing the supply of funds available for lending.

The 12 regional Federal Home Loan Banks provide loans to member banks in their regions and help to stabilize the available supply of residential mortgage credit. Every federal savings and loan association and savings bank and every state-chartered savings institution insured by the FSLIC is required to become a member of its regional Federal Home Loan Bank. Although the Home Loan Banks cannot regulate money supply as does the Federal Reserve System, they do lend funds, establish interest rates, and set other requirements for members. They are located in Atlanta, Boston, Chicago, Cincinnati, Dallas, Des Moines, Indianapolis, New York, Pittsburgh, San Francisco, Seattle, and Topeka.

Although savings and loan associations and savings banks are covered by the Federal Home Loan Bank System, credit unions are not. Federally chartered credit unions, however, are chartered, insured, supervised, and examined by the *National Credit Union* (*NCUA*) *Administration*.

It should be clear from this discussion that banks and thrifts are among the most heavily regulated and supervised institutions in the country. Many bankers, in fact, feel that they are constrained by provisions of post-Depression legislation and would like to expand the types of services offered so that they are more competitive with other, faster growing, segments of the financial services industry.

State Agencies

State-chartered banks and thrifts come under the control of state authorities. Although the structure of banking agencies varies from one state to another, most are established as separate departments or are parts of state departments of finance or commerce. Like their federal counterparts, state banking agencies charter, regulate, and monitor the banks and thrifts under their control. In addition, each state has the right to prohibit certain kinds of banking activities, such as branch banking, within its borders.

PUBLICATIONS

The financial services industry is well represented by publications and other types of information sources. This section examines materials relevant to banking and credit. Other segments of the financial services industry will be covered in the chapters that follow.

Bibliographies and Guides

Although the literature of banking is abundant, the same cannot be said of the bibliographies and guides representing the field. Most combine banking with such related subjects as finance and investment or economics, or focus on international and foreign as well as domestic banking. As a result, comprehensive bibliographies and guides to the U.S. banking industry are lacking. There are, however, several publications that provide good partial coverage.

Balachandran, M. **A Guide to Statistical Sources in Money, Banking, and Finance**. Phoenix, Ariz.: Oryx Press, 1988. 119p.

Daniells, Lorna. "Corporate Finance and Banking," **Business Information Sources**. 2nd ed. (Berkeley, Calif.: University of California Press, 1985), pp. 319-57.

Dicks, G. R. **Sources of World Financial and Banking Information**. Westport, Conn.: Greenwood Press, 1981. 720p.

One of the most useful is *A Guide to Statistical Sources in Money, Banking, and Finance*, a selected, annotated bibliography of sources that contain banking and monetary statistics. It is arranged by broad geographic categories (state, regional, national, foreign, and international), with a separate section for databases. Using it, one can identify printed and electronic sources that contain data on interest rates, consumer finance, bank deposits and loans, foreign exchange markets, and related topics. A directory of publishers and subject and title indexes are appended.

"Corporate Finance and Banking," in *Business Information Sources*, covers two interrelated areas of business finance: corporate finance, and money, banking, and credit. The section on money and banking lists and annotates basic texts, handbooks, legal services, banking and financial tables, dictionaries, statistical sources, and periodicals and newspapers. A list of major banking and credit associations is also included.

Sources of World Financial and Banking Information is considerably broader in scope. It is organized in three sections. Part 1, "Source Publications," is a listing, by country, of nearly 5,000 sources of data, comment, and interpretation of a financial, banking, or economic nature. In addition to the work's title and publisher, each entry contains a brief annotation and specifies the language of publication, country or countries covered, approximate number of pages, and price or subscription rate. Although a guide that covers the economic, financial, and banking publications of 140 countries is of necessity rather selective, *Sources of World Financial and Banking Information* is particularly useful for its coverage of publications that are not always featured in standard bibliographies. Newsletters issued by the Bank of America and Chase Manhattan Bank, for example, are included with other sources in the U.S. section. Publications of Federal Reserve Banks and relevant trade associations are also listed. Readers should be forewarned, however, that many major banking sources are not included. The *American Banker*, an important daily trade paper; basic banking directories; and many other works are missing.

Part 2, "Publishing Bodies," gives the addresses, telephone numbers, and, when possible, telex numbers of publishers listed in part 1. Finally, part 3, "Index of Sources by Subject and Country," classifies publications by seven different categories: general economic and financial information, national income accounts and public finance, money and banking, companies and stocks and shares, households and persons, balance of payments and energy, and prices. In the "Money and Banking" index, international titles and their corresponding entry numbers in the front of the volume are listed first, followed by similar listings for each of the 140 countries represented.

Other sources are considerably more specialized, focusing on specific types of publications or selecting materials intended for certain audiences.

U.S. Superintendent of Documents. **Banks and Banking.** Washington, D.C.: Government Printing Office, 1987 (Subject Bibliography 128). 3p.

Skeen, Molly M., and Deborah P. Wessell, comps. **A Basic Library for Savings Institutions**. 3rd ed. San Francisco, Calif.: Federal Home Loan Bank of San Francisco, 1986. 30p.

Ladley, Barbara, and Jane Wilford. **Money & Finance: Sources of Print and Nonprint Materials**. New York: Neal-Schuman, 1980. 208p.

Like other titles in the Superintendent of Documents "Subject Bibliographies" series, *Banks and Banking* selectively lists and annotates laws, congressional documents, and agency publications. For each item listed, title, number of pages, Superintendent of Documents classification, stock number, and price are included. An order blank is appended.

A Basic Library for Savings Institutions is an annotated list of books, journals, looseleaf services, and other sources appropriate for the libraries of savings and loan associations and other thrift institutions. Publications are arranged by broad subject category, including Accounting, Operations, Lending, and Financial Services Industry. A list of publishers and their addresses is also featured. Although *A Basic Library* was compiled with thrift institutions in mind, many of the titles it lists are appropriate to more general business collections as well.

Money & Finance lists and describes more than 500 organizations that provide information and publications relating to consumer finance. Organizations are grouped together by broad subject category, of which "Banking, Money, and Credit" is one. In it, such organizations as the American Bankers Association, American Express, and Federal Reserve and Federal Home Loan Banks are listed. Each entry includes the name, address, and telephone number of the organization covered, a description of its information-producing activities, and a list of representative books, pamphlets, newsletters, filmstrips, and other materials. Readers should be forewarned, however, that the publication lists are *not* inclusive; the focus is on consumer finance, and more sophisticated and scholarly works are excluded. It is useful, however, for publications that would be appropriate for vertical file collections and in libraries serving secondary school students, undergraduates, and the general public.

Dictionaries, Encyclopedias, Handbooks, and Yearbooks

DICTIONARIES

Banking dictionaries can be divided into two main categories: those intended for practitioners and students, and those written for consumers. Although a number of such dictionaries are available, the following are among the best.

American Bankers Association. **Banking Terminology**. Washington, D.C.: The Association, 1981. 260p.

Davids, Lewis E. **Dictionary of Banking and Finance**. Totowa, N.J.: Littlefield, Adams & Co., 1978. 229p.

Rosenberg, Jerry M. **Dictionary of Banking and Financial Services**. 2nd ed. New York: Wiley, 1985. 708p.

German, Don, and Joan German. **Money A to Z: A Consumer's Guide to the Language of Personal Finance**. New York: Facts on File, 1984. 265p.

Banking Terminology is a glossary of terms in current usage, intended as a desk reference tool for banking professionals and students of banking. It lists and defines terms ranging from *abandonment* to *zoning*, with numeric terms (*10-K reports, 78th methods of rebate*) following the alphabetical listing. Basic banking acronyms are also included.

The *Dictionary of Banking and Finance* is a standard reference work, presenting definitions for over 6,000 terms in banking and such related fields as accounting, law, taxation, and government. Although some of the definitions are original, many have been taken from basic banking reference works; in such instances, the definitions are attributed to the original sources, which are listed in the back of the *Dictionary*. Also appended are lists, addresses, and brief descriptions of U.S. banking, credit union, finance, insurance, investment, savings and loan, and federal and state government organizations. Although a bibliography of reference books is also featured, it is the least useful part of the dictionary; the list is too brief and too dated to be of much value.

The *Dictionary of Banking and Financial Services* is the most comprehensive of the dictionaries listed, defining approximately 15,000 terms. First published as the *Dictionary of Banking & Finance*, the title was changed to reflect the lessening differences between banks and thrift institutions and other components of the financial services industry. Another difference between editions is that the statistical and banking organization/operation appendixes featured in the first edition are no longer present.

Finally, *Money A to Z* is typical of dictionaries aimed at the general public. It is divided into two main parts: (1) definitions and consumer tips, and (2) financial planning, which summarizes and explains such financial topics as bank accounts, borrowing, retirement planning, and savings. The emphasis throughout is on "plain English" and topics of interest to ordinary people rather than to wealthy investors or banking institutions.

ENCYCLOPEDIAS

Two encyclopedias are considered standard reference works.

Munn, Glenn G. **Encyclopedia of Banking and Finance**. 8th ed., rev. and enl. Boston: Bankers Publishing, 1983. 1024p.

Rachlin, Harvey, ed. **Money Encyclopedia**. New York: Harper & Row, 1984. 669p.

The *Encyclopedia of Banking and Finance* is an authoritative, well-written source that combines brief definitions of basic banking terms with a series of encyclopedic articles on such varied topics as the Federal Reserve System and forgery. Statistics and bibliographies are frequently included, and definitions are often enhanced by examples illustrating proper usage. In addition, key concepts and terms from such related fields as finance and insurance are featured, and major banking legislation is described at length. The *Encyclopedia* is a basic reference work that belongs in every business collection.

Less essential but still very useful is the *Money Encyclopedia*. Directed at the general reader, it covers the whole field of personal finance, featuring signed articles on such topics as taxes, banking, and real estate. Although the *Money Encyclopedia* is shorter, less specialized, and lacks the bibliographies common to the *Encyclopedia of Banking and Finance*, it is nonetheless useful as an introduction to basic concepts in economics, banking, and personal finance.

HANDBOOKS

There are a myriad of handbooks that cover the banking industry and still others that combine coverage of banks and thrifts with the rest of the financial services industry. The titles that follow fall into the first category.

Baughn, William H., and Charls E. Walker. **The Bankers' Handbook**. Rev. ed. Homewood, Ill.: Dow Jones-Irwin, 1978. 1205p.

Cox, Edwin, et al. **The Bank Director's Handbook**. 2nd ed. Dover, Mass.: Auburn House Publishing, 1986. 294p.

The Bankers' Handbook is a basic banking source. Arranged by broad categories, such as "Organizing and Managing the Banking Corporation" and "Credit Policy Administration," it includes 104 articles by banking practitioners, academicians, and other experts. Although it is now somewhat dated—major legislation changing the shape of banking and the financial services industry has been enacted since it was published—it remains useful for its thorough coverage of many aspects of the business of banking.

While less comprehensive, the *Bank Director's Handbook* is also more current. Intended for directors with limited knowledge of banking, it covers an array of topics, including the changing role of banks in the financial services industry, banking functions and services, technology in banking, and the bank environment of the future. It also contains a glossary and an index. The *Bank Director's Handbook* is a useful source of background information, written by experts, about banking as it is presently being practiced and may be practiced in the future.

Other handbooks combine information about banking with broader coverage of economics and finance.

Logue, Dennis E., ed. **Handbook of Modern Finance**. Boston: Warren, Gorham & Lamont, 1984. [Various paginations]

Consolidated Capital Communications Group, Inc. **The Financial Desk Book**. Emeryville, Calif.: The Group, 1985. [Various paginations]

The *Handbook of Modern Finance* contains lengthy articles by experts grouped together under five broad categories: the financial system and markets, security analysis, pricing and portfolio management, short-term financial management, long-term financial management, and international dimensions of finance. Chapters frequently contain bibliographies, statistics, and mathematical tables, and are written for practitioners and academicians rather than the general public. An index is included.

The *Financial Desk Book* is intended for investors as well as financial professionals, and covers such topics as personal financial and tax planning. In addition, it presents an array of formulas and interest tables as well as data on key economic indicators, a glossary, and a directory of financial service associations and government agencies.

YEARBOOKS

One of the most popular U.S. banking yearbooks is described below.[17]

Cox, Edwin B. **Bank Performance Annual**. Boston: Warren, Gorham & Lamont, 1980- . [Title varies]

Formerly the *Bankers Desk Reference*, the *Bank Performance Annual* combines a review of the past year's banking activities with a series of essays by experts on topics of current interest. The 1987 edition, for example, includes articles on such topics as risk management in banking, contingency planning, and bank facility design. A third section presents statistics on commercial banks and thrift institutions, reprinted from such sources as the *American Banker, Business Week*, and the *Federal Reserve Bulletin*. Using it, one can identify the country's largest banks and thrifts, compare state laws regulating banking activities, and review the past year's interest rates. The last section is a directory of professional and trade associations, government regulatory organizations, special-purpose government agencies, and State Bankers Association executives. Each entry includes the organization's address and telephone number, the name of its chief officer, a brief description of its activities, and the titles of its principal publications.

Financial Manuals and Directories

Banking directories generally reflect the divisions between commercial banks, thrifts, and other financial service institutions. *Moody's Bank & Finance Manual*, however, is an exception.

Moody's Investors Service. **Moody's Bank & Finance Manual**. New York: The Service, 1900- . 3v. Annual, with semiweekly supplements.

The *Manual* is, in fact, both more and less than a directory. As a financial manual, it presents brief histories and descriptions of and current operating statistics for banks, thrifts, and other financial service organizations, far more information than most directories provide. As compared to the directories that follow, however, the *Manual* includes fewer banks and thrifts.

Volume 1 covers commercial banks and trust companies, mutual savings banks and savings and loan associations, and such federal credit agencies as the Federal Reserve System and the Federal Deposit Insurance Corporation. Volumes 2 and 3 focus on other components of the financial services industry, including mutual funds and investment companies, real estate companies, real estate investment trusts, finance and insurance companies, and unit investment trusts.

For research on banks and thrifts, the first volume is most useful. In it, some 3,000 of the largest banks are treated at length. Entries often exceed 10 pages, and generally include a corporate history, lists of subsidiaries and affiliates, a description of the bank, the names of its officers and directors, balance sheet and income statement data, and information on stocks and dividends. Approximately 3,600 additional banks are covered in less detail in a separate section. The entry for Ponchartrain State Bank shown in figure 11.5 is typical of the shorter entries. Similar information is presented for savings and loan associations and mutual savings banks.

The federal agency section of the *Manual* includes descriptions of the agencies listed, the names of officials, and, in many instances, balance sheets, income statements, and other data on operations. Finally, the blue pages in the center of volume 1 rank the largest banks by deposits and assets, and present data on business financing costs, thrift institutions, and related topics. Although the *Manual* is far from comprehensive, it presents a wealth of information for the banks and thrifts that are included. It is a basic business reference source.

For standard directory coverage, however, other publications are generally consulted. Commercial banks, for example, are listed in the following titles.

The Rand McNally Bankers Directory. Chicago: Rand McNally, 3v, 1872- . Semiannual. [Formerly *Rand McNally International Bankers Directory*]

Polk's World Bank Directory. Nashville, Tenn.: R. L. Polk, 1895- . Semiannual.

The Rand McNally Bankers Directory is a three-volume set that presents information about U.S. banks in volumes 1 and 2 and about international banks in volume 3. Arrangement in the first two volumes is by state, then by city, and then alphabetically by bank name. Although the length of the entries to a certain extent reflects the size of the bank, each generally includes (1) the name of the bank; (2) type of bank charter; (3) memberships in federal credit organizations, professional associations, and state banking organizations; (4) the name of the immediate holding company (when applicable); (5) parent company name; (6) state and national rankings for the head office; (7) officers and directors; (8) financial data for the head office; and (9) such operations-related information as the bank's routing

PONTCHARTRAIN STATE BANK
(Metairie, La.)
Established as a State bank Feb. 14, 1973. Conducts general banking business. Member Federal Deposit Insurance Corp. Operates a branch at Harahan, Gretna and Cypress Bend.

Officers
W.D. Womach, Jr., Chmn.
E.M. Reggie, Pres.
L.C. Hoffman, Senior'Vice-Pres.
Ronald Broussand, Vice-Pres.
Silvia Pons, Vice-Pres. & Cashier

Directors

W.D. Womach, Jr.	R.H. Creager
W.E. Beebe	J.D. Freeman
J.D. Boudreaux	Harry Lee
G.F. Burnsed	Frank Nicolodis
D.L. Bussell	Clayton Schexnaildre
H.L. Stram	E.M. Reggie
L.C. Hoffman	Uncas Favret
Carlo Ferrara	R.E. Steen

Office: 8923 Veterans Blvd., Metairie, LA 70003.
Tel.: (504)467-8923.

Statement, Dec. 31 (in thousand dollars):

Resources:	1986	1985
Cash & in bank	10,025	6,334
U.S. Gov't secur.	4,774	5,819
Fed. fds. sold	900	1,725
Loans & disc. (net)	36,147	26,320
Bank bldgs., etc.	2,427	2,621
Other assets...............	743	693
Total.................	55,016	43,512
Liabilities:		
Capital stk.	2,566	2,478
Surplus	3,191	2,908
Undivided profit & reserves ..	dr3,193	dr3,377
Deposits	51,493	40,930
Capital Deben..............	500	......
Other liabilities	459	573
Total.................	55,016	43,512
①Book val. per sh..........	$5.00	$4.05

①Includes reserves.

Capital Debentures: Outstanding Dec. 31, 1986, $500,000. Further details not reported.

Capital Stock: Outstg., $2,566,000; par $1.
Traded: OTC.
Price Range: 1986-85, 1½-½; 1984, ½-½.

Fig. 11.5. Typical bank entry, *Moody's Bank & Finance Manual*. Reprinted by permission from *Moody's Bank & Finance Manual*, Vol. 1, 1987.

number and the wire network services and clearinghouses to which the bank belongs. The entries shown in figure 11.6 (see page 294) are typical of listings for some of the smaller banks; entries for the larger banks usually fill an entire page.

Other features include a tabular comparison of financial services offered by banks, data on Federal Reserve and Federal Home Loan Banks and their districts, and lists of other government and regulatory agencies and world, national, and state banking associations. An alphabetical index by name of bank is also included.

Volume 3 lists international banks involved in foreign exchange or foreign trade. Listings are arranged by country, city, and bank name, and each contains relevant marketing, administrative, and operational information.

Polk's World Bank Directory also profiles banks and their branch offices. The two directories, in fact, duplicate each other to such an extent that it is unusual for any but the largest, most specialized, or most affluent libraries to subscribe to both.

▶ **PALM SPRINGS**   *Pop* 37,900   F5   *Riverside*   *Fed Dist* 12 L

Bank of America National Trust & Savings Association
Branch of San Francisco   *Rt No* 1220 0066 1   16-66/1220
101 N Palm Canyon Dr (92262)   *Mgr* NR
619/325-0011

Other City Branches 2355 Tahquitz-McCallum Way (92262), 619/325-0011, *Mgr* NR; 1801 E Palm Canyon
Dr (92262), 619/325-0011, *Mgr* NR

BANK Of PALM SPRINGS

BANK OF PALM SPRINGS   *Rt No* 1222 3738 2   90-3738/1222   *Fedwire on-line*

State	*Status* 110/455 State	2,207/14,531 U.S.	
601 E Tahquitz Way (92262);	*Financial Figures*	*12/31/86*	*12/31/85*
PO Box 2730 (92263)	*Total Assets*	133,279,000	93,941,000
619/323-4241 *Estb* 1979 *Memb* Fed, FDIC,	*Total Loans*	63,823,000	58,948,000
ABA, BAI, BMA, IBAA, RMA, CA Bnkrs Assn	*Total Deposits*	124,329,000	85,322,000
ACH CACHA, Los Angeles	*Total Equity*	6,931,000	6,038,000
Dishonored Items 323-4241 ext 201	*Net Income*	898,000	768,000
Holding Co NA			

Prin Corr Beverly Hills, CA: City Natl Bk; Los Angeles, CA: First Interstate Bk of California, Union Bk;
San Francisco, CA: Bk of America NT&SA

Chairman Roy Fey   *Loans* Reed A Mohney, EVP & Bus Dev
President Robert A Barley, CEO   *Marketing* Joanne F Shephard, Mktg/Card
Cashier NR   Services Off
                                                      Operations NR

City Branches NA
Other Branches Pasadena, Rancho Mirage

Fig. 11.6. Typical entries, *The Rand McNally Bankers Directory*. Reprinted with permission from *The Rand McNally Bankers Directory*, 1987 edition. Copyright © 1987 Rand McNally.

While the Polk and Rand McNally directories provide good coverage of commercial banks, they exclude savings and loan associations and credit unions. For listings of such institutions, other directories must be consulted.

Directory of American Savings and Loan Associations. Baltimore, Md.: T. K. Sanderson, 1955- . Annual.

The U.S. Savings and Loan Directory. Chicago: Rand McNally, 1982- . 2v. Annual.

Callahan's Credit Union Directory. Washington, D.C.: Callahan & Associates, 1986- . Annual.

The *Directory of American Savings and Loan Associations* is a comprehensive listing by state and city for all active S & Ls, building and loan associations, cooperative banks, and savings banks in the United States. Although most entries lack the detailed financial data contained in the banking directories described above, they do include standard directory information, indication of membership in the Federal Home Loan Bank system and the FSLIC, and the location and addresses of branch offices. The *Directory* also includes information on the members and staff of the Federal Home Loan Bank Board and the regional Federal Home Loan Banks.

The *U.S. Savings and Loan Directory* provides similar information, but is enhanced by the addition of comparative financial data, an alphabetical index by savings institutions, and lists of relevant federal and state government agencies and associations. Statistical data and ranked lists of top-rated S & Ls are also included.

Callahan's Credit Union Directory, described by its publisher as "a census of credit unions," is a comprehensive state-by-state listing. Its arrangement is somewhat different from the preceding directories, however. Each state listing begins with a summary page that lists the names, titles, and addresses of the state's major regulator of credit unions and the state's credit union league. Summary data on assets, shares, loans, reserves, and number of members of federally and state chartered credit unions follow. Also featured are lists of the top 10 credit unions in the state, ranked variously by total assets, reserves, loans/savings, number of members, investment/assets, and growth. Following the state summary page is a printout, arranged by institution name, that presents for each credit union its address and telephone number; the name of its chief executive officer; total assets, loans, investments, reserves, and number of members; and percent growth.

Callahan's also includes nationally ranked lists of the top 200 credit unions as well as brief articles and combined lists of state credit union officers, state credit union leagues, corporate credit unions, and national and regional credit union associations.

Although many of the directories that have been described above contain lists of the largest banks, often they are reprinted from other sources. Lists of largest banks are regular features of many different periodicals. *Business Week*, for example, publishes annually its "Bank Scoreboard" issue, which ranks by assets the 200 largest banks. *Fortune* includes top commercial banks in its "Fortune Service 500" issue. Perhaps the best source of such ranked lists, however, is the *American Banker*, an important daily trade paper that will be described in the section that follows.

Periodicals, Newspapers, Newsletters, and Indexes

PERIODICALS

Although personal finance magazines such as *Changing Times* and *Money* and such general business periodicals as *Business Week, Fortune*, and *Forbes* regularly report on the banking industry, most specialized banking periodicals are written for practitioners and scholars. Their number is impressive; 60 banking titles are listed in *Financial Journals and Serials*, the guide to periodicals described in chapter 3. Although comprehensive coverage is impossible in a work of this sort, the titles that follow are standard banking periodicals.

ABA Banking Journal. Washington, D.C.: American Bankers Association, 1908- . Monthly.

The Bankers Magazine. Boston: Warren, Gorham & Lamont, 1846- . Bimonthly.

Journal of Commercial Bank Lending. Philadelphia: Robert Morris Associates, 1918- . Monthly.

Journal of Retail Banking. Norcross, Ga.: Lafferty Publications, 1979- . Quarterly.

Savings Institutions. Chicago: United States League of Savings Institutions, 1926- . Monthly.

The *ABA Banking Journal* is the official publication of the American Bankers Association, the premier association for the commercial banking industry. It emphasizes current operations and practices in banking, recent developments, bank management, government regulation and legislation, and ABA-sponsored activities and services. Interviews with banking executives and government officials are frequently featured, as are reports on the implications of legislation enacted or being considered. Other articles cover the introduction of new financial products, and such management-related issues as personnel, customer relations, bank marketing, and security. Most articles are written by *Journal* staff.

The *Bankers Magazine*, on the other hand, publishes articles contributed by bankers, university faculty, and other experts. Its focus is somewhat broader than the *ABA Journal*'s, with articles about thrift institutions as well as commercial banks. Like the *Journal*, the *Magazine* emphasizes practice rather than theory. Clear and well written, it is useful for an overview of the entire banking industry. Each issue generally includes a "Special Report" section in which a series of articles focus on a specific topic. Recent series have, for example, examined "Banking's New Frontiers" and "Structural Issues in Banking." Other articles cover an array of topics, with regular columns on technology, community and international banking, marketing, and related fields. Lengthy, signed book reviews are also featured.

The *Journal of Commercial Bank Lending* is considerably more specialized. Published for commercial loan and credit officers and bank administrators by Robert Morris Associates (known mainly to librarians for its *Annual Statement Studies*), it emphasizes practical information pertaining to commercial lending. Articles cover such topics as creating a written loan policy, using information to make good credit decisions, and lending to specific types of businesses such as temporary service firms and health food stores. An annual subject index is published in the August issue, and the September issue includes an annual analysis of finance company ratios.

The *Journal of Retail Banking* combines theoretical research and practical applications. Its articles cover such topics as consumer attitudes and behavior, credit, credit cards, electronic banking, pricing and profitability, products and services development, service delivery, and technology. A separate "Research Notes" section contains brief descriptions of specialized research findings. The Spring issue includes author, title, and subject indexes for articles appearing in the previous year.

Savings Institutions focuses primarily on savings and loans, although other thrifts and banks receive some attention. It includes news and feature articles on industry developments, covering such topics as real estate financing, the Federal Home Loan Bank System and the FSLIC, automation, and the secondary mortgage market. Specific savings institutions are sometimes profiled, and interviews with noted practitioners and government officials are also featured.

The government's role in regulating and influencing financial activities is reflected in its periodical literature. The *Survey of Current Business*, for example, includes selective statistics on banking, credit, and money. Another government periodical provides even more comprehensive coverage.

U.S. Board of Governors of the Federal Reserve System. **Federal Reserve Bulletin**. Washington, D.C.: Government Printing Office, 1915- . Monthly.

The *Federal Reserve Bulletin* combines articles on the Fed and banking with the texts of reports and statements made by the Board of Governors to Congress; summaries of policy actions of the Federal Open Market Committee, staff research studies, and current legal developments; and announcements of Fed policy changes. Its "Financial and Business Statistics" section is an excellent source of current data on money, bank reserves, Federal Reserve and commercial banks, financial markets, federal finance, securities markets and corporate finance, mortgages, consumer credit, and related domestic and international banking activities. The section is, in fact, one of the best sources in which to locate information on monetary and financial conditions.

In addition, each issue of the *Bulletin* publishes a guide to special tables and statistical releases and the issues in which they appear, and lists of current members and official staff of the Board of Governors, the Federal Open Market Committee, and two advisory councils. Other lists contain the names and terms of people appointed to the Board of Governors since its beginning in 1913, and the locations, addresses, and officers of Federal Reserve Banks, branches, and offices. Finally, each issue cites a wide range of free or inexpensive publications available from the Board of Governors. The *Bulletin* is a basic business reference source.

Each of the 12 Federal Reserve Banks also publishes a free monthly periodical with articles on business, financial, and economic matters.[18] They are indexed in the *Fed in Print*, issued semiannually by the Federal Reserve Bank of Philadelphia, which provides subject access to the articles they contain as well as to other, selected periodical Bank publications.[19]

NEWSPAPERS

Although major daily newspapers such as the *New York Times* and the *Wall Street Journal* devote considerable attention to money, credit, and banking, another daily is even more important.

American Banker. New York: American Banker, 1836- . Daily, Monday through Friday.

The *American Banker* is basic reading for most professionals in the financial services industry. It covers current news and developments, analyzes trends, and profiles key companies, executives, and officials. All aspects of the industry are covered. Many issues include special sections focusing on such topics as marketing or telecommunications and financial networks. Ranked lists of the largest financial institutions are published regularly, and include the top commercial banks, ranked by deposits and assets; the top 100 thrift institutions and the top 100 credit unions; the largest bank holding companies and finance companies; and the world's largest banks. The *American Banker* is also available online as a full text database.

NEWSLETTERS

Most large commercial banks publish newsletters, often referred to as *bank letters*, that report on business conditions and the state of the economy. These publications are generally available free to customers, interested readers, and libraries and educational institutions. Although no single, comprehensive list of bank letters is available, many can be identified by scanning through the U.S. section of *Sources of World Financial and Banking Information* and by consulting *Data Sources for Business and Market Analysis, Business Information Sources*, and the *Statistical Reference Index*.

INDEXES

Major financial periodicals are indexed in many of the standard abstracting and indexing sources that were described in chapter 3. Another, more specialized, index is also available.

American Bankers Association. **Banking Literature Index**. Washington, D.C.: The Association, 1982- . Monthly, with annual cumulations.

The *Banking Literature Index* selectively indexes nearly 200 periodicals containing articles on banking trends, issues, operations, and related topics. The ABA distinguishes between core periodicals, which are indexed in depth, and other titles, which are more selectively covered. "Each article," the ABA notes, "is included on the basis of its substantive or statistical contribution to industry knowledge, such as discussion of the unique experiences of particular banks, new products and services, competition in financial services, and regulatory and compliance issues."[20] Banking periodicals are generally classed as core titles; periodicals from such related fields as economics, demography, and law, are not. (All core periodicals are designated by stars in the listing of periodicals indexed that begins each issue.)

The *Index* is arranged by subject, with brief entries limited to bibliographic citations (see figure 11.7 on page 298). The thesaurus of terms used is reprinted in the July and annual cumulative issues of the *Index*.

Competitive Equality Banking Act of 1987

"America's own minefield," *Economist*, Vol 304, Issue 7511, Aug 15 1987, pp. 60+.

"Band-aid banking law?" M. Kriz, *National Journal*, Vol 19, Issue 33-4, Aug 15 1987, pp. 2082-2086.

"Bank bill mauls FHLBB," J. Hutnyan, *Bottomline*, Vol 4, Issue 8, Aug 1987, pp. 48.

"Banking bill's grab-bag of exit fee requirements could evoke some protests," *BNA's Banking Report*, Vol 49, Issue 7, Aug 17 1987, pp. 297-299.

"Conference report (H. Rept 100-261) on HR 27 with joint explanatory statement (text)," *BNA's Banking Report*, Vol 49, Issue 6, Aug 10 1987, pp. 237-290.

"Congress sends final bill to President for signature, *ABA Bankers Weekly*, Vol 6, Issue 31, Aug 11 1987, pp. 1.

"Doing good by stealth," M. Mayer, *American Banker*, Vol 152, Issue 159, Aug 14 1987, pp. 1+.

Fig. 11.7. Sample entries, *Banking Literature Index*. Reprinted by permission of the publisher from the September 1987 issue of *Banking Literature Index*. Copyright © 1987 American Bankers Association.

Government Documents

Government involvement in regulating and monitoring banking activities is reflected in its documents output. The diversity and sheer number of documents on banking and the financial services industry are immediately apparent to anyone scanning through the subject index of the *Monthly Catalog of United States Government Publications*. Titles range from guides for consumers shopping for loans to congressional hearings on bank deregulation and Third World debt, from periodicals and news releases to statistical compendia. Although the need for such publications will vary considerably from one library to the next, the titles that follow point to their usefulness in many library settings.

U.S. Congress. House. Committee on Banking, Finance and Urban Affairs. **A Reference Guide to Banking and Finance**. 2nd ed. Committee print, prepared by the Congressional Research Service, 98th Congress, 1st session. Washington, D.C.: Government Printing Office, 1983. 102p.

_____. **Compilation of Selected Banking Laws, Revised Through January 1, 1984**. Committee print, 98th Congress, 2nd session. Washington, D.C.: Government Printing Office, 1984. 463p.

U.S. Federal Home Loan Bank Board. **A Director's Guide for the Savings and Loan Industry**. Washington, D.C.: Government Printing Office, 1980. 53p.

U.S. Small Business Administration. **The ABC's of Borrowing**. Washington, D.C.: Government Printing Office, 1982. 8p. (Management Aids series).

U.S. Federal Home Loan Bank Board. **Members of the Federal Home Loan Bank System**. Washington, D.C.: Government Printing Office. Annual.

U.S. National Credit Union Administration. **Directory of All Federally Insured Credit Unions**. Washington, D.C.: Government Printing Office. Annual.

U.S. Congress. House. Committee on Banking, Finance and Urban Affairs. **Bank Holding Companies and Their Subsidiary Banks**. Committee print, 99th Congress, 2nd session. Washington, D.C.: Government Printing Office, 1986. 287p.

Committee prints, publications prepared for the use of a specific congressional committee or for members of Congress, can be invaluable information sources. Although intended primarily for the use of the members of the House Committee on Banking, Finance and Urban Affairs, *A Reference Guide to Banking and Finance* is a useful and inexpensive quick reference tool. The *Guide* includes a glossary of economic and financial terms and organizations, a brief bibliography of relevant reference sources, and summaries of significant federal banking, housing, and securities laws. Entries in the banking laws section are arranged alphabetically; those in the housing and securities laws sections are chronologically arranged. In all three sections, however, entries include citations to the appropriate sections of the *U.S. Code*.

For even more thorough coverage of legislation enacted, another committee print is useful. *Compilation of Selected Banking Laws* reprints major statutes affecting banks and thrift institutions and laws pertaining to consumer credit protection in their entirety. The *Compilation* begins with the Federal Reserve Act and ends with the Electronic Fund Transfer Act, and is the first installment of a project designed to compile all banking statutes into a single document for the use of Congress. An index is included.

Other documents are intended for banking practitioners and the general public. *A Director's Guide for the Savings and Loan Industry*, for example, was published for newly appointed directors. It covers such topics as the operation, management, and examination of savings and loan associations, as well as the functions of S & L directors, and is useful for a general overview. *The ABC's of Borrowing*, on the other hand, was written for the small business person, and covers such topics as creditworthiness, types and amounts of loans, collateral, and the loan application process. Other, similar guides for consumers are discussed in the section on vertical file materials.

Many federal agencies publish directories of the institutions they serve. Thus, the Federal Home Loan Bank Board issues the annual *Members of the Federal Home Loan Bank System*, and the National Credit Union Administration, the annual *Directory of All Federally Insured Credit Unions*. Many of the same agencies publish statistical compilations, based on information submitted by member institutions. Representative compendia are discussed in the following section. Another directory was issued as a committee print. *Bank Holding Companies and Their Subsidiary Banks* lists, by state, all banks and bank holding companies with assets of $250 million or more. (A bank holding company is an organization that holds controlling stock interest in one or more commercial banks.)

Some of the most important and useful documents pertaining to banking, however, are not listed in the *Monthly Catalog*. Although they are prolific publishers, neither the Board of Governors of the Federal Reserve System nor the 12 regional Federal Reserve Banks make a practice of issuing documents through the Government Printing Office. Instead, libraries and interested individuals must identify these publications and order them from the issuing organizations. Fortunately, lists of Fed publications are not difficult to find. Each issue of the *Federal Reserve Bulletin*, for example, identifies publications available from the Board of Governors, and the *Fed in Print* lists and indexes by subject articles contained in Federal Reserve Bank periodicals, papers, staff reports, special studies, and other serial publications. In addition, each Reserve Bank maintains a public information department and generally issues publications lists. The addresses of the Federal Reserve Banks and the names of representative publications are included in appendix I.

Statistics

Government-issued periodicals are some of the best sources of current statistical information. As was mentioned earlier, the *Federal Reserve Bulletin* contains detailed monthly statistics on money, credit, and banking. Each of the Federal Reserve Banks publishes a monthly economic review and sometimes other serial titles as well. They are particularly useful for an overview of regional business and economic conditions. Similarly, each of the 12 regional Federal Home Loan Banks publishes at least one periodical that features analysis of area economic conditions as they relate to mortgage loans and the thrift industry. Articles in the *Bulletin* and in the Federal Reserve and Federal Home Loan Bank periodicals that contain statistics are indexed in the *American Statistics Index*, which is one of the best sources of information on the statistical output of independent federal agencies.

The Fed is the major publisher of federal financial data, issuing a number of periodicals, staff reports, annual publications, and other materials. The titles below are particularly useful for identifying and interpreting the statistics contained in selected Federal Reserve publications.

U.S. Board of Governors of the Federal Reserve System. **Concordance of Statistics Available in Selected Federal Reserve Publications**. Washington, D.C.: The Board. Annual.

Samansky, Arthur. **Statfacts: Understanding Federal Reserve Statistical Reports**. New York: Federal Reserve Bank of New York, 1981. 81p.

The *Concordance of Statistics* is a tabular list of statistics published monthly in the *Federal Reserve Bulletin*, showing for each statistic its corresponding location in the Fed's *Annual Statistical Digest*, described below. Arrangement is by order of appearance in the *Bulletin*, with an adjacent column indicating its location in the *Digest*. Free copies of the *Concordance* can be obtained by writing to the Board of Governors of the Federal Reserve System.[21]

The board also issues a series of weekly, monthly, and quarterly statistical releases, presenting time series data on such topics as measures of money stock and credit. *Statfacts: Understanding Federal Reserve Statistical Reports* provides a general explanation of the meaning and relationship of terms used in statistical releases. For each of six major releases, *Statfacts* reprints sample pages describing the data they contain and the underlying economic and financial concepts. *Statfacts* also includes an index to the terms it defines, a summary of major legislation enacted, and the names of security dealers reporting to the Federal Reserve Bank of New York.[22]

Although statistical releases and the *Federal Reserve Bulletin* are useful, sometimes the need is for earlier information or for graphic representations of financial and economic data. In such instances, the following publications are particularly helpful.

U.S. Board of Governors of the Federal Reserve System. **Annual Statistical Digest**. Washington, D.C.: The Board, 1975- . Annual.

_____. **Federal Reserve Chart Book**. Washington, D.C.: The Board, 1979- . Quarterly.

_____. **Historical Chart Book**. Washington, D.C.: The Board, 1965- . Annual.

The *Annual Statistical Digest* consolidates time series data from the *Federal Reserve Bulletin* for the preceding year, presenting information on Federal Reserve operations, the banking industry, credit, mortgages, and federal and international finance. Two earlier publications, *Banking and Monetary Statistics*, published in 1943 and covering 1914 to 1941, and *Banking and Monetary Statistics, 1941-1970* contain historical time series data that can be used in conjunction with the *Annual Statistical Digest* and the *Federal Reserve Bulletin*.

A somewhat different approach is followed in the *Federal Reserve Chart Book* and the *Historical Chart Book*. Both contain graphs illustrating financial and business conditions for designated time periods. The *Federal Reserve Chart Book* presents data for the current year and for the preceding eight years, while the *Historical Chart Book* graphs trends from as far back as 1800. Each includes data on money, measures of economic growth, industrial production, prices, debt and borrowing, government sectors, the corporate sector, households, mortgage debt and construction, commercial banks, financial institutions, the stock market, interest rates, and U.S. international transactions.

Although the Fed is undoubtedly the most prolific of federal financial publishers, other agencies issue important banking statistics as well.

U.S. Federal Home Loan Bank Board. **Savings & Home Financing Source Book**. Washington, D.C.: Government Printing Office, 1952- . Annual.

_____. **Combined Financial Statements, FSLIC-Insured Institutions**. Washington, D.C.: Government Printing Office, 1974- . Annual.

U.S. Federal Deposit Insurance Corporation. **Data Book: Operating Banks and Branches**. Washington, D.C.: Government Printing Office, 1980- . ca. 19v. Annual.

The *Savings & Home Financing Source Book* is an annual compilation of statistics on Federal Home Loan Banks, savings and loan associations, and mortgage markets. Although some tables date back more than 40 years, others cover recent years only. Data in many tables include breakdowns by Federal Home Loan Bank district and by state as well as U.S. summaries. Using the *Source Book*, one can track over time the number of mortgage foreclosures, interest rates for conventional mortgage loans, and the growth or decline of savings and loan facilities and their branches in each state. In addition, the *Source Book* presents composite S & L balance sheet data, including such items as assets, mortgage loans held, real estate owned, and deposit accounts, dating from 1935 to the present.

Another FHLBB publication, *Combined Financial Statements*, presents in summary form combined balance sheets and income and expense statements compiled from the quarterly reports of thrift institutions insured by the Federal Savings and Loan Insurance Corporation. Both national and state data are featured.

The *Data Book* is a multivolume statistical report on deposits held by commercial and mutual savings banks in the United States. Each volume begins with national summaries and SMSA data, including statistics on total number of banks and banking offices, total deposits, and deposits categorized as IPC (individuals, partnerships, and corporations) transaction accounts, IPC demand deposits, IPC nontransaction accounts, and all public (non-IPC) funds. The state listings in each volume present similar information, broken down by county, name of bank, and name and location of bank branches.

Other statistical compendia are published by professional and trade associations. The following titles are representative.

American Bankers Association. **Statistical Information on the Financial Services Industry**. 4th ed. Washington, D.C.: The Association, 1987.

National Council of Savings Institutions. **National Fact Book of Savings Institutions**. Washington, D.C.: The Council. Annual.

United States League of Savings Institutions. **Savings Institutions Sourcebook**. Chicago: The League, 1984- . Annual.

Statistical Information on the Financial Services Industry is a compilation of graphs and statistics. It begins with written "summary conclusions" based on data presented. Topics covered include economic trends affecting financial institutions; demographic and financial services marketing data; trends in assets, liabilities, and financial flows of nonfinancial sectors, nonfinancial business and public sectors; consumer attitudes and trends; financial institutions (sources and uses of funds, capital earnings, structure); payments system; international banking; and government credit operations. Most of the data are reprinted from publications issued by associations, research bureaus, and by the Fed, FDIC, and other government agencies. A bibliography of sources consulted is appended.

The *National Fact Book of Savings Institutions* briefly summarizes the past year's developments in the thrift industry, combining charts, graphs, and tables. The *Fact Book* includes national statistics grouped by the following categories: portfolio activity, deposit activities, mortgages and housing, and income and investment. A separate section contains selected state statistics arranged by the same broad categories. A glossary and an index are also included. Similar information is contained in the annual *Savings Institutions Sourcebook*, which summarizes mortgage lending, housing activity, savings institution operations, and related government activities.

Banking Tables

Basic to any banking reference collection is the presence of at least one compilation of banking and financial tables. A number of such sources are available, but one of the most comprehensive and popular works is listed below.

Thorndike, David. **Thorndike Encyclopedia of Banking and Financial Tables**. Rev. ed. Boston: Warren, Gorham & Lamont, 1980. [Various pagings]

The *Thorndike Encyclopedia of Banking and Financial Tables* groups tables by six broad categories: real estate, mortgage and depreciation; compound interest and annuity; interest; savings; installment loans, leasing and rebate; and investment. A general explanation precedes each table and describes its use, and each table begins with a summary of the rates, terms, payments, and yields that are shown in the table. A dictionary of financial terms is also included. A *Yearbook* brings the *Encyclopedia* up-to-date.

Warren, Gorham & Lamont publishes other useful collections of banking and financial tables, such as *Thorndike's Compound Interest and Annuity Tables* and *Consumer Credit Computation and Compliance Guide, with Annual Percentage Rate Tables*, but if only one such source is needed, the *Thorndike Encyclopedia of Banking and Financial Tables* is a good choice.

Vertical File Materials

An almost unlimited number of free and inexpensive publications on banking are available to enhance vertical file collections. Some of the sources that have already been described in this chapter are useful for identifying them. The *Federal Reserve Bulletin*, for example, lists materials issued by the Board of Governors, and *Sources of World Financial and Banking Information* identifies free publications issued by foreign and domestic commercial banks. Other indexes covered in earlier chapters are also useful. Both the *American Statistics Index* and the *Statistical Reference Index* include numerous free publications and the issuing organizations' names and addresses, while the *Consumer Information Catalog, PAIS*, and the *Vertical File Index* feature documents, pamphlets, and booklets on credit, banks, and the financial services industry.

Two sources described in chapter 7 are worth reexamining. *Public Information Materials of the Federal Reserve System* lists selected publications issued by the Board of Governors and each of the 12 Federal Reserve Banks. It is divided into two main sections: "general audience" materials intended for the general public, elementary and secondary school students, and college undergraduates, and "specialized audience" materials appropriate for undergraduate and graduate students and professionals. Within each category, the arrangement is by broad subject such as the Federal Reserve System, money, credit, banking, financial markets and instruments, and the economy. Each listing includes a brief annotation; publication date, number of pages, and issuing bank; and the audience for whom the publication is intended.

Other sections list filmstrips, films, and video cassettes for classroom use; periodicals and newsletters issued by Reserve Banks; and conference proceedings. An index is also included. *Public Information Materials*, however, is not comprehensive. It does not include more sophisticated staff studies and working papers or statistical releases. Librarians seeking to acquire such publications should contact the appropriate Federal Reserve Bank(s) or the Board of Governors.

Selected Federal Reserve and commercial bank publications are also identified in *Materials Available to Educators* (described in chapter 7), the Dow Jones list of free business publications.

Databases

Many of the databases mentioned in chapter 8 are directly relevant to the banking industry. *ABI/Inform* and *Management Contents*, for example, index and annotate articles on such topics as bank marketing and automatic teller machines, while numeric databases such as *PTS U.S. Forecasts* include statistics on interest rates and credit. There are, however, other databases whose main emphasis is on the financial services industry.

American Banker. New York: The Bond Buyer. Updated daily.

American Banker News (Banknews). New York: The Bond Buyer. Updated daily.

FINIS (Financial Industry Information Service). Chicago: Bank Marketing Association. Updated biweekly.

The *American Banker* is the full-text, online version of the daily trade paper of the same name. Like its printed counterpart, it includes articles on interest, credit, the economy, and financial institutions. It can be particularly useful to librarians seeking a specific bit of financial information, or lacking a subscription to the paper. A companion database, *American Banker News (Banknews)*, is a menu-driven system that allows searchers to retrieve data from the last five issues of the *American Banker*. Searchers are given seven options from which to choose: today's news, the previous day's news, Washington Monday (the week's schedule of bank-related events in Washington), executive changes, speeches and texts, opinion and analysis, and price and source information. Following selection of an option, the searcher is again presented with a menu. If "Today's News" were selected, for example, the searcher would be given a numbered list of the day's headlines from which to choose. By typing in the appropriate number, the full text of the article could be retrieved. *American Banker News*, however, does not permit printing of the records it contains. It is used primarily as a current awareness source and as a guide to items available in the *American Banker* database.

FINIS, or *Financial Industry Information Service*, provides marketing information on banks, thrifts, and other financial service organizations and on the products and services they offer. Included in the database are abstracts of articles in journals and of books, press releases, sample brochures, and outstanding student projects. The record shown in figure 11.8 (see page 304) is typical.

Another database, *BancBase*, is made available through Newport Associates. The menu-driven file contains numeric data culled from the Fed and other government organizations relating to banks and bank holding companies, thrift institutions, insurance and investment companies, real estate investment trusts, and other financial services. Although potentially quite useful, the high annual subscription rate makes *BancBase* inaccessible to all but the most affluent or highly specialized libraries.[23]

****

```
AN 0063759. 87094.
BM BMA NUMBER: HG3755-C67-1986.
AU Carlo-Carmen-J. Kohn-Ernest. Kaye-Bernard. Sismilich-Howard-F-Jr.
TI Consumer credit under deregulation.
SO New York State Banking Department, New York, December 1986, 124
   p.
PD 861200.
NT tables; charts; appendices.
NM OCLC: 16133624.
DE COMMERCIAL-BANKS. CREDIT-UNIONS. BOOK. CONSUMER-CREDIT.
   STATISTICS. LOANS. DEREGULATION.
GE New-York. Mid-Atlantic. USA.
AB The New York State Banking Department conducted a survey of
   financial institutions which extend credit to consumers in New York
   State, to provide information on consumer loan interest rates and
   the availability of consumer credit since 1983. The questionaire
   which was sent out covered the following areas: the most common
   annual percentage rate charged for various types of consumer
   lending, increases in outstanding amounts of consumer loans of
   various types and introduction of new consumer loan services. The
   survey findings are detailed in this paper.
```

****

Fig. 11.8. Typical record, *FINIS*. Reprinted by permission of the Bank Marketing Association.

NOTES

[1]Excerpts from Dun & Bradstreet's "Business Information Reports" are, however, available in *Dun's Financial Records*, an online database accessible through DIALOG and Dow Jones News/Retrieval Service. Although the high cost of searching the database (in January 1988, $135 per connect hour and $85 per full record) precludes its casual use, some firms that supplied information for the printed credit reports feel that by making even portions of their reports publicly available online, the spirit of confidentiality has been violated.

[2]Adam Snitzer, "Money for Nothing," *Forbes* 139, no. 7 (May 8, 1987): 212.

[3]Robin Gross and Jean V. Cullen, *Help! The Basics of Borrowing Money* (New York: Times Books, 1980), 41.

[4]Ibid.

[5]Thomas E. Van Dahm, *Money and Banking; An Introduction to the Financial System* (Lexington, Mass.: D. C. Heath, 1975), 48-49.

[6]Usually depositors can withdraw money from their savings accounts merely by presenting their passbooks. Banks do, however, have the (seldom exercised) right to require a 30-day written notification of any intended withdrawal. As a result, savings accounts are classified as time deposits.

[7]For an interesting and decidedly nonthreatening description of depository institutions and their role in creating money, see *The Story of Banks and Thrifts*. Free copies of the comic-style booklet and similar publications (*The Story of Checks and Electronic Payments, The Story of Consumer Credit, The Story of Foreign Trade and Exchange,* and *The Story of Inflation*) can be obtained by writing to:

Public Information Department
Federal Reserve Bank of New York
33 Liberty Street
New York, NY 10045

[8]William Gobble and Bruce Harwood, *North Carolina Real Estate*, 2nd ed. (Reston, Va.: Reston Publishing, 1984), 245-46.

[9]Marilu Hurt McCarty, *Money and Banking: Financial Institutions and Economic Policy* (Reading, Mass.: Addison-Wesley, 1982), 124.

[10]The president of the Federal Reserve Bank of New York serves as a permanent member of the Federal Open Market Committee. Of the remaining 11 Reserve Bank presidents, four rotate annually as members of the committee.

[11]McCarty, 243.

[12]*Federal Reserve Banks* (Washington, D.C.: Board of Governors of the Federal Reserve System, 1979), 2.

[13]*The Hats the Federal Reserve Wears* (Philadelphia: Federal Reserve Bank of Philadelphia, n.d.), 6.

[14]*Fed Points* (Boston: Federal Reserve Bank of Boston, n.d.), 5.

[15]*The 1986/87 United States Government Manual* (Washington, D.C.: Government Printing Office, 1986), 455.

[16]Ibid, 521.

[17]A new banking yearbook, the *American Banker Yearbook* was published for the first time in 1987; the author has not yet had the opportunity to examine it.

[18]For the titles of monthly periodicals issued by the 12 Federal Reserve Banks, see the appropriate Federal Reserve Bank entries in appendix I.

[19]To request a free subscription to the semiannual *Fed in Print*, write to:
Information Services and Research
Federal Reserve Bank of Philadelphia
P.O. Box 66
Philadelphia, PA 19105

[20]"Introduction," *American Bankers Association Banking Literature Index* 5, no. 8 (February 1987): 1.

[21]For a free copy of the *Concordance of Statistics Available in Selected Federal Reserve Publications*, write to:
Board of Governors of the Federal Reserve System
Publications Services
Mail Stop 138
Washington, DC 20551

[22]To request a free copy of *Statfacts: Understanding Federal Reserve Statistical Reports*, write to the address shown in #7.

[23]According to the Fall 1987 issue of the Special Libraries Association's *Business and Finance Division Bulletin*, access to the *BancBase* database requires a $7,500 yearly subscription fee as well as a $45/hour connect fee.

Wall Street is a narrow bituminous path running east and west across lower Manhattan, between Trinity Church and the East River. This strategic location provides heavenly guidance for those who come to the "Street" to make a "killing"; for those who are ruined, there's always the river. (The graveyard is filled.)

—Paul Sarnoff, *The Wall Street Thesaurus*

12

INVESTMENTS
An Introduction

As Americans become increasingly concerned with financial security, a growing number of them are seeking to find it through careful investment. The New York Stock Exchange's 1985 Share Ownership Survey determined that over 47 million people owned stocks in 1985, up from some 12.5 million in 1959.[1] But stocks are not the only investment medium.

Investment has many facets. It may involve putting money into banks, Treasury bills or notes, or common stocks, or paintings, or real estate, or mortgages, or oil ventures, or cattle, or the theater. It may involve speculating in bull markets or selling short in bear markets. It may involve choosing growth stocks, or blue chips, or defensive stocks, or income stocks, or even penny cats and dogs. It may involve options, straddles, rights, warrants, convertibles, margin, gold, silver, mutual funds, money market funds, index funds, tax exempt bond funds, and result in accumulation of wealth or dissipation of resources. Diversity and challenge characterize the field.[2]

In fact, as more people choose to invest, Wall Street has become increasingly ingenious in introducing new investment vehicles to the public. As a result, there are a myriad of investment opportunities for small, private investors. This chapter and the four that follow deal with the most common types of investments—stocks, bonds, mutual funds, futures, and options—and the basic types of information sources relevant to each.

INVESTORS AND THEIR INFORMATION NEEDS

Investors fall into two main categories: institutional and individual. *Institutional* investors include banks, insurance companies, mutual funds and investment companies, college endowment funds, corporate profit-sharing plans, and pension funds. They are organizations with considerable money to invest and large securities portfolios to manage. Frequently they have one or more departments that include securities analysts, portfolio managers, economists, and other experts to supply data and help make investment decisions. *Individual* investors, on the other hand, are private investors, people making their own, comparatively small, personal investments. Generally they lack the expertise available to institutional investors and are not usually full-time investors.

In order to be successful, such investors must be well informed. The astute investor who is considering purchase of stocks, for example, will not only attempt to learn as much as possible about the company itself, but also about the industry of which it is a part, the economy generally, and all of the factors that affect it. Some will look to their brokers to supply the needed information. Many others, however, will take a more active role, reading financial newspapers and business periodicals, advisory newsletters, textbooks, and all the latest get-rich-quick bestsellers.

Investment information can be categorized in many ways. It can, for example, be classified as either descriptive or analytical. Descriptive investment information is factual; statistics comprise a large part of the data presented, and the focus is on the recent past or on the historical performance of the company, industry, or economic development being considered. Analytical investment information, on the other hand, does not limit itself to historical data, but includes projections for future performance as well as investment recommendations. Both descriptive and analytical information sources belong in most business reference collections.

Before consulting these sources, prospective investors often need to learn more about specific types of investments. As a result, publications such as guides, encyclopedias, handbooks, and even textbooks are important because they provide broad coverage of the field.

Background Information Sources

Publications in this category introduce novice investors and librarians to specific types of investments, supply answers to quick reference questions, and often include lists and bibliographies for further reading. Although there are literally hundreds of such publications, the ones that follow are among the most highly regarded.

One good way to begin to understand the basics of investing in each of the major investment mediums is by consulting a personal finance guide.

Porter, Sylvia. **Sylvia Porter's New Money Book for the 80's**. Garden City, N.Y.: Doubleday, 1979. 1305p.

Donoghue, William E., and Dana Shilling. **William E. Donoghue's Lifetime Financial Planner: Straight Talk about Your Money Decisions**. New York: Harper & Row, 1987. 395p.

The best known personal finance manual is *Sylvia Porter's New Money Book for the 80's*. It covers many aspects of personal money management, ranging from the best times to buy new cars to how to read the fine print in mortgages, and includes considerable information on investing as well. More up-to-date but less comprehensive coverage is offered in *William E. Donoghue's Lifetime Financial Planner*. While an experienced investor might consider these manuals superficial or unsophisticated, they are a good starting point for librarians confronted for the first time with a reference question about the data contained in a newspaper stock table or on commodities trading. Somewhat more detailed information is contained in the following publications.

Little, Jeffrey B., and Lucien Rhodes. **Understanding Wall Street**. 2nd ed. Blue Ridge Summit, Pa.: Liberty House, 1987.

Siegel, Joel G., and Jae K. Shim. **Investments: A Self-Teaching Guide**. New York: Wiley, 1986. 216p.

Gitman, Lawrence J., and Michael D. Joehnk. **Fundamentals of Investing**. 2nd ed. New York: Harper & Row, 1984. 782p.

Understanding Wall Street is a good, basic guide to investments, written for the "individual who knows little or nothing about the stock market but has always wanted to understand it." It focuses on stocks primarily, but also covers bonds, preferred stocks, mutual funds, and stock options. Particularly useful is the chapter explaining the principles of technical analysis and describing how to read charts and use technical indicators. Again, coverage is fairly superficial, but the basics are presented in terms intelligible to lay people.

Investments: A Self-Teaching Guide covers a wide range of topics, including the investment process, fundamental and technical analysis, portfolio management, and securities valuation in addition to such investment mediums as stocks, bonds, options, commodities and financial futures, silver, and gold. Each chapter provides investor strategy sections, case studies and practical examples, and self-tests. Appendixes include "Investing with Personal Computers," a bibliography of general investment sources and professional journals, and future and present value tables. The *Guide* is an inexpensive, clearly written publication, well worth acquiring.

Some investment textbooks are also useful, one of which is Gitman's *Fundamentals of Investing*. It includes general information on investing, investment information sources, and specific types of investments. Each chapter features a list of key terms, case problems, and selected readings from such popular business periodicals as *Forbes, Barron's, Business Week,* and *Money*. Other textbooks provide similar information.

While these sources and others similar to them are not reference books per se, they provide good basic information and should not be overlooked by librarians beginning a search for information. Indeed, many libraries purchase reference as well as circulating copies.

Almanacs and Encyclopedias

Almanacs and single-volume encyclopedias constitute still another source of background information. Usually each chapter deals with a different aspect of investing or with a specific type of investment, and is often written by a specialist in the area being covered.

Crittenden, Alan, ed. **The Almanac of Investments**. Novato, Calif.: Crittenden Books, 1984. 514p.

Currier, Chet. **The Investor's Encyclopedia: Tax Reform Edition**. 2nd ed. New York: Franklin Watts, 1987. 469p.

Blume, Marshall E., and Jack P. Friedman, eds. **Encyclopedia of Investments**. Boston: Warren, Gorham & Lamont, 1982. 1041p.

Levine, Sumner N., ed. **Dow Jones-Irwin Business and Investment Almanac**. Homewood, Ill.: Dow Jones-Irwin, 1977- . Annual.

The Almanac of Investments lists and briefly describes traditional and nontraditional investments, including stocks and bonds, comic books, purebred cats and dogs, and beer cans. For each investment medium, a general description is supplemented by a brief history, consideration of "big versus small" investors, investment pros and cons, and a bibliography of relevant sources. An index is appended. Although many of the sources that follow provide more comprehensive information, the *Almanac* is useful for people in search of quick answers regarding the advantages and disadvantages of choosing to invest in tennis teams, movies, vineyards, and other unusual investment vehicles.

Like the *Almanac, The Investor's Encyclopedia* treats a number of investment products, most of which are fairly traditional. The *Encyclopedia* is divided into three main parts: investment vehicles, tools and techniques, and strategies. Arrangement within the first section is alphabetical, ranging from annuities to zero coupon investments. Each entry is several pages long, and includes a general description of the product, explains how and where to get investment information and how to invest, and discusses the costs of buying, owning, and selling. Investment risks and drawbacks are considered, as are the potential for income and capital gains. Finally, Currier discusses the product's liquidity—that is, the ease with which it can be converted into cash—as well as its tax advantages and disadvantages. The latter are an important consideration for many investors, but readers should be forewarned that tax law is not static, and that the tax consequences of a particular type of investment may change from one year to the next. As a result, unless a source has been newly published, such tax-related information is not always as useful as it might first seem.

The "Tools and Techniques" section describes such tools as investment advisory services and such techniques as fundamental and technical analysis, while the "Strategies" section covers hedging, index investing, investment clubs, social and ethical investing, and other topics. The *Encyclopedia* begins with a series of indexes that enable readers with certain investment goals—basic savings, maximum safety, current income, retirement, protection against inflation, liquidity, short-term gains, long-term growth, and tax advantages—to pinpoint the investment products, tools, techniques, and strategies most likely to be of interest to them.

While it is also intended for the general reader, the *Encyclopedia of Investments* is more scholarly and somewhat more technical than either the *Almanac* or the *Investor's Encyclopedia*. Each chapter, written by an expert, covers a different type of investment and outlines the factors determining its market value, how to buy and sell, tax implications, and representative types of investors. Glossaries and reading lists are also included. Like the *Almanac*, the *Encyclopedia of Investments* is particularly useful for quick information on nontraditional investments. Chapters on art deco, rare books, foreign equities, collectibles, leasing ventures, and motion pictures, for example, are included as well as chapters on more traditional investment mediums. Its coverage, however, is more substantial than the *Almanac*'s.

The *Dow Jones-Irwin Business and Investment Almanac* offers background information on securities as well. In addition to current business and economic statistics, it contains information on specific types of investments, and is particularly useful for its coverage of new investment mediums. Interest rate futures and stock options, for example, are covered as well as stocks, bonds, and mutual funds.

Dictionaries

Many of the publications already described contain glossaries, but for more detailed definitions or for a more comprehensive listing of terms, it may be necessary to consult an investment dictionary.

Sarnoff, Paul. **The Wall Street Thesaurus**. New York: Ivan Obolensky, 1963. 250p.

Rosenberg, Jerry M. **The Investor's Dictionary**. New York: Wiley, 1986. 513p.

Pessin, Allan H., and Joseph A. Ross. **Words of Wall Street: 2,000 Investment Terms Defined**. Homewood, Ill.: Dow Jones-Irwin, 1983. 297p.

———. **More Words of Wall Street**. Homewood, Ill.: Dow Jones-Irwin, 1986. 269p.

Quint, Barbara Gilder. **Wall Street Talk: How to Understand Your Broker**. New York: Walker and Co., 1983. 142p.

One of the classics is *The Wall Street Thesaurus*, which defines basic financial terms such as *arbitrage* and *odd lot*. While the definitions it includes are clear, often illustrated with specific examples, and frequently humorous, there are some drawbacks to the *Thesaurus*. The first is that it contains only a limited number of terms. The second is that it is over 20 years old. The nature of investing has changed tremendously during that time, and its vocabulary reflects these changes. As a result, current investment dictionaries are essential. Several such publications are available.

The Investor's Dictionary lists and defines some 8,000 terms, abbreviations, and acronyms, with numerous cross-references included. *Words of Wall Street* and *More Words of Wall Street* are similar to the *Investor's Dictionary*. They, too, include succinct but thorough definitions and numerous cross-references. Unlike the *Dictionary*, however, these two Dow Jones-Irwin publications frequently include examples illustrating usage, and contain more slang. Investment jargon is also covered in *Wall Street Talk: How to Understand Your Broker*, which defines such terms as *cats and dogs, cyanide capsules*, and *killer bees*, and is a useful and entertaining supplement to more traditional sources.

Many different types of publications—handbooks, textbooks, personal finance manuals, almanacs, and dictionaries—provide needed background information for prospective investors. Similar information is also available in the pamphlets, booklets, and brochures published by brokers, stock and commodity exchanges, mutual funds, and investment companies. Although specific examples are cited in the chapters that follow, it is worth noting that these free publications constitute an important resource for libraries. The *Wall Street Journal* often includes advertisements for such pamphlets. Another way to acquire these publications is by writing or calling the brokers themselves.

Standard & Poor's Security Dealers of North America. New York: Standard & Poor's. Semiannual.

Brokerage firms are listed in *Standard & Poor's Security Dealers of North America*, a sort of "Who's Who" of the financial community, which lists some 14,000 U.S. and Canadian securities firms. Arrangement is geographical, and the information provided for each firm includes its address, telephone number, identification number, and chief officers; for the firm's headquarters, it also includes the names of the exchanges of which the firm is a member, and the types of securities in which it specializes. A typical entry is shown in figure 12.1 (see page 312).

Also included in the *Directory* are the names and addresses of Canadian and U.S. exchanges and associations, major foreign stock exchanges, a listing of North American securities administrators by state and province, and a section listing firms that have been discontinued (that is, gone out of business, moved, or changed their name) since the last issue of the directory was published.

Not all investment firms publish pamphlets or newsletters for their clients, and not all brokerage houses have research departments. The level of service varies. In recent years, discount brokerage firms have become increasingly popular. A *discount brokerage firm* is one that concentrates solely on executing transactions for its clientele, on buying or selling securities at the client's direction. No research is conducted, no advice given, no informational literature published. In return for this "no frills" service, clients can expect to pay some 30 to 50 percent less in commission fees than they would pay to traditional full-service investment firms. People who use discount brokers tend to be thrifty do-it-yourselfers, and they often turn to the library for investment information contained in financial newspapers and advisory services.

KALB, VOORHIS & CO.
■ (NASD) (*) (+) (SIA) (N) (SIPC) (NSCC)
(MSRB) (1946) 27 William St. (10005)
Stock & Bond Brokers; Dealers in Corporate,
  Municipal & Over-the-Counter Securities &
  Convertible Stocks & Bonds
Branch—Miami, FL
Partners—Mark R. Feller, (*) Peter J. Dunn,
  (+) Kenneth A. Hipkins, Robert G. Gutenstein,
  (+) Neil F. Hayes, Jr., James A. Hunt, Bernard
  R. Relkin, (*) William W. Prager, Jr., William
  H. Herrman, Fred Bensinger, (+) Neil
  Rindlaub, (+) Wayne Wu; Celia L. Raumann,
  (Limited); Arthur Vare, (Limited)
Compliance Dept—William H. Herrman, Partner
Arbitrage & Convertible Dept—Herbert Hoffman
Over-the-Counter Trading Dept—Philip
  Hourwich
Research Dept—Bob Gutenstein, Partner-in-
  Charge
Telex—62833
NASDAQ—KALB
Employer's Ident. No.—13-5549000
Phone—212—804-0200

Fig. 12.1. Typical entry, *Standard & Poor's Security Dealers of North America*. Reprinted with permission from the Spring 1987 edition of *Standard & Poor's Security Dealers of North America*.

Investment Advisory Services

Investment advisory services provide current information on general market conditions and/or specific companies. Some of these services are factual, and some are interpretive, making recommendations on the purchase or sale of specific securities. Quality, particularly of the newsletters that sell investment advice, varies tremendously. Some are respectable, and others are no more than hucksters' appeals to the gullible and greedy. There are literally hundreds of these publications, some of which are quite expensive. Each has its own, often vocal, following. Clearly, libraries need to be highly selective and somewhat conservative in placing subscriptions to these publications. The service in vogue with investors one season may languish the next.

> Each quarter and each year, there are stars among the investment advisors and security analysts—individuals with a better record of picking winners than almost anyone else. Each year there are winners in the Irish Sweepstakes and the New York and Illinois state lotteries. No one, however, ever suggested that the winner of a million dollar grand slam prize in the Illinois state lottery had good insights. Few would pay for his advice on how to buy a winning ticket in the next year's lottery. The key question is whether the winners among the investment advisors have more skill and insight than the winners of the Irish Sweepstakes and the Illinois and New York Lotteries.[3]

The coverage in investment services varies. Some focus on particular types of investments, such as mutual funds or precious metals. Others use specific approaches or methods. Some rely on technical analysis, basing their recommendations on past patterns of market trading and price behavior. Some advocate "contrary opinion," theorizing that if all the *other* investment advisors are espousing a specific course of action, the sensible thing is to do the opposite. Perhaps one of the most unorthodox systems was that devised by

Frederick Goldsmith, who based his recommendations on the actions of Jiggs, a character in the comic strip, *Bringing Up Father.*

> If Jiggs was pictured with his right hand in his pocket, the market was a buy. If he was shown with two puffs of smoke rising from his cigar, this meant that the market would be strong in the second hour of trading.... When the strip showed Jiggs at the theater observing, "The intermissions are the only good thing about this show," Goldsmith advised his subscribers to buy Mission Oil.[4]

Almost anyone can publish an advisory letter. No special qualifications or preliminary tests are necessary. In fact, all that is required is that the publisher have no record of fraud and that he or she register with and periodically report to the Securities and Exchange Commission. (An annual report to the SEC on the service's financial condition that includes a brief description of the investment strategy being followed, information sources used, and methods of analysis employed is mandatory.) Publishers of such services have included people from a wide range of backgrounds, many of whom are not particularly well trained to give investment advice and who may not always hold their readers' financial well-being uppermost.

It is evident that library subscriptions to these services should be made with caution. Only a few publications, however, regularly list or evaluate advisory services.

Grant, Mary McNierney, and Riva Berleant-Schiller, eds. **Directory of Business and Financial Services.** 8th ed. New York: Special Libraries Association, 1984. 189p.

Hulbert Financial Digest. Baltimore, Md.: Agora, Inc., 1980- . Monthly.

Brimelow, Peter. **The Wall Street Gurus: How You Can Profit From Investment Newsletters.** New York: Random House, 1986. 238p.

The *Directory of Business and Financial Services* lists and annotates major investment advisory services. Each entry includes the name and address of the publisher, cost, frequency, and format, as well as a brief description of the contents. While useful for general information, the *Directory* makes no attempt to assess the effectiveness of the investment advice each service offers. Such ratings are, however, available.

The most current and comprehensive source is the *Hulbert Financial Digest* (*HFD*), a monthly that monitors more than 100 investment services and rates the performance of investment portfolios constructed on the basis of each service's recommendations.

> The core of *HFD* is a table listing the performances of hypothetical "paper" portfolios constructed by Hulbert on the basis of each letter's recommendations, as they would be understood by the average reasonable reader. Unless the letter says specifically to the contrary, Hulbert fully invests each paper portfolio, giving equal weight to each recommendation, rebalancing when new buy and sell recommendations are being made, or if stop-losses or other key points are reached. Where holding cash is the order of the month, Hulbert hypothetically invests in treasury bills, crediting the portfolio with interest. He also adds in dividend payments and commission costs. Each portfolio performance is calculated from scratch every year, so that every letter's record can be inspected either year by year, or cumulatively by multiplying (NOT adding) each year's percentage increase—or decrease.[5]

Librarians lacking access to the *Hulbert Financial Digest* can turn to the *Dow Jones-Irwin Business and Investment Almanac,* which reproduces annual *HFD* performance ratings for the past five years.

Also useful, although more for background than current information, is *The Wall Street Gurus,* which describes advisory services generally and highlights some of the best and worst-performing publications and the people who write them.

Some personal finance and general business magazines periodically evaluate investment services. *Money*, for example, regularly features articles on individual services such as *Value Line*, on specific types of services, and on advisory services generally. *Fortune* sometimes includes an assessment of services as a part of its "Investor's Guide" issue.[6]

The cost, sheer volume, widely differing quality, and rapidly fluctuating popularity with the investing public of investment advisory services are some of the main reasons why most libraries do not support extensive collections of such materials. Factual services—that is, those focusing on past performance, both recent and historical—are likely to be better represented in library collections. Some of the major advisory services are described in the chapters to follow on stocks, bonds, and mutual funds.

Securities Quotations

Investors turn to *quotations*, brief, numeric price reports, to attempt to determine the present market condition for specific securities. Although the amount of information included in quotations varies, usually most include closing (the last price paid on a particular trading day) and bid (the price someone is willing to pay) prices, the number of units traded, dividends, and high and low prices paid over a designated time period.

Basic to providing good business reference service is the ability to decipher the newspaper tables that contain quotations. Quotations within most tables are arranged alphabetically by company name or abbreviation. In most instances, it is easy to find the abbreviations assigned to companies, but in a few cases, the abbreviations may be ambiguous. It may not be immediately apparent, for example, that *AplDt* is the abbreviation for Applied Data Communications, while Applied Data Research is abbreviated *AplDta*. The publication that follows is extremely useful for its inclusion of Associated Press abbreviations for publicly traded companies.

> Warfield, Gerald. **The Investor's Guide to Stock Quotations and Other Financial Listings**. Rev. ed. New York: Harper & Row, 1986. 514p.

The ability to interpret the data contained in securities quotations tables is essential. Although the chapters that follow include sample quotations for stocks, bonds, mutual funds, futures, and options, even more detailed coverage is offered by *The Investor's Guide to Stock Quotations and Other Financial Listings*. It should be consulted by any librarian or investor seeking to better understand the data these tables contain.

Newspaper abbreviations are not the only alternative designations by which a company may be known. In addition, each company is assigned a *ticker symbol*, a one- to five-letter designation used by the exchanges on which a company is traded, in ticker quotations, and in some publications and databases. The ticker symbol for the Coca-Cola Company, for example, is *KO*; for American Telephone and Telegraph, *T*. Ticker symbols are included, with other information, in many directories, investment services, exchange reports, and other publications, but they are not used in newspaper tables.

Quotations in newspapers are for the preceding trading day, and are usually current enough for most individual investors. When more up-to-the-minute information is necessary, nonprint sources must be consulted. Often, the investor calls or visits his broker's office to view televised ticker quotations or quote terminals. Some libraries can also supply investors with current information. Those with access to the Dow Jones News/Retrieval Service, for example, can search an online database, *Dow Jones Enhanced Quotes*, for current stock, bond, and option quotations. Finally, as microcomputers become increasingly commonplace, many investors are accessing such databases at home.

Many individual investors are also using microcomputers and investment software to help manage personal finance and make investment decisions. Although such software falls outside the scope of most libraries' collections, the acquisition of one or two current directories of investment software can be helpful. Typical of such directories are Robert Schwaback's *The Dow Jones-Irwin Guide to Investment Software* (Homewood, Ill.: Dow

Jones-Irwin, 1986), an inexpensive paperback catalog of software for investment and portfolio management, and *The Individual Investor's Microcomputer Resource Guide* (Chicago: Longman Trade, 1987), which lists and describes investment software and financial databases and information services. Other, similar directories can be identified by consulting personal computing magazines and standard library book selection tools.

NOTES

[1] New York Stock Exchange, *Share Ownership 1985: The 10th National Survey* (New York: The Exchange, 1986), 3.

[2] Jerome B. Cohen, Edward D. Zinbarg, and Arthur Zeikel, *Guide to Intelligent Investing* (Homewood, Ill.: Dow Jones-Irwin, 1977), 3.

[3] Robert Aliber, *Your Money and Your Life* (New York: Basic Books, 1982), 107.

[4] Myron Kandel, *How to Cash in on the Coming Stock Market Boom: The Smart Investor's Guide to Making Money* (Indianapolis, Ind.: Bobbs-Merrill, 1982), 89-90.

[5] Peter Brimelow, *The Wall Street Gurus* (New York: Random House, 1986), 59.

[6] For brief descriptions of some of the top-rated investment advisory services, see "Rating the Newsletters," *Fortune Special Issue: The 1988 Investor's Guide* (Fall 1987): 225-28.

The market got clobbered
The market got mauled.
Investors on margin
Were frantically called.

It took just a fortnight.
The profits I'd racked
Were nicked, and then trimmed,
And then surgically hacked.

     —Andrew Tobias, "Elegy for the Bull Market"*

13

STOCKS

INTRODUCTION

  In the preceding chapter, basic investment guides, dictionaries, and handbooks were discussed. Before stock-related publications can be examined, however, it is first necessary to consider stocks themselves, the markets on which they are traded, and some of the ways in which stock market performance is measured.

  Most companies issue stock in order to raise capital. Each share of stock represents part ownership in a corporation. An investor, after buying stock in a company, may get a handsomely engraved certificate testifying that he or she has, in effect, become part owner. The share of the corporate pie may be small—one share of IBM, for example, endows the investor with the equivalent of 1/60,336,000 ownership—but the investor has, nonetheless, obtained that same fractional stake in everything the company owns—its plants and equipment, its patents and trademarks, even its management. Because stocks represent ownership, they are also known as *equity securities*, or *equities*.

Common and Preferred Stock

  Stocks are either *common* or *preferred*. If a company issues only one type of stock, it is usually common stock. Similarly, unless the abbreviation *pf* or *pfd* follows a stock listed in a newspaper stock table, one can assume that it is a common stock.

---

*Reprinted by permission of Sterling Lord Literistic, Inc. Copyright © 1978 by Andrew Tobias; first appeared in *Esquire* Magazine, December 1978.

With common stock ownership comes the opportunity to vote on corporate matters such as the election of company directors. Ordinarily each shareholder has one vote for each share he or she holds. This voting right is one of the ways in which common stock is different from preferred stock.

The other major difference pertains to dividends. A *dividend* is a payment — usually in cash, but occasionally in stock — make by a firm to its shareholders. Dividends are usually paid quarterly or semiannually. Newspaper stock tables include estimates of annual dividends, usually based on the most recent quarterly or semiannual payment, in stock tables for each common and preferred stock traded on the national and regional stock exchanges.

Dividends on common stocks are determined by the board of directors. They are often — although not always — a direct reflection of how well the company has done in terms of earnings. A significant increase in company profits may well be reflected in an increased dividend to common shareholders. On the other hand, if the board decides to plow its profits back into company expansion or increased research and development, or if business is bad, dividends may be reduced or even eliminated. With common stock, there are no guarantees: The potential for profit *or* loss is much greater than with preferred stock.

Preferred stock is given preferential treatment over common stock. Preferred stockholders are entitled to their dividends — if any are forthcoming — before common stockholders are paid theirs. Preferred stock, however, pays dividends at a specified rate, determined at the time the stock is issued; a holder of a preferred stock can expect no more than the specified dividend even if the company enjoys a banner year. In most corporations, preferred stockholders do not have the voting (or participation) rights enjoyed by common shareholders.

Convertible preferred stock is basically the same as regular preferred stock except that it can be converted into a certain number of shares of the company's common stock, determined at the time the convertible shares were placed on the market. To the investor, this is having the best of both worlds: The holder of the convertible preferred is promised a fixed dividend on the stock as long as he or she holds it, and at the same time enjoys the prospect of being able to, at a later date, convert the shares to take advantage of a rise in the value of the common stock. This conversion privilege, however, can only be exercised once.

Earnings per Share

Investors use a wide range of measures to help determine the value of a stock and to compare it with other stocks. One such measure is earnings per share, or EPS, which translates total corporate profits into profits on a per share basis. A simple formula is used to derive earnings per share.

$$\text{EPS} = \frac{\text{Net profit after taxes} - \text{preferred dividends paid}}{\text{Number of shares of common stock outstanding}}$$

Dividend Yield

Another measure is dividend yield, derived by dividing annual dividends paid per share by the market price per share of stock. Unlike earnings per share, which is expressed in dollars and cents, dividend yield is expressed in percentage points. A company that paid $3 per share in dividends to its stockholders, and whose stock was trading at $30, for example, would have a dividend yield of 10 percent, while one paying $2 in dividends and whose stock is traded at $25 per share, would have a dividend yield of 8 percent. Dividend yield is an indication of the rate of current income earned on the investment dollar, and is one of the items reported in newspaper stock tables and in other stock-related information sources.

Price-Earnings Ratio

The price-earnings ratio, also known as the price-earnings multiple, multiple, p/e ratio, or p/e, is one of the most commonly used measures of stock value, particularly in comparison with other stocks in the same industry. The price-earnings ratio of a stock is simply the price of the stock divided by its earnings, normally its earnings for the past 12 months. The formula for this is:

$$P/E = \frac{\text{Price of a share of stock}}{\text{Earnings per share of the stock for the most recent 12-month period}}$$

Thus, a share of Alberta Electronics, selling for $35, with an earnings of $7 per share in the past 12 months will have a p/e ratio of 5. In other words, the market is willing to buy a share of Alberta Electronics at a price five times greater than its current earnings.

Generally speaking, stocks in a given industry tend to have similar price-earnings ratios, and growth industries tend to have higher p/e ratios than more established industries. The p/e ratio is but one measure of stock value, but it is one of the most widely used. Price-earnings ratios are included in the newspaper stock tables for the New York and American Stock Exchanges.

Warrants

Warrants exist in a sort of financial netherworld. They are neither stock nor bond, have no book value, and pay no dividends. A warrant is a purchasable right that allows investors to buy corporate securities (usually common stock) for an extended time at a fixed price. When the designation *wt.* follows a corporate name (or abbreviation) in a newspaper stock table, it indicates that the security in question is a warrant.

STOCK EXCHANGES

A stock exchange is a central marketplace where shares of stock and other securities are bought and sold, using the auction system. There are two national exchanges in this country as well as several regional exchanges (see figure 13.1). Each exchange is a private organization that sets its own standards for the securities it will list (or trade); only securities that have been admitted to a specific exchange can be traded there, and then only by exchange members or their representatives. The two largest exchanges are the national exchanges, the New York Stock Exchange and the American Stock Exchange.

New York Stock Exchange

The New York Stock Exchange traces its origins back to 1792, when a group of 24 brokers gathered under a buttonwood tree on Wall Street to devise rules of conduct for the trade of stock—hitherto unregulated—and to take buy and sell orders for those who wanted to trade. From these modest beginnings, the New York Stock Exchange has become the world's leading securities exchange, with more than 141 million shares of stock traded daily.[1]

The standards for the stocks that it lists are also the most stringent. The NYSE requires that a company earn at least $2.5 million annually, that it have net tangible assets of at least $18 million, and that it have at least 1,100,000 shares of publicly held common stock. It is on this exchange that "blue-chip" stocks are traded—companies like Exxon and General Motors, IBM and AT&T. Although the companies that list shares on the exchange constitute

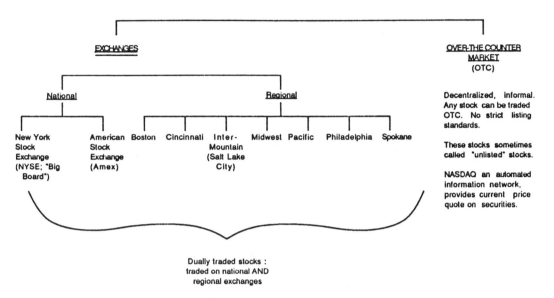

Fig. 13.1. Buying and selling stocks.

less than 1/10th of 1 percent of all U.S. corporations, they earn some 80 percent of the country's total corporate income.

Membership on the exchange, which has been described as an exclusive club, is costly and hard won. The number of "seats" or memberships on the exchange is limited to 1,366, most representing brokerage firms. The price of a seat on the exchange fluctuates; in recent years, it has ranged from $200,000 to more than half a million dollars. In addition, prospective members must be sponsored by two current members in good standing, and must be approved by the Board of Directors.

The New York Stock Exchange offers a wide range of informational and educational services. It sponsors, for example, the Investors Information Program, a countrywide offering of courses on investing offered by member brokerage firms. It also distributes free and inexpensive publications describing different types of investments. Some of these publications are available locally through member brokerage firms; others, such as the "Investors' Information Kit," a collection of four of the NYSE's most popular pamphlets, can be ordered directly from the exchange.[2] Another useful publication is listed below.

New York Stock Exchange. **Fact Book**. New York: The Exchange, 1956- . Annual.

The *Fact Book* is an annual compilation of current and historical statistics, with a summary of the previous year's activity and a description of the NYSE's organization and administration. It is an ideal quick reference source for people seeking answers to questions on the volume of shares traded, lists of stocks with largest market value, and the exchange's history.

American Stock Exchange

The American Stock Exchange, also known as Amex, is the second largest exchange in the country. Requirements for listing a stock on the Amex are not as stringent as on the New York Stock Exchange. As a result, it serves as the market for smaller, younger companies that grow, it has been said, from "new chips to blue chips."

Like the NYSE, Amex is strong on public relations and promotional activities. It makes publications and educational films available to libraries, schools, and prospective investors. It, too, publishes a statistical profile.

American Stock Exchange. **Amex Fact Book**. New York: The Exchange, 1968- . Annual. [Title varies]

The *Amex Fact Book* is similar to the New York Stock Exchange *Fact Book*. It, too, presents data on requirements for listing securities and for exchange membership, reviews the past year's trading activities, and presents current and historical statistics.

Regional Stock Exchanges

In addition to the national stock exchanges, there are seven major regional exchanges in the continental United States: the Boston, Cincinnati, Intermountain (Salt Lake City), Midwest (Chicago), Pacific (San Francisco and Los Angeles), Philadelphia, and Spokane. These exchanges were formed originally to help finance local corporations; because their standards are not as strict as those of the NYSE and Amex, many smaller companies are traded on the regional exchanges. At the same time, some stocks listed on the national exchanges are also listed on regional exchanges. These stocks are said to be *dually traded*.

Dually traded stocks are listed in the composite stock price tables for the New York and American Stock Exchanges in financial newspapers. Coverage of stocks that are traded only on regional exchanges, however, is rather sparse. It is limited for the most part to certain key issues, often no more than 10 or 20 for each exchange. More comprehensive information is, of course, available in the financial pages of the newspapers of the cities in which the regional exchanges are located.

Over-the-Counter Market

The over-the-counter market (OTC) is unlike any of the stock exchanges. It is a decentralized, informal market, a network of thousands of dealer-brokers across the country who do most of their business by telephone and computer. *Any* stock can be traded over-the-counter; unlike the exchanges described above, the OTC market is unencumbered by strict listing standards. The OTC market is second only to the New York Stock Exchange in volume of shares traded.

Often stocks traded on the OTC market are said to be *unlisted*, that is, not traded on one of the national exchanges. It is on the OTC market that most corporations sell shares to the public for the first time, and, as a result, investment in OTC-traded shares of these unproven companies tends to be more speculative than investment in companies listed on the organized exchanges. The OTC market offers more than the securities of small and growing companies, however. Shares of some large, established corporations are also traded OTC, and it is the principal market for federal and municipal government bonds, preferred stocks, and the stocks of insurance companies and banks.

The *National Association of Securities Dealers, Inc.*, or *NASD*, an association of OTC brokers and dealers, monitors the OTC market and sets standards for the ethical conduct of its members in much the same way the exchanges do. NASD is also responsible for the *NASDAQ* (National Association of Securities Dealers Automated Quotations), an automated information network which provides brokers and dealers with current price quotations on over 2,000 of the securities that are traded over-the-counter.

National Association of Securities Dealers, Inc. **The NASDAQ Fact Book**. Washington, D.C.: The Association, 1979- . Annual. [Formerly *NASDAQ Securities Fact Book*]

The *NASDAQ Fact Book* provides data on NASDAQ securities. It includes lists of the most active securities and of those with highest market value, as well as high, low, and closing prices for each of the securities listed on NASDAQ. Free copies of the *Fact Book* are available from the National Association of Securities Dealers.[3]

STOCK PRICES

The price of a share of stock fluctuates. It is dependent on what buyers are willing to pay and sellers are willing to take, and that in turn is directly affected by corporate and industrywide developments, by the economy, by the current political situation, by foreign exchanges, and by many other factors. Although stock price information is contained in many publications, the source most often consulted is the *Wall Street Journal*.

Reading a Newspaper Stock Table

The *Wall Street Journal* contains daily price information for stocks traded on the New York and American Stock Exchanges as well as for the most active stocks traded on some regional exchanges. The composite stock tables for the New York and American Stock Exchanges consolidate data on stocks that are traded both nationally and regionally as well as on those traded only nationally. The regional stock tables, on the other hand, list only a few stocks, and they are limited to those that are traded only on that exchange (that is, which are not dually traded).

Basic to the provision of good business reference is an understanding of the items contained in a newspaper stock table. The sample in figure 13.2 (see page 322) contains most information likely to be found in a stock price table.

Quotations for stocks traded in the over-the-counter market are listed separately from those traded on stock exchanges. Most newspapers, in fact, carry more than one OTC table. The *Wall Street Journal*, for example, contains three: "NASDAQ Over-the-Counter Markets: National Market Issues," "NASDAQ Bid and Asked Quotations," and "Additional OTC Quotes." The first of these includes information on some 2,600 OTC stocks reported via the National Market System, or NMS. Data featured in the "National Market Issues" table are fairly similar to those presented in the NYSE and Amex tables, except that yield and price-earnings ratios are less often included.

The other OTC tables feature less widely traded, lower-priced stocks, and bear less resemblance to standard stock price tables. "NASDAQ Bid and Asked Quotations" excludes yield, price-earnings ratios, and high, low, and closing prices (see figure 13.3 on page 323). Even less information is offered in the "Additional OTC Quotes" table, which includes only company names, bid, and asked prices.

Other Sources of Stock Price Information

The financial pages of the *New York Times*, the *Wall Street Journal*, and *Investor's Daily* are among the most popular sources of daily stock price information. Other less frequently issued financial newspapers—*Barron's*, the *Commercial and Financial Chronicle*, and *Media General Financial Weekly*—include stock price information as well, although it is given on a weekly rather than a daily basis. Many local newspapers contain stock price information in their business pages, but it is usually not as detailed or as comprehensive as that contained in the sources mentioned above. Finally, stock price information is also available online. A Dow Jones News/Retrieval database, *Enhanced Quotes*, makes stock quotes available only 15 minutes after they are reported for companies listed on the New York, American, Midwest, and Pacific Stock Exchanges and NASDAQ-OTC traded companies. Electronic versions of the *Wall Street Journal, Investor's Daily*, and *Media General Financial Weekly* are also available online.

| 52 Weeks | | | | Yld | P-E | Sales | | | | Net |
High	Low	Stock	Div	%	Ratio	100s	High	Low	Close	Chg
49	327/8	CocaCl[1]	1.12	2.5	18	4800	445/8	441/8	445/8	+1/4
89[2]	493/8	DowCh	2.20[3]	2.6	20	2802	851/4	891/2	85	+3/4
561/2	447/8	GTE pf[4]	2.50	4.8	. . .	6	513/4	515/8	515/8	-3/8
23/4	1	PanA wt[5]	. . . . . .		. . .	46688	61/8	53/4	61/8	+1/2
655/8	447/8	RJRNb	1.60	2.9[6]	13[7]	3437[8]	541/2[9]	54[10]	541/4[11]	-1/4[12]

1. Stock. Name of the corporation issuing the stock, usually abbreviated. In this example, "CocaCl" stands for Coca-Cola. Note that unless otherwise indicated, the stock listed is common stock.
2. High-Low. Highest and lowest prices paid for the stock during the past fifty-two weeks. During that time, for example, the highest price paid for a share of Dow Chemical common stock was $89.00; the lowest, $49.375. (Stock prices are listed in dollars and eighths of dollars, rather than in dollars and cents. One eighth of a dollar equals 12.5 cents.)
3. Div. Estimate of the annual dividend per share, based on the latest quarterly or semiannual dividend payment.
4. Pf. The listing for GTE Corp., followed by "pf" indicates that the stock listed is preferred rather than common stock.
5. Wt. The listing for Pan American World Airways followed by "wt" indicates that the security is a warrant and not a stock.
6. Yld %. Dividend yield, or the annual dividend divided by the current purchase price of the stock. The dividend yield for RJR Nabisco, for example, is 2.9%
7. P-E Ratio. The price-earnings ratio, or current market price divided by the previous year's per share earnings. The p-e ratio for RJR Nabisco is 13.
8. Sales 100s. Shows the number of shares in lots of 100 (or round lots) traded that day. On the trading day reported, 343,700 shares of RJR Nabisco (or 3437 lots of 100 shares) were traded.
9. High. Highest price paid for a share of stock on the trading day reported. The high for RJR Nabisco was 541/2 or $54.50.
10. Low. Lowest price paid that day. RJR Nabisco's low was $54.00.
11. Close. The price at which the stock sold during the day's last transactions. The closing price for RJR Nabisco was $54.25.
12. Net Chg. Net change refers to the change (if any) in price from the closing price paid that day and on the preceding day. A share of RJR Nabisco was down 1/4. In other words, today's closing price was 25 cents less than yesterday's.

Fig. 13.2. Daily stock price table.

	Sales			Net
Stock & Div	100s	Bid	Asked	Chg.
Beauty Labs[1]	139	6	61/2	+1/2
KC Lifeins .96[2]	1[3]	291/4[4]	293/4[5]	. . .[6]

1. Stock. Name of the company, usually abbreviated.
2. Div. Amount of the annual dividend, if any. Kansas City Life Insurance, for example, paid its shareholders annual dividends of 96 cents per share.
3. Sales 100s. Sales are expressed in hundreds (round lots). On the day being reported, 139 round lots, or 13,900 shares of Beauty Labs were sold, and 1 round lot, or 100 shares, of Kansas City Life was sold.
4. Bid. The price a dealer is willing to pay for a stock. (Newspaper quotes are always for the highest price available).
5. Asked. The price at which a dealer is willing to sell the stock. (Newspaper "asked" quotes are always for the lowest price available.).
6. Net Chg. Net change is the difference between bid prices on the day being reported and on the preceding trading day. The bid price for Beauty Labs increased by 1/2 (50 cents), but remained the same for Kansas City Life Insurance.

Fig. 13.3. OTC stock price table.

Sometimes historical stock prices may be required. Brokers, accountants, tax lawyers, and serious investors who need such data or want to study trends in the prices of specific stocks over a period of time can use either online or printed sources.

Historical Quotes. Dow Jones News/Retrieval. Daily updates.

Daily Stock Price Record. New York: Standard & Poor's. Quarterly. [Available in separate editions: *American Stock Exchange*, 1962- ; *New York Stock Exchange*, 1962- ; and *Over-the-Counter*, 1968- .]

Historical Quotes is an online database that provides daily high, low, and closing stock prices for the past year, as well as monthly summaries dating back to 1979, and quarterly summaries, to 1978.

Each printed edition of the *Daily Stock Price Record* includes both daily and weekly stock price and trading information for three-month periods. Separate volumes are issued each quarter for the American Stock Exchange, the New York Stock Exchange, and the Over-the-Counter Market. Although this publication may be too specialized for small and medium-sized libraries, librarians providing business reference service should know that it exists and that it provides a convenient alternative to painstakingly culling this information from the pages of daily or weekly financial newspapers.

STOCK PRICE INDEXES

While investors are interested in the performance of specific stocks, they are also concerned with general stock market trends. Stock price indexes or averages give an overview of general stock market conditions, enabling investors to spot the general direction in which prices are moving. There are several such market indicators, but the two best known are the Dow Jones Industrial Average and the Standard & Poor's Composite 500 Index.

Dow Jones Industrial Average

Anyone who watches network news has probably heard of the Dow Jones Industrial Average, which is given nightly along with other stock market information. The Dow Jones Industrial is a statistical compilation of the average prices of 30 well-known, blue-chip common stocks traded on the New York Stock Exchange. Although Dow Jones compiles averages for transportation and utilities as well, it is the Industrial Average that is Wall Street's most widely quoted measure of stock market performance.

Standard & Poor's 500 Index

More inclusive than the Dow Jones Industrial Average is the Standard & Poor's 500 Index, which measures the activities of 500 stocks traded on the New York Stock Exchange. The stocks are broken down into four main units: industrials, rails, utilities, and the 500 composite.

Other indexes commonly referred to by market analysts reflect the behavior of stocks on each of the three major markets on which they are traded. The *New York Stock Exchange Composite* includes all 2,100 stocks listed on the exchange, the *American Stock Exchange Index* covers all Amex stocks, and the *OTC Composite Index* is comprised of some 2,400 stocks traded in the OTC market.

Stock Index Information Sources

Information on stock price indexes is easy to find, particularly for the more popular indexes. It is contained in financial newpapers and in most sources that provide comprehensive stock market information. In addition to the standard statistical guides described in chapter 6, a more specialized guide lists sources that contain stock price indexes and averages.

Chapman, Karen J. **Investment Statistics Locator**. Phoenix, Ariz.: Oryx Press, 1988. 182p.

The *Investment Statistics Locator* lists by subject data available in 22 major investment serials. It cites the sources, for example, that publish half-hourly, hourly, daily, weekly, monthly, quarterly, and yearly versions of the Dow Jones Industrial Average. Less widely quoted market indicators and other types of investment statistics are also covered.

In addition, each issue of the *Wall Street Journal Index* includes closing Dow Jones averages for the month or year being indexed, and Standard & Poor's *Daily Stock Price Record* series include three-month compilations of stock price indexes and averages in the first part of each volume. A brief explanation of each indicator is also provided.

When historical information is being sought, two publications are particularly helpful.

Pierce, Phyllis, ed. **The Dow Jones Averages, 1885-1985**. Rev. ed. Homewood, Ill.: Dow Jones-Irwin, 1986. 410p.

Standard & Poor's. **Statistical Service**. New York: Standard & Poor's, 1978- . One-volume looseleaf service with monthly supplements.

The Dow Jones Averages, 1885-1985 is useful for its description of the history and development of the indexes created by Dow Jones as well as for daily stock averages from January 16, 1885, through December 31, 1985. Each daily listing includes data on the Dow Jones Industrial, Transportation, and Utilities Averages as well as daily sales figures.

Standard & Poor's *Statistical Service* provides similar data for indexes developed by Standard & Poor's. The most recent information, included in the monthly "Current Statistics" supplements, also presents summary monthly information for the Dow Jones averages for the current and preceding years as well as weekly information for an array of Standard & Poor's indexes for the same time period. In addition to the Standard & Poor's 500 Composite Index, for example, "Current Statistics" includes indexes for different types of stocks (capital goods versus consumer goods, high-grade versus low-price common stocks) and for such industry categories as aerospace, computer services, textile products, and toy manufacturers.

Data in the monthly "Current Statistics" section is enhanced by the *Security Price Index Record*, part of the *Statistical Service*. The *Record* presents the various S&P stock price indexes dating back to the 1920s, describes their history and development, and explains how they are computed. It is a key source of historical data for these and many other measures of stock performance and trading activity.

CORPORATE REPORTS

Astute investors require more than stock price and dividend information about the companies in which they are interested. They also want to know about company management, the products manufactured, and prospects for the future. Corporate reports, particularly those submitted to stockholders and the U.S. Securities and Exchange Commission, provide this information and are the primary data sources on which most published financial and investment advisory services are based.

Registration and Prospectus

The Securities and Exchange Commission (SEC), established by the Securities Exchange Act of 1934, serves as the government watchdog over the securities industry. Two of its major functions are to require that publicly traded companies make detailed financial reports to the SEC, and to make the information contained in these reports accessible to the public so that it can make informed investment decisions. This begins with the company registration.

Before most companies can make a public offering of new securities, they must file a registration statement with the SEC.[4] This document includes general business information such as corporate history, products, sales, number of employees, and an assessment of competition. It also includes detailed financial statements and balance sheet information, a description of the security being offered, and information about management.

The prospectus, a document intended for prospective investors, contains the highlights of the registration statement. The SEC is careful to point out that while the information contained in the prospectus is accurate, its approval of the document does not imply that the security being offered is necessarily a wise and prudent investment choice. Four key areas in the prospectus deserve the would-be investor's concentration: (1) "Company Business," (2) "Recent Developments," (3) "Use of Proceeds," and (4) "Litigation."

A copy of the prospectus can be obtained from the company itself, from brokers selling the stock, and from companies that are in the business of copying and selling the various SEC-required corporate reports to the public. At present, three such companies offer these reports: Bechtel, Disclosure, and Q-Data.

10-K Report

The 10-K report, so called because it is submitted on form 10-K, is a detailed annual report that all publicly traded companies must submit to the Securities and Exchange Commission. It is the most exhaustive source of current corporate information. The report is divided into two sections: (1) financial data and (2) supporting data. The financial section includes a statistical summary of operations for the last five years, financial statements for each line of business, legal proceedings, and a list or diagram of parents and subsidiaries. The supporting data in the second section of the report include a list of principal stockholders, security holdings of management, and a list of directors with specific background information and term of office for each.

The information contained in 10-K reports is basic to investment analysis. Major business reference collections may include microfiche copies of 10-K reports for all publicly traded companies, for Fortune 500 companies only, or for some specially designated category (perhaps by industry or state). Much of the information in 10-Ks is available in other sources. Comprehensive investment services, for example, routinely include information extracted from these reports. In some instances, the companies themselves duplicate the contents of their 10-K reports in their annual reports to shareholders. Finally, librarians and information specialists can search *Disclosure II*, an online database that extracts data from the 10-K and other SEC reports, or can use *Compact Disclosure* or *CD/Corporate*, compact disk databases. In one form or another, information contained in 10-K reports is accessible to virtually all libraries.

Annual Report to Shareholders

While a comprehensive collection of 10-K reports may be impractical for some libraries, a collection of the annual reports companies make to their shareholders is not. The reports are free and generally available to libraries upon request; the only costs involved are for the postcards to request them, the staff time to process them, and the file cabinets in which to store them.

Since annual reports to shareholders are not official SEC filings, there is considerable leeway in the depth of information they contain. One company's report may be little more than a glossy public relations effort; another's may essentially duplicate its 10-K report. Novice investors should be forewarned that annual reports do not always present the unvarnished truth. "Annual reports," writes *Forbes*, "are a lot like old-time strippers. They act like they're showing you everything. But there's still a lot hidden."[5] *Business Week* describes the tone that one report took.

> General Motors Corp. Chairman Roger B. Smith displays a penchant for casting bad news in the best possible light. GM's net income dropped 26% last year, its market share declined 1.5 points, and its costs are higher than any other U.S. producer. But the word "problem" never crops up in its report. Instead, there are references to a "carefully drawn strategy" and management that "has moved forward with careful planning and bold actions."[6]

Annual reports generally have two main parts. The first part summarizes the company's financial state, reviews its accomplishments for the past year, and discusses its plans and outlook for the future. The tone is positive, and problems or failures are seldom discussed.

The second part of the report consists of the corporate financial statements, described in chapter 10, that are prepared by the company and verified by independent auditors. It is an excellent source of financial statistics, including current assets; property, plants, and equipment; liabilities; stockholders' equity; earnings; per share data; and for most companies, a 10-year summary of financial highlights.

The four reports that have been mentioned thus far—the registration statement, the prospectus, the 10-K report, and the annual report to shareholders—are rich sources of corporate information. A comparison of the broad categories of information contained in each of these documents can be found in figure 13.4.

Types of Information	Type of Report			
	Registration	Prospectus	10-K	Ann. Rpt. to Shareholders
Auditor				
Name	A	A	A	A
Opinion			A	A
Compensation Plans				
Equity	F	F	S	
Monetary	F	F	S	
Company Information				
Nature of Business	A	A	A	S
History	A	A	F	S
Organization & Change	A	A	F	S
Debt Structure	A	A	A	A
Depreciation & Other Schedules	A	A	A	
Directors, Officers, Insiders				
Identification	A	A	F	S
Background	A	A	S	S
Holdings	A	A	S	
Compensation	A	A	S	
Earnings Per Share			A	A
Financial Information				
Annual Audited	F	F	A	A
Interim Audited	S	S	S	
Interim Unaudited	S	S	F	
Foreign Operations	A	A	A	S
Labor Contracts	F			
Legal Agreements	F		F	
Loan Agreements	F	F	F	
Plants & Properties	F	F	A	S
Product-Line Breakout	A	A	A	S
Securities Structure	A	A	A	
Subsidiaries	A	A	A	S

Legend:

A   Always included: included—if it occurred or significant.
F   Frequently included.
S   Special circumstances only.

Fig. 13.4. The information content of four major corporate reports. Extracted from *A Guide to SEC Corporate Filings* (Bethesda, Md.: Disclosure, 1986), pp. 12-13.

Other Reports

The reports described above are the most commonly consulted company filings, but they are not the only ones a company is required to make. Other reports must be filed with the Securities and Exchange Commission. The 8-K, for example, must be filed whenever unscheduled material events or significant corporate changes take place. Companies are also required to file listing application statements with national or regional stock exchanges whenever they propose to trade a new security on that exchange.

Finally, companies must file detailed reports with agencies of the state in which they are located. Three types of reports may be required.

1. *General Corporate Reports.* These will include the initial articles of incorporation (required in all states), notices of mergers and name changes, and, in most states, annual reports.

2. *Debt Reports.* Under the Uniform Commercial Code, a company must file a report whenever it borrows against any of its assets. A separate statement is filed for each debt and will usually show the name and address of the debtor and the lender, along with a description of the property used as collateral and the maturity date of the loan.

3. *Security Reports.* If a publicly traded company is listed on one of the national exchanges or if it is traded in more than one state, it must submit disclosure filings to the SEC. If its securities are traded in only one state, it is not required to report to the SEC, but must file similar disclosure statements with the state in which it is being traded.

These state-filed reports are valuable information sources, particularly for smaller companies that are not traded on the national exchanges. Copies of these reports are usually available from the state agencies where they are filed.

COMPREHENSIVE INVESTMENT SERVICES

Comprehensive investment services are used by people who want information about stocks and bonds and about specific companies and industries. Investment services fall into two categories. Some, which present facts and figures but contain no recommendations, are called *investment information services*. Others, which go one step further and advise readers regarding the investment outlook for the securities they list, are called *investment advisory services*. Investment information and advisory services, however, have several characteristics in common. Both are based on data compiled from the various SEC filings, annual reports, and other corporate releases, and may provide information on thousands of companies. Both are revised and updated on a regular basis. Finally, the cost of compiling these services is high, and as a result, subscriptions to them are expensive. They rank among many libraries' most costly reference sources.

Comprehensive Investment Information Services

The two major comprehensive investment information services are *Moody's Manuals* and *Standard Corporation Descriptions*. Each of these publications merits further consideration.

Moody's Investors Service. **Moody's Manuals**. New York: The Service. Annual. [7 different titles, described below]

Standard Corporation Descriptions. New York: Standard & Poor's, 1915- . Looseleaf service, updated by *Daily News*, 6v.

Moody's Manuals is the collective designation for a series of publications. Together, they cover approximately 19,000 American and foreign companies traded on the national and regional exchanges and over-the-counter, 5,000 major foreign companies, and some 15,000 municipalities. These listings are consolidated by type into the following seven manuals, issued annually.

1. Moody's Investors Service. **Moody's Bank & Finance Manual**. 1955- . Annual, supplemented by *Moody's Bank & Finance News Report*, issued twice weekly, 3v.

   Covers banks, insurance companies, real estate companies, real estate investment trusts, and miscellaneous financial enterprises.

2. _____. **Moody's Industrial Manual**. 1954- . Annual, supplemented by *Moody's Industrial News Report*, issued twice weekly, 2v.

   Covers industrial companies traded on the New York, American, and regional stock exchanges. Although coverage varies, each company listing generally includes history and background, a description of the business, a list of subsidiaries and of principal plants and properties, and names and titles of officers and directors. Statistical data include income accounts, financial and operating statistics, and long-term debt and capital stock.

   The "Special Features Section," a blue paper insert in volume 1, includes a classification of companies by products and industries, a geographic index, and several tables pertaining to industrial securities, many of which go back 20 years or more.

3. _____. **Moody's International Manual**. 1981- . Annual, supplemented by *Moody's International News Report*, issued semiweekly, 2v.

   Provides financial and business information on more than 5,000 major foreign corporations and national and transnational institutions in 100 countries. The "special features" section includes a classification of companies by industries and products and selected financial statistics.

4. _____. **Moody's OTC Industrial Manual**. 1970- . Annual, supplemented by *Moody's OTC Industrial News Report*, issued twice weekly.

   Information is very similar to that contained in the *Industrial Manual* except that the companies listed are those whose securities are traded over-the-counter.

5. _____. **Moody's Municipal & Government Manual**. 1955- . Annual, supplemented by *Moody's Municipal & Government News Report*, which is issued twice weekly, 2v.

   Includes federal, state, and local government bond issues as well as some foreign issues.

6. Moody's Investors Service. **Moody's Public Utility Manual**. 1954- . Annual, supplemented by *Moody's Public Utility News Report*, issued twice weekly, 2v.

   Domestic and foreign public utilities are covered, including electric and gas utilities, gas transmission companies, and water and telephone companies.

7. _____. **Moody's Transportation Manual**. 1954- . Annual. Supplemented by *Moody's Transportation News Report*, issued weekly.

   Includes railroads and airlines as well as other fields of transportation such as bus and truck lines, water transport, oil pipelines, private bridge, canal and tunnel companies, and car and truck rental companies. Its coverage of the railroad industry is outstanding.

The focus of each *Manual* determines the kind of specialized information it contains. Each listing, however, includes a history of the company or institution, a description of its business, its address, a list of its officers and directors, and basic financial data.

In addition to company-specific information, each *Manual* includes a blue "Special Features" section, which provides a wealth of current and historical statistical data and other information. This section in the *Bank & Finance Manual*, for example, lists the largest banks, savings and loan associations, and insurance companies in the country, while the one in the *Transportation Manual* includes a comprehensive statistical and analytical survey of the railroad industry.

Each of the *Manuals* is updated by a newsletter, which may include interim financial statements, merger proposals, litigation, personnel changes, description of new debt and stock issues, and announcement of new financings. These are filed in looseleaf notebooks which accompany the *Manuals*.

Moody's is a comprehensive service, and as a result, bonds as well as stocks and other securities are listed. For both bonds and preferred stocks, it assigns ratings so that relative investment qualities can be noted. For bonds, nine symbols are used, ranging from *Aaa* (highest investment quality, least risk) to *C* (lowest investment quality, highest risk). A variation of the bond rating symbols is used for Moody's preferred stock ratings, with *aaa* the designation for a top-quality preferred stock and *caa* the symbol for an issue that is likely to be in arrears on dividend payments. The blue pages in the front of each manual describe these ratings in some detail.

Moody's Complete Corporate Index, a triannual index that is included with a subscription to the *Manuals*, is a convenient alphabetical index to the companies listed in the six manuals that Moody's classifies as its corporate manuals. (The *Bank & Finance, Industrial, International, OTC Industrial, Public Utility* and *Transportation* manuals are included; the *Municipal & Government Manual* is not.)

Standard Corporation Descriptions, the second comprehensive investment service, is roughly comparable to *Moody's Manuals*. It, too, lists companies traded on the New York and American Stock Exchanges and the larger unlisted and regional exchange companies, and the information it contains is extracted from company reports and SEC filings. *Corporation Records*, however, is contained in six looseleaf volumes, and companies are listed alphabetically rather than segregated into broad industrial categories. Each volume includes two indexes: one is the general index, the other cross-indexes subsidiaries. Information for each company listed includes a description of the business, a list of plants and property, officers, and financial and operating data. *Records* is updated semimonthly.

The sixth volume of the set includes an index of leading companies by industry and several special tables, such as stock and bond offerings in the current and preceding year and important new registrations on file with the Securities and Exchange Commission.

Like Moody's, Standard & Poor's rates bonds for their investment safety. The highest rating is *AAA*, which indicates that the capacity to pay interest and repay principal is extremely strong. *D*, the lowest rating, indicates that the company is in arrears of paying interest and/or repaying the principal.

Standard Corporation Descriptions is updated by *Daily News*, which gives brief information about new offerings, changes in Standard & Poor's ratings, trading data, mergers and acquisitions, and other significant developments. *Daily News* issues are cumulated into *Corporation Records*.

Although Moody's and Standard & Poor's comprehensive investment information services are more alike than not, each has special features. *Corporation Descriptions* is updated more frequently, its company financial tables cover a wider range of years than do Moody's, and many small companies not included in Moody's are listed. On the other hand, far more companies are included in *Moody's Manuals*, the coverage of banks, the transportation industry, municipal bonds and public utilities is much stronger, and Moody's often covers corporate history and description of company products and operations in more depth than does its rival.[7]

Both *Moody's Manuals* and *Standard Corporation Descriptions* have online counterparts.

Moody's Corporate Profiles. New York: Moody's Investor Service. Weekly updates.

Standard & Poor's Corporate Descriptions. New York: Standard & Poor's. Biweekly updates.

Moody's Corporate Profiles provides descriptive and financial information on all companies traded on the New York and American Stock Exchanges, and some 1,300 of the most active companies traded over-the-counter. Most company records contain key statistics and five-year financial histories, and, for some 950 companies of high investor interest, also include analyses based on the most recent quarterly earnings, dividends, and other developments. *Moody's Corporate Profiles* is kept up-to-date by two current awareness files, *Moody's Corporate News—International*, and *Moody's Corporate News—U.S.* All three files include both textual and tabular records.

Standard & Poor's Corporate Descriptions provides similar information for nearly 11,000 publicly held U.S. companies, generally including data on corporate earnings, stocks and bonds issued, corporate histories, and other data. *Corporate Descriptions* is supplemented by *Standard & Poor's News*, which is updated daily.

Investment Advisory Services

In contrast to the Moody's and Standard & Poor's investment information services, *Value Line Investment Survey* is an investment *advisory* service.

Value Line Investment Survey. New York: Value Line, Inc., 1936- . Weekly.

Like the others, *Value Line* includes investment information, but it goes beyond presentation of factual material to include advice regarding the investment outlook for specific stocks and industries. "The operation is stumbling," the would-be investor may be warned, or, on a more hopeful note, "This stock is a worthwhile speculation." In addition, *Value Line* numerically ranks the stocks it lists for investment safety, for probable price performance and yield in the next 12 months, and for estimated appreciation potential in the next three to five years. These rankings are one of the reasons why *Value Line* is such a popular service.

There are three main parts to *Value Line*: an index and summary section, a newsletter, and the company and industry reports section. As shown in figure 13.5 (see page 332), the index includes the page citations to the companies listed. It also features tables for best and worst performing stocks, stocks with high three- to five-year appreciation potential, high yielding stocks, and lists of the companies whose stocks have been rated highest for safety and performance. Finally, for each company listed in the index, selected financial information, taken from the company reports section, is also included.

Every week, Value Line lists the 100 stocks currently ranked Number 1 for best year ahead performance.

In addition to NYSE issues, Value Line also ranks ASE and Over-The-Counter stocks.

Recent price per share is provided for comparison.

Stocks are ranked for relative long-term safety from 1 (most safe) to 5 (least safe).

A stock's Beta is its relative sensitivity to market fluctuation (NYSE average = 1.00).

Estimated Price to Earnings ratio is based on past 6 months' earnings plus estimated future 6 months' earnings.

Estimated Yield is based on estimated dividends for the next 12 months.

Each stock is grouped in one of 92 industry categories.

Industry Rank is based on the overall Timeliness ranks for all stocks in the industry.

TIMELY STOCKS
Stocks Ranked 1 (Highest) for Performance in the Next 12 Months

Page No.	Stock Name		Recent Price	Safety Rank	Beta	Current P/E Ratio	Est'd Yield	Industry Group	Industry Rank
2130	ADC Telecom.	(OTC)	21	3	1.00	13.5	NIL	Unassigned	—
853	AFG Inds.		30	3	1.30	13.8	0.5%	Building	26
2111	AGS Computers		27	4	1.20	14.4	NIL	Computer Software/Svcs	1
1813	Affiliated Publications		71	3	0.75	30.9	0.9%	Newspaper	2
347	Agency Rent-A-Car	(OTC)	21	3	1.15	21.2	NIL	Industrial Services	12
255	Air Express Int'l	(ASE)	13	5	1.35	14.1	NIL	Air Transport	16
1453	Alexander & Baldwin	(OTC)	47	3	0.55	12.0	3.3%	Food Processing	10
1455	Amer. Maize 'A'	(ASE)	20	4	0.85	11.6	2.6%	Food Processing	10
748	Amer. Water Works		43	2	0.70	11.4	2.9%	Electric Util.(Central)	33
276	Arkansas Best		25	4	1.05	12.0	1.5%	Trucking/Trans Leasing	5
2113	Ashton-Tate	(OTC)	42	3	1.50	15.8	NIL	Computer Software/Svcs	1
2003	Bank of Boston		28	2	1.05	7.7	3.6%	Bank	30
351	Banner Ind.		20	5	1.00	7.3	0.3%	Industrial Services	12
213	Bard (C.R.)		38	3	1.30	20.4	0.9%	Medical Supplies	13
1671	Barry (R.G.)	(ASE)	8⅞	5	0.90	9.1	NIL	Shoe	60
1429	Bindley Western	(OTC)	13	4	1.25	14.1	NIL	Unassigned	—
218	Biomet ■	(OTC)	18	3	0.80	27.7	NIL	Medical Supplies	13
352	Browning-Ferris Ind.		45	3	1.15	20.5	1.8%	Industrial Services	12
1754	CPI Corp.	(OTC)	37	3	1.15	17.3	0.8%	Recreation	71
1572	Caremark Inc.	(OTC)	24	4	1.60	28.2	NIL	Unassigned	—
1461	Castle & Cooke		19	4	0.80	12.2	NIL	Food Processing	10
931	Champion Int'l		32	3	1.30	13.4	1.6%	Paper & Forest Products	7
1640	Charming Shoppes	(OTC)	20	3	1.60	22.0	0.6%	Retail Store	25
1669	Circuit City Stores		31	4	1.50	19.0	0.3%	Retail (Special Lines)	65
1573	COMPAQ Computer		20	4	1.85	13.9	NIL	Unassigned	—
1463	ConAgra Inc.		31	3	0.85	16.3	1.9%	Food Processing	10
1100	Digital Equipment		107	3	1.25	16.5	NIL	Computer & Peripherals	46
1814	Dow Jones & Co.		40	2	1.20	23.8	1.6%	Newspaper	2
1045	Emerson Radio		9⅞	4	0.80	12.9	NIL	Electronics	79
1468	Federal Co.		41	2	0.70	10.3	2.9%	Food Processing	10
1255	Forest Labs.	(ASE)	21	4	1.45	26.9	NIL	Drug	8
1562	Fuji Photo ADR	(OTC)	45	3	0.95	19.8	0.4%	Japanese Diversified	22
511	Fuller (H.B.)	(OTC)	28	3	1.00	13.6	1.3%	Chemical (Specialty)	37
1893	GAF Corp.		39	3	1.00	16.4	0.3%	C...	
637	GEICO Corp.		103	3	0.95	13.6			
1647	Gap (The), Inc.								

Fig. 13.5. Typical index, *Value Line Investment Survey*. Copyright © 1987 Value Line, Inc.

The second section, "Selection & Opinion," includes general stock market information, investment strategies, and an in-depth analysis of a specially recommended stock in its "Stock Highlight" feature.

The "Ratings & Reports" section, however, comprises the bulk of the service. In all, some 1,700 companies are covered in detail. (A sample listing follows in figure 13.6.) Companies are grouped into broad industrial categories and then listed alphabetically. Particularly noteworthy for each company listing are the *Value Line* ratings; the Insider Decision Index, which compares the purchase versus the sale of stocks in the company by its officers, directors, and other "insiders"; detailed statistical analyses, including historical data and projections; and beta. *Beta*, also known as the *beta coefficient*, is a measure of the sensitivity of a specific stock's price to overall price fluctuations in the New York Stock Exchange Composite Average. It is essentially an index of riskiness, in which the Composite Average is assigned a value of 1.0. Individual securities may be assigned betas that are less than, the same as, or more than the Composite Average. Generally, the higher the beta, the more volatile the stock. A high-risk stock thus has a high beta, a low-risk one a low beta. Although betas are included in a few other printed and online sources, *Value Line* is one of the most widely held publications that contains betas.

Value Line, which is issued weekly, continuously analyzes the stocks it lists. Four times each year (or every 13th week), each stock is reevaluated, and a new analysis is printed.

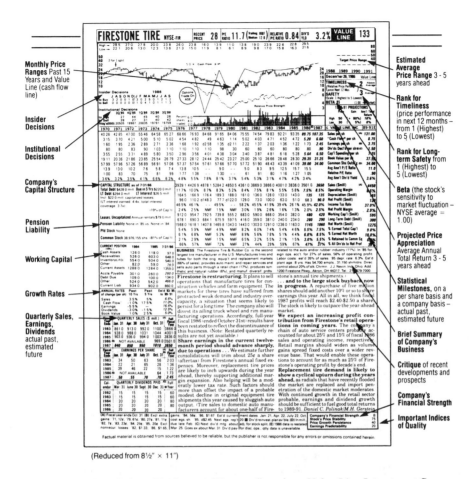

(Reduced from 8½" × 11")

Fig. 13.6. Typical listing, "Ratings and Reports" section, *Value Line Investment Survey*. Copyright © 1987 Value Line, Inc.

Unlike Moody's and Standard & Poor's, *Value Line* includes industry as well as company analyses. The listings for Coca-Cola and PepsiCo, for example, are preceded by a survey of the soft drink industry. Usually included in the industry analyses are a discussion of current political, economic, and technological developments that may affect the outlook for the industry, composite statistics, and *Value Line*'s assessment of investment opportunities in the industry. It also includes explicit rankings of the industry investment propsects. In all, 76 different industries are covered, ranging from advertising to trucking.

Although an online version of *Value Line* is available, it is not offered by any of the database vendors commonly used by libraries. A condensed version is, however, available on diskette.

Value/Screen Plus. New York: Value Line, Inc. Monthly or quarterly updates.

Value/Screen Plus reproduces 37 selected data items for each of the companies represented in *Value Line*. Using it, a researcher can identify companies with high or low ratings for timeliness and safety, or can compile data on earnings per share, dividends, price-earnings ratios, and other measures of stock performance. For many individual investors, the printed *Value Line* offers the quickest and most direct access to investment information. For researchers who would like to manipulate the data, follow several different investments, or create spreadsheets, however, *Value/Screen Plus* is a worthwhile alternative.

SOURCES OF INDUSTRY INFORMATION

Information on specific companies is vital to investors, but it needs to be supplemented with industrywide information. Someone contemplating purchase of stock in a large newspaper chain, for example, needs all available information about its financial well-being and the quality of its management. The person should also learn more about the outlook for the newspaper industry generally. Fortunately, there are many published industry studies. Depth of coverage varies, but usually includes a review of the industry's recent performance, a description of the present situation, and projections for the future. A survey of the newspaper industry, for example, may discuss the effects that automation and consolidation of ownership have had on the industry, consider the implications of the shift of advertising dollars from newspapers to television, or speculate about the development of some electronic technology that would replace newspapers as we know them. Considerable statistical data may be included.

Published sources of industry information fall into two categories: (1) those covering several industries and (2) those focusing on only one industry or on a closely related group of industries.

Multi-Industry Studies

The most comprehensive of all of the multi-industry studies are the economic censuses published every five years by the federal government. The Censuses of Construction Industries, Manufactures, Mineral Industries, Retail Trade, Service Industries, Transportation, and Wholesale Trade present detailed analyses of the economic sectors they cover, and include national, regional, state, and local statistics. The economic censuses, which are taken every five years, are supplemented by monthly, quarterly, and annual surveys. Both types of publications are available at regional depository and many research libraries.

In the preceding section, it was mentioned that *Value Line* contains industry as well as company analyses. Other sources, however, concentrate primarily on industry information.

Standard & Poor's. **Industry Surveys**. New York: Standard & Poor's, 1973- . Looseleaf, with weekly updates.

Moody's Investors Service. **Moody's Industry Review**. New York: The Service. Looseleaf, with weekly updates.

U.S. Dept. of Commerce. International Trade Administration. **U.S. Industrial Outlook**. Washington, D.C.: Government Printing Office, 1960- . Annual.

"Annual Report on American Industry," **Forbes**. Survey appearing in the first January issue each year.

Standard & Poor's. **Analyst's Handbook**. New York: Standard & Poor's, 1964- . Annual, with monthly supplements.

One of the most heavily used of these is Standard & Poor's *Industry Surveys*. This looseleaf service includes, for 22 industry categories, detailed analyses of each category and of the industries that comprise it. The categories are broad and may include several subsets. The "Leisure-Time" survey, for example, includes gambling, home entertainment, lodging, photography, restaurants, sporting goods, theatrical entertainment, and toys and games. In each survey, the investment outlook for the industry, comparisons of leading companies, and specific investment recommendations are featured, supplemented by statistical data, tables, and charts.

Two surveys are included for each industry, a "Basic Analysis" and a "Current Analysis." The "Basic Analysis" is the most comprehensive source of information, generally 30 to 40 pages long. The narrative descriptions are supplemented with numerous tables and graphs, frequently cite relevant trade publications and government documents, and include summary financial statistics for major companies. The "Basic Analysis" is brought up-to-date by the "Current Analysis." In addition to the basic and current surveys, a monthly bulletin, "Trends and Projections," is also included. It focuses on the current state of the economy, includes basic economic indicators, and presents industry and economic forecasts. Finally, both company and industry indexes are included. Standard & Poor's *Industry Surveys* is an excellent source of both factual and advisory information on many industries.

Moody's Industry Review focuses on specific companies within designated industries rather than on the industries themselves. It contains financial information, operating data, and financial ratios for approximately 4,000 companies, arranged in 145 industry groups. Each industry listing includes comparative statistics, annual rankings of companies by revenue, net income, return on capital, yield, and other categories, as well as price scores for the most recent 12 months and for the past 7 years. A chart of composite stock price movements is also included.

Unlike the *Industry Surveys* and *Moody's Industry Review*, the *U.S. Industrial Outlook* does not cover companies. The data it contains, however, are extremely useful. More than 200 manufacturing and nonmanufacturing industries are analyzed. For each, a brief description of the industry is followed by an examination of recent developments, a discussion of its size, trade position, and growth history. Projections for the future are also included. Statistics abound, many of them taken from the economic censuses and other government sources. Other useful features include brief bibliographies at the end of most sections, and the names, offices, and telephone numbers of the government experts who wrote the various industry reports, enabling librarians or library users to contact the specialists for additional information or for clarification.

Another industry information source, available in virtually all libraries, is the "Annual Report on American Industry," which appears in the first January issue of *Forbes* each year. Although coverage of industries is far more superficial than that in the preceding publications, it is useful. The "Annual Report" includes brief descriptions of 31 major industries, and ranks industries and 1,012 leading companies for profit, growth, and stock market performance.

For historical information, the *Analyst's Handbook* is useful. It contains financial statistics for the past 30 years for industries represented in the Standard & Poor's 500 Index. More than 80 broad industry categories are featured, including aerospace/defense, forest products, airlines, and life insurance companies. Coverage for each industry includes the names of companies represented in the Standard & Poor's index, the date(s) on which each was added to or dropped from the index, a chart comparing industry performance to the Standard & Poor's index, and approximately 20 financial statistics, most of them on a per-share basis. In addition, the *Handbook* contains selected financial ratios and income statement and balance sheet items for the past six years for most industry categories.

Commercial publishers and government agencies are not the only organizations that issue industry studies. Securities analysts and brokerage houses frequently publish substantial analyses of specific industries and companies. Three sources are particularly useful for such information.

Nelson's Directory of Wall Street Research. Port Chester, N.Y.: Nelson Publications, 1976- . Annual.

Corporate and Industry Research Reports. Eastchester, N.Y.: JA Micropublishing, 1982- . Quarterly or annual.

Investext. Boston: Business Research Corporation. Weekly updates.

Nelson's Directory of Wall Street Research, billed by its publishers as the "Who's Who" of investment research, is a six-part listing of companies and individuals involved in financial analyses of publicly traded companies and the industries they represent. Using it, research firms and key personnel can be identified, and the names and affiliations of analysts specializing in designated industries or U.S. and foreign companies can be determined. While the *Directory* is useful for identifying specialists, however, it does not list specific publications by name. Further, while such analyses contain a wealth of information, they are intended primarily for clients and until recently were not widely available to the public.

The introduction of *Corporate and Industry Research Reports (CIRR)* in 1982 greatly enhanced accessibility to these publications. *CIRR* is a microfiche collection of company, industry, and product-related reports originally issued by securities and institutional investment firms, copied and made available on microfiche. Publications range from newsletters that briefly assess the state of the economy or a specific industry to lengthy analyses of companies and industries. The publication described in figure 13.7, reprinted from the *CIRR Index*, is typical.

1986 Semiconductor Outlook: A Strenuous Climb Ahead.
Andrew J. Kessler; 02-14-86.
Technology Group; 11 p; Stats: EPS
   Estimates. Bookings & Billings.
   Industry Profitability Profile. For 7
   Companies-Sales, Cost of Sales,
   Restructuring Cost, Earnings,
   Dividends, Margins, Income, Tax .
   Rate, Gross Profit.
3674; Semiconductors & Related
   Devices.
Texas Instruments, Inc.; Advanced
   Micro Devices, Inc.
Fiche #PWI-04 (86-38) J.

Fig. 13.7. Typical entry, *Corporate and Industry Research Reports Index*. Reprinted with permission from the 1987 *Corporate and Industry Reports Index*.

The accompanying printed index to the collection, which can also be purchased separately, permits access by the issuing investment firms, company name, and by 600 different industry categories. The index is also available online and on compact disk. The electronic versions, in fact, contain abstracts, geographic locators, and product identification not included in the printed indexes.

Copies of investment reports can also be retrieved by using *Investext*, a full-text, online database that permits access to publications issued by investment houses, brokerage firms, and securities analysts.

Single-Industry Studies

For in-depth research on a particular industry, information contained in many of the multi-industry sources described above may be inadequate. Someone interested in the hotel business, for example, will discover that it is not even mentioned in the *Forbes* "Annual Report on American Industry," and that coverage in the *Industry Surveys and the U.S. Industrial Outlook* is brief. A single industry study may be the answer. Some are extremely expensive. Others, published by the federal government, trade associations, and other private organizations, are inexpensive or are sometimes even free.

Many of the privately published industry studies can be identified by using the sources listed in chapter 7. *Public Affairs Information Service Bulletin* and *What's New in Advertising and Marketing* list specific publications, while the *Encyclopedia of Business Information*

Sources identifies trade associations that may make industry information available to the public. Using it or the *Encyclopedia of Associations*, one can refer the researcher interested in hotels to the American Hotel and Motel Association in New York; if *PAIS* and *What's New in Advertising and Marketing* had been regularly searched for relevant industry publications, *Worldwide Lodging Industry, Trends in the Hotel Industry*, the *U.S. Lodging Industry*, and the *Annual Innkeeping Industry Financial Report* might be produced from the vertical file collection. Most of these publications are available to libraries for the asking, and they often contain information that is difficult to find elsewhere.

The guides to special issues of periodicals (see chapter 3) can also be used to identify special issues of trade journals and business periodicals that include statistical, directory, or forecast information for single industries.

The federal government is one of the most prolific publishers of single-industry studies. Government regulatory agencies produce detailed statistical analyses of the industries they monitor. The Interstate Commerce Commission, for example, annually compiles *Transport Statistics in the United States*, a comprehensive, multivolume series covering railroad companies, carriers by water, motor carriers, freight forwarders, and other types of transportation subject to the Interstate Commerce Act. The Departments of Commerce and Labor and the Bureau of the Census all regularly publish data that can be used when researching single industries, ranging from wage surveys to statistics on production and shipment. Libraries with a documents collection or with a depository nearby should not overlook this rich and often untapped information resource.

Finally, a number of the databases mentioned in chapter 8, including *FINDEX, PTS F&S Indexes, PTS PROMT*, and *Trade & Industry Index*, are useful for identifying sources of industry information.

OTHER PUBLICATIONS

Published financial and investment information is a highly marketable commodity. The quantity, variety, and expense of material in this field is almost overwhelming. This chapter concludes by examining a few of the general categories of investment materials not yet considered. It should be emphasized that it is a representative and not a comprehensive listing; for more specialized or esoteric publications or for a survey of the field as a whole, the appropriate chapters of Daniells's *Business Information Sources* should be consulted.

Stock Reporting Services

Stock reporting services, while somewhat narrower in scope and less detailed than the comprehensive investment information services described earlier, are useful for summary information and a quick overview of investments. Such publications are available in a variety of formats. Some are issued as looseleaf services, others as paperback books or booklets. The most widely used looseleaf services are those published by Standard & Poor's.

Standard & Poor's. **Stock Reports**. New York: Standard & Poor's. Looseleaf service, with weekly updates, 1973- . [Separate editions for the Amex, NYSE, and OTC]

The various editions of the *Stock Reports* provide current and background information on companies whose stock is traded on one of the national exchanges or on the over-the-counter market. A few companies traded on regional exchanges are also included. In each service, a two-page company report highlights the company's business, its sales and earnings, per share data, beta, and related information. A typical listing from the New York Stock Exchange edition is shown in figure 13.8 (see pages 338-39).

General Mills

976

NYSE Symbol GIS   Options on Pacific (Jan-Apr-Jul-Oct)   In S&P 500

Price	Range	P-E Ratio	Dividend	Yield	S&P Ranking	Beta
Jun. 17'87 56⅞	1987 58⅜-43	23	1.28	2.3%	A	0.71

Summary

Having completed its restructuring program in late 1985, GIS has major positions in the packaged food, restaurant and, to a lesser extent, specialty retailing industries. Earnings rebounded in fiscal 1985–6 and should trend higher in coming years, reflecting growth in all three business segments.

Current Outlook

Earnings for the fiscal year ending May, 1988 are expected to rise to $3.20 a share, from the $2.50 estimated for fiscal 1986–7.

The dividend of $0.32 quarterly is the minimum expectation over the near term.

Sales for fiscal 1987–8 are expected to continue to advance at a healthy pace, led by acceleration in cereals and restaurants. Mail order business, product line extensions and modest price hikes should also contribute to revenue growth of some 10%. Higher outlays for advertising and promotion activities are likely, but rising manufacturing efficiencies and tight controls on administrative costs should generate considerable profit expansion nonetheless. Despite stepped-up capital outlays, lower interest costs could be a positive factor. The company is also a major beneficiary of tax reform.

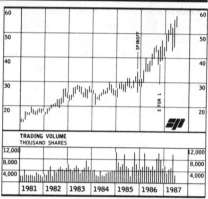

TRADING VOLUME
THOUSAND SHARES

Net Sales (Million $)

Quarter:	1987-8	1986-7	1985-6	1984-5
Aug.	---	1,193	1,068	1,017
Nov.	---	1,335	1,204	1,128
Feb.	---	1,311	1,154	1,069
May	---	---	1,161	1,070
	---	---	4,587	4,285

Sales from continuing operations for the nine months ended February 22, 1987 rose 14%, year to year, reflecting gains in all three major segments. Earnings from consumer foods advanced 26%, while restaurants were up 5.9% and specialty retailing more than doubled. Net earnings from continuing operations rose 28%, to $1.99 a share from $1.55 (adjusted), before income from discontinued furniture business of $0.10 a share, versus $0.04.

Common Share Earnings ($)

Quarter:	1987-8	1986-7	1985-6	1984-5
Aug.	E0.80	0.67	0.54	0.48
Nov.	E0.85	0.68	0.51	0.46
Feb.	E0.80	0.64	0.50	0.35
May	E0.75	E0.51	0.46	0.01
	E3.20	E2.50	2.01	1.29

Important Developments

Mar. '87—GIS attributed strong sales and earnings growth in the fiscal 1986–7 third quarter in large part to strong volume increases in the consumer foods segment. Restaurant operations were penalized by heavy start-up costs from new restaurants. The company opened 51 Canadian Red Lobster and Olive Garden restaurants in fiscal year to date, for a total of 591 units.

Next earnings report expected in mid-July.

Per Share Data ($)

Yr. End May 31	1987	1986	1985	1984	1983	1982	1981	1980	1979	¹1978
Book Value	NA	7.02	10.94	11.92	10.88	10.29	9.38	8.38	7.33	6.44
Earnings²	NA	2.01	1.29	2.49	2.45	2.23	1.95	1.69	1.46	1.29
Dividends	1.25	1.13	1.12	1.02	0.92	0.82	0.72	0.64	0.56	0.48½
Payout Ratio	NA	56%	86%	40%	36%	37%	37%	38%	38%	37%
Calendar Years	1986	1985	1984	1983	1982	1981	1980	1979	1978	1977
Prices—High	47⅜	34⅝	30	28⅞	27½	19⅞	15⅜	15¼	17⅛	17½
Low	28¼	23⅞	20⅞	22⅛	16½	13½	9½	11⅞	13⅜	13⅛
P/E Ratio—	NA	17-12	23-16	12-9	11-7	9-6	8-5	9-7	12-9	14-10

Data as orig. reptd. Adj. for stk. div(s). of 100% Nov. 1986. 1. Reflects merger or acquisition. 2. Bef. results of disc. opers. of +0.05 in 1986, −2.11 in 1985, +0.07 in 1978. NA-Not Available. E-Estimated.

Standard NYSE Stock Reports
Vol. 54/No. 120/Sec. 10

June 24, 1987

Standard & Poor's Corp.
25 Broadway, NY, NY 10004

976

General Mills, Inc.

Income Data (Million $)

Year Ended May 31	Revs.	Oper. Inc.	% Oper. Inc. of Revs.	Cap. Exp.	Depr.	Int. Exp.	Net Bef. Taxes	Eff. Tax Rate	[5]Net Inc.	% Net Inc. of Revs.
1986	4,587	477	10.4%	245	113	64.1	[4]324	43.3%	184	4.0%
[1]1985	4,285	442	10.3%	210	110	62.7	[4]196	41.1%	115	2.7%
1984	5,601	581	10.4%	282	129	67.0	[4]399	41.5%	233	4.2%
1983	5,551	591	10.6%	308	122	66.5	[4]410	40.2%	245	4.4%
1982	5,312	589	11.1%	287	107	82.9	[4]407	44.6%	[3]226	4.2%
1981	4,852	531	11.0%	247	100	[3]63.6	[4]374	47.5%	197	4.1%
1980	4,170	446	10.7%	197	81	48.6	[4]317	46.3%	170	4.1%
1979	3,745	372	9.9%	159	73	38.8	[4]264	44.3%	147	3.9%
[2]1978	3,243	333	10.3%	152	59	29.3	[4]245	47.5%	129	4.0%
1977	2,909	303	10.4%	117	48	26.7	[4]230	48.7%	117	4.0%

Balance Sheet Data (Million $)

May 31	Cash	Current Assets	Current Liab.	Ratio	Total Assets	Ret. on Assets	Long Term Debt	Common Equity	Total Cap.	% LT Debt of Cap.	Ret. on Equity
1986	190	804	763	1.1	2,086	7.7%	458	683	1,269	36.1%	21.4%
1985	67	1,287	1,057	1.2	2,663	4.2%	450	1,023	1,563	28.8%	10.4%
1984	66	1,390	1,145	1.2	2,858	8.3%	363	1,225	1,664	21.8%	19.6%
1983	58	1,358	1,123	1.2	2,944	8.9%	464	1,227	1,780	26.1%	20.4%
1982	33	1,259	1,048	1.2	2,702	9.0%	332	1,232	1,610	20.6%	19.0%
1981	39	1,076	739	1.5	2,301	9.1%	349	1,145	1,536	22.7%	18.1%
1980	39	986	570	1.7	2,012	8.8%	378	1,021	1,423	26.5%	17.6%
1979	97	936	495	1.9	1,835	8.5%	385	916	1,326	29.0%	16.9%
1978	20	788	503	1.6	1,613	8.4%	260	815	1,092	23.8%	16.7%
1977	22	713	415	1.7	1,447	8.4%	276	725	1,021	27.0%	17.1%

Data as orig. reptd. **1.** Excludes discontinued operations. **2.** Excl. disc. opers. and reflects merger or acquisition. **3.** Reflects accounting change. **4.** Incl. equity in earns. of nonconsol. subs. **5.** Bef. results of disc. opers. in 1985, 1978.

Business Summary

Having completed its restructuring program in late 1985, which included the spin-off of its toy and fashion units and the disposal of its nonapparel specialty retailing operations, General Mills is involved in the areas of packaged foods, restaurants and specialty retailing. Contributions by business segment in fiscal 1985-6 were:

	Sales	Profits
Consumer foods......................	67%	73%
Restaurants	23%	21%
Specialty retailing/other	10%	6%

Consumer foods operations include Big G ready-to-eat cereals, Betty Crocker desserts, main meals and side dishes, Yoplait yogurt, Bisquick baking mixes, Gold Medal flour, Nature Valley Granola Bars, Gorton's frozen seafood, and commercial foods.

The Restaurants segment is comprised of the Red Lobster seafood chain (389 units at fiscal 1985-6 year-end), York Steak Houses and York's Choices (114), and The Olive Garden Italian cafe-style concept (14).

Specialty retailing operations include The Talbots, a marketer of women's apparel through 84 stores and its mail-order business; and Eddie Bauer, which sells outdoor apparel and other products through 39 stores and catalogs.

Dividend Data

Dividends have been paid since 1898. A dividend reinvestment plan is available. A "poison pill" stock purchase right was issued in 1986.

Amt. of Div. $	Date Decl.	Ex-div. Date	Stock of Record	Payment Date
0.58	Jun. 23	Jul. 3	Jul. 10	Aug. 1'86
0.64	Sep. 22	Oct. 6	Oct. 10	Nov. 1'86
2-for-1	Sep. 22	Nov. 10	Oct. 10	Nov. 7'86
0.32	Dec. 16	Jan. 5	Jan. 9	Feb. 2'87
0.32	Feb. 23	Apr. 6	Apr. 10	May 1'87

Next dividend meeting: late Jun. '87.

Capitalization

Long Term Debt: $325,800,000.

Common Stock: 88,398,105 shs. (no par).
Institutions hold about 68%.
Shareholders of record: 25,377.

Office—9200 Wayzata Blvd., Minneapolis, Minn. 55440. Tel—(612) 540-2311. Chrmn & CEO—H. B. Atwater, Jr. Pres—M. H. Willes. VP-Secy—C. L. Whitehill. VP-Treas—D. E. Kelby. VP-Investor Contact—D. Belbas. Dirs—B. Ancker-Johnson, H. B. Atwater, Jr., F. C. Blodgett, R. M. Bressler, N. B. Grossman, J. R. Lee, L. W. Lehr, J. W. Morrison, G. A. Newkirk, W. F. Pounds, G. Putnam, E. S. Reid, M. D. Rose, A. R. Schulze, F. W. Smith, M. H. Willes, C. A. Wurtele. Transfer Agent & Registrar—First Trust Co, NYC, St. Paul, Minn. Incorporated in Delaware in 1928.

Information has been obtained from sources believed to be reliable, but its accuracy and completeness are not guaranteed.　Jane Collin

Fig. 13.8. Typical listing, Standard & Poor's *Stock Reports*. Reprinted with permission from Standard & Poor's *Stock Reports*.

Other stock reporting services are available in paperback and are considerably less expensive.

Moody's Investors Service. **Moody's Handbook of Common Stocks**. New York: The Service, 1965- . Quarterly.

Standard & Poor's. **Security Owner's Stock Guide**. New York: Standard & Poor's, 1947- . Monthly.

Moody's Handbook of Common Stocks, which is issued quarterly, gives basic financial information on over 900 stocks with high investor interest. The coverage of companies listed is somewhat less intensive than that offered by the *Stock Reports*, but the reviews of company background, recent developments, and investment prospects, supplemented by financial and operating statistics, make it particularly useful for a quick survey of the most popular stocks. Stocks are evaluated and assigned a rating of "High Grade," "Investment Grade," "Medium Grade," or "Speculative." The *Handbook*'s coverage of General Mills follows in figure 13.9.

The *Security Owner's Stock Guide* is a monthly summary of investment information on over 5,300 common and preferred stocks. Each listing features 48 different data items, including monthly high-low prices, volume traded, historical price ranges, dividends, earnings, and summaries of financial position. While the *Stock Guide* covers far more companies than *Moody's Handbook* and is updated more frequently, its format makes it less popular with many users, particularly novice investors. The *Guide* displays information for specific securities in a single line extending across two pages. People not familiar with it or the abbreviations used must frequently turn to the back of each issue for explanations of format and abbreviations. Although the emphasis in the *Guide* is on common and preferred stock, more than 425 mutual fund issues are also covered.

Investment Advisory Services

Investment advisory services are both more general and more specific than the stock reporting services described above. Their general coverage extends to economic and stock market conditions, discussing the past week's activity and predicting future stock market trends. They are more specific because they make judgments and recommendations regarding the investment prospects for particular stocks. The titles that follow are typical.

The Outlook. New York: Standard & Poor's, 1937- . Weekly.

Market Logic. Fort Lauderdale, Fla.: The Institute for Econometric Research, 1975- . Semimonthly.

Each issue of *The Outlook* generally considers stock trading during the past week and its outlook for the future, discusses the investment opportunities in a particular industry, and examines specific stocks. The analysis of Mobil Corporation, which follows in figure 13.10 (see page 342), is typical. Stocks that have been so analyzed are reexamined later in the regular "Current Advice on Earlier Selections" section.

Market Logic is another popular investment advisory service. It contains an abundance of information and advice, arranged according to an established format. The first page, for example, usually presents forecasts for expected stock market behavior, and the second reviews a number of trend indicators. Another page summarizes a recent article on investment research published in an academic journal, and still others present data on stocks comprising *Market Logic*'s "Master Portfolio." Like many similar investment advisory newsletters, *Market Logic* offers a telephone hotline service for more recent, supplementary information.

GENERAL MILLS, INC.

LISTED	SYM.	LTPS•	STPS•	IND. DIV.	REC. PRICE	RANGE (52-WKS.)	YLD.
NYSE	GIS	110.1	100.9	$1.28*	46	54 - 34	2.8%

INVESTMENT GRADE. THIS COMPANY IS PLACING GROWTH EMPHASIS PRIMARILY ON CONSUMER FOODS AND RESTAURANT OPERATIONS.

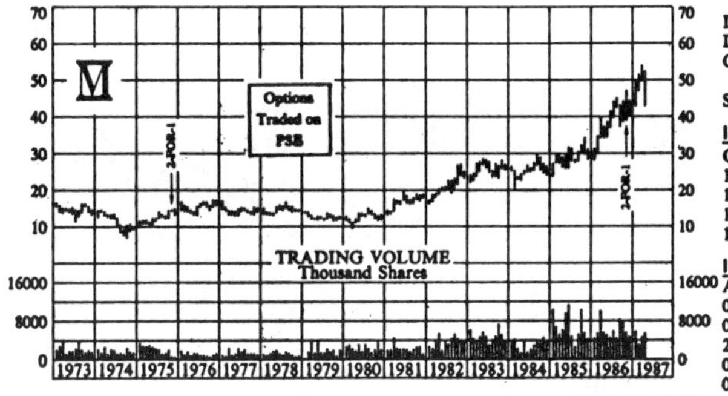

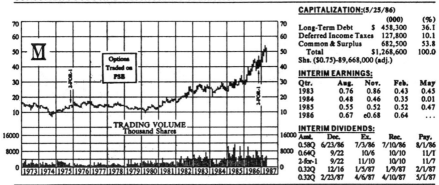

CAPITALIZATION:(5/25/86)

		(000)	(%)
Long-Term Debt	$	458,300	36.1
Deferred Income Taxes		127,800	10.1
Common & Surplus		682,500	53.8
Total		$1,268,600	100.0

Shs. ($0.75)-89,668,000 (adj.)

INTERIM EARNINGS:

Qtr.	Aug.	Nov.	Feb.	May
1983	0.76	0.86	0.43	0.45
1984	0.48	0.46	0.35	0.01
1985	0.55	0.52	0.52	0.47
1986	0.67	e0.68	0.64	...

INTERIM DIVIDENDS:

Amt.	Dec.	Ex.	Rec.	Pay.
0.58Q	6/23/86	7/3/86	7/10/86	8/1/86
0.64Q	9/22	10/6	10/10	11/1
2-for-1	9/22	11/10	10/10	11/7
0.32Q	12/16	1/5/87	1/9/87	2/1/87
0.32Q	2/23/87	4/6/87	4/10/87	5/1/87

BACKGROUND:

General Mills is a producer and marketer of consumer goods and services in three business areas: Consumer Foods, accounting for 67% of sales and (73% of operating profit), include breakfast and snack products, mixes and convenience foods, frozen seafood, yogurt, flour and frozen foods. Brand names include CHEERIOS, WHEATIES, LUCKY CHARMS, TOTAL, POP SECRET HAMBURGER HELPER, FRUIT CORNERS, BETTY CROCKER, BISQUICK, GOLD MEDAL, GORTON'S and YOPLAIT; Restaurants, 23% (21%); include Red Lobster specialty seafood restaurants and the Olive Garden Italian restaurants. Specialty Retailing 10% (6%) includes men's and women's apparel through Talbots and Eddie Bauer.

RECENT DEVELOPMENTS:

For the thirteen weeks ended 2/22/87, income from continuing operations advanced 27% to $56.9 million. Revenues were up 16%. Comparisons were made with restated prior-year figures. Consumer foods performed strongly due to volume gains and increased productivity. Operating profits were down 5% for the restaurant group due to heavy start-up costs for Canadian Red Lobster and Olive Garden restaurants. Specialty retailing achieved strong growth in the retail and mail order operations of both Talbots and Eddie Bauer.

PROSPECTS:

Earnings are expected to continue to increase. The Company has a strong base of established businesses, as well as many major growth businesses. Large marketing expenditures and new product introductions will continue to aid consumer food results. Despite the continued rapid expansion of the restaurant group in both domestic and international markets, operating profits are expected to rise. Specialty retailing will also expand and should benefit from the increasing number of consumers who shop by mail order catalogs.

STATISTICS:

YEAR	GROSS REVS. ($mill.)	OPER. PROFIT MARGIN %	RET. ON EQUITY %	NET INCOME ($mill.)	WORK CAP. ($mill.)	SENIOR CAPITAL ($mill.)	SHARES (000)	EARN. PER SH.$	DIV. PER SH.$	DIV. PAY. %	PRICE RANGE	P/E RATIO	AVG. YIELD %
a													
77	3,243	8.5	15.8	b128.8	285.1	259.9	100,470	b1.29	0.44	34	17½ - 13⅛	11.8	2.9
78	3,745	8.8	16.0	147.0	441.6	384.0	100,518	1.46	0.52	36	17⅛ - 13⅜	10.4	3.4
79	4,170	8.8	16.7	170.0	416.3	377.5	100,460	1.69	0.60	36	15¼ - 11¾	8.0	4.5
80	4,852	8.9	17.2	196.6	337.3	348.6	100,698	1.95	0.68	35	15¼ - 9½	6.4	5.5
81	5,312	9.1	18.3	225.5	210.7	331.9	100,572	2.23	0.78	35	19¾ - 13⅜	7.4	4.7
82	5,551	8.4	20.0	245.1	235.6	464.0	95,600	2.45	0.87	36	27⅜ - 16½	9.0	4.0
83	5,600	8.1	19.1	233.4	244.5	362.6	90,528	2.49	0.97	39	28⅞ - 22⅛	10.2	3.8
c84	4,285	7.7	11.3	b115.4	229.5	449.5	88,882	b1.29	1.07	60	30 - 20⅞	14.3	4.2
85	4,586	7.9	26.9	183.5	41.6	458.3	89,668	2.06	1.13	55	31½ - 21	12.7	4.3
86									1.18*		47¼ - 28¼		3.1

•Short-Term Price Score — Long-Term Price Score; see page 4a. STATISTICS ARE AS ORIGINALLY REPORTED. Adjusted for 2-for-1 split, 11/86. a-Fiscal year ends 5/31 of following year. b-From continuing operations. c-Reflects redeployment program. e-Includes gain of $5.2 million ($0.06 a sh.) from insurance settlement and an accounting change.

INCORPORATED:
June 20, 1928 – Delaware

PRINCIPAL OFFICE:
9200 Wayzata Blvd.
P.O. Box 1113
Minneapolis, Minn. 55440
Tel.: (612) 540-2311

ANNUAL MEETING:
Third Monday in September

NUMBER OF STOCKHOLDERS:
29,300

TRANSFER AGENT(S):
First Trust Company, Inc., NY, NY;
St. Paul, MN

REGISTRAR(S):
First Trust Company, Inc., NY, NY;
St. Paul, MN

INSTITUTIONAL HOLDINGS:
No. of Institutions: 378
Shares Held: 58,931,494

OFFICERS:
Chmn. & Ch. Exec. Off,
H.B. Atwater, Jr.
President
M.H. Willes
Sr. V.P., Gen. Coun. & Sec.
C.L. Whitehill
Sr. V.P. & Treas.
D.E. Kelby
Investor Contact
D. Belbas

Fig. 13.9. Typical listing, *Moody's Handbook of Common Stocks*. Reprinted with permission from the summer 1987 edition of *Moody's Handbook of Common Stocks*.

Mobil Corp.: attractive core investment

This major integrated international oil company is well positioned to take advantage of the fundamentally stronger oil price environment we expect to see over the next few years, while also benefiting near term as costs, prices and inventories come into better balance.

Through an aggressive program of cost reductions, staff cuts and internal consolidations, MOB has lowered its breakeven levels. At the same time, it has reduced debt incurred in the 1984 $5.7 billion acquisition of Superior Oil via sale of non-essential assets and marginal properties.

Beyond the improving industry fundamentals and MOBIL's important access to Saudi crude supplies as one of the four Aramco partners, representation in worldwide markets affords the company a large inventory of exploration and production properties that are profitable even during periods of low oil prices.

MOBIL's streamlined refining and marketing operations provide an assured market for its production, with retail gasoline outlets that occupy leading positions in important markets.

Earnings earlier this year were hurt by relatively low oil prices (though quotes were up sharply from their mid-1986 lows), while the refining business labored under stiff comparisons with unsustainably high year-earlier levels. With oil prices climbing, exploration and production earnings should strengthen, and refining/marketing margins (pinched by the lag in product prices relative to the rise in crude prices) should widen as the year progresses. Increasing profitability in the chemicals segment—initially because of lower feedstock costs and subsequently benefiting as healthy demand permits the recovery (pass-along) of higher costs—should also bolster the full-year performance.

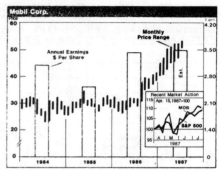

Meanwhile, the Montgomery Ward retail operation has shown a dramatic turnaround, thanks to concentration in its more profitable specialty stores. This bodes well even if the chain is eventually sold.

Over the longer term, MOBIL's efficiency in replacing reserves, financial flexibility and diversification of geographic and operational exposure should make the company an increasingly important player in a still-consolidating, essential industry. Toward the end of the decade, MOBIL's strong natural gas base in the U.S. and Canada should provide a growing contribution to earnings as the North American gas surplus dissipates.

The stock (MOB, 53, NYSE), selling at 15 times estimated 1987 earnings of $3.50 and yielding 4.2%, is a reasonably valued total-return investment for conservative investors seeking representation in the strategically situated oil industry. The shares are being added to Group 1 of the Master List.

—*Joanne Legomsky*

Fig. 13.10. Typical listing, *The Outlook*. Reprinted with permission from the July 22, 1987 issue of *The Outlook*.

Charting

Most of the reference sources that have been discussed in this chapter favor what is called the *fundamental approach* to investment analysis—that is, basing investment decisions upon the financial analysis of a company and examination of its management, the products or services which it sells, and the general well-being of the industry of which it is a part. These data are used to help the investor make judgments about the worth of a particular stock.

Not every investor uses the fundamental approach. Some favor *technical analysis*, in which the focus is on timing—when to buy and sell stocks. Technical analysts follow fluctuations in stock prices and volume of trading rather than the considerations mentioned above, and depend heavily on charts to help make investment decisions. Charts, the technicians contend, make it possible to tell in a glance what a stock's past performance has been and to make informed judgments about its future prospects.

In some libraries, a financial collection that does not include at least one charting service may be considered inadequate by patrons who are technically oriented. Although charts are included in several of the publications already mentioned — *Value Line, Moody's Handbook of Common Stocks,* and the stock reporting services — there are some sources that confine themselves to graphic presentation of stock and industry data. Typical of these are the bimonthly *OTC Chart Manual* and Standard & Poor's *Trendline's Current Market Perspectives,* a monthly publication that includes charts for over 1,400 stocks. (For *Trendline's* coverage of General Mills, see figure 13.11.) Charting services are regularly advertised in the *Wall Street Journal* and other financial newspapers.

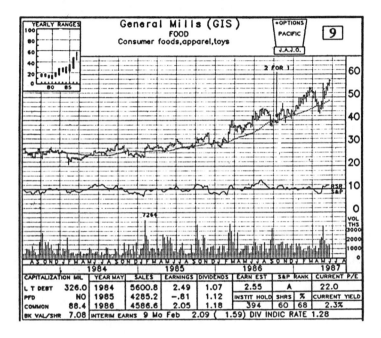

Fig. 13.11. Typical company chart, *Trendline's Current Market Perspectives.* Reprinted with permission from *Trendline's Current Market Perspectives,* June 1987.

Obsolete Securities

Occasionally, librarians are asked to help patrons determine the value of shares in companies that are no longer in business. Someone who has unearthed a yellowing stock certificate for 200 shares of Yum-Yum International Restaurant may want to know whether to plan a world cruise or use it as kindling. A search of the standard business directories and comprehensive investment services may fail to yield information on the elusive Yum-Yum Restaurant chain. There are, however, several sources of information on companies that are no longer in business.

Financial Stock Guide Service. **Directory of Obsolete Securities**. Jersey City, N.J.: The Service, 1927-. Annual.

The *Directory* lists companies and banks whose original identities have been lost because of name changes, mergers, acquisition, dissolution, reorganization, bankruptcy, or charter cancellation. Yum-Yum International Restaurant is listed in the *Directory*. "Charter cancelled and declared inoperative and void for nonpayment of taxes,"[8] the listing indicates, and assesses the current value of Yum-Yum common stock at one cent per share.

ONLINE DATABASES AND DISKS

Investment-related databases fall into two main categories: those that provide data for fundamental and/or technical analysis of stocks and other securities, and those that actually allow investors to instruct their brokers to make investments for them. Neither compact nor floppy disk databases permit investment transactions, but they do allow searchers to gather the information necessary to make informed investment decisions.

Online Databases

There are few online business databases whose contents are not directly relevant to investors. *ABI/Inform* and *Management Contents*, for example, permit access to articles on corporate policy and management decisions, while *Trade & Industry Index* and the Predicasts databases include information on products and industries. *Newsnet* offers the full text of selected investment newsletters, while *Investext* does the same for financial research reports. Almost every vendor offers an array of relevant databases.

One such vendor, Dow Jones News/Retrieval, is a leading supplier of financial information. It offers a series of business and financial databases, many of which are based upon its own publications. Some of its databases present stock price quotes and the Dow Jones averages, while others offer highlights or the full text of articles from *Barron's* and the *Wall Street Journal*. Other useful files include *Disclosure II*, which contains extracts from 10-K reports, company profiles, and related SEC data; *Media General Financial Services; Merrill Lynch Research Service;* and *Corporate Earnings Estimator. Words of Wall Street*, one of the investment dictionaries described in the preceding chapter, is also available online, as are the verbatim transcripts of the popular television program, "Wall Street Week." Dow Jones is, accordingly, a key supplier of online investment information. Other vendors supply similar data, but in many instances may offer fewer specialized databases from which to choose.

Some online databases permit investing. Generally, such files require that each individual user establish an investment account with a designated discount brokerage firm. Upon being assigned an account number, the individual can use the database to request the broker to execute buy and sell transactions for stocks and options. In addition, these databases can be used to maintain online, personalized portfolio records that are automatically revised as security prices and dividends change. Although libraries are not ordinarily involved in providing access to online investment services, they can collect publications that enable patrons to learn more about them. One such source is Thomas Meyers' *The Dow Jones Guide to On-Line Investing* (Homewood, Ill.: Dow Jones-Irwin, 1986), which describes databases and services offered by 13 different vendors of investing services and discusses general requirements for using such files.

Compact Disk Databases

Compact disk databases have become increasingly popular with business researchers and investors. Although their cost precludes their acquisition by some libraries, they increasingly are being offered by large public and academic business libraries and some special libraries.

The most widely held of such databases is *Compact Disclosure*, a CD-ROM version of the online *Disclosure II* offered through many database vendors. It permits searching in two different ways: by the DIALOG Emulation Mode, which is appropriate for librarians and other experienced DIALOG searchers, and the Easy Menu Mode, which is aimed at end-user searchers.

Using the Easy Menu Mode, searchers are presented with a series of menus, each offering a number of choices. One of the first menus, reproduced in figure 13.12, enables searchers to specify the types of information in which they are most interested.

```
IMMMMMMMMMMMMMMMMMMMMMMMMMMMMMMMMM;
:   Would you like to search by:    :
LMMMMMMMMMMMMMMMMMMMMMMMMMMMMMMMMMM9
: Company Name, Ticker or Number  :
: Type of Business                :
: Geographic Area                 :
: Annual Financial Information     :
: Quarterly Financial Information :
: Funds Source/Use Information     :
: Stock Price Information          :
: Ratio Analysis Information       :
: Owners, Officers, Directors      :
: Shares/Employees                 :
: Exchange(NYS,AMS,OTH,NMS,NDQ) , :
: More Choices                    :
HMMMMMMMMMMMMMMMMMMMMMMMMMMMMMMMMM<
```

Fig. 13.12. Typical menu, *Compact Disclosure.* Copyright © 1987 Disclosure Information Group.

Had the searcher chosen "Type of Business" from the menu displayed in figure 13.12, he or she would have been asked to specify whether subsequent searching should be by SIC code, primary SIC code, a textual description of the business, or the business segment. Each step of the search offers new choices, and culminates in the retrieval of the information being sought.

Compact Disclosure is popular with researchers because it is easy to use. In most instances, libraries absorb subscription costs and users have access to the database at no cost or for considerably less than an online search of *Disclosure II* would cost. Futher, because *Compact Disclosure* allows users to print out the full text of records retrieved, it offers a welcome alternative to many researchers who would otherwise have to look for the same information using the microfiche version of 10-K reports sold by Disclosure and other companies.

There are, however, some drawbacks to *Compact Disclosure*. It contains only extracts from the 10-K reports; some data are not included. Further, while useful for current information, it does not offer access to retrospective data. The researcher who needs to examine 10-K information for the past 10 years, for example, may still need to consult the reports on microfiche. As a result, most libraries must continue to subscribe to 10-K reports on microfiche even if they also choose to acquire *Compact Disclosure*.

Another producer, Datext, offers a whole family of CD-ROM business products. The most popular is *Datext Corporate Information Database*, an amalgam of many different databases. It includes the complete contents of *Disclosure II* and *Investext*, selected abstracts from *PTS PROMT* and *ABI/Inform,* biographical information from *Who's Who in Finance and Industry*, and stock price and trading data from Media General's *The Market File*. While *Datext* has much broader coverage than *Compact Disclosure*, it is also considerably more expensive.

Floppy Disks

Finally, an array of investment-related products are available on floppy disk. As was mentioned in the preceding chapter, however, most are more appropriate for home rather than library use.

NOTES

[1]New York Stock Exchange, *NYSE Factbook, 1987* (New York: The Exchange, 1987), 5.

[2]The pamphlets included in the "Investors Information Kit" are *Getting Help When You Invest, Glossary, Understanding Financial Statements*, and *Understanding Stocks and Bonds*. In 1987, the kit cost $4.00. It can be ordered from:

> Publications Office
> New York Stock Exchange
> 11 Wall Street
> New York, NY 10005

[3]To request a free copy of the annual *NASDAQ Fact Book*, write to:

> National Association of Securities Dealers, Inc.
> 1735 K Street, N.W.
> Washington, D.C. 20006

[4]Among the companies exempted from this registration requirement are those offerings that are limited to residents of the states in which the companies themselves are located, and companies proposing private offerings to a limited number of persons.

[5]"Beware of What You Don't See," *Forbes* 139, no. 6 (March 23, 1987): 102.

[6]"This Year's Annual Reports: Show Business As Usual," *Business Week* 2993 (April 13, 1987): 42.

[7]For a comparative review of these investment information services, see Thomas Rohmiller, "Through the Bull to the Bear Facts: A Comparison of the Library Packages of Moody's and Standard & Poor's," *Reference Services Review* (January/March 1981), 27-31.

[8]Financial Stock Guide Service, *Directory of Obsolete Securities* (Jersey City, N.J.: The Service, 1987), 1260.

This broker calls his customer for four straight years and each year puts him into some dreadful stock that drops right through the floor. The fifth year, the customer calls the broker and says, "Look, I don't know about all these stocks we've been buying—I think maybe I'd be better off in bonds." "Yeah, sure," says the broker, "but what do I know about bonds?"

—Old joke, quoted by Andrew Tobias, *The Only Investment Guide You'll Ever Need*

14

BONDS AND OTHER FIXED-INCOME SECURITIES

The preceding chapter examined stocks, the markets on which they are traded, and the use of stock-related publications by investors. This chapter deals in a similar way with another broad category of investments: bonds and fixed-income securities.

How do these securities differ from stocks? Stocks are equity securities; they represent partial ownership in the issuing organization. *Fixed-income securities*, on the other hand, are *debt securities*, representing money lent to the issuing organization for a designated time period. They are, in effect, IOUs.

Usually, the issuing organization agrees not only to repay the principal at some future date, but also to make regular, fixed interest payments for the use of the money. Some fixed-income securities are long-term loans, others are short term. Bonds fall into the first category.

BONDS

Bonds are long-term, fixed-income debt securities issued by corporations and governments to raise money. They can be as staid as U.S. savings bonds or as speculative as Mexican petrobonds paid in pesos, but most share certain characteristics. Bonds usually mature no earlier than 10 years after they are issued, and some are issued for as long as 30 years.

When a bond reaches maturity, the issuing organization is required to repay the *principal*, or *face value*, to the bondholder. Usually bonds are issued in $1,000 denominations or in multiples of $1,000. There are, for example, bonds with face values of $5,000 or even $10,000; others, called "baby bonds," have face values of only $100 or $500. Most, however, come in $1,000 denominations.

347

Interest

Bondholders are entitled to interest, usually paid semiannually. The amount of interest paid is determined in advance and is a fixed percentage of the face value of the bond. A 7⅛ percent $1,000 bond will earn its holder $72.50 per year, a 5½ percent bond, $55.00. The important thing to remember is that the rate of interest is set at the time the bonds are first sold to the public and remains fixed for the duration of the bond's life. While the prime interest rate may skyrocket or plummet according to the state of the economy, the rate of interest paid on a bond remains the same for its entire life span. As a result, bonds provide a steady, predictable income.

With certain bonds, interest is collected by clipping one of the coupons attached to the bond and presenting it for payment. Thus, the interest paid on a particular bond is often called its *coupon rate* or *coupon*, and bonds with coupons attached are called coupon bonds. They are also called *bearer bonds* because the holder of the bond is presumed to be its owner. If someone loses a bearer bond, the finder can sell it or hold it, collect interest on it, and redeem it at maturity.

In contrast, a *registered bond* is registered in the name of the bondholder, and only that person can sell it, receive semiannual interest payments on it, or redeem it. No coupons are attached to a registered bond; interest payments are automatically sent to the bondholder when they come due. Most bonds in the United States are now registered.

Prices

Although the interest rate is locked in for the life of the bond, the price of a bond fluctuates in much the same way as stock prices. What causes bond prices to rise or fall? Interest rates are the key.

When general interest rates rise, the interest rates on new bond issues must also be higher in order to attract investors. Interest rates on bonds already outstanding, however, are fixed and cannot be changed. As a result, an adjustment to the new interest rate takes place through a change in the prices of the outstanding bonds. When interest rates rise, the prices of outstanding bonds tend to decline. Conversely, if interest rates fall, bond prices rise.

If, for example, an investor paid $1,000 (*face value* or *par*) for an XYZ Corporation bond that paid 5 percent and subsequently the XYZ Corporation offered 7 percent interest on its new bond issues, the resale market for the 5 percent bond selling at par (or $1,000) would be nonexistent. Why accept 5 percent interest when 7 percent is available? If, however, the 5 percent bond was offered for $850 instead of $1,000, the bond would be more attractive because the buyer would be earning annual interest of $50 on an $850 investment as well as a $150 profit when the bond matured.

Bonds selling for less than face value are said to be selling at a *discount*, while bonds selling at a *premium* are those selling for more than face value. Thus investment advice to buy "deep discounted bonds" simply means to buy bonds selling for considerably less than their face value.

Yield

There are two different ways of expressing yield, or return on an investment. The first, *current yield*, measures the annual return on the price that the buyer actually pays for the bond. Current yield is derived by dividing the interest rate by the price paid for the bond. If the bond was bought at par ($1,000), the interest rate and current yield are the same. If, however, the bond was bought at premium or discount, the current yield will be different from the interest rate.

The 5 percent XYZ Corporation bond purchased for $850, for example, has a current yield of 5.88 percent (5 divided by 850), while a 9 percent bond bought at premium for $1,050 would have a current yield of 8.57 percent (9 divided by 1,050). Current yields are calculated and included in the bond tables in financial newspapers.

Yield to maturity, the other expression of bond yield, is the effective rate of return to the bondholder if the bond is held to maturity. It takes into account the amount paid for the bond, its par value, the interest rate, and the length of time to maturity. For a given interest rate, maturity, and price, yield to maturity can be determined by using tables from reference books commonly called basis books or yield books. Although libraries generally do not include these highly specialized sources in their collections, yield to maturity is one of the data elements included in major bond publications such as Standard & Poor's *Bond Guide* and *Moody's Bond Record*, which are discussed later in this chapter.

Call Provisions

When an investor buys bonds, he takes the risk that the issuing organization may default on interest payments or on repayment of the principal, or that spiraling inflation and general interest rates may make his long-term, fixed-interest bonds a poor investment. He may also have to risk recall of his bonds by the issuing organization before they reach maturity. This may result from two kinds of recall provisions: sinking fund and call.

A *sinking fund* is a pool of money put aside by the issuing organization so that, each year, it can recall and retire a certain percentage of the bond issue in advance of the actual maturity date. The rationale behind a sinking fund provision is that it is easier to retire the bond issue gradually than it is to pay the entire amount at maturity. The issuer usually has the option of buying the bonds on the open market or recalling them from bondholders. If the market price of the bonds is higher than the sinking fund call price, the issuer is entitled to recall a certain number of bonds from the bondholders, and to redeem them at the stated sinking fund price. Usually there is a 5- or 10-year grace period before the sinking fund provision goes into effect.

Although establishment of a sinking fund provision at least theoretically reduces the likelihood of default on repayment of principal, it can also work to the disadvantage of the investor whose bonds are redeemed before maturity, because the prospect of a steady source of fixed-interest income has been eliminated. As a result, one of the things that many prospective investors want to know about a particular bond is whether or not it contains a sinking fund provision. Many printed investment sources identify bond issues containing sinking fund provisions with the letters *s.f.*

Other bonds have call provisions which permit the issuer, after a lapse of 5 or 10 years, to redeem the bonds at any time prior to their maturity, at a set price. Such bonds are labeled, appropriately, as *callable bonds*. Generally the issuer will exercise the call provision whenever the fixed interest rate for their outstanding bond issues is significantly higher than the interest rate at which they could issue new bonds. Bonds that are called in under this provision are redeemed at face value plus a fixed payment, often equal to one year's interest rate. Call prices are included for callable bonds in *Moody's Bond Record,* Standard & Poor's *Bond Guide*, and many other investment publications.

Ratings

Close attention is paid by investors to the credit ratings assigned to bonds. The ratings most commonly consulted are those prepared by Moody's and Standard & Poor's, and they represent an assessment of the issuing organization's ability to pay interest and repay principal to bondholders. Not every bond is rated, but the major ones are.

Slightly different rating symbols are used by Moody's and Standard & Poor's, as evidenced by their rating categories shown in figure 14.1. Lists and explanations of the various bond rating symbols are contained in many of the Moody's and Standard & Poor's publications described later in this chapter.

General Description	Moody's	Standard & Poor's
Highest Quality	Aaa	AAA
High Quality	Aa	AA
Upper Medium Grade	A	A
Medium Grade	Baa	BBB
Somewhat Speculative	Ba	BB
Low Grade; Speculative	B	B
Poor Grade, Default Possible	Caa	CCC & CC
Default, Partial Recovery Possible	Ca	C
Default, Recovery Unlikely	C	D

Fig. 14.1. Bond rating categories.

Although each publisher is highly respected, some claim that Moody's surpasses Standard & Poor's in the value of its rating of municipal bond issues, while Standard & Poor's is more highly regarded for its rating of corporate bonds. In most instances, though, both services either assign the same rating to an issue or are within one rating level of each other. Neither service claims to be infallible. Both, for example, granted Penn Central high ratings just weeks before it declared bankruptcy.

Nevertheless, the ratings are useful. They give prospective investors an indication of the risk attached to each bond, and carry enough weight so that bonds with higher ratings (that is, those with less risk) have lower yields than bonds with lower ratings. New issues with the same maturity and face value may offer different interest rates, based on their ratings. A triple-A bond will have a lower coupon rate than a double-A bond, and so on. Ratings can change, and if they do, announcements are featured in financial newspapers and other publications.

If the rating assigned to an outstanding bond changes, its price in the resale market (discussed in the next section) will reflect this change. A lower rating will usually result in the lowering of a bond's price, and vice versa.

Secondary Bond Market

Not all investors hold newly issued bonds to maturity. As a result, there is a secondary arena for bonds, with most of it centered in the over-the-counter market. The OTC market is the primary market for trading of outstanding government and municipal bonds, and for many corporate bonds as well. The New York Stock Exchange lists about 3,800 bonds, most of them corporate, although some government, international bank, and foreign bonds are also traded. Finally, some trading of bonds is also done on the American Stock Exchange. Price and related trading information for many of the bonds traded in these markets are included in financial newspapers and bond-related publications and will be covered later in this chapter.

MONEY MARKET INSTRUMENTS

Bonds are long-term debt obligations. Corresponding short-term loans to various borrowers — federal and local governments, corporations, and banks — are known collectively as money market instruments. These short-term obligations are issued by organizations with high credit ratings, are highly liquid (easily convertible into cash), and are generally of less than one year's duration. Typical money market instruments include Treasury bills, commercial paper (short-term IOUs issued by corporations), and commercial bank certificates of deposit.[1]

Many of these securities require a substantial cash outlay and are thus of greater interest to institutional investors than to all but the wealthiest individuals. Commercial paper and commercial bank certificates of deposit, for example, are sold in minimum denominations of $100,000. When interest rates are high, however, there is widespread interest in money market funds, which are a type of mutual fund. For as little as $500, an investor can buy into a money market fund, which pools investors' money and buys these expensive short-term obligations. Money market funds are discussed briefly in the next chapter.

GOVERNMENT SECURITIES

The federal government issues a wide range of marketable securities.[2] Some, which are direct government obligations, are issued by the Treasury Department. These include Treasury bills, notes, and bonds. Others, such as the issues of federal agencies and government-sponsored agencies, are not considered direct obligations but enjoy credit ratings almost as impressive as those assigned to Treasury issues. The high rating given to government securities is based on the federal government's power to tax and print money; risk of default on a U.S. government bond is nonexistent. As a result, government securities offer lower interest rates than do corporate debt obligations, which compensate for their greater risk by offering higher interest rates.

Trading of government securities is active, with billions of dollars worth of short- and long-term securities bought and sold during a normal business day. Most of the trading of government issues is done in the vast over-the-counter market, although some trading is also done on the major exchanges. Trading activity is reported in the *Wall Street Journal*, in other financial newspapers and periodicals, and in the financial sections of many local newspapers.

Treasury Issues

One of the ways in which the Treasury Department finances the nation's debt is by issuing marketable securities. Three main types of Treasury issues, distinguished by their varying maturities, can be identified: Treasury bills, Treasury notes, and Treasury bonds.

Treasury bills (or *T-bills* or *bills*) are short-term securities, issued in maturities of 3, 6, and 12 months. T-bills do not pay interest. Instead, they are issued at a discount of their $10,000 face value. An investor may purchase a T-bill for $9,750, for example, and redeem it at maturity for the full $10,000, earning $250. The price at which the bills are discounted is determined by the market, more specifically by the investors and dealers who submit competitive bids at weekly and/or monthly auctions of Treasury bills. The highest bids determine the discount. Most of the competitive bidders are dealers in government securities, commercial banks, and other institutional investors.[3]

There is an active secondary market for T-bills, and the *Wall Street Journal* and many other newspapers report the daily prices of Treasury bills. The quotations look like those in figure 14.2.

U.S. Treas. Bills Mat. date[1]	Bid	Asked Discount	Yield
-1987-			
6-25	4.21	4.05	4.11
7-2	5.28[2]	5.24[3]	5.32[4]
7-9	5.54	5.50	5.59
7-16	5.28	5.24	5.33

1. <u>Mat. date</u>. Bills are listed chronologically in order of their maturity date, with those maturing soonest listed first.
2. <u>Bid</u>. Prices for Treasury bills are quoted as a percent of discount from their face value. The bid is the yield someone selling a bill would earn. Someone selling a $10,000 T-bill maturing on July 2nd, for example, would earn a yield of 5.28%.
3. <u>Asked</u>. The yield the buyer would earn. Someone buying a T-bill maturing on July 2nd, for example, would earn a yield of 5.24%.
4. <u>Yield</u>. Investment yield, the feature to be used in comparing the return on T-bills with other types of investments.

Fig. 14.2. Newspaper quotations for Treasury bills.

The table in figure 14.2 indicates that the buyer of a bill maturing on July 16th, for example, earns 5.24 percent; that is, the asked price provides a yield of 5.24 percent. The 5.28 in the *bid* column refers to the yield someone selling the bills would reap. Actual dollar prices are not quoted in this table, but can be determined by using a formula that takes into account discount rate and the number of days to maturity.[4] The last column, *Yield*, is investment yield, the figure to be used in comparing the return on Treasury bills with other types of investments.

Treasury notes and *bonds* have longer maturities than T-bills and are interest bearing. Bonds and notes come in denominations of $1,000, $5,000, $10,000, $100,000, and $1,000,000. Treasury notes range in maturity from 1 to 10 years, most falling in the 2- to 5-year range. Treasury bonds, on the other hand, generally mature in 10 years or more.

The Treasury follows essentially the same auction procedures for new note and bond issues as it does for bills. An offering is announced in advance of the issue date, and investors submit either competitive or noncompetitive bids and await the results.

Treasury notes and bonds are traded actively in the over-the-counter market, and OTC bond and note prices are included in the financial pages of most newspapers. The sample in figure 14.3 contains most information likely to be found in a government securities table.

The interest earned on Treasury securities is subject to federal income tax, but exempt from state and local taxes. The same exemptions apply to federal agency issues.

| Treasury Bonds and Notes | | | | | |
Rate	Mat. Date[2]	Bid	Asked	Bid Chg.	Yld.
113/4s[1]	1992 Apr	114.25	115.1	-.3	7.93
133/4s	1992 May n[3]	122.30	123.2	-.3	7.97[8]
71/4s	1992 Aug[4]	99.23[5]	99.31[6]	-.2[7]	7.26
85/8s	1993 Aug	102.17	102.25	-.5	8.04

1. Rate. Interest or coupon rate. The first security listed pays 11 3/4% interest.
2. Mat. Date. Maturity date, or the year and month in which the security matures. Securities maturing soonest are listed first.
3. N. The "n" following the maturity date indicates that the security is a Treasury note and not a Treasury bond.
4. [No n]. The absence of an "n" indicates that the security is a Treasury bond.
5. Bid. Dealer's bid quotation, or the price at which an investor could expect to sell the security. Prices in both the "Bid" and "Asked" columns are quoted in points, with one point equalling $10 for each $1,000 of face value. A quote of 105 means that a $1,000 security is selling at premium for $1,050, while a quote of 85 means that it is discounted at $850. Points are divided into 32nds so that any number to the right of the decimal point in the bid or asked column should be construed to mean 32nds rather than 10ths of a percent. The bid price for the 11 3/4% Treasury bond is 114.25. If it had a face value of $1,000, the bid price would be $1,147.81. (One thirty-second equals $.3125 for each $1,000 of face value; 25/32nds equal $7.8125.)[5]
6. Asked. The price at which the investor can buy the security, also expressed in 32nds of a point. The 7 1/4% Treasury bond is selling for 99 and 31/32nds or, if it is a $1,000 bond, $999.69.
7. Bid Chg. Change in bid price from the previous business day. Once again, the number to the right of the decimal point refers to 32nds.
8. Yld. Yield to maturity, which takes into account the price paid (the "Asked" column), the interest rate, and the length of time to maturity. This figure is highly useful to the potential investor who wants to know what kind of return he can expect. The yield to maturity on the note maturing in May, 1992, for example, is 7.97%, considerably less that its 13 3/4% coupon rate.

Fig. 14.3. Newspaper table, Treasury bonds and notes.

Federal Agency Issues

A wide range of government agencies, including federal agencies such as the Small Business Administration and the U.S. Postal Service, and government-sponsored enterprises, such as the Federal Home Loan Mortgage Corporation, are authorized to issue debt securities. Prime among these agency issues, or *agencies*, as they are collectively known, are those issued by the following organizations.

Banks for Cooperatives (Co-ops)

Federal Home Loan Mortgage Corporation (FHLMC or Freddie Mac)

Federal Intermediate Credit Bank (FICB)

Federal National Mortgage Association (FNMA or Fannie Mae)

Government National Mortgage Association (GNMA or Ginnie Mae)

Moody's Municipal & Government Manual describes agency issues in some detail. For each listing, fairly detailed financial and organizational information is given, including description and rating of outstanding debt obligations. A more superficial list of federal agencies and government-sponsored organizations, which does not include information on specific debt obligations, but which is, nonetheless, useful, can be ordered from the Federal Reserve Bank of New York.[6] It will tell the prospective investor the minimum investment required, and will give the address and telephone number of the organization itself, identify various types of distributors of the security, and indicate whether or not principal and interest are fully guaranteed by the federal government. Daily quotations for many agency issues are included in the *Wall Street Journal* and other newspapers. The format used for reporting is very similar to that used for Treasury notes and bonds.

MUNICIPAL ISSUES

Issuance of debt securities is not limited to the federal government. State, city, town, and other units of local government and political subdivisions also issue bonds, referred to collectively as *municipals* or *munis*. They are also known as *tax-exempts* because the interest earned on them is exempt from federal income tax and often from state and local income taxes where they are issued. Because of this tax-exempt feature, municipals can pay a lower rate of interest and still be competitive with taxable bonds paying a higher rate of interest.

Municipal securities are issued to help finance new roads, highways, bridges, schools, hospitals, libraries, sports and convention centers, airports, sewers, utilities, and other facilities. Unlike federal government securities, municipals are not sold directly to the public. Instead, municipals are sold to investment bankers or underwriters who in turn make them available to investors. There are two basic types of municipal bonds, based on the source of revenue used to repay the bond.

General Obligation Bonds

General obligation bonds are secured by the full and unlimited taxing power of the government issuing the bonds. Also known as *full faith and credit* bonds, these securities are ranked second in safety only to federal government issues. This is because the issuer of a general obligation bond is required by law to exercise its taxing power so that bondholders can be paid. Income from property tax or other locally levied taxes is used to pay local general obligation bonds, while holders of state general obligation bonds are paid with revenues generated from income, sales, gasoline, tobacco, corporation, or business taxes. Theoretically, at least, general obligation bonds have first claim on the revenue of the state or local government issuing the bond. "By law," writes *Wall Street Week* sage Louis Rukeyser, "such bondholders are right up there with the school teachers and the policemen in their claim on the community; in fact, in Chicago, during the Depression, municipal employees generally got scrip, bondholders got cash."[7]

Revenue Bonds

Revenue bonds, on the other hand, are backed only by revenues from a specific project, such as the tolls, fees, or rents paid by the users of the facility constructed with the proceeds from the bond. A typical example would be a bond issued to build a toll road, backed not by local taxpayers but by the income generated, in the form of tolls, from the motorists who use the road. Because payments to holders of revenue bonds are not guaranteed by the unlimited taxing power of the issuing government, revenue bonds are generally considered riskier than general obligation bonds and usually the investor is compensated for the added risk by receiving a higher rate of interest. Clearly, the investor contemplating purchase of revenue bonds should learn all he or she can about factors that might affect the profitability of the facility being constructed. While not common, default on revenue bonds does occur.

> The Chesapeake Bay Bridge and Tunnel District provides an example. The district first defaulted on its interest payments on a $100 million bond issue back in July 1970. Since then, it has met only two semiannual payments. Apparently, far fewer drivers use the 18-mile bridge tunnel across the lower Chesapeake Bay than had been expected. Investors in this issue not only lost income, but they also experienced a drastic decline in the value of their bonds. The price of the issue fell from $700 to $180 after the announcement of the default.[8]

Sources of Information on Municipal Bonds

Information on municipals is not always easy to locate, and in some instances may be completely unobtainable from the standard printed sources available in most libraries. Daily price quotations for municipal issues in the *Wall Street Journal*, for example, are limited to a few, select revenue bonds. The sheer volume and diversity of municipal bonds make it impractical for printed sources to list them all; the fact that many of them are serial bonds, each with a whole range of different maturities, makes it all but impossible. So, in many instances, an investor seeking current price and trading information for a specific municipal issue may well have to get it directly from a securities broker or a commercial bank.

Two major bond publications described later in this chapter, *Moody's Bond Record* and Standard & Poor's *Bond Guide*, list many municipal issues, but the information given is limited to the rating assigned to each. Somewhat more detailed information is contained in the weekly bond advisory newsletters issued by both publishers. Standard & Poor's publication is *CreditWeek*, while Moody's offering is *Moody's Bond Survey*. Each includes fairly detailed analyses of a few issues, similar to the one shown in figure 14.4 (see page 356), and each includes tables like the one in figure 14.5 (see page 356), which briefly summarize new tax-exempt issues.

The most comprehensive source of information is *Moody's Municipal & Government Manual*. Its arrangement is alphabetical by state, and then by city, town, and political subdivision. Information for each state includes a description of principal tax sources, financial, population, and industry statistics, a map of the state and its counties, and a list of outstanding issues. The listing for the California Student Loan Authority in figure 14.6 (see page 357) is typical.

After state government information is given, local government units are listed. The type of information provided varies according to the nature of the political subdivision. A town listing will include the name of the county in which it is located, date of incorporation, population in the most recent decennial census, assessed value of property, tax collected, Moody's rating, overdue taxes, and the name of the bank making interest payments. A school district listing might include the district's location in the state, average school attendance figures, assessed valuation of property in the school district, Moody's rating, and the name of the bank making semiannual interest payments to bondholders. The Hampden-Wilbraham Regional School District listing in figure 14.7 (see page 357) is typical.

The main drawback to *Moody's Municipal* is that the information becomes somewhat dated as the year progresses. This is offset by the publication of a semiweekly newsletter that updates the *Manual*. It includes listings of new and prospective issues, securities whose ratings have been changed or withdrawn, and a list of call notices posted by international, federal, and municipal organizations that are calling in some of their securities.

Tarrant County, Texas

$20 million general obligation bonds due 1988-2007
Competitive, June 15
Rated 'AA+'; outstanding rating affirmed

Rationale: An 'AA+' rating is assigned Tarrant County, Texas'
$20 million general obligation bonds series 1987, due 1988–
2007. The 'AA+' rating on $16.4 million outstanding parity
bonds is affirmed. The rating is based on continued growth in
the county's assessed value, employment, and income. Concerns over Texas' economic outlook and the county's earnings
dependency on defense-related spending also were rating factors. The county seat is Fort Worth, the fifth largest city in Texas, with a population of 439,000. Services provided by the
county include judicial, law enforcement, detention facilities,
welfare, and maintenance of county roads and bridges. This issue is the first stage of a $114 million authorization to build new
courts and detention facilities. Because most roads are currently maintained by the state or incorporated cities, projected
county capital needs are minimal. Despite significant increases
in operating expenditures as staffing levels have been increased, the county has maintained a stable financial position
through many years of strong revenue and budget growth.

Debt: The 1987 series brings gross debt to only $36.4 million.
Overall net debt, which includes county, cities', and school
debt, is high at $1,263 per capita, but represents only 3.4% of
true value. Because the county's direct debt accounts for only
2.9% of overall net debt, the additional $94 million issuable over
the next one and a half years will not significantly impact overall
net debt ratios. Historically, the county debt service burden has
represented a low 5%-6% of expenditures. Once full authoriza-
tion is issued, the county expects the burden to increase to approximately 15%, a higher but still manageable share.

Economy: The county's taxable assessed value base has
grown 144% over the past four years. This explosive growth
rate has moderated recently, but still maintains a 16% annual
average increase since 1985. There is little concentration exhib-
ited by the top 10 taxpayers which account for less than 5% of
total assessed value. Major employers, which include General
Dynamics Corp., Bell Helicopter Textron Inc., Tandy Corp., Mo-
torola Inc., and several military installations, reflect some de-
pendence on defense-related spending. A rising unemployment
rate is generated by rapid labor force growth which overshad-
ows strong employment gains of approximately 5% per year
since 1984. New area employers include transportation, food,

robotic, and electronic information companies. International
Business Machines Corp. is locating a four million square-foot
research and development complex in the county. Additionally,
Fort Worth is the site of the first U.S. Treasury currency printing
plant outside the District of Columbia. Wealth levels in the
county exceed metropolitan statistical area (MSA), state, and
national levels and trail only the consolidated MSA which includes Dallas County to the east.

Finances: General fund expenditures (85% of which are general government, law enforcement, and judicial) have grown
more rapidly than revenues. Higher personnel costs, both in
number of employees and compensation, helped boost general
fund expenditures 15% in 1986. In addition to a $3.2 million
salary package designed to make county salaries more competitive, 117 new positions were added, all related to law enforcement, courts, and jails. Continued expenditure growth is
expected in this area: Debt service expenditures will increase
with the completion of this project. In addition, four new criminal
district courts and one county court are now being considered
by the Texas legislature. These five new courts, if created,
would require a projected $3 million increase in operating funds.
The judicial and jail complex being built with proceeds of the
current sale should not significantly impact operating costs as
the new buildings are intended to replace less efficient facilities.
New hires are projected at approximately 110 over the next five
years. To provide for cost increases, the county will raise new
revenues, $6 million from new auto registration fees and $3 million from an increase in the operating levy. Although a small
operating and large debt service levy increase will be required
to meet new expenditure levels, the resultant tax rates are still
moderate. In addition, the county has larger-than-average cash
surpluses available going into fiscal 1988. As a result of the
county's change to an Oct. 1 fiscal year from Jan. 1, a one-time
cash flow gain of $5 million will accrue to the general fund in fis-
cal 1987. Due to this extra cash cushion and operating revenue
increases, the county appears well positioned for higher expenditure levels and plans to maintain ending general fund balances
around 13%.

Robert Swerdling
(212) 208-1962

Fig. 14.4. Analysis of a municipal bond offering, Standard & Poor's *CreditWeek*.
Reprinted with permission from the June 15, 1987 issue of Standard & Poor's
CreditWeek.

MUNICIPAL BOND OFFERINGS

GENERAL AND LIMITED LIABILITY OBLIGATIONS

Date Time Sale	Rating Amount ($000's)	Issue: (County) State	Population: Assessed Valuation (Est. % of Assessed to Market Value)	Net Direct & Over-all Debt: Over-all Equivalents	Comment
7/13 7:00 PM CDT	A1 15,000	Mesquite Independent School District (Dallas), Texas. Ser. 8/15/88-2007 (beg. 8/15/97 at par). School Construction, Various Renovations and Additions.	1987: 115,000 1980: 78,152 1987: $3,006,000 1986: $2,736,000 (100.0%)	$104,750,000 $160,582,000 $1,396 P.C. 5.3% of A.V. 5.3% of M.V.	Well managed finances and continued growth in taxable values provide broad security for moderate debt levels. Sizable additional borrowing noted.
7/13 5:00 PM CDT	A1 9,500	Waco Independent School District (McLennan), Texas. Ser. 8/1/89-2008 (beg. 8/1/97 at par). Construction, Remodeling and Additions to Existing Schools.	1987: 104,354 1980: 101,743 1987: $1,998,000 1986: $1,942,021 (100.0%)	$9,505,000 $38,047,000 $365 P.C. 1.9% of A.V. 1.9% of M.V.	Ample taxable resources and satisfactory finances provide upper medium grade security for modest debt. Significant additional borrowing is planned.
7/13 8:30 PM EDT	A1 3,910	New Milford (Bergen), New Jersey. Ser. 7/1/88-2002 (beg. 7/1/97 at 102). General Improvement Bonds.	1984: 16,627 1980: 16,876 1987: $280,748,000 1986: $279,044,000 (43.06%)	$3,910,000 $6,718,000 $404 P.C. 2.4% of A.V. 1.0% of M.V.	Generally affluent stable residential base and favorable debt position combine with satisfactory financial operations to provide upper medium grade security for rapidly amortized debt.

Fig. 14.5. Typical table, *Moody's Bond Survey*. Reprinted with permission from the July
13, 1987 issue of *Moody's Bond Survey*.

CALIFORNIA STUDENT LOAN AUTHORITY

History: The authority is a public instrumentality authorized to purchase and sell (or commit to do same) insured student loans. The state attorney general has issued an opinion that the authorized powers extend to loans to parents in the same manner as insured loans to students. The members of the authority are the state's treasurer, controller and director of finance and non-voting membership is extended to the directors of the California Student Aid Commission and the California Post Secondary Education Commission.

Bonded Debt: 1. California Student Loan Authority student and parent loan rev., 1983 Ser. A, 6¼s-8½s due serially 1984-89, term 8¾s due 1999 and term 9s due 1991:(Refunded)

Rating — Aaa
ISSUED — 1983 ser. A, $121,475,000; outstg., June 30, 1985, $117,660,000 ($7,405,000, 6.75s; $8,070,000, 7.25s; $10,220,000, 7.75s; $11,185,000, 8.25s; $10,805,000, 8.50s; $5,895,000, 8.75s, and $64,080,000, 9.00s).
DATED — Jan. 1, 1983.
MATURITY — Due Dec. 1 in annual amounts ranging from $3,815,000 in 1984 to $64,080,000 in 1991.
DENOMINATION — As fully registered $5,000 and multiples thereof; also as coupon $5,000.
INTEREST — J&D 1 (1st payment June 1, 1983) at Bank of America N.T. & S.A., San Francisco, or at Citibank, N.A., NYC (year and interest rate):

Year	%	Year	%	Year	%
1984	6.25	1985	6.75	1986	7.25
1987	7.75	1988	8.25	1989	8.50
1999	8.75	1991	9.00		

CALLABLE — As a whole on any interest date beginning Dec. 1, 1989 to Nov. 30: 1990 at 101; and thereafter at 100.
MANDATORY REDEMPTION — The bonds are subject to redemption, as a whole or in part, inversely and by lot within a maturity, on Dec. 1, 1985, at 100, plus interest accrued and unpaid to such date of redemption, from any amounts transferred to the surplus fund from amounts on deposit in the loan fund representing proceeds of the bonds not used to purchase eligible loans or to pay costs of issuance and from excess amounts on deposit in the loan reserve fund owing to any resulting reduction in the Loan Reserve requirement.

The bonds are also subject to redemption, as a whole or in part, inversely, by lot within a maturity at 100, on Dec. 1 of each year commencing Dec. 1, 1983 from all amounts then on deposit in the surplus fund in excess of $100,000. The Authority may apply amounts deposited in the surplus fund during the twelve-month period prior to Dec. 1 of each year commencing Dec. 1, 1984 to the purchase of additional eligible loans if the Authority has filed with the trustee at the commencement of such period a statement of projected revenues, giving effect to such purchases, that complies with the indenture and if such purchases are in compliance with the arbitrage provisions of the Internal Revenue Code of 1954.
SECURITY — Secured by U.S. Government securities, state and local Government Series, held in escrow, which will provide debt service for the bonds to their maturity from the revenues received under the terms of the indenture, including the payment of the principal of and interest on eligible loans acquired by the Authority and pledged to the trustee for the benefit of the bondholders.
PURPOSE — Proceeds will be used as follows: ($97,205,000) for the purchase of eligible student loans, ($1,673,370) for origination and commitment fees, ($12,147,500) for the debt service reserve fund, ($6,073,750) for the loan reserve fund, ($607,375) for the operating fund, and ($3,725,400) for the costs of issuance.
OFFERED — ($121,475,000) purchased thru negotiation on Jan. 6, 1983 by a group headed by L.F. Rothschild, Unterberg, Towbin; Shearson/American Express Inc., and Citibank, N.A., N.Y.C., reoffered at 100.

Fig. 14.6. Typical listing for a state-issued security, *Moody's Municipal & Government Manual*. Reprinted with permission from the 1987 edition of *Moody's Municipal & Government Manual*.

HAMPDEN-WILBRAHAM REGIONAL SCHOOL DISTRICT

P.O., Wilbraham. Located in Hampden County. Area 20 sq. miles. Organized in 1956 by towns of Hampden and Wilbraham to build a high school in Wilbraham.

Average Attendance: 1984-85, 1,306; population 1980 (est.), 17,007.

Assessed Value, etc. ($000):

	1985	1984	1983
All Property	110,216	110,216	101,219
Tax Rate per $1,000	19.32	20.79	19.64

Bonded Debt, Dec. 15, 1986, $1,230,000. Due within one year, $250,000.

Schedule of Bonded Debt, Dec. 15, 1986:
School
5s	'71 Ser. to 12-15-91 J&D 15	$1,230,000

RATING: General obligations A1

Interest Paid: At State Street Bank & Trust Co. Boston.

Fig. 14.7. Typical school district listing, *Moody's Municipal & Government Manual*. Reprinted with permission from the 1987 edition, *Moody's Municipal & Government Manual*.

CORPORATE SECURITIES

Corporations also issue bonds and other debt securities. As with government securities, corporate securities can be classified by length of time to maturity. Short-term corporate debt obligations, discussed earlier in the section on money market instruments, are called *commercial paper*. Generally, commercial paper has a maturity of from 90 to 180 days, and since it is traded in minimum denominations of $100,000, is only indirectly purchased by individual investors via money market funds.

Corporate bonds or *corporates*, on the other hand, are usually issued in denominations of $1,000, making them a more likely target for the individual investor. As on many government and municipal bonds, interest is generally issued semiannually. Corporate bonds usually have maturities of from 20 to 30 years, and many of them contain the sinking fund and call provisions described earlier in this chapter.

Types of Corporate Bonds

Corporate bonds can be categorized broadly by the type of collateral put up to secure the bond. Some bonds are unsecured, with no collateral pledged as security. Others may pledge specific equipment, facilities, or their own portfolios of stocks and bonds.

Debenture bonds or *debentures* are unsecured loans, backed only by the company's "full faith and credit." In other words, all that stands behind repayment of the loan is the company's own word that it will repay the principal and make the requisite number of semiannual interest payments. Obviously, the financial and managerial well-being of a company issuing debentures should be of prime interest to the prospective bond buyer, and careful attention should be paid to the ratings assigned by Moody's and Standard & Poor's.

Other bonds may be backed by some specific, tangible asset against the possibility of default. If the company fails to make interest payments or to repay the principal, the asset can be sold so that the bondholders will be paid. *Mortgage bonds*, for example, are secured by a specific piece of fixed property such as a company plant or laboratory. Still other bonds pledge movable equipment as security. They are called *equipment trust certificates*. Often issued by railroads, an equipment trust certificate will typically pledge a locomotive or freight cars as collateral. Finally, *collateral trust bonds* are those bonds backed by securities – usually the stocks and bonds of other companies – held by the issuing corporation.

Some bonds can be converted at the holder's option into a designated number of shares of common stock. These bonds are called *convertible bonds* or *convertibles*, and offer the investor the chance to do a little financial fence-straddling. If the company fails to prosper, the convertible bondholder can choose not to exercise the conversion privilege and can instead collect semiannual fixed-interest payments much as he would with any other bond. (The interest rate will be less, however, than for straight, nonconvertible bonds issued by the same company.) On the other hand, if the company should prosper, he has the option of converting the bond into common stock at a previously specified conversion price. Assume for example, that Placebo, Inc., a pharmaceutical company, issues a $1,000 convertible bond, giving its holders the option of converting the bond into 20 shares of its common stock. The conversion price per share of common stock would be $40, or $1,000 (the price of the bond) divided by 20 (the number of shares into which the bond can be converted). Suppose further that at the time the bond was issued, Placebo common was selling for $30 per share. No one would trade the bond for stock. But if Placebo should discover a cure for the common cold and its stock should zoom to $75 per share, the convertible bondholder would be able to tap into company profits by converting his $1,000 bond into 20 shares of stock, now worth a total of $1,500. Convertible bonds can be identified by the letters *cv* following the name, interest rate, and maturity date of bond listings in financial newspapers and other publications.

Trading of Corporate Bonds

Although the bulk of trading of corporate bonds is done on the OTC market, some corporates are also traded on the New York and American Stock Exchanges. Daily trading activity on the NYSE and Amex is reported in the *Wall Street Journal* and *New York Times*. A look at the information contained in the daily bond quotation tables may be helpful. The sample shown in figure 14.8 is typical.

Bonds	Cur Yld	Vol	High	Low	Close	Net Chg
IBM[1] 93/8[2]04[3]	9.3	62	1007/8	1001/4	1007/8-	1/8
IBM 77/804cv[4]		188	1231/2[7]	1221/2[8]	1231/2+[9]	1/4[10]
Wendy's 71/410	8.0[5]	32[6]	911/2	905/8	905/8-	5/8

1. Company Name. Abbreviated name of company issuing bond.
2. Interest or Coupon Rate. Immediately follows company name. The first IBM bond, for example, pays 9 3/8% interest.
3. Maturity Date. The two-digit number immediately following the interest rate indicates when the bond will mature. The 9 3/8% IBM bond, for example, will mature in 2004, the Wendy's bond, in 2010.
4. Cv. The "cv" following the name, coupon rate, and maturity date for the second IBM bond indicates that it is a convertible bond.
5. Cur Yld or Current Yield. Derived by dividing the bond's annual coupon rate by the closing price paid for the bond. The Wendy's bond, for example, has a current yield of 8%. Its current yield is greater than its interest rate because the $1,000 bond was purchased at a discount for $906.25.
6. Vol or Volume. The number of bonds traded that day. On the day being reported, 32 of Wendy's bonds were traded. [Note that if a bond is not traded on the day being reported, it will not be included in the table even though it is available through the exchange.]
7. High. Highest price paid for the bond that day, expressed in percent of the bond's face value. The highest price paid for the IBM convertible bond, for example, was 123 1/2% of the $1,000 face value, or $1,235.00.
8. Low. Lowest price paid for the bond that day.
9. Close. Price paid for the bond during the last transaction of the trading day.
10. Net Chg or Net Change. Comparison of closing price to the preceding day's closing price.

Fig. 14.8. Corporate bond table.

The quotation for the last item listed in figure 14.8, the Wendy's issue, means that 32 of its bonds, paying 7¼ percent interest and maturing in 2010, were traded. The bonds were selling at a discount (below their face value), and sold for $6.25 (⅝) less than on the previous trading day.

Weekly information on bond trading activity is given in *Barron's, Commercial and Financial Chronicle*, and *Media General Market Data Graphics*.

Sources of Information on Corporate Bonds

Various company-issued reports, such as the annual report to shareholders and the 10-K report will be of interest to investors, as will the comprehensive investment services described in the preceding chapter. *Standard Corporation Descriptions*, for example, and the various *Moody's Manuals*, particularly the *Industrial, OTC Industrial, Public Utility, Transportation*, and *Bank & Finance* manuals with their detailed financial statements, company histories, and descriptions and bond ratings, are basic corporate bond information sources.

Moody's Bond Record and Standard & Poor's *Bond Guide* include lengthy sections on corporate issues. The *Bond Guide* lists over 5,600 domestic and Canadian corporates, 275 foreign issues, and over 640 convertibles. General information is provided on each company, including its industry code and limited balance sheet data, as well as on each bond issued by the company. For each issue listed, data include the name of the exchange on which the security is traded, the type of bond, the rating assigned to the bond, interest payment dates, coupon and maturity, information on redemption provisions, both current yield and yield to maturity, and other financial data. All of this information is packed into a single line, so abbreviations and symbols are heavily used. Detailed explanations are given on the front and back inside covers of each issue.

Convertible bonds are listed separately from the other corporate issues in the *Bond Guide*. Information given for each convertible issue includes coupon rate and maturity, Standard & Poor's rating, expiration date of conversion privilege, number of shares of common stock into which each bond can be converted, the conversion price per share of common stock, and the dividend income per bond. In addition, current stock data – market price, price-earnings ratio, and earnings per share – are also included.

Moody's Bond Record provides similar information in a slightly different format, and includes Canadian provincial and municipal obligations and international listings as well as domestic corporate bonds in a single listing. Otherwise, the information is virtually identical, with coupon rate and maturity, dates of interest payments, ratings, current price, sinking fund and call provisions, yield to maturity, and other financial data given for each issue.

As in the *Bond Guide*, convertibles are listed separately in the *Bond Record*. Data include Moody's rating, conversion period and price, number of shares of common stock into which the bond can be converted, and current stock and bond data.

The bond advisory newsletters, discussed briefly in the section on municipals and at greater length in the forthcoming section on general information sources, include periodic in-depth analyses of specific corporate issues as well as brief tabular summaries of others.

GENERAL INFORMATION SOURCES

On the whole, information on bonds is more difficult to find than information on stocks. This is because of the diversity and complexity of bonds, because some bonds are traded only locally or have limited distribution, and because much of the published information is directed towards securities dealers and institutional investors rather than individual investors. Some publications – *The Blue List of Current Municipal Offerings*, for example – are available *only* to bond dealers.

This is not to say printed information sources are not available; they are. The *Directory of Business and Financial Services* lists several publications dealing with bonds in one form or another. Most can be categorized as (1) factual sources that provide summary statistical data and (2) advisory services. Both are deserving of attention, but it should be kept in mind that while the few titles mentioned below represent the types of publications available, they in no way comprise a comprehensive list. The *Directory* and *Business Information Sources* list major bond publications, and the librarian attempting to build a collection in this area would do well to consult them.

Factual Sources

Financial newspapers provide concise statistical data on bonds and other fixed-income securities. The *Wall Street Journal* has fairly comprehensive daily information on trading of federal government and corporate debt obligations, as does the *New York Times*. Weekly trading information is available in *Barron's, Commercial and Financial Chronicle*, and *Media General Market Data Graphics*. Two publications issued by Moody's and Standard & Poor's contain monthly trading information. Although each has been referred to in earlier parts of this chapter, an overview of both is useful.

Standard & Poor's. **Bond Guide**. New York: Standard & Poor's, 1938- . Monthly.

Moody's Investors Service. **Moody's Bond Record**. New York: The Service, 1932- . Monthly.

The *Bond Guide* is a monthly pocket guide to corporate, foreign, and municipal bonds. The bulk of each issue is devoted to corporate bonds, with 5,600 domestic and Canadian corporate offerings, 275 foreign issues, and over 640 convertible bonds listed. Information in these sections is condensed into one-line summaries, which include detailed information on both the issuing companies and the specific issues themselves. The municipal section, which is so densely packed that the print is difficult to read, is limited to the ratings assigned by Standard & Poor's to each issue.

The *Bond Guide* also includes a directory of underwriters of corporate bonds, a description of the S&P rating scheme, and a digest of investment security regulations. It briefly lists corporate and municipal bonds whose ratings have changed and recent issues registered with the Securities and Exchange Commission. Because of its compact format, abbreviations and symbols are heavily used, and the inner covers of each issue explain each item included in the table in some detail.

Moody's offering is *Moody's Bond Record*, another monthly. Like the *Bond Guide*, it provides most information on domestic, Canadian, and some foreign bonds as well as Canadian provincial and municipal obligations, all interfiled in a single listing. Convertible bonds are listed separately. In addition, it lists and rates commercial paper issued by companies. Separate rating and listing sections are also assigned to preferred stocks, industrial revenue bonds, environmental control revenue bonds, and municipal bonds and short-term loans. Finally, the *Bond Record* includes several charts: corporate bond yields by rating categories, yields of U.S. government securities, and weekly money market rates, among others.

Most small- and medium-sized libraries will not find it necessary to subscribe to both the *Bond Guide* and the *Bond Record*. Both are good, basic guides, each with its own special features. *Moody's Bond Record*'s format is more attractive and the print easier to read than that in Standard & Poor's *Bond Guide*. In addition, the *Bond Record*'s scope is somewhat broader; it provides information on short-term debt securities and government and federal agency obligations, while the Standard & Poor's publication does not. On the other hand, the corporate listings in Standard & Poor's *Bond Guide* feature more information about the companies themselves, assigning industry codes, and including balance sheet figures and other financial data. Furthermore, the *Bond Guide* lists corporate underwriters. Clearly, the choice of one or the other of these publications will be a reflection of the library's budget, its clientele and their preferences, and the type of information requests most commonly handled concerning bonds.

Advisory Services

Like weekly stock advisory services, bond services provide their readers with general information about the economy, the investment climate, and market trends as well as with analyses of specific issues. Typical of these publications are *CreditWeek* and *Moody's Bond Survey*.

CreditWeek. New York: Standard & Poor's, 1973- . Weekly.

Moody's Bond Survey. New York: Moody's Investors Service, 1932- . Weekly.

CreditWeek combines economic and credit market commentary with reviews and analyses of short- and long-term corporate issues, international bonds, and municipals. The listing for the Tarrant County, Texas, general obligation bonds in figure 14.4 in the section on municipals is typical.

The "CreditWatch" section lists bonds and other fixed-income securities under special surveillance for possible changes in S&P ratings. A company merger, for example, may positively or negatively affect the credit standing of a corporation, while a voter referendum reducing local property taxes would have the same effect on municipal obligations. Usually, Standard & Poor's makes a decision to revise or retain the issuer's present rating within 90 days.

Moody's Bond Survey presents similar information in a slightly different format. It, too, includes commentary on the economy, on specific industries, on business, and on technical matters. In addition, it includes a combination of fairly detailed analyses of specific issues along with brief listings of additional issues such as the "Municipal Bond Offerings" table in figure 14.5.

Although *Moody's* features a ratings section which lists new ratings, revised ratings, and ratings withdrawn for both long- and short-term securities, the section is merely a list and does not include the descriptions of issuers under review featured in *CreditWeek*. Both *Moody's Bond Survey* and *CreditWeek*, however, include detailed analyses of companies and municipalities whose ratings have changed in the appropriate sections of their publications.

The differences between *CreditWeek* and *Moody's Bond Survey* are not as great as their similarities. *CreditWeek*, with its format and content reflecting the findings of recent market research, is visually the more attractive and somewhat glossier, but if not purchased as part of Standard & Poor's "Complete Library Reference Shelf" is also considerably more expensive.

Moody's and Standard & Poor's are not the only publishers of bond advisory services. Fitch Investors Service, another New York-based credit rating firm, describes and rates municipal and corporate bonds in two of its publications, while *Value Line Convertibles* rates convertible bonds and preferred stocks. Since many libraries subscribe to one or the other or both of the library investment "packages" offered by Moody's and Standard & Poor's, however, their publications are the services most likely to be found in business reference collections.

Databases

Many of the databases described in the preceding chapter contain information about bonds and fixed-income securities as well as stocks. General financial information, for example, is available in files produced by Dow Jones and Media General. An even more specialized database is available through DIALOG.

The Bond Buyer. New York: Bond Buyer, Inc. Daily updates.

The Bond Buyer is the online, full-text version of two trade papers, the daily *Bond Buyer* and the weekly *Credit Markets*. It focuses on tax-exempt bonds and fixed-income securities, and it includes statistics on bond yields, prices, and sales; articles on federal laws and regulations affecting tax-exempt financing; Internal Revenue rulings; and also contains a complete record of municipal borrowings. Although *The Bond Buyer* is intended for institutional rather than private investors, the data it contains can be useful to scholars and researchers as well.

NOTES

[1]The Federal Reserve Bank of Richmond has compiled a series of articles, dealing with money market instruments and how they work, into a free and informative booklet, *Instruments of the Money Market*. A copy can be ordered from:

> Federal Reserve Bank of Richmond
> Bank and Public Relations Department
> P.O. Box 27622
> Richmond, VA 23261

[2]U.S. savings bonds, which are nonmarketable, nonnegotiable securities, are excluded from this discussion.

[3]Another free Federal Reserve Bank of Richmond publication, *Buying Treasury Securities at Federal Reserve Banks* describes this process in some detail and includes sample forms and general information on the purchase of government securities, all aimed at the individual investor. It is highly recommended for vertical file collections. The Bank's address is included in #1 above.

[4]The formula for converting the yield column to dollar price is:

$$\text{Price} = 100 - \frac{\text{Yield (Maturity)}}{360}$$

[5]Usually the prices in a Treasury securities table are divided in 32nds of a point to the right of the decimal point. Sometimes, however, prices are even more finely divided into 64ths of a point. A " + ," for example, indicates that 1/64th should be added to the figure, while a " − " indicates that 1/64th should be subtracted. A quote of 99.9 + , for example, equals 99 19/64 (9/32 + 1/64), while a quote of 99.9 − equals 99 17/64 (9/32 − 1/64).

[6]*Guide to the Securities of Federal Agencies, Government-Sponsored Corporations, and International Institutions* (1979). New York: Federal Reserve Bank of New York, 33 Liberty Street, New York, NY 10045. Free.

[7]Louis Rukeyser, *How to Make Money in Wall Street* (Garden City, N.Y.: Doubleday, 1974), 161.

[8]C. Robert Coates, *Investment Strategy* (New York: McGraw-Hill, 1978), 71.

Contrary to the tradition of the Pilgrims and the frontiersmen, and to the aspirations of manufacturers of electrical drills, not every American is by nature a do-it-yourselfer. In some areas, such as housekeeping and the assembly of children's Christmas toys, self-sufficiency has been rendered compulsory. In others, such as professional football and blue movies, spectatorial thrills are still available for those who prefer them. Mutual funds belong in the latter category.

—Louis Rukeyser, *How to Make Money in Wall Street*

15

MUTUAL FUNDS AND INVESTMENT COMPANIES

INTRODUCTION

Stocks and bonds are for those who prefer direct participation, the do-it-yourselfers to whom Rukeyser refers. *Investment companies*, that is, companies that sell shares in the investments held in diversified securities portfolios acquired with the pooled money of shareholders, are for those who prefer to relinquish responsibility for selection of securities and portfolio management to professional investment managers. The investor's responsibility ceases after he or she makes initial selection and purchase of shares in a chosen investment company, until such time as the investor decides to redeem the shares at current market value or switch to another fund.

The shares purchased may be in open- or closed-end investment companies. *Open-end investment companies*, also known as *mutual funds*, are those that will sell an unlimited number of shares to all interested investors; they stand ready to issue new shares or redeem old ones on a daily basis. As the number of shareholders increases, the pool of money to be invested grows proportionally and the securities portfolio expands. The shares are sold, or repurchased, at prices reflecting the value of the underlying securities.

Closed-end investment companies, on the other hand, issue and sell a fixed number of shares only once, at the time they are established. If new investors want to buy into a closed-end investment company, they must purchase some of the existing shares from another investor, using a stockbroker as an intermediary. Shares in these companies, also known as *publicly traded investment companies*, are traded on the major stock exchanges and over-the-counter, and their prices move up and down with investor demand.[1] Shares in open-end investment companies, on the other hand, are sold directly to the investor by the issuing company. This distinction is an important one to the librarian doing business reference, because information for both types of investment companies may not be given in the same place. Daily share price information, for example, is given separately for open- and closed-end investment companies in financial newspapers.

Mutual funds and closed-end investment companies, however, have two basic operating principles in common: They pool money from their investors to buy a broad range of stocks, bonds, and/or other investment vehicles, and they have professional investment managers who take full responsibility for all investment decisions.

Mutual funds and closed-end investment companies offer certain advantages to the investor with limited resources. Prime among these is diversification of investments. Although all investors routinely are counseled to minimize risk by diversifying their investments in a wide range of companies and industries, few individual investors can hope to achieve the variety found in most investment company portfolios. The Beacon Hill Mutual Fund is a case in point. Its investment portfolio recently featured stocks of 20 companies in 12 different industries. This is not unusual; many investment companies hold stocks issued by 50 companies or more, and some hold stocks from as many as 200.

Professional management is another advantage, particularly for the inexperienced or anxious investor. The professional manager handles basic investment decisions. In addition, he or she takes care of all of the paperwork and administrative details, including the preparation and distribution of quarterly reports to shareholders. In return for these services, an annual management fee—usually ½ of 1 percent of the total investment—is deducted from the company's assets.

A third advantage is that, as institutional investors dealing in large quantities, investment companies pay less in brokers' fees and commissions than do individual investors. An institutional investor might pay brokers' commissions of between 8 and 20 cents per share, for example, while an individual might pay from 25 to 40 cents per share.

Mutual funds are attractive because in most instances they require only relatively small minimum investments and dividends earned can be automatically reinvested in additional shares. Thus, it is possible for the small investor to steadily increase his or her holdings in a way that is difficult to match in other kinds of investments. Another significant advantage is the ease with which most investment company shares can be redeemed. This is particularly true of open-end investment companies or mutual funds, which stand ready to redeem shares at any time the securities markets are open. Shares are redeemed at *net asset value*, the value of the company's holdings minus its debt, divided by the number of shares outstanding. Net asset value is determined daily, so that market fluctuations in the price of the securities held by the fund can be taken into account. Closed-end investment companies, on the other hand, are traded on the securities exchanges, and their price is a reflection of supply and demand in the marketplace as well as of their net asset value.

Finally, many investment companies offer special services to their investors, including checkwriting privileges, special withdrawal plans, and the opportunity to switch from one company fund to another.

This is not to say that investment companies are without flaw. Some charge substantial sales commissions, some charge redemption fees, all levy management fees, and, in some instances, the return on these investments is not as great as one might earn from direct investment in stocks and bonds. Still, for many, the advantages they offer outweigh their drawbacks.

TYPES OF INVESTMENT COMPANIES

Investment companies, as we have seen, can be categorized as open- or closed-end. They can also be classified by the presence or absence of a sales fee, their investment objectives, and by their portfolio contents. Each of these classifications merits further consideration.

Load and No-Load Funds

Some mutual fund shares are sold using stockbrokers or securities dealers as middlemen. They promote the funds, handle the paperwork, and make it convenient for the investor to buy shares. These services, however, come dear. For each transaction, a sales charge, or *load*, ranging from 1½ to 8½ percent is deducted from the initial investment. Thus, a $10,000 investment in a fund charging an 8½ percent load is really only a $9,150 investment—the remaining $815 goes to the sales person. Further, an investor who puts $10,000 into a load fund from which the $815 load immediately is deducted must earn $815 on his or her investment just to break even.

Other funds must be purchased directly from the issuing investment company. Because no middlemen are involved, often no sales commission, or load, is deducted, and these funds are called, appropriately enough, *no-load funds*. The total amount of the investment goes directly into fund shares, which means that, over the long run and given the same initial investment, shareholders in no-load funds come out ahead.

> Let's assume two $10,000 investments: one in a load fund and the other in a no-load fund. In the case of the load fund, 8½ percent or $815 is deducted, the remaining $9,150 is invested. If both funds grow at the same rate—10% per year, for example—the no-load fund will be worth $11,000 at the end of the first year, while the load fund will be worth only $10,065. The no-load investor is now $1,000 ahead; the load fund investor is about even. But let's look closer. Originally the no-load investor had $850 more working for him than did the load fund investor. Now the differential is $935 ($11,000 versus $10,065). What has happened is that the $850 paid out as commission in one case but invested in the other, is also growing. And over the years this sum will continue to grow and compound, widening the differential. By the end of twenty years, the no-load investment will be worth $6,000 more.[2]

In terms of quality of professional investment management, neither load nor no-load funds are intrinsically superior. There are good, bad, and mediocre funds in both categories.

Purchase of no-load funds, however, requires more investor initiative, since it is the investor who must identify potential no-load fund investments, contact each company for additional information, and initiate the actual purchase of shares. (Securities brokers are understandably reluctant to promote funds on which they can make no sales commissions.) Although securities brokers are not ordinarily forthcoming with information on no-load funds, the investor can find these funds advertised in financial newspapers and publications, and listed in some of the basic reference sources described later in this chapter. Another way in which no-load funds can be identified is through the No-Load Mutual Fund Association's annual directory, which lists each fund by its investment objective and gives brief information on minimum investments required for initial and subsequent purchase of shares, procedures for redemption of shares, and services offered.[3]

Investment Objectives

Investment companies can also be differentiated by their investment objectives. Some funds, which stress immediate income and invest primarily in corporate bonds or high-dividend-yielding stocks, are *income funds. Growth funds*, on the other hand, look to long-term capital or income growth. Still other funds seek to attain a balance between income and growth. These are *balanced funds*. Many basic reference sources classify the various funds by their investment objectives; another source of this information is the prospectus issued by the fund itself. The 1987 prospectus for the Oppenheimer Special Fund, for example, states that it is an open-end, diversified "mutual fund whose investment objective is capital appreciation in its per share asset value. Current income is not a consideration in the selection of portfolio securities."[4] The Oppenheimer Special Fund, in other words, is a mutual fund whose primary investment objective is growth.

Portfolio Contents

Varying objectives necessitate the purchase of different types of securities for each investment portfolio. As a result, another way in which investment companies can be categorized is by the types of securities they hold. Although there are several variations, the basic categories are as follows.

1. Balanced Funds: bonds, preferred and common stocks included

2. Bond Funds

3. Commodity Funds

4. Common Stock Funds

5. Money Market Funds: short-term debt obligations, such as Treasury bills and commercial paper

6. Multifunds: portfolio composed of shares issued by other investment companies

7. Preferred Stock Funds

8. Specialty or Nondiversified Funds: portfolio limited to a specific industry, such as chemicals or electronics, or to a specific area, such as Japan or the sunbelt region of the United States

There is, of course, considerable variety within each of the above categories. One bond fund, for example, may invest only in double- and triple-A-rated bonds, while another fund's portfolio may include a mix of high- , medium- and low-rated bonds and even "junk" bonds. Similarly, a common stock fund can limit itself to conservative blue-chips, or it can gamble on speculative stocks. Many of the basic reference sources give an indication of portfolio contents, and this information is spelled out in detail in individual investment company prospectuses.

As the economy changes, so also does interest in specific types of funds. In years of spiraling interest rates, for example, money market funds enjoy tremendous popularity, with a resulting proliferation of guides, directories, and advisory letters, many of which are in great demand by library users. Some of these titles are discussed later in the section on information sources.

CURRENT PER-SHARE INFORMATION

Mutual Funds

Mutual funds stand ready to redeem their shares at net asset value whenever the securities markets are open. Net asset value for each fund is determined daily, and is listed in financial newspapers such as the *Wall Street Journal*. Compared to stock and bond tables, those for mutual funds are relatively easy to decipher – only three columns are included, and figures are in dollars and cents rather than eighths, sixteenths, or thirty-seconds. A sample follows in figure 15.1.

MUTUAL FUND QUOTATIONS			
	NAV	Offer Price	NAV Chg.
AcornFd[1]r[2]	45.00	N.L.+	.21
American Funds Group:[3]			
Am Bal	12.08[4]	13.20+[5]	.08[6]
Am Mutl	20.51	22.42+	.15
BondFdA	13.49	14.16	. . .
GthFdA	20.35	22.2+	.11
AmHeritg	1.72	N.L.+	.01
AmNtl Inc	23.68	25.88+	.19

1. Fund Name. Unless more than one fund is managed by the same investment company, funds are listed alphabetically.
2. "r." The "r" indicates that a redemption fee may be levied when investor shares are redeemed, or sold back to the issuing company.
3. Investment Advisory Organization. If an investment company sponsors more than one fund, all of its funds are listed under the name of the investment company. The American Funds Group, for example, sponsors several different funds, four of which are listed in this table. All funds are listed alphabetically.
4. NAV, or net asset value per share, derived by subtracting liabilities from assets and dividing the total number of outstanding shares into the remainder. This is the price at which a share will be redeemed; for the American Balanced Fund, $12.08.
5. Offer Price. The price the investor can expect to pay for each share. If there is a difference between the NAV and the offer price, the fund is a load fund. The load for the American Balanced Fund, for example, is $1.12, or $13.20, the offer price, minus $12.08, the net asset value. If the letters "N.L." appear in the offer price column, the fund listed is a no-load fund. This means that investors will buy and sell shares in that fund for the same amount, net asset value.
6. NAV Chg. Change in the net asset value from the preceding trading day.

Fig. 15.1. Daily mutual fund table.

Thus, in the example shown in figure 15.1, the last item listed, American National, Inc., a load fund, could be redeemed for $23.68 per share, its current net asset value. Someone wishing to buy a share of American National, however, would have to pay $25.88, the net asset value plus a sales commission of $2.20. The net asset value was up $.19 per share from the preceding trading day.

The growth of money market mutual funds in the past decade has led to the publication of a separate money market fund table in most financial papers. In addition to fund names, such tables generally include the average maturity time, in days, for each of the funds' money market portfolios, and yield averages for designated time periods.

Closed-End Investment Companies

Prices of shares in closed-end investment companies are shown in the stock tables of most financial newspapers, and the information given for both types of investments is fairly similar. Figure 15.2, which extracts information from a New York Stock Exchange table, illustrates how closed-end investment companies are listed.

52 Weeks				Yld	P-E	Sales				Net
High	Low	Stock	Div	%	Ratio	100s	High	Low	Close	Chg
237/8[2]	19	AdaEx[1]	3.42e[3]	15.5[4]	. . .[5]	204[6]	221/4[7]	217/8[8]	22-[9]	1/4[10]
213/8	17	GAInv	2.51e	12.0	. . .	176	21	203/4	21+	3/8

1. Stock. Name of the closed-end investment company is given, usually in abbreviated form. Here, "AdaEx" stands for Adams Express.
2. High-Low. Highest and lowest prices paid during the past year. During the past twelve months, for example, the highest price paid for a share of Adams Express was $23.88; the lowest, $19.00.
3. Div. Amount of the most recent dividend paid. In the past twelve months, Adams Express declared a dividend of $3.42. The letter "e" indicates that this is an annual, rather than a quarterly or semiannual dividend.
4. Yld %. Dividend yield, or the annual dividend divided by the cost of a share. The dividend yield on a share of Adams Express is 15.5%.
5. P-E Ratio. Price-earnings ratio information is not given for closed-end investment companies. This column is used for common stocks listed in the same table.
6. Sales 100s. The sales column shows the number of shares in 100s (or round lots) traded that day. On the day in question, 20,400 shares of Adams Express were traded.
7. High. Highest price paid for a share that day. $22.25 was the most paid for a share of Adams Express.
8. Low. Lowest price paid that day. Low for Adams Express was $21.88.
9. Close. Closing price that day.
10. Net Chg. Net change refers to the change (if any) in price from the closing price paid on that day and that paid on the preceding business day. A share of Adams Express was down 1/4, or $.25, from the preceding day.

Fig. 15.2. Closed-end investment company listings, daily newspaper stock tables.

Thus, the entry in figure 15.2 for General American Investment indicates that 17,600 shares were sold. The highest price paid that day was $21.00; the lowest price was $20.75, with the price up 37½ cents from the preceding trading day. The most paid for a share of General American in the past 12 months was $21.375; the least paid was $17.00. Its annual dividend was $2.51 per share, and its dividend yield, 12 percent.

INFORMATION SOURCES

A wide range of printed sources exists to help investors select and monitor investment companies in which they are interested, ranging from prospectuses and reports issued by the companies themselves to guides, directories, and specialized advisory newsletters. Some of the major reference tools, representative of the various types of information sources available, are described below.

Prospectuses and Company Reports

Investment companies are required by law to submit a prospectus to all prospective investors. This document describes the fund's investment objective, portfolio, management, special services offered, its assets and liabilities, and per-share income. This constitutes a summary of the registration statement filed with the Securities and Exchange Commission and provides an overview of a specific fund's investment philosophy and performance. Quarterly financial reports update the prospectus, and pinpoint the company's current financial status.

While most librarians will find it impractical to maintain a comprehensive collection of current investment company prospectuses and financial reports, they should know that these are readily available to anyone who expresses an interest, and that the information comprises the primary source on which most basic investment company reference publications are based.

Guides and Factbooks

Many of the general investment guides discussed in chapter 12 offer basic introductions to mutual funds and investment companies. More specialized guides are also available. Some are inexpensive booklets aimed at readers new to mutual funds. Others focus on specific types of mutual funds, such as money market funds or foreign equity funds. The type of mutual fund investment in vogue one season, however, may be in disfavor the next, and these specialized guides may remain unread on library shelves for years after a brief period of popularity. While such publications can be useful for the short term, libraries with limited book budgets should first acquire a core collection of general mutual fund guides. Some representative publications are listed below.

Rugg, Donald D. **The Dow Jones-Irwin Guide to Mutual Funds**. 3rd ed. Homewood, Ill.: Dow Jones-Irwin, 1986. 245p.

Dorf, Richard C. **The New Mutual Fund Investment Advisor**. Chicago: Probus Publishing, 1986. 256p.

The Dow Jones-Irwin Guide to Mutual Funds is a four-part guide to mutual fund investing, intended to help readers set up individually tailored investment programs based on the intermediate to long-term trading of no-load mutual funds. It begins by presenting guidelines to help readers analyze their own life situations and risk tolerance levels, and proceeds to a general discussion of mutual funds, including their history and development, advantages and disadvantages, and selection and evaluation. The third section deals with market timing, using monetary, psychological, and cyclical indicators to identify major turns in the stock market that will affect investment strategies. Finally, the fourth section focuses on tax-sheltered retirement plans. An appendix lists and briefly annotates major mutual fund information sources, beginning with *Barron's* and ending with *Wiesenberger Investment Companies Service*.

The New Mutual Fund Investment Advisor is similar. It introduces readers to mutual funds and also discusses such concepts as analysis and rating of funds, market timing, and selecting individualized portfolios. A glossary and appendixes that selectively list magazines and newspapers, computer programs and services, and mutual fund advisory services are included.

Although such guides are useful, they quickly become dated. For more current information about the mutual fund industry, another source is useful.

Investment Company Institute. **Mutual Fund Fact Book**. Washington, D.C.: The Institute, 1966- . Annual.

The *Mutual Fund Fact Book* provides an overview of the mutual funds industry, including its history, growth and development, composite industry statistics, and a glossary of key terms. It is useful for the researcher who wants to learn about mutual funds generally and does not require information on specific funds.

Directories

Many investors want composite information about open- and closed-end investment companies as well as details on specific funds. For them, the following titles will be particularly useful.

Wiesenberger Investment Companies Service. New York: Wiesenberger Financial Services, 1941- . Annual.

Moody's Investors Service. **Moody's Bank & Finance Manual**. New York: The Service, 1955- . 3v. Annual, supplemented by *Moody's Bank & Finance News Report*, issued twice weekly.

The most comprehensive source, and the one for which experienced investors are likely to ask, is *Wiesenberger Investment Companies Service*. It includes general background, management, and financial data, detailed information on specific companies, and a glossary. The first section covers such general topics as the difference between open- and closed-end investment companies, services offered, and how to select investment companies and appraise their management. The second section contains articles designed to help investors develop an individually tailored, long-range investment plan. One chapter, for example, discusses the types of investment programs that seem most appropriate to people in "average circumstances" at various stages of their lives, while another focuses on investing for retirement years.

The most frequently consulted sections, however, are those focusing on specific mutual funds and closed-end investment companies. Individual listings, such as the one shown in figure 15.3 (see page 372), describe the companies, their investment objectives, portfolio contents, and special services. Also included are the names of officers, directors, and investment advisors; frequency of dividend and capital gains payments; sales charge; and financial statistics for the past 10 years. *Investment Companies* also presents tables summarizing the results of a hypothetical $10,000 investment for each of the major funds for 5- , 10- , 15- , 20- , and 25-year periods. It is a basic reference source and belongs in every business reference collection.

Moody's Bank & Finance Manual is another source of detailed information. Volume 2 lists major U.S. and Canadian investment companies. Although it covers fewer companies, it includes some information not contained in *Wiesenberger*, and thus is a valuable supplement. As shown in figure 15.4 (see page 373), its entries lack the former's presentation of the results over time of a hypothetical $10,000 investment, but they do contain more detailed listings of portfolio contents and more thorough company histories. *Moody's* also includes a listing of the top 100 U.S. mutual funds, the top 25 domestic closed-end investment companies, and the 25 largest Canadian investment companies.

While *Wiesenberger Investment Companies Service* and *Moody's Bank & Finance Manual* provide information on both open- and closed-end investment companies, other publications are more specialized.[5] With the titles listed below, for example, the emphasis is on open-end companies.

Donoghue, William E., comp. **Donoghue's Mutual Funds Almanac**. Holliston, Mass.: The Donoghue Organization, 1969- . Annual.

Mutual Fund Directory. New York: Investment Dealer's Digest, Inc., 1938- . Semiannual.

The Handbook for No-Load Fund Investors. New York: McGraw-Hill, 1980- . Annual.

Donoghue's Mutual Funds Almanac is briefer, less technical, and omits coverage of closed-end companies. In other respects, however, it follows the format of *Wiesenberger Investment Companies Service*, first presenting general information and then fund-specific data. It is aimed primarily at prospective and novice investors, with separate chapters covering such topics as what to look for in a mutual fund; how to read a prospectus; and buying, selling, and switching fund shares. The detailed coverage of specific funds offered

THE DREYFUS THIRD CENTURY FUND, INC.

The fund seeks "capital growth through investment in companies which . . . not only meet traditional investment standards, but also show evidence in the conduct of their business, relative to other companies in the same industry or industries, of contributing to the enhancement of the quality of life in America as this nation enters the third century of its existence." Management will consider the performance of the companies in which the fund may invest in the areas of protection and improvement of the environment and the proper use of natural resources, occupational health and safety, consumer protection and product purity, and equal employment opportunity. Investments will normally be in common stocks or securities convertible into common stocks.

At the end of 1985, the fund had 38.7% of its assets in net cash and equivalent, 0.8% in senior securities and 60.5% in common stocks. Of equity holdings, the major industry commitments were railroads (7.8% of assets), chemicals (7.2%), paper & forest products (5.5%), entertainment (3.7%) and computer systems (3.4%). The five largest individual common stock positions were Santa Fe Southern Pacific Corp. (7.8% of assets), Scott Paper (5.5%), Dow Chemical (4.5%), Walt Disney (3.7%) and Wang Laboratories (3.2%). The rate of portfolio turnover in the latest fiscal year was 44.7% of average assets. Unrealized appreciation in the portfolio at the year-end was 10% of total net assets.

Statistical History

							% of Assets in								
			Net							ANNUAL DATA					
	Total	Number	Asset	Offer-			Cash &	Bonds &	Com-	Income	Capital				
	Net	of	Value	ing			Equiv-	Pre-	mon	Div-	Gains	Expense		Offering Price ($)	
	Assets	Share-	Per	Price	Yield		alent	ferreds	Stocks	idends	Distribu-	Ratio			
Year	($)	holders	Share ($)	($)	(%)					($)	tion ($)	(%)		High	Low
1985	182,481,337	19,147	7.50	—	2.6		39	1	60	0.205	0.51**	1.01		7.58	6.31
1984	133,564,974	20,218	6.39	—	2.9		18	2	80	0.20	0.53**	1.03		7.35	5.58
1983	131,086,846	21,428	7.10	—	3.3		4	2	94	0.255	0.55**	1.01		8.18	6.54
1982	116,781,511	20,241	6.58	—	4.6		26	1	73	0.32	0.445**	1.10		7.19	5.07
1981	101,342,343	18,905	7.19	—	2.7		14	1	85	0.205	0.475**	1.06		8.99	6.58
1980	107,279,025	14,177	8.78	—	4.4		14	2	84	0.158	0.677**	1.17		9.16	6.28
1979	48,492,579	5,091	6.92	—	1.3		17	2	81	0.10	0.55**	1.30		6.92	4.86
1978	24,867,745	4,630	4.84	—	1.3		9	—	91	0.065	0.228	1.30		5.88	4.20
1977	23,938,739	5,081	4.65	—†	1.6		8	—	92	0.077	0.055	1.10		4.94	4.02
1976	22,741,300	5,608	4.23	4.63	1.5		2	2	96	0.07	—	1.40		4.63	3.84
1975	20,104,546	6,221	3.48	3.82	1.2		27	6	67	0.047	—	1.50		4.06	2.56

Note: Initially offered 3/29/72 at $4.167 per share; continuous offering began 5/20/72.
** Includes $0.078 short-term capital gains in 1979; $0.095 in 1980; $0.475 in 1981;
$0.01 in 1982; $0.30 in 1983; $0.15 in 1984; $0.13 in 1985.
† On no-load basis, effective 7/18/77.

An assumed investment of $10,000 in this fund, with capital gains accepted in shares and income dividends reinvested, is illustrated below. The explanation in the introduction to this section must be read in conjunction with this illustration.

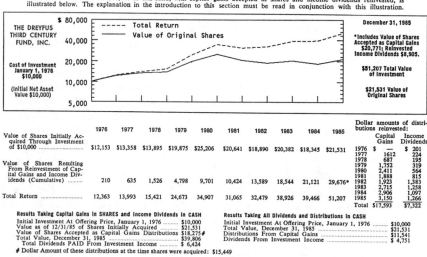

	1976	1977	1978	1979	1980	1981	1982	1983	1984	1985
Value of Shares Initially Acquired Through Investment of $10,000	$12,153	$13,358	$13,895	$19,875	$25,206	$20,641	$18,890	$20,382	$18,345	$21,531
Value of Shares Resulting From Reinvestment of Capital Gains and Income Dividends (Cumulative)	210	635	1,526	4,798	9,701	10,424	13,589	18,544	21,121	29,676*
Total Return	12,363	13,993	15,421	24,673	34,907	31,065	32,479	38,926	39,466	51,207

Dollar amounts of distributions reinvested:

	Capital Gains	Income Dividends
1976	$ —	$ 201
1977	1612	224
1978	687	195
1979	1,752	319
1980	2,411	564
1981	1,888	815
1982	1,923	1,383
1983	2,715	1,258
1984	2,906	1,097
1985	3,150	1,266
Total	$17,593	$7,322

Results Taking Capital Gains in SHARES and Income Dividends in CASH

Initial Investment At Offering Price, January 1, 1976	$10,000
Value as of 12/31/85 of Shares Initially Acquired	$21,531
Value of Shares Accepted as Capital Gains Distributions	$18,275#
Total Value, December 31, 1985	$39,806
Total Dividends PAID From Investment Income	$ 6,424

Results Taking All Dividends and Distributions in CASH

Initial Investment At Offering Price, January 1, 1976	$10,000
Total Value, December 31, 1985	$21,531
Distributions From Capital Gains	$11,541
Dividends From Investment Income	$ 4,751

Dollar Amount of these distributions at the time shares were acquired: $15,449

Fig. 15.3. Typical listing, *Wiesenberger Investment Companies Service*. Source: Wiesenberger Investment Companies Service, division of Warren, Gorham & Lamont, Inc.

4366 *MOODY'S BANK & FINANCE MANUAL*

50¢ for each withdrawal check. Automatic Withdrawal may be terminated at any time by the investor, or by the Fund or the Bank upon notice to shareholders. Shares for which stock certificates have been issued may not be redeemed pursuant to Automatic Withdrawal.
OFFERED—Continuously at net asset value. The minimum initial investment is $2,500, or $1,000 if the investor is a client of a securities dealer, investment advisor or bank which has made an aggregate minimum initial purchase for its customer of $2,500. Subsequent investments must be at least $100.
TRANSFER, DIVIDEND DISBURSING AGENT & REGISTRAR—Bank of New York.

PRICE RANGE	1985	1984	1983
High	14.63	13.55	13.44
Low	13.11	12.43	12.97

DREYFUS THIRD CENTURY FUND, INC.

History: Inc. in Del. May 6, 1971.

Business: A diversified, open-end management fund seeking capital growth.

Advisory Contract: Dreyfus Corp. advises and manages Fund for monthly fee at annual rate of ¾ of 1% of average value of its net assets.

Agreement provides that Advisor will reimburse Fund for expenses (excluding taxes, brokerage fees, interest on borrowings and extraordinary expenses) which exceed 1½% of average net assets during fiscal year.

Officers

Howard Stein, Chmn.
J.F. Friedman, Pres.
Mark Jacobs, Sec.
J.J. Pyburn, Treas.
F.J. Greene, Contr.

Directors

Alice P. Jones; J.J. McCloy
Howard Stein; Herbert Sturz
C.L. Alexander, Jr.

Custodian: Bank of New York, NYC.

Auditors: Ernst & Whinney.

General Counsel: Reavis & McGrath.

No. of Stockholders: May 31, 1984, 20,952.

Office: 600 Madison Ave., New York, NY 10022. **Tel.:** (212)935-3000.

Income Account, years ended May 31 ($000 omitted):

	1984	1983
Divs. & int. inc.	5,014	6,327
Inv. adv. fee	999	887
Expenses	377	309
[1]**Net income**	3,639	5,132
Dividends	5,015	4,730
[1]Balance	*d*1,376	402

[1]Before $9,745,695 (1983, $10,757,289) net gain secur. sold.

Balance Sheet, as of May 31 ($000 omitted):

Assets:	1984	1983
[1]Invest. (mkt.)	113,184	151,249
Cash	918	1,227
Rec. secur. sold	......	159
Divs. & int. rec.	710	668
Other assets	25	23
Rec. fd. shs. sold	22	......
Total	114,858	153,327
Liabilities:		
[2]Net assets	114,299	151,553
Pay. sec. purch.	30	35
Pay. shs. repurch.	339	1,538
Due to Co.	78	96
Accrued exps.	112	108
Total	114,858	153,327
Asset val. per sh.	$6.42	$7.86

[1]Cost: 1984, $120,416,693; 1983, $132,779,540.
[2]Par $1 shs.: 1984, 17,812,602; 1983, 19,275,080.

Record of Asset Value & Distributions (in $):

Yrs. to May 31	—Distribution Per Share— Invest. Income	Security Profits	Total	Asset Value May 31
1974	0.0267	...	0.0267	2.85
1975	0.05	...	0.05	3.40
1976	0.05	...	0.05	3.94
1977	0.07	...	0.07	4.34
1978	0.08	0.06	0.14	5.18
1979	0.06	0.23	0.29	5.70
1980	0.10	0.55	0.65	7.30
1981	0.16	0.68	0.84	8.93
1982	0.21	0.48	0.69	6.33
1983	0.32	0.45	0.77	7.86
1984	0.26	0.55	0.81	6.42

Note: Classification of dividends shown above does not necessarily represent their status for Federal income tax purposes.

Above adjusted for 3-for-1 split Nov., 1980.

Securities Owned, as of May 31, 1984:

Shares	Common Stocks	Mkt. Val.
200,000	Kaiser Alum. & Chem.	$2,850,000
100,000	Norton	3,587,500
50,000	U.S. Gypsum	2,662,500
224(c)	Industl. Vision Systems	100,990
38,400	Stauffer Chem.	648,000
100,000	AMAX	2,237,500
100,000	Cleve.-Cliffs Iron	2,062,500
80,000	SmithKline Beckman	4,310,000
120,000	Warner-Lambert	3,570,000
90,000	Dravo	1,068,750
80,000	Fluor	1,420,000
50,000	Morrison-Knudsen	1,500,000
135,000	Jerrico	1,890,000
100,000	Wendy's Intl.	1,537,500
100,000	Ahmanson (H.F.)	1,725,000
312,000	Alexander & Alexander Services	6,006,000
133,600	Golden West Financial	1,619,900
65,000	Transco Companies	2,551,250
80,000	U.S. Leasing Intl.	2,480,000
40,000	Caterpillar Tractor	1,630,000
100,000	Goulds Pumps	1,600,000
46,500	Raymond Corp.	1,557,750
60,000	Cameron Iron Works	1,065,000
60,000(a)	Crutcher Resources	180,000
60,000	Rowan Cos.	742,500
230,000	Scott Paper	6,037,500
160,000	Unocal	5,720,000
75,000	Addison-Wesley Publishing, Cl. B	1,650,000
120,000	Rio Grande Indust.	4,560,000
607,260	Santa Fe Southern Pac.	13,511,535
100,000	Macy (R.H.)	4,500,000
100,000	ITT	3,500,000
100,000	Applied Solar Energy	1,037,500
400,000	Dome Petrol.	950,000
56,000	Ionics	1,043,000
40,000	KMS Indust.	52,500
60,000	Magma Energy	356,250
40,000	Magma Power	312,500
15,168	Rockcor	163,056
200,000	Woodside Petrol., A.D.R.	178,000
50,000	Century Labs.	......
60,000	Coherent	1,425,000
40,000	DEKALB AgResearch, Cl. B	825,000
132,500	Genetic Systems	761,875
40,000	Gist-Brocades	1,735,200
160,000	Instrumentarium, Cl. B, A.D.R.	1,440,000
100,000	Pharmacia AB, A.D.R.	1,456,250
83,200	Ribi ImmunoChem Research	540,800
42,000	Ribi ImmunoChem Research (Wts.)	63,000
60,000	Sundance Oil	435,000
	Total common stocks	102,856,606
	Conv. Preferred Stocks	
3,182	Hansford Data Systems	87,505
4,545	Industrial Vision Systems	454,500
400	Laser Corp. of America	400,000
455	W.J. Schafer Assoc., Cl. A	45,500
	Conv. Notes & Bonds	
M Princ. Amt.		
$1,365	Mapco, sub. notes, 9s, 2003	1,699,425
1,000	Rockcor, sub. deb., 9s, 2000	840,000
	Short-Term Deposits	
6,800	Crocker Natl. Bank (London), $10^{11}/_{16}$s, 6/1/84	6,800,000
	Total investments	113,183,536
	Cash & rec., net	1,115,810
	Net assets	$114,299,346

Capital Stock: Dreyfus Third Century Fund Inc. common; par $0.33⅓:

Authorized, 60,000,000 shares; outstanding, May 31, 1984, 17,812,602 shares; par $0.33⅓:

Par changed from $1 to 0.33⅓ by 3-for-1 split Nov. 28, 1980.

Has one vote per sh. No preemptive rights.

Dividends Paid (calendar year):

1973 ......$0.08 1974 ....$0.15 1975 ......$0.14
1976 ....0.21 1977 .....0.39½ 1978 ....0.88
1979 ....1.95 1980 .....2.50½

On $0.33⅓ par shs.

1981 ....0.68 1982 .....0.77½ 1983 .....0.80½
1984 ....0.73 1985 .....0.71½

Note: Co. files Federal tax return as a regulated investment Co.

Redemption: Shs. of Fund are redeemable at net asset value.

Unless requested by holder in cash, all divs. and capital gains distributions will be reinvested in shs. of Fund at net asset value.

Exchange Privilege: Dreyfus Fund and Dreyfus Leverage Fund are sold to the public with a sales charge. The Fund, Dreyfus Special Income Fund, Dreyfus Money Market Instruments, Dreyfus A Bonds Plus, Dreyfus Number Nine, Dreyfus Tax Exempt Bond Fund and Dreyfus Liquid Assets are sold to the public without a sales charge. Shareholders of these nine funds have an Exchange Privilege whereby they may exchange, without paying any sales charge, all or part of their shares for shares of certain of the other funds on the basis of relative net asset value per share as described below:

(A) Shares of any of these funds which were purchased with a sales charge, may be exchanged for shares of any of the other funds;

(B) Shares of any of these funds which were acquired by means of an exchange of shares which had been purchased with a sales charge (and additional shares acquired through reinvestment of dividends or distributions may be exchanged for shares of any of the other funds;

(C) Shares of any of these funds may be exchanged for shares of the funds whose shares are offered without a sales charge.

When shares acquired without a sales are exchanged for shares sold with a sale, applicable sales charge will be deducted.

The shares exchanged must have a current offering price of at least $500. In order to accomplish an exchange under B, above, the shareholder must notify the Bank of his prior ownership of fund shares and account number.

The Exchange Privilege enables a shareholder in one of these funds to acquire shares in a fund with different investment objectives when he believes that a shift between funds is an appropriate investment decision. This privilege is available to shareholders resident in any state in which the fund being acquired may legally be sold. An exchange of shares is a sale for Federal income tax purposes and an exchanging shareholder may realize a taxable gain or loss.

Offered (2,500,000 shs.) at $12.50 a sh. on Mar. 23, 1972 thru Bache & Co., Inc., Reynolds Securities, Inc. and Kidder, Peabody & Co., Inc. and associates. Offering price was reduced in single transactions involving 400 or more shs.

Continuously thereafter by Dreyfus Sales Corp. at net asset value plus sales charge of 8¾% on purchases under $25,000; reduced rates apply to larger purchases. Shareholders have right to combine shares of Fund, Dreyfus Fund, Inc. (including shares purchased under a Dreyfus Investment Program), Dreyfus Leverage Fund, Inc., Dreyfus Liquid Assets and Dreyfus special Income Fund, Inc. purchased prior to the elimination of the sales charge, to qualify for reduced sales charge. Minimum initial purchase $500.

Transfer and Dividend Disbursing Agent: Bank of New York, NYC.

Price Range (bid prices):

	1985	1984	1983	1982	1981
High	7.58	7.35	8.20	7.19	8.99
Low	6.31	5.58	6.54	5.07	6.58

Fig. 15.4. Typical investment company listing, *Moody's Bank & Finance Manual*. Reprinted with permission from the 1986 edition of *Moody's Bank & Finance Manual*.

by *Wiesenberger* and *Moody's*, however, is missing. Instead, the *Almanac* presents data in tabular format, showing in a single line the fund's investment objective, date founded, annual gain or loss per share for the past 10 years, sales charge (for load funds), minimum investment required, total assets, net asset value per share, and capital gains and distributions. The table also shows, for each fund, how a $10,000 initial investment would have grown—or shrunk—over 5- and 10-year periods. Other tables list fund distributors and identify the top mutual funds.

Name changes in mutual funds are not uncommon, and usually reflect changes in investment objectives, new management, mergers, or takeovers. As a result, the section in the *Almanac* listing funds that changed their names, merged, split, or liquidated, can be particularly useful to librarians and investors attempting to track down seemingly elusive funds.

Similar information is also available in the *Mutual Fund Directory*, which offers somewhat more detailed information about specific funds than does the *Almanac*, but lacks some of the general explanatory material.

The Handbook for No-Load Fund Investors combines a review of the preceding year's mutual fund performance and sales with general information about funds and investing. Like many of the other sources described in this section, it includes comparative tables and a directory that lists and describes specific funds. For librarians and researchers with access to Dow Jones News/Retrieval, one useful feature is its access symbol for each fund. When the symbol is entered online, it enables searchers to retrieve fund-related financial data published by *Barron's*, the *Wall Street Journal*, and Media General Financial Services.

Although there are no widely held publications devoted specifically to closed-end investment companies, *Value Line* offers a quarterly summary of the investment company industry as well as detailed analyses of selected major closed-end investment companies whose shares are traded on national stock exchanges and over-the-counter.

Periodical Lists and Ratings

Many newspapers and periodicals regularly list and rate funds. One of the most comprehensive surveys is that offered by *Barron's*. Each quarter, with the assistance of Lipper Analytical Services, a fund-rating organization, *Barron's* presents the Barron's/Lipper Gauge, a table showing performance, yield, net asset value, capital gains and income dividends per share, and other financial information for nearly 1,200 mutual funds. In addition, articles on specific types of funds, investment strategies, and interviews with fund managers are supplemented by tables showing the best and worst performing funds, the top performers by investment objective, and average performance of mutual funds compared to such basic stock averages as the Standard & Poor's 500 and the Dow Jones Industrial.

Other business periodicals cover mutual funds as well, although not as often or as thoroughly. *Business Week*, for example, has added a mutual fund survey to its series of annual scoreboard issues, and *Forbes* combines brief articles with tables highlighting mutual fund performance as an annual special issue. Personal finance magazines also regularly include articles on mutual fund investments and comparisons of fund performance. *Changing Times* and *Money*, for example, cover mutual fund investment basics, specific funds' performance, and forecasts for the future.

Specialized Advisory Newsletters

In addition to the periodic coverage of mutual funds and investment companies in such standard sources as *Barron's* and *Money*, several advisory services and newsletters specializing in mutual funds are published. While a comprehensive collection of such material is impractical for most libraries, many will include one or two such sources in addition to mutual fund directories and guides. The titles listed below are typical.

United Mutual Fund Selector. Boston: Babson-United Investment Advisers, Inc., 1969- . Semimonthly.

Mutual Fund Forecaster. Fort Lauderdale, Fla.: The Institute for Econometric Research, 1985- . Monthly.

Donoghue's Moneyletter. Holliston, Mass.: The Donoghue Organization, Inc., 1980- . Biweekly.

Growth Fund Guide: The Investor's Guide to Dynamic Growth Funds. Rapid City, S.D.: Growth Fund Research, Inc., 1968- . Monthly.

The *United Mutual Fund Selector* combines general articles with comparative tables and charts, analyses of specific investment companies, and investment advice. A recent issue, for example, included an article that described bond funds, contained an interview with the portfolio manager of Century Shares Trust, answered inquiries on specific funds and investment tactics, and listed top-performing funds in 16 different investment strategy categories.

The *Mutual Fund Forecaster* also offers general surveys of fund-related activities, but is particularly popular for its tabular listing of some 500 mutual funds and closed-end investment companies, which includes current advice from the publisher ("avoid," "hold," "buy," or "best buy") and risk ratings and one-year profit projections as well as standard directory information and statistical data.

Donoghue's Moneyletter emphasizes funds likely to be of interest to individual investors, generally no- or low-load funds requiring initial investments of less than $10,000. Like the other services, it combines general information and investment advice with lists of top-performing funds and coverage of specific investment companies.

Some services are even more specialized, and concentrate on specific types of mutual funds. One of the most popular of these is the *Growth Fund Guide*, which focuses on no-load funds whose investment objective is growth. Each issue generally includes "personalized performance rating charts" for specific funds; current and historical statistics; and brief comments on trading, specific types of growth funds, and investment tactics. A separate list identifies the best-performing funds over the preceding 12 months. Also included are lists of new growth funds filed with the Securities and Exchange Commission and an investment forecast for the forthcoming month. In addition, each month the *Guide* rates some 30 equity funds and 4 money market funds on their potential for intermediate and long-term growth.

The *Growth Fund Guide* is a popular service, and is generally given high marks by investors, but it is only one of several such advisory publications. The librarian contemplating possible subscription to it or to other, similar advisory newsletters will need to be highly selective, since each has its ardent supporters and detractors. Further, all investment services recommend that people contemplating investing in specific funds acquire their prospectuses and study them carefully before making any investment decisions.

NOTES

[1] The Association of Publicly Traded Investment Funds publishes a list of major closed-end investment companies as well as a pamphlet listing companies that are Association members. For free copies, write to:

> Association of Publicly Traded Investment Funds
> 70 Niagara Street
> Buffalo, NY 14202

[2] Yale Hirsch, *Mutual Funds Almanac*, 11th ed. (Old Tappan, N.J.: The Hirsch Organization, 1980), 54.

[3] The annual *Investor's Guide and Mutual Fund Directory* is available for a small fee (in 1987, $5.00), and can be ordered from:

> No-Load Mutual Fund Association
> 11 Penn Plaza, #2204
> New York, NY 10001

[4] Oppenheimer Fund Management, Inc., *1987 Prospectus* (New York: Oppenheimer, 1987), 1.

[5] In December 1987, Standard & Poor's published its first issue of *Standard & Poor's/Lipper Mutual Fund Profiles*. Should it continue to be published, the *Mutual Fund Profiles*, which covers more than 750 equity-oriented mutual funds each quarter, will be a useful supplement to *Wiesenberger Investment Companies Service* and *Moody's Bank & Finance Manual*.

*A speculator who dies rich
has died before his time.*

— Anonymous

16

FUTURES AND OPTIONS

While stocks, bonds, and mutual funds are the most common investment mediums for individual investors, they are by no means the only ones. This chapter focuses on two increasingly popular types of investments, futures and options, and reviews information sources relevant to each.

FUTURES

In the futures market, investors trade *futures contracts*, which are agreements for the future delivery of designated quantities of given products for specified prices. Although futures trading in the United States began with agricultural commodities such as corn and wheat, items traded today are considerably more diverse. It is now possible to trade in precious and strategic metals, petroleum, foreign currency, and financial instruments as well as in such agricultural commodities as grain and livestock (see figure 16.1). Futures are usually divided into two broad categories: commodities and financial.

Commodities Futures

Commodities are sold in two different ways. Someone can buy sugar or wheat or pork bellies and take immediate possession of the product. Such a purchase is commonly referred to as a *cash*, or *spot*, *transaction*. Frequently, however, commodities are bought and sold for delivery at a later time by means of futures contracts. A *commodities futures contract* is a legal agreement between buyer and seller that a specified number of units of the commodity being traded on a particular futures exchange will be delivered at a certain place, during a certain month, for an agreed upon price. In July, someone who anticipates a rise in wheat prices, for example, may instruct his or her broker to buy one Minneapolis Grain Exchange wheat contract (5,000 bushels of wheat), to be delivered in December for $2.66 per bushel, or

376

COMMODITY FUTURES		FINANCIAL FUTURES	

COMMODITY FUTURES

Grains and Oilseeds

Barley	Sorghum
Corn	Soybean Meal
Flaxseed	Soybean Oil
Oats	Soybeans
Rapeseed	Wheat
Rye	

Wood

Lumber	Plywood

Metals and Petroleum

Aluminum	Petroleum
Copper	Platinum
Crude Oil	Propane
Gold	Silver
Heating Oil	Unleaded Gas
Palladium	

Livestock and Meat

Broilers	Hogs
Feeder Cattle	Live Cattle
Pork Bellies	

Food and Fiber

Cocoa	Orange Juice
Coffee	Potatoes
Cotton	Rice
Eggs	Sugar

FINANCIAL FUTURES

Interest Rates

Certificates of Deposit	T-bills
Commercial Paper	T-bonds
GNMA Certificates	T-notes

Foreign Currencies

British Pound	French Franc
Canadian Dollar	Japanese Yen
Deutschemark	Mexican Peso
Dutch Guilder	Swiss Franc

Indexes

Consumer Price Index (CPI-W)	Standard & Poor's 500 Index
CRB Futures Index	Standard & Poor's 100 Index
Municipal Bond Index	Standard & Poor's OTC Index
NYSE Index	U.S. Dollar Index
NYSE Beta Index	
Value Line Index	

Fig. 16.1. Major commodity and financial futures traded in the United States.

$13,300.00. If the market price of wheat rises from, say, $2.66 to $3.00 per bushel between the signing of the contract and the delivery date, the investor will have made a profit of $1,700.00. At this point, the purchaser of the wheat contract does not actually have physical possession of the 5,000 bushels of wheat. The purchaser is not required to accept delivery; he or she can offset the transaction at any time before the delivery month. In fact, actual delivery occurs in less than 5 percent of all commodities futures transactions.

Someone who expects wheat prices to fall might instruct his or her broker to execute a contract to sell wheat at the current prevailing price. If prices fall, the seller of the contract to deliver will have earned a profit; if they rise, the buyer of the contract will come out ahead.

If a wheat farmer thinks the price of his crop may fall by harvest time, he can sell wheat futures early in the season. If the price does fall, he will have a profit on the futures market to compensate for the lower price he receives for his wheat. This process is known as hedging. If wheat's price rises, the farmer loses money on his futures position, but makes up for that with higher-than-expected earnings from his crop. Either way, he comes out approximately even and he can use this knowledge to plan his business, because he knows early in the season how much he will get for his grain. The farmer needn't even deliver his crop against his futures market commitment. He can simply take his grain to a nearby elevator and sell it there; at the same time, he can tell his broker to buy enough wheat contracts to offset his futures commitment. This offsetting process, known as liquidation, is by far the most common way of ending a futures market commitment.[1]

As indicated above, most traders choose to liquidate their contracts before delivery by arranging offsetting transactions to reverse the original actions. Buyers, in other words, liquidate their contracts by executing a similar number of contracts to sell the same commodity, and sellers offset theirs by purchasing an equal quantity of contracts to buy the product. The difference between the first transaction and the second transaction is the amount of profit or loss (excluding broker's commission and other expenses) accruing to the trader. Each commodities exchange has a clearinghouse that oversees all buy and sell transactions, and stands ready to fulfill a contract in the event of buyer or seller default.

To this point, people who trade commodities have been referred to generically as *investors*. In fact, there are two main categories of commodities traders, speculators and hedgers. *Speculators* are traders who voluntarily assume high levels of risk in anticipation of equally high profits. The difference between speculating and investing is worth emphasizing. While investing offers the opportunity for making reasonable profit over the long term, speculating focuses on short-term trading and may involve considerable risk in the attempt to realize high profits.

> A speculator is a gambler who's out to make a killing at the risk of going broke. In contrast, an investor takes risks that won't endanger his financial health; he knows that the best way to go about doubling his money is never to risk losing half of it.[2]

The other main type of commodities trader is the hedger. *Hedgers* are often producers or major consumers of commodities who use futures contracts very conservatively to reduce risk and to protect themselves against adverse price fluctuations.

Commodities futures contracts appeal to individual investors who are willing to assume considerable risk in the hope of making a substantial profit in a short period of time. The risks should not be minimized—commodities prices fluctuate, affected by such unpredictable factors as world economic conditions, the weather, political developments, and the supply of the commodity being traded. Additional risk is introduced by the purchase of commodities futures contracts on margin. *Margin* simply means that the contract is not fully paid for in cash. Instead, the trader deposits earnest money—usually 5 to 20 percent of the cash value of the contract—with the broker. Buying on margin greatly increases the impact of commodities price fluctuations. With a 10 percent margin, for example, the commodities trader will realize a gross return of 50 percent if the futures profits are 5 percent. If, on the other hand, the prices move in the wrong direction and losses are 5 percent, the holder of a contract with a 10 percent margin will suffer losses of 50 percent. As a result, even minor price fluctuations may have disastrous consequences for some. Individual investors are usually counseled to avoid commodities futures trading unless they can absorb the losses and have a high tolerance for risk.

Futures Exchanges

Trading in commodities and financial futures is conducted on 12 major exchanges in the United States. In many respects, commodities exchanges are similar to stock exchanges. Both are membership organizations. In commodities exchanges, most members are either individuals representing brokerage firms (through which nonmembers trade) or those who are directly involved in producing, marketing, or processing commodities.

Like the stock exchanges, each commodity exchange has its own governing board which sets and enforces the rules under which the trading takes place, and like the stock exchanges, the commodities exchanges themselves do not buy or sell the product being traded or set prices.

Yet another similarity is the willingness of the exchanges to provide information to prospective investors about the mechanics of trading and about specific commodities. As a result, it is a fairly simple matter for a librarian wishing to build a comprehensive vertical file collection to acquire an impressive number of pamphlets from the exchanges, usually at no cost. Appendix J lists the major exchanges, their abbreviations, their addresses, and the futures they trade.

Each exchange sets certain standards for the goods it trades; a Minneapolis Grain Exchange wheat contract is always for 5,000 bushels of No. 2 Northern spring wheat, while the coffee "C" contract traded on the Coffee, Sugar & Cocoa Exchange is always for 37,500 pounds of "washed arabica coffee," and so on. The exchange also specifies delivery site(s) and the months in which delivery may take place. Figure 16.2 (see page 380) summarizes the regulations set by the Chicago Board of Trade pertaining to wheat futures contracts.

Each exchange also sets limits on the amounts by which prices can either rise or fall during a single trading day. The MidAmerica Commodity Exchange, for example, limits prices for its contracts in live hogs to a maximum rise or fall of 1½ cents per pound from the previous trading day's closing price, while the Coffee, Sugar & Cocoa Exchange sets limits of $88 per metric ton on its cocoa futures contracts. An exchange temporarily suspends trading of a particular delivery month in a commodity when it reaches the daily limit established by the exchange, thus controlling some of the wide swings that might otherwise develop in commodities prices.

Commodity Futures Trading Commission

Futures trading is regulated by the Commodity Futures Trading Commission (CFTC), an independent federal regulatory commission established by Congress in 1974.

> The Commission's regulatory and enforcement efforts are designed to ensure that the futures trading process is fair and that it protects both the rights of the customers and the financial integrity of the marketplace. The CFTC approves the rules under which an exchange proposes to operate and monitors exchange enforcement of those rules. It reviews the terms of proposed futures contracts, and registers companies and individuals who handle customer funds or give trading advice. The Commission also protects the public by enforcing rules that require that customer funds be kept in bank accounts separate from accounts maintained by firms for their own use, and that such customer accounts be marked to present market value at the close of each trading day.[3]

The CFTC also serves as an important source of commodities futures information, issuing periodic statistical compilations and reports on the trade of various commodities. In addition, it offers several publications for the individual investor considering trading in commodities. These can be ordered from the CFTC's Education Unit.[4] Copies are also available in most regional depository libraries.

Current Prices

Because of the volatility of the commodities market and its rapid price fluctuations, current price information is vital to traders. Professional investors may get up-to-the-minute information using tickers, wire services, and online databases. Small investors, on the other hand, may rely on the current daily price information found in the *Wall Street Journal, New York Times, Journal of Commerce,* and many local newspapers. A sample of the kind of information contained in daily futures tables is shown in figure 16.3 (see page 381).

Chicago Board of Trade
Wheat Futures
Highlights

Basic Trading Unit	5,000 bushels
Deliverable Grade	No. 2 Soft Red, No. 2 Hard Red Winter, No. 2 Dark Northern Spring, No. 1 Northern Spring and substitutions at differentials established by the Exchange
Price Quotation	Cents and quarter cents per bushel
Minimum Fluctuation	One-quarter ($\frac{1}{4}$) cent per bushel ($12.50 per contract)
Daily Price Limit	20 cents per bushel ($1,000 per contract) above and below the previous day's settlement price
Contract Months	July, September, December, March and May
Contract Year	Starts with July contracts and ends with May contracts
Trading Hours	9:30 a.m. to 1:15 p.m. (Chicago Time)
Last Trading Day	Seventh business day preceding the last business day of the month
Last Delivery Day	Last business day of the delivery month
Ticker Symbol	W
Date Trading Began	January 2, 1877

Fig. 16.2. Wheat futures contract specifications, Chicago Board of Trade. Copyright © 1985 Board of Trade of the City of Chicago.

FUTURES PRICES

	Open	High	Low	Settle	Change	Lifetime High	Low	Open Interest
				-GRAINS AND OILSEEDS-[1]				

[2]Corn (CBT)[3] 5,000 bu;[4] cents per bu[5]

	Open	High	Low	Settle	Change	High	Low	Open Interest
Sept[6]	1671/2[7]	168[8]	162[9]	1671/4-[10]	41/2[11]	208[12]	1571/4[13]	32,500[14]
Dec	1773/4	1781/4	1711/4	1711/2-	43/4	216	1631/4	61,800
Mr	1871/4	1871/2	1801/2	181-	43/4	2223/4	171	14,895

[15]Est vol 37,000; vol Tues 22,702;[16] open int 76,484, -342

1. Category of Commodity. Futures contracts are grouped into six categories: grains and oilseeds; livestock and meat; food and fiber; metals and petroleum; lumber; and financial.
2. Commodity Traded. Here, the commodity being traded is corn.
3. Exchange. Exchange on which the product is traded, usually presented in abbreviated form. Abbreviations are explained at the bottom of the futures price table in the Wall Street Journal. Here, "CBT" stands for Chicago Board of Trade.
4. Units Per Contract. Number of units comprising one futures contract. One CBT corn futures contract, for example, is comprised of 5,000 bushels of corn.
5. Unit of Measure for Which Price is Given. Corn, for example, is priced in cents per bushel.
6. Delivery Month. The left column shows the month during which deliveries in futures contracts must be made unless the contracts are offset.
7. Open. The price for the day's first trade; here, $1.675 per bushel.
8. High. Highest price at which the commodity sold that day.
9. Low. Lowest price at which the commodity sold.
10. Settle. Roughly equivalent to the closing price, usually based on a range of closing prices; here, $1.6725 per bushel.
11. Change. The difference between the price at close and the previous day's closing price.
12. Lifetime High. Highest price ever recorded for each contract maturity.
13. Lifetime Low. Lowest price ever recorded.
14. Open Interest. Number of outstanding contracts at the close of the day.
15. Volume of Trading. First figure is estimated volume for the trading day being reported, second figure is actual volume on preceding trading day.
16. Total Open Ineterest and Open Interest Change. First number is the total number of contracts outstanding, all maturities, for the commodity and exchange specified; second number compares the total number of contracts outstanding on the trading day reported with the preceding day.

Fig. 16.3. Typical listings, newspaper commodity futures table.

In this table, the opening price for Chicago Board of Trade corn futures contracts maturing in March was $1.8725 per bushel, or $9,362.50 per contract. The highest price paid that day was $1.875 per bushel ($9,375.00), the lowest was $1.805 per bushel ($9,025.00), with the settlement price estimated at $1.81 per bushel ($9,050.00). There was a decrease of 4¾ cents per bushel ($237.50 per contract) from the preceding trading day. The highest price ever paid for a March CBT corn futures contract was $2.2275 per bushel ($11,137.50), while the lowest price ever paid was $1.71 per bushel ($8,550.00). On the day being reported 14,895 March corn futures contracts were outstanding.

Less widely traded futures contracts are listed in separate tables, as are cash prices paid for the immediate delivery of various commodities. For more recent price quotes, a Dow Jones News/Retrieval database is particularly helpful.

Dow Jones Futures Quotes. Dow Jones News/Retrieval. Continuous updates.

This database offers current prices for more than 60 different commodities traded on major U.S. and Canadian exchanges. The quotes are constantly updated, and are displayed within 10 to 30 minutes after they are listed on the exchange. Information for each contract is similar to that provided in newspaper futures tables, and includes delivery month and year; daily open, high, low, last, and settlement prices; lifetime high and low; and daily volume and open interest. A help screen not only guides searchers through the database, but offers background information on commodities trading, directories of exchanges and their symbols, and an explanation of how to interpret price quotes.

Although prices for major commodities are easy enough to locate in key financial newspapers and databases such as *Dow Jones Futures Quotes*, there are several less widely traded commodities for which price information can be difficult to find.

Wasserman, Paul, and Diane Kemmerling. **Commodity Prices.** Detroit: Gale Research Co., 1974. 214p.

Wasserman's *Commodity Prices* lists 268 different American and Canadian sources which contain information on 5,000 different agricultural, commercial, industrial and consumer products. Although not necessary for all libraries, it is extremely useful to librarians who are asked for information about prices for fairly specialized commodities. The *Encyclopedia of Business Information Sources*, arranged by specific product, also lists sources of hard-to-find price information and has the advantage of being more current.

Financial Futures

Although commodities futures trading has been practiced for generations, financial futures are relatively new. Financial futures trading began in the 1970s with the trading of futures contracts on selected foreign currencies and fixed-income securities, such as Treasury bills. Since then, the diversity of products and trading volume have expanded considerably, and today financial futures comprise approximately three-fourths of all futures contracts traded in the United States.[5] As with commodity futures contracts, traders can use financial futures for hedging.

> In various ways, they provide borrowers, lenders, and users of foreign currencies with the same kind of protection against price variances as hedging in corn or wheat does. For example, an insurance company with a portfolio of bonds might worry that bond prices are due for a slump, to the detriment of its balance sheet. If the company sells Treasury bond futures, it will profit from such a slump and be able to use those profits to offset losses in the value of its portfolio.[6]

Financial futures can also be used for speculating. Someone who expects interest rates to increase can buy interest rate futures. If expecting the value of the Japanese yen to decline, the person can sell foreign currency futures. The most rapidly growing sector of the financial futures market, stock index futures, permits traders to try to profit from swings in the stock market by buying or selling futures contracts tied to such stock indexes as the Standard & Poor's 500 and the New York Stock Exchange Composite Index. Other index futures are tied to municipal bonds, the consumer price index, and commodity futures.

Financial futures are traded on the Chicago Board of Trade, International Monetary Market (part of the Chicago Mercantile Exchange), Kansas City Board of Trade, and the New York Futures Exchange, a subsidiary of the New York Stock Exchange.

Financial futures prices for major products are reported daily in futures price tables along with commodity price data, but researchers should be forewarned that the way in which prices are quoted will vary from one type of financial future to another. The quotations for Treasury bills, for example, are reported differently than those for Treasury bonds, and stock index futures quotations are different from those for foreign currencies. Although space does not permit inclusion of each type of newspaper financial futures table, readers can find examples and useful explanations by consulting "Financial and Stock Index Futures" in *The Investor's Guide to Stock Quotations and Other Listings*.

FUTURES INFORMATION SOURCES

Futures traders require current information to help them make sound investment decisions. They may acquire this information through brokerage firms, by reading financial newspapers and magazines, or from commodity exchanges, government agencies, commercial publishers, and database vendors. While only the largest and most specialized institutions will have a comprehensive collection of relevant reference materials, virtually every library should include selected publications. This section examines certain basic works.

Guides

Finding information on how futures trading works is easy. There are virtually hundreds of "how-to" books for erstwhile traders, ranging from flamboyant rags-to-riches-overnight sagas to weighty academic tomes, and almost all of them include descriptions of the mechanics of futures trading. Sometimes, however, a patron may want a brief introduction to futures trading. The titles listed below are particularly useful.

Chicago Board of Trade. **Commodity Trading Manual**. Chicago: The Board, 1985.

Gould, Bruce G. **The Dow Jones-Irwin Guide to Commodities Trading**. Rev. ed. Homewood, Ill.: Dow Jones-Irwin, 1981. 361p.

Powers, Mark J., and David J. Vogel. **Inside the Financial Futures Market**. 2nd ed. New York: Wiley, 1984. 369p.

Published by the Chicago Board of Trade, the *Commodity Trading Manual* includes chapters on the history and development of commodities trading, basic operations and trading strategies, and federal and exchange regulations. The major exchanges themselves are described in some detail.

For each of the commodities covered, the *Manual* includes a summary of past production, performance, supply, and demand. It lists the exchanges on which each is traded (and includes each exchange's regulations pertaining to delivery months, trading units, price and position limits, grades deliverable, delivery sites, and exchange trading hours) and cites selected sources of commercial, government, and trade information. The section on poultry, for example, lists books, Department of Agriculture reports, and trade reports from the Poultry and Egg Institute of America and the National Broiler Council.

The Dow Jones-Irwin Guide to Commodities Trading, written by a professional commodities speculator, includes some of the basic background material offered by the *Manual*, but also presents more detailed information on such technical aspects of futures trading as price forecasting, seasonal trends, and managing commodity accounts. Appendixes include a collection of sample commodity orders and a bibliography of relevant information sources.

Inside the Financial Futures Market includes general background information, as well as explanations of price analysis, interest rate and currency futures, stock index futures and options, recordkeeping, and trading techniques for hedgers and speculators.

A major problem with such guides is that they quickly become dated. One of the best ways to keep up with financial futures is by requesting brochures and pamphlets from the exchanges on which they are traded. These publications are more easily and inexpensively published than books, and can be valuable supplements to the guides listed above.

Bibliographies

A number of futures bibliographies are available; the titles below are typical.

Woy, James. **Commodity Futures Trading: A Bibliographic Guide**. New York: Bowker, 1976. 206p.

Nicholas, David. **Commodities Futures Trading: A Guide to Information Sources and Computerized Services**. London: Mansell, 1985. 144p.

Chicago Board of Trade. **Commodity Futures Trading: Bibliography**. Chicago: The Board, 1967- . Annual.

Woy's *Commodity Futures Trading* bridges the gap between guides and bibliographies. Intended for amateur investors and the librarians who serve them, it is a compendium of definitions, lists of books, descriptions of specific trading methods, and of many different commodities. Woy can serve both as a reference tool and as an aid in developing a good commodities collection. Using it, a librarian can find easy-to-understand definitions of such terms as the random walk theory; it can also be used to identify books on subjects as diverse as moon cycles, the oscillator method, and the psychology of commodities trading. A significant drawback is that Woy is dated, and coverage of financial futures is thus rather sparse. It remains useful, however, for the products it does cover.

More recent information is available in Nicholas's *Commodities Futures Trading: A Guide to Information Sources and Computerized Services*. Nicholas emphasizes the importance of up-to-the-minute information for commodities traders, focusing primarily on online trading systems, wire services, newspapers, and newsletter/telephone "hotline" combinations. Other reference sources, including books, periodicals and indexing services, yearbooks, and directories are also covered. Published in Great Britain, Nicholas combines descriptions of British and European sources with those published in North America.

Although not annotated, the *Commodity Futures Trading: Bibliography* is comprehensive, listing books, periodical articles, and commodity and trade press publications issued in the current year as well as material from earlier years. The annual bibliography supplements a cumulative bibliography, which is updated periodically and pulls together material contained in earlier annual bibliographies.

Dictionaries

Many of the publications that have already been described contain glossaries of key terms. In addition, the standard investment dictionaries listed in chapter 12 also include basic futures trading vocabulary. Another source is particularly useful for its coverage of commodities trading.

Steinbeck, George, and Rosemary Erickson. **The Language of Commodities: A Commodity Glossary**. New York: New York Institute of Finance, 1985. 198p.

The Language of Commodities defines terms ranging from *abandonment* to *zero plus tick*, some of which are too specialized to be included in standard business dictionaries. Explanations as well as definitions are frequently included, and both are enhanced by specific examples, charts, and *see also* references. Appendixes include "How to Read the Commodity Financial Quotes"; "Reference Guides," frequently used abbreviations for commodity exchanges and organizations; "Basic Calculations," which demonstrates the use of relevant formulas and calculations; and "How to Find a Commodity Factor," which explains how to translate data given in newspaper financial pages into *factor*, a component used in commodity formulas.

Periodicals, Newspapers, and Newsletters

Futures trading is covered to a certain extent in such general business periodicals as *Business Week* and *Forbes*, but may be too dated to be of much practical use to professional traders.

> Few journals are read by practitioners in the commodities world, who are much more interested in hard factual data (found in newspapers and the like) than in the research reports, product reviews, and methodological papers that are a feature of much of the journal literature. If investors hear of research at all, they will probably obtain it either orally or in filtered form in one of the popular newsletters; as for methods, these will generally be derived from work practice. Academics and researchers in the field, on the other hand, use journals to the exclusion of all else. Practitioners argue, perhaps a little unfairly, that these are the only people with the time and patience to wade through these publications.[7]

There is, however, one specialized commodity periodical that is popular with traders and researchers alike.

Futures: The Magazine of Commodities & Options. Cedar Falls, Iowa: Oster Communications, 1972- . Monthly. [Formerly *Commodities: The Magazine of Futures Trading*]

Futures offers its readers a series of articles on different aspects of futures and options trading. An issue may contain as many as 20 different articles dealing with such subjects as trading techniques, government policy affecting trading, the economy, and developments at specific exchanges. It periodically rates the performance of best-selling futures advisory services, and each month reviews microcomputer software packages relevant to futures trading. Other regular features include "My Position," editorial comment; "Trade Winds," news of major exchanges; "Option Strategy," techniques for options trading; "Pit Stops," which covers commodities; "Funds Review," for discussion of mutual funds trading in futures and/or options; "Commodity Alert," a calendar of important dates; and "Trader Profile" for biographical coverage of noted traders.

Although readers new to futures trading may find some articles difficult going, for the most part *Futures* is lively and well written and can be useful to novice investors as well as seasoned professionals.

Each year *Futures* issues a directory supplement, the *Annual Reference Guide to Futures Markets*. The *Guide*, which can be purchased separately, includes the names and addresses of the major brokerage, charting, computer, and advisory services, as well as weather services, commodity book and newsletter publishers, and consultants.

While not as popular as *Futures*, another periodical contains data of interest to academicians and other researchers.

The Journal of Futures Markets. New York: Wiley, 1981- . Quarterly.

Published in affiliation with the Center for the Study of Futures Markets of the Columbia Business School, *The Journal of Futures Markets* contains articles written by scholars on the technical and methodological aspects of futures trading and analysis. Each issue includes between 8 and 10 signed articles as well as book reviews, a bibliography of recent publications, and a brief treatment of legal and regulatory developments relating to futures trading.

Several financial newspapers contain information about commodities markets in addition to the price quotes that they regularly supply. The *Wall Street Journal*, for example, devotes at least one page of each issue to commodities, including features on specific products and the political, economic, industrial, and climatological factors that affect them, as well as summaries of significant developments in futures markets on the preceding trading day. *Barron's* column, "Commodities Corner," regularly features analysis of recent developments in the trade of specific products as well as more general information.

It is the *Journal of Commerce*, however, that provides the most comprehensive financial newspaper coverage of commodities. The daily price tables it includes for both futures and cash markets list more commodities than comparable tables in other newspapers, with data on foreign markets — London metals, Tokyo gold, Singapore rubber, and Sydney steer, among others — as well as domestic markets. It also includes articles on individual commodities, reviews of past trading, and projections for the future, all of which are included in the first section of the paper and indexed on page one. In addition, the *Journal of Commerce* covers all the major business and financial news that can affect commodities prices. Periodically, whole sections of the paper are devoted to specific industries, products, and commodities, or to special studies of supply and demand for each commodity. It is an important source of information for the serious commodities trader.

Other newspapers specialize in futures trading.

American Association of Commodity Traders. **Commodity Journal**. Concord, N.H.: The Association, 1965- . Bimonthly.

Consensus. Kansas City, Mo.: Consensus, 1971- . Weekly.

Commodity Journal is a sort of newspaper equivalent of *Futures*, covering both commodities and financial futures. Each issue contains signed articles ranging from the practical to the theoretical. Advertisements, many of them for newsletters, advisory services, and software packages, account for a substantial portion of the *Journal*.

Consensus focuses on commodities. Each weekly issue includes digests of current market letters, special studies, buy-sell recommendations issued by major brokerage firms, daily price quotations, and detailed price charts. Whether or not the cost of a highly specialized publication such as *Consensus* is offset by its anticipated use by library users must, of course, be determined by each library.

Commodities newsletters, weekly or monthly reviews of commodities trading and trends, are issued by several sources. Many are free, particularly those issued by banks, brokerage firms, and commodities exchanges. The titles listed below are typical.

Barclays Bank. Group Economics Department. **Barclays Commodities Survey**. London: The Bank, 1979- . Quarterly.

Kansas City Board of Trade. **KCBT Report**. Kansas City, Mo.: The Board. Bimonthly.

The Group Economics Department of Barclays Bank publishes a brief newsletter that surveys recent developments, makes projections, and offers a sector-by-sector commodity review. It is intended for the lay person, and is both authoritative and well written. The *KCBT Report*, published by the Kansas City Board of Trade, charts recent developments at the Board and in the products traded there. Occasionally, the *Report* also lists free publications that have recently been issued.

Statistics

A wide range of statistical publications is available, including those issued by commercial publishers, federal and state governments, and commodities exchanges. Some are highly specific, dealing with a particular commodity or group of commodities, such as the U.S. Department of Agriculture Crop Reporting Service's quarterly compilation, *Sugar Market Statistics*. Others are more general and cover the whole gamut of futures trading. Of these general sources, one of the most widely used and highly regarded is the *Commodity Year Book*.

Commodity Year Book. New York: Commodity Research Bureau, Inc., 1939- . Annual.

Commodity Year Book Statistical Abstract Service. New York: Commodity Research Bureau, Inc., 1964- . Triannual.

The *Commodity Year Book* provides detailed statistical data on over 100 commodities, ranging from alcohol to zinc. Coverage for each basic commodity generally includes a review of the past year's supply and demand and the conditions affecting both, a list of the exchanges on which the commodity is traded in the United States, and several tables on world production, domestic price support programs, domestic price supply, distribution, production, prices, exports, volume of trading, and other statistics. Most tables give information for at least 10 years, and some date back as far as 14 years. The *Year Book* also includes charts of cash prices for many commodities, with prices plotted on a monthly basis for the past 10 years. Each edition also features special research studies. The 1987 edition, for example, included articles on price trends, the U.S. agricultural dilemma, and financial futures. The *Commodity Year Book* is the single most important source of current and retrospective statistical data, and should be in most library reference collections. For those who require even more current information, the Commodity Research Bureau also publishes the *Commodity Year Book Statistical Abstract Service*, which updates monthly and annual tables and price charts contained in the *Year Book*.

Statistical compilations issued by the exchanges range from rather brief booklets to detailed, multivolume sets. The Chicago Board of Trade, for example, issues a statistical annual in two parts.

Chicago Board of Trade. **Statistical Annual: Grains, Options on Agricultural Futures**. Chicago: The Board, 1979- . Annual.

_____. **Statistical Annual: Interest Rates, Metals, Stock Indices, Options on Financial Futures, Options on Metal Futures**. Chicago: The Board, 1979- . Annual.

Each part of the *Statistical Annual* is indexed, and contains detailed price information for each commodity for each day of trade on the Chicago Board of Trade. The Chicago Mercantile Exchange also publishes a two-volume statistical annual that presents data on futures and option trading.

More specialized publications are also available, often from trade associations and the federal government.

Metal Statistics. New York: American Metal Markets, 1908- . Annual.

U.S. Dept. of the Interior. Bureau of Mines. **Minerals Yearbook**. Washington, D.C.: Government Printing Office, 1932/33- . 3v. Annual.

Typical of these are *Metal Statistics*, which compiles trade and production data on over 27 different metals, and the *Minerals Yearbook*, issued in three volumes by the U.S. Bureau of Mines.

The U.S. Department of Agriculture is a major supplier of data on agricultural commodities. Much of this information is available through the USDA's Crop Reporting Service, which periodically issues special reports on specific commodities. Another branch of the USDA, the Economic Research Service, publishes "Outlook and Situation" reports on individual commodities. Although these Agriculture Department publications are valuable information sources, they have not been immune to recent cutbacks in federal government publishing. As a result, some reports have been discontinued, and others, formerly free, now are available only by paid subscription.

Other sources of general and specialized commodities statistics can be found in the *American Statistics Index, Commodity Trading Manual, Encyclopedia of Business Information Sources, Statistical Reference Index, Statistics Sources*, and Woy's *Commodity Futures Trading*.

Advisory Services

Another source of market information is the futures advisory service. There are several such publications, some of which include detailed technical analyses and charts, while others contain only brief analyses and buy/sell recommendations. As with all investment advisory services, cost and quality vary, as do user opinions about the merits of each. Major advisory services are listed in the *Directory of Business and Financial Services* and in Nicholas's *Commodities Futures Trading*.

For many librarians, however, the decision will not be which of the many commodities advisory services to subscribe to, but whether to subscribe to any. The infrequent use of commodities advisory services by patrons compared to other investment services may mean that a subscription to such a publication cannot be justified, particularly with a limited serials budget. This is one instance in which users might be referred to nearby brokerage houses that trade commodities. These firms often subscribe to major advisory services and usually are not averse to making them available, even to those who are not presently clients.

Databases

Like the other investment mediums, a number of the general business databases contain information relevant to futures traders. Such files as *ABI/Inform, Trade & Industry Index*, and *PTS F&S Indexes*, for example, often yield valuable background information. Many product-oriented databases such as *Agribusiness U.S.A., Coffeeline*, and *Metadex* are useful for even more specialized commodities information. Finally, *Dow Jones Futures Quotes* is useful for current prices.

OPTIONS

Options give their holders the right to buy or sell certain securities—traditionally common stocks in 100-share units—at a set price by a certain, predetermined date regardless of how high or low the price of the underlying stock may move during that time.[8] An option holder may, for example, purchase the right to buy 100 shares of Acme Electronics for $60 per share anytime between date of purchase and, say, May. This means that, whatever the current market value of 100 shares of Acme may be, the holder can buy them for $6,000. If, for example, Acme shares soar to $106 (or $10,600 per 100 shares), the lucky option holder can either sell the option itself to another investor for a profit or can exercise the option and acquire Acme shares at a cost considerably below market value. If, on the other hand, the stock plummets to $50 per share (or $5,000 per 100 shares), the holder may choose not to exercise the option simply by allowing it to lapse; that is, by doing nothing until the contract expires in May. Why pay for the right to pay $6,000 for 100 shares of stock when it can be had for $5,000?

Holding an option is vastly different from owning the stock itself. Stock ownership represents part ownership in the issuing company, while an option merely gives its holder the right—which may or may not be exercised—to buy or sell stock at a predetermined price within a designated time period. An option holder has none of the rights of a stockholder; he or she cannot vote, owns no part of the company issuing the stock, and receives no dividends. Options are issued or written by individual investors and security dealers, who retain ultimate responsibility for carrying out the terms specified in the options contracts. They are *not* written by the companies issuing the underlying stock.

Options are attractive to many investors because they can be purchased for a fraction of the cost of the underlying stock and offer the opportunity for high profit with limited risk. Unlike the more speculative commodities trading, in options risk is limited to a predetermined amount, the amount paid for the option itself. If the market should go against an unlucky option trader, the worst that can happen is that the option will expire and become worthless. Finally, the action is fast. Most options expire at the end of three, six, or nine months.

Basic Features

Options contracts contain four basic features: (1) the striking price, or the price at which 100 shares of the underlying common stock can be bought or sold, (2) the exercise period, or the duration of the options contract, (3) the expiration date, and (4) the premium, or purchase price of the option itself. Each of these merits further attention.

The *striking price*, also known as the *exercise price*, is the price at which an option can be executed. In the above example, the striking price for a May option on Acme Electronics is $60 per share. (Note that while the striking price is listed on a per-share basis, the option contract itself is for 100 shares.) There are usually two or three different striking prices for options contracts expiring in a particular month.

The *exercise period* is the time during which an option can be executed. Listed options are written for periods of three, six, and nine months. For example, there are Acme options that expire in February, May, and August, and someone trading in Acme options could choose any of these exercise periods.

Closely allied to the exercise period is the *expiration date*. Three expiration date cycles have been created by the exchanges which list options, with each option assigned to one of the three cycles. There is a January-April-July-October cycle, a February-May-August-November cycle, and a March-June-September-December cycle. Prices are quoted for only three of the months listed in any cycle. For Acme, the February-May-August expiration dates would be quoted until the February options expired, then the May-August-November dates would be quoted, and so on.

The striking price, exercise period, and expiration date are all set at the time an option contract is written, and do not change for the duration of the contract. The *premium*, or cost of the option itself, however, fluctuates from day to day, reflecting the current market value of the underlying stock and investor expectations about its future value. Option premiums are quoted in newspaper option tables on a per-share basis. If, for example, the premium for Acme is listed at 30¼, the cost of an options contract would be $3,025 or $30.25 × 100.

Puts and Calls

There are two basic forms of options: puts and calls. A *call* gives its owner the right to buy 100 shares of common stock at a specified price (the striking price) within a given time (the exercise period) before the expiration date. A *put*, on the other hand, is an option to sell 100 shares of common stock for the striking price, exercise period, and expiration date designated in the contract. The purchaser of a put expects the value of the underlying stock to decline, while the purchaser of a call expects the stock's value to increase.

Exchanges

Prior to 1973, all options were traded in the over-the-counter market, with each option written to meet the specific requirement of the buyer. These *conventional options* were, in fact, so specialized that the secondary market for them was almost nonexistent. Holders of these conventional options could choose to exercise them and buy or sell the underlying stock at the striking price, or they could let the options expire; very seldom were they able to sell the options to other investors.

In 1973, the Chicago Board Options Exchange (CBOE) was opened by the Chicago Board of Trade, and *listed options* came into being. Unlike the conventional options traded over-the-counter, listed options are standardized, with systematic procedures for trading. As a result, there is a brisk secondary market in listed options, and while conventional options are still available in the OTC market, trading in listed options is far more active.

Although it was the first, the CBOE is not the only exchange that lists options. Puts and calls are also traded on the American, New York, Pacific, and Philadelphia Stock Exchanges, and major newspapers include options price tables for most of these exchanges.

Listed Options Quotations

Because options have such comparatively short life spans, and because the market for them can be extremely volatile, many professional traders follow price movements on an hour-by-hour or even a minute-by-minute basis. Smaller, private investors may find that the prices quoted in daily newspaper options tables are current enough. An extract from an options table is shown in figure 16.4.

LISTED OPTIONS QUOTATIONS						
CHICAGO BOARD[1]						
Option & NY Close	Strike Price	Calls - Last[2]			Puts - Last[3]		
		Aug	Sept	Oct	Aug	Sept	Oct[4]
Chryslr[5]							
393/4	35[6]	43/4[7]	51/4	51/2	1/8[8]	7/16	1/2
Pepsi							
387/8	35	37/8	43/8	41/2	r[9]	1/4	1/2
Xerox							
741/2	75	11/4	2	3	17/8	r	33/8

1. <u>Exchange</u>. Exchange on which the option is traded. Here, "Chicago Board" indicates that the option is traded on the Chicago Board Options Exchange.
2. <u>Calls - Last</u>. Last prices paid for options entitling the holder to buy 100 shares of the underlying common stock.
3. <u>Puts - Last</u>. Last prices paid for options entitling the holder to sell 100 shares of the underlying common stock.
4. <u>Options Cycle</u>. Quotes for both calls and puts are listed by expiration date cycles, with all options traded in one cycle listed first, and then followed by all options traded in the next cycle.
5. <u>Company Name and Current Market Value of Underlying Stock</u>. The company name is usually abbreviated. Here options for Chrysler common stock, currently selling at $39.75 per share, are listed.
6. <u>Striking Price</u>. The per share price at which the common stock can be bought or sold by the option holder. Here, the striking price is $35.00 per share.
7. <u>Last Price - Calls</u>. The last price paid, for each of the expiration months, listed for the right to buy 100 shares of common stock at the striking price. Here, the premium, or price paid, was 43/4, or $4.75 per share. To get the cost of the options contract, which is for 100 shares, multiply by 100.
8. <u>Last Price - Puts</u>. The last price paid, for each of the months listed, for the right to sell 100 shares of the underlying common stock. As with stocks, 1/8=121/2 cents, and as with calls, the price given must be multiplied by 100 to get the actual price of the options contract.
9. <u>"R"</u>. The "r" indicates that the option specified was not traded on the day being reported.

Fig. 16.4. Newspaper options table.

Thus, on the day being reported in figure 16.4, the current market value of Xerox common stock was $74.50 per share. Calls, or options to buy Xerox at a striking price of $75.00 per share were sold for $1.25 per share for the August expiration date. Puts, or options to sell Xerox at $75.00 per share for the August expiration date, sold for 1⅞ per share, approximately $1.88. No September Xerox puts were traded on the day being reported.

OPTIONS INFORMATION SOURCES

Decisions to purchase and trade in options are based primarily on the investor's opinion of the underlying stocks. As a result, the types of information sources described in chapter 13 will interest the person who speculates in options as much as the investor who buys stocks outright. Both will want to consult corporate reports, financial newspapers and journals, industry reports, stock charting, reporting and advisory services, and comprehensive investment services. There are, however, other more specialized publications.

Guides

Librarians and lay investors seeking to learn more about options trading can consult a wide assortment of introductory publications, ranging from pamphlets issued by brokers and exchanges to full-length texts outlining sophisticated trading techniques. In addition, sources that run the gamut of finance and investment often provide good basic information about options. The *Dow Jones-Irwin Business and Investment Almanac*, for example, covers put and call options, the reading of stock options quotations, and presents lists of the exchanges on which options are traded and the expiration date cycles they employ.

The Chicago Board Options Exchange publishes a number of pamphlets aimed at prospective investors. *Understanding Options*, for example, discusses the writing and trading of puts and calls, and outlines investor strategies for each. It is a good, basic introduction.[9]

Exchange-issued pamphlets are usually free or inexpensive and are simple to acquire. Further, since these pamphlets are revised fairly frequently, they tend to more accurately reflect the constantly growing and changing options market. Books that are only a year or two old may fail to indicate the breadth or volume of options trading today. Adding pamphlets to the vertical file collection is an inexpensive way to maintain up-to-date information on this rapidly changing field.

Periodicals and Newspapers

Options trading is covered periodically in *Business Week, Forbes, Money*, and other standard business serial titles. *Futures* contains a monthly column, "Options Strategy," that focuses on specific trading tactics and methods of analysis. In addition, articles on options are regularly featured, covering such topics as "How Option Traders Bet on Volatility," "Options and the Layman," and "How to Put a Portfolio on the Right Track."

Some of the best current coverage of options trading can be found in *Barron's*. Its "Options Trading" section provides complete statistical data on options activity of the Chicago Board Options Exchange and on the American, New York, Pacific, and Philadelphia Stock Exchanges, while the column, "The Striking Price," covers recent developments and trends in this fast-moving market.

Articles on new developments, trading coups and fiascos, and tax aspects of options trading are also regularly featured in the *Wall Street Journal*.

Statistics

Statistics on the options market are generally available from the exchanges on which they are traded. The Chicago Board Options Exchange, for example, publishes an annual brochure that gives quarterly, annual, and five-year data on stock prices and on options. The American and New York Stock Exchanges include options statistics in their annual *Fact Books*, while the Pacific and Philadelphia Stock Exchanges feature statistical data with their annual reports. Another source specializes in options.

Standard & Poor's. **Options Handbook**. New York: Standard & Poor's, 1982- . Semi-annual.

The *Options Handbook* includes two-page stock reports on stocks on which listed options are traded. Data presented for each stock include the exchange on which the option is traded, its recent price, price-earnings ratio, and historical data going back at least seven years. While much of the information in the *Options Handbook* is duplicated in other sources, such as Standard & Poor's *Security Owner's Stock Guide*, the *Handbook* is convenient and useful.

Advisory Services

Although prospective options traders may be content with some of the standard stock advisory services described in chapter 13, others may wish to consult special options services. While there are not as many options services as there are stock services, their number is growing, reflecting the increased interest in this area.

Daily Graphs. Stock Option Guide. Los Angeles, Calif.: William O'Neill & Co., Inc. Weekly.

Value Line Options. New York: Value Line, Inc., v. 12, no. 27, 1981- . Weekly.

Some are charting services, aimed at those who are technically oriented; these usually do not contain specific recommendations. Typical of these is *Stock Option Guide*, which provides graphic and statistical data on all active listed options and their underlying stocks.

Other services make specific recommendations. One of the most widely used of these is *Value Line Options*, a weekly that ranks options performance and evaluates risk levels for both writers and buyers of puts and calls. In addition to data on specific options, this service provides general information in its "Options Strategist" section, including basic background information and trading techniques and strategies.

There are other options advisory services, some similar in scope and content to the *Stock Option Guide* and *Value Line Options*, and others which are more like newsletters in tone and format. Some of these publications are listed in *Futures*, and the librarian seeking to build a representative collection of options advisory services would do well to consult it.

NOTES

[1]Robert D. Prinsky, *Understanding Futures: A Guide to Commodity and Financial Futures* (Princeton, N.J.: Dow Jones Educational Service Bureau, 1981), 1.

[2]Charles K. Rolo, "A Strategy for All Seasons," *Money* 11, no. 1 (January 1982): 38.

[3]U.S. Commodity Futures Trading Commission, *Annual Report, 1980* (Washington, D.C.: Government Printing Office, 1981), 12.

[4]Some of the Commodity Futures Trading Commission publications include *Basic Facts about Commodity Futures Trading, Before Trading Commodities — Get the Facts, Do's and Don't about Dealing in Commodities*, and *Economic Purposes of Futures Trading*. For a more detailed list of consumer-oriented publications, write for *CFTC Publications and General Bibliography* (CFTC Futures Fact Sheet No. 2). A free copy can be requested from:

> Commodity Futures Trading Commission
> Education Unit
> 2033 K Street, N.W.
> Washington, D.C. 20581

[5]"Volume Reflects Changing Thrust of Futures Industry," *Futures* 15, no. 3 (March 1986): 48.

[6]Prinsky, 7.

[7]David Nicholas, *Commodities Futures Trading* (London: Mansell, 1985), 87.

[8]In addition to stock options, options are also traded on Treasury notes, stock indexes, foreign currency, gold bullion, and futures.

[9]To request a free copy of *Understanding Options*, write to:

> Chicago Board Options Exchange
> LaSalle at Jackson
> Chicago, IL 60604

What is a surgically misplaced bellybutton worth?* ... *Eight hundred fifty-four thousand two hundred nineteen dollars and sixty-one cents, ruled the jury.

—Andrew Tobias, *The Invisible Bankers*

17

INSURANCE

This chapter describes basic concepts and identifies key information sources in insurance. It is an area in which information is sought by consumers as well as by investors and business people. Research inquiries may range from the investment performance of certain insurance companies to the computation of Social Security retirement benefits, from the number of unemployment insurance claims filed to the names of companies that insure against unusual risks. As a result, sources relevant to many different kinds of library users will be examined.

INSURANCE BASICS

We live in a world filled with risk. Headlines and news broadcasts daily trumpet disasters: explosions, droughts, floods, crashes. Lives are lost, property destroyed. Modern technology brings with it a new array of real and potential disasters. To automobile wrecks and airliner crashes have been added nuclear reactor accidents, toxic waste, even space shuttle explosions. At the same time, many of our lives are touched by less dramatically newsworthy but equally devastating events: the untimely death of a spouse or family member, the loss of a job, or unexpected disease or disability. Almost all of these events have severe financial consequences for the afflicted. Many people turn to insurance to reduce such financial risk.

Characteristics of Insurance

Insurance is a social mechanism that allows individuals, businesses, and other organizations to reduce financial risk by substituting a small but definite cost (the insurance payment, or premium) for a large, uncertain loss. Each of the insured pays a premium to the insurer for the promise that he or she will be reimbursed for losses up to the maximum amount indicated on the insurance policy.

Insurance, in other words, provides a certain measure of protection against major and minor catastrophes. It helps to protect against financial risk associated with death, disease, and property loss. It also may cover theft and embezzlement, professional malpractice, farm crops, ships' cargos, satellite launches, movie stars, hijackings, product liability, even the health of pets. Although different insurance companies (and government agencies) provide different types of insurance, certain characteristics are common to all.

The first of these is *risk transfer*. The insured pays premiums to the insurer, thus transferring financial risk within the limits stipulated by the insurance policy. The second is that of *pooling*. The premiums paid by all of the people cover the losses of the unlucky few to whom the insured-against disaster occurs.

Premium rates are in part based on the forecasts made by insurers regarding the number and severity of claims they will have to pay. Such forecasts are the responsibility of actuaries, experts in the mathematics of insurance. To determine premium rates, actuaries rely on the Law of Large Numbers to predict the amount they will have to pay over a given period. The *Law of Large Numbers* is a mathematical principle that states that as the number of exposures increases, the actual results tend to come closer to the expected results.

A practical illustration of the Law of Large Numbers is the National Safety Council's prediction of the number of auto deaths during a typical holiday weekend. Because millions of automobiles are on the road, the National Safety Council has been able to predict with great accuracy the number of motorists who will die during a typical July 4th holiday weekend.... Although individual motorists cannot be identified, the actual number of deaths for the group of motorists as a whole can be predicted with some accuracy.[1]

In the insurance industry, the Law of Large Numbers means that as the number of people and organizations choosing to insure against certain financial risks increases, the number and extent of loss claims filed with the insurer will more closely approach those predicted. Using statistical data from mortality tables, for example, actuaries are able to predict with reasonable accuracy the number of people in a given population who will die within a specified period, and whose beneficiaries might be expected to file life insurance claims.

A fourth characteristic of insurance is that policies enable the insured to be *indemnified* (either fully or partially reimbursed) for insured losses, but not to profit from such losses. The intent of this principle of indemnity is to eliminate or at least reduce the likelihood of intentional injury or destruction of property for profit. While the principle of indemnity does not, for example, preclude the possibility of arson to collect fire insurance, it means that fewer will be tempted to do so because the motive for profit will be missing.

The four basic characteristics of insurance, then, are that it transfers risk, pools losses, relies on the Law of Large Numbers to predict future losses, and utilizes the principle of indemnity to limit claims to no more than the actual losses incurred.

The terms of agreement between the insurer and the insured are set forth in the insurance policy, a legal contract that specifies types of coverage, amount and frequency of premiums, maximum coverage and amount deductible from coverage, exclusions, and the like. Although policies were once written in language unintelligible to all but lawyers and insurance professionals, many are now written so that lay people may understand them more easily.

Types of Insurance

Insurance can be classified in many different ways. One of the most common is by type of insurer. As shown in figure 17.1 (see page 396), there are two groups of insurers, private and public. Private insurers are primarily commercial insurance companies that sell policies;

public insurers are government agencies that provide compulsory or voluntary insurance. Each of these kinds of insurers can, in turn, be categorized by the type of insurance they offer.

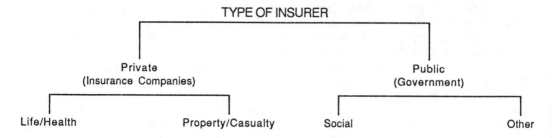

Fig. 17.1. Types of insurers and insurance.

INSURANCE SOLD BY PRIVATE INSURERS

Insurance sold by private insurers falls into two broad categories, life/health and property/casualty (see figure 17.2). Although some companies handle both types of insurance, many sell only one or the other. Life/health insurance and property/casualty insurance are, in fact, often treated as separate industries, as reflected in industry reports published in *Value Line,* Standard & Poor's *Industry Surveys*, and the *U.S. Industrial Outlook*.

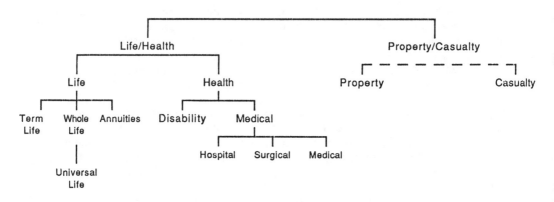

Fig. 17.2. Types of insurance sold by private insurers.

Life Insurance

Life insurance offers financial protection against the death of a family member, usually the major wage earner(s) and/or the person responsible for running and maintaining the home. Although coverage varies, all life insurance policies generally pay money to the beneficiary upon the insured's death.

There are two basic types of life insurance — *term* and *whole*. Term life, which is the least expensive type of life insurance, is often compared by insurance companies to renting, rather than buying, a house. In return for the payment of premiums, the insured is covered for a specified period, or term. The term may be as short as one year, or may extend for as long as 20 years or more. During that period, the insured is covered by the policy. Should he or she die while it is in force, the insurance company will pay the beneficiary the face amount of the policy. Should the insured live beyond the term covered, he or she will have to negotiate a new term life policy with the insurance company.

If term life is the insurance equivalent of renting, whole life is analogous to buying a house. Unlike the temporary coverage provided by term insurance, whole life provides insurance coverage over the entire life of the insured. There are other differences. The cost is determined by the insured's age at the time the policy is drawn up, based on actuarial tables that reflect the incidence and likelihood of death. Once the policy is in force, the premiums will remain the same, whatever the insured's health may be, or however long he or she may live.

Another difference between term life and whole life insurance is that the latter combines a forced savings plan with life insurance coverage. Part of each premium covers "pure" insurance, and part is diverted into a fund, called the *cash value*, which is similar to a savings account. The policyholder has two choices at any time: to continue paying the premiums at the rate originally agreed upon so that beneficiaries can receive death benefits, or to terminate the policy and be given the cash value and its accumulated interest. The interest earned by the cash value in most whole life policies, however, is generally significantly less than the same money would earn in savings accounts, and consumers are frequently counseled to consider alternative forms of investment.

> Insurance executives have traditionally believed in the whole life policy the way other people believe in God, the flag, and motherhood. It accounts for 43% of all life insurance sold, though the company that sells it frequently makes out better than the person who buys it. It is more expensive to buy than term coverage because its premiums are inflated by an amount that goes into a kind of savings account called the cash value. The industry has always promoted whole life as an investment, but the interest on the cash value is typically less than 6%.[2]

In 1979, a new variant of whole life insurance was developed. Like traditional whole life insurance, *universal life* divides premium payments into two parts, one covering the cost of insurance, the other into cash value. Universal life savings, however, are invested in short-term, money market securites that earn tax-free interest rates that are higher than the more conservative whole life cash value savings.

> Whole life remained utterly dominant until the inflation of the 1970s made the 4% to 6% yearly returns look pathetic. "Buy term and invest the difference" became the battle cry of a host of upstart companies. Term once again became dominant. And because it is much cheaper than whole life, total life insurance premiums stagnated despite healthy gains in the face amount of sales. To counter the crippling switch to term, universal life was developed and first marketed by E. F. Hutton in 1979. Universal life lets policyholders vary the amount of insurance protection and the size and timing of premium payments. The premium is split apart or unbundled, enabling buyers to see how much goes for the death benefit and how much to cash value. Moreover, the premiums are placed in separate accounts and invested in securities yielding far more than the old bonds in the company's general accounts.[3]

Universal life offers greater flexibility to its policyholders than does traditional whole life insurance. It permits them to adjust the size of premium payments and to determine when they are paid, subject to certain designated minimums. For these reasons, universal life has become increasingly popular with policyholders, and has accounted for steadily growing sales.

More recently, variant forms of whole life have been offered, permitting even greater flexibility and investment choice. Some, for example, permit choice of the types of securities in which cash value is invested. As opportunities for choice increase, or, as Standard & Poor's would have it, since "plain vanilla insurance" is no longer enough,[4] the availability of objective information about specific life insurance companies and the types of policies they offer has become more important than ever.

While the types of life insurance described above are intended primarily to cover the death of the policyholder and its financial consequences for the beneficiaries, *life annuities* focus on providing income payments to policyholders who have reached a certain age. Life insurance, in other words, provides protection for beneficiaries, while life annuities are designed to provide income for old age.

An annuity is a series of income payments guaranteed for a number of years or over a lifetime. There are two main types of annuities. An *immediate annuity* is one that is purchased with a single, lump-sum payment. The income starts one month from the purchase date if the income payments are to be made on a monthly basis, or one year from the purchase date if payments are made annually. Immediate annuities are usually purchased by the middle-aged or elderly who want annuity income to begin at once and to continue throughout the remainder of their lives.

A *deferred annuity* provides an income that begins at a future date. Although deferred annuities may be purchased with a single, lump-sum payment, more commonly they are paid for in installments over a number of years. The amount that the purchaser, or *annuitant*, receives is determined by the size of the premiums and the interest they earn as well as by the annuitant's age when payments to the insurance company began. The period of time between the first payment by the annuitant to the insurance company and the time the annuitant receives the first payment from the insurance company is known as the *accumulation period*. All interest earned on the accumulated payments during the accumulation period is currently tax-deferred; taxes are not levied on the interest until it is actually paid to the annuitant. This tax-deferred provision is one of the reasons that annuities are popular with many investors.

Health Insurance

Just as the death of a family's key provider can cause severe financial hardship, so also can unexpected disease or disability. Health insurance deals with two major types of financial loss. The first helps to cover medical expenses, including the cost of hospital stays, surgery, regular medical bills, and the major medical expenses caused by catastrophic illness or injury. The nature and extent of coverage of such health insurance policies varies considerably; most have some restrictions, contain certain deductibles, and set limits on coverage. As a result, sources that permit some comparison between companies are vital.

The other major type of loss is that caused by disability. Disability insurance provides periodic payments when the policyholder is unable to work owing to a covered injury, illness, or disease. While disability insurance helps to replace lost income, the principle of indemnity is very much in force. Companies, in fact, generally limit the amount of disability income to no more than 60 or 70 percent of the insured's earned income.

Although some health insurance policies provide both medical coverage and disability income payments, others offer only one or the other. Whatever the type of coverage offered, health insurance policies generally have certain provisions in common. The first of these is the *continuance provision*, which refers to the length of time that an individual policy may be in force and whether or not it will be renewed. A continuance provision may specify that the policy can be cancelled by its holder or, alternatively, that the insurer can refuse to renew the policy. It can also specify that the policy must be renewed or that it cannot be cancelled.

Health insurance policies usually contain a *preexisting conditions clause*, which states that mental or physical conditions that existed in the insured prior to the issuance of the health insurance policy are not covered until the policy has been in force for a specified period, usually a year or two.

Some policies also have a probationary period immediately following their issuance, during which time sickness is not covered by the policy. The probationary period, which is intended to eliminate coverage for sickness that existed before the policy went into effect, does not extend to accidents, which are covered even during the probationary period.

While much of the available health insurance is offered by private, commercial companies, they are by no means the only insurers in this field. Others include Blue Cross and Blue Shield and health maintenance organizations.

Blue Cross organizations are independent, nonprofit, membership corporations that provide protection against the cost of hospital care. Blue Shield organizations are similar in structure and membership, but focus on medical and surgical costs. The Blue Cross and Blue Shield Association provides guidance and direction to the "Blues," setting and enforcing standards for their operation. Originally, Blue Cross and Blue Shield organizations were represented by separate associations. Following their merger into the Blue Cross and Blue Shield Association in 1982, many local Blue Cross and Blue Shield organizations also merged.

A more recent alternative to traditional health insurance provided by for-profit and non-profit insurance companies is the coverage offered through membership in health maintenance organizations. A health maintenance organization, or HMO, is an organized system of health care that provides comprehensive health services to its members for a fixed, prepaid fee. By owning or leasing medical facilities, entering into agreements with hospitals and physicians to provide medical services, and hiring their own support staff, HMOs have greater managerial and financial control over the services offered. In return for a fee, usually paid monthly, HMO members are provided with a wide range of health services, most of which are covered in full even if an illness should reach catastrophic proportions.

Health maintenance organizations, however, have certain disadvantages. Although coverage is guaranteed to its members for the life of the HMO, not all health maintenance organizations survive. The membership in an HMO must be sufficient to support the cost of the services that are offered. When this is not the case (and sometimes, even when it is), HMOs may fail.

Another disadvantage is that members' selection of physicians and health care facilities is limited to those approved by the organization. Such limits to choice, some argue, may destroy the traditional physician-patient relationship or result in poorer quality health care. In spite of these real and perceived disadvantages, HMOs have become an increasingly popular alternative to traditional health insurance.

Property/Casualty Insurance

While some private insurers specialize in life/health insurance, others protect against property damage or liability caused by negligence and are categorized as property/casualty insurers. Although the distinction between property and casualty lines has become increasingly blurred, each has its own focus. Property insurance provides financial protection against loss of or damage to property caused by fire, theft, riots, natural disasters, or other calamities. It covers buildings, equipment, and inventories, as well as losses caused by interruptions in business operations. Casualty insurance is designed to protect against legal liability for injuries to others or damage to their property. Property and casualty insurance are further divided into specific types of insurance, known as *lines*. Property insurance, for example, includes such lines as crop-hail, ocean marine, and personal property insurance. Casualty insurance includes medical malpractice and product liability lines.

Property and casualty insurance can also be described as "first party" and "third party" insurance. Property insurance protects the policyholder, the first party, against damage to his or her property, while casualty insurance protects third parties (other people) against policyholder negligence. Often both property and casualty coverage are provided in a single policy, as in automobile and homeowners insurance.

Your homeowners policy is primarily a first-party contract: It protects your property. But it provides third-party coverage as well. If your second-story guest bedroom directly overlooks a deceptively shallow wading pool, and your guests enjoy an early morning dip, you could need it.[5]

Private insurers, as has been shown, can be classified according to the lines of insurance — life/health or property/casualty — that they write. Other classifications, based on the type of policyholder and the insurer's legal organization, are also possible.

Personal and Commercial Insurance Lines

The first of these categorizes insurance by the type of policyholder rather than by type of coverage, distinguishing between personal and commercial lines. Personal lines are sold to individuals; commercial lines, to businesses. Product liability insurance sold to a large pharmaceutical company is one of many commercial insurance lines. Many private insurers sell both personal and commercial lines.

Forms of Legal Organization for Private Insurers

Another way in which private insurers can be categorized is by form of legal organization. Most are either stock companies or mutual companies. Others are classified as fraternal insurers, reciprocal exchanges, and Lloyd's Associations.

Stock insurance companies are publicly traded corporations. Individual shareholders provide capital for the company in return for stock shares and the possibility of dividends. Most of the large property/casualty insurers are stock companies. The Travellers Insurance Corporation, for example, is traded on the New York Stock Exchange.

Mutual insurance companies, also known as *mutuals*, are owned by their policyholders rather than by shareholders. Just as shareholders earn dividends when stock companies have profitable years, policyholders benefit when mutuals have excess earnings, reaping benefits in the form of policyholder dividends or reduced policy renewal costs. While stock insurance companies are dominant in the property/casualty industry, mutuals are prevalent among life/health insurers.[6]

Although most private insurers are either stock companies or mutuals, there are also other forms of legal organization. They include *fraternal insurers*, fraternal benefit societies such as the Knights of Columbus and Aid Association for Lutherans that write insurance for their members. A *reciprocal exchange*, on the other hand, is a form of cooperative insurance, an association in which members insure one another.

To illustrate, assume each of ten business firms owns a building valued at $1 million. The ten firms could form an association and agree that each member would insure (and be insured by) each of the others in the amount of $100,000. If any of the buildings were damaged or destroyed the loss would be shared by all of the association members, each paying 10% of the loss. The advantage of this arrangement would be that each firm's loss exposure would be spread among the ten locations. Instead of standing to lose $1 million in a single loss, each would be exposed to a maximum $100,000 loss at each of the various locations. If the association grew to include 100 members the exposure of each would be lowered to $10,000 at each of the 100 locations.[7]

Another characteristic of reciprocal exchanges is that they are managed by an attorney-in-fact, an individual or corporation responsible for such administrative duties as collecting premiums, investing funds, handling claims, and seeking new members.

There are presently some 50 reciprocal exchanges. Most specialize in a limited number of insurance lines and account for only a small part of the insurance written. A few, however, are quite large. One of the largest automobile insurers in this country, Farmers Insurance Exchange, is a reciprocal exchange.

Insurance is also available through *Lloyd's Associations*, organizations comprised of individuals who underwrite insurance on a cooperative basis. There are two types of Lloyd's Associations: (1) Lloyd's of London and (2) American Lloyds.

Lloyd's of London is the most famous of all insurers. Most of the insurance that is sold at Lloyd's falls into property/casualty lines, and while it is best known for its unusual policies (covering, for example, Jimmy Durante's nose and Marlene Dietrich's legs), most of its policies are written to cover somewhat more mundane risks. Lloyd's of London is not an insurance company. It is an insurance *market*, roughly analogous to a stock exchange. Just as the New York Stock Exchange neither buys nor sells stock but provides a location for and services to its members who do, so also does Lloyd's provide a marketplace for its members to sell insurance. It is, in effect, an association whose members write and sell insurance, and it is unique in that its members accept — and are personally responsible for — risks as individuals rather than as corporations.

Lloyd's has a three-tiered structure, comprised of its members, insurance syndicates, and underwriters. The members, also known as *names*, are usually wealthy individuals who have pledged their personal assets to cover possible insurance losses. In return for taking such risks, they have the opportunity to earn handsome profits.

> As a member of Lloyd's — a "name," as Lloyd's calls its silent ("sleeping") partners — you would join thousands of others whose collective personal fortunes stand behind the association. "Individually we are underwriters," runs the classic explanation, "collectively we are Lloyd's." You would take tiny pieces of a great many risks.... You would be insuring against all manner of plague and disaster: the possibility of race horses going berserk in air cargo planes, of lottery ticket printers accidentally printing 5,000 winning tickets instead of 500, of Cutty Sark drinkers actually *finding* the Loch Ness monster and presenting it for the advertised $1 million reward. And you would hope that your share of the premiums (plus interest) in any given year exceeded your share of the claims, in which event you would have a profit. Should it go the other way round — should losses exceed premiums plus interest, as occasionally they do — you would be called on for your share, no matter how great.[8]

Because of this unlimited liability, prospective members are carefully screened. In addition to having liquid assets of at least $300,000, such people must come recommended by Lloyd's members, and must convince the admissions committee that they are suitable. There are presently over 18,000 members in Lloyd's of London.

Although members provide the financial backing, Lloyd's is operated by syndicates and underwriters. The insurance is written by *syndicates*, groups of members organized under the heading of an underwriter. There are over 400 different syndicates, each specializing in certain insurance lines. Some, for example, write marine insurance, and others, aviation or product liability insurance.

Underwriters, each with his or her own area of expertise, head the syndicates. *Underwriters* decide whether or not to accept certain risks, how policies should be written, and what the premium rates should be. In most situations, more than one syndicate will participate. A syndicate specializing in the insured-against risk will act as the lead syndicate, underwriting the largest share of the insurance. It, in turn, will contact as many additional syndicates as are needed to underwrite the face value of the insurance policy.

> To illustrate in a simplified fashion how Lloyd's operates, consider the following example. Jack Wilhoft is going into business and wants $1 million of products liability insurance on a new roller skate that he is manufacturing. An agent locates a company in the United States that will sell him $100,000 of products liability insurance. Since another American company cannot be found to under-write the remaining insurance, the agent contacts a surplus line broker who arranges to place the remaining $900,000 of products liability insurance with

Lloyd's of London. Information about Jack's roller skating business is submitted to a Lloyd's broker, who then presents the proposal to a syndicate specializing in high-risk products liability insurance. A lead underwriter then determines the initial premium rate. Let us assume that the lead syndicate takes $100,000 of the desired $900,000 of insurance. Each member of the syndicate will take his or her agreed-upon share. The Lloyd's broker will then contact the other syndicates as well. The second syndicate may take $50,000, the third, $10,000, and so on, until the entire $900,000 is placed. Each member of the various syndicates takes his or her share of the insurance, and pays his or her share of any loss. Finally, the policy is prepared, issued, and the insurance is in force.[9]

Although private underwriters in the United States have tried to form associations similar to Lloyd's of London, these "American Lloyds" have been largely unsuccessful. Most have limited financial resources. A few have failed. Some states, in fact, refuse to license them. None of the American Lloyds are connected to Lloyd's of London.

INSURANCE PROVIDED BY PUBLIC INSURERS

While the private insurance industry handles billions of dollars annually, it is by no means the only source of insurance coverage. Many federal and some state and municipal government agencies provide voluntary or compulsory protection against financial risk associated with unemployment, old age, death, and other perils. As shown in figure 17.3, the insurance provided by public insurers falls into two broad categories: social insurance and all other types of insurance.

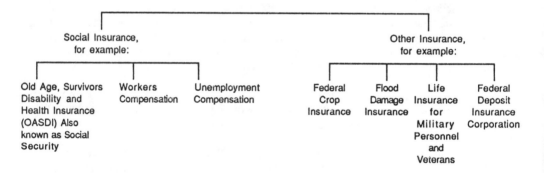

Fig. 17.3. Government insurance programs.

Social Insurance

Social insurance is publicly financed insurance, usually compulsory, enacted into law to achieve certain social goals or to provide coverage that private insurers are unwilling or unable to offer. Social Security, for example, came into existence as an attempt to deal with the widespread unemployment and poverty of the Great Depression.

Certain characteristics distinguish social from private insurance. First, social insurance is based on law rather than contract, with eligibility requirements and benefits prescribed by law. Second, coverage is compulsory for all people to whom the law applies. As a rule, it covers only those who are or have been employed, their spouses, and their dependents. Third, social insurance programs are intended to be financially self-supporting, with specific payroll taxes designated to fund them. Fourth, social objectives are paramount. The purpose is to guarantee a minimum level of economic security, but not to subsidize fully all living expenses.

The philosophy is that, in an economic system that stresses free enterprise and individual initiative, people should not rely entirely upon governmental programs. Social insurance is designed to guarantee economic security at minimal levels; those who want more adequate benefits obtain them through personal savings and private insurance.[10]

Finally, benefits are paid as a matter of course to anyone who meets certain eligibility requirements; an eligible millionaire, for example, receives Social Security benefits whether or not he or she actually needs them.

The most important social insurance programs in the United States are the Old Age, Survivors, Disability and Health Insurance program, commonly known as Social Security, unemployment insurance, and workers' compensation.

Enacted into law as a result of the Social Security Act of 1935, *Old Age, Survivors, Disability and Health Insurance* (OASDI) provides most workers with retirement, survivor, disability, and Medicare benefits.[11] Eligibility requirements for these benefits vary, but are based to a very large extent on credit earned for the length of covered employment, with the amount of credit required in turn affected by the type of benefit being sought.

Unemployment insurance programs provide short-term financial protection to workers who are involuntarily unemployed. Such programs pay workers weekly cash benefits; in addition, by requiring applicants for benefits to register for work at local employment offices, they help the unemployed find jobs. Each state has its own unemployment insurance program, subsidized by special payroll taxes paid by employers to the federal government.

Workers' compensation programs are state-authorized social insurance programs that help to protect employees from the financial consequences of job-related injuries and disease. Workers' compensation provides medical care, disability income, rehabilitation services, and death benefits. Coverage varies from state to state. Most programs are compulsory, cover most occupations, and are limited to injuries or diseases that are job connected. Some states operate their own workers' compensation funds, while others allow approved employers to self-insure their workers or permit private insurers to provide coverage.

Other Government Insurance Programs

In addition to social insurance, the government oversees many other types of insurance programs. These include insurance on checking and savings accounts provided by the Federal Deposit Insurance Corporation and the Federal Savings and Loan Insurance Corporation, federal crime insurance for property owners and businesses in high crime areas, and riot reinsurance, known as the Fair Access to Insurance Requirements (FAIR) plan, for property owners unable to obtain property coverage through private insurers. Further, the government offers some programs, such as life insurance for members of the armed forces and veterans, that are similar to coverage provided by private insurers.

Insurance Associations

The insurance industry is represented by several different associations. Some of the most important are the Alliance of American Insurers, the American Insurance Association, and the National Association of Independent Insurers. In terms of the information they make available to the public and to libraries, however, two of the most important are the American Council of Life Insurance and the Insurance Information Institute.

The American Council of Life Insurance, the major trade association for the industry, serves almost 600 member companies who handle more than 95 percent of this country's life insurance business.[12] In addition to member services, this council lobbies legislators and government officials, and collects and dispenses data about the life insurance industry. Its publications range from booklets for consumers to actuarial, economic, legal, social, and statistical research studies.

The Insurance Information Institute is the property/casualty industry's counterpart. Supported by more than 300 major companies, it focuses on public relations, research, and publishing. Many of the booklets and reports it publishes are available to the public and contain useful industry data.

Regulation of the Insurance Industry

Government regulation of the insurance industry is intended to protect against insurer insolvency and fraud, to ensure reasonable premium rates, and to make insurance protection widely available. It is carried on at the state level by state insurance departments, usually under the direction of appointed insurance commissioners. In addition to the broad regulatory responsibilities outlined above, state insurance departments must review new kinds of policies, license insurance agents, and settle policyholder disputes.

The National Association of Insurance Commissioners (NAIC), an association of state insurance commissioners, imposes some influence on self-regulation of the insurance industry. In addition, the NAIC has drafted model legislation for different portions of insurance regulation which some states have chosen to adopt.

There is, however, growing sentiment for centralized federal regulation of insurance companies. Proponents of such a move point to the inefficiency and inconsistency of 50 different sets of insurance regulations. Some claim that state insurance officials, many of whom are former or future insurance company employees, may be too accommodating to the companies they regulate.

> Richard Schweiker, the former GOP senator from Pennsylvania who now heads the American Council of Life Insurance, on fears that the incoming Democratic Congress will move toward federal rather than state regulation of the insurance industry: "Most insurance companies would rather have 50 monkeys on their back than one big gorilla."[13]

Others argue that the National Association of Insurance Commissioners already provides guidance and standards for state regulations, and that a federal system of regulation would be detrimental to many of the smaller insurance companies operating in only a few states.

INSURANCE INFORMATION SOURCES

This section considers materials in a wide variety of formats, listing for each the key insurance information sources available.

Guides, Bibliographies, and Dictionaries

The most comprehensive guide to insurance, Roy Edwin Thomas's *Insurance Information Sources* (Detroit: Gale Research Co., 1971), is too old to be useful as a guide to current insurance publications. It is still in print, however, and libraries holding copies should consider retaining them until a successor is published. Many of the explanatory sections which precede the listing of titles in each chapter are still useful.

More current, although less comprehensive, coverage is provided in "Insurance and Real Estate," chapter 15 in *Business Information Sources*. In it, Daniells annotates key handbooks, textbooks, and services available in the fields of risk and insurance, and life/health and property/liability insurance, as well as bibliographies and indexes, law and legal services, sources of information about insurance companies, and statistics, periodicals, and directories. A list of insurance associations is also included.

For insurance-related documents, however, another bibliography must be consulted.

U.S. Superintendent of Documents. **Insurance**. Washington, D.C.: Government Printing Office, 1986 (Subject Bibliography 294). 5p.

Insurance selectively lists and annotates federal documents pertaining to health insurance and health care, liability coverage for small business, unemployment insurance, Medicare, Social Security, and related topics. As with all the subject bibliographies, GPO stock numbers and prices are included in addition to Superintendent of Documents classifications.

Two bibliographies selectively identify current titles.

Special Libraries Association. Insurance and Employee Benefits Division. **Insurance and Employee Benefits Literature**. New York: The Division, 1950- . Bimonthly.

Insurance Information Institute. **Books in Insurance: Property, Liability, Marine, Surety**. New York: The Institute. Irregular.

Insurance and Employee Benefits Literature lists and briefly annotates selected books, pamphlets, and documents. Arrangement is by subject, with both consumer- and industry-oriented titles included. Many of the publications cited are free. As a result, it is useful for supplementing vertical file collections as well as in collection development.

More specialized coverage of the property/casualty industry is provided by the Insurance Information Institute's free *Books in Insurance*. Although it is issued less frequently than the SLA publication, it, too, selectively lists and annotates current titles in the field.[14]

Insurance vocabulary can, at times, baffle those within the profession as much as those outside it. Not all insurance professionals have agreed on the exact meaning of terms.

It was Humpty-Dumpty of Alice in Wonderland fame who said: "When I use a word, it means just what I choose it to mean—neither more nor less." Perhaps insurance people have individually and collectively humpty-dumptied the special language of this business to the extent that it is hard even to understand each other. Pity the poor public![15]

In an attempt to deal with such "terminological inexactitude" a Commission on Insurance Terminology (CIT) was formed by the American Risk and Insurance Association.[16] The commission has since prepared definitions for many terms; in insurance, the letters *CIT* indicate such a commission-issued definition. Many such definitions are included in the two most widely used insurance dictionaries, listed below.

Davids, Lewis E. **Dictionary of Insurance**. 6th rev. ed. Totowa, N.J.: Rowman & Allanheld, 1983. 338p.

Green, Thomas E., Robert W. Osler, and John S. Bickley, eds. **Glossary of Insurance Terms**. Santa Monica, Calif.: Merritt Co., 1980. 234p.

The *Dictionary of Insurance*, long a standard reference work, briefly defines terms and phrases connected with all phases of the insurance industry. CIT definitions are so indicated. Also included are insurance acronyms, a directory of state commissioners of insurance, and of U.S. and Canadian organizations ("agencies, associations, bureaus, conferences, councils, forums, foundations, institutes, schools, services, and societies") relating to the insurance industry.

The *Glossary of Insurance Terms* also includes CIT-approved definitions and, in addition, features a brief glossary of terms on pensions and profit-sharing defined by the American Risk and Insurance Association's Committee on Pension and Profit Sharing Terminology. As in the *Dictionary*, definitions are practical, concise, and usually can be understood by lay people.

Handbooks and Consumer Guides

Insurance handbooks generally fall into two categories: those written for insurance professionals and those intended for lay people. The following titles are representative of each.

> Castle, Gray, Robert F. Cushman, and Peter R. Kensicki. **The Business Insurance Handbook**. Homewood, Ill.: Dow Jones-Irwin, 1981. 753p.

> Gregg, David W., and Vane B. Lucas. **Life and Health Insurance Handbook**. 3rd ed. Homewood, Ill.: Dow Jones-Irwin, 1973. 1366p.

> U.S. Department of Health and Human Services. Social Security Administration. **Social Security Handbook**. 9th ed. Washington, D.C.: Government Printing Office, 1986. 456p.

The *Business Insurance Handbook* is a comprehensive, practical guide for business people. Chapters, which are written by legal experts and insurance professionals, cover such phases of insurance as business insurance cost, property, liability, specialized, and unique risk exposures, combining several kinds of insurance coverage in one policy, and providing for business continuation through insurance and selected employee benefits. The *Handbook* is indexed, and a variety of risk management checklists are appended.

More focused treatment is provided in the *Life and Health Insurance Handbook*, which covers all phases of that industry. Written and edited by 123 experts, the chapters are grouped into 10 sections covering economic security and insurance, individual and group insurance, government benefits, annuities, estate planning, business uses of life and health insurance, company operations and institutional aspects of insurance, and various types of life and health insurance. Chapters frequently include bibliographies, tables, graphs, and statistical data. In addition, appendixes containing sample forms and policies, life expectancy and death rate tables, and historic dates in the development of life and health insurance in the United States are also included. Subject and name indexes are provided.

Although the *Life and Health Insurance Handbook* is a standard reference work, it is too dated for coverage of certain types of insurance policies and practices. For example, universal life insurance, now one of the most popular types of life insurance, was developed after the present edition was published. As a result, while the *Handbook* is useful for an overview of the industry and its development, it is too old to treat fully the range of life insurance coverage now available. Until a more recent edition is published it should be used with caution.

The *Social Security Handbook* is the basic reference for social insurance programs and benefits, as well as social assistance programs, made available through the Social Security Administration. It describes federal retirement, survivors, disability, and black lung benefits, supplemental security income programs, health insurance, and public assistance programs. It also stipulates the evidence necessary to establish rights for specific benefits, lists the procedures for applying for benefits or filing claims, and describes the appeals review process. Each chapter covers a specific program or set of procedures, and is subdivided into numbered paragraphs (see figure 17.4). An index, with citations to paragraph numbers, is also included.

719.   AFTER MAY 1975, BENEFITS MAY BE AUTOMATICALLY INCREASED to keep pace with increases in the cost-of-living if laws providing general benefit increases are not passed. Depending on the condition of the Social Security Trust Funds, the increase will be based on either the Consumer Price Index as published by the Department of Labor or the average wage index which is the average of the annual total wages used for computing a PIA. Where the appropriate index for a base quarter shows an increase of at least 3 percent over the same index for the last base quarter, the following will happen: Each PIA (except the special minimum PIA see § 717), each related maximum family benefit, each transitionally insured benefit, and each special age 72 payment will be raised to reflect the same percentage of increase (rounded to the nearest one-tenth of 1 percent). The base quarter is the third calendar quarter of each year after 1974, or a later calendar quarter within which a general benefit increase became effective. This cost-of-living benefit increase will be effective beginning with December of the year which contains the base quarter for the index increase. The cost-of-living increase is published in the *Federal Register* on or about November 1 of the year preceding the year the benefits are payable.

Fig. 17.4. Sample entry, *Social Security Handbook*. Reprinted from the *Social Security Handbook 1986*, 9th edition.

In addition to the handbooks described above, consumer guides periodically are published to help lay people make decisions about insurance coverage or about specific insurance companies. Although the number of companies in the insurance business and the types of policies they write are too numerous to lend themselves to more than brief coverage in such sources, consumer guidebooks can nonetheless be useful for simplifying and providing a basic introduction to insurance.

Belth, Joseph M. **Life Insurance: A Consumer's Handbook**. 2nd ed. Bloomington, Ind.: Indiana University Press, 1985. 240p.

Consumers Union of the United States. **The Consumers Union Report on Life Insurance: A Guide to Planning and Buying the Protection You Need**. 4th ed. New York: Holt, Rinehart, and Winston, 1980. 383p.

Life Insurance: A Consumer's Handbook is a guide to life insurance and its variant forms. The *Handbook* provides more than a general introduction, however. It also contains instructions on how to examine policies already held and how to obtain information and make calculations in determining the best type of life insurance coverage for special individual needs. Appendixes include a listing of companies with 10 consecutive years of top ratings, addresses of state insurance regulatory officials, and instructions for calculating the yearly price of life insurance protection and for computing present value, the amount of funds required to produce specified yearly payments at some time in the future.

The *Consumers Union Report on Life Insurance* is somewhat less technical than *Life Insurance*. Like other Consumers Union publications, it succinctly describes and tells how to evaluate an important consumer product. Although it lists companies selling highest and lowest cost life insurance policies in 1980, this information is dated, and is not as useful as the general discussion of factors to consider when purchasing life insurance.

Directories

Two directories dominate the insurance field.

The Insurance Almanac; Who, What, When, and Where in Insurance, An Annual of Insurance Facts. Englewood, N.J.: Underwriter Printing and Publishing, 1912- . Annual.

Who's Who in Insurance. Englewood, N.J.: Underwriter Printing and Publishing, 1948- . Annual.

The Insurance Almanac is a compilation of lists by categories of insurance companies and practitioners. Insurance companies, for example, are organized by form of legal organization and lines of insurance written. The company entries are fairly brief, including company address and telephone number, date and state in which the company was established, officers' names, types of insurance coverage written, and territory covered. Most entries, as shown in figure 17.5, also include the names of the executives in charge of advertising and claims. Entries for some of the largest insurance companies may also feature a brief corporate history and operating statistics.

```
COUNTRY-WIDE INSURANCE COMPANY, 141 E. 8th St., New York, NY 10003. (212) 425-3800.
Licensed April 15, 1964, under the laws of New York.
     OFFICERS - Pres., Philip D. Held; Exec. V.P. & Sec., Raymond Cheven; Asst. Treas.,
William Menza.
     IN CH. OF ADV.- Raymond Cheven, Exec. V. Pres. & Sec.
     IN CH. OF CLAIMS - Walter Convery, Claims Mgr.
     WRITES - Licensed to write Multiple Lines; writes Fire, Miscellaneous Property,
Water Damage, Burglary and Theft, Glass and Inland Marine; primary emphasis is on Auto-
mobile Liability, specializing in Full Coverage Liability and Physical Damage Insurance
for large automobile and trucking fleets.
     TERRITORY COVERED - NJ, NY.
```

Fig. 17.5. Typical company entry, *The Insurance Almanac*. Reprinted with permission from the 1986 edition, *The Insurance Almanac*.

The Insurance Almanac also lists agents and brokers in principal cities, insurance adjusters, and insurance inspection and investigation services. Finally, the *Almanac* identifies organizations related to various types of insurance, assigned risk plans and rating bureaus, and state insurance officials. It is a basic insurance reference work and belongs in most business reference collections.

Who's Who in Insurance provides biographical information on over 5,000 insurance officials, brokers, agents, and buyers. Each entry generally includes the biographee's address, educational background, positions held, club and association memberships, and other personal data.

Other biographical directories, published by professional organizations, include the American Academy of Actuaries *Yearbook*, the *Yearbook* of the Society of Actuaries, and the *Member Roster* of the Life Insurance Marketing and Research Association (LIMRA). Such specialized lists of members, however, are less widely available and thus less frequently consulted than *Who's Who in Insurance*.

Both *The Insurance Almanac* and *Who's Who in Insurance* are published by Underwriter Printing and Publishing, one of the firms dominating the insurance reference marketplace. Publications of two others, A. M. Best and National Underwriter, will be discussed in the sections that follow on company and policy information.

Information about Insurance Companies

One of the major considerations in selecting an insurer is the company's financial strength. All other things being equal, it is better to insure with a company that is financially sound—and likely to be so at some unknown time in the future when a claim may be filed—than it is to buy insurance from a company that lacks financial strength or stability. As a result, publications that document and permit financial comparison of insurers are vital. Most reflect the traditional industry division between life/health and property/casualty insurers, but one does not.

Moody's Investors Service. **Moody's Bank & Finance Manual**. New York: The Service, 1900- . 3v. Annual.

Volume 2 of *Moody's Bank & Finance Manual* permits comparison of some of the largest U.S. and Canadian insurance companies. As with the other Moody's manuals, length of coverage varies and to a certain extent depends upon the fee paid by the company to Moody's. At a minimum, however, a listing includes the corporate address, number of employees, officers and directors, types of insurance written, and states in which the company is licensed to operate. Each entry also features comparative financial statistics for the current and preceding year, as well as investment and stock ownership information (see figure 17.6).

CONNECTICUT NATIONAL LIFE INSURANCE CO. (Somerville, N.J.)

Incorporated in New Jersey Nov. 4, 1981 as Covenant Life insurance Co.; present name adopted Jan. 1, 1985.

Life, accident and health, and hospitalization insurance on a non-participating basis.

Operates in D.C. and all states except N.Y.

Control: NEN Life Insurance Co. (a wholly-owned subsidiary of New England Mutual Life Insurance Co.) owns 100% of Co.'s stock.

Officers

C.S. Hohengarten, Pres. & Chief Exec. Off.
S.R. Fawber, Senior Vice-Pres., Sec., Treas. & Contr.
D.W. Sleeper, Senior Vice-Pres.
W.E. Sweeny, Senior Vice-Pres.
W.M. Holmes, Vice-Pres. & Actuary

Vice-Presidents

M.P. Lucafo	R.C. Armstrong
F.W. Menold	F.G. Dranginis
P.J. Smith	H.C. Reed

Directors

R.F. Verni	J.A. Fibiger
E.E. Phillips	J.S. Caras
C.S. Hohengarten	R.A. Shafto
S.R. Fawber	E.K. Leaton
W.E. Sweeney	

Home Office: 50 West Main St., Somerville, NJ 08876.

Administrative Office: 175 Powder Forest Dr., Simsbury, CT 06070. **Tel.:** (203)651-0931.

Mailing Address: P.O. Box 1169, Hartford, CT 06101.

Comparative Statistics ($000):

Years to Dec. 31:	1984	1983
Insurance written ...	1,433,553	1,776,325
Life prem. income ...	32,033	20,846
A. & H. premiums ...	15,710	9,236
Invest. income	4,879	3,584
Total income	61,698	44,681
Net to surp.........	dr2,058	dr6,198
Net cap. gain (loss) ..	dr248	dr221
Incr. in surplus......	1,981	dr6,753
As of Dec. 31:		
Admitted assets	78,296	55,612
Bonds	43,819	29,694
Preferred stock......	62	62
Surp. & vol. res.	9,714	8,754
Net life res.	28,026	14,818
Net A. & H. reserve..	2,936	2,060
Insurance in force ...	5,291,011	5,130,770

Capital Stock: Auth., 800,000 shs.; Outstg. Dec. 31, 1984, 300,000 shs.; par $8.40.

NEN Life Insurance Co. owns 100% of stock.

Fig. 17.6. Typical insurance company listing, *Moody's Bank & Finance Manual*. Reprinted with permission from *Moody's Bank & Finance Manual*, 1986 edition.

The center blue pages provide data on the distribution and dollar value of assets (government securities, stocks, bonds, mortgages, real estate, and policy loans) held by U.S. life insurance companies, and ranked listings of the 300 largest life insurance companies and the 50 leading property-casualty companies and groups. Data for compiling the lists of largest insurance companies are supplied by A. M. Best.

Although *Moody's* provides useful financial and background information about many insurance companies, its coverage is neither as detailed nor as broad as that made available in more specialized sources. Some of the most widely used titles are described below.

> A. M. Best Company. **Best's Insurance Reports: Life-Health**. Oldwick, N.J.: A. M. Best, 1906- . Annual.

> National Underwriter Company. **Life Financial Reports**. Cincinnati, Ohio: National Underwriter, 1976- . Annual.

> _____. **Argus Chart of Health Insurance**. Cincinnati, Ohio: National Underwriter, 1962- . Annual.

Best's Insurance Reports are published annually in two editions: one for the life/health industry, and one for property/casualty insurers. The *Life-Health* edition provides detailed information on some 1,650 U.S. and Canadian life and health insurance companies. Each report summarizes the company's history and describes its management and operation. It also presents key balance sheet and income statement data, and includes statistics on the value of new business issued, insurance in force, and company development (see figure 17.7). Although each company report focuses on the past year's performance, many of the statistical tables provide historical data as well. In addition, most companies are assigned a financial size category and are rated on the basis of their financial strength and ability to meet contractual obligations. Company performance is compared to industry norms established by Best in the areas of profitability, leverage, and liquidity. In addition, Best's evaluation includes a qualitative review, focusing on such factors as "the amount and soundness of a company's reinsurance, the quality and diversification of investments, the valuation basis of policy reserves, and the experience of management."[17]

Based on these factors, most companies are assigned one of the following ratings.

A +	Superior
A	Excellent
B +	Very Good
B	Good
C +	Fairly Good
C	Fair

Not all companies are rated. Those that are excluded are usually either inactive, are too small, lack sufficient experience, or fall below minimum standards. In all, there are 10 main categories for exclusion, each of which is listed and described in the *Reports'* preface.

People consulting *Best's Reports* for the first time are advised to read it with care. As shown above, Best does not assign ratings below C. Companies failing to meet the minimum requirements for a C rating are simply not graded; consequently, firms with C and even B ratings are considered risky and should be avoided. Consumers, in fact, frequently are advised to select from only those companies receiving a rating of A+ from Best for the past 10 years.[18] A certain amount of reading between the lines in company reports is necessary. Best seldom overtly condemns a company for bad management or investment policies. Either the comments are favorable, or none are included. As a result, Best's assessments must be interpreted with caution.

AMBASSADOR LIFE INSURANCE COMPANY

AMBASSADOR LIFE INSURANCE COMPANY
6101 Southwest Freeway, Suite 127
Houston, Texas 77057
Tel.–713-432-0595
Data Bank Number: 09172

ASSETS AND LIABILITIES — DECEMBER 31, 1985

Assets		Liabilities	
Policy loans	$17,916	†Net policy reserves	$83,827
Cash	16,075	Policy claims	13,070
Short-term investments	411,959	Comm taxes expenses	3,233
Life & annty prems due	5,109	Other liabilities	486
Acc & health prems due	1,947		
		Total Liabilities	$100,616
		Common stock ($1 par)	100,000
		Paid in & contrib surpl	100,000
		Unassigned surplus	152,390
Admitted Assets	$453,006	Total	$453,006

† Analysis of reserves: Life, $78,085; miscellaneous reserves, $255; accident & health, $5,487.

SUMMARY OF OPERATIONS (ACCRUAL BASIS)

Premiums:			
		Death benefits	$12,998
Ordinary life	$4,179	Surrender benefits	21,018
Credit life	25,693	Acc & health benefits	-3,082
Acc & health credit	9,705	Incr life reserves	-7,026
		Incr a & h reserves	-12,496
Total prems	$39,577	Comm exp reins assumed	17,946
Net investment income	31,579	Insur taxes lic & fees	4,520
		General ins expenses	37,895
Total	$71,156	Total	$71,773

Gain from operations before FIT & div to policyholders	-617
Dividends to policyholders:life	-210
Gain from operations after dividends to policyholders	$-407
Federal income taxes incurred	-3,062
*Net gain from operations after FIT and dividends	$2,655

*Byline breakdown: Ordinary life, $950; credit life, $-11,597; acc & health credit, $13,302.

Direct premium writings by line: Ordinary life, $4,758; reinsurance assumed, $35,398; reinsurance ceded, $579; net premiums, $39,577.

CAPITAL SURPLUS ACCOUNT

Net operating gain	$2,655	Incr cap & surplus fund	$2,655
Total	$2,655	Total	$2,655

CASH FLOW ANALYSIS

Funds Provided		Funds Applied	
Gross cash from oper	$79,229	Benefits paid	$33,582
Decr pol loan, prem note	8,074	Comm, taxes, expenses	66,831
Decr cash & short-term	17,318	Other cash applied	4,208
Total	$104,621	Total	$104,621

Life business in force: Non-participating, $2,407,000; total, $2,407,000. The foregoing includes: Ordinary reinsurance ceded, $116,000; total reinsurance ceded, $116,000.

INVESTMENT DATA

Bonds: No bonds owned.

Stocks: No stocks owned.

Mortgages: No mortgages owned.

Real estate: No real estate owned.

Short-term (91% of admitted assets): Certificates of deposit, $411,959.

HISTORY

The company, incorporated under the laws of Texas March 21, 1980, was licensed and commenced business April 3, 1980. Initial resources of $200,000 (capital $100,000 and surplus $100,000) were provided through the sale of 100,000 shares of common stock, par value $1, at $2 each.

Present authorized capital is $200,000, comprising 200,000 shares of common stock, par value $1, of which 100,000 shares are issued and outstanding.

MANAGEMENT AND OPERATION

Control of the company (100%) is held by Ambassador Corporation, a Texas holding company, which in turn is wholly owned by Jerry E. Finger. Mr. Finger serves as president of the life company and with one affiliated carrier, Charter Insurance Company, Texas.

Marketing activities are conducted only in Texas where the company specializes in the acceptance of reinsurance of credit life and credit accident and health coverages. The company also services a nominal amount of ordinary life policies which were issued during 1981, however no new business has been issued since that time.

An examination of the company's affairs and condition was conducted as of December 31, 1984 by the Texas Insurance Department.

Affiliates/Subsidiaries: Life insurance members of the Charter Insurance Group include Ambassador Life Insurance Company; and Charter Insurance Company.

Reserve basis: (Current ordinary business): 1958 CSO 3 1/2%; CRVM and Net Level valuation. (Current credit business): 1958 CET 3 1/2%; Net Level valuation.

Officers: President and treasurer, Jerry E. Finger; vice president, Richard B. Finger; secretary, Patricia W. Thomas; consulting actuary, John Gorman.

Directors: Jerry E. Finger, Nanette B. Finger, Richard B. Finger, Victor C. Moore, Patricia W. Thomas.

Territory: Licensed in Texas.

OPERATING COMMENTS

To date activities of Ambassador Life have been concentrated in the specialized field of credit life and credit accident and health reinsurance in which only a modest volume of business has been transacted. While net premium writings have declined significantly since 1981, operating gains have enabled the company to increase capital and surplus funds 7% to its year end level of $352,390. Due to its credit insurance operations, Ambassador Life has traditionally maintained a very liquid investment position as is evidenced by the fact that cash balances and short-term certificates of deposit comprised 94% of admitted assets at year end.

BEST'S RATING

Under our rating policy and procedure, a Best's Rating is Not Assigned as the insurer does not meet our minimum size requirement for rating purposes. For an "Explanation of Best's Rating System" see Preface.

NEW BUSINESS ISSUED
(in thousands of dollars)

Year	Whole Life & Endow.	Term	Credit	Group	Industrial	Total Insurance Issued	Non-Par (%)	Par (%)
1981	317	....	....	....	....	....	100	..

INSURANCE IN FORCE
(in thousands of dollars)

Year	Whole Life Endow.& Adds	Term	Credit	Group	Industrial	Total Insurance In Force
1980	....	....	25,474	6,449	....	31,923
1981	317	....	22,174	....	....	22,491
1982	284	....	11,583	....	....	11,867
1983	193	....	15,429	....	....	15,622
1984	265	....	3,293	....	....	3,558
1985	144	....	2,263	....	....	2,407

COMPANY DEVELOPMENT
(in thousands of dollars)

Year	Admitted Assets	Capital Surplus Funds	Condit'l Reserve Funds	Net Premiums Written	Net Invest Income	Net Gain
1980	452	200	....	665	....	....
1981	558	266	....	258	....	....
1982	518	311	....	320	52	33
1983	468	314	....	123	35	10
1984	482	350	....	56	38	28
1985	453	352	....	40	32	3

Note: Virtually all business is reinsurance assumed.

		Profitability Tests			Leverage Tests			Liquidity Tests	
Year	Best's Rating	NOG to NPW	Return on Equity	Chng in C&S	Chng in NPW	DPW to C&S	NPW to C&S	Com Stk & R.E. to C&S	Curr Liquidity
1981		....	....	33.0	-61.2	....	1.0	....	....
1982	NA-3	10.3	12.4	16.9	24.0	0.0	1.0	....	217.9
1983	NA-2	8.1	3.2	1.0	-61.6	0.0	0.4	....	290.3
1984	NA-2	50.0	8.9	11.5	-54.5	0.0	0.2	....	356.8
1985	NA-2	7.5	0.9	0.6	-28.6	0.0	0.1	....	441.6

———————◆———————

Fig. 17.7. Sample entry, *Best's Insurance Reports: Life-Health.* Copyright © A. M. Best Company, Inc., Oldwick, New Jersey.

To illustrate Best's "code," consider the discussion of the quality of a company's investment portfolio. For many companies, the statement is made that "We consider the bond portfolio to be of excellent quality." If it is described as "of very good quality" or "of good quality," or even worse, if nothing is said about its quality, watch out.[19]

In addition to detailed reports on over 1,600 companies, *Best's Insurance Reports: Life-Health* presents summary financial information on an additional 200 life and health insurance companies, lists state insurance commissioners, and appends tables showing the distribution of assets of U.S. life insurance companies and the growth of life insurance in the United States from the late 19th century to the present. The preface describes Best's rating system and financial size categories in detail, and explains each of the items contained in company reports. In addition, each edition includes the group affiliations of life/health and property/casualty insurers, lists legal reserve life insurance companies by state, and cites recent name changes, mergers, and dissolutions.

In spite of its limitations, *Best's Insurance Reports: Life-Health* and its companion volume for property-casualty insurance are useful to insurance professionals, librarians, and researchers. While *Best's* is the most comprehensive source, its cost precludes its addition to many libraries. A less expensive alternative, *Life Financial Reports: Financial and Operating Results of Life Insurers* is produced by another major insurance publisher, National Underwriter Publishing Company. Although it lists fewer companies and lacks the ratings and financial size categories assigned by *Best's*, it does provide basic financial information on over 1,000 of the largest insurance companies, with financial and operating statistics for more than half of the insurers listed (see figure 17.8). It also includes a ranked list of the largest life insurance companies for the current and preceding year, and lists company changes for the past five years.

Summary information about health insurers is available in the *Argus Chart of Health Insurance*. As in the other publications described above, the data presented are compiled from annual statements filed by insurance companies with state insurance departments and from special questionnaires prepared by the publisher. Information is presented in tabular format, with data for several different companies shown on the same pages.

Each entry provides year-end data about the insurer for the past two years, including such items as assets, liabilities, reserves, dividends to policyholders or stockholders, and net gain; health insurance results, featuring statistics on health reserves, premiums written and earned, claims and expenses incurred; analysis of individual business (premiums earned, claims incurred, and ratios for five classes of business); and group health premiums and underwriting results.

The *Chart* also presents financial and operating results for Blue Cross and Blue Shield plans, ranks insurance groups and individual insurance companies by premiums earned, and includes tables that compare claims incurred to premiums earned for companies and by type of insurance.

Financial information about property and casualty insurers is equally important and can be found in the following publications.

A. M. Best Company. **Best's Insurance Reports: Property-Casualty**. Oldwick, N.J.: A. M. Best, 1976- . Annual.

_____. **Best's Key Rating Guide: Property-Casualty**. Oldwick, N.J.: A. M. Best, 1976- . Annual.

A companion volume to the *Life-Health* edition, *Best's Insurance Reports: Property-Casualty* presents detailed financial information on over 1,800 companies. Each entry includes a brief corporate history, a description of operations and management, corporate assets and liabilities, investment data, reinsurance information, and, when available, financial and operating statistics. Financial size categories and Best's ratings are assigned to most companies, and are described at length in the preface. The *Property-Casualty* edition also lists state insurance commissioners, mutual insurance companies, underwriting

LUMBERMENS LIFE
H.O., 9101 WESLEYAN ROAD, INDIANAPOLIS, IN 46268 TEL: 317-875-0142

Statistics (000 Omitted)

12/31	Admitted Assets	Net Reserve	Capital & Surplus	Insurance Paid For	Insurance in Force
1984	$17,028	$7,740	$3,219	$283,149	$524,490
1985	$17,695	$7,631	$4,056	$184,544	$537,024

INDUST IN FORCE 3,502

12/31	Invest Income Ratio	Premium Income	Total Income	Policyholder Dividends	Net Gain	Total Paid Policy-Holders
1984	9.11	$25,987	$27,298	$42	$1,070	$18,704
1985	7.98	$28,569	$29,782	$39	$1,140	$17,532

Business in Force (000 Omitted)

Life, Endt, Adds	$24,153	Participating	$8,262
Term & Other	96,881	Guaranteed Cost	528,762
Group	412,488		
Credit		Total	$537,024
		Annuity Annual Payments	$319
Total	$533,522		

CURRENT RESERVE BASIS: 1958 CSO 3%, 4% CRVM, 3% NL; 1980 CSO 6% CRVM; ANNUITIES: VARIOUS.

Balance Sheet, Operations & Surplus for the Current Year (000 Omitted)

ASSETS		DEDUCTIONS	
Bonds	7,736	Death Benefits	1,118
Preferred Stocks	119	Matured Endowments	
Common Stocks		Annuity Benefits	2,298
Mortgages	101	Disability & A & H Benefits	13,690
Real Estate	2,092	Surrender Benefits	387
Policy Loans	518	Reserve Increase	113-
Separate Accounts		Commissions	3,270
Other	7,129	General Insurance Exps	6,956
Total	$17,695	Taxes, Licenses & Fees	561
LIABILITIES		Other	317
Net Policy Reserves	7,631	Total	28,483
Policy Claims	4,206	Operations Gain	1,299
Dividend Accumulations	176	Policyholder Dividends	39
Dividend Apportioned	40	Federal Income Taxes	121
Separate Accounts		Net Gain	$1,140
Other Liabilities	1,586		
Total	$13,639	**CAPITAL & SURPLUS**	
INCOME		Balance Previous Yr.	3,219
		Net Gain •	1,140
Life Premiums	2,742	Capital Gains	11
Annuity Premiums	2,279	Non-Admitted Items	471
A & H Premiums	23,548	Security Valuation Res	29-
Net Investment Income	1,141	Capital & Surplus Changes	
Other	72	Stockholder Dividend	300
		Other	456-
Total	$29,782	Balance Current Year	$4,056

1985: INDUST 50; ORD 25; ANNUITIES -188; SUPP CONTR -61; GRP 619; GRP A&H 684; OTHER A&H 10.
1984: INDUST 68; ORD -41; ANNUITIES -177; SUPP CONTR -7; GRP 649; GRP A&H 634; OTHER A&H 4.

HISTORY: INCORPORATED 1965; 1984 PURCHASED BY SOCIETY NATIONAL CORP AND SOCIETY NATIONAL LIFE INS CO, SOCIETY NATIONAL LIFE INS CO MERGED INTO LUMBERMEN'S LIFE INS CO. WRITES: GTD COST LIFE, ANNUITIES, GROUP L&H. STOCKHOLDER DIVIDENDS: PER SHARE 1983 NIL, 1984 $.20; 1985 $.30. CORPORATE AFFILIATIONS: SOCIETY NATIONAL CORP AND REX UNDERWRITERS, INC, SOCIETY NATIONAL CORP. OFFICERS: LOUIS R BOLOGNA, PRES; PATRICK J WACK, SECY; DENNIS W HOUCHENS, VP & TREAS; VP'S: JAMES E PUTKA, HENRY F GARMAN, KAY F PAULEY. LICENSED: AR,FL,IL,IN,IA,KS,LA,MS,MO,NE,OH,OK,SC,TN,TX. 1985 REINSURANCE CEDED: ORD 98,018; GRP 58,644; TOTAL 156,662. 1984 REINSURANCE CEDED: ORD 117,615; GRP 50,542; TOTAL 168,157.

Fig. 17.8. Typical entry, *Life Financial Reports*. Reprinted from 1986 edition of *Life Financial Reports*, published by National Underwriter Co., Cincinnati, Ohio.

organizations, and companies that have merged or are no longer in business. Also featured are lists of company groups and insurance companies by state and a statistical review of state workers' compensation funds.

Best's Key Rating Guide is intended primarily for insurance professionals. It presents summary financial information, operating ratios, and Best's ratings for some 1,700 property and casualty insurers in tabular format. Other tables list insurance groups, states in which companies are licensed to do business, and companies and associations that have retired. As in *Best's Reports*, principal underwriting and advisory organizations are briefly described.

Information about Insurance Policies

Requests for information about insurance policies generally fall into two categories: identifying companies that write policies offering special coverage, and comparing policies written by different companies. An insurance agent, for example, may want to compile a list of companies writing ocean marine insurance or selling health coverage for hemophiliacs. The head of a family may want to compare the provisions of life insurance policies sold by Baltimore Life with those offered by Northwestern Mutual Life. Although precise comparison is impossible, the sources listed below provide a good base for identifying companies offering special coverage and for comparing the basic provisions of many insurance policies.

> **Who Writes What in Life and Health Insurance**. Cincinnati, Ohio: National Underwriter. Annual.
>
> **The Insurance Marketplace**. Indianapolis, Ind.: Rough Notes, 1962- . Annual.
>
> **Agent's and Buyer's Market Service "Shortcut."** Cincinnati, Ohio: National Underwriter, 1987- . Quarterly updates. [Machine-readable data file]

Who Writes What in Life and Health Insurance lists insurance companies and brokers that provide hard-to-place, unusual, substandard, or new types of life and health insurance coverage. The directory is divided into two main sections: life insurance and health and accident insurance. Each section is further divided into specific policy features. The life insurance section, for example, is subdivided into the following categories: benefit limits, renewal and conversion features, distribution of proceeds, unusual insureds, modified or discount premium plans, and multiple line.

Many of the categories are preceded by an introductory statement describing the coverage. The section on occupations normally excluded from standard life insurance coverage, for example, includes the following statement.

Excluded Occupations — Individual

These occupations are frequently on company prohibited lists. But as in most situations, some companies find classes such as these acceptable when properly underwritten.[20]

The section goes on to identify occupations that may require special coverage, including such risk-prone workers as motorcycle racers, movie stuntpeople, and wild animal trainers. For each listing, companies providing special coverage are identified. The entry shown in figure 17.9 for sky divers is typical.

In addition, *Who Writes What* includes a directory showing in which states a company is licensed to operate as well as the address and telephone number of its corporate headquarters and the title of the person to whom correspondence about special coverage should be directed.

Similar information is available about property-casualty insurers. *The Insurance Marketplace*, for example, annually identifies companies that write policies for unusual or hard-to-place risks. Even more current coverage is available through the *Agent's and Buyer's Market Service "Shortcut,"* a collection of data diskettes, updated quarterly, that provide information on both personal and commercial property and liability insurance lines. The *"Shortcut"* replaces a standard printed source, the *Agent's and Buyer's Guide*, and while it is more up-to-date and somewhat more comprehensive, it is also more expensive.

UNUSUAL INSUREDS   63

Sky divers — free fall exhibitions

Many companies will write life only protection for persons in this hazardous occupation. The companies listed offer one or more of the additional coverages associated
with life policies.

020935

AID ASSOCIATION FOR LUTHERANS	1,3,4	SECURITY BENEFIT LIFE	1,4
AMERICAN-AMICABLE LIFE	1-4	SECURITY-CONNECTICUT LIFE	1
AMERICAN CROWN LIFE	1,3,4	STANDARD SECURITY LIFE OF N Y	+1
AMERICAN GENERAL LIFE COS	1,2,3,4	SUN LIFE OF AMERICA	1,3,4
AMERICAN MAYFLOWER LIFE	1,3,4	WESTERN LIFE, MN	1,3,4
CONFEDERATION LIFE	1,3	ZURICH AMERICAN LIFE INS CO	1,3,4
CROWN LIFE, CAN	1,3,4	AMERICAN INSURANCE DYNAMICS-AID	1,3,4
FIRST COLONY LIFE	1,3,4	AMERICAN INSURANCE MARKETERS-AIM	1,3,4
GREAT-WEST LIFE ASSURANCE	+1	DWORKIN ASSOCIATES, INC (DAI)	1,4
LONE STAR LIFE		ESCO LIFE CONSULTANTS, INC	1
PAN AMERICAN LIFE	1	PROFESSIONAL LIFE UNDWTRS SERV	
PRUDENTIAL INS OF AMER	1,3,4	UNDERWRITING SPECIALISTS, INC	

Fig. 17.9. Sample entry, *Who Writes What in Life and Health Insurance.*
Reprinted from 1985 edition of *Who Writes What in Life and Health Insurance,*
published by National Underwriter Co., Cincinnati, Ohio.

Although a line-by-line comparison of insurance policy provisions is almost impossible,
the sources listed below permit examination of the basic provisions of many of the standard
policies that are sold today.

A. M. Best Company. **Best's Flitcraft Compend**. Oldwick, N.J.: A. M. Best. Annual,
   with optional quarterly updates on universal life.

National Underwriter Company. **Life Rates & Data**. Cincinnati, Ohio: National
   Underwriter, 1971- . Annual.

Best's Flitcraft Compend provides information on life insurance policies, rates, values,
and dividends. Although not all insurers are included, the companies that are write over 90
percent of the life insurance in force. Each company entry includes a brief corporate profile,
an analysis of major policy provisions, limitations and restrictions, and premium, cash
value, and dividend tables. Entries may vary from a single page to five or more pages,
depending on the company's size and the types of policies it writes. The entry for The Paul
Revere Companies, shown in figure 17.10 (see page 416), is typical.

The *Compend* includes instructions in the interpretation and use of data presented for
each company. In addition, a "Reference Section" provides annuity data and settlement
options for leading insurance companies as well as mortality, cash value, and compound
interest tables, mortgage amortization schedules, and an explanation and summary of
Medicare provisions. *Best's Flitcraft Compend* is a basic reference work, particularly useful
in libraries serving insurance practitioners or students of insurance or where interest in
detailed comparison of policy features is strong. Researchers should be forewarned,
however, that its effective use requires careful reading of the instructions in the front of the
manual.

Life Rates & Data condenses and presents information on policy rates and provisions.
For each company listed, it highlights policy premiums, cash values, paid-up insurance
values, and dividends. As shown in figure 17.11 (see page 417), its frequent use of abbreviations and symbols can be somewhat confusing to the uninitiated, but the publication's
introductory section explains most of them. *Life Rates & Data* includes settlement options,
annuities, compound interest, mortgage amortization, and mortality tables. Also featured
are numbered listings of activities—loss of life while participating in an insurrection, for
example, or after taking poison—normally excluded from insurance coverage.

THE PAUL REVERE COMPANIES
18 Chestnut St., Worcester, MA 01608   (617) 799-4441

THE PAUL REVERE PROTECTIVE LIFE INSURANCE COMPANY
THE PAUL REVERE VARIABLE ANNUITY INSURANCE COMPANY
THE PAUL REVERE LIFE INSURANCE COMPANY

OPERATIONS

Affiliation: Textron

Brokerage: Accepted; Individual life, group life, A&H, annuities.

Equity Products: Variable annuity, individual and group.

Marketing Operations: General agency, career agents, and brokerage.

Retention Limit: Standard, $300,000 ages 0-17, $500,000 ages 18-65, $300,000 over 65. Retention limits decrease as mortality increases.

Substandard: 500%.

Leading Term Plan: ART

Leading Specialty Plan: Excelerator, Interest Sensitive Whole Life.

POLICY ANALYSIS

Accidental Death Benefit: Up to 5 times face amt. of policy for accidental death within 90 days of injury and before age 70, provided death did not occur as a result of (see page 11) 50, 51, 53, 54, 55, 56, 58, 69, 70, 73.

All plans, except Excelerator, payable to age 70 plus: $.90 per $1,000 ages 0-35 (18-35 ART); $1.11 age 45, $1.41 age 55.

Age Limits: Vary by plan.

Amount Limits: Generally none. ADB for up to 5 times the base coverage ($200,000 max.).

Aviation: No restrictions in policy. If aviation hazard excessive, extra premium or aviation exclusion endorsement required.

Cash Values: May be deferred 6 months; if deferred 30 days or more, interest at 3.5% guaranteed (present crediting rate 5.5%) allowed during deferred period. For basis see page 10.

Change of Plan: Policy provides that portion of insurance may be changed to higher premium form without evidence of insurability upon payment of difference in cash values; to lower premium plan upon evidence of insurability with adjustment of difference in cash values.

Disability Benefits: After 6 months' or 3 months' disability before age 65, premiums will be waived, retroactively. Recognized disability 1 (see page 11); restrictions 5 and 6.

Incontestability: After 2 years during the lifetime of the insured, except for non-payment of premiums and for disability and accidental death benefits.

Loan Values: To the amount of the cash value; interest at 8% payable at end of policy year. Payment may be deferred 6 months except to pay premiums.

Non-Forfeiture Provisions: Policy provides for cash, paid-up insurance with cash and loan values, extended term insurance with cash values; fractional premium increases values; grace period 31 days without interest.

Non-Medical Limits: Ages 0-30, $300,000; 31-35, $200,000; 36-40, $100,000; 41-45; $25,000.

Premiums: May be paid annually, semi-annually (x.51 + $45.00 Excelerator; $22.50 ART, quarterly (X.26 + $25.00 Excelerator; + $15.00 ART), or monthly advance check (X.085 + $7.50 Excelerator; + $3.75 ART). Any premiums paid beyond the policy month of death are added to the proceeds payable to the beneficiary.

Reinstatements: By providing evidence of insurability policy may be reinstated subject to payment of past due premiums with interest of 6% compounded yearly, and payment or reinstatement of any policy loan balance with interest of 6% compounded yearly.

Reserve Basis: (current issue) 1958 CSO 4.5%.

Restrictions: Suicide, sane or insane, within 2 years limits liability to premiums paid.

Settlement Options: (1) Monthly income for specified period, 1 to 30 years (3.5% guaranteed).* Monthly instalments per 1,000: 1 yr., $84.65; 5 yrs., $18.12 10 yrs., $9.83; 20 yrs., $5.75. (2) Monthly income of specified amount (3.5% guaranteed).* (3) Life income for the lifetime of the payee with 10 or 20 years certain (3.5% guaranteed).* (4) Monthly interest income with proceeds subject to withdrawal or change (3.5% guaranteed).* (5) Monthly life income, joint and survivor (3.5% guaranteed).* (6) Monthly life income (increased by 3%) purchased by current single premium annuity rates in effect at time the option becomes operative.

Women: All rates are Unisex.

*Present rate 5.5%.

Interest-Adj. Surr. Cost Index (Non-Par) Guar.
(Prem. = Pay't. Index) (5% Basis)

	Excelerator-NS, Opt. 3 ($100,000 Basis)			
Age	25	35	45	55
Premium	6.37	10.38	18.96	35.45
10 Year Cost	3.09	3.99	8.66	20.53
20 Year Cost	2.10	3.61	9.30	22.97

NON-PAR. PREMIUMS PER $1,000

Note: Prems. shown are per $1,000 excluding the policy fee. Add $75 per policy to Excelerator. Add $35 per policy to ART.

	Excelerator (a) Interest Sensitive Whole Life			ART (b)		
			Non-Smoker			
Male Age	Opt. 1	Opt. 2	Opt. 3	$50M	$100M	$250M
18	6.11	4.97	4.30	1.37	1.19	.98
19	6.31	5.13	4.44	1.37	1.19	.98
20	6.53	5.31	4.59	1.37	1.19	.98
21	6.77	5.50	4.76	1.37	1.19	.98
22	7.03	5.72	4.95	1.37	1.19	.98
23	7.33	5.96	5.15	1.37	1.19	.98
24	7.64	6.21	5.38	1.37	1.19	.98
25	7.99	6.50	5.62	1.37	1.19	.98
26	8.37	6.80	5.89	1.37	1.19	.98
27	8.78	7.14	6.18	1.37	1.20	.99
28	9.23	7.51	6.49	1.38	1.21	1.00
29	9.72	7.90	6.84	1.40	1.22	1.01
30	10.25	8.34	7.21	1.42	1.23	1.02
31	10.83	8.81	7.62	1.45	1.25	1.04
32	11.45	9.32	8.06	1.49	1.27	1.08
33	12.14	9.87	8.54	1.54	1.29	1.12
34	12.88	10.47	9.06	1.60	1.33	1.17
35	13.68	11.13	9.63	1.67	1.39	1.23
36	14.54	11.83	10.24	1.76	1.47	1.29
37	15.48	12.59	10.90	1.87	1.58	1.37
38	16.48	13.41	11.61	1.99	1.70	1.45
39	17.56	14.29	12.37	2.12	1.83	1.54
40	18.71	15.23	13.19	2.26	1.96	1.65
41	19.94	16.24	14.07	2.42	2.10	1.78
42	21.26	17.31	15.00	2.59	2.29	2.01
43	22.66	18.46	16.00	2.78	2.49	2.26
44	24.16	19.69	17.07	2.99	2.72	2.53
45	25.76	21.00	18.21	3.24	2.97	2.80
46	27.47	22.40	19.43	3.50	3.24	3.08
47	29.28	23.88	20.73	3.78	3.53	3.38
48	31.22	25.47	22.12	4.06	3.85	3.71
49	33.26	27.16	23.60	4.37	4.19	4.06
50	35.44	28.95	25.17	4.71	4.57	4.45
51	37.75	30.86	26.85	5.09	5.03	4.92
52	40.19	32.88	28.63	5.61	5.55	5.45
53	42.78	35.03	30.53	6.22	6.16	6.06
54	45.52	37.31	32.55	6.87	6.82	6.73
55	48.41	39.72	34.70	7.61	7.56	7.48
60	65.05	53.76	47.31	12.78	12.74	12.70
70	85.38	71.37	63.51	21.10	21.09	21.08
75				34.33	34.33	34.33
				54.33	54.33	54.33

Waiver of Premium Disability

25	.28	.20	.14	.08	.08
35	.66	.46	.33	.13	.13
45	1.72	1.18	.82	.45	.45
55	4.63	3.26	2.36	1.35	1.35

(a) Min. $25,000. Higher prem. rates are available for smokers, age 0-75. Option to vanish premiums after approx. 6 yrs. (Option 1), 8 yrs. (Option 2), 10 yrs. (Option 3) is available. (b) Non-guaranteed prem. rates. Higher prem. rates are available for smokers.

CASH VALUES PER $1,000
Excelerator (Proj. @ 10.5%)

	End of Year						At Age	
Age	2	3	4	5	10	15	20	60	65

Option 1

Age	2	3	4	5	10	15	20	60	65
20	11	17	24	32	84	171	310	2158	3252
25	14	22	31	41	108	219	394	1703	2584
30	19	30	42	55	145	290	518	1384	2122
35	26	41	57	75	197	392	693	1140	1780
40	36	56	79	104	270	534	928	928	1495
45	49	77	108	142	368	719	1226	716	1226
50	66	104	146	191	497	953	1590	497	953
55	87	137	192	251	652	1231	2016	251	652
60	110	173	242	318	832	1550	2510	....	318
65	133	209	293	387	1026	1906	3054	....	

Option 2

Age	2	3	4	5	10	15	20	60	65
20	8	13	18	24	63	128	234	1647	2484
25	11	17	24	31	83	166	301	1314	1995
30	15	23	32	43	112	222	400	1076	1652
35	20	32	45	59	152	303	538	889	1391
40	28	44	62	81	209	413	723	723	1169
45	38	60	84	110	284	558	958	558	958
50	52	81	113	149	380	738	1241	380	738
55	68	106	148	193	495	951	1571	193	495
60	85	132	184	240	624	1192	1952	....	240
65	101	157	218	286	762	1461	2375	....	

Option 3

Age	2	3	4	5	10	15	20	60	65
20	7	10	14	19	51	102	187	1335	2015
25	9	14	19	26	67	135	245	1076	1636
30	12	19	27	35	92	183	327	887	1364
35	17	27	37	49	127	249	444	736	1153
40	24	37	52	68	173	340	598	598	970
45	32	51	70	92	235	458	792	458	792
50	43	68	95	124	311	605	1025	311	605
55	57	89	123	160	399	775	1294	160	399
60	70	109	151	196	493	965	1602	....	196
65	83	128	176	229	588	1175	1945	....	

Excelerator (Guaranteed)

	End of Year						At Age	
Age	2	3	4	5	10	15	20	60	65

Option 1

Age	2	3	4	5	10	15	20	60	65
20	....	5	10	15	50	90	130	383	465
25	....	7	13	20	64	114	161	369	453
30	1	10	19	28	85	147	205	349	435
35	2	14	26	38	113	194	267	338	411
40	3	19	35	51	151	258	355	355	453
45	8	29	51	73	203	346	481	346	481
50	18	46	75	104	272	467	658	272	467
55	30	68	106	145	362	632	879	145	362
60	48	96	145	196	475	831	1146	....	196
65	69	127	187	249	615	1058	1447	....	

Option 2

Age	2	3	4	5	10	15	20	60	65
20	....	3	7	11	36	66	112	383	465
25	....	4	9	14	47	91	148	369	453
30	....	7	13	20	63	121	189	349	435
35	1	10	19	28	84	155	235	321	411
40	1	13	25	37	111	193	284	284	379
45	3	18	34	50	146	240	335	240	335
50	5	25	46	68	192	314	405	192	314
55	12	39	67	96	249	410	550	96	249
60	24	59	94	130	315	533	773	....	130
65	38	80	122	164	384	693	1020	....	

Option 3

Age	2	3	4	5	10	15	20	60	65
20	....	2	5	8	26	66	112	383	465
25	....	3	7	11	43	91	148	369	453
30	....	5	10	16	63	121	189	349	435
35	....	7	15	23	84	155	235	321	411
40	....	9	20	34	109	193	284	284	379
45	1	13	24	46	166	234	335	234	335
50	2	19	39	60	166	277	386	166	277
55	3	26	50	74	197	319	433	74	197
60	11	38	65	93	230	360	484	....	93
65	21	53	85	115	262	405	532	....	

Projected and guaranteed cash values assume vanishing prem. option not elected.

Fig. 17.10. Sample entry, *Best's Flitcraft Compend.* Copyright © A. M. Best Company, Inc. Oldwick, New Jersey 08858.

PYRAMID LIFE

ANB
Add $10 per policy except where otherwise noted

WL PAR 5MIN

M	P	**0** 8.97	**20** 14.15	**25** 16.26	**30** 18.91	**35** 22.29	**40** 26.65	**45** 32.27	**50** 39.60 / **55** 49.23
A	R	**5** 9.77	**21** 14.54	**26** 16.74	**31** 19.52	**36** 23.08	**41** 27.67	**46** 33.59	**51** 41.32 / **56** 51.51
L	E	**10** 10.97	**22** 14.94	**27** 17.24	**32** 20.16	**37** 23.90	**42** 28.73	**47** 34.97	**52** 43.13 / **60** 62.09
E	M	**15** 12.42	**23** 15.36	**28** 17.77	**33** 20.83	**38** 24.78	**43** 29.85	**48** 36.43	**53** 45.05 / **65** 79.40
	S	**18** 13.42	**24** 15.80	**29** 18.33	**34** 21.54	**39** 25.69	**44** 31.03	**49** 37.97	**54** 47.08 / **70** 102.61

	AGE 20	AGE 25	AGE 30	AGE 35	AGE 40	AGE 45	AGE 50	AGE 55
Male Dis Waiver	.33	.41	.52	.69	.96	1.39	2.17	3.64
CASH VALUES Yr 20	233.00	270.00	310.00	353.00	397.00	443.00	486.00	525.00
At Age 65	613.00	593.00	568.00	536.00	495.00	443.00	360.00	257.00
PAID-UP INS								
20 Yrs	499.00	522.00	544.00	566.00	586.00	607.00	624.00	640.00
Age 65	839.00	812.00	778.00	734.00	678.00	607.00	493.00	352.00
DIVS Acc 20 Yrs	108.89	119.97	134.33	151.71	177.26	210.35	254.53	314.05
Acc at 65	689.48	565.40	458.18	362.71	282.33	210.35	145.95	87.71
SUMMARY—20 YEARS								
20 Premiums	303.00	345.20	398.20	465.80	553.00	665.40	812.00	1004.60
Total 20 Divs	82.23	90.67	101.56	114.71	133.39	157.33	189.26	232.06
Net Payment—20	220.77	254.53	296.64	351.09	419.61	508.07	622.74	772.54
								($10,000 BASIS)

WL GTD COST 10MIN, $25-49999 PREMS BELOW, $15 POL FEE

M	P	**0** 6.04	**20** 9.28	**25** 10.63	**30** 12.61	**35** 15.77	**40** 19.79	**45** 24.67	**50** 30.75 / **55** 38.71
A	R	**5** 6.46	**21** 9.55	**26** 10.90	**31** 13.16	**36** 16.51	**41** 20.69	**46** 25.77	**51** 32.17 / **56** 40.61
L	E	**10** 7.12	**22** 9.82	**27** 11.24	**32** 13.76	**37** 17.28	**42** 21.63	**47** 26.93	**52** 33.66 / **60** 49.55
E	M	**15** 8.04	**23** 10.09	**28** 11.64	**33** 14.39	**38** 18.09	**43** 22.60	**48** 28.14	**53** 35.25 / **65** 64.61
	S	**18** 8.76	**24** 10.36	**29** 12.10	**34** 15.06	**39** 18.92	**44** 23.61	**49** 29.41	**54** 36.93 / **70** 87.84

	AGE 20	AGE 25	AGE 30	AGE 35	AGE 40	AGE 45	AGE 50	AGE 55
Female Prems	8.51	9.82	11.24	13.76	17.28	21.63	26.93	32.66
Male Dis Waiver	.23	.28	.34	.49	.70	1.06	1.65	2.86
Male Accid Death	1.05	1.05	1.05	1.05	1.10	1.16	1.22	1.32
CASH VALUES								
Year 1	....	....	....	....	....			
2	....	....	....	....	....	2.00	5.00	7.00
5	9.00	16.00	25.00	36.00	47.00	60.00	73.00	88.00
10	49.00	66.00	87.00	110.00	135.00	162.00	191.00	221.00
20	177.00	214.00	256.00	301.00	348.00	398.00	446.00	489.00
At Age 65	542.00	526.00	506.00	479.00	444.00	398.00	310.00	221.00
PAID-UP INS								
20 Yrs	568.00	587.00	605.00	620.00	632.00	645.00	656.00	664.00
Age 65	879.00	853.00	820.00	777.00	720.00	645.00	503.00	359.00

WLNCS ADJ PREM $25-49999, CURRENT PREMS GTD 1 YR, $20 POL FEE

M	P	**0** 2.88	**20** 5.81	**25** 6.80	**30** 8.69	**35** 11.26	**40** 14.07	**45** 17.70	**50** 22.33 / **55** 28.35
A	R	**5** 3.20	**21** 5.98	**26** 7.11	**31** 9.16	**36** 11.79	**41** 14.73	**46** 18.54	**51** 23.41 / **56** 29.78
L	E	**10** 3.98	**22** 6.15	**27** 7.46	**32** 9.66	**37** 12.33	**42** 15.41	**47** 19.41	**52** 24.54 / **60** 36.38
E	M	**15** 5.00	**23** 6.33	**28** 7.84	**33** 10.18	**38** 12.88	**43** 16.14	**48** 20.33	**53** 25.73 / **65** 47.11
	S	**18** 5.48	**24** 6.54	**29** 8.25	**34** 10.72	**39** 13.45	**44** 16.90	**49** 21.30	**54** 27.00 / **70** 66.11

	AGE 20	AGE 25	AGE 30	AGE 35	AGE 40	AGE 45	AGE 50	AGE 55
Female Prems	5.33	6.15	7.46	9.66	12.33	15.41	19.41	24.54
Male Dis Waiver	.20	.24	.31	.41	.60	.90	1.49	2.47
Male Accid Death	1.05	1.05	1.05	1.05	1.10	1.16	1.22	1.32
CASH VALUES								
Year 1	....	....	....	....	....	....	....	....
2								3.00
5	....	5.00	14.00	24.00	34.00	47.00	60.00	74.00
10	28.00	44.00	63.00	85.00	109.00	136.00	166.00	197.00
20	113.00	149.00	190.00	235.00	284.00	336.00	386.00	432.00
At Age 65	465.00	453.00	435.00	412.00	379.00	336.00	277.00	197.00
PAID-UP INS								
20 Yrs	521.00	561.00	589.00	608.00	624.00	637.00	645.00	649.00
Age 65	881.00	859.00	824.00	781.00	718.00	637.00	525.00	374.00

C1YTNCS ADJ PREM $100-249999 CURRENT PREMS GTD 1 YR, ALB, $20 POL FEE

M	P	**0**	**20** 1.42	**25** 1.42	**30** 1.59	**35** 1.83	**40** 2.60	**45** 3.84	**50** 5.32 / **55** 7.85
A	R	**5**	**21** 1.42	**26** 1.44	**31** 1.63	**36** 1.94	**41** 2.81	**46** 4.10	**51** 5.74 / **56** 8.48
L	E	**10**	**22** 1.42	**27** 1.47	**32** 1.66	**37** 2.08	**42** 3.05	**47** 4.36	**52** 6.20 / **60** 11.59
E	M	**15** 1.42	**23** 1.42	**28** 1.51	**33** 1.69	**38** 2.23	**43** 3.30	**48** 4.64	**53** 6.70 / **65** 17.57
	S	**18** 1.42	**24** 1.42	**29** 1.55	**34** 1.75	**39** 2.41	**44** 3.57	**49** 4.95	**54** 7.25 / **70**

C 1YT (CONTINUED) $100-249999 CURRENT PREMS

M	P	**0**	**20** 1.80	**25** 1.80	**30** 2.04	**35** 2.45	**40** 3.72	**45** 5.84	**50** 7.87 / **55** 11.49
A	R	**5**	**21** 1.80	**26** 1.83	**31** 2.10	**36** 2.64	**41** 4.09	**46** 6.23	**51** 8.48 / **56** 12.29
L	E	**10**	**22** 1.80	**27** 1.87	**32** 2.15	**37** 2.86	**42** 4.51	**47** 6.58	**52** 9.16 / **60** 15.93
E	M	**15** 1.80	**23** 1.80	**28** 1.92	**33** 2.22	**38** 3.11	**43** 4.96	**48** 6.95	**53** 9.91 / **65** 22.58
	S	**18** 1.80	**24** 1.80	**29** 1.98	**34** 2.31	**39** 3.40	**44** 5.41	**49** 7.36	**54** 10.69 / **70**

C 1YTNCSBOF (CONTINUED) $100-249999 CURRENT PREMS

M	P	**0**	**20** 1.19	**25** 1.19	**30** 1.30	**35** 1.48	**40** 2.11	**45** 3.12	**50** 4.32 / **55** 6.36
A	R	**5**	**21** 1.19	**26** 1.20	**31** 1.32	**36** 1.57	**41** 2.28	**46** 3.33	**51** 4.66 / **56** 6.87
L	E	**10**	**22** 1.19	**27** 1.22	**32** 1.35	**37** 1.68	**42** 2.48	**47** 3.55	**52** 5.03 / **60** 9.39
E	M	**15** 1.19	**23** 1.19	**28** 1.25	**33** 1.37	**38** 1.81	**43** 2.68	**48** 3.77	**53** 5.43 / **65** 14.18
	S	**18** 1.19	**24** 1.19	**29** 1.27	**34** 1.41	**39** 1.95	**44** 2.90	**49** 4.02	**54** 5.88 / **70** ....

Fig. 17.11. Sample entry, *Life Rates & Data*. Reprinted from 1986 edition of *Life Rates & Data*, published by National Underwriter Co., Cincinnati, Ohio.

Insurance Periodicals

Periodicals relating to the insurance industry are generally either trade publications aimed at insurance practitioners or scholarly journals focusing on the study of insurance, risk management, and actuarial science. The titles that follow are typical trade publications.

Best's Review: Life/Health Insurance Edition. Oldwick, N.J.: A. M. Best, 1899- . Monthly.

Best's Review: Property/Casualty Insurance Edition. Oldwick, N.J.: A. M. Best, 1899- . Monthly.

National Underwriter: Life & Health/Financial Services Edition. Cincinnati, Ohio: National Underwriter, 1897- . Weekly.

National Underwriter: Property & Casualty/Employee Benefits Edition. Cincinnati, Ohio: National Underwriter, 1896- . Weekly.

Each of the two major insurance publishers, A. M. Best and National Underwriter, publishes trade magazines in two editions for the life/health and property/casualty insurance industries. Best's offering is *Best's Review*. Published since 1899, it contains news of industry and company developments, new types of policies, and prominent practitioners who have changed companies, been promoted, or retired. In addition, it covers regulation of the insurance industry, sales and marketing, and tax policies as they affect insurance. Regular features include "New Publications," which lists and reviews selected books, proceedings, and booklets; "Reports on Companies," "Company Reports Index," which indexes companies and organizations mentioned in *Best's Review* in the last six months; and "Insurance Stocks," which provides stock price and trading information on publicly traded insurance companies.

Further, each edition of *Best's Review* provides more specialized coverage. Recent issues of the *Life/Health Insurance Edition*, for example, have included articles on how health insurers can provide comprehensive coverage for AIDS victims and how advances on life insurance policies can help to pay for organ transplants. Annual statistical surveys are common. One major survey covers annuity premiums, another, policy dividends, and a third, leading life insurance companies. Other special issues can be identified by consulting the *Special Issues Index* or the *Guide to Special Issues*.

The companion periodical is *Best's Review: Property/Casualty Insurance Edition*. A typical issue includes some 10 articles dealing with different facets of the industry. As with the *Life/Health* edition, the *Property/Casualty* edition includes many special reports, such as an annual industry review and preview, an insurance salary survey, an auto insurance issue, and the top 200 property and casualty insurance companies.

Similar coverage is provided in both editions of the *National Underwriter*, a weekly trade paper that reports on recent developments in the insurance industry. Articles may focus on commercial or personal insurance, group and employee benefits, sales, management, current legislation, and regulation. Special issues in the *Life & Health/Financial Services Edition* include an industry forecast and review, rankings of health insurance companies, an insurance marketing review, and reports on several professional conferences. The *Property & Casualty/Employee Benefits Edition* includes reviews of auto, marine, and international insurance, insurance-in-force rankings, and summaries of professional meetings. The *National Underwriter* and *Best's Reviews* are the most widely read and circulated of all such trade journals.

Scholarly treatment is provided in several periodicals; two of the most highly regarded follow.

American Risk Insurance Association. **The Journal of Risk and Insurance**. Athens, Ga.: The Association, University of Georgia, 1932- . Quarterly.

American Society of CLU and ChFC. **Journal of the American Society of CLU & ChFC**. Bryn Mawr, Pa.: The Society, 1946- . Bimonthly.

The Journal of Risk and Insurance is the most scholarly and quantitative of all insurance periodicals. Articles are usually written by academicians rather than insurance practitioners, and frequently include formulas, statistics, and lengthy footnotes. Typical titles include "A Regression-Based Methodology for Solvency Surveillance in the Property-Liability Insurance Industry," and "Risk Aversion in the Theory of Life Insurance." Each issue also contains "Recent Court Decisions," which briefly describes important legal actions, "From the Library Shelf," which annotates significant new titles, and "Book Reviews," which features lengthier signed reviews. The Journal reproduces the table of contents pages from two related publications, Insurance: Mathematics and Economics and the ASTIN Bulletin, a journal of the International Actuarial Association. An annual index is published as part of one issue, with a cumulative subject, author, and book review index published as a separate volume every few years. The most recent Periodic Index, published in 1986, covers 1981 through 1985, and is next scheduled to be published in 1991.

The Journal of the American Society of CLU & ChFC (Chartered Life Underwriters and Chartered Financial Consultants) focuses on the life/health insurance industry. Regular columns include ones on estate, financial, and tax planning, information management, economic trends, and "Strictly Speaking," which discusses current ethical, legal, and social issues relating to the profession. The articles themselves are written by insurance professionals as well as by academicians and are generally less theoretical and quantitative than those appearing in The Journal of Risk and Insurance.

Current information about the insurance industry is as important to consumers as it is to agents and brokers. Although no consumer-oriented serial is devoted entirely to insurance, some periodically describe or evaluate specific types of insurance coverage and insurance companies. Consumer Reports, Changing Times, and Money, for example, frequently include articles intended to help consumers keep abreast of industry developments and make wise insurance decisions.[21]

The above periodicals focus primarily on private, rather than public, insurance. One key government periodical, however, contains current information on social insurance programs provided by the federal government.

U.S. Dept. of Health and Human Services. Social Security Administration. **Social Security Bulletin**. Washington, D.C.: Government Printing Office, 1938- . Monthly.

Each issue of the Social Security Bulletin includes summaries of recent research, notes and brief reports, and two or three articles treating some aspect of social insurance or public assistance. Recent issues, for example, have included articles on worldwide trends and developments in social security, the pension status of recently retired workers, and a study of 35 years of cash benefits for short-term sickness. The articles are often written by the Social Security Administration research staff, and usually include statistics, tables, and graphs, some of which are extremely useful for reference. "Fast Facts and Figures about Social Security," for example, was written to answer the questions most frequently received by the Social Security Administration. It provides data on OASDI programs, Medicare, Medicaid, Supplemental Security Income, and Aid to Families with Dependent Children. General information about social insurance tax rates, benefits, and the income of the aged population is also included.[22]

The Bulletin's "Current Operating Statistics" section contains several pages of statistics pertaining to Social Security Administration programs as well as economic indicators relating to personal income and prices paid for medical care. An annual statistical supplement is included with the subscription.

Periodical Indexes

Major insurance periodicals are indexed in such standard business sources as *Business Periodicals Index* and *Business Index*. In many instances, these sources will suffice. One specialized index, however, is also available.

Insurance Periodicals Index. Chatworth, Calif.: NILS Publishing, 1964- . Annual.

The *Insurance Periodicals Index* indexes the articles, product announcements, book reviews, statistics, letters to the editor, and obituaries included in 36 major insurance periodicals. The *Index* is arranged in two parts, a subject index and an author index.

The *Insurance Periodicals Index* was originally compiled by members of the Special Libraries Association's Insurance and Employee Benefits Division from monthly lists in both editions of *Best's Reviews*. In 1982, the NILS Publishing Company joined with the division to help them develop the computerized database out of which the annual *Index* is now published. *IPI* is available as an online database through LEXIS and NEXIS.

Government Documents

Insurance is regulated at the state level. As a result, the federally published statistical compilations, consumer guides, and information sources so common to federally regulated industries are not generally available for private insurance. Congressional hearings regarding the insurance industry are held periodically and are subsequently published and distributed by the Government Printing Office. Most federal documents, however, deal with social insurance programs. Many are written for program beneficiaries. One such source, the *Social Security Handbook*, has already been described. Other booklets and brochures deal with specific types of social insurance coverage. Some of the most useful and popular of these documents are listed below.

> U.S. Dept. of Health and Human Services. Social Security Administration. **Your Social Security Rights and Responsibilities: Retirement and Survivors Benefits**. Washington, D.C.: Government Printing Office, 1986. 23p.
>
> _____. **Your Medicare Handbook**. Washington, D.C.: Government Printing Office. Annual.
>
> _____. **Guide to Health Insurance for People with Medicare**. Washington, D.C.: Government Printing Office. Annual.

Written for people who have recently become eligible for retirement or survivors' benefits, *Your Social Security Rights and Responsibilities* describes the schedule for issuing Social Security checks, explains what to do when checks are lost or stolen or fail to arrive, and includes instructions for reporting events that may affect social security payments.[23] A similar publication, *Your Medicare Handbook*, describes the Medicare program, lists medical care services and supplies included under or excluded from Medicare coverage, and explains how to file medical insurance claims. A list of Medicare carriers by state is also included. The *Guide to Health Insurance for People with Medicare* focuses on situations in which it is advisable to obtain private insurance to supplement Medicare coverage, with tips for selecting insurers and supplemental insurance. These and other similar documents are often free or very inexpensive; public and state-supported libraries can provide a useful service by keeping circulating copies of them on hand in their vertical file collections.[24]

Although such consumer-oriented booklets are the most common type of federal document, other insurance-related sources are also available. Some present statistics relating to social insurance programs, others describe supplementary state programs, and still others, produced by the Small Business Administration, cover insurance as it relates to business. Some representative documents follow.

U.S. Dept. of Health and Human Services. Social Security Administration. **Income and Resources of the Population 65 and Older**. Washington, D.C.: Government Printing Office, 1986. 20p.

_____. **Characteristics of Social Security Disability Insurance Beneficiaries**. Washington, D.C.: Government Printing Office, 1987. 330p.

U.S. Small Business Administration. **Insurance and Risk Management for Small Business,** by Mark R. Greene. 3rd ed. Washington, D.C.: Government Printing Office, 1986. 93p.

Income and Resources of the Population 65 and Older is a chartbook based on data collected by the Social Security Administration and the Census Bureau. It is a graphic depiction of statistics on retirement benefits and pensions, income size, health benefits, and the importance of social security income payments to the aged. More detailed and specialized statistics are available in *Characteristics of Social Security Disability Insurance Beneficiaries*. Based on disability determination records of the Social Security Administration, it presents statistics on selected demographic, socioeconomic, and medical characteristics of persons who receive benefits as disabled workers.

Not all federal documents focus on social insurance. *Insurance and Risk Management for Small Business*, produced by the SBA, provides an introduction to all types of business insurance. It offers pointers on buying insurance, explanations of common insurance terms, and descriptions of different types of insurance coverage. Chapters on the settlement of losses and managing insurance programs are also included, as is a bibliography of titles for suggested further reading.

Many state government agencies also issue insurance-related documents. They range from consumer guides such as *Alaska's Consumer Guide to Automobile Insurance* and the *Florida Consumer's Guide to Mobile Home Insurance* to statistical compilations, fact books, and manuals. Such publications are frequently produced by state insurance departments, and can be identified by consulting state documents checklists, the Library of Congress's *Monthly Checklist of State Documents*, or by contacting the agency itself. Some of the most detailed information on the insurance industry and on specific companies can be found in the annual reports issued by state insurance departments. The reports are available from the departments themselves, state document depository libraries, and through the SRI Microfiche Library. They are usually quite long, contain extensive statistical information, and are one of the primary sources from which data presented in the statistical sources listed in the following section are derived.

Statistics

Insurance statistics are plentiful. Many of the sources already described contain valuable statistical information. Such trade publications as *Best's Review* regularly publish annual surveys of company and industry financial performance, while federal publications such as the *Social Security Bulletin* present detailed statistics on social insurance programs and benefits. State insurance departments publish statistics as well, based primarily on the reports submitted to them by insurance companies.

While these sources are useful, however, they are by no means the only publications in which statistics are available. Although there is no single source that presents comprehensive information on all types of commercial and social insurance, several titles focus on specific insurance lines. Most reflect the traditional division between the life/health and property/casualty industries.

The life/health industry is represented by several different sources. The two most widely consulted sources follow.

American Council of Life Insurance. **Life Insurance Fact Book**. Washington, D.C.: The Council, 1946- . Annual.

Health Insurance Institute. **Source Book of Health Insurance Data**. New York: The Institute, 1959- . Biennial, with an *Update* published in the interim year.

The *Life Insurance Fact Book* is a basic source. Based on data compiled from annual statements provided by life insurance companies, council surveys, and other organizations, it summarizes industry trends and developments, presenting information on life insurance purchases and ownership, annuities, life insurance and annuity benefit payments, pension and retirement programs, policy lapses and surrenders, life insurance assets, and other aspects of the life insurance business. For the most part, it emphasizes the current and preceding year, with data in tables, charts, and graphs supplemented by brief, narrative descriptions. Some historical data are presented. Additional sections identify key state insurance officials and present mortality tables, historic dates, and name and describe important trade and professional life insurance associations. A glossary and index are also included.[25]

Similar coverage is provided in the *Source Book of Health Insurance Data*. Like the *Fact Book*, it includes an index, glossary, and list of historic dates. Its main sections present tables on the extent of private health insurance coverage, benefit payments, premium income, government health care programs, medical care costs, disability and health care utilization, and health manpower. Formerly an annual, the *Source Book* is now published biennially, with a supplementary update published in interim years. The *Update*, it should be noted, is selective; not all tables included in the *Source Book* are brought up-to-date. Both the *Source Book* and the *Update* are available from the Health Insurance Association.[26]

Although the *Fact Book* and the *Source Book* are perhaps the most widely used statistical sources, others are also available. The Metropolitan Life Insurance Company, for example, publishes a quarterly *Statistical Bulletin*, which presents articles and statistical analyses of leading causes of death, demographic trends, and regional variations in health and health-related behavior. The Health Insurance Association of America publishes two biennials, *New Group Health Insurance* and *New Group Disability Insurance*, that briefly summarize new group insurance policies written.[27]

The Life Insurance Marketing and Research Association (LIMRA) is one of the most prolific publishers of statistics on the life insurance industry. It conducts research, produces a wide range of publications, and is a principal source of industry sales and marketing statistics. It regularly surveys life insurance companies, agencies, agents, and brokers, and publishes its findings in such studies as *Agent Production and Survival, Agency Expenses and Performance, Survey of Agency Opinion*, and *The Buyer Study*. It also publishes a brief *Monthly Survey of Life Insurance Sales in the United States* that includes data on sales, policy characteristics, and premiums. In addition, LIMRA publishes an annual *Index to Publications* and *LIMRA Research*, which provides an overview of the projects, products, and services of the Research Division. Like other insurance trade associations, LIMRA makes most of its publications available free of charge to libraries and educational institutions.[28]

The property/casualty industry is also well represented by statistical publications. Two of the most useful follow.

Insurance Information Institute. **Insurance Facts; Property-Casualty Fact Book**. New York: The Institute, 1961- . Annual.

A. M. Best Company. **Best's Aggregates & Averages: Property-Casualty**. Oldwick, N.J.: A. M. Best, 1976- . Annual.

Insurance Facts is another association-published fact book. Like the others, it includes detailed current and historic industry statistics, grouped under the following broad categories: Scope of the Business, Dollars and Cents of the Business, Shared Markets, Government Insurance Programs, Factors Affecting Costs, Losses by Category, and Laws Affecting Motorists. A general information section describes the regulation of insurance and lists state insurance commissioners, insurance and service organizations, and companies that are members of the institute. A brief glossary and an index are also appended.[29]

Best's Aggregates & Averages: Property-Casualty includes composite industry data as well as information on specific companies. It is particularly useful for researchers who need to compare the performance of one company with others in the same line or with the industry aggregate. It presents consolidated industry totals as well as totals for companies categorized by type of organization and by predominant type of insurance written. Each of these listings presents aggregate balance sheet and operating statistics, showing assets and liabilities for the current and preceding year, average yield on company investments, premiums written, premiums earned and collected, commissions, expenses, and other operating data.

In addition, *Best's Aggregates & Averages* features time series data on industry resources and operating results, loss and expense ratios, and an extensive "Lines of Business" section that provides statistics on leading companies and insurance groups. Also included are lists of leading companies and of underwriting expenses by company.

Other publications are more specialized. The All-Industry Research Advisory Council (AIRAC), an industry-sponsored organization, conducts research, publishes the findings, and makes them available to the public. *Uninsured Motorist Facts and Figures*, for example, presents detailed demographic information on the characteristics of uninsured drivers and the cars they drive, accident claims, and state laws on uninsured motorist coverage.[30]

Another industry-sponsored organization, the Highway Loss Data Institute, publishes reports on theft, insurance losses, and collision coverages of automobiles, vans, pickup trucks, and utility vehicles, as well as on accident-related injuries. Reports analyze insurance claims by such factors as the use of seat belts or the frequency with which different models and years of automobiles and vans are involved in accidents.[31]

Other statistics relating to the life/health and property/casualty insurance industries can be identified by consulting *Statistics Sources*, the *American Statistics Index*, and the *Statistical Reference Index*.

Vertical File Materials

The insurance industry is well represented by materials appropriate for vertical file collections. Many of the trade associations already described have active publishing programs, issuing educational and promotional pamphlets as well as professional publications. In addition to the *Life Insurance Fact Book*, for example, the American Council of Life Insurance publishes such titles as *Understanding Your Life Insurance, A Consumer's Guide to Life Insurance*, and *Planning with Your Beneficiaries*. The Insurance Information Institute, representing the property-casualty industry, issues such consumer-oriented leaflets as *Home Insurance Basics, Auto Insurance Basics*, and *Risk Management and Business Insurance*. Both associations also issue publications catalogs and sample policies for different lines of insurance.[32]

Many major insurance companies publish similar types of booklets, intended to educate and inform and to promote the products they are selling. *How Much Life Insurance Do I Need? How Much Life Insurance Can I Afford?* and *How to Choose a Life Insurance Plan Best for You* are available from Bankers Life Company, and *Exercise Your Right to Live*, from Transamerica Occidental Life Insurance Company. Although such materials are promotional, most also contain useful information and are suitable for vertical file collections.

Other booklets are intended primarily for insurance practitioners. The Life Insurance Marketing and Research Association, for example, publishes a series of reports and studies focusing on specific life insurance markets and products. Typical of such LIMRA publications are *The Retirement Markets: Overview and Outlook, Variable Universal Life: To Market or Not?*, and *The Baby Boomers; a Market in the Making*. The American Council of Life Insurance publishes a series called *DataTrack*, reports that compile and interpret demographic information of interest to life insurance executives. Titles in the *DataTrack* series include *Blacks and Hispanics in the United States, Women in the Labor*

Force, and *Above-Average Income Households and Families.* Another trade association, the Life Office Management Association (LOMA), issues pamphlets and reports promoting management excellence in life and health insurance companies. Its publications include reports on financial planning and control, human resources, and operations and systems, as well as a *Manager's Guide* series that focuses on such topics as employee selection and employee relations.[33]

Trade association publications can be acquired easily. For a more balanced collection of insurance pamphlets, however, it may be necessary to scan such sources as *Public Affairs Information Service Bulletin, Vertical File Index,* and *Insurance and Employee Benefits Literature.*

Databases

In many library settings, access to online bibliographic insurance information will be through such standard business databases as *ABI/Inform, Business Periodicals Index,* and *Management Contents. Insurance Periodicals Index* is, however, available as an online database through LEXIS and NEXIS. Finally, some of the major insurance publishers are also vendors of electronic business information. A. M. Best, for example, offers *Best's Online Database,* a database that contains current and historical financial and marketing information on some 4,000 insurers. It also sells more specialized databases on diskettes and computer tape. Such products, however, are costly and are best suited to large insurance companies and the libraries that serve them.

NOTES

[1]George E. Rejda, *Principles of Insurance* (Glenview, Ill.: Scott, Foresman and Co., 1982), 24.

[2]"Current Accounts," *Money* (March 1982): 6.

[3]"Upheaval in Life Insurance," *Business Week* (June 25, 1984): 61.

[4]"Insurance and Investment: Basic Analysis," *Standard & Poor's Industry Surveys* (May 8, 1986): I-15.

[5]Andrew Tobias, *The Invisible Bankers* (New York: Linden Press/Simon & Schuster, 1982), 303.

[6]Although most property/casualty insurers are stock companies, there are some exceptions. State Farm Insurance, a mutual insurance company, is perhaps the most notable.

[7]Frederick G. Crane, *Insurance Principles and Practices* (New York: Wiley, 1980), 427.

[8]Tobias, 82.

[9]Rejda, 505.

[10]Crane, 303.

[11]Most federal civilian employees and some employees of state and local governments and nonprofit organizations are not covered by Old Age, Survivors, Disability and Health Insurance (Social Security).

[12]American Council of Life Insurance, *Who We Are, What We Do* (Washington, D.C.: The Council, n.d.), 1.

[13]"Quote, Unquote," *Forbes* 139, no. 2 (January 12, 1987): 17.

[14]To request a complimentary copy of *Books in Insurance*, write to:
>Insurance Information Institute
>110 William Street
>New York, NY 10038

[15]David W. Gregg, "A Note on Insurance Terminology," in Lewis E. Davids, *Dictionary of Insurance*. 6th rev. ed. (Totowa, N.J.: Rowman & Allanheld, 1983), xiii.

[16]Lewis E. Davids, *Dictionary of Insurance*. 6th rev. ed. (Totowa, N.J.: Rowman & Allanheld, 1983), x.

[17]"Explanation of Best's Rating System," *Best's Insurance Reports: Life-Health* (Oldwick, N.J.: A. M. Best, 1986), ix.

[18]Joseph M. Belth, *Life Insurance: A Consumer's Handbook*. 2nd ed. (Bloomington, Ind.: Indiana University Press, 1985), 71-72.

[19]Ibid, 72.

[20]*Who Writes What in Life and Health Insurance* (Cincinnati, Ohio: National Underwriter, 1986), 59.

[21]The February 1987 issue of *Money*, for example, includes a special section that features advice on determining the amount of insurance coverage required, dealing with insurance agents, and using insurance as a tax shelter.

[22]"Fast Facts and Figures about Social Security," *Social Security Bulletin* 49, no. 6 (June 1986): 5-19.

[23]A companion publication, *Your Social Security Rights and Responsibilities: Disabilities* is also available from the Government Printing Office.

[24]Pamphlets available free from the Consumer Information Center are:

>*A Brief Explanation of Medicare* (511R)

>*A Woman's Guide to Social Security* (512R)

>*Your Social Security* (513R)

>*Guide to Health Insurance for People with Medicare* (528R)

To order them, write to:
>S. James
>Consumer Information Center-A
>P.O. Box 100
>Pueblo, CO 81002

Note that, as with any multiple orders for free materials submitted to the Consumer Information Center, any requests for more than one item must be accompanied by $1 per order.

[25]For a free copy of the *Life Insurance Fact Book*, write to:

> American Council of Life Insurance
> 1001 Pennsylvania Avenue, N.W.
> Washington, DC 20004-2502

[26]For complimentary copies of the biennial *Source Book of Health Insurance* and the *Update*, write to:

> Public Relations Division
> Health Insurance Association of America
> 1850 K Street, N.W.
> Washington, DC 20006-2284

[27]Free copies of *New Group Disability Insurance* and *New Group Health Insurance* can be acquired by writing to the address in #26 above.

[28]Librarians and researchers interested in the life insurance industry might benefit from contacting and obtaining publications from:

> Life Insurance Marketing and Research Association
> P.O. Box 208
> Hartford, CT 06141

[29]For a free copy of *Insurance Facts*, write to the address in #14.

[30]To request a copy of *Uninsured Motorist Facts & Figures*, write to:

> All-Industry Research Advisory Council
> 1200 Harger Road, Suite 222
> Oak Brook, IL 60521

[31]To request a list of reports available to the public, write to:

> Highway Loss Data Institute
> 600 Watergate
> Washington, DC 20037

[32]The American Council of Life Insurance and the Health Insurance Association of America jointly publish an annual catalog, *Resources for the Education Community*, that lists and annotates pamphlets, booklets, and videocassettes likely to be of interest to high school and college educators. It includes materials on financial planning, insurance, and health and wellness. For a free copy, write to the address in #25.

The Insurance Information Institute publishes *A Guide to the Services of the Insurance Information Institute*, which lists professional, educational, and promotional materials. It, too, is free (see #14).

[33]The Life Office Management Association's annual *Price List* can be ordered from:

> LOMA
> 5770 Powers Ferry Road
> Atlanta, GA 30327

The best investment on earth *is earth.*

— Louis Glickman

18

REAL ESTATE

Earlier chapters have covered such traditional and speculative investments as stocks, bonds, mutual funds, commodities futures, and options. This chapter examines another investment medium, real estate. Its importance is difficult to overestimate.

Each of us uses real estate every day. Real estate provides shelter, protection, comfort, convenience, privacy, and many other things. Business firms need a place of business — a store, office, plant, or other parcel of real estate — in order to carry on operations. Farms and ranches, of course, rely heavily on real estate. Governmental, educational, religious, and cultural institutions all make use of real estate. Our real estate resources — the homes, factories, office buildings, stores, shopping centers, farms, rights of way, roads, streets, parks, recreational areas, and other kinds — represent more than half of our national wealth.[1]

This chapter explains basic real estate concepts and describes reference sources of potential interest to homeowners, business people, investors, realtors, and real estate practitioners.

BASIC REAL ESTATE CONCEPTS

Real estate means land and the attachments to it that are intended to be permanent. Such attachments, also known as improvements, may include fences, landscaping, bridges, and pipelines as well as buildings. Automobiles parked on the land or possessions stored in the buildings, however, are personal rather than real property. The distinction is an important one. Personal property includes items of a temporary or movable nature, and real property, land and its permanent structures. Land includes more than the earth's surface. It begins at the earth's center, and continues through to the surface and beyond it into space; rights to the subsurface, surface, and airspace for the same plot of land may, in fact, be separately held.

Categories of Real Estate

Real estate can be categorized in many different ways. It can, for example, be classified as urban or rural or as residential, commercial, or industrial. It can also be categorized as property purchased primarily for occupancy (a house, store, or factory) by its owner, or for investment purposes (an apartment building, a syndicated real estate partnership). A brief discussion of each of these classifications is in order.

As the population has grown and become increasingly urban, so also has the proportion of urban real estate increased. Even so, such real estate accounts for less than 2 percent of the total land area in the United States. Most other land can be classified as rural. It includes not only farms, ranches, and the land they occupy, but also commercial forests, wildlife refuges, reservoirs, and recreational and wilderness areas. Finally, some real estate can be categorized as both urban and rural; interstate highways and railroad rights-of-way fall into this classification.

Real estate is often described by the uses for which it is intended (see figure 18.1). Owner- and renter-occupied housing, for example, is generally referred to as *residential property*, while real estate used for wholesale, retail, and service industries is considered *commercial property*. Shopping centers, office buildings, resorts, restaurants, and hotels and motels are all categorized as commercial property. Real estate used primarily for manufacturing or warehouses is referred to as *industrial property*, and includes factories, warehouses, and industrial parks. Two additional categories, agricultural and governmental, are less immediately relevant to business research and are thus excluded from discussion in this chapter.

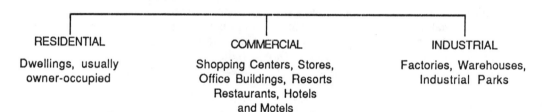

RESIDENTIAL	COMMERCIAL	INDUSTRIAL
Dwellings, usually owner-occupied	Shopping Centers, Stores, Office Buildings, Resorts Restaurants, Hotels and Motels	Factories, Warehouses, Industrial Parks

Fig. 18.1. Types of real estate.

All real estate ownership represents investment, some of it considerable. Not all real estate, however, is purchased primarily for investment purposes. Although the homeowner hopes that his or her property will appreciate in value, usually the primary goal is to enjoy other benefits—shelter, privacy, convenience, status—that homeownership may bring. The same is true for the small business person who owns the buildings and land occupied by his or her business. The emphasis in these situations is on ownership of real property for occupancy rather than for any immediate investment returns. Others, however, buy property primarily for investment. Land developers and contractors who routinely buy and sell real estate and institutional investors, such as insurance companies that invest heavily in buildings and land, fall into this category. So also do a growing number of small, private investors. Some purchase real property directly; a person who has recently inherited money, for example, may choose to buy rental property rather than stocks or bonds. Other investors share ownership of real estate through limited partnerships and real estate investment trusts.

A *real estate limited partnership*, or *RELP*, enables member investors to share ownership in more extensive and diverse real estate holdings than they would be able to afford individually. Membership in such syndicates consists of limited and general partners. Limited partners put up the capital. General partners seek the investors, make the investment decisions, and act as the syndicate managers. In addition, general partners assume greater risk than limited partners; while limited partners chance loss of capital, their liability is limited to the amount of their investment. General partners, on the other hand, must personally assume all other liabilities of ownership and financing. In return for their services and their assumption of greater risk, general partners receive fees from the limited partners, much as investment company managers receive them from shareholders.

> A real estate syndicator arranges to buy property with a bunch of dentists and airline pilots. The syndicator, a general partner, puts together the deal; the dentists and airline pilots [limited partners] put up the money. Whatever profit or loss the property generates, after certain fees to the general partner, gets passed through to the limited partners.[2]

RELPs may be either private (that is, not open to the public) or public. Public real estate limited partnerships, also known as master limited partnerships or MLPs, are publicly traded on the major stock exchanges and in the over-the-counter market. Like other publicly traded securities, master limited partnerships are under the regulation of the Securities and Exchange Commission and are required to report to it on a regular basis.

Real estate investment trusts (REITs) are related investment mediums. Like limited partnerships, real estate investment trusts pool the money of several investors for the purchase of real property (or mortgages on such property) and are generally considered long-term investments. Like master limited partnerships, REITs are publicly traded. REITs, however, are organized and function as corporations rather than partnerships; REIT investors are exempt from the risk of liability that limited partners must assume. As a rule, REITs have fewer restrictions attached to them and are more easily traded than MLPs. Some MLPs and REITs are marketed as if they were mutual funds. A column in *Money* describes two such offerings.

> T. Rowe Price's new Realty Income Fund III is actually a limited partnership. It is designed to last seven to 10 years, after which its holdings will be sold and the proceeds distributed. If you want out sooner, there's no guarantee that you will be able to find a buyer for your partnership unit. Minimum investment is $5,000.

> Vanguard's Real Estate Fund I, also new, is a real estate investment trust. REITs are fixed portfolios of properties, and shares in them trade on the exchanges like other stocks. But this one won't start trading for two years during which it will be hard to cash in your holdings. Minimum investment: $2,500.[3]

Genuine mutual funds, however, are generally more easily traded than either MLPs or REITs and can be redeemed at any time.

Prospective investors are counseled to learn all they can about specific MLPs and REITs before they invest. Some sources discussed in preceding chapters are useful. *Value Line*, for example, presents an industry analysis of real estate investment trusts as well as reports on and ratings of specific trusts. "Insurance and Investment," a Standard & Poor's *Industry Survey*, includes a section on REITs as well, and the second volume of *Moody's Bank & Finance Manual* incorporates one section on REITs and another on real estate companies and related securities.

Real Estate Industry

Discussion of real estate to this point has focused on the property holder—the homeowner, business person, or investor—rather than on the business of real estate. Real estate is, however, a major industry. It includes a wide variety of businesses, most of which can be categorized as marketing, producing, or financing enterprises. In addition, several related industries and professions are frequently directly involved in the real estate industry.

MARKETING

Marketing enterprises include two main types of business: brokerage and property management. *Real estate brokerage* involves selling, leasing, buying, or exchanging property for others on a commission basis. Brokerage firms, or real estate agencies, may range in size from small, one- or two-person operations to large national firms. They may handle all types of real estate or they may specialize in residential, commercial, industrial, or farm property. All, however, serve as intermediaries and all charge commissions. Owners of brokerage firms are usually referred to as *brokers*, while other employees assisting in marketing real estate are usually called *sales persons*. Both brokers and sales persons must pass examinations in order to be licensed to practice in the states in which they are located.

Often the term *realtor* is used by lay people to designate brokers and sales people. Not all such real estate practitioners, however, are realtors. A *realtor* is a broker who is affiliated with a local real estate board that is a member of the National Association of Realtors (NAR). The term is copyrighted by the NAR, and only those with the stipulated membership ties are allowed to use it.

The National Association of Realtors is, in fact, the most important national real estate organization. It is comprised of many local and state boards as well as of such subsidiary organizations as the Society of Industrial Realtors, the American Institute of Real Estate Appraisers, and the Realtors National Marketing Institute. The NAR performs many of the activities characteristic of trade and professional associations. It offers seminars and other continuing education opportunities, promotes the interests of the real estate industry, and has an active public relations program. The creation and support of its Code of Ethics, however, is generally regarded as its most important contribution to the profession and to the public. In 1916, the NAR voted to use the term *realtor* to designate member brokers and to distinguish them from other brokers who, it was felt, might not always adhere to the high standards set forth in the Code of Ethics. More recently, the National Association of Realtors has adopted the designation *Realtor-Associate* for sales persons working for member brokers.

Property management is the other main type of real estate marketing enterprise. As the number of properties owned by absentee landlords and groups of people or organizations (including, for example, life insurance companies and pension funds, limited partnerships and real estate investment trusts) increases, so also has the demand for professional property management. A property manager acts as the owner's agent, performing such duties as negotiating leases, collecting rent, supervising maintenance, repair, and upkeep of the property, and providing accounting and financial services. The property manager reports periodically to the owner(s), and carries out any additional duties specified in his or her contract. These may include preparing and filing tax returns and arranging for insurance coverage. Although property management is available—usually through brokerage firms— for single-family dwellings, more often it is characteristic of larger properties such as condominiums and apartment complexes, shopping centers and stores, and office and industrial buildings. In return for such services, the property manager or the property management firm is usually paid a fixed percentage of rents collected from the occupants of the property.

PRODUCTION

Another major functional division of the real estate industry is generally referred to as production. Production begins with land development. It, in turn, consists of three phases: preliminary analysis, implementation, and evaluation. During the first phase, the developer attempts to determine the market for his proposed development. This will include consideration of local economic conditions, demographic factors likely to affect demand, the existence and occupancy rates of similar types of property, and the availability of land for development. During this phase, developers may seek information from local government agencies, chambers of commerce, and trade organizations. Although sometimes overlooked, libraries can also provide valuable information. The economic censuses, the *Census of Population* and *Census of Population and Housing, County Business Patterns, Sales & Marketing Management*'s "Survey of Buying Power" and "Survey of Industrial Purchasing Power," and many other government, trade, and commercial publications can help developers analyze the local market. If market research indicates that conditions are favorable, further study is required. It will include identification and analysis of possible tracts of land, subsequent selection of the site to be developed, and analysis of local, state, and possibly even federal government regulations that may affect the project.

During the second phase, the developer negotiates with and secures the approval of various government agencies, purchases and finances the land, and, with the aid of engineers and other specialists, draws up a complete layout and design for the tract. Someone developing land for a shopping center, for example, will use topographic maps, surveys, and the results of soil and drainage tests to designate space for the building itself, and for parking, access roads, and landscaped areas. Implementation also includes the establishment of land use restrictions for future occupants, acquiring the necessary liability insurance and performance bonds to ensure completion of site improvements, and the actual installation of improvements on the site. The final step in the implementation phase involves marketing the new development to prospective buyers.

The third phase is one of feedback and evaluation. It involves assessment of development costs, sales performance, and other factors that helped the project succeed or fail.

Following land development comes the building process. Many of the builder's tasks parallel those of the developer. Both begin with preliminary analyses. Like the developer, the builder wants to be certain that there will be a market for the finished product. Accordingly, the astute builder will also be interested in learning as much as possible about local market conditions and can benefit from consulting Census Bureau publications and other library information sources.

The preliminary phase also includes drawing up the building design and engineering plans. Other steps in the building process include securing the necessary financing, constructing the building(s), and, finally, marketing the finished product.

Sometimes the same company handles both land development and building. Whether the operations are combined or separate, however, the phases most closely tied to library resources and research are the preliminary planning phase when economic and demographic information is being sought, and the phase in which the finished project is about to be marketed to prospective buyers or lessees. Both are marketing research-oriented, and many of the sources described in chapter 9 will be useful.

FINANCING

Few purchasers of real estate, whether they are individuals or businesses, have the capital to purchase property outright. Most must borrow from banks, savings and loan associations, or other financial institutions. These institutions, in fact, comprise the third main type of real estate enterprise: organizations involved in the financing of real estate purchases.

Although many lending institutions and practices were covered at length in chapter 11, certain special characteristics of real estate financing are worth noting. First, most real estate financing is long-term; home mortgage loans, for example, may be for 20, 25, or even 30 years. Second, real estate loans are typically made with the property itself as collateral. For this reason, such loans require that the property be evaluated by a professional appraiser to arrive at an objective estimate of its current market value. Finally, the amount and terms of credit available for real estate financing are based to a large extent on the state of the economy and general money market conditions. When, for example, money is tight, real estate financing, particularly for residential properties, is more difficult to obtain.

The mortgage loan is the most common form of real estate financing. A *mortgage* is a legal instrument that allows the borrower to pledge the real property as collateral in order to secure the debt with the lender. It consists of two separate documents: the mortgage agreement, also known as the deed of trust, which sets forth the terms of the loan and pledges the property as security; and the promissory note, or deed of trust note, in which the borrower is made personally responsible for the debt.

Although the number and types of mortgage loans have increased tremendously in recent years, the amortized loan remains one of the most common types of mortgage. An *amortized loan* is one that is spread out over a period of time and repaid periodically in payments that include both principal and interest. The loan, in other words, is paid off gradually.

> The payment, made monthly, quarterly, or semiannually, is usually a fixed amount. Interest has first claim in the installments, and the balance is credited toward repayment of debt, which is reduced with every payment. Because the debt is less than it was the time before, the amount of money paid each payment on interest decreases. The amount applied to the principal increases.[4]

Loan amortization tables are used to determine the size of the payments needed to repay a loan. Since library users often request such information, an examination of the amortization table shown in figure 18.2 is in order.

A loan amortization table, or schedule, includes four main pieces of information: (1) the amount of the loan, (2) the rate of interest being charged, (3) the length of time to maturity, and (4) the amount of the periodic payments. The table in figure 18.2, for example, shows loans of from $5 to $100,000 made at 9.8 percent interest. The schedule is for monthly payments, and maturity dates range from 15 to 40 years. Using it, it is possible to determine that monthly payments of $4.32 would be required to amortize a 30-year, 9.8 percent loan of $500.00, and that payments of $647.13 per month would be necessary to pay off a $75,000 loan for the same period. Amortization tables are also used to determine the maximum amount of loans that can be afforded. Someone who is borrowing money at 9.8 percent and who can make maximum monthly payments of $400, for example, can use the table in figure 18.2 to find the maximum amount that can be borrowed.

Although loan amortization schedules are available at banks and thrift institutions, most libraries include one or two in their business collections as well. Two representative publications are listed below.

Estes, Jack. **Handbook of Loan Payment Tables**. New York: McGraw-Hill, 1976. 659p.

Thorndike, David. **Thorndike Encyclopedia of Banking and Financial Tables**. Rev. ed. Boston: Warren, Gorham & Lamont, 1980. 1700p.

The *Handbook of Loan Payment Tables* includes monthly amortization schedules for 329 interest rates from 5 to 25.5 percent, in increments of 8ths and 10ths of a percent. Terms are from 1 to 25 years in one-year increments, and then for 30, 35, and 40 years. As shown in figure 18.2, amounts covered in the *Handbook* range from $5 to $100,000.

The *Thorndike Encyclopedia of Banking and Financial Tables*, described in chapter 11, contains a whole series of mortgage and real estate tables, including monthly and quarterly amortization schedules, constant annual percent tables, mortgage loan payment tables, percent paid off tables, and depreciation schedules.

Amortized mortgages are not the only types of mortgage loans that are made. Others include *variable rate mortgages*, in which interest rates fluctuate within a specified range, *straight term mortgages*, in which repayment of the principal is made in one lump sum at the date of maturity, and *flexible payment mortgages*, which enable borrowers to adjust their payments so that they will be less in the beginning and will become progressively greater, reflecting expected increases in the borrowers' incomes.

MONTHLY PAYMENT
REQUIRED TO AMORTIZE A LOAN
9.800%

TERM AMOUNT	15 Years	16 Years	17 Years	18 Years	19 Years	20 Years	21 Years	22 Years	23 Years	24 Years	25 Years	30 Years	35 Years	40 Years
5	.06	.06	.06	.05	.05	.05	.05	.05	.05	.05	.05	.05	.05	.05
10	.11	.11	.11	.10	.10	.10	.10	.10	.10	.10	.09	.09	.09	.09
15	.16	.16	.16	.15	.15	.15	.15	.14	.14	.14	.14	.13	.13	.13
25	.27	.26	.26	.25	.25	.24	.24	.24	.23	.23	.23	.22	.22	.21
50	.54	.52	.51	.50	.49	.48	.47	.47	.46	.46	.45	.44	.43	.42
75	.80	.78	.76	.75	.73	.72	.71	.70	.69	.68	.68	.65	.64	.63
100	1.07	1.04	1.01	.99	.97	.96	.94	.93	.92	.91	.90	.87	.85	.84
200	2.13	2.07	2.02	1.98	1.94	1.91	1.88	1.85	1.83	1.61	1.79	1.73	1.69	1.67
300	3.19	3.11	3.03	2.97	2.91	2.86	2.82	2.78	2.75	2.72	2.69	2.59	2.54	2.51
400	4.25	4.14	4.04	3.95	3.88	3.81	3.75	3.70	3.66	3.62	3.58	3.46	3.38	3.34
500	5.32	5.17	5.05	4.94	4.85	4.76	4.69	4.63	4.57	4.52	4.48	4.32	4.23	4.17
600	6.38	6.21	6.06	5.93	5.81	5.72	5.63	5.55	5.49	5.43	5.37	5.18	5.07	5.01
700	7.44	7.24	7.07	6.91	6.78	6.67	6.57	6.48	6.40	6.33	6.27	6.04	5.92	5.84
800	8.50	8.27	8.07	7.90	7.75	7.62	7.50	7.40	7.31	7.23	7.16	6.91	6.76	6.67
900	9.57	9.31	9.08	8.89	8.72	8.57	8.44	8.33	8.23	8.14	8.06	7.77	7.60	7.51
1000	10.63	10.34	10.09	9.88	9.69	9.52	9.38	9.25	9.14	9.04	8.95	8.63	8.45	8.34
2000	21.25	20.67	20.18	19.75	19.37	19.04	18.75	18.50	18.27	18.07	17.90	17.26	16.89	16.67
3000	31.88	31.01	30.26	29.62	29.05	28.56	28.13	27.75	27.41	27.11	26.84	25.89	25.34	25.01
4000	42.50	41.34	40.35	39.49	38.73	38.08	37.50	36.99	36.54	36.14	35.79	34.52	33.78	33.34
5000	53.13	51.68	50.43	49.36	48.42	47.60	46.87	46.24	45.68	45.18	44.74	43.15	42.22	41.68
6000	63.75	62.01	60.52	59.23	58.10	57.11	56.25	55.49	54.81	54.21	53.68	51.77	50.67	50.01
7000	74.37	72.35	70.61	69.10	67.78	66.63	65.62	64.73	63.95	63.25	62.63	60.40	59.11	58.35
8000	85.00	82.68	80.69	78.97	77.46	76.15	75.00	73.98	73.08	72.28	71.58	69.03	67.56	66.68
9000	95.62	93.02	90.78	88.84	87.15	85.67	84.37	83.23	82.21	81.32	80.52	77.66	76.00	75.02
10000	106.25	103.35	100.86	98.71	96.83	95.19	93.74	92.47	91.35	90.35	89.47	86.29	84.44	83.35
11000	116.87	113.69	110.95	108.58	106.51	104.70	103.12	101.72	100.48	99.39	98.42	94.92	92.89	91.69
12000	127.49	124.02	121.04	118.45	116.19	114.22	112.49	110.97	109.62	108.42	107.36	103.54	101.33	100.02
13000	138.12	134.36	131.12	128.32	125.88	123.74	121.86	120.21	118.75	117.46	116.31	112.17	109.78	108.36
14000	148.74	144.69	141.21	138.19	135.56	133.26	131.24	129.46	127.89	126.49	125.25	120.80	118.22	116.69
15000	159.37	155.03	151.29	148.06	145.24	142.78	140.61	138.71	137.02	135.53	134.20	129.43	126.66	125.03
16000	169.99	165.36	161.38	157.93	154.92	152.29	149.99	147.95	146.16	144.56	143.15	138.06	135.11	133.36
17000	180.61	175.70	171.46	167.80	164.60	161.81	159.36	157.20	155.29	153.60	152.09	146.69	143.55	141.69
18000	191.24	186.03	181.55	177.67	174.29	171.33	168.73	166.45	164.42	162.63	161.04	155.31	152.00	150.03
19000	201.86	196.37	191.64	187.54	183.97	180.85	178.11	175.69	173.56	171.67	169.99	163.94	160.44	158.36
20000	212.49	206.70	201.72	197.41	193.65	190.37	187.48	184.94	182.69	180.70	178.93	172.57	168.88	166.70
21000	223.11	217.04	211.81	207.28	203.33	199.88	196.86	194.19	191.83	189.74	187.88	181.20	177.33	175.03
22000	233.73	227.37	221.89	217.15	213.02	209.40	206.23	203.43	200.96	198.77	196.83	189.83	185.77	183.37
23000	244.36	237.71	231.98	227.02	222.70	218.92	215.60	212.68	210.10	207.81	205.77	198.46	194.22	191.70
24000	254.98	248.04	242.07	236.89	232.38	228.44	224.98	221.93	219.23	216.84	214.72	207.08	202.66	200.04
25000	265.61	258.38	252.15	246.76	242.06	237.96	234.35	231.17	228.37	225.88	223.67	215.71	211.10	208.37
26000	276.23	268.71	262.24	256.63	251.75	247.48	243.72	240.42	237.50	234.91	232.61	224.34	219.55	216.71
27000	286.85	279.05	272.32	266.50	261.43	256.99	253.10	249.67	246.63	243.95	241.56	232.97	227.99	225.04
28000	297.48	289.38	282.41	276.37	271.11	266.51	262.47	258.91	255.77	252.98	250.50	241.60	236.44	233.38
29000	308.10	299.72	292.49	286.24	280.79	276.03	271.85	268.16	264.90	262.02	259.45	250.23	244.88	241.71
30000	318.73	310.05	302.58	296.11	290.48	285.55	281.22	277.41	274.04	271.05	268.40	258.85	253.32	250.05
31000	329.35	320.39	312.67	305.98	300.16	295.07	290.59	286.65	283.17	280.09	277.34	267.48	261.77	258.38
32000	339.97	330.72	322.75	315.85	309.84	304.58	299.97	295.90	292.31	289.12	286.29	276.11	270.21	266.72
33000	350.60	341.06	332.84	325.72	319.52	314.10	309.34	305.15	301.44	298.15	295.24	284.74	278.66	275.05
34000	361.22	351.39	342.92	335.59	329.20	323.62	318.72	314.39	310.57	307.19	304.18	293.37	287.10	283.38
35000	371.85	361.72	353.01	345.46	338.89	333.14	328.09	323.64	319.71	316.22	313.13	302.00	295.54	291.72
36000	382.47	372.06	363.10	355.33	348.57	342.66	337.46	332.89	328.84	325.26	322.08	310.62	303.99	300.05
37000	393.09	382.39	373.18	365.20	358.25	352.17	346.84	342.13	337.98	334.29	331.02	319.25	312.43	308.39
38000	403.72	392.73	383.27	375.07	367.93	361.69	356.21	351.38	347.11	343.33	339.97	327.88	320.88	316.72
39000	414.34	403.06	393.35	384.94	377.62	371.21	365.58	360.63	356.25	352.36	348.91	336.51	329.32	325.06
40000	424.97	413.40	403.44	394.81	387.30	380.73	374.96	369.87	365.38	361.40	357.86	345.14	337.76	333.39
41000	435.59	423.73	413.52	404.68	396.98	390.25	384.33	379.12	374.52	370.43	366.81	353.76	346.21	341.73
42000	446.21	434.07	423.61	414.55	406.66	399.76	393.71	388.37	383.65	379.47	375.75	362.39	354.65	350.06
43000	456.84	444.40	433.70	424.42	416.35	409.28	403.08	397.61	392.78	388.50	384.70	371.02	363.10	358.40
44000	467.46	454.74	443.78	434.29	426.03	418.80	412.45	406.86	401.92	397.54	393.65	379.65	371.54	366.73
45000	478.09	465.07	453.87	444.16	435.71	428.32	421.83	416.11	411.05	406.57	402.59	388.28	379.98	375.07
46000	488.71	475.41	463.95	454.03	445.39	437.84	431.20	425.35	420.19	415.61	411.54	396.91	388.43	383.40
47000	499.33	485.74	474.04	463.90	455.08	447.35	440.58	434.60	429.32	424.64	420.49	405.53	396.87	391.74
48000	509.96	496.08	484.13	473.77	464.76	456.87	449.95	443.85	438.46	433.68	429.43	414.16	405.32	400.07
49000	520.58	506.41	494.21	483.64	474.44	466.39	459.32	453.10	447.59	442.71	438.38	422.79	413.76	408.40
50000	531.21	516.75	504.30	493.51	484.12	475.91	468.70	462.34	456.73	451.75	447.33	431.42	422.20	416.74
55000	584.33	568.42	554.73	542.86	532.53	523.50	515.57	508.58	502.40	496.92	492.06	474.56	464.42	458.41
60000	637.45	620.10	605.16	592.21	580.95	571.09	562.44	554.81	548.07	542.10	536.79	517.70	506.64	500.09
65000	690.57	671.77	655.59	641.57	629.36	618.68	609.30	601.04	593.74	587.27	581.52	560.84	548.86	541.76
70000	743.69	723.44	706.01	690.92	677.77	666.27	656.17	647.28	639.41	632.44	626.25	603.99	591.08	583.43
75000	796.81	775.12	756.44	740.27	726.18	713.86	703.04	693.51	685.09	677.62	670.99	647.13	633.30	625.11
80000	849.93	826.79	806.87	789.62	774.59	761.45	749.91	739.74	730.76	722.79	715.72	690.27	675.52	666.78
85000	903.05	878.47	857.30	838.97	823.00	809.04	796.78	785.98	776.43	767.97	760.45	733.41	717.74	708.45
90000	956.17	930.14	907.73	888.32	871.42	856.63	843.65	832.21	822.10	813.14	805.18	776.55	759.96	750.13
95000	1009.29	981.82	958.16	937.67	919.83	904.22	890.52	878.45	867.77	858.32	849.91	819.69	802.18	791.80
100000	1062.41	1033.49	1008.59	987.02	968.24	951.81	937.39	924.68	913.45	903.49	894.65	862.83	844.40	833.47

Fig. 18.2. Typical loan amortization table. Reprinted by permission from Jack Estes, *Handbook of Loan Payment Tables* (New York: McGraw-Hill, 1976).

Frequently points are attached to mortgage loans. In finance, a *point* is 1 percent of the amount of the loan. On a $50,000 loan, a point is $500; on a $100,000 loan, $1,000. Points are used in real estate financing to increase the return on loans.

Financing for the purchase of real estate is available from both private and public organizations. In the private sector, thrift institutions such as savings and loan associations have been most important as sources of funds for the purchase of residential property, while commercial banks traditionally have provided commercial and industrial property loans. Since most commercial bank deposits come from checking rather than savings accounts, the emphasis is on short-term construction loans rather than on long-term mortgages. Life insurance companies also offer real estate financing, particularly for large-scale projects such as shopping centers, apartment complexes, and office buildings. Finally, two special organizations are involved in real estate financing. They are mortgage banking companies and mortgage brokers.

A *mortgage banking company* makes mortgage loans to borrowers and subsequently sells them as long-term investments to such institutional investors as life insurance companies, pension funds, savings institutions, and government agencies. The mortgage company handles the preliminaries: It assesses the creditworthiness of the borrower and the value of the property, prepares the necessary papers, and makes the loan. After it sells the mortgage, the mortgage company is usually retained by the purchaser to collect the monthly payments, handle additional paperwork, and to deal with any borrower-related problems.

Mortgage brokers, in contrast, act as middlemen only. They neither lend money nor service the mortgages they help to arrange. Instead, they act as agents, bringing together prospective borrowers and lenders. In return, brokers are paid a fee, usually expressed in points, for each loan that they help to arrange.

In addition to the private organizations mentioned above, some federal government agencies are also either directly or indirectly involved in real estate financing. Although space does not permit consideration of all such agencies, two are particularly important to prospective home buyers: the Veterans Administration and the Federal Housing Administration.

The Veterans Administration (VA) helps to finance home ownership by guaranteeing loans made by private lenders to eligible veterans. The Federal Housing Administration (FHA), a part of the Department of Housing and Urban Development, insures mortgage loans made by private lenders against possible borrower default. By so doing, it lessens risk for private lenders and thus increases the supply of credit available for home financing. Veterans Administration and Federal Housing Administration-insured loans are known respectively as VA and FHA loans; loans made by private lenders without government backing or insurance are called conventional loans.

Discussion of real estate financing to this point has focused on what is known as the *primary mortgage market*, consisting of lenders and borrowers directly involved in the financing and purchase of real estate. In addition to the primary market, however, there is an active *secondary mortgage market*, in which existing mortgages are sold by lenders to other investors. The secondary mortgage market helps to increase the amount of credit available for real estate loans in all parts of the country.

Three government or quasi-government agencies and one private corporation are actively involved in the secondary mortgage market. The oldest of these is the *Federal National Mortgage Association*, also known as the *FNMA* or "Fannie Mae." Established by the government in 1938, the FNMA was rechartered as a private corporation in 1968 in order to provide secondary market support for the private residential mortgage market. Fannie Mae issues publicly traded stocks, bonds, and notes, and uses the funds from their sale to finance the purchase of FHA, VA, and conventional mortgage loans. Described as "a private corporation with a public purpose,"[5] the FNMA encourages home ownership by buying more mortgages when money is tight, so that the original lenders can use the money from mortgage sales to issue new mortgage loans.

The *Government National Mortgage Association* (*GNMA* or "Ginnie Mae") operates as a corporation within the Department of Housing and Urban Development and is responsible for two major secondary market operations. The first of these is its Tandem Plan, a subsidy program in which the GNMA buys government-insured and conventional mortgages from lenders at full market value, and then resells them on the open market at a lower price. The GNMA absorbs the difference between purchase and sales prices in order to subsidize mortgages that might not otherwise be marketable within the private sector and to stimulate housing production and purchase.

Another way in which the Government National Mortgage Association indirectly promotes home ownership is through its Mortgage-Backed Securities (MBS) Program. Mortgages for similar types of property are pooled and used to back publicly traded GNMA securities. The securities pass through to the investors monthly payments of principal and interest on mortgaged property held in the pool. The MBS Program's purpose is to increase the availability of mortgage credit by attracting new sources of funds for the mortgage market. Since its securities are backed by the full faith and credit of the U.S. government, the program has been successful in attracting both institutional and individual investors.

The *Federal Home Loan Mortgage Corporation*, also known as the *FHLMC* or "Freddie Mac," is a quasi-public corporation that provides for a secondary market for conventional mortgage loans.[6] It buys individual mortgages from savings and loan associations and banks that meet its requirements for loan applications, appraisal methods, and that use standardized forms that it has developed. The loans are subsequently packaged into pools of several million dollars each and resold to investors.

> The Federal Home Loan Mortgage Corporation (FHLMC) issues and guarantees pass-through securities backed by pools of unsubsidized conventional residential mortgages. The mortgage pools consist of loans acquired by FHLMC through various purchase programs, primarily from savings and loan associations. Most of the securities are marketed to private investors through a syndicate of securities dealers. Although savings and loans were the primary investors in FHLMC-guaranteed pass-throughs in the early days of the program, a variety of capital market participants—including retirement and pension funds—now purchase substantial amounts of these instruments.[7]

The MGIC Investment Corporation (MGIC), also buys and sells conventional loans. Unlike the Federal National Mortgage Association, the Government National Mortgage Association, and the Federal Home Loan Mortgage Association, the MGIC has no direct ties to the federal government; it is a private corporation. It does, however, share a common purpose with the FNMA, GNMA, and FHLMC: It attracts investors who might not otherwise invest in mortgage loans.

In summary, the real estate industry consists of three main elements: marketing, land development and construction (production), and financing. Financing, as has been shown, consists not only of providing direct loans to borrowers, but also of participating in the secondary mortgage market.

Government and Real Estate

Private ownership and control of real estate in this country is a right that is subject to certain government restrictions. Although private citizens have the right to own buildings and land, the government has certain property rights as well—of taxation, police power, and eminent domain.

Property taxes are levied to help support community services and facilities such as roads, sewers, schools, and libraries. In order to encourage citizens to pay such taxes promptly and in full, the government has the power to seize any property for which taxes are delinquent and to sell it to recover the unpaid taxes. Property taxes are collected primarily at the local level, and local property tax rates and assessed value of real property are published in the municipal listings in *Moody's Municipal & Government Manual*.

Each state government has the right of police power, to enact and enforce laws and regulations for the common good. Such power can be exercised at the state level or delegated to local governments. Police power as it applies to real estate enables state and local governments to set minimum structural requirements for buildings by establishing building codes, to enact planning and zoning ordinances, and to draw up other related regulations. These might, for example, include regulations relating to the maximum height of buildings or to the minimum distance houses must be set back from the street. Since the right of police power affects how land can be used, it has a significant impact on property values. Local zoning laws, for example, may decree that land in a certain area be excluded from commercial or industrial use and will thus affect the value of that land as well as the uses to which it can be put.

Whenever the government or a public utility needs land for public use or for the construction of public facilities, it has the right to take ownership of privately held real estate. This right of eminent domain empowers the government to buy the property at fair market value whether or not its owner actually wants to sell it.

In addition to the activities tied to the rights of taxation, police power, and eminent domain, many federal, state, and local government insured agencies are involved with real estate. At the federal level, the Department of Housing and Urban Development is perhaps the best known of all such agencies.

The Department of Housing and Urban Development (HUD) was established in 1965 as the first cabinet-level department to oversee housing matters. It administers federal programs concerned with housing needs, fair housing opportunities, and community development. HUD also administers FHA mortgage insurance programs, facilitates construction and rehabilitation of rental units, and offers rent subsidy programs to low-income families. In addition, it oversees homebuyer consumer protection and education programs and publications, and supports neighborhood preservation and development programs. Many of the documents published by HUD are extremely useful to real estate researchers; some key titles will be described later in this chapter.

Another important federal organization is the Federal Home Loan Bank Board. An independent, self-sustaining agency, this board supervises and regulates savings and loan associations and operates the Federal Savings and Loan Insurance Corporation (FSLIC) which insures savings accounts in FSLIC-insured savings and loan associations. It also directs the Federal Home Loan Bank System, described in chapter 11.

Other federal departments and agencies are also involved in real estate. The Departments of Agriculture and the Interior, for example, include agencies responsible for the nation's system of forests and parks, and the Government National Mortgage Association and the Federal Home Loan Mortgage Association, as we have seen, are active participants in the secondary mortgage market. Other agencies are less directly involved or focus on some narrower aspect of real estate activity. Researchers seeking information on government involvement in real estate are advised to begin by consulting the *Monthly Catalog*, the *United States Government Manual*, and some of the sources described in the publications section that follows.

State and local governments are similarly involved in promoting and protecting the public interest in real estate. Most states have agencies responsible for housing and land development programs, and many local governments have planning boards and related agencies. Although state and local government regulations and publications are extremely important to the business of real estate, such sources often are not held by libraries. In many instances, the library is more useful for referral to such agencies than it is for its collection of representative state and local documents.

REAL ESTATE INFORMATION SOURCES

The literature of real estate ranges from pamphlets for prospective homebuyers to valuation manuals for real estate practitioners. Some sources are so specialized that they are not widely available. Other, more frequently consulted, titles can be found in many different library settings. The remainder of this chapter focuses mainly on sources that fall into the second category, listing and describing bibliographies, dictionaries and handbooks, directories, government documents, statistical compilations, vertical file materials, and other sources.

Bibliographies

There are several bibliographies that touch upon specific aspects of real estate marketing, production, or finance, or that focus on such related activities as land management and planning. For comprehensive coverage, however, the following are among the best.

Burrows, Arthur J., and John M. Clapp. **Data Sources for Real Estate Decisions**. Storrs, Conn.: Center for Real Estate and Urban Studies, School of Business Administration, University of Connecticut, 1985. 121p.

Harris, Laura A. **The Real Estate Industry; An Information Sourcebook**. Phoenix, Ariz.: Oryx Press, 1987. 170p.

Haikalis, Peter D., and Jean K. Freeman. **Real Estate; A Bibliography of the Monographic Literature**. Westport, Conn.: Greenwood Press, 1983. 317p.

Data Sources for Real Estate Decisions lists and annotates publications of interest and use to real estate analysts. Arrangement is by subject, covering such topics as "Taxes on Real Property, Sales and Income," "Trends and Forecasts," and "Cost of Construction or Operation." Each entry includes the frequency of publication, price range (titles are classed as free, inexpensive, moderate, or expensive), a brief summary of contents, and the publisher's address and telephone number. Both government and commercial publications are included, and an index permits access by subject, title, and, in some instances, publisher. Although not inclusive, *Data Sources* is extremely useful, both for identification and description of major reference works and for its inclusion of free titles that are suitable for vertical file collections.

The Real Estate Industry is a select, annotated list of books, journals, quick reference sources, and other materials relevant to real estate practitioners, students, and librarians. It begins with a list of 135 core publications considered basic to any real estate collection, followed by a general literature section that lists titles by such broad subject categories as appraisal, finance, market analysis, and property management. Key real estate journals are listed in a separate section, followed by "Other Sources of Information," which describes and includes the addresses for associations, government agencies, and other organizations as well as the names and addresses of relevant special libraries and state real estate boards. Brief author, title, and subject indexes are also included.

The Real Estate Industry is complemented by *Real Estate*, which lists more than 2,600 monographic titles. Each chapter treats a different aspect of real estate, covering land use, real estate business and investment, housing, finance and insurance, taxation of property, and law. A list of bibliographies and author and title indexes are appended. Although *Real Estate* lacks annotations, it lists more titles than either *The Real Estate Industry* or *Data Sources for Real Estate Decisions*.

Other bibliographies are somewhat narrower in scope. The Council of Planning Librarians, for example, regularly publishes bibliographies relating to housing, land use and development, real estate finance, and related topics. *Business Information Sources* selectively lists and annotates texts pertaining to real estate principles and practices, management and appraisal, finance and investing, and law, as well as key periodicals, bibliographies and indexes, dictionaries, operating statistics, housing and real estate statistics, and directories. Several useful government publications are identified in the following GPO subject bibliographies.

U.S. Superintendent of Documents. **Construction Industry**. Washington, D.C.: Government Printing Office, 1987 (Subject Bibliography 216). 9p.

_____. **The Home**. Washington, D.C.: Government Printing Office, 1987 (Subject Bibliography 41). 4p.

Construction Industry lists and selectively annotates federal publications pertaining to building and design. Included are documents that specify standards for building materials and for the safety of workers as well as competitive assessments of the construction equipment and international construction industries. Particularly useful to real estate researchers are the construction reports issued by the Bureau of the Census and the bimonthly periodical, *Construction Review*, which will be described later in this chapter.

The Home lists documents pertaining to construction and maintenance and selecting and financing a home. Although several of the titles focus on care and upkeep of property, many sources in the "Selecting and Financing" section are good basic guides to real estate fundamentals and will be particularly useful in libraries serving the public. As with other GPO subject bibliographies, both *Construction Industry* and *The Home* include prices and Superintendent of Documents classification and stock numbers in addition to standard bibliographic information.

Dictionaries, Encyclopedias, and Handbooks

A wide range of general and specialized real estate dictionaries are available. Although space does not permit consideration of them all, the following are typical.

Bagby, Joseph R., and Martha L. Bagby. **Real Estate Dictionary**. Englewood Cliffs, N.J.: Institute for Business Planning, 1981. 188p.

Allen, Robert D., and Thomas E. Wolfe. **The Allen and Wolfe Illustrated Dictionary of Real Estate**. New York: Wiley, 1983. 266p.

Gross, Jerome S. **Webster's New World Illustrated Encyclopedic Dictionary of Real Estate**. 3rd ed. New York: Prentice-Hall, 1987. 418p.

Intended primarily for practitioners but useful also for lay people, the *Real Estate Dictionary* briefly defines over 2,000 terms in real estate and allied fields. In addition to standard real estate vocabulary, the *Dictionary* also includes jargon, slang, abbreviations, and acronyms. Tables commonly used in real estate transactions are also featured, including measurement, simple and compound interest, present worth, and comparative depreciation. Although useful, the *Dictionary* and other, similar works need to be supplemented by titles that feature illustrations as well as definitions. The new real estate salesperson who cannot distinguish between mansard and gambrel roofs, for example, requires pictures as well as words to fully comprehend the difference between the two. As a result, illustrated dictionaries are particularly important in real estate reference collections.

Representative of such dictionaries are *The Allen and Wolfe Illustrated Dictionary of Real Estate* and *Webster's New World Illustrated Encyclopedic Dictionary of Real Estate*. The Allen and Wolfe *Dictionary* lists and defines over 3,000 terms. In addition, it includes reproductions of commonly used real estate forms, sample statistics, maps, charts, illustrations, graphs, tables, a list of national real estate organizations, and the Code of Ethics of the National Association of Realtors.

Webster's New World Illustrated Encyclopedic Dictionary of Real Estate combines an illustrated glossary with a portfolio of real estate forms and a directory of national real estate organizations. Definitions are clear and concise, making this a useful source for lay people as well as practitioners.

Sometimes more specialized dictionaries, particularly as they relate to appraising and investment, are required.

Boyce, Byrl N. **Real Estate Appraisal Terminology**. Rev. ed. Cambridge, Mass.: Ballinger, 1981. 384p.

Lyons, Paul J., and Matthew J. Bowker. **Real Estate Investor's Desk Encyclopedia**. Reston, Va.: Reston Publishing, 1982. 267p.

Real Estate Appraisal Terminology is intended primarily for appraisers and other real estate professionals. Although the focus is on appraisal, terms in the areas of finance, statistics, and energy are also included. Definitions are generally brief, ranging in length from a sentence or two to an entire paragraph. Illustrations are appended (including different types of roofs, windows, masonry, arches, and interior trim). In addition, lists of acronyms and of electric and plumbing symbols are also included. It features descriptions of and formulas for simple linear regression, depreciation methods, and valuation models, as well as lists and descriptions of soil and vegetation types. A bibliography is appended. *Real Estate Appraisal Terminology* is a basic reference source and belongs in most business reference collections.

The *Real Estate Investor's Desk Encyclopedia* is intended primarily for lay people who are relatively new to real estate. Its strength is its coverage of investment-related terms ("real estate investment trust," "specified fund syndicate," and "secondary mortgage market" are included), but some general terms and current slang are also featured.

More detailed information is available in encyclopedias and handbooks.

Arnold, Alvin L., and Jack Kusnet. **The Arnold Encyclopedia of Real Estate**. Boston: Warren, Gorham & Lamont, 1978. 901p.

Friedman, Edith J. **Encyclopedia of Real Estate Appraising**. 3rd ed. Englewood Cliffs, N.J.: Prentice-Hall, 1978. 1283p.

Described by its publisher as "a comprehensive one-volume real estate library," *The Arnold Encyclopedia of Real Estate* lists, defines, and explains basic concepts in real estate, law, banking, and taxation. Arrangement is alphabetical, and the entries range in length from a sentence or two to several pages. Most, however, are one or two paragraphs long. A topical entry finder classifies and lists terms under 12 major subject areas, including "Acquisition, Disposition, and Ownership," "Investment and Appraisal," and "Land Development, Building, and Construction." Also appended is a collection of tables and charts including mortgage rate and depreciation tables and statistics on new construction, housing inventory, housing units sold or rented, home improvement expenditures, interest rates, nonresidential real estate, demographics, price and cost indexes, and personal income. Although the data in these tables are no longer current, the government agencies and trade organizations responsible for collecting and publishing the statistics contained in each table are identified, giving researchers a start in finding more comprehensive and up-to-date information.

The *Encyclopedia of Real Estate Appraising* features articles by experts dealing with the various aspects of appraisal theory and practice, appraisal of specific types of property, appraisal of "special-use" property (including, for example, churches, golf courses, funeral homes, and automatic car washes), special branches of appraisal practice, and appraisal as a business or profession. Each chapter begins with an outline of its scope, defines key terms, and concludes with a brief summary. Chapters are well organized and the text is supplemented with diagrams, statistics, and sample forms. A detailed subject index enhances access to the *Encyclopedia*.

Real estate handbooks are commonplace. For general information, the following is one of the best.

Seldin, Maury, ed. **The Real Estate Handbook**. Homewood, Ill.: Dow Jones-Irwin, 1980. 1186p.

The Real Estate Handbook presents 67 chapters, written by industry experts, classed under broad subject headings: Real Estate Transactions, Real Estate Analyses, Real Estate Marketing, Real Estate Financing, and Real Estate Investment. An appendix lists and describes various professional designations, including for each the offering organization and educational, experiential, and other requirements necessary to qualify. The *Handbook* is indexed.

Other handbooks focus on specific segments of the real estate industry. One area in which interest is particularly strong is the purchase and sale of real estate for investment.

Mader, Chris, and John Bortz. **The Dow Jones-Irwin Guide to Real Estate Investing**. Rev. ed. Homewood, Ill.: Dow Jones-Irwin, 1983. 291p.

Tanzer, Milt. **Commercial Real Estate Desk Book**. Englewood Cliffs, N.J.: Institute for Business Planning, 1981. 414p.

The Dow Jones-Irwin Guide to Real Estate Investing is intended for use by prospective investors rather than seasoned professionals. Written for the lay person, it discusses real estate as an investment medium, describes various types of real estate—including home and condominium, residential income, commercial and industrial, and land and development property—and the advantages and disadvantages of investing in each. Techniques for the analysis of specific investments are explained, and statistical tables presenting salient information about investing in each type of property are also included.

The *Commercial Real Estate Desk Book* is a "how-to" book for investors interested in commercial property. Sections cover the selection, management, and selling of commercial property as well as key investment considerations and government regulations affecting such investments. Sample forms, brief formulas, checklists, charts, and graphs are also included.

Directories

A wide range of general and specialized directories are available. This section lists and describes some of the most widely used titles, beginning with general real estate directories.

Real Estate Review's Who's Who in Real Estate. Boston: Warren, Gorham & Lamont, 1983.

National Roster of Realtors. Cedar Rapids, Iowa: Stamats Communications, 1962- . 2v. Annual.

"National Real Estate Investor Directory," **National Real Estate Investor** (June 15th issue). Atlanta, Ga.: Communications Channels, Inc. Annual.

The most detailed biographical information is presented in *Real Estate Review's Who's Who in Real Estate*. Some 12,000 real estate professionals are listed, including developers and syndicators, state and federal government officials, mortgage and real estate brokers and consultants, real estate executives from Fortune 1000 firms, and attorneys and bankers specializing in real estate. The main section is an alphabetical "Biographies" listing. Entries include business and home addresses, professional affiliations and honors, and other standard biographical information. The sample entry shown in figure 18.3 is typical. An "Index by Geographic Area and Primary Professional Activity" is also included.

The *National Roster of Realtors* is arranged by state, then by city and by the real estate board serving that city. The listing for each local board includes the names and addresses of the president and executive officer and is followed by the names and addresses of realtors who are members of the local board. The entry for Valley Center, California, shown in figure 18.4, is typical.

For more than 25 years, the monthly *National Real Estate Investor* has been publishing a special issue, its "National Real Estate Investor Directory." The directory, published in mid-June, lists more than 7,000 leading companies and individuals in 16 categories of real estate. Included are entries for appraisers; national associations; builders, contractors, and developers; corporate real estate managers; economic and industrial development authorities; equity investors and investment companies; industrial properties and parks; investment and pension fund advisers; mortgage sources; office parks; property managers; real estate brokers and agents; real estate consultants and counselors; syndicators; and title insurance companies. Entries are brief, including only name, address, and telephone number, but the wide array of businesses represented and the low price of the directory, which can be purchased as a separate issue, make it an inexpensive and useful addition to business reference collections.

① **SMITH, John Downing, Jr.** — ② **B:** Dec. 4, 1940, Philadelphia, PA, ③ *Vice Pres.*–Site Acquisition,④ Liebermann Development Corp.;⑤ **PRIM RE ACT:** Developer, Investor, Property Manager, Syndicator; ⑥ **OTHER RE ACT:** Consultant; ⑦ **SERVICES:** Investment counseling, valuation, development and syndication of commercial properties, property management; ⑧ **REP CLIENTS:** Lenders and individual or institutional investors in commercial properties; ⑨ **PREV EMPLOY:** Dept. of Housing and Urban Development, 1966-70; ⑩ **PROFL AFFIL & HONORS:** NYC Planning Commission, RESSI, Consultant to the Society for the Preservation of NYC Landmarks, Recipient of the Donnelly Investment Award, 1977; ⑪ **EDUC:** BA, Urban Planning, NY Univ., 1962; ⑫ **GRAD EDUC:** MBA, Harvard Bus. School, 1966; ⑬ **EDUC HONORS:** President's List, Magna Cum Laude; ⑭ **MIL SERV:** US Army, Sgt., 1962-64; ⑮ **OTHER ACT & HONORS:** Board of Advisers of the NYC Boys Clubs, Inc.; ⑯ **HOME ADD:** 240 W. 57 St., New York, NY 10019, (212) 543-5686; ⑰ **BUS ADD:** 203 Broadway, New York, NY 10007, (212) 337-5794;⑱ *

① Name
② Date and place of birth
③ Current title and division
④ Current firm affiliation
⑤ Primary real estate activities
⑥ Other real estate activities
⑦ Services offered
⑧ Representative clients
⑨ Previous employment
⑩ Professional affiliations and honors
⑪ Undergraduate education
⑫ Graduate education
⑬ Educational honors
⑭ Military service
⑮ Other activities and honors
⑯ Home address and phone
⑰ Business address and phone
⑱ Biography not verified by individual

Fig. 18.3. Sample entry, *Real Estate Review's Who's Who in Real Estate*. Reprinted by permission from *Real Estate Review's Who's Who in Real Estate*.

Valley Center
Board of REALTORS

President: Ken Knust, P O Box 529, Valley Center, 92082.
Executive Officer: Barbara Brodie, P O Box 529, Valley Center, 92082 619/749-1637.

Atkinson, W. R., 30683 Persimmon 92082.
Buddin, Thomas Daniel, 32255 Cole Grade Rd. 92082.
Campbell, James R., 31029 Oak Glen Lane 92082.
Carter, Dora, P. O. Box 867 92082.
Demeaux, David Benedict, 27301 Valley Center Rd. 92082.
Dodson, Harlene, P. O. Box 10 92082.
Elder, Robert W., P. O. Box 794 92082.
Farmer, Garry, P. O. Box 10 92082.
Gravett, Donald, 27301 Valley Center Rd. 92082.
Handa, Susan, 28714 Valley Center Rd. 92082.
Hartman, Margie, 27959 Valley Center Rd. 92082.
Hartman, Randall J., 27959 Valley Ctr. Rd. 92082.
Haskell, Bette Allene, 14305 Woods Valley Rd. 92082.
Hill, Edna M., P. O. Box 346 92082.
Horn, William George, III, 11101 Berry Rd. 92082.
Israel, Tonia Barclay, 29143 Valley Center Rd. 92082.
Jackson, Charles W., P O Box 10 92082.
Jonker, Mary Geraldine, P. O. Box 808 92082.
Knust, Kenneth, 27301 Valley Center Rd. 92082.
Kruger, Ellen, 13275 Blueberry Hill Ln 92082.
Last, Elsie R., 29143 Valley Center Rd. 92082.
Mahan, Ruth, P.O. Box 206, Pauma Valley 92063.
Mc Kinely, Forrest S., 27011 Banburg Drive 92082.
Mitchell, John, P.O. Box 821 92082.
Neschke, Ada Mae, 28634 Sunset Road 92082.
O'Donnell, Patrick I., 27930 Valley Center Rd. 92082.
Parsons, Ruth R., P. O. Box 808 92082.
Roberts, Ethel, P.O. Box 808 92082.
Rozelle, Richard K., 27357 Valley Center Rd. 92082.
Thomas, Dorothy, 28481 Gordon Hill Rd. 92082.
Tilton, Kenneth G., 28215 Valley Center Rd 92082.
Turnbull, Susan Jae, 28215 Valley Center Rd. 92082.

Fig. 18.4. Typical entry, *National Roster of Realtors*. Reprinted from May 1986 *National Roster of Realtors*®.

Other directories are aimed at individuals and corporations or other organizations contemplating relocation in another part of the country.

Employee Relocation Council. **E-R-C Directory**. Washington, D.C.: The Council, 1964- . Annual.

The *E-R-C Directory* lists real estate professionals "who are prepared to give particular attention to the sale and/or acquisition of homes when employees are transferred from one location to another."[8] It gives separate, color-coded listings for appraisers and brokers, with each section geographically arranged. Also featured is an alphabetical listing of relocation service companies, including areas of specialization, as well as name, address, and telephone number. In addition, the *Directory* reproduces Rand McNally state market maps showing counties, metropolitan areas, cities, and towns for each state.

Other directories are even more specialized. Although space does not permit consideration of them all, the following is typical.

National Research Bureau, Inc. **Directory of Shopping Centers in the United States**. Chicago: The Bureau, 1977- . Annual, published in four regional editions (Eastern, Midwestern, Southern, and Western) plus a fifth national summary volume.

The *Directory of Shopping Centers in the United States* contains detailed listings and summary statistics for shopping centers. Each regional edition is arranged by state, city, and name of shopping center. As shown in figure 18.5, an entry generally includes the center's address and telephone number, a brief description of the center, and the names of the owner(s), leasing agent, architect/engineer, anchor stores, and other tenants.

The *Directory* also includes a glossary; regional summary statistics; metro area and city indexes; as well as an alphabetical index of shopping centers; state fact sheets; indexes of centers by gross leasable area; market positioning strategy; and centers that are planned, under construction, or have expanded or are being renovated. A list of centers with space available for lease is also included.

Periodicals and Periodical Indexes

The diversity of the real estate industry is reflected in such periodicals as *Appraisal Journal, Builder, Constructor, Mortgage Banker*, and *Secondary Mortgage Market Analysis*. Although a comprehensive collection of such serials is rare in all but the largest or most specialized business collections, some real estate periodicals are more commonly held. They include the following titles.

Real Estate Forum. New York: Real Estate Forum, 1946- . Monthly, with an additional issue in November.

New York University. Real Estate Institute. **Real Estate Review**. Boston: Warren, Gorham & Lamont, 1971- . Quarterly.

National Real Estate Investor. Atlanta, Ga.: Communication Channels, 1959- . Monthly, with an additional issue in June.

Real Estate Forum is a commercially published trade magazine that focuses primarily on recent developments in commercial and industrial real estate. A typical issue contains one or two articles; recent issues, for example, have included articles on title insurance and real estate syndication. The bulk of each issue, however, consists of brief announcements in such regular columns as "National Round-Up," "Construction/Modernization," "Loans and Leases," and "Shopping Centers/Industrial." The February issue contains its annual review of the industry, examining market conditions across the country and identifying in each state residential, commercial, and industrial markets that are unusually strong or weak. Although some statistics are included, the annual review lacks the detailed statistics that are common to many industry reviews and forecasts.

PEACHTREE CENTER
231 Peachtree St.
Atlanta GA 30303
Telephone: (404) 659-0800
Mailing Addr.: Peachtree Center Mgmt. Co.
225 Peachtree, #610, S. Twr.
Atlanta GA 30303

Description of Center

Type: Community	Mkt. Strategy: Traditional Mix
Year First Opened: 1974	Strip Center: No
Mixed Use Dev.: Yes	Food Court: Yes
Space Available: Yes	Hours: 10AM-6PM M-Sa

Center Physical Configuration

GLA, incl. Anchors: 134,000	Enclosed: Yes
Levels: 3	Shape: Other
Acres: 12	Stores: 56
Parking Spaces: 6,000	

Construction Activity
Current: Existing Center Renovating
Completion Date: 1986

Ownership
John Portman, Dev.
225 Peachtree St., Ste. 201, Atlanta GA 30303
Telephone: (404) 522-8811

Prudential Insurance Co. of America, The
1 Ravinia Dr., Ste. 1400, Atlanta GA 30346
Telephone: (404) 395-8600

Leasing Agent
Peachtree Center Management Company
225 Peachtree, #610, S. Twr., Atlanta GA 30303
Telephone: (404) 659-0800
Contact: Penelope K. Cheroff, Director of Leasing

Center Management
General Manager......................Tom Tabor
Marketing Director ....Susan Guerrero

Architect/Engineer
John Portman & Assoc.
225 Peachtree St., NE, Atlanta GA 30303

Anchors
Rich's II, GLA: 8,266

Tenants

A Taste Of China	Alan's Photography
American Lunch	Athlete's Foot
B. Dalton Bookseller	Benihana of Tokyo
C & S Bank	Charlie & Barney's Chili Parlor
Cheese Villa	Chez Jackie
Chick - Fil - A	Circle Cafe
Coffee Port, The	Continental Collection, The
Continental Styles, Hair Salon	Cookie's, Etc.
Eastern Newsstand	Eastern Newsstand II
Executive Shine	Extron Corp.
Federal Express	Fidelity Natl. Bank
Fitzgerald's, Liquor	Flower Garden, The
Frabel Gallery	Gorin's Ice Cream
Grampa's Cookies	Grandma's Biscuits
International Records & Tapes	J. Brenners
La Grande Convenience Store	Ladies Samples by Howard
Lindsay's Drugstore	Louise Light Jewelry
Naturalizer Shoes	Occasion Flower
Pat Burgess Couture	Peachtree Center Mail Room
Roman Delight	Salle's Opticians
Shipfeifers Gyro Wrap	Toy Box, The
Trust Co. Bank	

Fig. 18.5. Sample entry, *Directory of Shopping Centers in the United States*. Reprinted by permission from the 1987 edition of the *Directory of Shopping Centers in the United States*, National Research Bureau, 1986.

While *Real Estate Forum* is essentially a news magazine, *Real Estate Review*, a publication of the Real Estate Institute of New York University, contains articles on a wide range of topics. Recent issues have included articles on such subjects as the reemergence of real estate investment trusts, residential real estate marketing, and the development of retirement communities. Contributors include real estate executives and practitioners as well as scholars, and the emphasis is on practical information and problem-solving. Recurring features include "Stanger Syndication Sales Data," which presents statistics on sales of public and private real estate partnerships and syndicates, "Syndication Topics," "Real Estate Dealing," "Real Estate Compensation," and "Legal Opinion."

The *National Real Estate Investor* is another trade publication. It covers construction, development, finance, investment, and management, and combines news and announcements with articles. Each issue also includes "City/Area Reviews," which provides intensive analyses of three or four selected real estate markets. Each issue also has a theme, such as corporate real estate, shopping centers, industrial/high technology development, and real estate renovation. Regular columns include "Computers in Real Estate," "Financing Today," "Smart Building," "Purchase and Sale Language," "Tax Notes," and "Washington Wire." Finally, as noted in the preceding section, *National Real Estate Investor* publishes a special directory issue each June.

Some periodicals are particularly useful for the statistics they contain. Representative of these are *U.S. Housing Markets* and *Construction Review*.

U.S. Housing Markets. Detroit: U.S. Housing Markets, 1966- . Quarterly.

U.S. Dept. of Commerce. International Trade Administration. **Construction Review**. Washington, D.C.: Government Printing Office, 1955- . Bimonthly.

U.S. Housing Markets surveys housing for 45 metropolitan areas, 8 regions, and the United States. Data on private housing permits for single and multifamily units are provided, along with additional information on multifamily housing units completed or under construction, rental vacancy rates, household formats, and U.S. households by age groups. Also covered are trends for existing home sales and mortgage markets, with mid-year and year-end issues including editorial analyses and forecasts. In addition to the quarterly surveys, a subscription includes a series of special reports, released throughout the year, that examine emerging housing trends. In past years, special reports have analyzed home cost trends, condominiums, local housing markets, land and lot costs, and demographic trends.

Construction Review consists primarily of statistical tables. Although each issue includes one article, it is generally no more than 5 to 10 pages long; the statistical tables, on the other hand, fill 20 pages or more. Tables are grouped together under: construction put in place; housing; building permits; contract awards; costs, prices, and interest rates; construction materials; and contract construction employment. Indexes provide access to statistics presented in each issue and to articles in earlier issues.

Real estate periodicals are indexed in such standard sources as *Business Index, Predicasts F&S Index United States*, and *Business Periodicals Index*. *BPI*, for example, indexes articles contained in *Appraisal Journal, Journal of the American Real Estate and Urban Economics Association, National Real Estate Investor*, and *Real Estate Review*. *Public Affairs Information Service Bulletin*, in turn, is particularly strong for planning and development issues, both in the United States and in other countries.

Government Documents

Federal real estate publications are rich and diverse. They include hearings on real estate development and financing, GNMA manuals for institutional investors, reports on new housing technology, statistics, and market analysis. The field is so broad that it is all but impossible to list even selectively documents likely to interest real estate brokers and sales people, developers, builders, financiers, and investors. Each library will want to collect documents that reflect its users' interests and needs. At a minimum, however, libraries should be able to refer users to nearby depository libraries housing documents published by such agencies as the Department of Housing and Urban Development, the Veterans Administration, the Departments of Commerce and Labor, and Congress.

One area in which there is widespread interest in most public and many academic libraries is the purchase of residential property.

U.S. Dept. of Housing and Urban Development. **Homebuyer's Information Package**. Washington, D.C.: Government Printing Office, 1979.

U.S. Dept. of Agriculture. **Selecting and Financing a Home**. Rev. ed. Washington, D.C.: Government Printing Office, 1986. 16p.

U.S. Federal Trade Commission. **The Mortgage Money Guide**. Washington, D.C.: Government Printing Office, 1986. 16p.

U.S. Dept. of Housing and Urban Development. **Settlement Costs**. Washington, D.C.: Government Printing Office, 1983. 46p.

The *Homebuyer's Information Package* is a guidebook for prospective homeowners. Sections discuss the advantages and disadvantages of owning a home, selecting a house, purchase contracts, home financing, the closing process, money management, and home maintenance and repair. A glossary is appended, and worksheets, checklists, and sample forms are also included. Although some readers may find the language and style somewhat simplistic, for others the nontechnical, heavily illustrated approach will help to defuse some of the anxiety attached to buying a house. *Selecting and Financing a Home* contains information similar to that published in the *Information Package*, minus the illustrations, forms, and worksheets. Many users, however, will find the smaller size and less elementary approach more convenient and appealing.

The *Mortgage Money Guide* is intended as a manual to "creative home financing." Basic mortgage types are listed and defined. Advantages, disadvantages, and major considerations for each are discussed, and brief mortgage payment tables for loans from $25,000 to $100,000 at interest rates of from 8 to 12 percent are included.

Settlement Costs describes the settlement process, including the costs involved and the types of questions to ask lenders, attorneys, brokers, and others. Sample forms and worksheets are included. Many financial institutions give copies of this document to their clients when they apply for loans. By stocking copies, libraries can help users anticipate and answer many questions before they begin the loan application process.

Statistics

Statistics pertaining to real estate are abundant. They include data gathered and published by a wide range of sources and provide information on construction and sale of housing, growth of shopping centers and industrial plants, operating costs, and vacancy rates. In addition, general demographic, social, and economic statistics are of direct importance to real estate operations of all kinds. Although space does not permit coverage of every pertinent statistic, some of the most important ones are discussed below.

On the most basic level, most people pay rent or monthly mortgage loan installments. Costs for housing are, in fact, one of the major components of the consumer price index, which presents data on rent, owners' equivalent rent, homeowners' or tenants' insurance, and maintenance and repair. Such information is included in the *CPI Detailed Report* and the *Inter-City Cost of Living Index*, both of which were described in chapter 6.

Data on construction and building costs are also compiled and reported. In all, there are 10 major construction cost indexes, some produced by the government, others by private organizations. The Census Bureau, for example, issues the Bureau of the Census Index of New One-Family Houses Sold Excluding Census Lot Value and the Department of Commerce Composite Cost Index, which reflects the changes for all types of construction. The Federal Highway Administration publishes quarterly indexes relating to highway construction, and the Department of the Interior issues a Bureau of Reclamation Composite Index, which measures the costs of constructing dams and reclamation projects sponsored by the department. The Federal Energy Regulatory Commission (FERC) issues a Federal Energy Regulatory Commission Pipeline Index that presents data on construction costs reported by pipeline companies regulated by the commission.

Some of the most widely cited indexes are issued by private sources. Key among these are the Boeckh Indexes, issued monthly by the American Appraisal Company. The Boeckh Indexes include Total Construction Costs; Residences; Apartments, Hotels, and Office Buildings; and Commercial and Factory Buildings. The *Engineering News-Record*, a trade paper for the construction industry, publishes national cost indexes for construction and building. Others include the Turner Construction Company Index, which measures building construction costs in eastern cities; the Handy-Whitman Indexes, which present building costs for utility buildings, gas plants, and electric light and power plants; and, finally, the Bell System Telephone Indexes, which measure cost changes for construction of telephone company buildings and "outside plants" (including telephone poles, cables, aerial wires, and underground conduits).[9] Each issue of the bimonthly *Construction Review*, described earlier in this chapter, publishes all 10 indexes (see figure 18.6 on pages 448 and 449). In addition, selected construction cost indexes are included in each issue of the *Survey of Current Business*.

The most detailed and comprehensive statistics on the construction industry are those published by the Census Bureau. Such data include a series of monthly, quarterly, and annual surveys known collectively as *Construction Reports* and the *Census of Construction Industries*.

> U.S. Dept. of Commerce. Bureau of the Census. **Construction Statistics Data Finder**. Washington, D.C.: Government Printing Office, 1986. 16p.

The *Construction Statistics Data Finder*, a free Census Bureau guide, lists and briefly describes construction statistics, most of which are published by the Bureau.[10] The *Data Finder* also includes tables for the various *Construction Reports*, special reports (usually historical composites of *Construction Reports*), the *Census of Construction Industries*, and other statistical reports. For each, it notes the title, series number, subject content, level of geographic detail, and frequency of issuance.

A brief consideration of some of the publications included in the *Data Finder* may be useful.

> U.S. Dept. of Commerce. Bureau of the Census. **Census of Construction Industries**. Washington, D.C.: Government Printing Office. Quinquennial, taken in years ending in -2 and -7.

The *Census of Construction Industries* enumerates construction establishments that operate as general and special trade contractors, builders, and land subdividers and developers. It consists primarily of two main series, an *Industry Series*, which includes reports on some 27 different construction industries, and the *Geographic Area Series*, which presents data for selected metropolitan areas, all 50 states, nine census divisions, and the United States as a whole.

While the census covers only those establishments considered to be a part of the construction industry, *Construction Reports* pertain to all construction activities regardless of who performs the work. In all, there are nine such reports, each dealing with a different activity. Some cover construction and sale of new houses, and others, the value of recent construction. Each of the reports is listed and briefly described in appendix K.

Although many libraries lack direct access to *Construction Reports* and the *Census of Construction Industries*, these publications are available at all regional and many selective depository libraries. In addition, some of the most useful information they contain is published in other sources as well, including the *Statistical Abstract of the United States, Survey of Current Business*, and *Construction Review*.

The Census Bureau also issues a series of statistical publications relating to housing. Key among these are the *Census of Housing*, the *Census of Population and Housing, Current Housing Reports*, and the *Annual Housing Survey*.

> U.S. Dept. of Commerce. Bureau of the Census. **Census of Housing**. Washington, D.C.: Government Printing Office. Decennial.

> _____. **Census of Population and Housing**. Washington, D.C.: Government Printing Office. Decennial.

Every 10 years, the Bureau of the Census collects detailed demographic and economic information about the United States' inhabitants and their dwellings. The decennial census, known collectively as the *Census of Population and Housing*, is published as three separate censuses: the *Census of Population*, the *Census of Housing*, and the *Census of Population and Housing*.

The *Census of Housing* presents housing and occupancy information, published in separate series volumes. *General Housing Characteristics, Detailed Housing Characteristics*, and *Metropolitan Housing Characteristics* comprise the bulk of the *Census*, while the *Subject Reports, Components of Inventory Change*, and *Residential Finance* provide additional information. The contents and geographic coverage of these publications are described briefly in appendix L, but it is worth noting here that by using the *Census of Housing*, researchers can obtain valuable information about the physical and financial characteristics of housing units. They can, for example, determine the number of condominium- and renter-occupied units, housing vacant and for sale, and housing lacking complete plumbing facilities. Data are available for each state and for designated metropolitan areas, as well as for the United States as a whole.

Also useful is the *Census of Population and Housing*, which combines data taken from the *Census of Population* with *Census of Housing* statistics. The *Census of Population and Housing* is particularly popular with researchers seeking information for smaller geographical units. It presents population and housing data on a block-by-block basis in its *Block Statistics* series, and by census tracts, cities, and counties in its *Census Tracts* series.

While complete collections of the *Census of Housing* and the *Census of Population and Housing* may be limited to depository and research libraries, librarians in other settings may want to consider acquiring selected volumes for the cities and states in which their libraries are located.

The *Annual Housing Survey*, conducted by the Bureau of the Census for the Department of Housing and Urban Development, supplements the *Census of Housing* by providing current information on housing characteristics.

> U.S. Dept. of Commerce. Bureau of the Census. **Annual Housing Survey**. Washington, D.C.: Government Printing Office. Biennial.

The *Survey* is published in six subject reports: *General Housing Characteristics, Indicators of Housing and Neighborhood Quality by Financial Characteristics of the Housing Inventory, Housing Characteristics of Recent Movers, Urban and Rural Housing Characteristics*, and *Energy-Related Housing Characteristics*. In each report, data are shown for the United States and for the Northeast, Midwest, South, and West. In addition, the *Survey* includes statistics on housing for 13 selected standard metropolitan statistical areas, published as separate reports.[11] The *Annual Housing Survey* is part of the bureau's *Current Housing Reports* series, which also includes *Housing Vacancies, Marketing Absorption of Apartments*, and *Characteristics of Apartments Completed*.

CONSTRUCTION REVIEW

COSTS, PRICES, AND INTEREST RATES

Table E-1.—Construction Cost Indexes
[1982 = 100]

Period	Department of Commerce composite cost index	Engineering News-Record		"Boeckh Indexes," The American Appraisal Company, Inc.		
		Building	Construction	Residences	Apartments, hotels, and office buildings	Commercial and factory buildings
Annual average						
1981	97.0	94.0	92.5	92.2	91.6	92.2
1982	100.0	100.0	100.0	100.0	100.0	100.0
1983	102.7	105.7	105.3	105.9	106.4	105.3
1984	106.3	106.2	106.4	111.9	111.2	106.4
1985	106.4	106.6	106.3	115.1	113.0	111.3
Monthly Indexes					**Bimonthly Indexes**	
1985: January	106.1	107.9	106.4	114.1	112.3	110.4
February	106.1	108.1	106.6			
March	106.6	107.7	106.5	114.3	112.5	110.5
April	106.4	107.7	106.5			
May	106.9	106.0	106.0	114.7	112.6	110.8
June	106.4	106.8	106.8			
July	106.6	106.6	110.3	115.5	113.1	111.5
August	106.7	106.2	110.0			
September	110.0	106.9	106.6	115.9	113.5	112.2
October	110.2	106.0	106.5			
November	110.3	106.2	106.8	116.3	113.9	112.4
December	110.3	106.9	110.0			
1986: January	110.6	108.9	108.9	116.5	114.1	112.6
February	110.6	109.3	110.2			
March	110.9	109.4	110.3	116.5	114.2	112.8
April	112.0	109.9	110.6			
May	112.8	110.0	111.4	116.8	114.4	112.9
June	112.9	112.1	112.2			
July	112.4	111.9	113.2	117.3	114.9	113.3
August	112.3	111.8	113.2			
September	112.4	112.1	113.3	118.1	115.8	113.8
October	112.3	112.3	113.5			
November	112.4	111.8	112.8	118.6	116.1	114.0
December	112.6	112.4	113.7			

46

Period	Federal Highway Administration Composite	Bureau of the Census new one family houses excluding Census lot value	Bureau of Reclamation	Turner Construction Company	Handy-Whitman Public Utility Buildings	Handy-Whitman Public Utility Electric light and power	Bell System Telephone Plant Telephone and telegraph Buildings	Bell System Telephone Plant Telephone and telegraph Outside plant	Federal Energy Regulatory Commission Pipeline
Annual average									
1981	106.7	97.0	95	92	100	95	83.1	85.8	98
1982	100.0	100.0	100	100	100	100	100.0	100.0	100
1983	99.8	102.6	101	105	103	103	n.a.	n.a.	101
1984	105.8	106.2	103	111	107	105	n.a.	n.a.	103
1985	117.2	108.4	105	115	110	107	n.a.	n.a.	n.a.
Quarterly indexes				**Semiannual indexes**			**Annual indexes**		
1985: 1st quarter	114.5	107.9	104	114	111	107	n.a.	n.a.	n.a.
2nd quarter	118.5	107.8	104	115					
3rd quarter	119.4	108.9	105	116	110	106	n.a.	n.a.	n.a.
4th quarter	116.8	109.4	105	116					
1986: 1st quarter	119.7	109.7	105	r 116	r 110	107	n.a.	n.a.	n.a.
2nd quarter	115.1	112.4	105	r 117					
3rd quarter	119.9	111.6	106	r 118	113	r 107	n.a.	n.a.	n.a.
4th quarter			106	119					

* An implicit price deflator, computed by the Bureau of the Census, which is the ratio of the estimate of total new construction put in place in current dollars (seasonally adjusted) to the corresponding estimate in 1982 dollars. In form, the index is a weighted harmonic mean of the deflators used for various categories of construction (and, hence, of the basic cost indexes which make up these deflators), with weights proportionate to the value-put-in-place estimates (seasonally adjusted) for these categories. Since this "implicit price deflator" is in the form of a changing weight index, it measures the combined result of cost changes as well as monthly changes in the weights of different types of construction in the current-dollar construction activity aggregate.   Sources as stated.   n.a Not available   Revised

Fig. 18.6. Construction cost indexes presented in *Construction Review*. Reprinted from the January/February 1987 *Construction Review*.

The government issues other statistics as well. Although many of the series formerly published by the Department of Housing and Urban Development, including its *Statistical Yearbook*, are no longer available, it still publishes data on FHA-insured mortgages. The Energy Information Administration issues statistics on characteristics of commercial buildings, while the Bureau of Labor Statistics' monthly *Producer Price Indexes* highlights changes in the cost of such building materials as plumbing fixtures, lumber, and insulation materials. In addition, the *Federal Reserve Bulletin* presents information on primary and secondary mortgage market activity and on outstanding residential, commercial, and farm mortgage debt. In some libraries, however, the "Construction and Housing Section" of the *Statistical Abstract of the United States*, which contains excerpts from many of the sources described above, will suffice.

Other statistics are available from trade associations, private organizations, and commercial publishers.

National Association of Realtors. **Outlook for the Economy and Real Estate**. Washington, D.C.: The Association. Monthly.

———. **Existing Home Sales**. Washington, D.C.: The Association, 1976- . Monthly.

United States League of Savings Institutions. **Savings Institutions Sourcebook**. Chicago: The League, 1984- . Annual.

Society of Industrial and Office Realtors. **Industrial Real Estate Market Survey**. Washington, D.C.: The Society, 1980- . Semiannual.

The *Outlook for the Economy and Real Estate* is a brief report on current and projected economic conditions as they affect residential, commercial, and industrial real estate markets. Each issue, generally no more than 10 pages long, presents a few pages of introduction, followed by two main tables. The first includes statistics on the economy, presenting such measures as gross national product, manufacturing capacity utilization, the trade deficit, employment and unemployment, and price indexes. The second table covers real estate markets and prices and financial markets. The section on real estate includes statistics on housing starts, new commercial and industrial buildings constructed, mobile home shipments, and office building vacancy rates. The financial markets section includes general financial measures such as money supply and the value of the dollar and such specialized indicators as residential and nonresidential investment. Special supplements are occasionally featured; one recent issue, for example, included a supplement on the U.S. merchandise trade deficit.

More specialized information is available in *Existing Home Sales*, which is a compilation of data received by the National Association of Realtors from over 275 boards of realtors and multiple listing systems from all parts of the country. Again, a brief narrative section precedes the tables and graphs, which include data on the sales of existing one-family houses, the supply of such houses, and housing affordability. Although some information is included for selected metropolitan areas, most summarize trends for the United States or for the Northeast, Midwest, South, and West.

The *Savings Institution Sourcebook* includes an overview of the savings institutions business and data on savings, mortgage lending, housing, and federal government agencies. The mortgage lending section, for example, includes tables on types of mortgage loans outstanding, interest rates, private and government mortgage insurance, and foreclosures. In addition, the *Sourcebook* includes a brief description of major federal laws affecting savings institutions, a glossary, and an index.

The *Industrial Real Estate Market Survey* covers construction, financing, sales, and leasing of industrial property in nearly 100 major metropolitan areas. Although it emphasizes the United States, it does include some foreign cities.

Information on construction and operating costs is vital to real estate professionals. Several sources provide such data, and while usually only the most specialized or largest libraries have comprehensive collections of these sources, it may be useful to consider a representative title.

Dodge Cost Calculator and Valuation Guide. New York: McGraw-Hill Information Systems Company, 1971- . Looseleaf, with quarterly updates.

Contractors submitting bids on all types of construction projects routinely are asked to submit estimates of how much it will cost to erect the proposed structure or remodel an existing one. These estimates are usually based on past experience and reflect anticipated labor and building materials costs. Sometimes published building cost estimators are also used.

Typical of these sources is the *Dodge Cost Calculator and Valuation Guide*, which provides average construction costs per square and cubic foot for more than 100 types of residential, commercial, industrial, public, medical, educational, and religious buildings. Each entry is generally two pages long: The first page consists of photographs of representative buildings, and the second page presents such information as the type and quality of the structure, exterior material used, and brief descriptions of the building's structure, its functional use, and plumbing, electrical, air conditioning, and other specifications. Also included are average construction costs, supplemental costs, and instructions for computing costs. Figure 18.7 (see page 452), which is the entry for concrete and steel high-rise office buildings of good quality, is typical. The *Cost Calculator* also includes indexes that permit cost adjustments for specific locations and time periods.

Other publications provide operating statistics for different categories of commercial, industrial, or residential property, showing income and expense data for each. By consulting these sources, building owners, property managers, developers, investors, and others can compare their operations to the national, regional, or local norms for that type of property.

Institute of Real Estate Management. **Income/Expense Analysis: Apartments**. Chicago: The Institute, 1954- . Annual.

_____. **Expense Analysis: Condominiums, Cooperatives, and Planned Unit Developments**. Chicago: The Institute. Annual.

_____. **Income/Expense Analysis: Office Buildings Downtown and Suburban**. Chicago: The Institute, 1976- . Annual.

Building Owners and Managers Association International. **BOMA Experience Exchange Report: Income/Expense Analysis for Office Buildings**. Washington, D.C.: The Association, 1920- . Annual.

Urban Land Institute. **Dollars & Cents of Shopping Centers: A Study of the Receipts & Expenses in Shopping Center Operations**. Washington, D.C.: The Institute, 1961- . Triennial.

Each year, the Institute of Real Estate Management's Experience Exchange Department compiles and analyzes financial operating data contributed by its members for over 6,500 buildings and developments. These data are published as three separate titles: *Income/Expense Analysis: Apartments; Income/Expense Analysis: Office Buildings Downtown and Suburban;* and *Expense Analysis: Condominiums, Cooperatives, and Planned Unit Developments.* Coverage varies, but each publication charts recent trends in building operations, covers income by source, and presents data for different building types. The *Apartments* report, for example, features information on such expenses as utilities, security, repairs, grounds maintenance, and real estate taxes, and presents median income and operating costs for high-rise, low-rise, and garden-apartment buildings.

COMMERCIAL/INDUSTRIAL 2

Specifications

BUILDING	OFFICE BUILDING HIGH-RISE
CONSTRUCTION	CONCRETE AND STEEL
QUALITY	GOOD

STRUCTURE
Reinforced concrete foundation, footings, walls and slabs. Structural steel framing, encased in concrete or fireproofed. Metal decking with concrete fill or cast concrete reinforced.

EXTERIOR WALL:
Glass with metal extrusions or precast concrete panels, stone, or marble panels set between glass or curtain wall finishes, or masonry exterior walls with block backup, ornate trim and exterior finishes of stone, brick or terra cotta.

PLUMBING
Good quality fixtures, water coolers utility and service sinks. Standpipe.

HEATING VENTILATION
Baseboard hot water heating system or boiler fired system.

AIR CONDITIONING
Chilled water system, perimeter fan coil units ventilation system, 2-4 pipe system.

ELECTRICAL
Fluorescent lighting fixtures integrated with good quality suspended acoustical ceiling panels, underfloor ductwork.

FLOORING
General areas: Vinyl floor covering, ceramic tile in toilets, terrazzo or

SPECIAL
(Vertical Transportation)
Passenger elevators—High speed type, adequate transportation. marble in corridors and public areas.

LOBBY

FUNCTIONAL USE
Single use tenant. Special interior partition requirements and distinctive type use rooms with custom design requirements.

Cost Factors (per floor)

HIGH-RISE OFFICE BUILDING CONCRETE AND STEEL GOOD QUALITY					THOUSANDS OF SQUARE FEET		
	16m	18m	20m	22m	24m	26m	28m
	$36.90	$34.82	$33.11	$31.29	$30.13	$29.86	$29.30

To Compute the value of the high-rise office building do as follows:

1. Assign the quality rating from the narrative given in the specifications above.

2. Compute the total gross area of one typical floor and apply the square foot cost (or interpolated cost between the 2000 SF increments), then multiply the result by the number of indentical floors.

3. (a) Exclusions: For high-rise office buildings that may have one or more floors of parking garage areas refer to page 2-69 Commercial/Industrial—Parking Garage, concrete frame, for cost per square foot by the assigned quality rating of either average or good.

   (b) Refer to page A-3 for cost inclusions and exclusions.

Additives and Variables

	16m	18m	20m	22m	24m	26m	28m
Concrete Basement	$6.00	$6.55	$6.45	$6.40	$6.33	$6.27	$6.15

The above costs may not be used without first applying an appropriate Local Cost Multiplier. See page A-14.

2-15

Fig. 18.7. Typical entry, *Dodge Cost Calculator and Valuation Guide*. Reprinted by permission from the *Dodge Cost Calculator and Valuation Guide*.

Operating statistics for U.S. and Canadian office buildings are also available in the annual *BOMA Experience Exchange Report*. The *Report* presents income and expenses for different types of private and public office buildings and also includes building occupancy rates, year-end rent, and space per tenant and worker. Data on selected areas by major city and regions and by size, story height, and age of building are included.

Dollars & Cents of Shopping Centers reports on shopping center operations. Based on responses made by shopping centers to periodic surveys by the Urban Land Institute, *Dollars & Cents* includes operating receipts and expenses, sales, rent, and detailed tenant information. Data are by type of shopping center (super regional, regional, community, and neighborhood) and cover the United States and Canada.

Vertical File Materials

While not abundant, real estate pamphlets and booklets appropriate for vertical file collections are available from a number of sources. Some have already been mentioned. Federal government publications such as *Settlement Costs* and *The Mortgage Money Guide*, for example, are ideally suited for such collections. Other documents can be identified by consulting the *Consumer Information Catalog*. Such titles as *Buying Lots from Developers, Are There Any Public Lands for Sale?*, and *Refinancing Your Home* are inexpensive, worthwhile vertical file candidates, and another, *Sales of Federal Surplus Real Estate*, which tells when, where, and how surplus government property will be sold during the next three month period, is free.[12]

Consumer finance magazines periodically publish inexpensive guides for homeowners. Typical of these is *Money Guide: Your Home* (New York: Time, Inc., 1985), which includes articles on buying, financing, improving, and investing in houses, as well as a glossary of basic housing terms.

Other pamphlets are available from associations and corporations. The American Council of Life Insurance, for example, publishes the quarterly *Mortgage Commitments on Multifamily and Nonresidential Properties Reported by 20 Life Insurance Companies;*[13] and Coldwell Banker issues another quarterly, *Office Building Vacancy Index of the United States,*[14] which summarizes and graphs downtown and suburban office vacancy rates for the United States and selected cities. By consulting the indexes and other sources described in chapter 7, additional vertical file titles can be identified.

Online Databases

Most of the general online business databases provide access to literature in real estate and related fields. One specialized database is also available.

HUD User Online. Germantown, Md.: HUD User. Quarterly updates.

HUD User Online includes abstracts of reports, documents, and other sources dealing with affordable housing, housing finance, building technology, economic development, housing for special groups such as the elderly and disabled, energy conservation, assisted housing, and other topics. Although most of the titles abstracted are issued by the Department of Housing and Urban Development, documents from other government organizations and some journal articles are indexed as well. Most of the documents cited in *HUD User Online* are available from HUD User, a service provided by the Department's Office of Policy Development and Research.

NOTES

[1]George F. Bloom, Arthur M. Weimer, and Jeffrey D. Fisher, *Real Estate*, 8th ed. (New York: Wiley, 1982), 3.

[2]Andrew Tobias, "Quarterly Report," *Playboy* 34, no. 4 (April 1987): 120.

[3]"Pushing Property," *Money* 16, no. 2 (February 1987): 33.

[4]Joseph R. Bagby, *Real Estate Financing Desk Book*, 3rd ed. (Englewood Cliffs, N.J.: Institute for Business Planning, 1981), 16.

[5]Ibid., 233.

[6]Although the Federal Home Loan Mortgage Corporation buys some VA and FHA mortgages, it has concentrated on conventional loans.

[7]U.S. President's Commission on Housing, *The Report of the President's Commission on Housing* (Washington, D.C.: Government Printing Office, 1982), 113.

[8]*1985 E-R-C Directory* (Washington, D.C.: Employee Relocation Council, 1985), 9.

[9]For a more thorough treatment of these construction cost indexes, see Elliot Levy, "Construction Cost Indexes, 1915-76," *Construction Review* 23, no. 4 (June/July 1977): 4-17.

[10]To request a free copy of the *Construction Statistics Data Finder*, write to:

> Customer Services
> Data User Services Division
> U.S. Bureau of the Census
> Washington, DC 20233

[11]The SMSAs covered in separate reports for the *Annual Housing Survey* vary from one *Survey* to the next. In 1983, for example, the SMSAs included were as follows: Baltimore, Chicago, Hartford (Conn.), Honolulu, Houston, Louisville, Miami, New York, Portland (Oreg.), Sacramento, St. Louis, and Seattle.

[12]To request a single free copy of *Sales of Federal Surplus Real Estate*, ask for booklet 567R from:

> Consumer Information Center−Y
> P.O. Box 100
> Pueblo, CO 81002

[13]For a free copy of *Mortgage Commitments on Multifamily and Nonresidential Properties Reported by 20 Life Insurance Companies*, write to:

> American Council of Life Insurance
> 1001 Pennsylvania Avenue
> Washington, DC 20006-2284

[14]Free copies of the *Office Vacancy Index of the United States* can be obtained by writing to:

> Corporation Communications
> Coldwell Banker
> 533 Freemont Avenue
> Los Angeles, CA 90071

APPENDIX A
Business Acronyms and Abbreviations

AACSB	American Assembly of Collegiate Schools of Business
ABA	American Bankers Association
ABC	Audit Bureau of Circulations
ABI	*Abstracted Business Information* (variant name for the database, *ABI/Inform*)
ACCRA	American Chamber of Commerce Researchers Association
ACE	Active Corps of Executives
AICPA	American Institute of Certified Public Accountants
AID	Agency for International Development (U.S.)
AIRAC	All-Industry Research Advisory Council (insurance organization)
AMA	American Management Association
AMA	American Marketing Association
AMEX	American Stock Exchange
APB	Accounting Principles Board
APR	Annual Percentage Rate
ARB	*Accounting Research Bulletin*
ARBA	*American Reference Books Annual*
ARF	Advertising Research Foundation
ARM	Adjustable Rate Mortgage
ARS	Annual Report to Shareholders
ASB	Auditing Standards Board (AICPA)
ASR	*Accounting Series Releases* (SEC)
ASI	*American Statistics Index*
ATM	Automated Teller Machine
BEA	Bureau of Economic Analysis (U.S.)
BLS	Bureau of Labor Statistics (U.S.)
BNA	Bureau of National Affairs, Inc.
BPA	Business Publications Audit of Circulation

455

BPI	*Business Periodicals Index*
BPI	Buying Power Index
BRASS	Business Reference and Services Section, American Library Association
BRS	BRS Information Technologies, formerly Bibliographic Retrieval Services, Inc.
CBOE	Chicago Board Options Exchange
CBT	Chicago Board of Trade
CCPA	Consumer Credit Protection Act
CCH	Commerce Clearing House, Inc.
CD	Compact Disk
CD-ROM	Compact Disk, Read-Only-Memory
CEA	Council of Economic Advisers (U.S.)
CFTC	Commodity Futures Trading Commission (U.S.)
ChFA	Chartered Financial Analyst
CIS	Congressional Information Service, Inc.
CIT	Commission on Insurance Terminology (of the American Risk and Insurance Association)
CLU	Chartered Life Underwriter
CME	Chicago Mercantile Exchange
CMX	Commodity Exchange, Inc.
CPA	Certified Public Accountant
CPI	Consumer Price Index
CPI-U	Consumer Price Index for All Urban Consumers
CPI-W	Consumer Price Index for Urban Wage Earners and Clerical Workers
CRS	Congressional Research Service (U.S.)
CSCE	Coffee, Sugar & Cocoa Exchange
CV	Convertible Security (i.e., convertible preferred stock or convertible bond)
D & B	Dun & Bradstreet, Inc.
DBC	DIALOG Business Connection
DCAA	Defense Contract Audit Agency (U.S.)
DDA	Demand Deposit Accounts
DOD	Department of Defense (U.S.)
DOL	Department of Labor (U.S.)
D-U-N-S	Dun's Universal Numbering System
EBI	Effective Buying Income
ECOA	Equal Credit Opportunity Act
EPA	Environmental Protection Agency (U.S.)

EPS	Earnings per Share
ERC	Employee Relocation Council
ERS	Economic Research Service (U.S.)
ESA	Employment Standards Administration (U.S.)
ETA	Employment Training Administration (U.S.)
EYP	*Electronic Yellow Pages*
F&S	*Predicasts F&S Index United States*
FAA	Federal Aviation Administration (U.S.)
FAIR	Fair Access to Insurance Requirements
FASB	Financial Accounting Standards Board
FCC	Federal Communications Commission (U.S.)
FCRA	Fair Credit Reporting Act
FDA	Food and Drug Administration (U.S.)
FDIC	Federal Deposit Insurance Corporation (U.S.)
Fed	Federal Reserve System (U.S.)
FERC	Federal Energy Regulatory Commission (U.S.)
FHA	Federal Highway Administration (U.S.)
FHA	Federal Housing Administration (U.S.)
FHLB	Federal Home Loan Bank
FHLBB	Federal Home Loan Bank Board
FHLBS	Federal Home Loan Bank System
FHLMC	Federal Home Loan Mortgage Corporation (U.S.)
FICB	Federal Intermediate Credit Bank (U.S.)
FINIS	*Financial Industry Information Service*
FNMA	Federal National Mortgage Association (U.S.)
FOMC	Federal Open Market Committee, Federal Reserve System (U.S.)
FSLIC	Federal Savings and Loan Insurance Corporation (U.S.)
FTC	Federal Trade Commission (U.S.)
GAAP	Generally Accepted Accounting Principles
GAAS	Generally Accepted Auditing Standards
GAO	General Accounting Office (U.S.)
GNMA	Government National Mortgage Association (U.S.)
GNP	Gross National Product
GPO	Government Printing Office (U.S.)
GRA&I	*Government Reports Announcements & Index*
GSA	General Services Administration (U.S.)
HBR	*Harvard Business Review*
HFD	*Hulbert Financial Digest*

HMO	Health Maintenance Organization
HUD	Housing and Urban Development Department (U.S.)
HUT	Households Using Television
IAC	Information Access Company
ICC	International Chamber of Commerce
ICC	Interstate Commerce Commission (U.S.)
IMM	International Monetary Market
IPC	Individuals, Partnerships, and Corporations
IRS	Internal Revenue Service (U.S.)
ISBN	International Standard Book Number
ISSN	International Standard Serial Number
ITA	International Trade Administration (U.S.)
ITS	Intermarket Trading System
KCBT	Kansas City Board of Trade
LIMRA	Life Insurance Marketing and Research Association
LMS	Labor Management Standards Office (U.S.)
LNA	Leading National Advertisers
LOMA	Life Office Management Association
MACE	MidAmerica Commodity Exchange
MBS	Mortgage-Backed Securities Program
MGE	Minneapolis Grain Exchange
MGIC	MGIC Investment Corporation
MLP	Master Limited Partnership (real estate)
MRDF	Machine-Readable Data File
MVMA	Motor Vehicle Manufacturers Association
NAIC	National Association of Insurance Commissioners
NAR	National Association of Realtors
NASD	National Association of Securities Dealers, Inc.
NASDA	National Association of State Department Agencies
NASDAQ	National Association of Securities Dealers Automated Quotations
NAV	Net Asset Value
NBS	National Bureau of Standards (U.S.)
NCHS	National Center for Health Statistics (U.S.)
NCUA	National Credit Union Administration (U.S.)
NLRB	National Labor Relations Board (U.S.)
NMS	National Market System
NTIS	National Technical Information Service (U.S.)

NYCE	New York Cotton Exchange
NYFE	New York Futures Exchange
NYME	New York Mercantile Exchange
NYSE	New York Stock Exchange
OASDI	Old Age, Survivors, Disability and Health Insurance
OBA	Office of Business Analysis (U.S.)
ODDD	Optical Digital Data Disk
OMB	Office of Management and Budget (U.S.)
OSHA	Occupational Safety and Health Administration (U.S.)
OTA	Office of Technology Assessment (U.S.)
OTC	Over-the-Counter
PAIS	*Public Affairs Information Service Bulletin*
P/E	Price/Earnings Ratio
PF	Preferred Stock
PFD	Preferred Stock
P-H	Prentice-Hall, Inc.
PPI	Producer Price Index
PROMT	*Predicasts Overview of Markets and Technology*
PTS	Predicasts Terminal System
R & D	Research and Development
REIT	Real Estate Investment Trust
RELP	Real Estate Limited Partnership
RMA	Robert Morris Associates
ROM	Read-Only-Memory
S & L	Savings and Loan Association
S & P	Standard & Poor's Corporation
SBA	Small Business Administration (U.S.)
SBW	Small Business Workshop (IRS)
SCORE	Service Corps of Retired Executives
SCSA	Standard Consolidated Statistical Area
SDA	*Standard Directory of Advertisers*
SEC	Securities and Exchange Commission (U.S.)
SF	Sinking Fund
SFAS	*Statement of Financial Accounting Standards*
SIC	Standard Industrial Classification
SLA	Special Libraries Association
SMSA	Standard Metropolitan Statistical Area
S/N	Stock Number (U.S. Superintendent of Documents)

SRDS	Standard Rate & Data Service
SRI	*Statistical Reference Index*
SRIM	*Selected Research in Microfiche*
SUDOCS	Superintendent of Documents (U.S.)
T BILL	Treasury Bill
TCE	Tax Counseling for the Elderly
UPI	United Press International
USDA	Department of Agriculture (U.S.)
UT	Understanding Taxes (IRS)
VA	Veterans Administration (U.S.)
VITA	Volunteer Income Tax Assistance
WORM	Write Once, Read-Only-Memory
WSJ	*Wall Street Journal*
WT	Warrant

APPENDIX B
Federal Executive Departments and
Selected Agencies and Publications

Department or Agency	Functions	Representative Publications	Information Office
Agriculture	Works to improve farm income, develop markets for agricultural products, and to help curb hunger, poverty, and malnutrition. Helps landowners protect soil, water, forests, and other natural resources. Through inspection and grading, ensures quality of daily food supply. Responsible for rural development, credit, and conservation programs.	*Agricultural Statistics*	Office of Governmental and Public Affairs 202/447-2791
Economic Research Service	Provides economic information to aid in the development of agricultural policies and programs. Information made available through monographs, reports, situation and outlook periodicals, and databases.	*Agricultural Outlook; Impact of Land Degredation on Future World Food Production; National Food Review; Wheat Outlook and Situation Yearbook.*	Information Division, Economics Management Staff 202/786-1504
National Agricultural Statistics Service	Prepares estimates and reports on production, supply, and prices of agricultural products.	*Agricultural Prices; Dairy Products*	Information Division, Economics Management Staff 202/786-1504
Commerce	Encourages, serves, and promotes the free enterprise system, economic growth, international trade, and technological advancement. Provides assistance and information to domestic and international business; publishes social and economic analyses and statistics.	*Commerce Publications Update*	Office of Public Affairs 202/377-4901
Bureau of the Census	Collects, tabulates, and publishes demographic and socioeconomic statistical data.	*Census of Population; Census of Retail Trade: Statistical Abstract*	Public Information Office 301/763-4040

461

Department or Agency	Functions	Representative Publications	Information Office
Bureau of Economic Analysis	Develops and interprets measures of U.S. economic activities such as balance of payments, gross national product, and personal wealth.	*Business Conditions Digest; Business Statistics; Local Area Personal Income; Survey of Current Business*	Public Information Office 202/523-0777
International Trade Administration	Promotes world trade, strengthens U.S. international trade and investment position.	*Business America; Foreign Economic Trends; Franchise Opportunities Handbook; U.S. Industrial Outlook*	ITA 202/377-3808
Patent and Trademark Office	Examines, registers, and administers national system of patents and trademarks.	*Official Gazette ... Patents; Official Gazette ... Trademarks*	Office of Public Affairs 703/557-3341
Defense	Provides military forces needed to deter war and protect national security.	*Defense Management Journal; Guide to the Preparation of Offers for Selling to the Military*	Public Correspondence Division 202/697-5737
Defense Logistics Agency	Works with current and potential suppliers of weapon systems and other DOD materials; administers defense contracts and other support services.	*Military Standard Billing System; NATO Supply Code for Manufacturers; Classes of Surplus Personal Property*	DLA 202/274-6115
Education	Establishes policy for federal assistance to education; supports educational research.	*American Education; Computer Literacy; Education Around the World Series*	Information Center 202/245-3192
Office of Educational Research and Improvement	Focuses on educational research, development, demonstration, and assessment. Collects and disseminates statistics pertaining to U.S. and foreign education.	*Digest of Education Statistics; College Costs; Education Directory*	(No separate information center listed)
Energy	Coordinates and administers the government's energy functions; sponsors energy technology research and development; administers energy data collection and analysis programs.	*Contractor Research & Development Reports; Energy & Technology Review*	DOE 202/586-5000

Department or Agency	Functions	Representative Publications	Information Office
Energy Information Administration	Collects, processes, and publishes data in the areas of energy resources and reserves, and energy production, demand, consumption, distribution, and technology.	*Annual Energy Outlook; Annual Energy Review; Energy Conservation Indicators; Energy Data; Financial Statistics of Selected Electric Utilities*	National Energy Information Center 202/252-2363
Health and Human Services	Administers government programs in the areas of health, welfare, and income security; collects, analyzes, and publishes data relating to these programs.	*Grants Administration Manual; Working Papers on Long-Term Care*	Information Center 202/475-0257
Food and Drug Administration	Works to protect against impure and unsafe foods, drugs, cosmetics, and other hazards.	*Evidence and Proof; FDA Consumer; FDA Drug Bulletin; The Quack Attack*	FDA 301/443-2894
National Center for Health Statistics	Collects, analyzes, and disseminates health statistics; promotes and conducts research in health data systems and statistical methodology.	*Charting the Nation's Health; Data on Licensed Pharmacists; Vital and Health Statistics*	NCHS 301/436-8500
Social Security Administration	Administers national program of contributory social welfare; conducts research relating to poverty, financial insecurity, and health care for the aged, blind, and disabled.	*AFDC and Related Income Maintenance Programs; Social Security Bulletin; Social Security Handbook; Your Medicare Handbook*	Office of Public Inquiries 301/594-7700
Housing and Urban Development	Responsible for programs concerned with housing needs and assistance, community development, mortgage lending and rent subsidies, and encouraging private homebuilding.	*Affordable Housing Demonstration Case Studies; Directory of Public Housing Agencies; Housing Inspection Manual; Quality of Life*	Program Information Center, Publication Service Center 202/755-6420
Interior	Responsible for nationally owned public lands and natural resources; protects fish and wildlife; assesses mineral resources and works to assure that their development is in the public interest.	*Doing Business in the American Pacific; Decisions of the Dept. of the Interior; Final Environmental Impact Statement Series; National Aquaculture Development Plan*	(No public information office listed) 202/343-3171

Department or Agency	Functions	Representative Publications	Information Office
Bureau of Mines	A research and fact-finding agency. Helps ensure that the country has adequate supplies of nonfuel minerals.	*Domestic Supply of Critical Materials; Mineral Commodity Profiles; Minerals Yearbook*	Office of Technical Information 202/634-1004
Fish and Wildlife Service	Conserves, protects, and enhances fish and wildlife and their habitats.	*Biological Reports; Coast Ecological Inventory; Endangered Species Technical Bulletin*	Office of Public Affairs 202/343-5634
Geological Survey	Identifies the nation's land, water, energy, and mineral resources; classifies federally owned land for minerals, energy, resources, and water power potential; investigates natural hazards; and conducts the National Mapping Program.	*Earthquake Information Bulletin; Guidelines for Communicating Local Flood Warning and Response Systems; Professional Papers*	Public Affairs Officer 703/648-4460
Office of Surface Mining Reclamation and Enforcement	Assists states in developing a nationwide program that protects the environment from adverse effects of coal mining, while ensuring that such mining can be done without damage to land and water resources.	*National Inventory of Abandoned Mine Land Problems; Technical Services and Research Series*	Office of Public Affairs 202/343-4719
Justice	Enforces law in the public interest, including law relating to drugs, immigration, and naturalization. Promotes effective law enforcement, crime prevention and detection, and prosecution and rehabilitation of offenders.	*Attorneys General of the U.S.; Methods of Proof; Proving Federal Crimes; Prison Gangs*	Office of Public Affairs 202/633-2007
Federal Bureau of Investigation	Investigates all violations of federal law except those assigned to another agency.	*Gambling Technology; Uniform Crime Reports*	Office of Congressional and Public Affairs 202/324-3691
Immigration and Naturalization Service	Responsible for administering laws relating to admission, deportation, exclusion, and naturalization.	*Guide to Immigration Benefits; Statistical Yearbook; U.S. Naturalization Requirements*	Office of Information 202/633-4316 -4330 or -4354

Department or Agency	Functions	Representative Publications	Information Office
Labor	Administers federal labor laws and monitors changes in employment, prices, and other measures of the national economy.	*Employment and Training Report of the President; Quality of Work Life*	Office of Information and Public Affairs 202/523-7316
Bureau of Labor Statistics	Collects, analyzes, processes, and disseminates data relating to employment, wages, and prices.	*Area Wage Surveys; CPI Detailed Report; Employment and Earnings; Handbook of Labor Statistics; Monthly Labor Review*	Office of Publications 202/523-1327
Employment and Training Administration	Fulfills DOL responsibilities relating to employment services, job training, and unemployment insurance.	*Area Trends in Employment and Unemployment; Interviewing Guide for Specific Disabilities*	(No public information office listed)
Employment Standards Administration	Administers and directs employment standards programs dealing with minimum wages, overtime, farm labor, and nondiscriminatory and affirmative action for workers on government contracts and subcontracts.	*Groups with Historically High Incidences of Unemployment; State Workers' Compensation; Vietnam Veterans and Disabled Veterans in Business and Industry*	(No public information office listed)
Labor Management Standards Office	Regulates certain internal union procedures, including the handling of union funds and the election of officers; protects the rights of union members.	*Union Investigations under the LMRDA: Union Officer Elections and Trusteeships*	LMS 202/523-7320
Occupational Safety and Health Administration	Develops and promotes occupational safety and health standards; issues regulations; conducts investigations and inspections to determine compliance with safety and health standards; issues citations and proposes penalties for noncompliance.	*Employer Rights and Responsibilities Following an OSHA Inspection; How to Prepare for Workplace Emergencies; Job Hazard Analysis; Workplace Health Programs*	OSHA 202/523-8017
State	Provides the president with advice in formulating and executing foreign policy.	*Background Notes Series; Department of State Bulletin*	Office of Public Communication 202/647-6575

Department or Agency	Functions	Representative Publications	Information Office
Transportation	Establishes and administers national transportation policies and programs, including those relating to highways, mass transit, railroads, and aviation.	*Alternatives Available to Accelerate Commercial Aircraft Fleet Modernization; How Ride Sharing Can Help Your Company*	Office of the Assistant Secretary for Public Affairs, Public Information 202/366-5580
Federal Aviation Administration	Regulates air commerce; controls the use of navigable air space; promotes, encourages, and develops civil aeronautics.	*Airman's Information Manual; Census of U.S. Civil Aircraft; FAA Statistical Handbook of Aviation*	Office of Public Affairs 202/267-3484
Federal Highway Administration	Operates and administers highway transportation programs relating to highway development and travel, transportation needs, and engineering and safety aspects.	*Highway Statistics; Highway Taxes and Fees; Managing Highway Maintenance*	Office of Management Systems 202/366-0630
Federal Railroad Administration	Promulgates and enforces rail safety regulations; administers financial assistance programs; conducts research and development.	*Rail Passenger Corridors; Railroad Freight Traffic Flows*	Public Affairs Officer 202/366-0881
Maritime Administration	Administers programs to aid in the development, promotion, and operation of the U.S. merchant marine.	*Containerized Cargo Statistics; Domestic Waterborne Trade of the U.S.; Guide to Stowage of Cargo in Marine Containers*	Office of External Affairs 202/366-5807
National Highway Traffic Safety Administration	Carries out programs relating to safety and performance of motor vehicles, their occupants, and pedestrians.	*Federal Motor Vehicle Safety Standards and Regulations; Auto Safety Problems; Profit in Seat Belts*	Office of Public and Consumer Affairs 202/366-9550
Treasury	Formulates and recommends economic, financial, tax, and fiscal policies; serves as financial agent for the U.S. government; and manufactures coins and currency.	*Treasury Bulletin; Monthly Statement of Receipts and Outlays of the U.S. Government*	Public Affairs Office 202/566-2041
Bureau of Alcohol, Tobacco, and Firearms	Enforces and administers firearms and explosives laws, as well as those governing the production, use, and distribution of alcohol and tobacco products.	*Alcohol and Tobacco Statistics; Alcohol, Tobacco, and Firearms Bulletin; Explosives Incidents; Tax Compliance Handbook*	Public Affairs Branch 202/566-7135

Department or Agency	Functions	Representative Publications	Information Office
Internal Revenue Service	Administers and enforces internal revenue laws excluding those relating to alcohol, tobacco, firearms and explosives; determines, assesses, and collects taxes; educates and advises the public.	*Internal Revenue Bulletin; Statistics of Income, Corporation Income Tax Returns; Statistics of Income, Individual Income Tax Returns*	IRS 202/566-5000
United States Customs Service	Assesses and collects customs duties, excise taxes, fees, and penalties due on imported merchandise; seizes contraband; processes persons, carriers, cargo, and mail into and out of the United States.	*Customs Bulletin; Computerized Electronic Import Processing; Role of the Import Specialist*	Public Affairs Office 202/566-8195

Note: Telephone numbers given in appendix B are those published in the 1987/88 issue of the *United States Government Manual*. Verification of all telephone numbers in the most recent edition of the *Manual* is advised before placing any calls to government agencies.

APPENDIX C
Federal Government Corporations and
Independent Agencies Relevant to Business

Organization	Functions	Representative Publications	Information Office
Commodity Futures Trading Commission	Regulates and oversees the trading of commodity futures and options.	*Annual Report; Glossary of Some Terms Commonly Used in the Futures Trading Industry*	Office of Communication & Education Services 202/254-8630
Consumer Product Safety Commission	Protects the public against risk of injury from consumer products; develops uniform safety standards; promotes research and investigation.	*Alert Sheet: Safety Rules for Using Kerosene Heaters; Fact Sheet—Enforcement Policy on Children's Sleepwear; Poison Lookout Checklist*	Office of Information and Public Affairs 301/492-6580
Environmental Protection Agency	Protects and enhances the environment by controlling and abating air, water, solid waste, radiation, and toxic substance pollution.	*Assessment of Hazardous Waste Mismanagement Damage Case Histories; Ecological Research Series; Environmental Health Effects Series*	Office of Public Affairs 202/382-4361
Equal Employment Opportunity Commission	Responsible for compliance and enforcement activities relating to equal employment opportunities among federal employees; promotes voluntary action programs by employers, unions, and community organizations.	*Annual Report on the Employment of Minorities, Women, and Handicapped Individuals in the Federal Government; Job Patterns for Minorities and Women in Private Industry*	Office of Program Operations 202/634-6922
Export-Import Bank of the United States	Facilitates and aids in financing exports of U.S. goods and services.	*Annual Report; Statement of Active Loans and Financial Guarantees*	Public Affairs Officer 202/566-8990

Organization	Functions	Representative Publications	Information Office
Federal Communications Commission	Regulates interstate and foreign communications by radio, television, wire, and cable.	*FCC Rules and Regulations; Purchasing a Broadcast Station; Statistics of Communications, Common Carriers*	Office of Congressional and Public Affairs 202/632-5050
Federal Deposit Insurance Corporation	Promotes and preserves public confidence in banks; protects the money supply through provision of insurance coverage for bank deposits.	*Annual Report; FDIC Bank Operating Statistics; Changes among Operating Banks and Branches*	Corporate Communications Officer 202/898-6996
Federal Home Loan Bank Board	Supervises and regulates savings institutions specializing in the financing of residential real estate.	*Annual Report; Combined Financial Statements, FSLIC-Insured Savings and Loan Associations*	Communications Office 202/377-6677
Federal Maritime Commission	Regulates waterborne foreign and domestic offshore commerce of the United States.	*Annual Report; Approved Conference, Rate, and Interconference Agreements of Steamship Lines...*	Office of the Chairman 202/523-5911
Federal Mediation and Conciliation Service	Provides mediators to help labor and management settle work stoppages and other disputes.	*Annual Report; Arbitration*	Office of Information/ Public Affairs 202/653-5290
Federal Reserve System	Central bank of the United States; responsible for administering and policymaking for U.S. credit and monetary affairs.	*Federal Reserve Bulletin; Federal Reserve Chart Book; Staff Studies*	Office of Public Affairs, Board of Governors 202/452-3204 or -3215
Federal Trade Commission	Promotes the free enterprise system; ensures that it is not hindered by monopoly, restraints on trade, or unfair or deceptive trade practices.	*Court Decisions; Facts for Consumers; Guide to the FTC Funeral Rule; Writing Readable Warranties*	Office of Public Affairs 202/326-2180
General Services Administration	Responsible for providing the government with an economic and efficient system for managing its property and records.	*Consolidated List of Debarred, Suspended, and Ineligible Contractors; Contract Opportunities for Maintenance and Repair of Equipment*	Office of Public Affairs 202/566-0705

Organization	Functions	Representative Publications	Information Office
Interstate Commerce Commission	Regulates interstate surface transportation, including buses, trains, trucks, water carriers, and transportation brokers.	*Coal Rate Guidelines; Railroad ... Monitoring Study; Rules and Regulations*	Office of Government and Public Affairs 202/275-7119
National Aeronautics and Space Administration	Supports, conducts, and promotes peaceful activities in space.	*Announcement of Opportunities for Participation ...; NASA Contractor Reports; Technical Papers; Space Technology Trends and Forecasts*	Headquarters Information Center 202/453-1000
National Credit Union Administration	Charters, insures, supervises, and examines federal credit unions.	*Accounting Manual for Federal Credit Unions; Chartering and Organization of Federal Credit Unions*	Office of Public and Congressional Affairs 202/357-1050
National Labor Relations Board	Administers federal labor law; prevents and remedies unfair labor practices.	*Annual Report; The NLRB: What It Is, What It Does; Decisions and Orders*	Information Division 202/632-4950
National Mediation Board	Resolves air and railway disputes that might disrupt travel or threaten the economy.	*Annual Report*	Executive Director 202/523-5920
National Science Foundation	Promotes science and engineering through the support of research and education programs.	*Federal Funds for Research and Development; Five-Year Outlook on Science and Technology*	Public Affairs Group 202/357-9498
National Transportation Safety Board	Investigates accidents, conducts studies, and makes recommendations on safety measures and practices.	*Annual Review of Aircraft Accident Data; Highway Accident Reports; Special Investigation Reports*	Office of Government and Public Affairs 202/382-6600
Nuclear Regulatory Commission	Licenses and regulates civilian use of nuclear energy.	*Contractor Reports; Information Report on State Legislation; Licensed Operating Reactors*	Office of Governmental and Public Affairs 301/492-7715

Organization	Functions	Representative Publications	Information Office
Occupational Safety and Health Review Commission	Reviews and rules on disputed Occupational Safety and Health Administration (OSHA) decisions.	*Administrative Law Judge and Commission Decisions; Occupational Information System Handbook*	Public Information Specialist 202/634-7943
Securities and Exchange Commission	Provides information to the investing public; protects against securities fraud and malpractice.	*Directory of Companies Filing Annual Reports with the SEC; SEC Docket; SEC Monthly Statistics Review*	Office of Public Affairs 202/272-2650
Small Business Administration	Aids, counsels, assists, and protects the interests of small business.	*Advertising; Directory of State Small Business Issues; Inventory Management*	Office of Public Communications 202/653-6832
United States International Development Cooperation Agency	Policy planning, policymaking, and coordination of international economic issues affecting developing countries.	*Creating Rural Employment; Selected Statistical Data by Sex; Women in Development*	Bureau for External Affairs 202/647-1850
United States International Trade Commission	Furnishes studies, reports, and recommendations involving international trade and tariffs to the president, Congress, and other government agencies.	*Determination of (Likelihood of) Injury Series; U.S. Automotive Trade Statistics; U.S. Import of Textile and Apparel Products*	Secretary 202/523-0161

APPENDIX D
Regional Depository Libraries as of May 1987

FEDERAL DEPOSITORY LIBRARY PROGRAM

The Federal Depository Library Program provides Government publications to designated libraries throughout the United States. The Regional Depository Libraries listed below receive and retain at least one copy of nearly every Federal Government publication, either in printed or microfilm form for use by the general public. These libraries provide reference services and inter-library loans; however, they are *not* sales outlets. You may wish to ask your local library to contact a Regional Depository to help you locate specific publications, or you may contact the Regional Depository yourself.

ARKANSAS STATE LIBRARY
One Capitol Mall
Little Rock, AR 72201
(501) 371-2326
AUBURN UNIV. AT MONTGOMERY LIBRARY
Documents Department
Montgomery, AL 36193
(205) 271-9650
UNIV. OF ALABAMA LIBRARY
Documents Dept.—Box S
University, AL 35486
(205) 348-6046
DEPT. OF LIBRARY, ARCHIVES AND PUBLIC RECORDS
Third Floor—State Capitol
1700 West Washington
Phoenix, AZ 85007
(602) 255-4121
UNIVERSITY OF ARIZONA LIB.
Government Documents Dept.
Tucson, AZ 85721
(602) 621-6433
CALIFORNIA STATE LIBRARY
Govt. Publications Section
P.O. Box 2037
Sacramento, CA 95809
(916) 324-4863
UNIV. OF COLORADO LIB.
Government Pub. Division
Campus Box 184
Boulder, CO 80309
(303) 492-8834
DENVER PUBLIC LIBRARY
Govt. Pub. Department
1357 Broadway
Denver, CO 80203
(303) 571-2131
CONNECTICUT STATE LIBRARY
Government Documents Unit
231 Capitol Avenue
Hartford, CT 06106
(203) 566-7029
UNIV. OF FLORIDA LIBRARIES
Library West
Documents Department
Gainesville, FL 32611
(904) 392-0367
UNIV. OF GEORGIA LIBRARIES
Government Reference Dept.
Athens, GA 30602
(404) 542-8949
UNIV. OF HAWAII LIBRARY
Govt. Documents Collection
2550 The Mall
Honolulu, HI 96822
(808) 948-8230
UNIV. OF IDAHO LIBRARY
Documents Section
Moscow, ID 83843
(208) 885-6344

ILLINOIS STATE LIBRARY
Information Services Branch
Centennial Building
Springfield, IL 62756
(217) 782-5185
INDIANA STATE LIBRARY
Serials Documents Section
140 North Senate Avenue
Indianapolis, IN 46204
(317) 232-3686
UNIV. OF IOWA LIBRARIES
Govt. Documents Department
Iowa City, IA 52242
(319) 353-3318
UNIVERSITY OF KANSAS
Doc. Collect.—Spencer Lib.
Lawrence, KS 66045-2800
(913) 864-4662
UNIV. OF KENTUCKY LIBRARIES
Govt. Pub. Department
Lexington, KY 40506-0039
(606) 257-3139
LOUISIANA STATE UNIVERSITY
Middleton Library
Govt. Docs. Dept.
Baton Rouge, LA 70803
(504) 388-2570
LOUISIANA TECHNICAL UNIV. LIBRARY
Documents Department
Ruston, LA 71272-0046
(318) 257-4962
UNIVERSITY OF MAINE
Raymond H. Fogler Library
Tri-State Regional Documents Depository
Orono, ME 04469
(207) 581-1680
UNIVERSITY OF MARYLAND
McKeldin Lib.—Doc. Div.
College Park, MD 20742
(301) 454-3034
BOSTON PUBLIC LIBRARY
Government Docs. Dept.
Boston, MA 02117
(617) 536-5400 ext. 226
DETROIT PUBLIC LIBRARY
Sociology Department
5201 Woodward Avenue
Detroit, MI 48202-4093
(313) 833-1409
MICHIGAN STATE LIBRARY
P.O. Box 30007
Lansing, MI 48909
(517) 373-1593
UNIVERSITY OF MINNESOTA
Government Pubs. Division
409 Wilson Library
309 19th Avenue South
Minneapolis, MN 55455
(612) 373-7870

UNIV. OF MISSISSIPPI LIB.
Documents Department
University, MS 38677
(601) 232-5857
UNIV. OF MONTANA
Mansfield Library
Documents Division
Missoula, MT 59812
(406) 243-6700
UNIVERSITY OF NEBRASKA-LINCOLN
Love Library
Documents Dept.
Lincoln, NE 68588-0410
(402) 472-2562
UNIVERSITY OF NEVADA LIB.
Govt. Pub. Department
Reno, NV 89557-0044
(702) 784-6579
NEWARK PUBLIC LIBRARY
5 Washington Street
Newark, NJ 07101-0630
(201) 733-7812
UNIVERSITY OF NEW MEXICO
Zimmerman Library
Government Pub. Dept.
Albuquerque, NM 87131
(505) 277-5441
NEW MEXICO STATE LIBRARY
Reference Department
325 Don Gaspar Avenue
Santa Fe, NM 87503
(505) 827-3826
NEW YORK STATE LIBRARY
Empire State Plaza
Albany, NY 12230
(518) 474-5563
UNIVERSITY OF NORTH CAROLINA AT CHAPEL HILL
Davis Library
BA/SS Division
Chapel Hill, NC 27514
(919) 962-1151
UNIVERSITY OF NORTH DAKOTA
Chester Fritz Library
Documents Department
Grand Forks, ND 58202
(701) 777-4629
(In cooperation with North Dakota State Univ. Library)
STATE LIBRARY OF OHIO
Documents Department
65 South Front Street
Columbus, OH 43266-0334
(614) 462-7051

OKLAHOMA DEPT. OF LIBRARIES
Government Documents
200 NE 18th Street
Oklahoma City, OK 73105
(405) 521-2502, ext. 252
OKLAHOMA STATE UNIV. LIB.
Documents Department
Stillwater, OK 74078
(405) 624-6546
PORTLAND STATE UNIV. LIB.
Documents Department
P.O. Box 1151
Portland, OR 97207
(503) 229-3673
STATE LIBRARY OF PENN.
Government Pub. Section
P.O. Box 1601
Harrisburg, PA 17105
(717) 787-3752
TEXAS STATE LIBRARY
Public Services Department
P.O. Box 12927—Cap. Sta.
Austin, TX 78711
(512) 475-2996
TEXAS TECH UNIV. LIBRARY
Govt. Documents Department
Lubbock, TX 79409
(806) 742-2268
UTAH STATE UNIVERSITY
Merrill Library, U.M.C. 30
Logan, UT 84322
(801) 750-2682
UNIVERSITY OF VIRGINIA
Alderman Lib.—Public Doc.
Charlottesville, VA 22903-2498
(804) 924-3133
WASHINGTON STATE LIBRARY
Documents Section
Olympia, WA 98504
(206) 753-4027
WEST VIRGINIA UNIV. LIB.
Documents Department
Morgantown, WV 26506-6069
(304) 293-3640
MILWAUKEE PUBLIC LIBRARY
814 West Wisconsin Avenue
Milwaukee, WI 53233
(414) 278-3065
ST. HIST. LIB. OF WISCONSIN
Government Pub. Section
816 State Street
Madison, WI 53706
(608) 262-4347
WYOMING STATE LIBRARY
Supreme Ct. & Library Bldg.
Cheyenne, WY 82002
(307) 777-5919

PRELIM. 18

APPENDIX E
Representative Types of Business Information
Published by State Government Agencies

Department/Agency*	*Types of Publications*
Agriculture	Crop production and demand; agricultural statistics; market surveys; consumer guides
Commerce/Business	Business and economic statistics; directories; surveys and assessments; economic indicators
Economic Development/Planning	Promotional literature; directories; bibliographies, forecasts and projections
Education	Public and private education statistics; school enrollment; directories; bibliographies
Energy	Energy statistics; alternative energy sources; energy conservation
Insurance	Annual reports; insurance statistics; lists of authorized insurance companies; consumer guides
Labor/Employment	Hour and wage statistics; cost of living; unemployment compensation; occupational safety and health; local labor market information
Taxation/Revenue	Income statistics; sales of certain taxed products; tax guides; statistical reports
Tourism	Guides and brochures; maps; calendars of events
Transportation	Traffic statistics; transit development plans; research studies; traffic safety

*Agency name varies.

APPENDIX F
Periodic Censuses and Programs Authorized by Law

Name of Census	Description	Years Taken
Population and Housing		
Population	Tallies general, social, and economic characteristics of the population.	Every 10 years (for years ending in "0")
Housing	Tallies general and detailed housing characteristics, including such items as value, persons per unit, and plumbing facilities.	Every 10 years (for years ending in "0")
Population and Housing	Combined population and housing data.	Every 10 years (for years ending in "0")
Economic		
Retail Trade	Focuses on establishments engaged in selling merchandise to the general public for personal or household consumption. Includes statistics on the number of establishments, sales, payroll, number of proprietorships and partnerships, employment, and size of establishments by type of retail business (includes SIC Major Groups 52-59).	Every 5 years (for years ending in "2" and "7")
Wholesale Trade	Contains information similar to the *Census of Retail Trade* except for wholesale establishments engaged in selling to retailers, industrial, commercial, and institutional users, or to other wholesalers (includes SIC Major Groups 50-51).	Every 5 years (for years ending in "2" and "7")
Service Industries	Contains information similar to that listed above, except for establishments that provide service to individuals, business, and government establishments, and other organizations (includes SIC Major Groups 70, 72-73, 75-76, 78-79, 80-84, 86, and 89).	Every 5 years (for years ending in "2" and "7")
Construction Industries	Enumerates construction establishments operating as general contractors and builders, special trade contractors, and land subdividers and developers (includes SIC Major Groups 15-17 and SIC 6552).	Every 5 years (for years ending in "2" and "7")

474

Name of Census	Description	Years Taken
Manufactures	Focuses on establishments involved in the mechanical or chemical transformation of materials or substances into new products. Provides information on employment, payroll, inventories, capital expenditures, and selected manufacturing costs (includes SIC Major Groups 20-37).	Every 5 years (for years ending in "2" and "7")
Mineral Industries	Focuses on establishments primarily engaged in mining, including extracting minerals, preparing them on-site as necessary, and exploring and developing mineral properties. Provides employment, payroll, man-hours, costs, capital expenditures, energy consumption, and other data (includes SIC Major Groups 10-14).	Every 5 years (for years ending in "2" and "7")
Transportation	Consists of three separate surveys providing data on truck inventory and use, travel, and intercity commodity shipments (includes SIC Major Groups 42-47).	Every 5 years (for years ending in "2" and "7")
Economic Censuses of Outlying Areas	Economic censuses of retail trade, wholesale trade, selected service industries, construction industries, and manufactures (but not mineral industries or transportation) for Puerto Rico, the Virgin Islands, Guam, and the Northern Marianas.	Every 5 years (for years ending in "2" and "7")
Enterprise Statistics	Regroups economic census data for establishments under common ownership or control to show various economic characteristics of the owning or controlling firm.	Every 5 years (for years ending in "2" and "7")
Minority- and Women-Owned Businesses	Determines extent of business ownership by specific minority groups in the United States.	Every 5 years (for years ending in "2" and "7")
Other Censuses and Programs		
Agriculture	Presents data on such items as number and size of farms, cropland harvested, land irrigated, livestock, labor costs, and selected production expenses.	Every 5 years (for years ending in "2" and "7")
Governments	Covers state and local governmental units, focusing on governmental organization, taxable property values, public employment, and government finance.	Every 5 years (for years ending in "2" and "7")
Foreign Trade	Export and import statistics showing the physical movement of merchandise to and from U.S. trade zones, the U.S. customs territory, and the U.S. Virgin Islands.	Monthly and annual compilations

APPENDIX G
Key Economic Indicators

Indicator	Description	Gov't Agency	Frequency	When Announced in *Wall Street Journal**
Gross National Product (GNP)	GNP is the dollar value of the nation's goods and services produced each year. It is the broadest measure of the economy's performance, and movement in many areas of the economy is closely related to the GNP.	Bureau of Economic Analysis, Commerce Department	Quarterly	Usually published about 3 weeks after the close of the quarter, around the 20th of month
Industrial Production Index	An index measuring changes in the output of the mining, manufacturing, and gas and utilities sector of the economy.	Board of Governors of the Federal Reserve System	Monthly	Usually published midmonth
Leading Indicators	An index that is a composite of 12 different economic statistics that are averaged together and converted into a monthly index. If the index moves in one direction for several months, the economy is predicted to follow a similar pattern.	Bureau of Economic Analysis, Commerce Department	Monthly	Usually published on the first day of the month
Personal Income	Shows before-tax income received in the form of wages, salaries, tips, fringe benefits, interest and dividends, rents, profit, and social security, pension, and unemployment payments. Used as a measure of individuals' purchasing power and to follow trends in consumer buying.	Bureau of Economic Analysis, Commerce Department	Monthly	Published during the 3rd week of the month

*Information on appearance of these indicators in the *Wall Street Journal* is based on data in Michael B. Lehmann's *The Dow Jones-Irwin Guide to Using the Wall Street Journal*. Homewood, Ill.: Dow Jones-Irwin, 1984.

Indicator	Description	Gov't Agency	Frequency	When Announced in *Wall Street Journal*
Retail Sales	An estimate, based on a sample of retail establish-ments, of total retail sales. Often used to follow changes in consumer attitudes toward specific products.	Bureau of the Census and Bureau of Economic Analysis, Commerce Department	Monthly	Published during the 2nd week of the month
Consumer Price Index (CPI)	Shows changes in prices for a fixed market based of consumer goods and services.	Bureau of Labor Statistics, Labor Department	Monthly	Published during the 4th week of the month
Producer Price Index (PPI)	Shows average price changes of goods at various stages of production, from crude materials to finished goods.	Bureau of Labor Statistics, Labor Department	Monthly	Published on the 3rd Monday of the month
Unemploy-ment	Percentage of the work force that is involuntarily out of work.	Bureau of Labor Statistics, Labor Department	Monthly	Published on the 2nd Monday of the month
Housing Starts	Based on building permits issued each month for con-struction of new residential housing units. Increase in the number of housing starts is an indicator of improvement in the state of the economy.	Census Bureau, Commerce Department	Monthly	Published between the 17th and the 20th of the month

APPENDIX H
Ten Key Monthly Federal Periodicals
and the Statistics They Contain

Title	Issuing Agency	Statistics
Business Conditions Digest	Bureau of Economic Analysis, Dept. of Commerce	Contains economic time series, arranged in two broad categories, "Cyclical Indicators" and "Other Economic Measures." Data for each category are presented in tables and in charts. Emphasis is on the cyclical indicators, which include employment and unemployment; production and income; consumption, trade, orders, and deliveries; fixed capital investment; inventories and inventory investment; prices, costs, and profit; and money and credit.
CPI Detailed Report	Bureau of Labor Statistics, Dept. of Labor	Reports CPI price changes (both the CPI-U and the CPI-W). Statistics are presented for the U.S. city average, 28 Standard Metropolitan Statistical Areas, and 4 regions. Products are grouped by broad category, such as food and beverages, housing, and transportation.
Economic Indicators	Prepared for the Joint Economic Committee by the Council of Economic Advisers	Presents current information on such economic indicators as total output; income and spending; employment, unemployment and wages; production and business activity; prices; and money, credit, and security markets.
Employment and Earnings	Bureau of Labor Statistics, Dept. of Labor	Presents current statistics on domestic employment, unemployment, hours, and earnings.
Federal Reserve Bulletin	Board of Governors of the Federal Reserve System	Current domestic business and financial statistics include money stock and bank credit; policy instruments; monetary and credit aggregates; commercial banking institutions; financial markets; federal finance; securities markets and corporate finance; real estate; consumer installment credit; and flow of funds. International financial statistics include securities holdings and transactions; interest and exchange rates; and international statistics reported by banks and nonbanking business enterprises in the United States.

478

Title	Issuing Agency	Statistics
Monthly Energy Review	Energy Information Administration, Dept. of Energy	Includes statistics on energy consumption; petroleum; natural gas; oil and gas resource development; coal; electric utilities; nuclear energy; fuel prices; and international nuclear electricity generation and petroleum production and consumption.
Monthly Labor Review	Bureau of Labor Statistics, Dept. of Labor	Statistics on the labor force; labor compensation and collective bargaining; prices; productivity; and injury and illness.
Producer Price Indexes	Bureau of Labor Statistics, Dept. of Labor	Includes indexes for specific industrial commodities and/or by stage of processing.
Social Security Bulletin	Social Security Administration, Dept. of Health and Human Services	Includes tables on income maintenance programs; Social Security trust funds, OASDI cash benefits; supplemental security income; public assistance; black lung benefits; unemployment insurance; and economic indicators.
Survey of Current Business	Bureau of Economic Analysis, Dept. of Commerce	Presents monthly data for general business indicators; commodity prices; construction and real estate; domestic trade; labor force, employment, and earnings; finance; foreign trade; and specific industries.

APPENDIX I
Free Vertical File Materials for Business Collections

Vertical file materials are ephemeral. Although the following titles were available at the time that the manuscript for this book was being prepared, it is likely that some may no longer be in print. This list is intended as much to identify organizations that typically issue free materials as it is to pinpoint specific titles.

Air Transport Association of America
1709 New York Avenue, N.W.
Washington, DC 20006

   Air Transport

All-Industry Research Advisory Council
1200 Harger Road, Suite 222
Oak Brook, IL 60521

   Catastrophic Losses

   Evaluation of Motor Vehicle Records as a Source of Information on Driver Accidents and Convictions

   Patterns of Shopping Behavior in Auto Insurance

   Pollution Liability Claims Administration

   Pollution Liability; the Evolution of a Difficult Insurance Market

   Risk Assessment for Pollution Liability

   A Survey of Public Attitudes toward Trends in Personal Injury Lawsuits, the Civil Justice System, Drunk Driving and Other Topics

   Surveys on Investigative Units: Surveys on Insurance Company Use of SIUs for Fraud Investigations

   Surveys on Liability Insurance for Government Entities

   Uninsured Motorist Facts & Figures

American Bus Association
1025 Connecticut Avenue, N.W.
Washington, DC 20036

   Annual Report

American Council of Life Insurance
1001 Pennsylvania Avenue
Washington, DC 20004-2502

A Consumer's Guide to Life Insurance

Investment Bulletin

A List of Worthwhile Life and Health Insurance Books

Mortgage Commitments on Multifamily and Nonresidential Properties Reported by 20 Life Insurance Companies

Resources for the Education Community

American Institute of Certified Public Accountants
1211 Avenue of the Americas
New York, NY 10036-8775

Academic Preparation for Professional Accounting Careers (No. 876744)

Accounting Education—A Statistical Survey (No. G00020)

Accounting: It Figures in Your Future (No. 870091)

Careers in Accounting (No. 870104)

Choosing the CPA That's Right for You

Education Requirements for Entry into the Accounting Profession

Implementation of the Postbaccalaureate Education Requirement (No. 870265)

Information for CPA Candidates

A Postbaccalaureate Education Requirement for the CPA Profession (No. 870250)

Supply of Accounting Graduates and Demand for Recruits (No. G00091)

What Does a CPA Do?

Why Graduate School for Professional Careers in Accounting (No. 872364)

American Stock Exchange
Publications Department
86 Trinity Place
New York, NY 10006

Gold Options

Interest Rate Options Study Guide

Options on the Airline Index

Options on the Computer Technology Index

Options on the Major Market Index

Options on the Oil Index

Armstrong World Industries, Inc.
Public Relations and Public Affairs Department
Armstrong World Industries, Inc.
P.O. Box 3001
Lancaster, PA 17604

Special Edition Annual Report

Arthur Andersen & Co.
69 W. Washington Street
Chicago, IL 60602

Accounting News Briefs

Banking News Briefs

International Trends in Retailing

Tax Economics of Charitable Giving

Tax Shelters—the Basics

Yearend Tax Strategy for Individuals

Association of Publicly Traded Investment Funds
70 Niagara Street
Buffalo, NY 14202

Closed-End Fund List, Association of Publicly Traded Investment Funds

Publicly Traded Investment Funds; Membership Directory

Bankers Life Company
711 High Street
Des Moines, IA 50307

How to Choose a Life Insurance Plan ... Best for You

Barclays Bank
Group Economics Department
54 Lombard Street
London EC3P 3AH England

Barclays Commodities Survey

Brunswick Corporation
Bowling Division
1 Brunswick Plaza
Skokie, IL 60077

Are You Running Your Business ... Or, Is It Running You?

The Name of the Game Is: How to Make Money

Your Bowling Business; What It Is (and Can Be) Worth

Bureau of National Affairs
1231 25th Street, N.W.
Washington, DC 20037

Reporter Services and Their Use (single copies only)

Chicago Board of Trade
Education and Marketing Services
LaSalle at Jackson
Chicago, IL 60604

Action in the Marketplace (EM42-2)

Agricultural Options: A Home Study Course (EM272)

Agricultural Options: A New Dimension in Risk Management for Farmers (EM234)

CBOT Interest Rate Futures Review (monthly)

CBOT Long-Term Treasury Note Options (EM276)

CBOT 1000-oz. Silver Futures and Options on Futures (EM51-1)

CBOT Options on Agricultural Futures (EM261)

CBOT Options on U.S. Treasury Bond Futures (EM262)

CBOT Stock Index Update (monthly)

CBOT 10-Year U.S. Treasury Note Futures (EM235)

Chicago Board of Trade Conversion Factors (EM253)

Corn Futures (EM222)

The Delivery Process in Brief: Treasury Bond and Treasury Note Futures (EM32-1)

Do's and Don'ts of Commodities Futures Trading (EM249)

Interest Rate Futures for Institutional Investors (EM286)

An Introduction to Agricultural Hedging: A Home Study Course (EM12-1)

Introduction to Financial Futures (EM32-2)

An Introduction to Options on Treasury Bond Futures (EM24)

Long-Term U.S. Treasury Bond Price/Yield Calculator (EM32-5)

Major Market Index Futures (EM260)

Margins for Options on Treasury Bond and Treasury Note Futures (EM273)

MMI: A Series of Trading Strategies (EM31-1)

Municipal Bond Index Futures (EM31-2)

Municipal Bond Index Futures Overview (EM32-3)

Oats Futures (EM230)

One Kilo Gold Futures (EM51-2)

Options on Agricultural Futures (EM280)

Options on Corn Futures (EM271)

Options on Soybean Futures (EM270)

Options on Treasury Note Futures Trading Strategies Report (EM292)

Options on U.S. Treasury Bond Futures for Institutional Investors (EM244)

Soybean Futures (EM224)

Speculating in Futures (EM20)

Stock Index Futures: A Home Study Course (EM62-1)

Strategies for Buying and Writing Options on Treasury Bond Futures (EM266)

Trading in Corn Futures (EM22)

Trading in Metals (EM54)

Trading in Soybean Complex Futures (EM26)

Two New Options for You (EM11-1)

Understanding Basis—The Economics of Where and When (EM12-4)

Wheat Futures (EM223)

Wheat Options Trading Manual (EM12-3)

Chicago Board Options Exchange
Marketing Services Department
LaSalle at Jackson, Room 2200
Chicago, IL 60604

Market Statistics

Understanding Options

Understanding the Risks and Uses of Listed Options

Chicago Mercantile Exchange
30 S. Wacker Drive
Chicago, IL 60606

CME Sources

CME Trader's Scorecard

Futures Trading in Frozen Pork Bellies

Futures Trading in Live Cattle: Contract Specifications

How to Make Livestock Futures Work for You

Trading in Tomorrows: Your Guide to Futures

Using Interest Rate Futures and Options

Using S&P 500 Index Futures and Options

Cleveland Trust Company
P.O. Box 5937
Cleveland, OH 44101

Cleveland Trust Business Bulletin (monthly)

Coffee, Sugar, & Cocoa Exchange
Four World Trade Center
New York, NY 10048

CPI-W Futures Contract: Questions and Answers

Inflation: Volatile, Unpredictable, Costly, but Now Manageable

Options on Cocoa Futures

Options on Coffee Futures

Trading in Coffee Futures

Trading in Sugar Futures

Coldwell Banker
533 Fremont Avenue
Los Angeles, CA 90071

Office Vacancy Index of the United States

Commerce Clearing House
4025 W. Peterson Avenue
Chicago, IL 60646

Finding the Answers to Federal Tax Questions

Today's Business and Tax Law

Congressional Information Service, Inc.
4520 East-West Highway, Suite 800
Bethesda, MD 20814

ASI Search Guide

IIS Search Guide

SRI Search Guide

Corn Refiners Association, Inc.
1001 Connecticut Avenue, N.W.
Washington, DC 20036

Corn Annual

Deloitte Haskins & Sells
1114 Avenue of the Americas
New York, NY 10036

Exporting: Small and Growing Businesses

Financing: Small and Growing Businesses

Forming R & D Partnerships

Raising Venture Capital

Strategies for Going Public

Dow Jones Educational Service Bureau
(Has 5 regional bureaus, listed below)

Eastern
P.O. Box 300
Princeton, NJ 08540

Southern
3525 Piedmont Road, NE, Suite 309
Six Piedmont Center
Atlanta, GA 30305

Midwestern
One South Wacker Drive
Chicago, IL 60606

Western
1701 Page Mill Road
Palo Alto, CA 94304

Pacific
201 California Street, 6th Floor
San Francisco, CA 94111

The ABC's of Market Forecasting: How to Use Barron's Laboratory Report

The ABC's of Options Trading

Barron's Educational Edition

The Dow Jones Averages

How to Read Stock Market Quotations

Materials Available to Educators

Understanding Financial Data in the Wall Street Journal

Wall Street Journal Educational Edition

Dun & Bradstreet
99 Church Street
New York, NY 10007

Business Failure Record

Cost of Doing Business: Corporations

Cost of Doing Business: Partnerships and Proprietorships

The Pitfalls in Managing a Small Business

Eli Lilly and Company
Pharmaceutical Division
General Office and Principal Laboratories
Indianapolis, IN 46285

Lilly Digest

Lilly Pharmacy Supply

FIND/SVP
625 Avenue of the Americas
New York, NY 10011

The Information Catalog

First Hawaiian Bank
Research Department
P.O. Box 3200
Honolulu, HI 96847

Economic Indicators, Hawaii

Neighbor Island Profiles

First National Bank of Chicago
Group D
One First National Plaza, Suite 0084
Chicago, IL 60670

Consumer Finance (Direct Cash Lending) Company Ratios

Diversified Finance Company Ratios

Health Insurance Association of America
1850 K Street, N.W.
Washington, DC 20006-2284

New Group Disability Insurance

New Group Health Insurance

Source Book of Health Insurance

Update

Insurance Information Institute
110 William Street
New York, NY 10038

Books in Insurance

Clean away Those Fire Hazards

Don't Give Invitations to Car Thieves

Family Escape Plan

A Guide to the Services of the Insurance Information Institute

How Much Is Your Home Really Worth?

Insurance Facts

Inventory: The Other Step

On Car Insurance Premiums

Six Steps to Auto Safety

Smoke Detectors for the Extra Minutes You Need

Those Rising Auto Insurance Costs

Your Homeowners Deductible: A Source of Saving

Kansas City Board of Trade
Marketing Department
4800 Main Street, Suite 303
Kansas City, MO 64112

Annual Statistical Report

KCBT Report

Laventhol & Horwath
Executive Offices
1845 Walnut Street
Philadelphia, PA 19103

U.S. Lodging Industry

Worldwide Lodging Industry

Life Insurance Marketing and Research Association, Inc.
P.O. Box 208
Hartford, CT 06141

The Baby Boomers: A Market in the Making

The Retirement Markets: Overview and Outlook

Variable Universal Life: To Market or Not

Life Office Management Association
5770 Powers Ferry Road
Atlanta, GA 30327

Price List

Manufacturers Hanover Trust Co.
Economics Department, Financial Digest
270 Park Avenue
17th Floor
New York, NY 10017

Financial Digest

Merrill Lynch, Pierce, Fenner, & Smith, Inc.
One Liberty Plaza
165 Broadway
New York, NY 10080

How to Read a Financial Report

National Association of Securities Dealers, Inc.
1735 K Street, N.W.
Washington, DC 20006

The NASDAQ Fact Book

National Automatic Merchandising Association
20 N. Wacker Drive, Suite 3500
Chicago, IL 60606

Cost and Profit Ratios for Vending Operators: Summary

Prentice-Hall Information Services
240 Frisch Court
Paramus, NJ 07652

Research in Federal Taxation

Price Waterhouse & Co.
1251 Avenue of the Americas
New York, NY 10020

Accounting for Sales of Real Estate

The Accounting Interview

The Audit Committee, the Board of Directors, and the Independent Accountant

Basic Accounting Library

Building a Better World of Financial Reporting

Coping with Bank Regulation: A Guide to Compliance

Cost Accounting for Real Estate

Cost Accounting Standards: A Guide to the Pronouncements of the Cost Accounting Standards Board and Their Implementation

Developing a Competitive Edge in Professional Accounting

Does Your Internal Audit Department Measure Up?

Electronic Banking — Where It Is Now ... Where It Is Going ... A Survey

Enhancing Government Accountability

The 15 Key Steps to Reducing Inventory Shrinkage

Foreign Exchange Information

Microcomputers: Their Use and Misuse in Your Business

No Big Brother Wanted Here: The Mood of High Tech Companies in the 1980s

Personal Tax Strategy

Price Waterhouse—A Tradition and a Future

Price Waterhouse in Print

A Program for the Support of Accounting Education

Questions Which May Be Asked at Shareholders Meetings

The "Real" Profits of Business—Big and Small

Recommended Supplementary List (to *Basic Accounting Library)*

Tax Calendar

Tax Incentives for Exporters

Tax Releases

U.S. Citizens Abroad

The World's Major Stock Exchanges

Security Pacific National Bank
Economics Department
H8-13
P.O. Box 2097
Terminal Annex
Los Angeles, CA 90051

Economic Report: California Economic Outlook and U.S. Economic Update

Society of Industrial Realtors
777 14th Street, N.W., Suite 400
Washington, DC 20005-3271

The Executive Guide to Specialists in Industrial and Office Real Estate

Tax Foundation
One Thomas Circle, N.W., Suite 500
Washington, DC 20005

Tax Features

U.S. Commodity Futures Trading Commission
2033 K Street, N.W.
Washington, DC 20581

Basic Facts about Commodity Futures Trading

CFTC Publications (CFTC Futures Fact Sheet No. 2)

U.S. Consumer Information Center
Consumer Information Center-C
P.O. Box 100
Pueblo, CO 81002

Before You Say Yes: Fifteen Questions to Ask About Investments (570R)

A Brief Explanation of Medicare (511R)

Choosing a Credit Card (587R)

A Consumer's Guide to Life Insurance (592R)

Consumer's Resource Handbook (560R)

The Federal Oil and Gas Lottery (575R)

Guide to Health Insurance for People with Medicare

How to Choose and Use a Lawyer (586R)

Mail Order Rights (577R)

Sales of Federal Surplus Real Estate (567R)

Trade, Trade-Offs, and Consumers (605R)

What You Should Know about Medicare (511R)

A Woman's Guide to Social Security (512R)

Your Social Security (513R)

Note that any order of more than one item requires the inclusion of $1 for handling.

U.S. Department of Commerce. Bureau of the Census
User Training Branch
Data User Services Division
Washington, DC 20233

Construction Statistics Data Finder

Monthly Product Announcements

Telephone Contacts for Data Users

U.S. Department of Commerce. National Technical Information Service
NTIS
5285 Port Royal Road
Springfield, VA 22161

Data Files Directory (PR629/154)

Data Files List (PR700/154)

Directory of Computer Software (PR261/154)

Diskette Titles List (PR771-1/154)

General Information Catalog (PR154/154)

NTIS Bibliographic Database Guide (PR253/154)

Published Search Catalog (PR186/154)

U.S. Department of Commerce. Office of Business Liaison
Room 5898-C
Washington, DC 20230

Business Service Directory

Lost? Need Directions? Roadmap Leads Business to the Answers in the Federal Government Maze

U.S. Department of Defense
Directors of Small and Disadvantaged Business Utilization
Office of the Secretary of Defense
Room 2A330, Pentagon
Washington, DC 20301-3061

Selling to Air Force Prime Contractors

Subcontracting Directory

U.S. Federal Home Loan Bank of Atlanta
Coastal States Building
260 Peachtree Street, N.W.
Atlanta, GA 30303

Data Digest

Financial Characteristics of Member Savings Institutions

Quarterly Statistics

Review

U.S. Federal Home Loan Bank of Boston
One Federal Street, 30th Floor
Boston, MA 02106

First District Facts

New England Thrift Industry

U.S. Federal Home Loan Bank of Cincinnati
2000 Atrium Two
Cincinnati, OH 45202

Economic Trends and Cycles

Highlights

U.S. Federal Home Loan Bank of Chicago
111 E. Wacker Drive, Suite 800
Chicago, IL 60601-4360

Home Mortgage Commitment Rates in Illinois

Home Mortgage Commitment Rates in Wisconsin

Housing Vacancy Survey

Index Report

U.S. Federal Home Loan Bank of Dallas
500 E. John Carpenter Freeway
Irving, TX 75062

District Data Highlights

Quarterly Trends

U.S. Federal Home Loan Bank of Indianapolis
1350 Merchants Plaza, South Tower
115 E. Washington Street
Indianapolis, IN 46204

Financial Information Report

U.S. Federal Home Loan Bank of New York
One World Trade Center, Floor 103
New York, NY 10048

Member Activity Report

U.S. Federal Home Loan Bank of San Francisco
600 California Street
San Francisco, CA 94108

Evaluation and Outlook for Manufactured Housing

Model for Pricing Adjustable-Rate Mortgages

Perspectives

Quarterly Report

U.S. Federal Home Loan Bank of Seattle
600 Stewart Street
Seattle, WA 98101

Twelfth District Summary

U.S. Federal Home Loan Bank of Topeka
No. 3 Townsite Plaza, 120 E. 6th Street
Topeka, KS 66603

Economic Indicators

Monthly Financial Data

U.S. Federal Reserve Bank of Atlanta
Research Department, Publications Unit
104 Marietta Street
Atlanta, GA 30303-2713

Economic Review (Monthly)

Federal Reserve Operations

Federal Reserve Structure

Fundamental Facts about United States Money

Southeastern Economic Insight (Monthly)

U.S. Federal Reserve Bank of Boston
Bank and Public Services Department
600 Atlantic Avenue
Boston, MA 02106

Consumer Education Catalog

The Depository Institutions Deregulation and Monetary Control Act of 1980

Dollar Points

Electronic Funds Transfer

Fed Points

Federal Funds Market

The Federal Reserve in Electronic Payments

Float on the Checkstream

Historical Beginnings ... the Federal Reserve

New England Economic Indicators (Monthly)

New England Economic Review (Bimonthly)

Putting It Simply

Reserve Position: Methods of Adjustment

U.S. Federal Reserve Bank of Chicago
Public Information Center
230 South LaSalle Street
Chicago, IL 60690

The ABC's of Figuring Interest

Agricultural Letter (Biweekly)

Credit Guide

Economic Perspectives (Bimonthly)

A Guide to Banking Markets

Leveling the Playing Field

Midwest Update

Modern Money Mechanics

On Reserve (3 per year)

Seventh District Economic Data (Annual)

Two Faces of Debt

U.S. Federal Reserve Bank of Cleveland
Public Information Center
P.O. Box 6387
Cleveland, OH 44101

Economic Commentary

Economic Review (Quarterly)

Economic Trends (Monthly)

Employment and Unemployment

Effects of Unions (Working Paper 8601)

Financial Institutions in Transition

Forecasting and Seasonal Adjustment (Working Paper 8507)

Forum (Quarterly)

Fragments of Transition

Origins of Commercial Banking in the Fourth Federal Reserve District

Your Federal Reserve Bank

U.S. Federal Reserve Bank of Dallas
Public Affairs Department
Station K
Dallas, TX 75222

Agricultural Highlights (Quarterly)

District Highlights (Quarterly)

Economic Review (Bimonthly)

Energy Highlights (Quarterly)

Quarterly Survey of Agricultural Credit Conditions

Roundup (Monthly)

Selected Interest Rates

Through the Discount Window of the Federal Reserve

United States Treasury Securities

U.S. Federal Reserve Bank of Kansas City
Public Affairs Department
925 Grand Avenue
Kansas City, MO 64198

Banking Regulation: Its Purposes, Implementation, and Effects

Banking Studies (Annual)

Competing in the World Marketplace: The Challenge for American Agriculture

Economic Review (Monthly)

Fed Letter (Bimonthly)

Financial Letter (Monthly)

Financing Modern Agriculture: Banking's Problems and Challenges

Price Stability and Public Policy

Tenth District Depository Institutions and Large Commercial Bank Statistics

U.S. Dollar: Recent Developments, Outlook, and Policy Options

U.S. Federal Reserve Bank of Minneapolis
Office of Public Information
250 Marquette Avenue
Minneapolis, MN 55480

Agricultural Credit Conditions (Quarterly)

Are Banks Special?

District Economic Conditions (Quarterly)

Employment and Unemployment

Meeting the Challenges of a New Banking Era

Money, Banking and the Federal Reserve System

A New Law, a New Era

Quarterly Review (Quarterly)

The Transition to Low Inflation: Progress and Pressures

Your Credit Rights

U.S. Federal Reserve Bank of New York
Public Information Department
33 Liberty Street
New York, NY 10045

ACHs (Fedpoints 31) (Automated Clearinghouses)

The Arithmetic of Interest Rates

Bankers' Acceptances (Fedpoints 12)

Basic Information on Treasury Bills

Basic Information on Treasury Notes and Bonds

Book-Entry Procedure (Fedpoints 5)

Coins and Currency

Commercial Paper (Fedpoints 29)

Consumer Credit Terminology Handbook

Currency Processing and Destruction (Fedpoints 11)

A Day at the Fed

Debts and Deficits

Depository Institutions and Their Regulators

Discount Borrowing Surcharges (Fedpoints 33)

Discount Rates (Fedpoints 30)

The Discount Window (Fedpoints 18)

Estimating Return on Treasury Issues (Fedpoints 28)

Federal Reserve System Public Information Materials

Financial Institution Regulators (Fedpoints 9)

Float (Fedpoints 8)

How Currency Gets Into Circulation (Fedpoints 1)

How the Federal Reserve Is Audited (Fedpoints 35)

How to Read U.S. Government Securities Quotes (Fedpoints 7)

Keeping Our Money Healthy

Key to the Gold Vault

The New York Fed (Fedpoints 13)

Open Market Operations

Presenting ... "The Fed"

A Primer on Inflation

Quarterly Review (Quarterly)

Reading and Viewing; Public Information Materials from the Federal Reserve Bank of New York

Regional Check Centers (Fedpoints 3)

The Role of Reserve Bank Directors (Fedpoints 10)

Seasonal Borrowing (Fedpoints 16)

Special Treasury Borrowing from the Fed (Fedpoints 23)

Statfacts: Understanding Federal Reserve Statistical Reports

The Story of Banks and Thrifts

The Story of Checks and Electronic Payments

The Story of Consumer Credit

The Story of Money

Strategic Groups and the Profitability of Banking (Research Paper 8507)

System Open Market Account (Fedpoints 27)

Techniques of Open Market Operations (Fedpoints 32)

Treasury Auctions (Fedpoints 41)

Treasury Tax and Loan Program (Fedpoints 21)

What's All This about the M's?

U.S. Federal Reserve Bank of Philadelphia
Public Information Department
P.O. Box 66
Philadelphia, PA 19105

A Banker's Day

Banking Legislation and Policy (5 per year)

Business Outlook Survey (Monthly)

Business Review (Bimonthly)

Charting Mortgages

The Fed in Print (Semiannual)

How the New Equal Credit Opportunity Act Affects You

How to Establish and Use Credit

IRA & Keogh—New Opportunities for Retirement Income

The Men Who Made the Fed

Money Matters (6 per year)

Options for Savers

Plastic Money

Quarterly Regional Economic Report

Regional Economic Highlights (Monthly)

The Rule of 78s

Your Credit Rating

U.S. Federal Reserve Bank of Richmond
Bank and Public Relations Department
P.O. Box 27622
Richmond, VA 23261

Black Banks

Borrowers, Lenders, and Interest Rates

Business Forecasts (Annual)

Consolidated Reports of Condition and Income

Cross Sections: A Review of Business and Economic Developments (Quarterly)

Economic Review (Bimonthly)

Essays on Inflation

Farm Credit Conditions in the Fifth District

Instruments of the Money Market

Keys for Business Forecasting

The Relevance of Adam Smith

Where Banks Get Their Money

U.S. Federal Reserve Bank of St. Louis
Bank Relations and Public Information Department
P.O. Box 442
St. Louis, MO 63166

Agriculture: An Eighth District Perspective (Quarterly)

Annual U.S. Economic Data

Banking and Finance: An Eighth District Perspective (Quarterly)

Business: An Eighth District Perspective (Quarterly)

Economic Activity and Markets

International Economic Conditions (Annual)

Monetary Trends (Monthly)

National Economic Trends (Monthly)

Review (10 per year)

Role of Government in U.S. Economy ... Fiscal Policy

U.S. Financial Data (Weekly)

Who We Are and What We Do

U.S. Federal Reserve Bank of San Francisco
Public Information Department
P.O. Box 7702
San Francisco, CA 94120

Economic Review (Quarterly)

The Federal Reserve System in Brief

Money in the Economy

Weekly Letter

U.S. Federal Reserve System, Board of Governors
Publications Services
Mail Stop 138
Washington, DC 20551

The Board of Governors of the Federal Reserve System

Capacity Utilization: Manufacturing and Materials (Monthly)

Concordance of Statistics Available in Federal Reserve Publications

Consolidated Condition Report of Large Commercial Banks and Domestic Subsidiaries (Weekly)

Consumer Handbook on Adjustable Rate Mortgages

Consumer Handbook to Consumer Protection Laws

Consumer Installment Credit (Monthly)

Fair Credit Billing

The Federal Open Market Committee

Federal Reserve Bank Board of Directors

Federal Reserve Banks

Federal Reserve Glossary

The Federal Reserve System: Purposes and Functions

A Guide to Business Credit and the Equal Credit Opportunity Act

Guide to Federal Reserve Regulations

How to File a Consumer Credit Complaint

If You Borrow to Buy Stock

If You Use a Credit Card

U.S. Currency

Welcome to the Federal Reserve

What Truth in Lending Means to You

U.S. Federal Trade Commission
6th and Pennsylvania Avenue, N.W.
Washington, DC 20580

Best Sellers for Business

Facts for Consumers

FTC 'Best Sellers'

What's Going On at the FTC?

U.S. General Accounting Office
Documents Handling & Information Services Facility
P.O. Box 6015
Gaithersburg, MD 20877

Auto Insurance: State Regulation Affects Costs and Availability (GAO/OCE-86-2)

A Glossary of Terms Used in the Federal Budget Process and Related Accounting, Economic, and Tax Terms

Managers, Your Accounting System Can Do a Lot for You; Accountants, You Can Do a Lot for Your Managers (09110)

Publications Issued....

United States General Accounting Office: Answers to Frequently Asked Questions (091614)

U.S. Superintendent of Documents
Government Printing Office
Washington, DC 20402

Accounting and Auditing (Subj. Bibl. 42)

Agricultural Research, Statistics, and Economic Reports (Subj. Bibl. 162)

Banks and Banking (Subj. Bibl. 128)

Business and Business Management (Subj. Bibl. 4)

Employment and Occupations (Subj. Bibl. 44)

Energy Management for Consumers and Business (Subj. Bibl. 303)

Foreign Investments (Subj. Bibl. 275)

Foreign Trade and Tariff (Subj. Bibl. 123)

Government Regulations and Standards (Subj. Bibl. 231)

How to Sell to Government Agencies (Subj. Bibl. 171)

Labor-Management Relations (Subj. Bibl. 64)

Marketing Research (Subj. Bibl. 125)

New Books

Occupational Safety and Health (Subj. Bibl. 213)

Patents and Trademarks (Subj. Bibl. 21)

Prices, Wages, and the Cost of Living (Subj. Bibl. 226)

Shipping and Transportation (Subj. Bibl. 40)

Small Business (Subj. Bibl. 307)

Statistical Publications (Subj. Bibl. 273)

Subject Bibliography Index

Taxes and Taxation (Subj. Bibl. 195)

U.S. Government Books

United States Telephone Association
1801 K Street, N.W.
Washington, DC 20006

Phonefacts

United Van Lines
One United Drive
Fenton, MO 63026

United Van Lines Migration Study

APPENDIX J
Commodities Exchanges

Chicago Board of Trade (CBT)
141 W. Jackson Blvd.
Chicago, IL 60604

Corn, GNMA certificates, GNMA-CDR's, Gold, Major Market Index-Maxi, Municipal Bond Index, NASDAQ-100 Index, Oats, Silver, Soybean Meal, Soybean Oil, Soybeans, U.S. Treasury Bonds, U.S. Treasury Notes.

Chicago Mercantile Exchange (CME)
30 S. Wacker Drive
Chicago, IL 60606

Feeder Cattle, Fresh Eggs, Live Cattle, Live Hogs, Pork Bellies; offered through *International Monetary Market Division*: British Pound, Canadian Dollar, Deutsche Mark, Domestic Certificates of Deposit, Eurodollar Time Deposit, Japanese Yen, Mexican Peso, Swiss Franc, Treasury Bills. Offered through *Index and Option Market Division*: Lumber, Standard & Poor's 500 Stock Index, Standard & Poor's 100 Index, Standard & Poor's Over-the-Counter Index.

Chicago Rice and Cotton Exchange (CRCE)
444 W. Jackson Blvd.
Chicago, IL 60606

Cotton, Rough Rice.

Coffee, Sugar & Cocoa Exchange (CSCE)
4 World Trade Center
New York, NY 10048

Cocoa, Coffee "C", Consumer Price Index (CPI-W), Sugar No. 11, Sugar No. 14.

Commodity Exchange, Inc. (COMEX)
4 World Trade Center
New York, NY 10048

Aluminum, Copper, Gold, Silver.

Kansas City Board of Trade (KCBT)
4800 Main Street, Suite 303
Kansas City, MO 64112

Mini Value Line Stock Index, Value Line Stock Index, Wheat.

MidAmerica Commodity Exchange (MACE)
444 W. Jackson Blvd.
Chicago, IL 60606

British Pound, Canadian Dollar, Copper, Corn, Deutsche Mark, Japanese Yen, Live Cattle, Live Hogs, New York Gold, New York Silver, Oats, Platinum, Soybean Meal, Soybeans, Swiss Franc, U.S. Treasury Bills, U.S. Treasury Bonds, Wheat.

Minneapolis Grain Exchange (MGE)
400 S. Fourth Street
Minneapolis, MN 55415

Wheat.

500

New York Cotton Exchange (NYCE)
4 World Trade Center
New York, NY 10048

Cotton, European Currency Unit, Five-Year U.S. Treasury Index, Orange Juice, Propane Gas, U.S. Dollar Index.

New York Futures Exchange (NYFE)
20 Broad Street
New York, NY 10005

CRB Futures Price Index, NYSE Beta Index, NYSE Composite Stock Index.

New York Mercantile Exchange (NYME)
4 World Trade Center
New York, NY 10048

Crude Oil, Heating Oil, Palladium, Platinum, Potatoes, Unleaded Gasoline.

Philadelphia Board of Trade
1900 Market Street
Philadelphia, PA 19103

British Pound, Canadian Dollar, Deutsche Mark, European Currency Unit, French Franc, Japanese Yen, National Over-the-Counter Index, Swiss Franc.

APPENDIX K
Census Bureau *Construction Reports*

Title	Series No.	Description
Housing Starts	C20	Monthly. Presents data on new single and multifamily housing units started under private and public ownership. Includes type of structure and purpose of construction, backlog of unused permits, manufacturers' shipments of mobile homes to dealers and placements for residential use, annual data seasonally adjusted by month, and selected characteristics of apartment buildings. Covers the United States, census regions, and selected SMSAs (inside and outside SMSAs).
New Residential Construction in Selected Standard Metropolitan Statistical Areas	C21	Quarterly. Contains statistics on new housing authorized; authorized but not started; started, under construction; and completed. Covers 20 SMSAs.
Housing Completions	C22	Monthly. Provides information on the number of housing units completed each month, by type of structure; the number completed in permit-issuing places; and privately owned units under construction. Covers the U.S., census regions, and selected SMSAs (inside and outside SMSAs).
New One-Family Houses Sold and for Sale	C25	Monthly. Contains U.S. totals for new privately owned one-family houses sold during the reporting month and for sale at the end of the month. Data include the ratio of houses for sale to those sold; the number sold and for sale, by stage of construction; and median and average sales prices. Quarterly supplements provide additional information on type of financing, by region.
Characteristics of New Housing	C25	Annual. Contains detailed information on selected physical and financial characteristics of new one-family houses completed or sold, including square footage area, number of bedrooms and bathrooms, type of fuel used, heating facilities, prices, and downpayment. Selected characteristics of multifamily buildings are also included. Covers the U.S., census regions, and SMSAs.
Price Index of New One-Family Houses Sold	C27	Quarterly. Provides a measure of changes over time in the national sales prices of new one-family houses (including land).

Title	Series No.	Description
Value of New Construction Put in Place	C30	Monthly. Presents information on the total value of new private and public construction put in place, including value for residential and nonresidential buildings, public utilities, non-building construction, and residential additions and alterations.
Housing Authorized by Building Permits and Public Contracts	C40	Monthly, with annual cumulation. Provides information on new housing units authorized. (Mobile homes, hotels, motels, and other group dwellings are not included.) Covers the U.S., census regions, and divisions, states, and selected SMSAs, as well as some 4,700 of the most active permit-issuing places.
Residential Alterations and Repairs	C50	Quarterly and annual. Quarterly report covers expenditures of residential property owners, by number of units on the property; annual report shows expenditures made by owners of all types of residential properties and by owner-occupants of one-housing-unit properties, by type of construction, type of property, and by region.

APPENDIX L
Components of the 1980 *Census of Housing*

Title	Geographic Coverage	Description
General Housing Characteristics	U.S., regions, divisions, states, counties, county subdivisions, SMSAs, SCSAs, places of 1,000 or more, and Indian reservations and Alaska Native villages	Covers total housing units, total year-round housing units, total occupied housing units, owner-occupied housing units, units at address, median rooms, persons in unit, median number of persons, and persons per room. Also covers condominium status, tenure, vacancy status and duration of vacancy, vacancy rate, value, price asked, contract rent, rent asked, percent lacking complete plumbing for exclusive use, and percent with 1.01 or more persons per room (based on full-count items). Contained in 58 volumes.
Detailed Housing Characteristics	U.S., regions, divisions, states, counties, county subdivisions, SMSAs, SCSAs, places of 2,500 or more, and Indian reservations and Alaska Native villages	Covers total housing units, occupied housing units, year householder moved into unit, tenure, vacant housing units, rooms, size of household, persons per room, bedrooms, year built, units in structure, stories in structure, and passenger elevators. Also covered are plumbing facilities, bathrooms, source of water, sewage disposal, kitchen facilities, heating equipment, vehicles available, air conditioning, telephones in unit, fuels used for heating, fuels used for heating water and cooking, value, mortgage status and selected monthly owner costs, contract rent, and gross rent (based on sample items). 58 volumes.
Metropolitan Housing Characteristics	U.S., regions, SMSAs, central cities of SMSAs, and places of 50,000 or more	Covers tenure, condominium identification, duration of vacancy, year moved into unit, housing units, rooms, persons in unit, bedrooms, median rooms, units in structure, year structure built, and number of stories in structure. Also covered are plumbing facilities, heating equipment, air conditioning, vehicles available, house heating fuel, water heating fuel, value, price asked, mortgage status and monthly owner costs, contract rent, gross rent, and rent asked. Includes 375 reports.

504

Title	Geographic Coverage	Description
Subject Reports	U.S., regions, divisions, states, SCSAs, SMSAs	Each covers a separate topic. 1. [not published] 2. *Mobile Homes* 3. *Condominium Housing* 4. *Structural Characteristics of the Housing Inventory* 5. *Space Utilization of the Housing Inventory* 6. *Mover Households*
Components of Inventory Change	U.S. and regions	Presents data on changes in housing characteristics between 1973 and 1980.
Residential Finance	U.S. and regions	Presents data on the financing of nonfarm home-owner, homeowner condominium, and rental properties, including characteristics of the mortgages, properties, and owners.

INDEX

This index combines authors, titles, and subjects. In order to conserve space, the following conventions have been observed:

Authors: When more than one author or editor has contributed to a publication, only the first author is listed in the index. For corporate authors, indexing is to the highest level of specificity.

Titles: In most instances, subtitles are not used.

Depth of coverage: When more than one entry is listed, page numbers in boldface indicate that the work receives major coverage in the pages so designated. The letter "n" following page numbers indicates that the work receives only passing mention on the pages cited. Note also that the names of organizations, publications, and authors used only for illustrative purposes are excluded from the index.

Health insurance, 398-99
Health Insurance Institute, 422
Health maintenance organizations (HMOs), 399
Hedgers, 378
Hendrickson, Robert, 15
Heyel, Carl, 18
Highway Loss Data Institute, 423
Historical Chart Book, 300-301
Historical Quotes, 323
Historical Statistics of the United States, 121, **133, 135-36**, 138
Hoel, Arlene, 124-26
Home, 437-38
Homebuyer's Information Package, 445
Hoover, Ryan E., 176-77
Households Using Television Index, 217
Housing Authorized by Building Permits and Public Contracts, 503
Housing Completions, 502
Housing starts, 477
Housing Starts, 502
How Accounting Works, 245
How to Find Information about Companies, 10
How to Read a Financial Report (Merrill Lynch, Pierce, Fenner & Smith), 147n, 234
How to Read a Financial Report (Penton/IPC), 234
How to Read Stock Market Quotations, 148n
How to Use the Business Library, 9
Howitt, Doran, 164n, 176-77
HUD User Online, 453
Hulbert Financial Digest, 313

Imber, Jane, 200
Immediate annuities, 398
Inc. Magazine's Databasics, 164n, 176-77
Income and Resources of the Population 65 and Older, 421
Income/Expense Analysis: Apartments, 451
Income/Expense Analysis: Office Buildings Downtown and Suburban, 451
Income funds, 366
Income, personal (economic indicator), 476
Income statements, 231-32
Income statistics, 205
Income tax guides, 259-61
Indemnity, principle of, 395
Independent agencies, federal government, 83, 468-71
Index numbers, 121-24. *See also* Construction cost indexes; Consumer Price Index; Producer Price Index
Index to International Statistics, 132
Index to U.S. Government Periodicals, 97-98, 167n
Indexes. *See* Newspaper indexes; Periodical indexes and abstracts

Indicators, economic, 124-26, 476-77
Individual Income Tax Returns, 266-67
Individual investors, 308
Individual Investor's Microcomputer Resource Guide, 315
Industrial Equipment News, 160n
Industrial Production Index, 476
Industrial property, 428
Industrial Real Estate Market Survey, 450
Industry Audit Guides, 229n
Industry Data Sources, 222
Industry information, 334-37
  government experts, 100
Industry Norms and Key Business Ratios, 239, 242
Industry Surveys, 334-35, 336n, 429
Inflation, Federal Reserve System's role in preventing, 285-86
Information Catalog, 192-93
Information clearinghouses, federal, 94. *See also* U.S. National Technical Information Service
Information for CPA Candidates, 228
"Information Guide" series, 254
Information Sources in Management and Business, 5-6
Information U.S.A., 100-101, 104
InfoTrac, 157n, 166, **174-75**
InfoTrac II, 175n
Ingham, John, 40
Inside the Financial Futures Market, 383
Institute of Real Estate Management, 451
Institutional investors, 308
Insurance, 394-426
  associations, 403-4
  basics of, 394-404
  characteristics of, 394-95
  information sources, 404-24
    bibliographies, 404-5
    consumer guides, 406-7
    databases, 424
    dictionaries, 405-6
    directories, 408
    government documents, 420-21
    guides, 404-5
    handbooks, 406-7
    information about insurance companies, 408-13
    periodical indexes, 420
    periodicals, 418-19
    policy information sources, 414-17
    statistics, 421-23
    vertical file materials, 420, 423-24
  policies, 395, 414-17
  regulation of, 404
  types of, 395-403. *See also* names of specific kinds of insurance
Insurance, 90n, 405
Insurance Almanac, 408